Journal of Anatomy and Physiology
by Anatomical Society of Great Britain and Ireland

Address:
HardPress
8345 NW 66TH ST #2561
MIAMI FL 33166-2626
USA
Email: info@hardpress.net

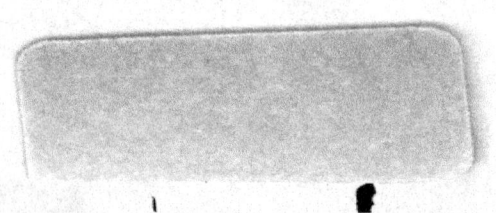

THE

JOURNAL

OF

ANATOMY AND PHYSIOLOGY

CONDUCTED BY

G. M. HUMPHRY, M.D. F.R.S.
PROFESSOR OF ANATOMY IN THE UNIVERSITY OF CAMBRIDGE;
HONORARY FELLOW OF DOWNING COLLEGE.

AND

WM. TURNER, M.B.
PROFESSOR OF ANATOMY IN THE UNIVERSITY OF EDINBURGH.

VOLUME III.
(*SECOND SERIES, VOL. II.*)

MACMILLAN AND CO.
Cambridge and London.
1869.

Cambridge:

PRINTED BY C. J. CLAY, M.A.
AT THE UNIVERSITY PRESS.

15
1

CONTENTS.

FIRST PART. NOVEMBER, 1868.

CONTENTS.

SECOND PART. MAY, 1869.

ERRATA *in Professor Rolleston's paper in last Number.*

At p. 258, line 17, "Firstly the dolichocephalic Celt" should have been "Finally the dolichocephalic Celt"

At p. 258, lines 35 and 36, "Sometimes characteristic and sometimes not (*Pruner Bey*)" should have been "Sometimes characteristic and sometimes not of the Celt (Pruner Bey)"

And, after 1868, the page, viz. p. 319, and after 1864, the page, viz. p. 283, of the volume referred to should have been given in each case.

Journal of Anatomy and Physiology.

ON THE TOPOGRAPHICAL RELATIONS OF THE ARCH OF THE AORTA AND THE POSTERIOR MEDIASTINUM TO THE SPINAL COLUMN. By JOHN WOOD, F.R.C.S. *Examiner in Anatomy to the University of London.* (Pl. I. Fig. 1.)

IT happens occasionally that some out of the way corner of a science remains, after years of investigation, the retreat of a curious error which has escaped the detection of successive generations of observers. This seems sometimes to have originated in a mistaken assumption on the part of some of the earlier writers of authority, and to have been continued by the tendency of successive commentators to take for granted a point not assuming a position of especial importance, and to follow in the wake of the established authority without applying to it the test of observation.

The parietal relations of the aortic arch, and even its very definition, as well as those of the limits of the posterior mediastinum, are points of this kind, where we observe, in comparing the various standard anatomical works, a want of uniformity of description and a great vagueness of definition. This is, no doubt, owing, in some degree, to the varieties affecting Nature herself at different ages and in different individuals; and partly, to the absence of salient outlines in the region under consideration. Although there is but small practical application of an exact anatomical knowledge at present apparent here, yet the progress of discovery may bring about a change in this respect; and, even if it be not so, it is always of importance, in a science aiming at exactness, to clear away even the smallest error or obscurity, whether important or no.

In the last edition of *Quain's Elements of Anatomy* by Professors Sharpey, Thomson and Cleland, 1867, I. 332, we find as follows. "The arch of the aorta commences at the upper part or base of the left ventricle of the heart, behind the pulmonary artery. At first it passes upwards and to the right side, somewhat in the direction of the heart itself, and crosses obliquely behind the sternum, approaching at the same time more nearly to that bone. Having gained the level of the upper border of the *second* costal cartilage of the *right* side the vessel alters its course, and is directed upwards, backwards, and to the left side, then directly backwards, in contact with the trachea, *to the left side of the body of the second dorsal vertebra.* Arrived at that point, it tends downwards, inclining at the same time a little towards the median line, and, *at the lower border of the body of the third dorsal vertebra* on its left side, *the arch terminates* in the descending portion of the vessel."

Again, at page 335 :—"The ascending portion of the arch of the aorta is placed at its commencement behind the sternum, *on a level with the lower border of the third costal cartilage* of the *left* side, and it rises as high as the upper border of the *second* costal cartilage of the *right* side;" and at page 336 :—"The descending portion of the arch rests against *the left side of the body of the third dorsal vertebra.*" In fig. 224 of this work the arch of the aorta is represented as reaching to a level with the hinder end of the *second* rib. *Three mediastina* are described ; the *middle* one including the heart and pericardia and the roots of the great vessels. The posterior is not limited, nor its boundaries, above and below, defined.

Professor Ellis in his *Demonstrations of Anatomy*, 1852 (page 362), states that the ascending aorta commences "close below the junction of the cartilage of the third *rib* on the left side with the sternum." The first or ascending part "reaches as high as the upper border of the cartilage of the *second rib on the right side.*" "The second or transverse piece crosses behind the sternum, and reaches from the second right costal cartilage to the *left side of the body of the second dorsal vertebra.* The third or descending part of the arch is very short, extending only from the *second* to the lower part of the *third dorsal vertebra.*" The thoracic aorta is described (page 380) as the "part of the great systemic vessel which is above the diaphragm. Its extent is from the lower border of the *third* dorsal vertebra (the left side) where the arch ceases, to the front of the last dorsal vertebra."

This author describes *no middle* mediastinum, and he enumerates among the other contents of the *posterior* mediastinum more usually described, the *bifurcation of the trachea.* (p. 340.)

In his *Manual of the Dissection of the Human Body*, 1851, Mr Luther Holden describes (p. 196) the aorta as arising "nearly opposite to the upper border of the *fourth* costal cartilage of the left side at its junction with the sternum. The vessel ascends forwards and to the right side as high as the upper border of the *second* costal cartilage on the right side; it then curves backwards towards the left side of the body of the *second* dorsal vertebra, and turning downwards over the *third*, completes the arch." Again in describing the descending portion he says (p. 197), "This part of the arch lies upon the left side of the body of the *third* dorsal vertebra;" and, at page 207, he again states that the descending thoracic aorta begins on the left side of the body of the *third* dorsal vertebra.

At page 198, he states that in a well formed adult, the ascending aorta is about five-eighths of an inch distant from the first bone of the sternum; and the highest part of the arch is on a plane about 1½ *inches below the upper edge of the sternum.* In infants it is relatively higher, in consequence of the incomplete development of the bone, and also in the aged, in consequence of dilatation of the arch. He mentions, moreover, that in the exceptional case of a young female who died of phthisis the aortic valves were on a level with the middle of the second costal articulation, and the highest part of the arch was on a level with the upper border of the sternum.

This author makes no mention of a *middle* mediastinum, and does not define the limits of the *posterior* at all.

In the last edition of *The Dublin Dissector*, Mr Harrison says (II. p. 406), "The arch of the aorta, though not very accurately defined, may be considered as extending from the left ventricle to the *fourth* dorsal vertebra." Treating of the third or descending portion, he says again (p. 407), "its right side corresponds to the œsophagus, thoracic duct, and *left* side of the *third dorsal vertebra.*" No middle mediastinum is described.

In the *Anatomy, Descriptive and Surgical*, of the late Mr Henry Gray, F.R.S. (p. 310), the ascending portion of the arch of the aorta is described as commencing opposite the middle of the sternum on a line with its junction to the *third* costal cartilage; the transverse portion as commencing "at the upper border of the *second* costo-sternal articulation of the right side in front, and passes from right to left, and from before backwards, to the left side of the *second* dorsal vertebra behind," and that "its upper border is usually about an inch below the upper margin of the sternum." The thoracic aorta is said (p. 311) to commence at the lower border of the left side of the body of the *third* dorsal vertebra.

This author describes a *middle mediastinum*, containing the heart enclosed in the pericardia, the ascending aorta, the superior vena cava, the pulmonary arteries and veins, the phrenic nerves, and the *bifurcation of the trachea.* He does not limit the upper and lower boundaries of the *posterior* mediastinum, nor mention its exact relation to the spinal column or aortic arch.

In Wilson's *Anatomist's Vade Mecum* (p. 310) it is stated that

1—2

"the arch of the aorta, commencing at a point corresponding with the articulation of the cartilage of the *fourth* rib with the sternum on the left side, crosses behind and near the sternum to a point corresponding with the upper border of the articulation of the *second* rib with the sternum on the right side. It then curves backwards and to the left, and descends to the left side of the body of the *third* dorsal vertebra, and at the lower border becomes the thoracic aorta." No *middle* mediastinum is described by this author, and the *posterior* is not defined.

Among the foreign authorities consulted upon this subject J. Cruveilhier in his *Anatomie Descriptive, Angeiologie*, 1834, pp. 55 and 56, describes the aorta as follows. "Sortie du pericarde, elle change de direction, se recourbe brusquement pour se porter presque horizontalement de droit à gauche et d'avant en arrière sur la partie laterale gauche de la colonne vertebrale, au *niveau de la troisième vertèbre dorsale;* là, elle se recourbe une troisième fois, pour devenir verticale et descendante." This author defines the "Crosse de l'aorte" (p. 57) as follows. "Je donnerai ce nom à toute la partie de l'aorte comprise entre l'origine de cette artère au ventricle gauche et le point où le vaisseau est coupé perpendiculairement par la bronche gauche." In a foot-note it is remarked, "Les limites de la crosse de l'aorte ne sont pas bien definies.—Suivant un grand nombre (des auteurs), la limite inférieure est marquée par l'articulation de la *quatrième* avec la *cinquième* dorsale."

In the *Handbuch der Gefässlehre des Menschen*, 1868, Henle divides the aortic curve into "aorta adscendens," "arcus aortae," and the "aorta descendens," calling it, below the last, the "aorta thoracica." At s. 79 he says, "befindet sich das Ende des Aortenbogens entweder in *einer Horizontalebene mit der Synchondrose zwischen dem zweiten und dritten Brustwirbel*, oder zur *linken Seite des dritten Brustwirbels*, und von demselben Umstande hängt es ab, ob die absteigende Aorta mit der linken Hälfte des Bogens oder sogleich in einer geraden Linie beginnt, die fast vertical, aber in der Art steil schräg absteigt dass sie die Strecke *vom dritten Brustwirbel* bis zum vierten Bauchwirbel braucht," &c. &c.

Dr C. Langer in *Lehrbuch der Anatomie des Menschen*, 1865, Vienna, says respecting the aortic arch (s. 323), "Die aufsteigende Aorta kreuzt die hintere Wand des Lungen-arterienstammes,—der Bogen, dessen scheitel sich bis *zur Ebene des 2 Brustwirbelkörpers* erhebt,—und das absteigende Stück *geht vom 3 Brustwirbel*," &c. &c.

The last three authors do not describe a *middle* mediastinum, and the *posterior* is mentioned but not defined.

Among the notes of my observations taken from 32 subjects, viz. 14 male and 18 female, in the dissecting rooms at King's College, London, for my article on the "Pelvis" in Todd's *Encyclopedia of Anatomy and Physiology*, in the year 1859, the inclination of the ribs to the spinal column and to its transverse vertical plane is compared with the inclination of the pelvis to the same plane which is published in that work.

In these subjects an antero-posterior vertical section of the spinal column from top to bottom was made, with the principal pelvic and thoracic viscera *in situ*. My observations then made upon the position of the aortic arch have been taught every winter session since that time, in my demonstrations to the anatomical class at King's College, London. They differ in many important particulars from the descriptions above quoted from the various English, French, and German authorities.

I found that a perpendicular line, drawn on the face of the antero-posterior vertical section of the spinal column, thorax and pelvis, from the centre of the body of the axis to that of the last lumbar vertebra at its articulation with the sacrum, would, in a perfectly well formed young adult male, pass through the centre also of the body of the 1st dorsal and 2nd lumbar vertebræ, and would indicate the line of gravity of the head and trunk in a perfectly upright and balanced position, traversing the pelvis midway between the cotylo-femoral joints and falling between the bases of support.

In the accompanying figure, which is taken from the main outlines of a diagram of the natural size which I made at that time for the use of the dissecting room, and which is still in use there, the dotted vertical line *ab* expresses the course of this *transverse vertical plane* of the spinal column. It will be seen that the dorsal incurvature of the thoracic cavity lies altogether behind that line, and that it indicates pretty closely the anterior limits of the posterior mediastinum.

I found, also, that the inclination of the first rib or plane of the upper thoracic opening, as expressed by a line drawn from the upper part of the body of the first dorsal vertebra, in the median line, to the top of the sternum, (the line *cd* in the figure,) in the condition of complete expiration of the thoracic air usually present in the dead subject, (when not affected by any special disease of the thoracic organs,) formed, with the transverse vertical plane, an angle which varied from

115° to 120° in the adult male of middle age; and that it was usually a little larger (120° to 125°) in the adult female. The line passed out behind at the 7th cervical spine.

Under the same conditions, I found that the upper border of the sternum was placed in the horizontal level of the lower border of the body of the *second* dorsal vertebra, and that the horizontal plane, extended backward, would emerge near the tip of the *third* dorsal spine (in the line *ef* in the figure).

Further, the raised line on the sternum between the articulations of the *second* rib cartilage was on a level with the lower border of the body of the *fourth* dorsal vertebra, the plane emerging posteriorly near the point of the *fourth* dorsal spine (in the line *gh*).

This apparently great anterior depression was seen to arise chiefly from the oblique direction of the ribs ; but, in part, from the much greater width in vertical direction, of the first intercostal space in front than behind, at which latter point its width was extended more in the horizontal direction than in the vertical.

Another horizontal plane drawn through the centre of the *third* piece of the sternum, and passing midway between the *third* and *fourth* rib cartilages, was found to pass out behind about the tip of the *sixth* dorsal spinous process (in the line *ik*). In this horizontal plane, or very near it, in well formed and healthy subjects, were found the cardiac openings of the aortic and pulmonary arteries and their semilunar valves, each lying in its own respective plane, inclined in different directions from the horizontal plane, the plane of the aortic opening having an inclination downwards, slightly forwards and towards the right side, and the pulmonary, downwards, backwards and towards the left. From this point the ascending aorta passed upwards, a little forwards, and towards the right border of the sternum; its upper part lying from three-fourths of an inch to an inch, from the posterior wall of the second piece of that bone, close to its right border, and to the inner side of the joint between the *second right* rib cartilage and the sternum. At this place the aortic arch forms its most prominent bulge, and is usually opened for the purpose of injecting the subjects.

The arch then turns obliquely across the cavity of the thorax, crossing the trachea just above its bifurcation, and lying at its highest point or culm in the horizontal plane *gh*. Here it gives off its innominate, carotid and subclavian branches. Just before the latter is given off, however, the artery, when not over injected, is seen to turn more directly backwards, as it arches also more downwards. Here it is in contact, posteriorly towards the median line, with the œsophagus and thoracic duct, both of which cross behind it. Finally it approaches the lower border of the left side of the *fourth* dorsal vertebra, and *first touches the spine* usually about the intervertebral substance *between the fourth and fifth* vertebræ. It then assumes a more vertical direction, and lies against the left side of the body of the *fifth* dorsal vertebra, which is, in fact, *the uppermost vertebra, which shews on its body the impression or flattening produced by contact with the aorta*. The curve of the aortic arch was found to cease fairly at the intervertebral substance between the fifth and sixth dorsal vertebræ, i. e. about the depth of one vertebra above the horizontal plane *ik*, from which point the straight descending portion, usually defined, curiously enough, as the "thoracic aorta," takes its departure.

By inflating forcibly the lungs of the entire subject, and correcting the results by comparison with the living subject in full and deep inspiration, I concluded that the rise and fall of the front end of the four upper ribs and sternum range usually along the depth of the body of one dorsal vertebra in the adult male, and rather more in the adult female. Thus, in a deep inspiration, the relation of the *aortic arch* to the *front* chest wall will be altered nearly to this extent.

Again, a plane horizontal to the transverse vertical plane and drawn at the level of the central tendon of the diaphragm upon which the heart rests, was found, under the same conditions of complete expiration, to emerge anteriorly about the junction of the xiphoid cartilage with the sternum, and posteriorly about the tip of the eighth dorsal spine (in the dotted line *lm*, in the fig.).

On each side of this line, however, and especially on the right side, the muscular fibres of the diaphragm rise in a sort of double dome shape considerably higher than this point, reaching usually, on the right side, as high as the middle of the shaft of the 6th rib or the 5th intercostal space. About the level of the upper part of the 10th dorsal vertebra, or the intervertebral substance between it and the 9th, the œsophagus passes through its opening in the diaphragm. During a deep inspiration the dome of the diaphragm becomes flattened, both at the sides, where the chief alteration ensues, and in the median line at the central tendon also, but to a much less extent. The apex of the heart is thus lowered a little absolutely, as well as relatively to the front wall of the chest; and this may have a limited influence in lowering also in a slight degree the position of the aortic arch during extreme inspiration. The attachments of the fibrous pericardium and its continuity with the cervical fascia will, however, prevent any very considerable movement in a vertical direction.

When, however, as is frequently the case in old age, the arch of the aorta is absolutely dilated and hypertrophied; or if, as frequently happens in preparing subjects for the dissecting rooms, the aorta is over-injected, then the arch of the aorta will rise considerably above the normal level herein indicated.

Again, another common consequence of senility is an increase in the dorsal incurvature of the thoracic cavity, which has a marked effect in elevating the relative position of the aortic arch, by causing the upper dorsal vertebræ to assume a lower position in the chest. In the normal adult subjects examined, it was found that the dorsal thoracic incurvature culminated about the 6th dorsal vertebra (about the plane *ik*), and that an *axial line* traversing as nearly as possible to the centres of the bodies of the five upper dorsal vertebræ, cut the transverse vertical plane (*ab*) at the centre of the body of the first dorsal vertebra, and formed there with the *plane of the superior thoracic opening* (*cd*) an angle of about 100° in the male, and rather more, on an average, in the female. The axial line of the bodies of the six lower dorsal vertebræ, gradually approaching downwards and forwards the transverse vertical plane, *ab*, usually cuts it about the middle of the *second lumbar* vertebra.

In infants and young children, this dorsal incurvature, in common with the other spinal curves, was uniformly less marked or flatter; but in subjects past the middle period of life, it becomes gradually increased, the upper dorsal vertebra assuming a lower position, the plane of the superior thoracic opening becoming more horizontal, and the play of the ribs less free; while at the same time the aortic arch is rising under the distending influence of the circulatory forces.

Under such circumstances, common enough among the subjects of our dissecting rooms, the arch of the aorta may reach as high as the *third* dorsal vertebra. But under no conditions short of humpbacked deformity of the spine or extreme dilatation of the artery have I found the arch of the aorta to rise as high as the horizontal level of the *second dorsal vertebra*, as described in the text-books already quoted. In fact, such a position of the arch would cause it to appear *above the level of the upper border of the sternum* and to encroach upon the root of the neck, which is normally occupied by the first or intra-thoracic portions of the innominate, left carotid and subclavian arteries. It should, under such circumstances, clearly be classed as abnormal, and not described as a normal condition. To do so is entirely inconsistent with the descriptions of the relations of the last-named arteries in the upper part of the thorax, and with those of the lower part of the trachea, the corresponding portions of the œsophagus and thoracic duct, and of the brachio-cephalic and superior caval veins, found in the same works by the authors already quoted.

In the useful anatomical Manual of my friend and former pupil and assistant demonstrator, Mr Chr. Heath, it is gratifying to find under this head the token of my own teaching in former years. At page 385 this author describes the ascending portion of the aorta as beginning opposite the *third* costal cartilage of the left side, and reaching as high as the *second* costal cartilage of the right side; the horizontal or transverse part, as reaching from the *second* costal cartilage on the right side to the left side of the *fourth* dorsal vertebra; and the descending portion, (p. 387) as extending to the lower border of the *fifth* dorsal vertebra.

Upon consulting the plates in the *Anatome Topographica* of the Russian surgeon Nicolao Pirogoff, *sectionibus per corpus humanum congelatum*, Petropoli, 1859, I find a complete general corroboration of the above remarks as to the position of the sternum and rib cartilages, as well as of the aortic arch to the spinal column.

In Fascic. 1A, Tab. 12 and 13, is shown the longitudinal antero-posterior section of the spine and sternum of an adult male frozen stiff in a perfectly upright position. The upper border of the sternum in this figure is in the same horizontal plane with the middle of the body of the *third* dorsal vertebra; and the sterno-xiphoid joint is opposite to the upper border of the *ninth dorsal* vertebra, and to the tip of the eighth dorsal spinous process. In the next plate (Tab. 14) of an adult male subject frozen in an extremely flexed condition, the upper border of the sternum is opposite to the lower margin of the *second* dorsal vertebra; and the sterno-xiphoid joint opposite to the lower margin of the *ninth dorsal* vertebra. The same general position is found also in the following plate of the series (Tab. 15). In Tab. 10 of the same (Fascic. 1A), the longitudinal section seems to have been made upon a male body which had been subjected to much antero-posterior compression, since the upper border of the sternum is found as low down as the *fourth dorsal vertebra*, and the costo-xiphoid joint is opposite to the *twelfth* dorsal, both the sternal and vertebral curves being very much flattened. This illustrates the care necessary in drawing conclusions from bodies observed under such extremely abnormal conditions as those illustrated in this eminent surgeon's valuable and laborious work, unless corrected by other observations made upon the living or recently dead and unaltered subject. Of course, in all these subjects, the natural depression of the ribs in complete expiration is increased by the act of congelation, and the shrinking induced by it. In the next table of the same Fascic. (Tab. 11), a longitudinal section of the trunk of a female subject shows the upper margin of the sternum placed opposite the upper border of the *third dorsal vertebra;* and the sterno-xiphoid joint opposite the lower margin of the *tenth* dorsal vertebra. The straighter curves of the spinal column and the increased curve of the sternum in the child and infant are well compared in Fasc. 1A Tab. 16 of Pirogoff's work.

In Fasc. 2A (cavum thoracis in longitudinem diffissum) Tab. 7, figs. 1 and 2, the longitudinal section of the trunk of an adult with the contained viscera undisturbed exhibits the section of *the end of the aortic arch* placed on a level with or opposite to the *fifth* dorsal vertebra.

In Fasc. 2, Tab. 3, figs. 3 and 4, a transverse section of the chest with its contained viscera, made on a level with the front part of the first intercostal space and the body of the *fourth* dorsal vertebra behind, dividing the 2nd, 3rd, 4th and 5th ribs, in the body of a youth of 16, cuts exactly through the *horizontal portion* of the aortic arch just below the origin of the large ascending branches.

In fig. 2 of the same plate, a transverse section through the *first* intercostal space in front, and two lines above the lower margin of the *third* dorsal vertebra behind, in an adult male subject affected with pneumothorax of the left side, shows the upper part or culm of the aortic arch just sliced off where the great branches arise.

In Fasc. 2, Tab. 4, fig. 1, a transverse section on a level with the *lower* border of the *fourth* dorsal vertebra is seen to divide the aortic arch in two places, viz. the ascending and the descending parts, leaving a very narrow part of the lower wall between them, thus proving that the section has barely escaped the transverse part. In fig. 3 of the same plate a similar section, made on the level of the upper margin of the *second* costal cartilage in front and the body of the *fifth* dorsal vertebra behind, in a healthy male subject, shows a section of "transitus arcus aortæ in aortam descendentem" (7) and the section of the bronchi close below the bifurcation. In figures 4 and 5 the same general arrangement is also shown.

It is to be observed that the discrepancies which exist between the observations of Pirogoff and those of myself, made under different and more normal conditions, are invariably in the downward direction or opposite extreme to those found in the anatomical writers quoted in the earlier part of this paper. Allowance must be made for individual peculiarities and the manner of preparation in the comparatively small number of cases quoted from Pirogoff; but the fact of their being all in one direction, and that direction favourable to the deductions drawn from the mean average of the 32 instances in which I have examined the point, is at least significant, and supports the position I have brought forward in the present paper.

In my demonstrations to the Anatomical Class at King's College, I have been in the habit of dividing the thorax into two pleural cavities, separated, in the lower four-fifths of the chest, by three mediastina; and in the upper fifth or thereabouts, by the region of the great branches of the aortic arch, which I have called the "Superior" or "Cervico-thoracic" regions or "root of the neck".

The latter falls between the oblique plane, *cd*, of the accompanying figure, i.e. *the plane of the superior thoracic outlet*, and the horizontal plane *gh*, i.e. *the plane of the aortic arch;* the three upper dorsal vertebræ and their intervertebral substances, together with that between the third and fourth vertebra, being the posterior wall; and the manubrium sterni, and upper fourth or fifth of the anterior mediastinum,—the anterior limit of the region; while the apices of the lungs and pleuræ form the sides thereof. In this I give the relations of the innominate, left carotid and left subclavian artery, the brachio-cephalic veins, the lower part of the trachea and adjacent œsophagus and thoracic duct, &c.

The *anterior mediastinum* is limited in front (as usually described in anatomical text-books) by the sternum and left costal cartilages; behind, by the pericardium contained in the middle mediastinum for the lower three-fourths or four-fifths, and for the remainder of the posterior part by the cervico-thoracic region; and at the sides by the pleura.

The *middle mediastinum* contains the heart and great vessels, including the ascending part of the aorta and aortic arch invested by the serous and fibrous pericardia, and also containing, between the latter and the pleuræ, the phrenic nerves and their accompanying vessels. The limits of the middle mediastinum behind, I make the hinder wall of the fibrous pericardium, and the fibrous cord of the obliterated "ductus arteriosus". This leaves as the *posterior mediastinum*, the descending portion of the aortic arch, and all the parts usually described therein, with the addition of the bifurcation of the trachea, including the bronchi and hinder part of the root of the lung and the recurrent laryngeal nerve of the left side. Its upper limit would thus be the hinder or left portion of the aortic arch limited by the plane, *gh*, impinging on the second rib cartilage in front, and behind on the body of the *fourth* dorsal vertebra, and passing out behind at the fourth dorsal spine. Its lower limit would be the lesser muscle of the diaphragm inclosing the aortic, œsophageal and splanchnic openings; and its sides, as usually described, the pleural cavities, the roots of the lungs, and the "ligamenta lata pulmonum". The whole of the region will be seen, on inspecting the figure, to fall within the segment described by the curved *arc* of the spine from the *fourth* to the *twelfth* dorsal vertebra; and by the *chord* of the transverse vertical plane in the line *ab*, limited only above by the segment cut off by the horizontal plane *gh*.

The advantage of making a *middle* mediastinum is, that it gives a definite "locus" to the phrenic nerves, so often placed wrongly by students in the anterior or posterior mediastina, as well as to the fibrous pericardium, and the great vessels up to their first branchings. That of limiting the posterior mediastinum above so definitely as I have done, is to give a place to the bifurcation of the trachea and bronchi, and to the left recurrent laryngeal nerve so doubtfully, obscurely, and even contradictorily placed by anatomical writers; the attachment of the obliterated "ductus arteriosus" to the aortic arch giving a definite outline to the region above.

Torsion of Arteries.

Figures 2 to 7, inclusive, on Plate I. represent arteries which have been subjected to torsion in the dead subject. They show the mode in which the inner coats of the vessel become divided across and separated from the outer coat, and, in consequence of the pressure exercised upon them by the latter during the twisting, are reflected or squeezed up in a funnel, or cup-like, manner into the vessel. The extent to which this upturning takes place depends upon the amount of twisting which the outer coat bears before it gives way; and the resistance which the twisted artery offers to the pressure of the blood-current is porportionate, partly, to the depth of this funnel-like valve, but, still more, to the firmness with which the position of the valve is maintained, and the closeness with which the end of the artery, is sealed by the tight twisting together of the torn fibres of the outer coat.

Figures 2, 3, and 4 are from a young woman. In 3 and 4 the vessel has been laid open: the inner coat is inverted like a cup in 3; and the twisted outer coat extends some distance below it. In 4 the inversion is not distinct.

Fig. 5 is the twisted carotid of a man which bore a column of 20 inches of mercury. The mercury passed through the funnel of the inner coat and distended and partially unfurled the outer coat. It would probably soon have quite unfurled the outer coat and escaped through the end. More commonly it finds its way through some weak point or rent in the outer coat.

Figures 6 and 7 are from the carotid artery of a bullock. The inner coats are reflected downwards as well as upwards, having given way at some little distance above the point seized with the forceps, and the vessel not being quite divided by the torsion.

G. M. HUMPHRY.

OBSERVATIONS ON THE CILIARY MUSCLE IN FISH, BIRDS, AND QUADRUPEDS. By R. J. LEE, M.B. Cantab.

IN the year 1813 Sir Philip Crampton described in Thompson's *Annals of Philosophy* a structure in the eye of the ostrich which had previously escaped the notice of anatomists.

The observation attracted at the time considerable attention from the promise it offered of explaining the means by which the eye is enabled to adjust itself for various distances. The reason why the line of research thus indicated has been neglected by many who have attempted the solution of that difficult and undecided question I hope to be able to explain satisfactorily in the following remarks on the structure and functions of the Ciliary Muscle.

On comparing the eye of the fish, the mammal, and the bird, the ciliary muscle is found to vary in so many respects that it is not surprising that Crampton failed to recognise it as the ciliary ligament or muscle of anatomists; and to the same cause is to be attributed in some degree the reason of its being considered by some a ligament, by others a muscle. Without entering into a minute account of its intimate structure, it is here proposed to adopt the general term of ciliary muscle under whatever conditions that structure is met with in the eyes of different animals.

Its absence in the eye of the fish, whose range of vision is more limited than that of any of the higher vertebrate animals; its perfect development in the bird, which possesses the most accurate and extensive range of sight; and its intermediate degree of development in the mammalia, led me to examine the eyes of various animals with a view to finding the true explanation of those remarkable differences and to determine if possible the function performed by the ciliary muscle in affording the varied power of vision with which the eye is endowed. A most accurate description has been given of the muscle in the eye of the bird by Mr Rainey in the *Lancet*, 1851. It is only the want of illustration to render the description more easy to understand that has prevented his account from receiving the attention it deserves. The illustrations which accompany this communication were made from dissections at various times repeated as opportunity offered for obtaining different specimens. Those who are interested in such investigations may be willing to adopt the same mode of dissection that I have found most suitable for demonstrating the structures we are considering. The eye should be placed in water as soon after the animal is killed as possible, and exposed to the influence of a gentle flow from a tap in order to wash away all trace of blood from the tissues. After being treated for three days in this way, it should be immersed in pure alcohol, or methylic alcohol, in which it may remain for any length of time until the dissection is commenced. Even after many months have elapsed no material change will be found to have taken place in the structures.

The instruments required are a small pair of straight scissors, which are superior in most respects to a knife or razor; two pairs of finely pointed curved forceps, two needles properly mounted in handles, and a magnifying glass of one or two inch focus arranged on a moveable arm, and lastly a thin piece of cork affixed to a solid basis of lead, on which a section may be fixed and examined under alcohol or water. It is difficult to describe the great advantages of this mode over every other. Decomposition is prevented and any degree of labour may be bestowed upon one dissection; while the aid of a powerful magnifying glass and the great facility of separating the tissues when floating in fluid considerably assist the dissector.

Some have certainly found that the evaporation of alcohol is attended with unpleasant effects, and others object to the long continued use of so powerful a lens, yet a very little practice will accustom to the vapour of the spirit, while the sight will really be found to be improved instead of injured by the assistance of the lens; indeed such dissection ought not to be attempted without it.

Three views may be obtained of the ciliary muscle according to the mode of dissection. The surface which lies in contact with the sclerotic may be shewn by removing that membrane close to the cornea. Similarly the choroidal or internal surface is exposed by detaching the iris and choroid from the internal surface of the eyeball when divided into equal parts.

The third method allows the structures to be seen in their relative position, and is the only one by which the origin and insertion of the ciliary muscle are both preserved. The eye is divided into lateral halves by a section through the centre of the cornea, and from either of the parts, sections may be made of not less than a line in thickness with the scissors, and which may be fixed on the cork by means of needles, so that the cut surfaces of the cornea and sclerotic, the choroid and iris with the ciliary muscle interposed, are presented to the view. The dissection must be continued under alcohol or water with the assistance of the lens, one needle and a pair of forceps. The iris is to be drawn away from the cornea as far as possible without destroying its attachment, and fixed by means of the needle. In the same way the choroid is drawn from the sclerotic and similarly fixed to the cork. The ciliary muscle is thus exposed in its whole extent and may be examined under the inch object glass of the microscope with great advantage. ·

In order to understand the remark which has been made respecting the degree of development of the ciliary muscle in various animals, attention is directed to the woodcuts, 1, 2, 3.

The eye of the cod fish (Fig. 1) may be taken as an example of the general condition of the structures in the class of fishes.

The line from E to where the sclerotic passes into the cornea, and the choroid into the iris, points out the situation where the ciliary muscle would be found if it existed, but in all the species of fish which are common in this country there is no vestige of any structure corresponding to it. ' The iris in fish,' says Haller, 'does not move,' and where this is the case it

Fig. 1.

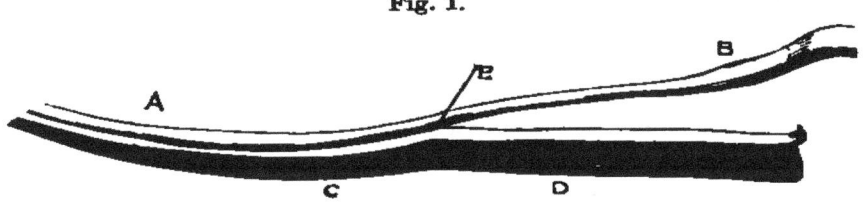

From a dissection of the membranes of the eye of the Cod Fish.

A.   Sclerotic.   B.   Cornea.   C.   Choroid.   D.   Iris.
E.   Position of Ciliary Muscle in mammalia and birds.

will be found that the ciliary muscle does not exist; a conclusion which is one part of a general
law I have observed, that the activity
of the iris is directly proportional to the
degree of development of the ciliary
muscle.

Fig. 2.

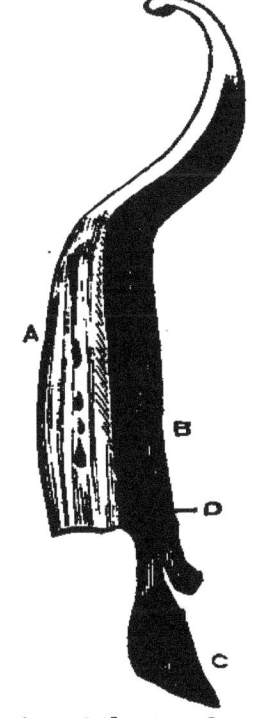

The next illustration (Fig. 2) is taken
from a section of the eye of the cat.
There is a peculiarity in the structure of
the ciliary muscle in this animal which,
at first, induced me to choose that of one
of the larger quadrupeds; but as the
reader will find such illustrations in most
works on physiology, and as the muscle
in the feline species is chiefly remarkable
for its size, no objection can be made to
it for the purpose of comparison.

The muscle is seen to arise from the
anterior border of the sclerotic close to
the margin of the cornea which has been
removed in the dissection, and to pass
backwards to the choroid, forming so intimate a connexion with it as to appear
really a part of that membrane.   I have
reasons for believing that its chief function in this class of animals is to increase
or diminish in a remarkable manner the

Section of the membranes
of the eye of the Cat.

A. Sclerotic. B. Choroid.
C. Iris. D. Ciliary Muscle.

the flow of blood to the erectile tissue of the iris on which the size of the pupil depends.

The third illustration.(Fig. 3) is made from a dissection of the eye of the common fowl, in which the mode of arrangement of the membranes above described has been adopted. A needle was passed through the cornea at C by which it was held firmly fixed to the cork. Another needle was inserted between the choroid and sclerotic near F so that the iris could be drawn away from the cornea, and fixed by a third needle. The choroid A was then drawn away from the sclerotic D, so that the fibres at F were stretched in the same manner as those at E. By means of a mounted needle the ciliary muscle was carefully cleaned and exposed in its whole extent.

Illustration 4 is made from a similar dissection to the last, in which the section obtained was thinner and more highly magnified.

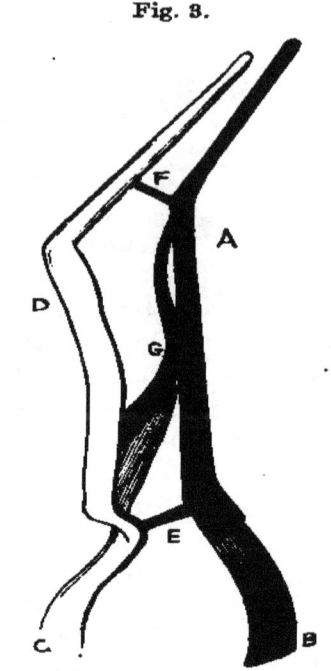

Fig. 3.

From a dissection of the Ciliary Muscle of the Fowl.

A. Choroid. B. Iris. C. Cornea. D. Sclerotic. E. Elastic Fibres passing between C and A. F. Elastic Fibres between D and A.

In the dissection illustrated. in Fig. 5 the elastic fibres which pass between the cornea and choroid have been cut away. Those which attach the sclerotic and choroid remain (F). The ciliary muscle has been divided and a part of the sclerotic removed.

There are thus seen to be three structures in the eye of the bird which demand attention before considering the functions which they are intended to perform.

The first set of fibres which attach the choroid to the sclerotic or to the outer margin of the cornea are composed of soft filamentous structure of great delicacy and of less elasticity than those which attach the two membranes posteriorly.

By gently drawing the iris away from the cornea the degree of elasticity they possess is easily ascertained, while the filaments are separately exhibited.

They differ to some extent in various species of birds, but exist in all that I have examined. In none however are the fibres so much developed as in the eye of the owl, of which an illustration is subjoined.

The dissection was made by removing the cornea to within a line of the sclerotic, thus exhibiting the iris, which is attached to the margin of the sclerotic by the elastic fibres. By drawing the iris away from the sclerotic the fibres are clearly seen.

The figure, however, does not represent with sufficient accuracy this simple and

Fig. 4.

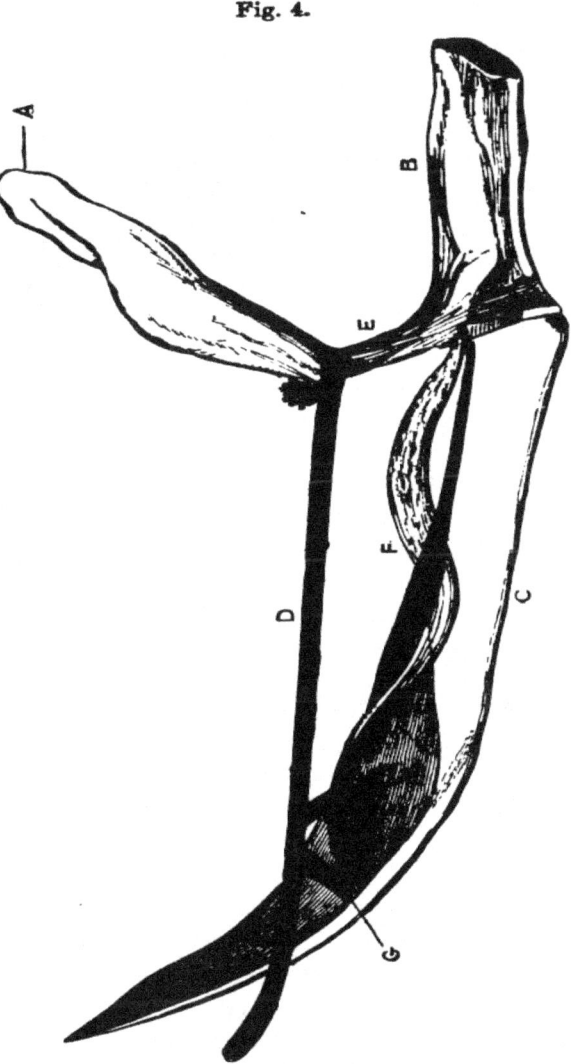

A. Iris.   B. Cornea.   C. Sclerotic.   D. Choroid.
E. Elastic Fibres attaching Choroid to Cornea.
F. Ciliary Muscle.   G. Elastic Fibres attaching the Choroid to the Sclerotic.

2—2

beautiful mode of arrangement, nor the delicate structure of the tissues.

The posterior elastic fibres (Fig. 3, F) are composed of a different kind of tissue. Indeed they appear to form a distinct membranous band, somewhat resembling elastic ligamentous tissue in composition, and are possessed of considerable strength and great elasticity. It is important that this peculiar property should be distinctly exhibited in order to understand the function the structure performs. This may be done in the following manner. In the dissection (Fig. 3) the iris (B) is held by the forceps, and drawn in such a direction as to extend the fibres (F), and if carefully done it is not difficult to stretch them to more than double their length. On relaxing the tension they immediately resume their former condition.

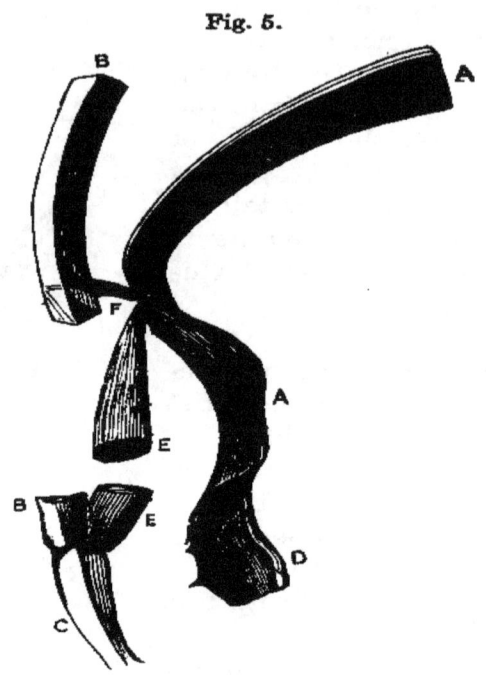

Fig. 5.

A. Choroid.   B. Sclerotic.   C. Cornea. D. Iris.   E. Ciliary Muscle.   F. Elastic Fibres connecting B and A.

So much information is derived from this experiment that it should be frequently repeated and carefully considered. It is evident that this structure is intended to counteract the ciliary muscle, and to restore to their natural position those parts on which the muscle exerts its influence.

The dissections of the eyes of the owl and the falcon exhibit a different arrangement of the elastic fibres required by the shape of the eye-ball in these species of birds.

In the above illustration, the ciliary muscle (*d*) is seen to lie upon the sclerotic, which presents a convexity of surface requiring no special means of attachment for the choroid.

As a substitute for the elastic fibres, and to oppose the muscle, that part of the choroid (*R*) which lies between *k* and the insertion of the ciliary muscle is itself composed of highly elastic tissue. In the eye of the falcon, which is intermediate in form to the globular and pyramidal, there is a certain variation in the length of the ciliary muscle adapted to the shape of the eyeball.

As it is not intended to enter into the subject of the minute structure of the parts of the eye which have been described, a few remarks will suffice for the ciliary muscle itself.

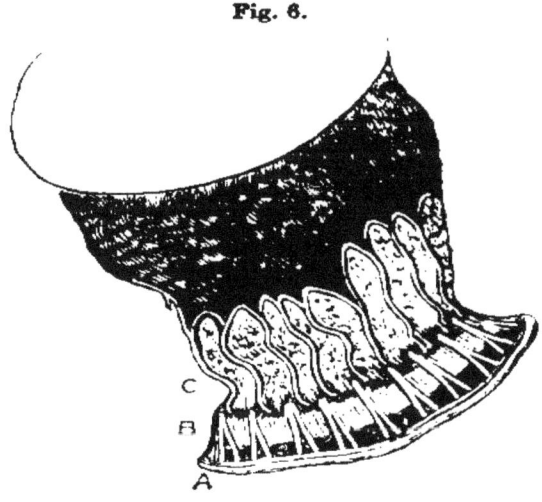

Fig. 6.

Iris of the Owl.

A. Edge of Cornea.   B. Elastic Fibres.
C. Choroidal Filaments expanding to form the Iris.

It arises generally from the margin of the cornea, or from the cornea and sclerotic where those membranes unite. In the eye of the owl (Fig. 6) the fibres of the muscle are attached to the strong tissue which lies between the cornea and osseous ring of the sclerotic. The insertion of the muscle however, that is to say, the full extent of its muscular and tendinous structure, was not known to Sir P. Crampton; and the same cause has led many physiologists to misunderstand its functions. It was supposed by Crampton that the origin of the muscle was the inner surface of the sclerotic quite close to the cornea, and that the muscle was inserted into the cornea so as to produce by its contraction such changes in the convexity of the cornea as would adjust the sight to objects at various distances.

In illustration 7 it is seen that the chief portion of the ciliary muscle lies between the point designated by *h* and the edge of the cornea. Similarly in Fig. 4 it can easily be conceived that the muscle might appear to extend only from the sclerotic at the point F to the edge of the cornea.

By separating the parts in the manner described the whole extent of the muscle is exhibited, which is not the case when a simple section is examined without this preparation. There are thus seen to be three structures of a peculiar and remarkable character in the eye of the bird. By means of two rows of elastic fibres with a muscle interposed, the choroid is so attached to the sclerotic that a certain degree of movement may take place between them. That part of the choroid which is thus attached to the sclerotic is the portion which is supplied with the ciliary processes on its internal surface, and to which the crystalline lens is affixed; that is to say, the whole arrangement described is intended for the alteration of the position of the crystalline lens.

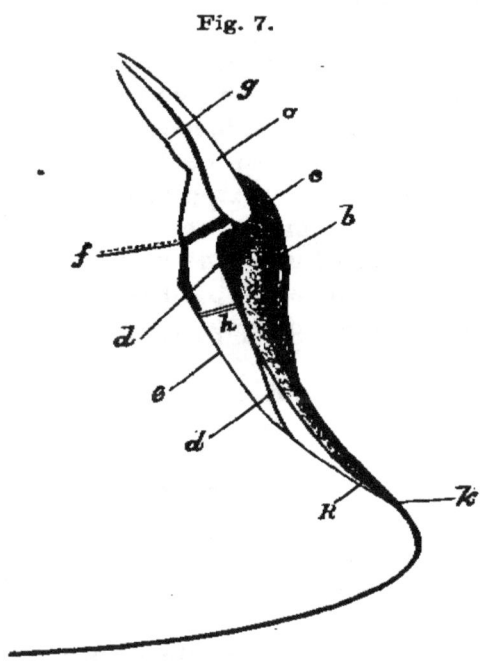

Fig. 7.

Section of the eye of the Owl.

a. Cornea.   *b.* Osseous ring in Sclerotic.
c. Cartilaginous portion of Sclerotic.
d. Ciliary muscle.   *e.* Choroid.
f. Elastic fibres.   *g.* Iris.   *R.* Elastic portion of Choroid.

The result of the numerous dissections which I have made leads me to consider that the various theories which have been advanced at different times to explain the means by which the eye is enabled to adjust itself for distance are inconsistent with the anatomy of the organ of vision, and I trust that it will not be thought presumptuous to express my belief that this phenomenon will be found to be explicable by the simple law of optical science which requires nothing more than a change in the relative position of the lens and the retina to accommodate the sight to near and distant objects.

Fig. 8.

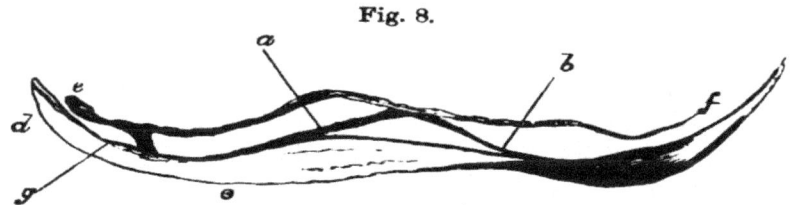

Section of the eye of a species of falcon.

a. Ciliary muscle.   *b.* Posterior elastic fibres.   *c.* Sclerotic.
d. Cornea.   *e.* Iris.   *f.* Choroid.   *g.* Anterior elastic fibres.

The last illustration is introduced for the purpose of exhibiting the view obtained of the ciliary muscle by removing the sclerotic and cornea in such a way as to expose the muscle lying on the choroid. The iris, the ciliary muscle, and the choroid form three distinct bands in the accompanying drawing.

Fig. 9.

Ciliary Muscle of the Pheasant's Eye.

ON THE ACTION OF THE SALTS OF IRON WHEN INTRODUCED DIRECTLY INTO THE BLOOD. By JAMES BLAKE, M.D., F.R.C.S. *San Francisco, California.*

SOME years ago I performed a series of experiments to ascertain the effects produced on living animals by the introduction of inorganic compounds directly into the blood; and although the results arrived at were I think interesting as pointing out the existence of a new law governing the reactions between living elements and inorganic compounds, these results have, I believe, remained unnoticed by physiologists up to the present time.

It is not my intention at present to enter fully on the subject, but I would state that after a series of observations made with compounds of twenty-nine of the elementary bodies, and involving some hundreds of experiments on living animals, the result arrived at was, that these inorganic compounds when introduced directly into the blood, give rise to reactions connected with their isomorphous relations, or that isomorphous substances produce analogous reactions. This law was verified as regards all the more important isomorphous groups, including compounds; in the magnesian group, of iron, zinc, manganese, copper, cadmium, lime and magnesia; in the platinum group, of platinum, palladium, osmium and iridium; in the arsenic group, of arsenic, antimony and phosphorus; in the chlorine group, of chlorine, bromine and iodine; in the potassium group, of potassa, ammonia, soda and silver; in the baryta group, of baryta, strontia and lead; in the alumina group, of alumina, ferric oxide and glucina; in the sulphur group, of sulphur and selenium. Some of these experiments were published in the proceedings of the British Association for the Advancement of Science, about 1844 to 1848, and a résumé in the American Journal of Medical Science for January, 1848[1].

The experiments I now have to bring forward were performed with the salts of iron. The fact that this metal forms

---

[1] The only marked exception to this law was found in the potassa group, the salts of potassa differing from those of ammonia in their action on the nervous system, and also from the salts of silver and soda in their action on the heart, and on the pulmonary circulation.

oxides, the salts of which are widely different in their iso-morphous relations, renders the investigation of its action in connection with the above law of considerable importance, and the part that this metal plays in the physiology of the blood, adds a still greater interest to any facts connected with its reactions.

Ex. 1.   A tube was introduced into the jugular vein of a strong healthy dog weighing about 20 lbs.   A hæmadynamometer was con-nected with the femoral artery—pressure in the arteries from 4 to 6 inches, heart's action regular ; 10 grains of sulphate of iron dissolved in ¾ oz. of water was injected into the jugular vein, in 12″ the heart was affected, its pulsations rendered weaker, and the arterial pressure became diminished; at 30″ it had fallen to 2 inches, oscillations only 0·2 in.   The pressure in the arteries soon again rose, at 1′. 30″ it was at 4 in., oscillations slight.   The animal did not appear to suffer any pain, the respiration and heart's action slower; at 5′ after the injec-tion the pressure in the arteries had again reached its natural level, although the pulse oscillations were not so great; respiration and heart's action normal.

Fifteen grains of the salt in the same quantity of water was again injected into the vein ; in 13″ the pressure in the arteries had fallen to 3 in., in 15″ to 1 in. ; it then began to rise, so that at 30″ after the injection it was 3 in., respiration slower but regular; at 1′. 30″ the pressure in the arteries was up to 5 in., heart's action regular, vomiting at 2 min., at 5 min. pressure 5 in., oscillations slight.

Inject 28 grs.   In 13″ heart's action stopped, the pressure fell rapidly to zero, nor were any more pulse oscillations observed, respi-ratory movements continued and efforts to vomit took place 2 min. after the heart had stopped; the animal was then dead.   The thorax was immediately opened.   The right auricle was found pulsating, the right cavities were much distended with dark fluid blood, the left contained about 1 oz. of blood, brighter than that in the right cavi-ties, but still not of a bright scarlet; it was quite fluid.   The heart was slightly irritable after the blood had been let out.   The blood did not coagulate, no clot having been formed after it had stood 48 hours[1].

Ex. 2.   In order to ascertain more accurately the general effects produced by the introduction of the sulphate of iron into the blood, a tube was inserted into the jugular vein, and immediately on the injection being made the animal was set at liberty.

The animal was a strong healthy dog weighing about 20 lbs.

Ten grains of sulphate of iron dissolved in half an ounce of water was injected into the jugular.   The animal showed no sign of suffer-ing, but after a few minutes appeared rather dull; 15 grs. in the

---

[1] The absence of or imperfect coagulability in the blood is found after the injection of the salts of zinc, nickel, cobalt and copper, in fact of all the metallic salts of the magnesian family.

same quantity of water was injected, in a few seconds the respiration appeared disturbed, the animal was dull and not inclined to move, but there was no expression of pain.

After a few minutes 20 grs. was injected—no expression of pain ; after three minutes vomiting, and the animal was dull and listless. After an interval of ten minutes, 25 grs. of the salt dissolved in six drachms of water was injected. In 15″ the animal fell down, and in 48″ respiratory movements had ceased and the animal lay to all appearance dead; no pulsations of the heart could be felt. After it had remained about a minute in this state, respiratory movements again commenced and the heart could be felt beating. The animal gradually recovered, and soon regained consciousness. It did not appear to suffer, but lay on the side perfectly sensible and wagged its tail when caressed. After about a quarter of an hour it could stand and even walk about when lifted on its legs, although 70 grs. of sulphate of iron dissolved in about 2 oz. of water had been introduced into the blood in twenty minutes. The animal was killed by injecting a solution containing 40 grs. of the salt into the veins—in a few seconds the heart was stopped. On opening the thorax, the appearances presented were the same as in the last experiment. The blood remained fluid.

Ex. 3. In order to ascertain the effect of the salt on the passage of the blood through the systemic capillaries, a tube was inserted into the axillary artery of a dog, the point looking towards the heart. The hæmadynamometer was connected with the femoral artery On injecting a solution containing 15 grs. of the salt through the axillary artery into the aorta, there was a slight general spasm. In a few seconds the animal was quiet; and the pressure in the arteries 30″ after the injection was about half an inch less than before. On injecting a stronger solution the respiration was suspended, and the heart stopped by asphyxia.

The following experiments have been performed with the sulphate of the peroxide of iron, the general conditions being the same as in the former experiments :—

Ex. 4. Two grains of the salt dissolved in 2 oz. of water was injected into the jugular vein of a strong healthy dog weighing about 20 lbs. Twelve seconds after the injection the pressure in the arteries, which before the injection was at 5-6 inches, began to diminish rapidly : at 45″ it was only 1½ inches, although the heart was felt beating and slight oscillations caused by its action were noticed; 2 min. after the injection the pressure in the arteries began to rise, and in another minute it was up to 6 inches, action of the heart regular, respiratory movements rather laboured ; the animal apparently not much affected.

After an interval of fifteen minutes, 3 grs. of the salt in 2 oz. of water was injected into the vein. In 12″ the pressure began to diminish, and in 45″ it was nearly at zero, although oscillations caused by the action of the heart and violent respiratory efforts still took place. At 45″ the respiration became much affected and there were violent struggles. At 3 min. the respiration stopped; and at 3′. 30″ the animal was dead. Convulsive movements of the diaphragm continued for 2″. At 4 min. after the injection the thorax was opened. The left auricle and ventricle were found still contracting; the right cavities were so distended with blood that they would not contract; but on letting out the blood rhythmical contractions again took place. There was a small quantity of scarlet blood in the left cavities, which coagulated. The blood from the right side was dark, and coagulated firmly after it had been let out. The lungs were of a bright scarlet colour and very much contracted. There can be no doubt but that in this experiment death was caused by the blood containing the salt causing contraction of the pulmonary capillaries, so that no blood reached the left side of the heart.

Ex. 5. In order to ascertain if the presence of the salt in the blood caused contraction of the systemic capillaries or arteries, tubes were introduced as in Ex. 3. The pressure before the injection was 6-7 inches. A solution containing 5 grs. of the salt in 2 oz. of water was injected through the axillary artery; in 4″ after the injection the pressure in the arteries began to rise, and in 45″ it was equal to 12 inches of mercury; heart's action much quickened, oscillations slight; respiratory movements ceased at 1′, but the action of the heart seemed unaffected. The respiratory movements remained suspended for 1′. 30″, the animal being to all appearance dead, but the pressure in the arteries still kept up to 12 inches. After being suspended for 1′. 30″ respiration again commenced, it was slow (10 in a minute) but regular and not laboured. At 3′. 30″ after the injection, the pressure in the arteries had fallen to 10 inches; the heart's action slower. At 4′. 30″ heart stopped for 5″ and then recommenced beating, the pressure rising from 7 to 10 inches. At 5′. 30″ heart's action slower, pressure diminishing. At 8′ pressure still 10 inches, the animal to all appearance dead, with the exception of the respiratory movements, which were slow and regular. At 9′ respiration ceased, and the pressure fell rapidly, although the heart continued beating. On opening the thorax, the heart was found contracting. Both cavities contained dark blood, which coagulated firmly. These experiments will suffice to show the marked difference there is between the action of the proto- and persalts of iron, when introduced directly into the blood; for whilst large quantities (as much as forty or fifty grains) of the former can be mixed with the blood without affecting its passage either through the systemic or pulmonary capillaries, two or three grains of the persalt is enough to arrest the passage of the blood through the capillaries of the lungs, or to cause such a contraction in the systemic capillaries or smaller arteries as to require a pressure equal to 12 inches of mercury to overcome the resistance[1].

[1] It might be that this obstruction to the circulation is caused by a physical change produced in the blood, rather than by contraction of the vessels themselves; but I am inclined to think that the quantity of the salt required is too small to cause any marked physical change in the blood; besides the same

The quantity of the different salts required to produce death is extremely different, for whilst 60 to 70 grs. of the protosalt can be circulating in the blood without producing any fatal symptoms, four or five grains of the persalt will destroy life[1].

As regards the action of the salts of iron on the heart, the protosalts evidently tend to diminish its irritability, as the pulsations become slower and the pressure in the arteries diminishes. In larger doses, the action of the heart is arrested. The persalts on the other hand appear not to exert any direct action on the heart; they certainly do not diminish the strength of its contractions, or it would not go on beating under the enormous pressure to which its internal surface must be submitted, when the arterial pressure is equal to 12 inches of mercury.

The action of the protosalts on the nervous system shows itself in slower respiration, a peculiar state of quietness, in which the animal does not wish to move, although it has the power and is perfectly sensible, and by inducing vomiting. When introduced directly into the arteries, death is caused by its action on the nervous system. It is probable that the general effects produced by the persalts are owing to the important changes caused in the circulation. On first injecting it into the veins, the pulmonary circulation is arrested and venous congestion results: the supply of blood to the left side of the heart being cut off, the circulation of arterial blood through the body is almost suspended. When injected directly into the arteries the curious nervous phenomena that result are probably owing to the great pressure to which the nervous centres are submitted, and which appears to abolish entirely the functions of the encephalon, although respiration and heart-

effect is produced by substances which have no physical effect on the blood. An infusion of digitalis will cause quite as great an obstacle to the passage of the blood through the capillaries, and yet it does not give rise to any recognizable physical change in the blood. The known hæmastatic properties of the persalts of iron and of digitalis are probably connected with this action on the blood-vessels.

[1] The poisonous properties of the persalts of iron should lead to caution in their employment. I have seen deaths recorded after the use of these salts for the destruction of nævi in which I have no doubt the hæmadynamometer would have showed obstruction in the pulmonary circulation. In the *Berlin Allgemeine Med. Cent. Zeitung* for January 11th, 1868, a death is recorded in which the symptoms plainly indicate fatal pulmonary obstruction.

pulsation are kept up for some minutes. As to the cause of the final cessation of the respiratory movements, I am inclined to think that it is owing to the effect of continued pressure producing some state of the nervous tissue which interferes with its reflexibility and not owing to any chemical changes caused by the presence of the salt in the blood. In the more appreciable physical changes produced in the blood the two classes of salts are as different in their action as in every other respect. The protosalts give rise to changes in the blood which prevent its coagulation after death, whilst the salts of the peroxide do not at all interfere with its coagulation, but I believe render the clot firmer. Such are the more striking facts caused by the introduction of the ferrous and ferric salts directly into the blood. The difference in the physiological reactions produced by two classes of salts of the same metal is in itself a curious fact, but it becomes I think far more interesting when we find that these two classes of salts of the same metal, differing so strongly in their physiological action, yet have their strict physiological analogues in salts of other metals very different from iron. Thus the substances which when introduced directly into the blood produce effects analogous to the protosalts of iron, are the salts of magnesia, zinc, nickel, copper and cadmium ; whilst the salts that are analogous to the ferric salts in their physiological action are the salts of alumina and glucina. On the important bearing of these facts on the question of isomorphism and physiological reactions it is needless to enlarge. As regards the chemistry of respiration, the above experiments would show that the salts of the protoxide of iron, although so readily passing to a higher degree of oxidation when out of the body, are in some way preserved from the action of oxygen when mixed with the blood. Were not this the case a sufficient quantity of the persalt to prove fatal would soon be formed when fifty to seventy grains of the sulphate had been introduced into the blood. On the other hand it would seem that the salts of the peroxide cannot be rapidly reduced whilst circulating with the blood, otherwise the effects of the small quantities used in some of my experiments would not have been so persistent.

ON THE ANAL FIN APPENDAGES OF EMBIOTOCOID FISHES. By James Blake, M.D., F.R.C.S., *Professor of Obstetrics in Toland Medical College, St Francisco, California.* (Pl. II. figs. 1 and 2.)

In the class of fishes in which the ovum is retained in the body of the female during developement, it is evident that some anatomical arrangement must exist by which the semen can be conveyed into the interior of the ovisac. In the embiotocoid fishes the ovisac opens on the surface by a narrow canal or oviduct, the lower parts of the canal being surrounded by a sphincter, so that the ingress of water containing spermatozoa would be extremely difficult, if not impossible. The male is furnished with a very rudimentary tubercular penis; and as the orifice of the oviduct forms but a very slight depression on the ventral edge of the fish, it is difficult to imagine how impregnation could take place, unless pretty close contact could be maintained during coition. From the direction of the orifices of the oviduct and penis, coition must take place whilst the male and female are in reversed positions, so that the head of one points to the tail of the other. In this position when the penis is in contact with the mouth of the oviduct, the ventral fins of one fish will be in contact with or near the anal fin of the other. In all the embiotocoid fishes I have examined, the anal fin of the male is furnished, particularly during the season of coition, with certain appendages by which the ventral fins of the female can take a firm hold of the male and thus secure perfect contact whilst insemination takes place. These appendages consist of a groove along the base of the anterior part of the fin, a mammary protuberance on each side of the fin, transverse bony plates with serrated edges and cartilaginous ridges, and tubercles with roughened surfaces. The groove at the base of the fin has been found in all the species I have examined. It is formed by a thickening of the substance of the anterior border of the fin, and by the secretion of a layer of tenacious epithelium on the surface of the fin membrane. This secretion is formed generally over the anterior part of the surface of the fin, being much greater about the season of impregnation, in fact almost disappearing when the generative organs are quiescent. In the larger species it is fully an eighth of an inch thick, and as it terminates rather suddenly at a short distance from the body it leaves a well marked groove in which the edges of the ventral fins of the female are received, and thus the ventral surfaces can be held together. As before stated, this groove has been found in all the species I have examined. In addition to this there is found in all the species some arrangement for steadying the bodies in the longitudinal direction. This differs in different species. In Embiotica—Damolichthys Toeniotaca—Hypsurus and Cymatogaster, we find mammary appendages projecting from each side of the front part of the anal fin. They are formed of a tough external membrane enclosing a cavity containing base cellular tissue well supplied by blood-vessels: from the front part there projects a tubular prolongation like a teat; in fact so close a resemblance does the organ bear to a cow's udder, that it has served to give the specific name *vacca* to one of the order Damolichthys. In the genera Holconatus Amphisticus and Hyperprosopion these mammary protuberances are not found, but their place is supplied by transverse bony plates with serrated edges, extending from the base to the edge of the fin, parallel to the fin rays, and situated farther back on the fin. In front of these plates, and near the edge of the fin, are two cartilaginous ridges, one on each side. They run for some distance nearly parallel to the edge of the fin, and then posteriorly turn upwards towards the belly. As the ridges are inclined upwards and forwards a sort of *cul de sac* is formed at the bend, which may serve to receive the ends of the ventral fin rays. It is during the season at which insemination takes place that these fin appendages become most developed. After this has passed and *pari passu* with the diminution in the size of the testicles, these appendages become smaller; in two or three months the thickened epithelium has almost disappeared, and the mammary pouches are so reduced in size as to be barely discoverable; but even in its most undeveloped state the anal fin of the male can always be distinguished from that of the female[1]. In the genera with the bony plates no change takes place in these appendages, but the cartilaginous ridges become smaller, and the thickened epithelium disappears.

The only peculiarity in the structure of the female fish that can assist in maintaining contact during coition, is the existence of a thin membranous abdominal wall immediately in front of the ventral fin; this could easily be forced in so as to form a groove, in which the thickened anterior edge of the anal fin of the male would be received and possibly clasped during coition.

[Figs. 1 and 2 in Pl. II. are representations of the testes and anal fins of the male Damolicthys vacca at different periods of the year, drawn from specimens kindly sent by Dr Blake to the Museum of the University of Cambridge. In fig. 1, taken at spawning time, the testes (TT) are large, and the mammary protuberance with its tubular teat-like process on the side of the fin is well seen. The anterior edge of the fin is also thick. In fig. 2, taken at another time of the year, the testes are smaller; a slight thickening and scar-like appearance are the only relic of the mammary protuberance; and the anterior edge of the fin is sharp.

I may observe that specimens shewing the delicate fringe-like membranous appendages to the fins in the fœtus of embiotocoid fishes, described by Dr Blake in the last No. of this Journal, have also been forwarded by him to Cambridge, and are placed in the Museum of Comparative Anatomy. G. M. H.]

---

[1] In the *Ann. des Sc. Nat.* Mai et Juin 1867, M. Baudelot describes the formation of epithelial tubercles on the heads and bodies of certain fishes. They appear to be analogous to the thickened epithelium found on the fins of the embiotocoid fishes, particularly as regards their temporary character. The author of the paper considers their shedding analogous to the moulting of birds.

AN ATTEMPT TO APPLY CHEMICAL PRINCIPLES IN EXPLANATION OF THE ACTION OF REMEDIES AND POISONS. By W. H. BROADBENT, M.D.

THE object of the present communication is sufficiently indicated by the title, as is also the method of investigation which has been followed, viz. the deductive. In the establishment of the relation between Chemical properties and Physiological action, the final step by which the effects of a given substance on the animal organism are referred to the laws of Chemistry and Physics must necessarily be a deduction; and, this being the case, it seems reasonable to expect that by starting from these laws in the first instance, and endeavouring to apply them to the explanation of the vast array of facts, already well established, some insight may be obtained into the problem which awaits solution. In any case, deductive reasoning is the best guide to experiment.

The two following propositions, then, are taken as axioms, or at any rate as postulates. 1. That there must be some relation between the organism and the substance administered on which the effects depend. 2. That so far as the substance is concerned, the basis of this relation can only be its chemical properties, using the term chemical in its widest sense. From these certain corollaries follow, the one most important for the present purpose being, that the action of Food, Remedies, and Poisons, must be capable of explanation on the same principles, and that the difference in their effects is to be referred to, and may be explained by, differences in their chemical composition.

It would not be difficult to show that the gradation between food and poison which, on this view, should be traceable, actually exists; but the proposition is taken as a guide in another way. The various substances comprised in food may be arranged in classes; and much is known of the uses of each class in the economy, and of the mode in which these uses are subserved. This knowledge furnishes a clue to the action of bodies not usually taken as food, but which, in larger or smaller doses, are poisons or remedies.

In order to follow out this clue it is necessary to consider very generally the operations taking place in the animal organism. They may be divided into two great classes, (a) for maintenance of structure, (β) for evolution of force, which, while mutually interdependent, going on at the same time in every part and inextricably mixed up in every function, are yet distinct, and in character essentially antagonistic—the one constructive—the other destructive. In the maintenance of structure or the nutritive operations (which consist essentially of the conversion of amorphous pabulum into tissue), the direction of the processes is towards the formation of highly specialised structures and of complex chemical molecules, which implies latency of energy. The evolution of force, on the other hand, implies oxidation, the breaking up of complex molecules and the disintegration of tissue or blood.

Considering foods in the same general way, the primary division of the substances used as food is into organic and mineral; and there may be traced a striking relation between the two classes of food on the one hand and the two classes of physiological operations on the other. The organic foods constitute the mass of the solid matters of the blood and the bulk of the tissues; but ultimately their destination is to undergo oxidation with evolution of force. The mineral constituents of food, on the contrary, form a small proportion of the blood and (except the lime-salts of bone) take an insignificant part in the construction of the textures. They cannot yield force by their oxidation; but in some way they influence the nutritive operations.

These statements are made broadly, and much time would be required for their full development and exemplification. A certain degree of qualification also would be necessary; but in the main they hold good and are true when extended to poisons. Inorganic poisons, like inorganic food, act primarily on the organic processes and affect the structural integrity of the tissues. Organic poisons affect primarily the evolution of force; and any structural lesions which may occur are secondary. Direct chemical action, such as corrosion by acids and alkalies, which may be compared to traumatic injury, is excluded from the consideration. As illustrations, let arsenic and mercury be taken on one side, strychnine and opium on the other.

From these preliminary considerations it is clear that the action of organic and inorganic remedies and poisons must be investigated apart. I have endeavoured elsewhere to show that the explanation of the action of mineral matters is to be sought mainly in the varying affinity of these substances for the different organic proximate principles, especially albumen, and in the influence which is exerted on cell growth by the combination of the mineral salts, &c. with the organic principle. In the present paper, an attempt is made to trace a relation between the organic substances which affect the evolution of that form of force manifested by the nervous system, and the chemical action by which this force is evolved, which may in some measure explain their action.

The forms of force manifested in the animal organism are heat, motion, and nervous action, and the common source of all is oxidation or some equivalent change. It is sufficiently well established to need no discussion here, that the oxidation which evolves heat takes place in the tissues generally—that evolving motion in the muscles, the instruments of motion—that evolving nerve-force in the nervous structures. In the case of muscle and nerve, physiologists are not agreed whether the matter oxidized is furnished exclusively by the blood or partly by the structures.

As the special subject of investigation is the action of poisons on the nervous system, it will be necessary to realize, as far as possible, the chemical conditions attending the evolution of nerve-force: but, first, what are the poisons primarily and directly affecting the nervous system? Almost any poison capable of destroying life rapidly without the intervention of local corrosion or local inflammation, must appear to act on the nervous system. The effects are necessarily manifested through the nervous functions. For example, suppose the blood corpuscles to be so changed as to cease to carry oxygen, or to act as the medium of interchange between the air and the tissues ; the *obvious* effect would be suspension of the nervous functions. This is thoroughly recognized, and indeed most attempts to explain the action of the more powerful organic poisons have turned on antecedent effects on the blood. It will be a distinct step gained when we are able to distinguish clearly between those poisons which act directly on the nervous structures and those in which the action on the nervous centres is secondary to and consequent upon changes induced in the blood. Without attempting to do this in an absolute manner, it may be concluded that the action on the nervous system is direct (1) when the effects are almost instantaneous, (2) when the poisonous dose is externally small, (3) when the nervous system is affected unequally in its different parts. It must not always be concluded that because the blood presents naked-eye changes after death the cause of death lies in an altered condition of the blood. The action of chloroform and of ether is on the nervous system and is essentially the same ; but one, ether, renders the blood dark, the other leaves it red ; a difference which, no doubt, accounts for some of the subordinate differences observed in their effects, but does not destroy the essential similarity in their main action. So again too much weight must not be attached to the changes detected by spectrum analysis without a due consideration of all the circumstances of the experiment : e.g.—if the blood has been taken after death by the poison, whether the mode of death might not have had some influence ; if the poison has been added to blood drawn from the living animal, whether the proportion of poison to blood is not more than would have been necessary to produce a fatal result.

In endeavouring to obtain an approximate idea of the kind of chemical change by means of which nerve-force is evolved, we may compare the circumstances attending its manifestation with those which accompany the liberation of heat. The following peculiarities are noted. (1) While heat is evolved in the tissues generally the nervous force requires for its manifestation specialized structures. (2) Whereas the liberation of heat is continuous and comparatively equable, nerve-action is irregular and intermittent in point of time, taking place only in obedience to some so-called stimulus or impulse either from without or from some other part of the nervous system, and varying in intensity with the stimulus. Translated into chemical language, this means that for the oxidation to take place by which nerve-force is evolved it is not sufficient for the oxygen and the oxidizable substance to be in presence of each other. Some impulse from without is required to determine the combination, like the electric spark for the mixture of oxygen and hydrogen, flame for gunpowder and concussion for nitro-glycerine. (3) While the blood and all the structures of the body (the nervous perhaps excepted, see Chossat's exps.) constitute a store of potential energy from which heat can be evolved, the storing of potential nervous energy takes place in the nervous structures only. For example, a nerve submitted to the interrupted current for a length of time ceases to respond, or is exhausted, and recovers its properties only by repose and a due supply of blood. Again, there is the sense of fatigue and exhaustion after prolonged physical or mental exertion. Still another example is found in the need for sleep which is experienced not only after bodily labour, when the store of force-yielding material in the blood might be supposed to be exhausted, but without any such drain. The demand for repose and repair is local and is mainly in the cerebral hemispheres and sensory ganglia. Accumulated potential energy means chemically the storing up of a substance usually of complex constitution, by oxidation of which the energy becomes active. (4) Finally, it is to be noted that while oxygen is in the highest degree necessary for the action of every part of the nervous system, the urgency of the demand is different in the different centres. The immediate cause of death in asphyxia is suspension of nervous action from want of oxygen; and the order in which the functions are suspended is from above downwards. So in the slow asphyxia seen in the last stage of some diseases of the lungs, there is somnolence passing into coma while the reflex function of the cord persists.

Putting together the conclusions derived from these consi-derations, it would appear that there is accumulated in the nervous structures by nutrition a substance which, in the pre-sence of duly oxygenated blood and on the application of a given impulse, undergoes oxidation proportionate to the impulse and yields the peculiar form of force which constitutes nerve-action. But the fact that an impulse from without is required to determine the occurrence of the oxidation, and that the amount of oxida-tion as indicated by the force evolved, varies with the intensity of the impulse, points to a peculiarity in the oxidizable matter, a peculiarity which I have ventured to call 'chemical tension.' This property I shall endeavour to define and explain more fully later. For the present it is sufficient to say that it is due to the presence of nitrogen or of some body having similar chemical relations, but that it does not necessarily belong to all nitrogenized matter, and is not met with in any combinations of C, H and O only. An extreme example of this chemical tension is furnished by nitro-glycerine, which may for the pre-sent serve as an illustration. The tension here is manifested by the well-known explosive property of nitro-glycerine. It is stable in the sense of not undergoing gradual decomposition and will even resist the application of flame, but concussion deter-mines instantly a change in the arrangement of its elementary constituents, which is attended with violent explosion.

It will be understood that this is tentative hypothesis, and that nothing higher is claimed for it. It derives a certain amount of support however from the fact that the Protagon of Liebreich, and the derivative of this, Neurine, recently identified by Wurtz with Hydrate of Trimethyl-Oxethyl-Ammonium, have the property of chemical tension in a certain degree. -

Turning now to the poisons which act directly and power-fully on the nervous system, it is found that they vary greatly in chemical properties. A large proportion of them are alka-loids, either crystalline, like strychnia, morphia, &c. or fluid and volatile, like nicotine or conia; but others are acid, prussic acid for example; others again are neutral, such as nitro-glycerine. Two points are however common to the entire group; they all contain nitrogen or some equivalent, and they all possess the property of chemical tension. The mere presence of nitrogen cannot be the source of the poisonous influence. It possesses no chemical energy which could endow it with such powers. It is so devoid of positive properties as to act as the diluent for oxygen in the atmosphere ; and it is present in almost all proportions in substances which are inert as well as in the albuminoid foods. Nitrogen is nevertheless the pivot on which the deadly influence turns, as it is the source of the chemical tension.

Nitrogen is pre-eminently the mobile element. Its affinities for the other elementary bodies which are present in organic matter are feeble as compared with the affinity these have for each other. When therefore in a molecule containing C, H and N or C, H, N and O the arrangement of the elementary bodies is not such that the mutual affinities of C, H and O co-operate to maintain the integrity of the molecule, there may be a more or less powerful tendency on the part of the C, H and O to re-arrange themselves without regard to the N, or to combine with O or H_2O when these are presented. This is what is meant by chemical tension ; and it differs from mere instability, which may be described as a readiness to yield to the disintegrating influence of forces acting from without, in the fact that there exists an internal or intrinsic force or tendency which, under appropriate conditions, determines change in a certain definite direction and with a certain degree of energy. A body in a state of chemical tension may be perfectly stable in the absence of the special conditions which liberate its atoms from the existing state of combination ; and in the act of change it is capable of exercising influence on surrounding matter, while an unstable substance is simply passive. In the case of nitro-glycerine, the example previously given, the source of the tension is the introduction into the molecule of glycerine $C_3 H_8 O_3$ of 3 equivalents of NO_2 in the place of 3H, giving $C_3 H_5 (NO_2)_3 O_3$. The large amount of O thus imported into the molecule in combination with N, upon which it has a comparatively feeble hold, deranges the balance of affinities. On concussion it leaves the N to combine with C and H, which it does with explosive violence.

Dislocation of C and H from N cannot be illustrated by such striking examples as are presented when O takes part in the process (unless one is found in the explanation given later in this paper of the poisonous action of prussic acid); nor is it easy in all cases to point out the exact way in which the chemical tension is produced. One very important manner however in which the balance of affinities is deranged and the condition of tension brought about is by departure from a stable type of constitution. Such a type is ammonia or an ammonium salt, and to one or other of these a great number of organic substances are referred, either by substitution of a complex carbo-hydrogen molecule for one, two, or more of the atoms of H; or as residues in which successive atoms of H are removed in combination with the O of an oxyacid by a process of dehydration, leaving amides, imides, or nitriles. When the type remains unbroken and the new compound is formed simply by substitution it usually retains some of the characters of the type, and tension is not always induced; but in the residues, and especially the nitriles, there is a complete departure from the typical constitution and characters. Now, most, if not all, of the markedly poisonous alkaloids belong to the class of nitrile bases; and the relation between this feature in their constitution and their physiological action has been most opportunely and conclusively demonstrated by the remarkable researches of Drs Crum Brown and Fraser published in this Journal, in which they have shown that by the introduction of methyl-iodide into the nitrile molecule of poisons the effects of which are so diverse as those of morphia, strychnia, nicotine, &c. by which the constitution is carried back a step towards the ammonium type, a similar modification of their action is produced, their poisonous properties being greatly diminished and entirely altered in character. It is interesting also to note that conia, which is an imide base and therefore less condensed or less removed from the normal type, is a much less powerful poison than nicotine, the nitrile which it most resembles, and that its action is mainly on the motor nervous apparatus (Dr John Harley, *Gulstonian Lectures*, 1868). The condensation of Drs Crum Brown and Fraser is a particular case of chemical tension. That it is not the sole source of poisonous action is shown by such examples as nitroglycerine, and there are numerous examples of condensed bodies which are not poisonous.

If, as seems to be the case, chemical tension is common to the entire group of poisons acting directly on the nervous system, and if they have no other property in common, if further the poisonous energy varies with the degree of tension, as is indicated by the experiments of Drs Brown and Fraser, there is established a relationship of coincidence between the chemical property and the physiological effect. Further, this relationship is conceivably, and even probably, one of causation. A substance cannot by its mere presence in the blood or nervous centres produce the results which follow the administration of these poisons. It must induce change or undergo change ; and it scarcely needs elaborate argument to show that the probability is that it undergoes change, while the comparative constancy of the effect of the same substance indicates that the direction of the change is determined by the constitution of the particular poison. Let the deduction which points to chemical tension as the cause of the peculiarity in the mode of evolution of nerve-force be accepted, and we have, in the introduction into the blood and presence in the nervous centres of substances having varying degrees and different directions of chemical tension which will have different relations with the tension of the nervous matter, a means of influencing the manifestation of nerve-action which is in a certain degree capable of being understood.

There is much that is vague in the conclusion as it stands. Some little additional light will be thrown upon it in the further course of this paper ; and it will be expanded, defined and more or less modified by deeper knowledge and more extended experiment. But a wider area of speculation may be taken. Looking at nerve action as a result of oxidation it is possible to trace in the various methods by which this oxidation may be influenced analogies with the conditions which affect ordinary combustion. Probably still closer analogies might be found in the oxidation which, taking place in the cells of the galvanic battery, evolves the form of force known as Galvanism.

The conditions which influence combustion are, (1) the supply of oxygen, (2) the composition and state of aggregation of the combustible, (3) the degree in which the process of oxidation is interfered with by products of combustion or bodies having a similar influence. CO_2 and H_2O are often looked upon as specially antagonistic to combustion, because they are its products, while N is considered merely obstructive. The difference is however due only to their higher vapour density, or in other words, to the greater weight of matter to be set in motion.

In pursuing the analogy suggested, it is of course necessary to bear in mind the differences between combustion and oxidation in the moist state, the modifying conditions present in the animal economy, and the peculiarity of the oxidation which yields nerve-force. For example, while death by asphyxia is perfectly comparable to arrest of combustion by the shutting off of oxygen, respiration of undiluted oxygen is by no means equivalent to the supply of pure oxygen in combustion. When an animal is placed in an atmosphere of oxygen there are no signs of excitement, no evidences of intensification of nerve-action, and eventually it dies comatose. Apparently the energy of the undiluted oxygen is expended on the blood, which is oxidized and spoiled instead of being merely oxygenated.

The analogies to the conditions enumerated which are traceable in the action of poisons on the nervous system are as follows:

1. Deprivation of oxygen has its presumed analogue in poisoning by prussic acid. By the dislocating influence of N, C and H are supposed to be set free in the nascent state in the nervous centres and to appropriate the O brought by the blood for the oxidation which should yield nerve-force. The converse of this, liberation of O, is not likely to take place, as O is never present in an organic compound in excess of the proportion required for the full oxidation of the other elemetary constituents. 2. The influence on the energy of combustion by the composition and character of the combustible is, in some

sort, represented by the presence in the nervous structures of substances having chemical tension, holding varying relations to the tension of nervous matter. 3. The action of the anæsthetic vapours and gases furnishes a strict parallel to the influence of CO_2 &c. on combustion. This last analogy may be taken as completely established. It constitutes the rationale of the action of anæsthetics originated by Dr Snow, now generally accepted.

Considerable importance is attached to the establishment of the explanation here given of the mode of action of prussic acid. Stated more fully and explicitly this theory is as follows. The prussic acid is carried by the blood to the nerve-centres ; under the influence of the affinities here in operation, which normally determine the oxidation which evolves nerve-force, its elements are dislocated from each other ; and the carbon and hydrogen, liberated in the nascent condition, appropriate the oxygen destined for the evolution of nerve-force which is thus arrested. The dislocation is permitted by the feebleness of the bond of union formed by nitrogen, the pivot of the molecule. The prussic acid does not deoxidise the entire mass of blood. The quantity which constitutes a fatal dose would be utterly insufficient. It does not kill by preventing the oxidation of the blood, the time in which it can destroy life being too short.

It is not necessary to describe minutely the phenomena of poisoning by prussic acid. The animal staggers, then falls and is convulsed. The respiration, at first frequent and deep, becomes slow and gasping, and finally ceases; while after apparent death the heart continues to beat for some minutes. (I have found no exception to the rule that the heart's action thus persists even when overwhelming doses of the poison have been used.) Most observers have noted the essential similarity between death by hydrocyanic acid and death by asphyxia. Again, the remedy for asphyxia is also the remedy for prussic acid poisoning, viz. artificial respiration ; and oxygen is said to be more efficacious than air. It may almost be considered as generally recognized that the cause of death is the same in both, i.e. arrest of the oxidation which evolves nerve-force. The point to be determined then is, how this arrest is brought about. One explanation given has been that the respiratory movements are paralyzed. This is disproved by the merest observation of the phenomena. The respiratory movements are the last to cease except those of the heart; and were it otherwise the cause of the paralysis of the respiratory apparatus would be still to seek. Another, the most recent and plausible, is that prussic acid deoxidizes the blood without itself combining with the oxygen (Preyer). This again only throws the explanation a step further back. It must be shown how this deoxidization is effected. To accept it as an ultimate fact would leave us still quite in the dark as to the real mode of action. The minuteness of the fatal dose in proportion to the mass of blood on which the effect is supposed to be produced also renders this explanation inherently improbable, in the highest degree, from a scientific point of view.

Examining now the hypothesis here advanced, it will be admitted that so far as it is an explanation at all, it is a real and sufficient one, i.e. it refers the action of the poison to known chemical laws. Nascent carbon and hydrogen set free in the nervous structure to exercise their affinity for oxygen, would seize it and anticipate the normal oxidation. Again, if (as we may almost say science demands) a body producing effects on the organism does so in virtue of some change which itself undergoes, the simple composition of prussic acid HCN scarcely permits of any other change than a resolution into its elements and their individual combination with oxygen, a reducing action comparable to that of cyanide of potassium KCy or KCN, which is much employed as a deoxidizing agent in chemistry. That prussic acid will undergo change is rendered probable by its constitution as a nitrile (formio-nitrile); and that it is by means of such a change that it acts is apparent from the fact that when the elements are held together by some supporting affinity, as in the ferrocyanides, no poisonous influence is present. A more remarkable example is furnished by hydrosulphocyanic acid, which is poisonous (i.e. undergoes change), but reinforced by a base is innocent (Miller). The destruction of prussic acid implied by this hypothesis is not at all incompatible with its presence in the blood after death and its escape in the excretions. It is mingled uniformly with the blood but undergoes decomposition only in the nervous structures. A certain proportion only of the blood passes through these; that consequently which has circulated in the rest of the body will contain it unchanged.

Experiments have been made for the purpose of ascertaining whether the previous respiration of undiluted oxygen would in any measure prevent or retard the action of prussic acid. The animals employed were frogs and rats.

The following abstract of the notes of the principal experiments on the rats shows that the results obtained were by no means uniform, but in some of the cases the effects of the poison were retarded in a degree quite beyond the action of mere accidental causes. It may be stated that the oxygen in which the rats were placed was constantly renewed by a current passing through the chamber—that a screw syringe was employed in the injections, and every precaution taken to equalize the conditions in comparative experiments: no excitement or discomfort was manifested by the rats on being placed in oxygen, but unless they were disturbed the respirations became more shallow and less rapid.

1. Prussic acid (pharmacopœial strength, large dose) 10 drops. Symptoms at once. Apparent death in $1\frac{1}{2}'$. Heart continued to beat $4\frac{1}{2}'$.

2. Similar dose after being in oxygen for 11'. First symptoms in $2\frac{1}{4}'$. Apparent death at 6'. Heart beat up to 11'.

3. Similar dose after 20' inhalation of oxygen. Death apparently not delayed.

4. Prussic acid, (moderate dose) 3 drops. Apparent death in 1'. 30".

5. Inhalation of oxygen 15'. Prussic acid, same dose. Symptoms in 50". Apparent death in 2'.

(The notes of 3, 4 and 5, and of other experiments made at the same time, were dictated to an assistant, and proved on examination to be imperfect and confused. The general result however was that no important retardation of the action was observed.)

A minimum fatal dose was now sought, and it was found that while one drop was usually fatal after about 8 or 10 minutes, one rat survived it with the following train of symptoms.

6. Prussic acid one drop at 2°. 51". From 55" to 1'. 45" afterwards, staggering at times. At 2' falls on abdomen, at 2'. 25" rolls over on side, 2'. 35" convulsed, 2'. 45" quiet. At 4' lies on side

gasping at long intervals as if just about to die. At 5′ the gasps replaced by a kind of snort. From this gradual recovery. At 3°. 5′ i. e. 14′ after the injection, lying on side breathing deeply, still unable to stand.

Two out of three rats which had been in oxygen died, but one had made his escape while being removed from the oxygen, and was only secured after a chase. In the other symptoms appeared at 1′. 25″, at 4′ he was gasping, at 5′ snorting, the precise moment at which death occurred was not noted.

7. The precise time this rat was in oxygen was not noted, but he was frequently disturbed and made to move about. Prussic acid one drop at 4°. 41′. Seen to pant soon after being put down, and up to 3′ after the injection had the alarmed aspect observed in other rats just before the access of symptoms. None however occurred, and in 6 minutes he seemed quite well. Some time after he was put under a glass shade and a little of the poison was diffused in the atmosphere. Symptoms at once came on, showing that he was amenable to its influence.

Experiments were also made with a view to ascertain the comparative effects of inhalation of the acid in air on the one hand and oxygen on the other.

8. Rat placed under a glass shade fitting closely to the table, 2 drops of prussic acid introduced under the margin by means of the syringe. Uneasy at once. In 1′ staggering ; in 1′. 30″ lying on side panting. At 2′, when apparently all but dead, removed. No response when tail violently pinched. At 10′ lies on side panting and trembling. Respiration 48 in 15″ very shallow. No response when tail pinched. Up to 21′ had remained on side trembling, but now when placed on feet remained, and got up when turned over. Gradually recovered.

9. Another rat, rather smaller, placed under same shade with an atmosphere of oxygen. Two drops of prussic acid introduced as before. Very little immediate effect. Rubbing nose and washing face at 3′. At 3′. 15″ very decided symptoms, staggering, &c. At 4′ still on his legs but looking very ill. The symptoms did not go beyond this, and on a little more oxygen being introduced he was soon quite recovered.

It might be claimed that these results, such as they are, support equally the hypothesis which attributes the action of prussic acid to deoxidation of the blood. The question will be decided on other grounds than such as are furnished by these experiments, and discussion of it with reference to them would do little to settle it. Again, were the hypothesis dependent on these experiments, much might be said to account for the variable results. The most constant effect of the inhalation of oxygen was the retardation of the access of symptoms, and this is theoretically the most important, since supposing the blood to contain an excess of oxygen, this would be appropriated by the tissues generally while, *ex hypothesi*, the prussic acid is destroyed only in the nervous structures.

In the case of frogs the results were for a time unaccountably irregular, and were explained only by the discovery that prussic acid has little effect upon them. The most convenient method of administering a poison to these animals is to apply it in the fluid form to the skin, when it is rapidly absorbed; but hydrocyanic acid being so volatile that it evaporates before absorption can take place, a glass shade was placed over the frog, and the poison was really taken by respiration. Usually restlessness was manifest from the first, but about 4 minutes elapsed before any symptom due to the action of the poison was manifested, when the respiratory movements became irregular, and sooner or later the mouth was opened. In an experiment made for the purpose, in which a frog was drenched with the poison, and shut up in the vapour, ten minutes was found to be the shortest time in which apparent death could be induced. But the time at which symptoms appeared, and at which very decided effects manifested themselves, either with or without oxygen, varied so greatly that no conclusion of any kind was possible. At length it was discovered that the presence of water retarded the effects, no doubt by removing some of the acid from the atmosphere. When the acid was injected under the skin, and the frog was placed under a glass shade, so as to be conveniently observed, the course of events was much the same, except that there was at first violent leaping, apparently excited by pain. Finally it was discovered, that if after the injection of the acid the frog were allowed to hop about freely, no appreciable effects of any kind followed, at any rate for an hour. This was tried successively with half a drop, one, two, four, and eight drops, with the same result. Half an hour after the injection of 4 or 8 drops, if the frog were placed for a minute or two under cover, the odour of prussic acid was very distinct; and in five minutes, not only the injected frogs, but uninjected companions shut up with them, began to manifest the usual symptoms of prussic acid poisoning, recovering speedily on exposure to fresh air. About half an hour later still, the two frogs, which had had one 4 the other 8 drops under the skin, were placed with others in a covered vessel during my absence, and on my return after some time, one was dead the other not, and one or two others had also perished.

The interpretation I have ventured to put upon these facts is that the energy of the changes going on in the nervous system of the frog is not adequate to determine the decomposition of the HCN, and that its action when breathed is partly comparable to that of the class of anæsthetics, partly due to some effect on the blood.

Some 40 experiments were made in all; a *résumé* of them is given here rather on account of their interest than because they bear immediately on the explanation of the action of prussic acid which has been advanced.

Before the second analogy—that in which the introduction into the blood of substances having different degrees and directions of chemical tension is likened to the influence on the energy of combustion of the composition of the combustible—can be followed out, a very comprehensive enquiry will be needed, on the one hand, as to the conditions of the nervous system associated with convulsions, tetanus, delirium &c. and, on the other, as to the chemical relations of substances which give rise to these symptoms. Only a short time ago all tetanic or convulsive movement would unhesitatingly have been ascribed to stimulation of some part of the motor nervous system. Spasm and paralysis are however nearly related, and until the state of the nervous centres which gives rise to or permits of irregular and violent movements is better understood, it would be premature to attempt to settle how this state is induced by poisons.

In connexion with this presumed analogy two suggestive points may be noted. 1. That as compared with prussic acid and the class of anæsthetics, which arrest or suspend all the nervous functions from above downwards, like asphyxia, in the order of their demand for oxygen, the alkaloids have for the most part a special influence on some particular part of the nervous apparatus. 2. That while prussic acid and the anæsthetics manifest their influence immediately on their reaching the nervous centres in sufficient amount, a certain time intervenes between the introduction into the blood of the poisonous alkaloids and the full development of their action.

The lines of investigation to be pursued for the elucidation of the relation between chemical tension and physiological action, in addition to the admirable method of research originated by Drs Crum Brown and Fraser, which unfortunately can be carried out only by the most advanced chemists, having special opportunities, are ; 1st, experiments on the same class of animals with substances of simple composition and known constitution (the various compounds of the great Cyanogen group offer a tempting field) ; 2nd, experiments with bodies in which the direction of the chemical tension is manifestly different, the results to be compared (the class of compounds for example formed by substitution of NO_2 for H as compared with the condensed ammoniums) ; 3rd, experiments on different classes of animals with the same poison.

From experiments on frogs with nitro-picric acid $H_1C_6H_2(NO_2)_3$ O, and nitro-glycerine $C_6H_5(NO_2)_3$ O_3 as compared with aniline C_6H_5, H_2N, it would appear that the action on these animals of the bodies into which oxygen is introduced largely by substitution of NO_2 for H is to induce convulsion, while the effect of the reduced ammoniums is to cause paralysis. Again, the action of nitro-glycerine, in which the proportion of O to C is very large and the tension extreme, is excessively violent as compared with nitro-picric acid, in which there is less O and less tension. Again, nitro-benzol $C_6H_5(NO_2)$ has a much slower and far less powerful action on frogs than aniline C_6H_5, H_2N, and, so far as could be judged, stupefying rather than paralyzing. These are facts as regards the substances named. The details of the experiments made are not given here because a more extended series, yet to be made, would be required to establish the suggested relation between different directions of chemical tension and different physiological action as a general law.

In the third line of investigation specified, comparative experiments on rats and frogs have yielded interesting results. The difference in the action of prussic acid has already been given. A still more striking difference is observed when nitroglycerine is the poison employed. In frogs the action is speedy and the effect most violent tetanic convulsion. In rats the action is slow and the effect a gradual motor paralysis without loss of sensation. A single experiment will suffice as an illustration.

A. Rat. Five drops of a solution of nitro-glycerine in methylic alcohol (strength one to four) were injected under the skin of a small rat at 2°. 24′ P.M. Pain was evidently caused by the injection, but afterwards for some time no effect could be perceived. An hour after the injection the rat seemed quite well, ran about, took food, &c. Somewhat later he gave evidence of weakness, which gradually increased, so that at 5°. 30′ he could scarcely crawl. He cried feebly when the tail was pinched. Respirations shallow and feeble, heart's action weak. At 5°. 40′ P.M. he could not move, gasped at long intervals, and the heart's action was not perceptible. Soon after this he died. There was never any convulsive movement, and as long as any movements were possible there was a feeble cry when the tail was pinched.

B. Frog. One drop of the same solution of nitro-glycerine placed on the back of a frog at 12°. 35′ M. Vigorous attempts to remove it with foot and to escape. At 12°. 40′ movements stiff, limbs apparently rigid and attitude peculiar. At 12°. 48′ moves with great difficulty, much urine ejected, then a leap and a tetanic spasm of extreme violence, gradually relaxing in about two minutes. The spasms usually recurred at intervals of about a minute for some time, becoming at length less severe with longer intervals. During the intervals the frog could draw up and move his limbs, but a touch would bring on a paroxysm. After one drop the duration of symptoms was usually about 12 hours.

Nitro-glycerine was at first employed under the idea that oxygen might be set free in the nervous centres. Subsequent consideration showed that this would not be the case, the fact however remains, that nitro-glycerine contains a proportion of oxygen altogether exceptional, and in a state of combination easily disturbed ; and there can be little doubt that this stands in some relation with the difference of effects observed in rats and frogs, representing warm and cold-blooded animals respectively.

One or two other interesting points may be mentioned before leaving nitro-glycerine and prussic acid.

In rats, if nitro-glycerine or strychnine be injected, and 5 or 10 minutes later prussic acid, the effects of prussic acid are apparently retarded. On the other hand, either the puncture with the handling attending an injection, or the prussic acid, hastens the appearance of symptoms of strychnine poisoning, probably the latter, for a rat with a small dose of strychnine in his blood manifests symptoms when placed in an atmosphere containing prussic acid, while he is otherwise free from any apparent effects ; slight symptoms have been thus induced several times in a rat while under the influence of the same dose of strychnine. In frogs an atmosphere containing prussic acid precipitates greatly the access of the tetanus of strychnia or nitro-glycerine, but afterwards induces relaxation of the spasm, the frog lying sometimes for hours apparently dead, but ultimately recovering. I have found it impossible by any amount of prussic acid to obtain this relaxation without the occurrence of the tetanic symptoms if nitro-glycerine or strychnine had been applied.

There are two points which cannot be passed over in any

attempt to apply the principles of Chemistry and Physics to the operation of poisons, or in any explanation of their action which claims to be rational. One is, the minuteness of the fatal dose; the other, the special action on particular nerve centres.

That a few drops of dilute prussic acid or a fraction of a grain of strychnine should suffice to destroy life so speedily, must always be matter for astonishment and constitute a difficulty in any rational explanation of the action of these and other powerful poisons. It is not sufficient to indicate the nature of their operation. It is necessary also to show its adequacy. Quantitative as well as qualitative relation must be established between the cause and the effect.

Some experimenters have thought to elude this difficulty by tracing all the consequences to a primary action on some particular nerve, as for instance, on the pneumogastric in poisoning by prussic acid. But the poison is present in the blood which reaches the nerve-filaments only in the same proportion as in that distributed to the nervous centres in general; and its effect on the particular nerve is not a whit less wonderful or difficult to understand than an action on the nervous system as a whole.

From whatever point of view the action of poisons may be regarded, it seems to me that the first step towards the removal of this difficulty or even its right appreciation, is to endeavour to estimate the equivalency of nerve-force or, in other words, the amount of chemical change involved in its evolution. Every consideration points to the conclusion that nerve-force is characterized by intensity as distinguished from quantity, and that its equivalency is extremely small. The physical force with which it presents the greatest analogy is electricity either galvanic or frictional. Now, the mere contact of a warm hand with the thermo-electric pile will develope a galvanic current; and Faraday calculated that the liberation of a single grain of hydrogen by decomposition of water or conversely the turning of this quantity into water was equivalent to 800,000 discharges of a large Leyden battery. If, as is probable, the analogy between nerve-force and either of the forms of electricity extends to relative quantivalence, this indicates that the equivalence of nerve-force may possibly be extremely low.

4—2

Again, the lightest touch of a feather on the skin, a few rays of light impinging upon the retina, may set in motion almost the entire nervous apparatus. Unless there is a tremendous disproportion between the force applied and the force called into operation, this would point to an equivalency so low as to elude calculation altogether[1].

These are mere conjectures; one or two out of very many which point in the same direction, and they cannot be taken as doing more than to establish a probability that nerve-force has a small equivalency; a consequence of which would be that the chemical change necessary for its development or arrest is small.

On the other hand, the maximum of force to be obtained from an organic body is through the exercise of the affinities of its individual elements, as in the explanation given of the action of prussic acid.

The second point mentioned as requiring notice, is the special action of different poisons on particular divisions of the nervous system; strychnia on the cord, opium on the brain, curare on the end organs of the nerves, &c. The poison being conveyed by the blood equally to every part of the nervous system, the nervous structures having presumably a similar chemical composition and the action of the poison being referred to chemical laws, it is absolutely necessary to explain how it is that some parts of the nervous apparatus are untouched by a substance which profoundly affects others.

It is said in the above statement that the chemical composition of the nervous structures is presumably everywhere similar, but if chemical composition have anything to do with the

---

[1] Unfortunately there are no data for a calculation which, taking the amount of force obtainable from the food and deducting that which is expended in the form of heat and mechanical work, might leave a residuum for nerve-action. Nerve-force like the mechanical work of the heart is again expended in the system, and consequently either again becomes latent, or changes its form probably into heat; just as the mechanical work of the heart is delivered up in the capillaries as heat from obstructed motion. We cannot state the problem thus: latent energy of food = animal heat + external mechanical work + work of heart and respiratory muscles + vital action? + nerve action. Nerve action, vital action, whatever this may be understood to include, the force exerted in the circulation of the blood and much of that of respiration are all included as unknown quantities in the animal heat.

evolution of nerve-force, it cannot be everywhere identical. The difference in functional activity of different centres implies a difference of chemical tension and therefore of chemical composition and, more particularly, a difference of relation with the tension of the various poisons. For example, the brain requires sleep, the cord does not or, at any rate, not in the same degree. The brain is occupied with mental processes and has only a mediate relation through the sensori motor ganglia with the outer world. The cord receives the shock of contact with external nature and is the instrument of the brain. The brain suffers first from the absence of oxygen in asphyxia and from obstruction to oxidation by the anæsthetic vapours : all facts which point to a difference in intensity of the force, and of chemical tension in the matter.

Again, the entire sensory apparatus which receives, transmits and recognises impressions of all kinds and degrees must have a far more varied and extensive range of operation than the motor apparatus, which has simply to transmit impulses to the muscles, and this implies a difference in chemical tension.

The special action of different poisons on different nervous centres can thus be explained without the assumption of a specific influence or virtue. A similar explanation applies to the different action of the same poison on different classes of animals ; a difference in the functional energy and activity of the same centres in the various kinds of animals implies a difference in their chemical tension and, therefore, in their relation with poisons. The following facts are interesting in connexion with this point.

1. The anæsthetics affect all animals alike. In these the action is simply general arrest of oxidation.

2. Strychnine, which acts on the cord, affects all animals alike. The spinal system is that part of the nervous apparatus which has similar endowments in all classes of animals.

3. The poisons which have the most diverse action on different classes of animals are such as affect the cerebral ganglia, the functions and endowments of which vary so greatly in the animal series.

NOTES ON THE HOMOLOGIES AND COMPARATIVE ANATOMY OF THE ATLAS AND AXIS.

By ALEXANDER MACALISTER, L.R.C.S., *Demonstrator of Anatomy, Royal College of Surgeons, Ireland, Hon. Professor of Anatomy, Royal Dublin Society, &c.* (Read before the Physiological Section of the British Association in Norwich. August, 1868.)

IT seems to be a principle in morphology that the greater the amount of specialization of function manifested by any organ, the farther does the structure so specialized depart from the form of the primordial type to which it belongs. This principle is particularly exemplified in the case of the two upper cervical vertebræ, the atlas and the axis, as, on account of the special varieties of motion in this region, the different parts are so modified that it is in some instances difficult to assign to the processes of these bones their exact positions as serial homologues of the processes in other vertebral segments. We owe much of our knowledge of the relations of these bones to Owen[1], Rathke[2], Cleland[3], and Robin[4]; but a few points yet require to be wrought out with regard to them, so as to enable us to understand more clearly the homologies of their several portions. In order to present a complete series of relationships between these bones and the ordinary cervical vertebræ, the points to be considered are the following:—1st, the nature and homologies of the body of the axis, and of the odontoid process; 2nd, the nature of the pre-odontoid half-arch of the atlas; 3rd, the serial homologies of the transverse atlantal ligament and of the occipito-axial or check ligament; 4th, the third occipital condyle of Meckel and Halbertsma; 5th, the articular processes of the atlas and axis; and 6th, the transverse processes of the cervical vertebræ in general, and of these two in particular.

1. The body of the axis taken by itself departs in no respect from the typical vertebrate body. In its development it

---

[1] *Homologies of Vertebrate Skeletons*, p. 93.
[2] *Ueber die Entwickelung der schildkröten, &c.*
[3] *Nat. Hist. Review*, April, 1861.
[4] *Journal de l'Anat. et de Physiologie*, 1864, p. 274, and pl. 7, et seq.

has, at least in some animals, a lower epiphysary disk, a central ossific point, and occasionally an upper disk. In the adult it is united to the odontoid process, whose appearance and position naturally suggest to the mind of any thoughtful observer, that it belongs to the atlas more distinctly than to the axis, that it is the separated body of the atlas; and this theory, put forward by Blandin[1], Rathke, and Owen, is deserving of our best attention; lying in the direct line of the chain of centra, being ossified around the notochord, being developed in the topmost somatome of the primordial vertebral column in immediate contact with the atlas, and being in the young turtle a detached ossicle occupying the hollow of the atlas where a body should be. All these indicate the probability of its corporeal nature and atlantal relations. Comparative Anatomy supplies us with many evidences in confirmation of this theory, and one of the most striking of these is furnished by the axis of the piked whale, *Balœnoptera rostrata.* This, as I have elsewhere described[2], is a flattened bone, separate from the other cervical vertebræ, with a hemispherical elevation on its forward side which occupies the anterior or inferior hollow of the atlas and is the true odontoid process, degenerated however in point of height, as is usually the case with cetaceans, and covered, in part, with an extension inwards of the lateral cartilaginous articular surfaces. In a young specimen of this species, which I have examined in conjunction with Dr Carte, the accomplished curator of the Royal Dublin Society's Museum, the upper or neural side of the body displayed a short shallow slit running transversely, dividing the posterior part of the true odontoid process from the body of the axis proper. The odontoid portion exhibits a small apical epiphysary crust imbedded in the middle of its prominent convexity, irregular and unconsolidated with the rest of the process; the central portion of this segment is perfectly continuous with the true body of the axis on its ventral and lateral aspects, but behind or towards the neural side is separated by the posterior transverse fissure or slit above mentioned, the remains of the primitive interver-

---

[1] *Nouveaux Élémens d'Anatomie*, Tom. I. p. 49 note.
[2] *Phil. Trans.* 1868.

tebral separation remaining partially unossified, as one often sees in the consolidated vertebræ forming the sacrum. This fissure is bounded by two epiphysary laminæ, one an inferior surface-crust belonging to the underside of the odontoid process and placed on the cranial side of the fissure, and a superior disk which is evidently the upper epiphysis of the axis forming the posterior wall of the groove. Thus it is evident that in this cetacean the body of the axis has three centres of ossification, and that the odontoid process has likewise three centres from which it is developed, as in the case of the centra of other vertebræ. Of these it will be seen in the specimen under notice, that the contiguous epiphysary crusts are but small and coalesce at their inferior border, in front of which the bodies of the two segments are confluent. In other animals the development of the odontoid process from three centres is not always clearly marked, but in every instance which I have examined the embryonic axis presents a dilatation of the notochord between the odontoid process and the body of the axis, as has been described by Robin, similar to the dilatation found in other intercentra. In the human subject the ossification of the centrum of the axis is usually accomplished in the following manner: a central nucleus appears for the body proper, and this is surmounted by two lateral nuclei for the odontoid process, which soon consolidating present the appearance of a bifid single point, and hence some anatomists, as Harrison, have referred the tooth-like process to a single centre. The notch in the summit is filled up with cartilage, in which occasionally an apical ossific point may appear, frequently overlooked owing to its variable, often diminutive, size, and by no means constant. In many cases in the progress of ossification the centre of the odontoid process and nucleus of the axial body rapidly approach each other, bony development spreading quickly downwards from the former point, and hence the appearance described by Robert Knox, and Sömmerring, that the odontoid process seems to be sunk or embedded into the body proper. In some cases however the cartilage surrounding the intercentral dilatation of the notochord displays two supplementary centres of ossification similar to those in the *Balænoptera*, an inferior odontal lamina and an upper axoid epiphysary disk, making up five out of the six typical points of the two bodies. Still later in the progress of development two small nuclei appear in the interval between the neuro-central suture, the body proper, and the odontoid process *on the level, not of the body of either vertebra, but of the intercentrum;* these were noticed by Meckel, Nesbitt, and Humphry, and have been considered by the last-named authority (*The Human Skeleton,* p. 131) as inward prolongations of the lateral masses, but being placed in the intervertebral space they claim affinity more closely with the nuclei of the costiform epiphyses of the lower cervical vertebræ than with any part of the pedicle. The only point requiring remark in the method of development is the presence of a double corporeal centre, which favours the hypothesis of Humphry, that the typical vertebral body probably possesses twin centres from which it is developed; however, as far as my observations have gone, they have accorded with the conclusion of Robin, that nowhere else in the chain of human vertebral centra does a double or twin body-nucleus appear. The human axis does not present to us an inferior surface disk as we find in cetacea; at least I have failed in every case, and in immature axes of all ages, to determine the existence of a separate bony nucleus or lamina below the centrum. The fœtal *rabbit* and fœtal *horse* exhibit a single lamina on the upper side of the axis and beneath the odontoid process, but I have not in either found the double lamina above mentioned in this interspace.

2. Having decided the affinities of the odontoid process of the axis, it becomes an important point to determine the precise nature of the anterior half-arch of the atlas, which is thus removed from the category of vertebral bodies. To explain its serial homologies several theories have been advanced, to all of which, I think, we must take exception. The first, or that of Blandin, regards the double ossific nuclei of this part of the atlas as the upper and lower epiphysial crusts of the body of the atlas consolidated and displaced, leaving the middle nucleus as the odontoid process. To this there are the objections that in man and *Balænoptera,* as before mentioned, the three centres are present in the odontoid process while the anterior atlantal

arch coexists, while rarely in man and other animals the anterior arch is ossified from a single centre, a condition which I have seen in an African elephant, as well as in a child of a few years old, and it is described and figured in the human subject in Rambaud and Renault's observations, *Sur l'origine et le developpement des os.* The second theory, or that of Professor Owen, refers this half-arch to the category of exogenous cortical formations, a hypo-apophysis: but to this Prof. Robin objects that it is not developed in the tissue immediately surrounding the notochord; and there is to it likewise the objection that it is of a fibrous nature in the *wallaby, wombat, thylacinus, koala,* &c. and human fœtus; so if we accept it as true that in no case can a bone developed in a fibrous basis be the homologue of one formed in cartilage, the anterior half-arch is thus virtually removed from the number of central parts. The third theory, or that of Prof. Humphry, regards it as a dependence of the lateral mass of the vertebræ extended inwards, a sub-central prolongation of the pedicles. That it is in truth, as suggested by Robin, intimately connected with the lateral masses of the atlas, admits of no question; but to what structures it is related, and with what parts it is immediately united, are questions difficult of solution. It is plainly not a mere prolongation inward of the pedicle, or else it would not be provided with double special points of ossification, nor could it on this hypothesis ever present to us a single centre, as I have seen in the human subject, or as occurs in some reptiles and batrachians. The fourth theory, or that of Koster, that it is a hæmal arch, is less probable than the last, as it contains in its grasp neither blood-vessels nor any visceral structure, conditions which would exist were the hæmal arch of this vertebra developed; on the contrary, the parts developed from the inner layer and from the lamina intermedia of the blastoderm are in front of and not within the arch. The points then to be noted as distinguishing the anterior half-arch from the other parts of the vertebra are, 1st, its being placed on the plane of the intercentrum; 2nd, its having separate centres of ossification; 3rd, its being fibro-cartilaginous, and not truly cartilaginous in its primary stage; 4th, its being late in ossification: I have found it unossified even up to the second year. Meckel mentions that out of thirty fœtuses and new-born children, only one had a nucleus of bone in this arch, and that the usual time for the commencement of ossification is six months; 5th, the part of the vertebra with which it is connected is that at the base of the costiform epiphysis or anterior root of the transverse process. When carefully compared with the portions of other vertebræ there is but one structure to which it seems related, and that is the ligament which, in all vertebræ possessing costal appendages, stretches from the intercentrum to the front of the rib, the hæmal equivalent of the ligamentum conjugale of Meyer, or the anterior costo-vertebral ligament. To this structure, all the peculiarities possessed by this half-arch, and noted above, indicate its relations. In the thorax of many animals this ligament is stronger and more complete than in man, in whom the mesial portion is deficient, and its lateral parts stellately expanded; but in other mammals, as some of the larger ruminants, it presents to us the appearance of a strong firm band crossing from the intervertebral substance and edge of the bone to the front of the rib, similar to the modification of its antithesis—the conjugal ligament, in the sheep. Comparative Anatomy furnishes to us a very valuable confirmation of this theory, in the examples before quoted, of the larger marsupials, in whom the arch never gets beyond the fibrous or fibro-cartilaginous stage.

3. The transverse ligament of the atlas has been made the subject of remark by Prof. Cleland, of Galway, in a paper on the serial homologies of the articular surfaces of the atlas, axis, and occipital bone, published in the *Natural History Review*, April, 1861. He has shown, with reason, that it is in series with the ligamentum conjugale before mentioned. To the remarks in his paper I have nothing to add as the affinity seems to be clear, and it confers an additional probability on my theory of the nature of the anterior half-arch. In many cetaceans, as the cervical vertebræ are all soldered together, this ligament becomes an ossified part of the general mass forming a ridge, which in the common *Porpoise* is very early consolidated with the back of the odontoid process. In *Hyperoodon* and *Delphinus* this ridge exists, and is easily discriminated in a young

bone from the rest of the vertebral mass. If then the ligamentum conjugale is capable, for the accomplishment of special purposes, of being thus modified, surely it is not too much to assume that the anterior costo-vertebral ligament, a corresponding structure, should, for a particular end, undergo an alteration as simple as that of calcification. That the anterior and posterior girdle of the odontoid process should resemble the anterior and posterior girdle of any vertebra presenting costal appendages is what we might expect, if we can determine the presence of such processes in the atlas. The moderator or occipito-axial ligaments are, as suggested by Dr Cleland, likewise members of the same series, conjugal ligaments. Occasionally the fibres are not all attached to the odontoid process, but pass from side to side, not bound down in the middle. In their ordinary condition, however, they represent the conjugal ligament severed in the middle, and with each part attached to the upper edge of the centrum below—a variety analogous to the common arrangement in vertebrates of the anterior rib-girdle or the stellate ligament[1].

4. An anomalous process of great interest often occurs on the occipital bone projecting backwards to articulate with the summit of the odontoid process; its degree of frequency seems to be about once in sixty crania: it was described and figured by Meckel as a third condyle, and was likewise made the subject of remark by the late Professor H. Halbertsma. This process is of interest as it consists of a continuation downward of the ossification along the tissue surrounding the notochord, and is in fact a central prolongation uniting the basilar process to the chain of true vertebral bodies. When we compare the occipital condyle of man with that of the *turtle*, and find that in the latter the condyle is partly formed on the basi-occipital and partly on the ex-occipitals, we can see then the bearing of an instance of this kind exhibiting a mesial typical condyle with the delicate suspensorium representing the last of the chain of intercentra, for although the basi-cranial axis does not undergo

---

[1] In some birds, as the *raven*, the atlas presents a complete osseous ring around the ligamentum suspensorium, the anterior part of which is the anterior semi-arc of the atlas, and the posterior is the ossified transverse ligament. In the *ostrich* and *rhea*, on the other hand, the transverse ligament is truly fibrous.

a primordial division into somatomes, yet its occipital portion is clearly in series with the segments of the vertebral column.

The laminæ of the atlas and axis are distinctly homologous with the laminæ of the other vertebræ, and the spine of the axis and the posterior tubercle of the atlas are in series with the true spines. The latter prominence is rarely developed, as the function of the atlas to rotate on the axis, carrying the head along with it, would be seriously interfered with if there were a prominent spur in this position. Occasionally a separate ossific point is detectible in the spine of the atlas; and I have even seen two nuclei, as in some of the lower cervicals. The atlas of the Pig shows a longer spine than usual. In the Dog, and many other mammals, the spine of the axis is very large and projects as far forwards as the top of the atlas, giving the appearance as though the spine of the atlas had shared the fate of its centrum, and had been severed from its proper segment and joined to the spine of the axis.

5. The posterior edge of the groove for the vertebral artery and sub-occipital nerve on the upper side of the lamina of the atlas in man is often projected into a ridge; which sometimes is sufficiently large to convert that groove into a foramen, and when well developed it is united to the back part of the upper articular process; this is well known to all osteologists, and has been described by Sömmerring, Meckel, and Henle. The value of this process has been recognized by Dr Cleland, who describes it correctly as an oblique process, as it arises from the lamina behind the exit-point of the spinal nerve and in series with the other cervical oblique processes. Now, the upper articular process of the atlas, though frequently uniform and undivided on each side, yet is as often separated into anterior and posterior parts placed at very different inclinations with regard to each other, being separated by a rough non-articular space, and by a line continued outwards from the plane of the insertion of the transverse ligament. This division is seen so frequently in the human atlas as to indicate that it is not a mere anomaly, and often, as represented by Harrison, this line of division parts the atlantic condyle into two completely separate articular surfaces. The importance of this division can

be easily understood in the light of an example of the former variety, where the hinder part of the atlantic condyle can be seen to surmount a lateral offshoot from the neural arch, or in other words a true oblique process. It indicates that the posterior part of the atlantic condyle is in reality the summit of an oblique process, whose base usually has become absorbed. This process is present in some *monkeys* and in the *lemur* among quadrumana, in the *bear, lion, leopard, civet, otter* and most carnivores, in *sheep, deer, goat, llama* and other ruminants, and in the *pig, horse,* &c. among pachyderms. In the young *pig, camel* and *seal* I have seen the oblique-process-nature of the posterior part of the atlantic condyle most clearly shown, as in these the separation of the two parts seems to be most obvious. The hinder extremity of the articular surface on the upper part of the atlas, according to this theory, would be of a nature distinct from the anterior ; but as oblique processes, except in the case of a few of the lower dorsal and upper lumbar vertebræ, have not separate points of ossification, we would not necessarily find special centres for the development of these parts. However, even this mark of distinctness is not invariably absent, as, according to the illustration of Professor Turner's paper in Vol. II. p. 78 of this *Journal,* in *Globiocephalus svineval* there are separate ossific nuclei for the anterior and posterior parts of the articular surface—a fact which I have confirmed from the examination of a young individual of this species. The lower oblique processes of the atlas are suppressed in ordinary cases in mammalians, but I have ound them present in chelonians, as in *Testudo sulcata,* also in the *Iguana* and other Saurian and Loricate reptiles. In these animals the upper oblique processes of the axis are also well marked, although in the majority of mammals these processes have become suppressed or modified. In the *goat, pig,* and *deer* they have undergone the same mutation as the corresponding processes of the atlas, being bent forward to join the articular process.

6. In the transverse processes of the atlas and axis, as in the corresponding parts of the other cervical vertebræ, we have a complex system of elements not easily understood. The parts entering into the composition of each process are

an anterior or inferior lateral process and a posterior or superior lateral process, parapophyses and diapophyses of Owen. The superior is generally the longest and largest, and is in series with the true dorsal transverse processes and with the mammillary process of the lumbar vertebra. This pair of processes in the atlas displays nothing remarkable except that occasionally a spur is continued from it to the edge of the articular surface, making a species of second arch. In some rare cases it is contiguous to a projecting paramastoid process from the cranium. The anterior lateral processes—the costiform epiphyses of Blandin—are usually smaller than the preceding; and in the lower cervical vertebra they are continuous with that part of the body which is elevated into the lateral ridge, a portion of the vertebra developed not from the centrum but from the base of the pedicle, and so they always are placed external to the neuro-central suture. They are ossified from distinct centres as described by Blandin, and as I have verified by repeated observations. Hunauld, Sue, Nesbitt, Meckel, Beclard, and Cruveilhier describe this as the condition of the seventh alone, or as a variety not constantly present; but my own observations convince me that these costiform epiphyses have in most cases separate centres; the processes of the upper vertebræ being much later in development than the lower. This process is to be regarded then as a separate segment, articulating internally in the vicinity of the neuro-central suture and uniting externally to the front of the true transverse process : hence we may infer that it is the neck of a true cervical rib in rudiment. This idea is still farther strengthened by the appearance seen in those cases in which cervical ribs are present, for there the neck of the rib usually forms the anterior root of the foramen for the vertebral vessels. I say usually, for in a few cases, as in the example figured by Professor Humphry (see *Human Skeleton*, Plate VI. fig. 2), a thin scale of bone intervenes between the true transverse process and the rib-neck subdividing the vascular canal ; but this does not invalidate the costal claims of the anterior limb of the so-called transverse process, because in the sixth and seventh cervical vertebræ a ridge not unusually subdivides the foramen into two canals.

I have traced this in an eighth-month fœtus, and have found that this intermediate process was ossified from the posterior root, quite independently of the costiform epiphysis. I have found many specimens of this spur in the lower pair of vertebræ, and in all cases they are precisely of the same nature as the mesial lamina, coexisting with the cervical rib in the case mentioned above. Prof. L. Stieda, of Dorpat, figures an instance of a cervical rib in which the correspondence of the anterior root and the neck of the rib can be plainly seen, although they are not directly continuous (*Virchow's Archiv*, 1866, p. 425, and Pl. 11, Fig. 1). Sometimes in the adult human subject this costiform epiphysis or rib segment in the atlas is undeveloped or remains permanently as cartilage; the former condition is exemplified in a female skeleton in the Dublin College of Surgeons Museum. The theory of the ligamentous nature of the anterior half-arch of the atlas derives an additional support from the adoption of the costal theory of the anterior root of the transverse process; for it is always of this portion of the lateral mass that it is a dependent, and, even when attached to the root of the pedicle proper, it is not necessarily removed from the category of rib ligaments, for the conjugal ligament, its fellow member of the vertebral girdle, is in some instances attached to the angles of the centrum and not to the rib.

The articular plates of the occipital bone, atlas, and axis have been carefully considered by Prof. Cleland in the paper before referred to, and their serial homologues have been demonstrated in the minute cervical joint of Luschka and the costo-vertebral articulation. I have, however, given above reasons why the posterior part of the atlantal condyle may be excepted from this category.

COMPLETE OBLITERATION OF THE CŒLIAC AND MESENTERIC ARTERIES: THE VISCERA RECEIVING THEIR BLOOD-SUPPLY THROUGH THE EXTRA-PERITONEAL SYSTEM OF VESSELS. By JOHN CHIENE, M.D., F.R.C.S.E., *Demonstrator of Anatomy, University of Edinburgh.* (Read at the Oxford Meeting of the British Medical Association. August, 1868.)

THE body of a female, aged sixty-five, which had been injected with lard and vermilion from the femoral artery, was dissected in the Practical Anatomy Rooms of the University of Edinburgh, in the month of May of the present year. The cause of death, as stated in the certificate accompanying the body, was paralysis. During the dissection required for displaying the vessels supplying the abdominal viscera it was observed that, although the branches of the cœliac and mesenteric arteries were fully injected, the main trunks were completely obliterated at their origins, the obliteration in each case extending to the first branch.

The ABDOMINAL AORTA was extensively diseased. A large pear-shaped aneurism extended from its bifurcation upwards to the crossing of the left renal vein, in length 4½ inches, in breadth, inferiorly where its transverse diameter was greatest, 2½ inches. The inferior mesenteric artery arose from the lower part of the aneurism. Above the renal vein the aorta was enlarged. Atheromatous plates were scattered here and there throughout its whole extent. The iliac vessels were perfectly healthy.

The CŒLIAC AXIS arose in the usual position; it was a fibrous cord for the first half inch of its extent; past that point it was of the normal size, dividing almost immediately into the hepatic, splenic, gastric, and left phrenic arteries; they and their branches were fully injected. The gastro-duodenal branch of the hepatic gave off three large pancreatico-duodenal arteries to the pancreas and duodenum. A well-marked branch from the splenic supplied the splenic flexure of the colon ana-

stomosing with the arterial loop formed by the colica media
and colica sinistra. This junction was uninjected. No other
anastomosis with the mesenteric system could be found. The
left phrenic, equal in size to the radial, ramified in the left half
of the diaphragm, there inosculating with branches from the
lower intercostals. These inosculations were filled with injection. A plexus of tortuous well-injected arteries, situated on
the left side of the aorta above the renal artery, connected the
left phrenic and pancreatico-duodenal with the renal and supra-
renal arteries. As these anastomosing vessels were filled with
injection presumably the blood had entered the cœliac system
through them. No other injected communication could be discovered; it is quite possible, however, that such may have existed, escaping notice owing to the fluidity of the injection, due
to the very warm weather at the time of the dissection.

MESENTERIC VESSELS. Both these arteries were obliterated
at their origin; their branches were filled with injection from
the pelvis through the superior hæmorrhoidal, which equalled
in size the femoral at Poupart's ligament. The blood reached
the superior mesenteric through the left and middle colic arteries, which were more than double their ordinary size; the ileo-
colic and right colic were of normal calibre. The last dorsal
artery on the right side gave off opposite the apex of the last
rib a branch, equal in size to the anterior temporal, which
helped to supply the caput cæcum and the commencement of
the large intestine, inosculating with the ileo-colic; this inoscu-
lation was not injected. The lumbar arteries were large, inosculating freely with each other, and with the ileo-lumbar and
circumflex-ilii arteries. The supra-renal arteries were enlarged,
sending branches to the fat around the kidneys. On each side
a well-marked artery pierced the capsule of the kidney at the
upper part, supplying the fat around the organ. These enlarged vessels communicated freely with the lumbar arteries.
The right phrenic was absent, its place being taken by branches
from the supra-renal on the same side. The epigastric and circumflex-ilii arteries were increased in size.

The AORTA was carefully removed; it was adherent to the
anterior surface of the body of the 4th lumbar vertebra; the

pressure of the aneurism had caused absorption of the bone at that point. The walls of the artery were thickened and atheromatous, studded with calcareous plates of various sizes. It was laid open from behind: anteriorly its canal was filled throughout the whole length with laminar clots, evidently of long standing. A channel for the passage of the blood to the iliacs remained patent behind this fibrinous layer, which, in the lower part of the cavity of the aneurism, was nearly an inch in thickness. A careful dissection of the origins of the cœliac axis and mesenteric vessels showed organized clots firmly adherent to the edges of their openings, completely obliterating them. The closure of these arteries was not of recent date.

The superior hæmorrhoidal artery was traced into the pelvis, and its inosculations with the internal iliacs were dissected with care. The presence of a large abscess, filled with fœtid pus, surrounding the lower end of the rectum, and the resulting induration of the tissues around, rendered the dissection difficult. The uterus was fixed, and the rectum adherent to the anterior surface of the sacrum.

The SUPERIOR HÆMORRHOIDAL, as large as the femoral at Poupart's ligament, passed into the pelvis a little to the left of the middle line, and, opposite the 2nd sacral vertebra, divided into two primary branches. 1. The smaller or left division, equal in size to the brachial, coursed down the side of the rectum, and there bifurcated; its anterior branch, anastomosed with a branch from the ischiatic, and with the lateral sacral of the gluteal; while its posterior branch joined a plexus around the rectum, and anastomosed with the middle and inferior hæmorrhoidal arteries. 2. The larger or right division, as large as the axillary, also bifurcated. The anterior branch anastomosed by numerous branches with the right pudic and right middle hæmorrhoidal, forming a dense plexus of tortuous vessels resembling closely an "aneurism by anastomosis." This plexus lay to the right side of the rectum, opposite the third sacral vertebra. The arteries forming it were twisted and tortuous, similar to the curling arteries of the gravid uterus. After sending branches to this plexus, it divided into two vessels, which ended in the plexus round the rectum. The posterior branch, a very tortuous vessel, after giving off a branch to each plexus, anastomosed with a large branch from the right pudic. This was the principal channel by which the blood passed from the parietal to the visceral arteries, a direct communication existing between the two systems equal in size to the brachial. The main branches of the right division were connected by a transverse vessel. From this description, and from a reference to the diagram, it will be seen that the blood was conveyed from the in-

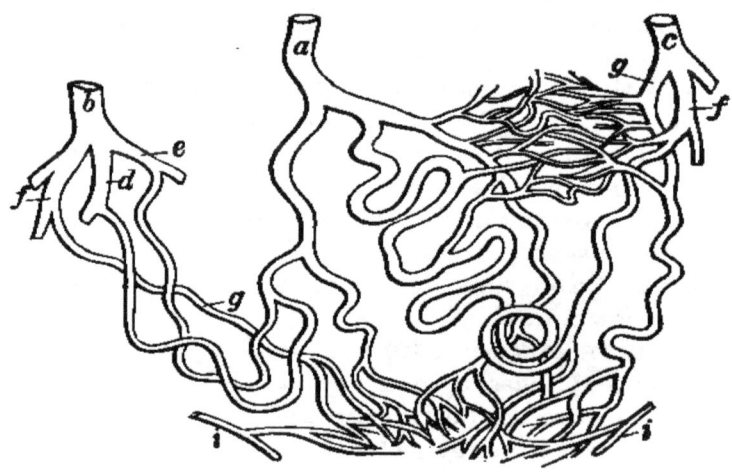

Diagram of Pelvic Plexus, seen from behind, the sacrum having been removed.

- *a.* Superior hæmorrhoidal.
- *b.* Left internal iliac.
- *c.* Right internal iliac.
- *d.* Ischiatic.
- *e.* Gluteal.
- *f.* Pudic.
- *g.* Middle hæmorrhoidal.
- *i.* Pudic in perineum, giving off sup. hæmorrhoidal.

ternal iliacs to the mesenteric vessels; first, through two large plexuses, one situated round the lower end of the rectum, the other at a higher level and to the right; secondly, by three large anastomosing vessels: the whole forming a dense mass of tortuous arteries closely aggregated together on the posterior aspect and sides of the rectum. I could trace no anastomosis in front of the gut. The remaining branches of the internal iliacs were normal. The viscera were normal.

Remarks. This case is probably the only recorded example of an obliteration of the three anterior visceral branches of the abdominal aorta at their origin, and of a consequent enlargement of the secondary anastomoses for the supply of the viscera: the stomach, liver, spleen, pancreas and duodenum being supplied from the left lower intercostals, and from the left renal and supra-renal arteries which inosculated with the lumbar arteries on the same side; the remainder of the intestines receiving its supply from the internal iliacs through a large plexus surrounding the rectum, except the cæcum and ascending colon, which received blood from the last dorsal artery on the right side.

This case presents several interesting practical aspects.

1. It confirms the statement that, between the visceral and parietal branches of the abdominal aorta, a free communication exists through the sub- or extra-peritoneal system of arteries, first systematically described by Prof. Turner, in the *Brit. and For. Med. Ch. Rev.* for July, 1863.

2. Enlargement of this system of arteries, not only in the abdomen proper but in the pelvis, may take place to such an extent as to become the channel of blood supply to the abdominal viscera when their main arterial trunks are obliterated.

3. It establishes the important practical point that a direct arterial channel exists by which the blood can be drawn directly from the abdominal viscera by the employment of depletory measures to the walls of the abdomen. Thus, in inflammation of the cæcum, the arterial anastomosis between the last dorsal artery and the ileo-colic branch of the superior mesenteric, enlarged in this instance but always present, enables the physician, if he considers it advisable, to draw blood directly from the inflamed viscus: and in inflammation of the kidneys the anastomoses between the renal and lumbar arteries (specially those branches of the renal which, passing through the substance of the organ, pierce the capsule and supply the surrounding fat), explain easily and satisfactorily why cupping over the loins in inflammation of the kidneys is of such undoubted benefit.

4. It is evident that the anastomoses in the pelvis between the internal iliac and mesenteric vessels, enlarged in this instance for the supply of the viscera, would be one of the principal channels of blood-supply to the lower limbs in occlusion of the lower part of the aorta from disease, or as the result of ligature. Here the current of blood was reversed, the blood flowing from the pelvis to the viscera, while in occlusion of the aorta the blood would pass through the mesenterics into the pelvis, and thence into the internal iliacs to the lower limbs. In ligature of the common iliac, this anastomosis between the mesenterics and internal iliacs would probably be enlarged.

This case is therefore interesting to the surgeon in reference to ligature of the aorta. It does not, I apprehend, bear directly on the important question: Is there any rational hope of recovery after this operation? The arterial changes consequent on disease are gradual, and they therefore do not give us much assistance in estimating the effect that would be produced by the sudden stoppage of the current of blood, as in ligature. It will, however, help to solve the as yet unsettled point—By what channel does the blood reach the pelvis and lower limbs after obliteration of the aorta? That it does so cannot be doubted. There are four cases on record which place this fact beyond dispute. 1. In the *Dublin Hosp. Reports*, II. 1818, Dr Goodisson of Wicklow describes a case in which, as a consequence of disease, the lower part of the aorta and the common iliacs were obliterated. The obliteration was of long standing. The intercostal arteries, and "in particular that one which takes its course along the last rib," were "much increased in size," the spermatic arteries were "immensely increased," the mammary, lumbar, and circumflex ilii were "much enlarged." The inferior mesenteric was occluded, but the viscera had been removed before the diseased condition was noticed, so that no description of their arterial supply could be obtained. 2. In a pamphlet on *Aneurism of the Abdominal Aorta*, Ed. 1827, Dr A. Monro relates a case of closure of that vessel at the bifurcation in consequence of an aneurism. The patient died of phthisis, and there were no symptoms referable during life to the abdominal lesion. Dr Monro distinctly says that the cœliac axis, mesenteric, renal and lumbar arteries were of normal size ; and adds that probably the blood reached the limbs by anastomoses between the phrenic, lumbar, ileo-lumbar and circumflex-ilii arteries, between the gluteal and lumbar, and lastly, between the internal mammary and epigastric arteries. In neither of these cases, owing to the vessels being uninjected during the *post mortem* examination, have we a complete or satisfactory account of the enlarged anastomoses which must have been present. 3. The abdominal aorta has been ligatured five times in man, by Sir Astley Cooper in 1817[1], by James in 1829[2], by Murray in 1834[3], by Monteiro in 1842[4], by South in 1856[5]. There has not yet been a successful case; but Dr Monteiro's patient lived for ten days after the operation; we may therefore conclude that the blood must have reached and nourished the lower limbs. A *post mortem* examination was made, but special attention does not seem to have been paid to, and no attempt made to discover, the new channels through which the blood reached the extremities. 4. A description will be found in the *Med. Chir. Trans.* XXIX, of a case in which Dr William Murray of Newcastle cured, by pressure with a tourniquet on the aorta above the tumour, an abdominal aneurism the size of a large orange. The aneurism was situated below the origin of the superior mesenteric artery, the pulsation being felt on a level with, and a little to the left of, the umbilicus. Two attempts were made, under chloroform—the first for two hours, the second for five; the latter was completely successful. Five months after the operation Dr Murray notes, " Patient looks well, works as engine-fitter from 6 a.m. to 8 p.m. Lives two miles from his work. No pulsation in the aorta below the tumour, which is now small and hard. Distinct pulsation in right femoral, none in left." The man is, as far as I am aware, still alive, and the condition of the abdominal vessels cannot be definitely settled; the present case will, I think, aid us in coming to a conclusion. Is it not highly probable that the extra-peritoneal vessels around the kidneys and in the pel-

[1] Cooper and Travers, *Surg. Essays*, I. 1818, p. 101.
[2] *Med. Chir. Trans.* XVI. 1.
[3] *Lond. Med. Gazette*, XIV. 68.
[4] Schmidt's *Jahrbuch*, 1843.
[5] *Lancet*, 1856, p. 222.

vis are enlarged; and that through them the blood is conveyed to the pelvis and lower limbs? This view is strengthened by a note taken on the 4th day after the compression. "Running over the right border of the tumour a vessel can be felt pulsating, which, from its position and size, is probably the superior mesenteric artery." Eleven weeks after there is no pulsation to be felt in the iliacs or femorals. Pulsation is not noticed in the right femoral until five months have elapsed. Is not this significant fact explained by supposing that the anastomoses between the lumbar arteries and ascending branches of the gluteal are enlarged; also that the blood having reached the ischiatic and gluteal through the pelvic plexus, is thence poured into the circumflex and perforating branches of the profunda of the femoral; and that the pulsation in the right femoral, five months after the consolidation of the aneurism, is a regurgitant one?

To sum up: these four cases distinctly prove that the circulation can be carried on after the aorta is occluded. In none have we a satisfactory explanation by what channel it reaches the lower limbs. Does not the present case fill up the blank? Can it not now be said that it is through the anastomoses between the parietal and visceral branches of the aorta; in other words, through the extra-peritoneal system of vessels in the region of the kidneys, and more especially in the pelvis, that the blood, for the most part, finds its way to the lower extremities?

ON THE NOMENCLATURE OF MAMMALIAN TEETH, AND ON THE DENTITION OF THE MOLE (*Talpa Europæa*) AND THE BADGER (*Meles taxus*). By HENRY N. MOSELEY, B.A., *Exeter College*, and E. RAY LANKESTER, *Christ Church, Oxford.* (Pl. II. figs. 5 and 6.)

I. THE object of this communication is to draw attention to the unsatisfactory nature of the divisions of the dental series in mammals now in use, especially as to the "canine tooth," and to propose a nomenclature based upon structural relation rather than upon superinduced form. In studying the dentition of Insectivora in the fine osteological collection of the Oxford University Museum, we have had especial occasion to observe the deceptive and arbitrary nature of the rules which have been laid down for determining the homologies of teeth in different animals, and in the upper and lower series of the same individual. With regard to the latter point, we may state at once that the arbitrary determination of the homology of a tooth of the lower series with a tooth of the upper series by the shutting of the former in front of the latter seems to have very little to justify it, excepting that it is convenient, and enables one to write dental formulæ. The desire to use "dental formulæ" has caused a great deal of the unnatural and misguiding divisions of the teeth of mammals, which we call in question. Formulæ are absolutely of no use in the majority of cases, without description; and truth is sometimes greatly strained in order to make a particular case fit in with the typical formula. The existence of any homology at all between upper and lower jaw teeth must be denied; it could only have a theoretical existence in connection with that view of the structure of the vertebrate skull which placed the upper and lower jaws as homologous parts of a vertebra. The only correspondence between the teeth of the upper and lower series is a general one as to their function, certain teeth in the one acting with certain teeth in the other. To take a particular case, in the Lemurs there is a group of six median teeth in the lower jaw directed forwards, and obviously acting with the four upper teeth of the præmaxillary bone. But because the outer of the six median lower teeth shuts immediately in front of the first tooth implanted in the maxilla—the so-called "canine"—it receives the name of canine also, a title which it in no way deserves, but which is far more applicable to the tooth behind it. In the higher monkeys the tooth in this same position is undoubtedly large and caniniform, but this is surely no reason for giving so incongruous a name to the Lemur's tooth. With equal reason or want of reason, might both the teeth be termed incisors. An exactly similar case is seen in the median teeth of the lower jaw of Ruminants, where, as in the sheep, the outermost of the eight median incisiform teeth receives the name of canine, for no other reason than that, in the allied Camelidæ, there is a tooth in this position which is conical and caniniform. It is apparent that the teeth of the upper and lower series cannot be described by the same terms, if those terms are to have any real homological signification; and hence the system of numerator and denominator which has been in vogue, ought to be abandoned.

With regard to the teeth of the upper series, we would remark that the use of terms descriptive of mere form, and of distinctions based upon such adaptations, cannot serve any real use in homological anatomy. The most conspicuous case of the fallacy of this method is in the recognition of the tooth which is implanted in the maxilla next to the præmaxilla, as a distinct *kind* of tooth having a recognisable homologue, more or less, throughout the class mammalia. Professor Owen, in his *Odontography*, thus defines the canine: "When the tooth which succeeds the incisors (the teeth of the præmaxillary bone) is conical, pointed, and longer than the rest, it is called a canine:" it is also generally stated that the canine is late in its development and succession, and that it has but one fang. In these characters, there is not one—we submit—which is possibly a test of homology, excepting the position of the tooth in the maxillary bone, and obviously the distinctive character of this position is no greater than that which belongs to the second, third, or fourth maxillary teeth, and cannot be logically assigned the same value as divisions based upon the method of development (molars and præmolars) or position in distinct bones (maxillaries and præmaxillaries).

It is true that in a large number of familiar mammalia, it is this first maxillary tooth which, together with a tooth shutting in front of it in the lower jaw, becomes modified into a conical organ for purposes of punching and stabbing, and taking the Dog as presenting the typical form of this modification, the word 'canine' is a useful descriptive term in particular cases. But this is by no means invariably the case. In the Anoplotheria the first maxillary tooth is no more differentiated in size or shape than are the succeeding præmolar and preceding incisor. In the Camel three teeth become caniniform, one præmaxillary, and two maxillary, the second maxillary tooth being further remarkable in that it is implanted by only one fang, though the rest of the præmolars have two. In this we have it proved, that this asserted characteristic of the canine tooth may be assumed by a so-called præmolar tooth in adaptation to external conditions, thus shewing the failure of form-definition as applied to the classification of the teeth. In the Vicugna the caniniform tooth of the *intermaxillary* bone is larger and projects further from the jaw than the caniniform first *maxillary* tooth—*the* so-called canine. In the mole—as the researches of Mr Spence Bate shew—the first maxillary tooth is small and insignificant, whilst the large superior caniniform tooth is developed in the intermaxillary, and not in the maxillary bone. Other similar cases, such as the *Otariæ*, might be enumerated. With regard to the development and succession being a definite characteristic of the 'canine,' it seems clear that this lateness is due simply to the greater or less elaboration required in the development of the tooth in each particular case: for Professor Rolleston has shewn that in the female Gorilla, in which the canine is much smaller than in the male, this tooth is developed proportionately earlier, and is fully in its place before the 'wisdom teeth' have cut the gum. This point is well shewn in a fine skeleton of this species in the Oxford University Museum.

From the foregoing considerations we submit, that the use

of the term canine in any but a descriptive sense (when it is better to substitute 'caniniform') is injurious to the progress of this branch of anatomy. The marked differentiation of the tooth in the Carnivora is perhaps some justification for the use of the term in that case; but when we come to the Insectivora and other groups, it is simply futile to enter into long discussions as to which tooth is *the* canine, or whether it is present or absent, since so many teeth in these animals are caniniform. Prof. Owen, we notice, calls in a 'canine' at discretion in these cases. Mr St George Mivart, in his Essay on the Osteology of the Insectivora, published in this Journal says, in speaking of Potamogale, "Professor Allman considers that the tooth, which I prefer to call canine, should rather be considered as a præmolar, on account of its extreme similarity in form to the præmolar behind it. But the two incisors have also very nearly the same shape, and unless a tooth developed in the maxilla, but close behind the maxillary suture, be in all cases called 'a canine,' *whatever its shape*, great uncertainty and inconvenience would result in dental nomenclature." In this passage we have a good example of the trouble which this term 'canine' gives. The conclusion which Mr Mivart comes to has certainly the merit of consistency, but most clearly demonstrates the uselessness and futility of the division 'canines.' In place then of the terms 'molar,' 'canine,' and 'incisor' teeth, which are based upon functional modifications of form, and which are troublesome and mis-guiding where it is desirable to indicate homology, we propose to divide the mammalian dentition thus:—firstly, into (A) the Præmaxillary group[1], (B) the Maxillary group, and (C) the Mandibular group. The maxillary and præmaxillary groups form the upper series, the mandibular forms the lower series, and cannot be sharply divided as those of the upper series; but for convenience, and not with any reference to homology, may be grouped into (1) lateral teeth, and (2) median teeth. In a very large majority of the

---

[1] In some cases there is difficulty in deciding the limits of this group on account of the obliteration of the sutures or the squamous growth of the bone. The Mole and Insectivora are cases of the first cause, whilst in two *Phalangista* skulls at Oxford, one has the first maxillary tooth normal, whilst in the other it is overlapped by the præmaxillary bone.

Diphyodonts (but not in all, since Mr Flower's discovery in the Armadilloes) the maxillary teeth of the upper series and the lateral teeth of the lower series are divisible at a certain point, demarcated by that constantly successional tooth which is known as the fourth præmolar, into an anterior and a posterior series, the anterior series, including that first maxillary tooth which is so frequently caniniform, and which has been called *the* canine, besides other teeth which are frequently preceded by an earlier set of representatives, the posterior group being in some cases wanting, but comprising those unpreceded teeth known as 'true molars.' Since the term 'molar' is objectionable, we should wish to supplant the terms 'molar' and 'præmolar' by the terms 'posterior' and 'anterior' teeth of the maxillary group, or of the mandibular lateral series. The teeth thus primarily divided into groups, which are clearly recognisable as homological identities in the different orders of mammals, may be further particularized by the use of descriptive terms. Incisiform, caniniform, molariform, conoid, bicuspid, tricuspid, sectorial, laniariform, and similar terms may be applied to the teeth, according to their special modifications, in various animals. Thus we should say, that the præmaxillary teeth in man are incisiform, whilst the first anterior maxillary tooth has a tendency to that caniniform development which its position in the angle of the mouth subjects it to in the pugnacious male apes, and in the prædatory Carnivora. In Galeopithecus—we may say—the first anterior maxillary (called by Prof. Owen and others the canine) is foliaceous like the præmaxillaries, and is implanted in the bone by a double fang.

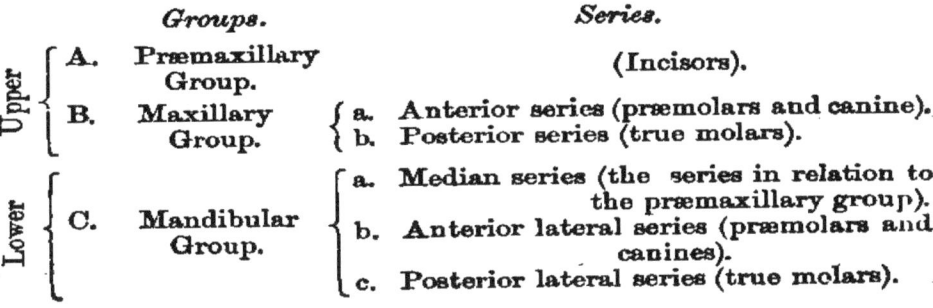

	Groups.	Series.
Upper {	A. Præmaxillary Group.	(Incisors).
	B. Maxillary Group.	{ a. Anterior series (præmolars and canine). { b. Posterior series (true molars).
Lower {	C. Mandibular Group.	{ a. Median series (the series in relation to the præmaxillary group). { b. Anterior lateral series (præmolars and canines). { c. Posterior lateral series (true molars).

II.   The dentition of the common Mole (*Talpa Europœa*) which has been so variously stated, and for the true determination of which Mr Spence Bate (in a paper of great value, published by the Odontological Society of London) has furnished the necessary data, may serve as a particular case by which to illustrate the above views.

Mr Spence Bate shews that in the upper series of its teeth, the mole presents *four* implanted in the præmaxillary bone on either side: *four* anterior maxillary teeth which have milk predecessors, and *three* posterior maxillary teeth or 'true molars.' In the lower series each ramus of the mandible exhibits an anterior group of *four* median teeth of small size, and similar shape; next to these is *one* large caniniform tooth, and behind this are *six* molariform teeth, of which the three posterior have no milk predecessors. According to Professor Owen and Mr Spence Bate, whose statement is accepted by Mr St George Mivart, in his Essay in this Journal, the large outer intermaxillary tooth is *the* 'canine.'   Mr Bate says simply and plainly, *because* it is in the intermaxillary bone[1], but this is, as we need not remark, the very thing which makes it *not* the canine, according to Professor Owen's definition.   De Blainville calls the tooth next behind this tooth *the* canine; and, by a curious insight, groups together all the intermaxillary teeth, though he probably never saw the sutures of the adjacent bones.   De Blainville's canine is a diminutive tooth, which has clearly no claim to such distinction, as Professor Allman remarks with regard to the similarly placed tooth in Potamogale.   Coming to the lower jaw, we find that Professor Owen's rule for determining the names (for it can determine nothing more) of the lower series of teeth leads him to call the simple little tooth belonging to the median group—the lower canine—whilst the large caniniform next to it is reckoned a præmolar.   Professors Bell and De Blainville both count *four* lower incisors

---

[1] "This tooth is implanted within the limits of the præmaxillary bones, the suture separating them passing through the posterior portion of its alveolus: thus demonstrating that this deciduous tooth is the true homologue of that of the canine in the mammalian type," p. 273; and again, "In these bones are situated, on each side of the central suture, the four anterior deciduous teeth," p. 272.

(our median group) to each ramus, and take Owen's first præ-molar for *the* 'canine.' The shortest way in which we can express the chief facts of relation in the mole's dentition is as follows. We should be sorry to call this a formula.

PRÆMAX. 4. MAX. ant. 4. post. 3. MANDIB. med. 4. ant. lat. 4. post. lat. 3. or, to avoid futile discussion as to the grouping of the median and lateral mandibular teeth, we may write MAN-DIB. med. and ant. lat. 8. post. lat. 3.

Apart from the questions of nomenclature which we have been discussing, we have above pointed out a most unexpected and unprecedented fact with regard to the mole's dentition. It is the only placental mammal in which eight intermaxillary teeth occur. Mr Spence Bate has the merit of observing and illustrating this fact, though he appears to have not appreciated it. The existence of a double fang to the tooth, called canine by Prof. Owen and Mr Spence Bate, and which is now shewn to belong to the intermaxillary group, acquires an additional in-terest. It has its parallel in the case of the outermost inter-maxillary of the *Galeopithecus*, in which animal the first ante-rior maxillary (so-called canine) has also a double fang.

III. Mr Flower, in his recent admirable paper on the Den-tition of the Marsupials, has laid some stress on the fact that, in several diphyodont mammalia, some of the anterior maxillary teeth never have predecessors, as in the case of the second an-terior maxillary teeth of the dog, and the corresponding lateral mandibular teeth, and in the hog also. We are led to believe, from the examination of a fine series of Badgers' skulls in the University Museum, that this animal furnishes an additional example. In three skulls, possessing the permanent dentition, we found a small peg-like tooth implanted in the jaw imme-diately behind the caniniform maxillary, and somewhat inter-nally to the general line of the teeth, and obviously correspond-ing to the small anterior lateral tooth (præmolar) of the lower series abutting against the large caniniform. We found no trace of this tooth in a young skull with the perfect deciduous dentition, nor in De Blainville's figure of the same. It is de-scribed neither by Owen nor De Blainville, and is evidently easily lost, since it had dropped out of one skull, leaving only its alveolus as evidence of its former presence; and in two other skulls no traces of it were to be seen at all. The addition of this tooth makes the dentition of the Badger the same as that of the Glutton.

Figs 5 and 6 on Pl. II. give a representation of the development of the Mole's dentition after Spence Bate (*Trans. Odon. Soc.* Vol. v.) lettered and numbered according to the views in this paper.

THE VALVE OF THE FORAMEN OVALE.

Fig. 3 on Pl. II. represents part of the wall of the left auricle of a foetal calf, at about three months, with the valve of the foramen ovale projecting into it. The valve, resembling one half of a funnel longitudinally bisected, is attached, in the greater part of its circumference, to the right-auricular side of the thick edge which surrounds the 'foramen'. Towards the part most distant from the vena cava inferior it creeps upon the left side of the edge of the foramen and, finally, is attached quite within the left auricle. The extremity of its attachment here is in the form of two columns. These are nearly united where they are blended with the lining membrane of the auricle, then separate and form the margins of the aperture between the two auricles. The valve is very loose ; and the part near the aperture has a beautifully cribriform structure composed of fine interlacing fibres hanging into the left auricle and permitting the blood to pass through it as well as through the aperture.

Fig. 4 represents the corresponding part of a human foetus at about three months. The half-funnel-like valve is attached more to the margin of the 'foramen' than it is in the calf; but the columns bounding its aperture extend some distance upon the surface of the left auricle, so that when the valve falls to, it quite closes the foramen. The anterior edge of the valve, however, is very loose, so that when pressed towards the left it separates from the edge of the foramen, and an oblique opening of considerable size is formed for the passage of blood from the vena cava. There is none of the cribriform appearance so marked in the calf and which is also shown in a preparation from a foetal horse in the anatomical museum of this University. The preparations were made by Mr Gedge of Caius College.

G. M. HUMPHRY.

THE DISSECTION OF A CASE OF ECTOPIA VESICÆ.

By Professor Humphry.   (Pl. III.)

A YOUNG man with this malformation, who had long been under my notice, died during the present year; and I am indebted to Mr Carver for removing the parts, and for assistance in dissecting them.

There was, as usual in such cases, a deficiency of the lower and fore part of the abdominal wall; so that the mucous surface of the hinder part of the bladder was exposed and on a level with the surrounding skin, and the orifices of the ureters, from which the urine continually trickled away during life, could be easily seen. The surface of the bladder was partially concealed by the penis, which was short, inclined upwards and flat, or nearly flat, upon the upper surface where it presented a slight median longitudinal groove. The mucous membrane of the bladder was continued along the upper surface of the penis to the glans penis which was smaller and flatter than usual : it was encrusted with urinary salts and otherwise altered so as to create a difficulty in defining its precise limits; but it appeared to be continuous with the adjacent skin of the abdominal wall and of the penis. The scrotum was wide and flat with a slight fullness at the sides indicating the position of the testicles.

The symphysial margins of the pubes were separated—écarté—nearly three inches. Between them was extended a fibrous membrane which may be regarded as the representative of the 'symphysial structure' and the 'triangular ligament' for it was continued, unbroken and without any orifice for the urethra, across the under part of the pelvis from the upper level of the pubic bones, between the pubic and ischiatic rami, upon the fore part of the rectum. It was a tolerably firm structure, and constituted a chief support of the pelvic and abdominal organs.

The 'crura penis' (fig. 1, C. c.), attached as usual to the rami of the ischiatic and pubic bones, were long. They met in the middle line beneath the membrane just described and were continued on into the 'corpus cavernosum,' terminating in round ends beneath the glans penis which was reflected over them from above, instead of, as it usually is, from beneath. At the angle of their union there was no 'bulb' or only a slight trace of it; and along the under surface of the corpus cavernosum there was no trace of corpus spongiosum. This indeed, or its representative—the membrane covering the groove before mentioned—was situated above, extending from the bladder, or prostate, along the upper surface of the corpus cavernosum to the glans penis.

The 'erectores penis' muscles were disposed as usual; also the 'transversi perinei,' but these were many times larger than usual. The 'acceleratores urinæ' were composed of strong bundles passed from the rami of the pubic and ischiatic bones to the middle line. They were connected, behind, with the transversi perinei by the 'central tendinous point' and, in front, with the converging crura penis. Thus they, with the transversi perinei and the crura penis, constituted a powerful aid to the symphysial membrane in supporting the viscera.

The 'Prostate' (fig. 1, P) was oblong, bilobed, and open, much resembling, in form, an ordinary prostate, the anterior part of which has been divided longitudinally in the usual mode of opening the bladder from the urethra. The kidneys and ureters were natural. The 'testes' (T. T) were natural, but small. The 'vasa deferentia' (v. d), rather dilated as they approached the prostate, passed through it, and opened much as usual. The orifices of their ducts were about a quarter of an inch from the bladder, and an inch and half from the extremity of the penis. They were, of course, exposed during life. The 'vesiculæ seminales' were absent or represented only by the slight dilatation of the vasa deferentia just mentioned.

The prostate was close to the corpus cavernosum, there being no intervening membranous portion of the urethra; and the mucous membrane was continued directly from the bladder, over the superior surface of the prostate, upon the superior surface of the corpus cavernosum above the symphysial membrane. This latter intervened between the prostate and the crura penis, but stopped just short of the union of the crura penis in the corpus cavernosum.

It will be perceived, therefore, that the urinary tract, instead of being continued forwards as a tube perforating the triangular ligament, passing under the angle formed by the uniting crura penis and running upon the under surface of the corpus cavernosum, was continued directly forwards from the prostate, over the anterior edge of the triangular ligament and the anterior surface of the penis, to the glans penis.

The 'recti abdominis' muscles as they descended to the hinder margins of the pubes were widely separated, the interval being occupied by the 'linea alba' unusually wide and unusually strong. Beneath the lower edge of the linea alba was the space occupied by the hinder wall of the bladder.

There was no visible navel. The round ligament of the liver was traced to the upper edge of the membrane of the bladder; and the hypogastric cords passed to the same point which must be regarded as the representative of the umbilicus. There did not appear to be any distinct space, such as has been described in some cases, between the wall of the bladder and the situation for the navel; but the outline of the mucous surface of the bladder was not sufficiently defined, in consequence of deposit upon it and other changes preceding death, to permit of this being positively determined.

The external inguinal ring was formed as usual, the inner column being continued, partly, into the symphysial ligament. A hernial sac of peritoneum (fig. 1, H. h) extended, on each side, through the inguinal canal into the scrotum to near the testis; and a narrow channel of the tunica vaginalis ran up into close contact with the hernial sac; but there was no communication between the two.

The pelvis (fig. 4) presents very remarkable features, the most important being the interval between the pubic bones which measures at the narrowest part $2\frac{3}{4}$ inches[1]. In the recent state it was, as described, traversed by a fibrous membrane representing the symphysial tissue and extending between the pubic bones. The interval is due, chiefly, to the direction of the pelvic bones, which is such that the pubic bones and the

---

[1] I remember a similar specimen in the Musée Dupuytren in Paris.

ascending rami of the ischium, instead of inclining to the middle line, are continued almost straight forwards. In addition to this the anterior part of the pubes—that between the spine and the symphysis (usually called the crest) and between the obturator hole and the symphysis—is about a third less broad than usual; and the edge of the bone is here thinner than natural, in short, a proper amount of growth has not taken place in this situation. The obturator hole is of the ordinary size; and the tubera ischii and other parts of the innominate bones are as well developed as usual.

The other peculiarities appear to be dependent on this ecartement of the pubic bones—this incompleteness of the fore part of the pelvic circle. The sacrum (fig. 3) instead of being concave in front from above downwards, is convex, or, rather, forms a projecting angle between the second and third sacral vertebræ; and the intervertebral space is, in this instance, ossified over. Transversely also the sacrum is slightly convex, i. e. the bodies of the several vertebræ project in front of the lateral parts. This arching of the sacrum forwards makes the upper surface, upon which the body of the last vertebra rests, to look a little backwards, causing the vertebra to be set further backwards than natural; so that it does not overhang the pelvis so much as usual. The lower part of the sacrum is also directed backwards; and it is only in the body of the last sacral vertebra that we observe any trace of the ordinary curve which is continued in the coccyx. In this limited space the curve is sharper than usual.

The surfaces of the sacro-iliac symphysis have nearly their usual form; but that on the ilium is shifted forwards and rendered more vertical, thus diminishing, by nearly one half, the extent of surface which the iliac bone of each side usually contributes to the brim of the pelvis, and narrowing greatly the ischiatic notch. For the same reason the projection of the iliac bones behind the symphysial surfaces is greatly increased, and they nearly meet in the middle line, behind, over the sacrum. The condition may be roughly imitated in the skeleton of an ordinary pelvis by pressing the sacrum forwards half way to the acetabula and separating the pubic bones. The iliac bones will then project posteriorly and be inclined towards one another so as nearly to meet, in the middle line, behind the sacrum. This forward advance of the sacrum, diminishing the distance between it and the acetabula, is obviously a provision, in the absence of the fore part of the pelvic circle, for preventing the thrusting of the acetabula inwards, that is, towards one another; and the anterior convexity of the sacrum, together with its vertical position, and the greater overhanging of the iliac bones, behind, contribute to the same purpose.

The approximation of the acetabula to the plane of the vertebral column, which in this specimen has been effected by the advance of the sacrum forwards, is observable in most animals, as Birds, Bats, the Hedgehog, and others, in which the lower part of the pelvic arch is weak or incomplete. Whereas in those animals—Ruminants, Solipeds, the Tortoise, and many others—in which the lower or pubic and ischiatic part of the arch is strong, the acetabula are placed at a greater distance from the spine. In short the distancing of the acetabula from the pubes bears, as a general rule, a relation to the strength of the fore, or under, part of the pelvic arch.

This malformation is by no means uncommon; and many instances of it have been recorded[1], though not often with a description of the pelvis, and of the dissection of the soft parts. It depends, probably, as supposed by Vrolik and others, upon a deficiency in the development of the fore part of that inferior portion of the allantoic sac which extends from the bowel to the umbilicus, and which is, under ordinary circumstances, covered by the abdominal parietes. The allantois, as is well known, is developed from the hinder part of the visceral layer of the embryo, and is early covered in by the other more superficial layers which form the abdominal wall and which, growing from opposite sides, meet in the linea alba over it. Nevertheless, it does not, like most other portions of the visceral tract, become separated from the abdominal wall, but grows up in close con-

[1] Under the name 'prolapse.' 'inversion,' or 'fissure' of the bladder. See Vrolik in *Cyclopedia Anat.* IV. 950, Martels in *Archiv für Anat.* 1868, p. 165 &c. Both these give instances in which the development of the hinder wall of the allantois failed as well as the anterior, and the bladder consequently was represented by two lateral pieces.

nection with it. A failure in the development of a part or of the whole length of the anterior surface of this part of the allantois is very liable to occur; and when it does take place it affects the entire thickness of the abdominal wall which is contiguous to and connected with it. The umbilicus is at the one extremity of the allantoic tract, and the glans penis at the other; for the urethra is a prolongation of one part of the allantois, as is the urachus of another. Thus we may have an open urachus, a cleft on the upper surface of the penis into the urethra, i.e. epispadius; or, as in the case before us, the deficiency may extend along the whole line of the allantoic tract, and the urinary passage may be laid open from the umbilicus to the extremity of the penis.

What determines this particular defect of development in a part or the whole of the anterior wall of the allantois, and of the tissues that should cover it, we do not know. We can imagine a preternatural distension of the allantoic sac under an accumulation of secretions poured into it, or in other ways, causing it to bulge, and so interfering with the formation of tissues in and upon it in a manner similar to that which appears to take place in spina bifida; but there is no evidence of such a cause. Being at the greatest distance from the starting line of growth of the abdominal plates, the anterior median line is at some disadvantage; and the tissues produced along it are, under ordinary circumstances, of less variety, and of lower grade than in other parts of the abdominal wall; and we might, à priori, have inferred that a failure of development would be more likely to be witnessed here than elsewhere. Perhaps in this topical disability, added to variations in the conditions of the allantois or the amount of its contents, we may recognise a cause of the not unfrequent presence of congenital fissure or opening into the urethro-vesical tract.

When such a gap occurs and the integumental and other strata of the abdominal plates fail to close over the urinary tract, the anterior wall of the pelvis, and the several structures connected with it (the symphysial ligament, the corpus cavernosum, &c.) can be formed only behind, instead of in front of, the urinary tract, and the approximation of the pubic bones is liable to be prevented. The separation of the pubic bones will of itself tend to cause an approximation of the iliac bones behind the sacrum, and to promote the advance of this bone forwards towards the acetabula.

The absence of vesiculæ seminales may have relation to the open state of the urethra. They are commonly absent in those animals, Birds and Reptiles, in which the urethra is a groove. These organs vary, however, a good deal even in members of the same class.

DESCRIPTION OF PLATE II.

Fig. 1. A view, from behind, of the urinary and genital organs with part of the abdominal wall.—*B*, the hinder surface of the bladder with its peritoneal covering.— *U*, *U*, the ureters.—*T*. *T*, the testes of which the right has been exposed by cutting the tunica vaginalis; and a pin has been inserted into the cul-de-sac, which is prolonged from the cavity of the tunica vaginalis, close up to but not quite into the hernial sac (*H. h*).—*H. H*, are rods passed into the hernial pouches.— *V. d*, vas deferens: the dotted line runs to the slight dilatation near the prostate which constitutes the only representative of the vesicula seminalis.

Fig. 2. A normal sacrum with two lumbar vertebræ to contrast with those from the specimen (Fig. 3).

Fig. 4. The pelvis and two lower lumbar vertebræ, shewing the interval between the pubic bones, the advanced position of the sacrum, the narrowness of the sciatic notches, &c.

ON THE CHANGES IN THE NERVOUS SYSTEM WHICH FOLLOW THE AMPUTATION OF LIMBS.

By W. H. Dickinson, M.D. Cantab. F.R.C.P., *Assistant Physician to St George's Hospital, and to the Hospital for Sick Children.* (Pl. IV.)

Some years ago, in the hope of throwing light upon a conclusion which I had formed to the effect that the cerebellum directed its influences in an especial manner to the lower limbs, I sought opportunities of examining the brain after amputation of the extremities in the vain expectation of finding that the portion of the encephalon which regulated the movements of each limb would be declared by a localized atrophy consequent upon its removal.

After weighing and examining with the microscope the various parts of the brain, in several cases in which one or more limbs had long been absent, I was driven to the conclusion that loss of the extremities was not followed by loss of weight, or by appreciable change of structure, either in the cerebellum or in the hemispheres or great ganglia of the cerebrum[1].

Failing to find atrophy within the cranium as the result of

[1] This statement rests upon the examination of four cases of amputation of one leg, and one of amputation of both. In the four cases, one leg had been removed at periods varying from two years to fifty-three years before death. In each instance I divided the cerebrum and cerebellum as carefully as possible along the median plane and then weighed the separated halves of each structure. The inequality of weight was very small, such only as must necessarily have resulted from accidental unfairness of section, and the loss was sometimes on the side of the amputation, sometimes on the opposite side. With regard to the cerebellum in particular I found that the lobe on the side of the operation appeared in three of the cases to have lost weight to the amount of about 30 grains, while in the fourth case that lobe was heavier than its fellow by 8 grains. I judged therefore that neither cerebrum nor cerebellum acquired any lateral inequality of bulk as the result of the removal of one leg.

In the case in which both legs had been removed, the operation had been performed on both limbs just below the knee, twenty-five years before death. As there was no reason to expect any difference between the two sides, the halves of the brain were not divided. The cerebrum weighed 46½ ounces; the cerebellum 4 ounces 300 grains; the cerebellum having a proportion to the encephalon of 1 to 10·2, a proportion which could not be looked upon as abnormal. I may add that the microscope shewed nothing unnatural in the structure of any part of the encephalon, and that in the four cases previously mentioned, the same instrument gave similar negative results.

these mutilations I next sought to trace evidences of change by commencing at the stump and working upwards, hoping by this means to secure evidence of a more positive kind.

I will give a brief statement of the facts I have obtained. The subjects of the following observations were seamen who died in Greenwich Hospital.

CASE 1.—A seaman who was fighting on board the *Dictator* Frigate, in an action with the Danes, on the sixth of July, 1812, had his left leg carried away by a cannon shot. Amputation was performed at the junction of the upper and middle thirds of the thigh, and a wooden leg subsequently provided. He died in the year 1865 at the age of 74, having survived the loss of his limb for 53 years. Through the kindness of Dr Maclaurin I was enabled to attend the post-mortem examination.

The stump was conical and much wasted, the muscles being very soft and fatty. At the end of the sciatic nerve was a large globular neuroma. The nerve was dissected out up to the pelvis, as also was the corresponding portion of the sciatic nerve on the right side. The two nerves laid side by side looked almost exactly alike, no difference being observed in bulk, texture, or colour. They were hardened in chromic acid, and transverse sections were examined with the following results.

The bundles of nerve-fibres were not perceptibly altered in size or arrangement, and to the naked eye no difference could be discerned save that in the left sciatic nerve the contents of the fasciculi became more deeply coloured with carmine than those on the right side. Under the microscope, however, a most striking difference was found.

In the nerve of the right, or sound limb, the nerve-bundles, each surrounded by the natural thin envelope of fibrous tissue, consisted of a close regular arrangement of nerve-tubes, each of which shewed distinctly the outer white matter and the central grey cylinder. The nerve-tubes were comparatively uniform in size, and were in contact with each other, excepting where they were separated by minute blood-vessels or by the fine fibrous septa by which those structures are naturally supported.

In the nerve of the stump the characteristic structure had

undergone so complete a disorganization that the nervous structure could scarcely be recognized. While the nerve-bundles retained their natural bulk and external conformation, the uniform tubular arrangement proper to their interior was replaced by a material which, under a low power of the microscope, presented merely a coarse granulation which absorbed carmine more freely than the natural nerve structure. A higher power (300 diameters) shewed that the coarse granules were for the most part minute circles, which differed from the sections of nerve-tubes not only in their exceeding minuteness, but in the fact that they presented no distinction between white and grey matter. These dwindled representatives of nerve-fibres were not, like the healthy tubes, in contact with each other, but were separated by, and imbedded in, a structureless material, which from its power of imbibing carmine was the means of imparting the peculiar pink tint to the section which has been referred to.

Some of the bundles composing the nerve consisted wholly of the disorganized structure described; in others a few normal nerve-tubes could be detected. All were surrounded by an envelope of connective tissue somewhat thicker than existed in the normal nerve[1].

The perfect preservation of the outer aspect and larger anatomy of the nerve is interesting, and would, had not the microscope been used, have led to the belief that the essential structure was natural.

Sections from the two nerves are represented in Figs. 1 and 2, and I may also refer to the representation of the same preparations which is given by Mr Lockhart Clarke in the current Vol. (LI) of the *Medico-Chirurgical Transactions*.

The spinal cord was examined in section after hardening in chromic acid, and the changes traced from below upwards.

In the portion between the lower extremity and the lumbar enlargement, the grey matter was somewhat smaller on the left

---

[1] I may here state by way of parenthesis that in the case of another Greenwich Pensioner who had suffered amputation of the thigh many years before death, precisely the same destruction of the fibres of the sciatic nerve was found, with the same retention of external appearance. I have not given this case in detail as I had no opportunity of examining the cord.

side than the right. The difference was very slight and might easily have escaped observation. No difference was observed in the shape of the grey crescent, or in its intimate structure. The nerve-cells were apparently the same on both sides. In this situation the white matter was symmetrical.

In the lumbar enlargement there was a decided loss of thickness in the left posterior column (Fig. 3, L), which was sufficient to cause distortion of the cord, giving in particular a slanting direction to the transverse commissure, in the neighbourhood of which the wasting of the posterior column was greater than nearer the circumference of the cord. The wasted column shewed a relative increase in connective tissue, as if this material had fallen together on the removal of nerve-tubes. The nerve-tubes which remained exactly resembled those of the opposite side in the corresponding situation. The atrophy of the left posterior column was traced up through the dorsal region. Here as in the lumbar enlargement the grey matter was symmetrical and apparently unaltered. No change was found in the white matter excepting what has been described as affecting the left posterior column. It was roughly estimated that this portion of the cord had lost, in the lumbar region rather more, in the dorsal region rather less, than a quarter of its bulk. (Fig. 4, L.)

The cervical part of the cord was not obtained for examination. Various sections however were made through the medulla oblongata, the two sides of which proved to be perfectly symmetrical and natural in all respects. The brain was examined with the negative result which has been already stated.

CASE 2.—In the year 1865, I examined the body of a Greenwich pensioner who had lost the left arm 23 years previously. In the year 1842 he had fallen from the rigging of his ship and so injured the limb that amputation had to be performed two inches from the shoulder-joint.

It is only necessary to describe the changes in the nervous system.

At the lower end of the cervical region, for the space of about two inches, there was a striking diminution of the left posterior nerve-roots. The strands of nerve-fibres were less than half the thickness of those on the right side; and were also considerably thinner than the anterior roots on the same side. No change in their colour or texture was evident to the naked eye.

On making transparent sections of the roots in different situations the following facts were apparent.

The dwindled posterior roots were materially altered in minute structure. The nerve-tubes instead of being uniformly packed in contact with each other were here and there separated by irregular masses of a carmine tinted material in which a high magnifying power shewed the shrivelled remains of nerve-tubes—minute circles with a central speck. The tubes which retained their bulk were not unnatural.

The left anterior roots corresponding to the atrophied posterior roots, though they were not appreciably altered in thickness, shewed under the microscope traces of the same partial destruction of nerve-fibres. In the anterior roots however the amount of the change was much smaller than in the posterior.

The spinal cord, examined after hardening in chromic acid, proved to be natural excepting in the cervical region.

In the cervical enlargement the left posterior column (Fig. 5, L) was reduced in thickness, presenting in section about two-thirds the surface shewn by its fellow. The loss of bulk chiefly affected the anterior part of the column, the part, that is, towards the commissure, where it had a very pointed outline compared with the column on the opposite side.

Beside the mere loss of bulk the wasted column was traversed by a line of altered structure, which passed from the circumference towards the centre in a radiating direction so as to divide the column into two nearly equal parts. Nerve-tubes were nowhere unnatural or totally absent, but the line of change was indicated by a condensation of areolar tissue, as if nerve-tubes had, at some period, been withdrawn from the structure.

The change described extended through the whole of the cervical region, being however more declared in the enlargement than elsewhere.

There was a slight diminution of bulk in the grey matter of the cervical enlargement. The crescent retained its shape, every part being apparently slightly and uniformly shrunk. The change was very trifling and might easily have escaped notice. It shewed no change in its microscopic characters, the cells being unchanged in appearance.

In the medulla oblongata it was found that on a level with the decussation of the pyramids there was the same wasting of the left posterior column (Fig. 6, L) as has been described in the cord, the change being continuous from the cervical region to the upper limit of the decussation. The loss of bulk and alteration of structure which has been described in the left posterior column of the cord was equally evident in the corresponding portion of the medulla in the position stated. Above the decussation all traces of the atrophy were lost, the medulla being symmetrical and natural in all respects.

CASE 3.—Last year I received from Dr Middelton the cord of an old Greenwich pensioner who had in consequence of an accident suffered amputation of the right forearm, in the year 1845. The cord had been placed in spirit before I obtained it, and did not yield such satisfactory sections as did the preparations which have been heretofore dwelt upon. The following points however were clearly made out.

In the cervical enlargement the right posterior column was narrowed especially towards the commissure. This column at the point of greatest loss presented about two-thirds of the bulk of the column of the left side. The grey matter had also suffered a slight diminution in bulk on the same side, the anterior horn being decidedly narrowed from before backwards. As in the preceding cases no change of structure could be detected in the grey matter. (Fig. 7, R.)

The medulla was not obtained for examination.

Placing together the several observations, it appears that when a limb has been absent, as the result of operation, for 20 or more years, the following changes have been found in the nervous system.

First, atrophy of the nerves of the stump, of which a large proportion of the fibres have perished, notwithstanding that,

supported by the fibrous tissue which enters into their structure, they retain their bulk and external appearance almost
without alteration.

Secondly, wasting of the nerve-roots, especially the posterior. The wasting of the tubes, in the absence of such fibrous
investure as belongs to the mixed nerves, produces an attenuation, which in the case of the posterior root is very conspicuous.

Thirdly, a slight loss of bulk in the grey matter of the
cord, on the side of the lost member, near the origin of its
nerves, without any intimate change discernible by the microscope.

Lastly, a remarkable shrinking of the posterior column of
the cord on the side of the mutilation, attended by a condensation of areolar tissue. The atrophy extends upwards,
and in the case of the loss of an arm can be traced into the
medulla oblongata as far as the upper limit of the decussation
of the pyramids.

The cerebrum and cerebellum remain unchanged.

I am aware that many details relating to this subject remain to be worked out, and I should have waited for further
opportunities had not my purpose been forestalled by M. Vulpian, who has, since these observations were made, published
two similar cases.

His results differ very materially from mine. Both the
cases he reports were of amputation of the leg, a little distance
above the ancle. In one case the leg had been removed for
47 years, in the other for 20 years. In both cases M. Vulpian
describes the spinal cord as slightly lessened in bulk on the
side of the amputation. This diminution affected the grey
matter generally, the white matter *with the exception of the
posterior column.*

The cells of grey matter were not altered in character, or
appreciably in number. In one of the cases some spots of disintegration were supposed to exist in the grey horn. No
changes were detected in the nerves or nerve-roots.

My results differ from those of M. Vulpian in the atrophy
of the nerves, posterior nerve-roots, and posterior columns of
the cord, which were found in my cases but not in his. His

cases and mine coincide in attributing a slight loss of bulk to the grey matter on the side of the mutilation.

Dr Waller long ago pointed out that nerves separated from their centres rapidly became atrophied. With regard to the spinal roots in particular he found that when an anterior root was cut the part retaining its connection with the cord remained unaltered, while the outer extremity wasted. After dividing a posterior root the reverse took place; the central end wasted, the peripheral end retained its structure. From these and other experiments, Dr Waller was led to conclude that the outer portion of the severed posterior root owed its retention of structure to the ganglion to which it was attached, while the nutrition of the motor root depended on the cord.

The facts brought forward in this paper appear to shew that these conclusions need modification. It would seem that the posterior root may waste though still in connection with the ganglion, the anterior though still in connection with the cord. The ganglion therefore is not the sole controller of the nutrition of one root, or the cord of the other. It appears that long disuse of a nerve is sufficient to lead to its atrophy notwithstanding that those nervous structures which more immediately regulate its nutrition are complete.

There are some points which as yet must be left without explanation, namely the greater atrophy of the sensory than of the motor roots, and the peculiar wasting of the posterior columns, passing vertically up the cord, and in the case of loss of the arm affecting the medulla, a course not corresponding with that of the sensory fibres, which soon lose themselves in the grey matter.

I hope to pursue some of the questions which the subject suggests to a more complete issue, and to this end should be much obliged to anyone who has the opportunity of doing so, and is willing to be at the trouble, if they would send me the cord and medulla from any case in which amputation of a limb has been survived for several years.

I must in conclusion convey my thanks to the gentlemen who have assisted me on the present occasion, more especially to Sir Alexander Bryson, the Director General of the Navy Medical Department, and to Sir Edward Hilditch, Dr Maclaurin and Dr Middelton, formerly Officers at Greenwich Hospital.

DESCRIPTION OF PLATE IV.

Fig. 1 represents a transverse section of the normal sciatic nerve, magnified 300 diameters.

Fig. 2 represents a transverse section of the sciatic nerve from the stump of the same person fifty-three years after amputation, also magnified 300 diameters.

Fig. 3. A transverse section of the lumbar part of the spinal cord from the same person. L, the left posterior column rather smaller than the right.

Fig. 4. A transverse section of the dorsal part of spinal cord from the same person. L, the left posterior column, is distinctly smaller than the right.

Fig. 5. A transverse section of the cervical part of the spinal cord from a man whose left arm had been amputated twenty-three years before death. The left posterior column (L) is smaller than the right.

Fig. 6. Transverse section of the medulla oblongata from the same patient, shewing the left posterior column (L) smaller than the right.

Fig. 7. Transverse section of the cervical portion of the spinal cord from a man who had undergone amputation in the right forearm twenty-two years before death. R, the right posterior column, is smaller than the left.

ON THE QUESTION WHETHER THE EUSTACHIAN TUBE IS OPENED OR CLOSED IN SWALLOWING.

By Professor Cleland, *Galway*.

In the year 1853 Mr Toynbee laid before the Royal Society a paper the object of which was, as he afterwards stated it in the Report of the meeting of the British Association in 1861, "To demonstrate, *firstly*, that the faucial orifice of the Eustachian tube is always closed, except momentarily during the act of deglutition, or when air is forcibly blown through it; *secondly*, that the Eustachian tube is opened by the muscles of the palate, the *tensor* and *levator palati; thirdly*, that, contrary to the preconceived opinion of physiologists that if the Eustachian tube is closed the hearing is lost at once, in order that the function of hearing may be duly performed it is absolutely necessary for the Eustachian tube to be closed, otherwise the sonorous undulations which ought to be confined to the tympanic cavity in order that they may be concentrated upon the membrana fenestræ rotundæ, are lost in the fauces, and the sounds from the fauces also enter the tympanum and produce the most distressing discord."

In proof that the faucial orifice of the Eustachian tube remains closed after the act of swallowing, Mr Toynbee referred to the sensation in the ears produced by swallowing while the nostrils are closed by the finger and thumb, and the persistence of that sensation until the act of swallowing is repeated, also to the relief which the act of swallowing gives from the sensation of pressure in the ears felt during descent in a diving bell; and further stated that in cases in which the membrana tympani is lax it is seen to move outwards when air is blown into the tympanic cavity, and it returns to its natural position only on the act of swallowing being performed. On the occasion already alluded to, Mr Toynbee also exhibited an instrument contrived by Dr Politzer of Vienna by which it could be demonstrated that air blown into the tympanum pressed the membrana tympani outwards, and that the membrane continued pressed outwards until the next act of swallowing.

Mr Toynbee's view has obtained very general credence in this country; and although Hyrtl in his *Topographische Anatomie* writes in 1857, that while "Toynbee calls the Eustachian tube a closed canal, Kramer contends that it is open throughout, and in this shares the opinion of most physiologists," the manner in which more recently the anatomy of the parts is handled in the classic works of Henle and Luschka, to which I shall again refer, seems to show that among the Germans it is now generally considered that the tube is usually closed. I believe, however, that the evidence which I shall now adduce conclusively proves that it is usually open, and is momentarily closed in swallowing.

A man named Anthony Browne was admitted to hospital for ulcerative disease of the palate. The whole velum palati was considerably thickened, and immediately in front of it on the right side was an ulcerated aperture larger than a sixpenny piece, so situated that the orifice of the Eustachian tube could be distinctly seen. Being anxious to ascertain what really was the condition of the orifice in the act of swallowing, I caused the man to practise swallowing with his mouth open, and had the satisfaction of observing and of pointing out to others that the lower margin of the orifice of the tube, instead of being pulled down, as Toynbee believed, was spasmodically twitched up. So much in harmony did this movement seem with the spasmodic elevation of all the surrounding parts, that it struck one as a matter of course which ought to have been appreciated before. The larynx, hyoid bone and tongue, the pharynx and velum palati are all suddenly jerked upwards in swallowing; and the fixed basis from which the styloid muscles, tensor and levator palati, and superior constrictor muscle act to produce this effect is the skull; hence it happens that the pharynx, palate and tongue in their elevation push up the lower margin of the Eustachian orifice. It may be judged probable that when the act of swallowing is performed effectually and completely, this pushing upwards of the lower margin will be so great as altogether to close the Eustachian orifice. This was not observed in the case of the patient; but it is to be remembered that in his case the palate was stiff with morbid thickening, and that the depression of the lower jaw in keeping the mouth open rendered it more difficult to raise the hyoid bone and the adjoining parts than in ordinary swallowing.

The patient's hearing was unimpaired; and he heard the ticking of a watch as well with the one ear as with the other. A probe being passed into the exposed Eustachian tube, it was ascertained that the sides of the tube were certainly not in contact, at least for a considerable distance back from the orifice. A gutta-percha stopper pushed lightly into the tube for more than half an inch made no observable difference in hearing through the external meatus of the ear.

The observations just recorded would, I think, be sufficient to warrant an explicit denial of the Toynbee theory, but if we proceed to enquire into the supposed action of the levator and tensor palati muscles, additional light will be thrown on the subject.

If a dissection be made from the interior of the pharynx, and if the tensor and levator palati be pulled in the direction of their muscular fibres, it will be easily seen that no change is made on the orifice of the Eustachian tube; and indeed a careful examination will show that the tensor palati when contracted, so far from pulling the tube open, must block it by its increased thickness. The walls of the tube after its exit from the temporal bone are protected by a strong cartilage which bounds it above and passes down on the inner side and on the upper part of the outer side. Examining the walls of the tube from below, a groove is seen to lie along its whole extent. If now the tube be slit open from above, its lumen will be found to have the form of a vertical fissure, excepting only in the immediate neighbourhood of the guttural orifice; and the floor of the fissure will be observed to correspond with the inner margin of the inferior groove. In this position a small tendinous band exists, making the margin of the groove more defined: it is fixed to the temporal bone behind, and tapers away as its passes forwards: it may be termed the inferior tendon of the Eustachian tube. The groove is bounded externally by fibrous membrane which forms the inferior half of the internal wall of the tube; and internally it is bounded by the lower edge of the cartilage, which therefore enters into the formation of no more than the upper half of the inner wall of the tube, and stands out from it below. Near the guttural orifice, however, this is no longer the case, but the whole breadth of the groove is bounded inferiorly by fibrous membrane which forms a moveable convex floor. Now the levator palati arises somewhat tendinously from the apex of the petrous portion of the temporal bone, and by scattered fibres from the inner margin of the inferior tendon of the Eustachian tube, and from the groove; and it occupies the groove in its whole extent, filling it up. Its fibres run parallel with the Eustachian tube, in contact

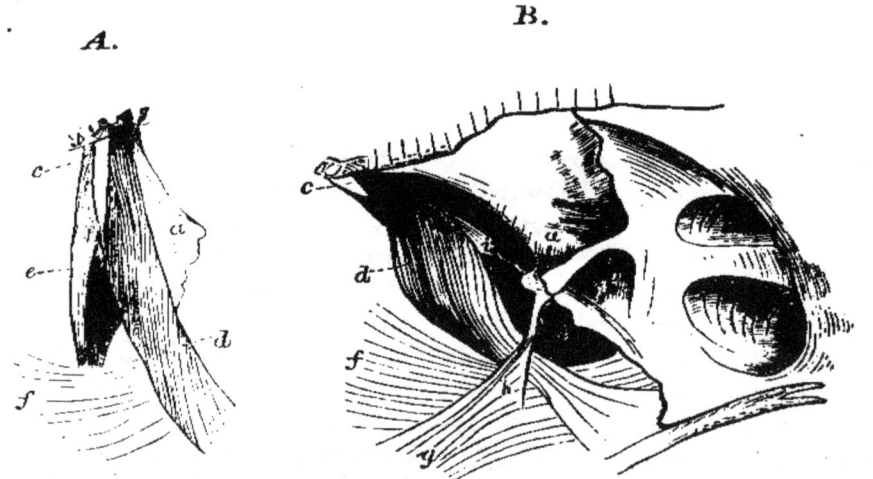

A. The Eustachian tube from beneath and behind, with the levator palati lying in the groove.

B. View from the interior of the pharynx, the levator palati withdrawn from the groove.

a, The cartilage of the Eustachian tube; b, the guttural orifice; c, the inferior tendon; d, the levator palati; e, the tensor palati; f, the superior constrictor of the pharynx; g, the palato-pharyngeus; h, the salpyngo-pharyngeus; i, the groove beneath the Eustachian tube.

with it, but very few of them attached to it; and therefore it cannot possibly pull the tube open, but, on the contrary, when it is contracted its thickness is increased, and it must obviously elevate the floor of the orifice precisely after the fashion in which it was observed to be elevated in the man Browne when he swallowed. It is very remarkable that Luschka has beautifully described this function of the levator palati, and yet so completely has he been misled by the prevalent notion that the surfaces of the tube are usually in contact, that, taking no account of the action of swallowing, he imagines that the object gained by the levator palati compressing the Eustachian tube is merely "so to press the yielding under side against the firm wall as completely to obliterate the opening during coughing, sneezing, and vomiting[1]."

Those fibres of the tensor palati muscle which take origin from the Eustachian tube are attached on its outer side to the perichondrium of the imperfect cartilaginous wall; and it is now admitted that this muscle cannot pull the membranous outer wall of the tube away from the inner, seeing that none of the muscular fibres take origin from the membranous part, and that the direction of the muscle being downwards it could not in any case pull the wall outwards. But a new view has sprung up, originating with Rüdinger[2], and held by both Henle and Luschka, that the cartilaginous part of the external wall of the tube is somewhat rolled in, and that the fibres of the tensor palati being partly attached to the edge of the cartilage pull it down and unroll it, and thereby open the tube. Rüdinger, it would appear, considers that the upper part of the lumen, contained in the fold of the cartilage, is permanently open, but that the remaining part can only be opened by the unrolling of the inner edge of the cartilage as described. Laying open, by means of a slit in the roof, the otherwise uninjured Eustachian tube, I find little rolling in of the external wall such as has been described; and on pulling the fibres of the tensor palati muscle in the line of their direction, I have seen none of the unrolling action which is alleged. It seems probable that the writers named have been misled by the transverse sections which they used. In these the cartilage was loosened from its surrounding connections, and it is not wonderful that it should in these circumstances have fallen into the position

---

[1] Luschka, *Anatomie des Menschen*, III. 466.
[2] Rüdinger, *Beitrag zur Anatomie und Histologie der Tuba Eustachii*, 1865; referred to by Luschka, and in Henle's *Bericht* for 1865, p. 107.

which they have described as normal. On pulling the most posterior fibres of the tensor palati I find that there is actually a slight driving inwards of the wall of the tube, which leads me to think that at the same moment when the faucial orifice is closed by the spasmodic elevation of its floor, the commencement of the cartilaginous part of the tube has its outer and inner walls brought into momentary contact. It is curious to observe that the possibility of this action occurred to Henle when writing his description of the tensor palati; but that afterwards when he came to the description of the Eustachian tube, the influence of the notion that the tube is opened in the act of swallowing was such that he took up the idea of the muscle unrolling the cartilage[1]. There is little inducement to strive for that idea, when once the two points are made out, that the levator palati closes the Eustachian orifice, and that it does so in the act of swallowing.

Perhaps one ought to take notice of the small and inconstant salpyngo-pharyngeus which might be supposed to act on the Eustachian tube; but it is attached not to the membranous floor of the orifice but to the thick extremity of the cartilage; it is also an extremely minute slip, and its lower attachment is mobile, so that it has obviously no action but to assist the palato-pharyngeus and superior constrictor in elevating the pharynx. There is a muscle, however, which assists the levator palati in closing the orifice of the Eustachian tube, viz. the superior constrictor of the pharynx. The arched upper border of that muscle, extending from the internal pterygoid plate to the body of the sphenoid bone, lies immediately beneath the trumpet-shaped opening, and when made tense and straight in swallowing must inevitably press the levator palati against it.

Having now appealed to the anatomy of the parts as well as to observation on the living subject to disprove the theory that the Eustachian tube is usually closed, and is opened in swallowing, we have yet to seek an explanation of the phenomena on which the theory is based, and particularly of the circumstance that when air is blown into the tympanum dis-

[1] Henle, *Handbuch der Systematischen Anatomie des Menschen*, II. 117 and 755.

placement of the membrana tympani continues until the act of swallowing is performed. The explanation that a film of moisture occludes the tube, an explanation which must have forced itself on every uninitiated person suffering from coryza, is, I believe, the right one. The propulsion of air through the nares acts powerfully in setting the moisture of the mucous membrane in motion; and in the Eustachian tube it sends it back in the contrary direction to that in which it is normally carried by the cilia of the epithelial lining. The transverse diameter of the tube is extremely small, and a very slight accumulation of moisture in any part of it will cause by capillary attraction an obstruction sufficiently strong to resist a considerable pressure of air, or possibly may even cause its sides to adhere with the action of a sucker. The sudden closure and alteration of the form of the tube in swallowing, and the equally sudden recovery of its natural form is precisely the operation most likely to burst such an obstruction, expel superabundant moisture, and allow the escape of pent-up air. The disagreeable sensation in the ears in descending in a diving bell seems to depend on more than one cause; but engorgement of the mucous lining of the Eustachian tube and atmospheric pressure at its pharyngeal extremity are things very likely to occasion obstructions of the lumen; and once such obstruction is formed, and the freedom of communication of the tympanic cavity with the external air is checked, discomfort may be expected immediately to begin.

A point in favour of this view, and fatal to the Toynbee theory, is to be found in the circumstance that when the sensation of pressure on the tympanum has been accidentally produced by blowing the nose or in some other way, if it be allowed to remain, or if swallowing is ineffectual to remove it, it will often, after a little, suddenly disappear with a slight noise when no act of swallowing is being performed.

NOTES ON SOME POINTS IN THE ANATOMY OF THE PERINEUM. By GEORGE W. CALLENDER, *Lecturer on Anatomy at St Bartholomew's Hospital.*

THE anterior portion of the outlet of the pelvis which bounds the perineum is formed by the bone extending on either side from the lower angle of the symphysis pubis to the tuberosity of the ischium. The space within these limits, and a line drawn from one tuberosity to its fellow, triangular in shape, has its several sides nearly equal; and although it is possible that some differences may exist, yet I find, from measuring the pelvis in various adult male skeletons, that material differences must be rare, whether in the side length of the perineum, or in its transverse measurement.

In twenty-four adult male skeletons, each side of the perineal triangle has an average length of 3·2 inches; in two cases the length is 3·7, in two cases it is 3·1 inches; but in each of those remaining it is 3·2. In the same skeletons the distance intermediate to the tuberosities averages 3·3 inches, but in fourteen instances it is either 3·4 or 3·5 inches, the average being affected by four cases in which the line measures from 2·7 to 2·9 inches. The distance is greatest (3·7) with a length of perineum of 3·2 inches; with the minimum length of 3·1, the breadth is 2·7 inches in one case, and 3·2 in the second; with the maximum length of 3·7 inches, the breadth is 3·5.

Twelve of the measurements referred to are given in the following table :—

Perineal division of pelvic outlet.

Length of side.	Breadth.
3·1 inches............	2·7 inches
3·1 "	3·2 "
3·2 "	3·7 "
3·2 "	3·5 "
3·2 "	3·5 "
3·2 "	3 "
3·2 "	3·5 "

Length of side.	Breadth.
3·2 inches ....3·4 inches.
3·2 " ....2·9 "
3·2 " ....3·5 "
3·7 " ....3·5 "
3·7 " ....3·5 "

Dupuytren in twenty-three subjects found that the distance between the tuberosities varied from two inches to three and a half inches. Velpeau in forty subjects met with one in which the distance was only one inch and three quarters, whilst in another they were four inches apart. I believe the figures I have given fairly represent the measurements with which, for this country, we are concerned.

In a male skeleton twenty-nine inches long, the length of either side of the perineum is 1·2 inches, the width 1·2 inches; in one of thirty inches I find the measurements fractionally less than the preceding. In a male skeleton of thirty-six inches the length is 1·7, the width 1·8 inches; in one of forty-four inches the length is 2·2, the width 2·5 inches; in one of forty-eight inches the length is 2·2, the width 2·6 inches. The boundaries of the perineum, it will be observed, having much the same relative proportions as in the adult.

The structures connected with the perineum shew their mutual relations more distinctly perhaps when examined in a mature fœtus than when dissected in the adult From some dissections I had to make of various fœtuses I was led to note the following points.

Looking from the pelvis towards the perineum, and after removing the peritoneum, a delicate fascia, spreading from the front and sides of the pelvis over the base of the bladder, and over the front and sides of the rectum, is brought into view. The only parts of this fascia stronger than the rest are two narrow bands; which pass from behind the pubes, on either side of the symphysis, to the front and sides of the bladder, in the tissues of which they are lost. If these bands (to call them ligaments of the bladder only complicates matters) are removed with the intermediate fascia, the fibres uniting the pubic bones below the symphysis are seen closing the upper angle of the perineal triangle, and these form the only triangular ligament properly so called, beneath, not through which the urethra passes out. To write of the fascia which lines the pelvis, part of which dips in beneath the front of the levator ani, and which extends over the front and base of the bladder, as connected with the triangular ligament, is incorrect. This fascia covers the triangular ligament on the side of the pelvis, simply as it covers the pelvic surface of the levator ani muscle.

If the pelvic fascia is wholly removed, then on either side of the triangular ligament, and thence backwards, the levator ani muscle is in view. The anterior fibres of this muscle extend in a direction backwards and upwards to the side of the prostate (levator prostatæ), on which some are lost, but others are continued into the adjacent wall of the bladder, just about and above the trigone, whilst others pass between the bladder and the rectum. These fibres doubtless assist in supporting the prostate and the bladder.

Removing the anterior part of the levator ani, the muscular fibres which are placed below the triangular ligament, and which surround the urethra between the prostate and the bulb, known collectively as the constrictor urethræ, may be examined; they ought to be regarded in some sort as a continuation of the levator ani. Arising from the upper part of either pubic ramus, the fibres pass both above and below the membranous portion of the urethra, forming a plane of muscular tissue which reaches in front of and sustains the prostate gland, to which, and through which to the bladder, it serves the purpose of a sustaining muscle, and resists, when necessary, the forcible bearing down of these structures towards the perineum. As the direction of its fibres is from behind forwards, that is towards the surface, its contraction tends to draw the membranous portion of the urethra and the prostate backwards. I doubt very much if this muscle causes any constriction of the urethra; it should be known as the levator prostatæ. Its relations are fairly represented in Santorini's plate, from which the method of its action is sufficiently evident. Its fibres, reaching forward in waving lines, mix from opposite sides in a kind of raphe, above and below the urethra, a very small number being traceable from one side to the opposite, whilst a few are prolonged by the side of, and below the bulb, to the tendinous centre of the perineum.

The other muscles of this region to which I would refer, are the transversus perinæi of either side, and the superficial sphincter.

Taking the transverse muscles collectively, and recognising the great irregularity of the deeper fibres, we find that the latter are directed inwards from the pubic arch to meet from opposite sides behind the bulb at the centre of the perineum. In this passage some of the fibres pass well nigh horizontally, others have a direction forwards, but the fibres of the superficial transversus perinæi, arising from the lower part of the inner surface of the pubic arch, are all directed forwards, that is towards the symphysis, and inwards, to unite at the centre of the perineum with the muscle of the opposite side. Thus we have fibres converging to the perineal centre, some horizontal, some ascending; and as all of these are more deeply placed at their origin from the bones than at their insertion, for the central tendon is superficial as compared with the inner surface of the rami, their action is first to steady the perineum, and secondly, to draw its centre backwards towards the pelvis.

The superficial sphincter coming from the tip and back of the coccyx, passing forward on each side of the anus, joins with the transverse muscles at the central point or tendon, and thus, in addition to other services, helps to support the perineum, and to draw its centre backwards.

In an ordinary description of the perineum, either the parts are dissected from the surface towards the deeper regions, or are written of with reference to various surgical operations, and very properly so. But either plan fails to illustrate the purposes served by the structures to which I have briefly referred. These structures are beautifully adapted to support and to hold in place the viscera against which they are applied. Acting after the fashion of the levator ani, they are associated with that muscle in various secondary actions, but their primary use is this; the superficial external sphincter, and the various transverse fibres stretch, like so much rigging, from the bony boundaries of the pelvic outlet to the centre of the perineum, fix it and sustain it against downward pressure, and by their contraction draw it up towards the pelvis. The constrictor urethræ, inappropriately so named, forms the second line of support, acting more immediately to sustain the membranous urethra and the prostate gland, and as some of its fibres may be traced, as already stated, to the central tendon, its retracting power must be very considerable. Supplementing these lesser structures, the levator ani completes the series of muscles which sustain and brace up the viscera which rest upon the perineum.

SESAMOID BONE IN THE TENDON OF THE SUPINATOR BREVIS.

In the arm of a thin female subject, dissected in the Anatomy Hall of the College of Surgeons during the winter of 1867, I found a small round sesamoid bone in the tendon of the origin of the supinator brevis. The muscle arose from the external condyle above, and a little in front of, the origin of the external lateral ligament, and the small bony nodule lay upon the outer surface of the condyle with a small synovial bursa beneath it. The muscle had a supplemental origin from the external ligament, but it mainly arose from the tendon below the sesamoid bone. The existence of a nodule in this situation has not been before recognized to my knowledge, and it confers an additional probability on the theory which I put forward in a previous number of this Journal, that the supinator brevis is the serial homologue of the popliteus, as in the long tendon of that muscle winding over the external condyle of the femur a small cartilaginous or bony tubercle has been described, and the presence of a synovial sac under its tendon is the normal condition in the thigh.

ALEXANDER MACALISTER.

DUBLIN, *Sept.* 1868.

ON THE SKULL OF AN OTARIA (OTARIA ULLOÆ?) FROM THE CHINCHA ISLANDS. By JAMES M°BAIN, M.D., R.N.

THE osteological characters of this skull correspond to the genus Otaria, sub-family Arctocephalina of the British Museum Catalogue for 1866.

There is a well-marked post-orbital process and a distinct alisphenoid canal. The mastoid process stands aloof from the auditory bulla and forms a lateral ridge of about 1¾ths of an inch, extending from the meatus auditorius externus backwards and inwards to a level with the anterior part of the occipital condyle. The horizontal plates of the bones of the palate are concave below, and the palate reaches nearly as far back as the articulation of the lower jaw. The hinder edge of the palate is transversely truncated and in a line with the pterygoid processes of the sphenoid, immediately under the anterior opening of the alisphenoid canal, and from the centre of the posterior edge of each horizontal plate of the palate bone, a minute process projects directly backwards.

The posterior palate process of each superior maxilla extends 1½ inch behind the transverse palato-maxillary suture, i. e. half-way between it and the pterygoid process, whilst in my specimen of *Arctocephalus Gillespii* (*Proc. Roy. Phys. Soc. Edinburgh*, 1858) it only passes ⅓rd that distance.

The carotid canal is situated just in front of the foramen lacerum jugulare, and again appears at the anterior part of the tympanic bulla, and the foramina condyloidea are placed behind and internal to each foramen jugulare. The posterior palatine foramina are well marked, and instead of being formed in the palate bone as in *A. Gillespii*, they are placed as in *Callocephalus vitulinus* in the palatine plate of the superior maxillary bone about an inch anterior to the transverse palatal suture. The anterior palatine foramina are large and occupy the entire palatine plate of the premaxillary bones, whilst in *A. Gillespii* these foramina are comparatively small. The orbito-sphenoids are greatly compressed, so that the optic foramina have almost coalesced. The nasal bones are an inch and a half in length,

and somewhat broader in front than behind, with a small inner
and outer nasal process at the anterior border of each bone.
The posterior margins are separated by a short triangular process of the frontal bone, and the nasal process of the superior
maxilla reaches as far back as the posterior extremities of the
nasal bones.   This appears to be an osteological character of
considerable importance, for in all the skulls belonging to the
inauriculate section of the seals that I have examined, for
example, in that of *Stenorhynchus leptonyx, Callocephalus vitulinus, Pagophilus groenlandicus, Phoca barbata, Halichœrus
grypus*, and *Cystophora cristata*, the nasal process of the upper
jaw does not extend so far back as the posterior extremity of
the nasal bone.

The nasal aperture is $1\frac{7}{10}$ths of an inch in length, and $1\frac{1}{10}$th
of an inch in breadth, and slopes at an angle of 45°.   In the
upper jaw the teeth are twenty in number, the formula being
3—3 in; 1—1 c; 6—6 m.
The two outer incisors large, like canines, and the crown of the
only remaining central incisor distinctly bifid.   The canines
are 2 inches in length and $\frac{1}{2}$ an inch in breadth.   The molars
somewhat unequal, with a strong conical tubercle in the centre
of each crown.   There are traces of tubercles before and behind
in each molar tooth, with enlargement at the base of the corona.
The teeth are all single rooted.   The last molar teeth are in a
line with the transverse palato-maxillary suture, and with the
zygomatic arches where they spring from the superior maxillæ.
A vertical line from the process on the anterior orbital margin
falls on the centre of the 4th molar.   The skull was presented
to me by William Flockhart, Esq., Lomond House, Trinity,
who found it amongst a quantity of guano imported from the
Chincha Islands, which are situated in the Pacific Ocean, in
Lat. 13° and 14° S., at a distance of about twelve miles off the
coast of Peru.   It wants the right half of the cranium, and the
lower jaw is absent, otherwise it is in a good state of preservation.

At first, when the skull was exhibited to the Royal Physical
Society of Edinburgh, 27 February, 1867, I considered it to be
a specimen of a young *Otaria leonina* (perhaps a female), the

only known species of the genus *Otaria* mentioned in the British Museum Catalogue. The sutures of the face and palate are open, the skull is light, and without very strongly marked muscular impressions, but the occipito-sphenoid, parietal and coronal sutures are completely obliterated, and an extended anatomical comparison of this skull with other skulls of the Phocidæ proves that this condition of the cranial sutures in them indicates a full-grown animal.

The canine teeth are scarcely half the size of those of an adult marked *Otaria jubata* in the Edinburgh Museum of Science and Art, and Professor Peters of Berlin states, that in a cranium of a young *Otaria jubata* (Blainville) the canine teeth are just as large as in the old animal.

Professor Peters has read two papers, May 17, Nov. 1, 1866, on the *Otaria ulloæ* of Von Tschudi, before the Berlin Academy. (*Monatsbericht der Akademie der Wissenschaften zu Berlin*, 1867, pp. 270, 667.)

He there describes and figures the cranium of Von Tschudi's original specimen of this species of *Otaria*. The plate shows that the palate of the skull extends nearly to the glenoid cavity, and by comparing the following measurements of the skull from the Chincha Islands with those given by Professor Peters of *Otaria ulloæ*, reduced to inches and tenths, it will be observed that though they approximate in some, yet they differ in other dimensions.

	O. ulloæ Peters.	O. ulloæ ? Mc Bain.
Total length of skull	9·4	9·3
Length of hard palate.....................	5·1	5·6
From the last molar tooth to the point of the hamular process	2·5	3·
From the posterior border of the palate to the point of the hamular process	·8	·8
Distance between the points of the upper canine teeth	1·7	1·7
Breadth of the skull at the zygomata	5·	5·5
Breadth at mastoid processes............		4·7

Provisionally I place this skull with *O. ulloœ*, but as Professor Peters only gives a very brief description of his specimen, and as the data for a comparison of my specimen with his are, therefore, limited, it is possible that if an opportunity occurred for comparing the two side by side, anatomical differences might be found sufficient to justify the elevation of this Chincha Island cranium into a distinct species, and if so I would suggest that it should receive the name of *Otaria graii* in honour of Dr John Edward Gray of the British Museum for his eminent services in elucidating this difficult department of Zoology.

ON THE CRANIUM OF AN APPARENTLY NEW SPECIES OF ARCTO-CEPHALUS. By PROFESSOR TURNER.

IN the Osteological Collection of the Anatomical Museum of the University of Edinburgh is the cranium of a seal, which was presented to the late Professor Goodsir, along with the cranium of a Caffre, by Mr C. Bell, and is marked 'Seal's head from Cape of Good Hope.' The skull has not been described, and no attempt apparently had been made by Mr Goodsir to identify it.

By the presence of an alisphenoid canal, a post-orbital process, and the separation of the mastoid process from the tympanic bulla (H. N. Turner), and by the nasal process of the superior maxilla articulating with the nasal bone as far back as its posterior border (M'Bain), the cranium belongs to one of the eared seals. By the slightly concave surface of the hard palate, its deep posterior emargination, and the posterior border not reaching so far back as the middle of the zygomatic arch (Gray), it belongs to the genus Arcto-cephalus.

The skull is adult, but not aged, for the teeth are fully erupted, though little worn, the basi-cranial synchondrosis is ossified, the cranial sutures have almost entirely disappeared, and sagittal and lambdoidal ridges are fairly marked, though not large. A very distinct constriction separates the box of the skull from the broad flattened post-orbital processes. A sharp triangular process, which is in vertical line with the 3rd upper molar, projects from the orbital border of the superior maxilla close to the fronto-maxillary suture. Forehead slightly convex.

The dental formula is

$$\frac{3-3}{2-2} \text{ in.} : \quad \frac{1-1}{1-1} \text{ c.} : \quad \frac{6-6}{5-5} \text{ m.} = 36.$$

The crowns of the 1st and 2nd upper incisors are transversely divided into anterior and posterior cusps: the 3rd incisor, much longer, approximates in shape to a canine. The lower central incisors have simple crowns, whilst the lateral possess an external tubercle, which in closure of the jaws fits between the 2nd and 3rd upper incisors. The canines project $\frac{8}{10}$ ths of an inch beyond the alveoli, and the surface of the crown is longitudinally striped. The five lower grinders interlock with the five anterior upper grinders and the canine. The crowns of the molars possess a large middle cusp, and a more or less strongly marked anterior and posterior cusp. A very decided diastema separates the 5th and 6th upper grinders, the latter of which lies immediately opposite the transverse part of the palato-maxillary suture, and somewhat behind the spot where the zygoma springs from the superior maxilla. The fangs of the teeth are simple. The palate is elongated and narrow, a little more concave in front than behind. Its posterior border is deeply emarginate, and though the horizontal plates of the palate bones gradually approximate from behind forward, yet they do not articulate in the middle line, so that a cleft extends as far as the transverse palato-maxillary suture. The cleft is clearly not occasioned by a fracture, and as the skull is in every way most symmetrically formed and has no appearance

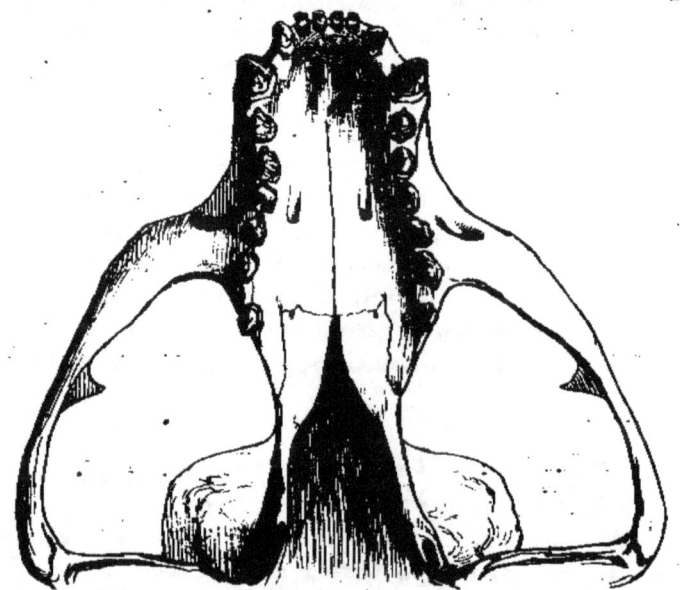

Camera lucida sketch, one-half the size of nature, of the hard palate of
Arcto-cephalus schist-hyperöes.

of imperfect development, this remarkable condition of the palate constitutes a most distinctive character of the cranium. The posterior palatine foramina are $\frac{9}{10}$ ths of an inch in front of the transverse palato-maxillary suture, and the posterior palate process of the superior maxilla extends for an equal distance behind the suture: the anterior palatine foramina are distinct. The internal process of the lower jaw is $\frac{9}{10}$ ths of an inch long, and quadrangular in form.

When in London, during the month of August, I obtained permission to compare this skull with the very extensive collection of Seals' crania in the British Museum, and, in the absence of Dr Gray, was most kindly aided by Mr Gerrard. I failed however to find a specimen presenting the same form and characters. No similar specimen was seen in the collection of the College of Surgeons. In the literature of the subject the described skull which most closely approaches it in size and form is that of a seal from Juan Fernandez, to which Prof. Peters of Berlin has recently given the name of Otaria Philippii[1]; but, in addition to the more perfect construction of the palate in Peters's specimen, there are other important characters which sufficiently distinguish them. Thus in Otaria (Arcto-cephalus) Philippii the upper molar formula is only 5—5, and these teeth are separated from each other by larger interspaces, the chief diastema is between the 4th and 5th molars, the accessory cusps also are less strongly marked: the root of the zygoma below the infra-orbital foramen is broader, the tympanic bullæ are flatter, and the lower jaw has even less of the appearance of an angle.

Though far from disposed unnecessarily to multiply species, yet as this cranium differs in various particulars, more especially in the form of the hinder part of the palate, from all other described seals, in accordance with recognized principles of classification it will have to be regarded as a distinct species. I propose the name of *Arcto-cephalus schist-hyperöes* (σχιστὸς ὑπερῴη).

[1] *Monatsbericht der Akademie zu Berlin,* 1867, pp. 276 e. s. Plates 2 A, B, C. Peters describes all the eared seals under the common generic name of Otaria. If the classification of Dr Gray were followed O. Philippii should be called Arcto-cephalus Philippii.

The chief dimensions of the cranium are given in the following table in inches and tenths:—

Length from basi-occipital to tip of snout . . . 8·1
From anterior border of orbit to tip of snout . . 2·5
From central incisor to tip of hamular process . 5·2
From last molar to tip of hamular process . . . 2·2
Breadth at mastoid processes . . . . 4·4
Breadth at zygomata. . . . . 5·1
Breadth at mandibular condyles . . . . . . 4·6
Breadth of anterior nares . . . . 1·1
Height of anterior nares . . . . 1·3
Between points of upper canines . . . . . . 1·3
Between points of lower canines . . . . . . 1·3
Length of lower jaw . . . . 6·1

If these measurements are compared with those corresponding to them given by Dr Gray in his Catalogue, p. 55, it will be seen that in its length this cranium most closely approaches his *A. nigrescens*, but the transverse diameters of the skull of the latter are greater; and, moreover, the hinder edge of the palate possesses a different form.

The osteological collection also possesses an imperfect skeleton of a young seal found in the Chincha Islands imbedded in guano. The cranial characters show it to be the young of an eared seal. The cranial synchondroses and sutures are unossified, the milk canines still in situ, the lower and 1st and 2nd upper permanent incisors erupted, the 3rd upper lateral incisors and the 1st pair of upper and lower molars partially erupted, the 3rd, 4th, and 5th molars yet concealed in their alveoli. The incisor and canine formulæ in the upper jaw is 3—3; 1—1, but as the hinder part of the palate is broken off and lost, it is impossible to say whether or not a 6th upper molar had been present. The lower dental formula is in. 2—2: c. 1—1: m. 5—5. The edges of the crowns of the lower central incisors are tri-serrated, whilst the lateral possess pointed crowns.

Owing to the immaturity of the cranium and the broken

condition of the palate, it is difficult to say in which of the two genera Dr Gray and other British naturalists subdivide the family Arcto-cephalina it should be placed. Two species of the genus Otaria from the Chincha Islands have now been described by Zoologists, one the Otaria Godeffroyi of Peters (*op. cit.* p. 266, Plate I.), the other the Otaria Ulloae, recorded by my friend Dr M'Bain in the preceding article. This young cranium, in addition to other points in which it differs from O. Godeffroyi, possesses bi-cuspidate crowns to the 1st and 2nd upper incisors, whilst in the latter the crowns are simple. From Dr M'Bain's specimen it differs in the almost entire absence of a constriction behind the post-orbital processes; in the greater relative breadth of the cranium than at the zygomata; in the more vertical form of the occiput; in the shortness of the face; and in the zygomata springing from the superior maxillæ opposite the 5th upper molars. Whether or not it is to be regarded as a new species cannot be at present decided. The consideration of this question must be deferred until the opportunity for a more extended comparison with other specimens is obtained.

Length of skull	5·2
Breadth at zygomata . .	3·5
Breadth of cranium . . .	3·6
Length of lower jaw . . .	3·6
Breadth at condyles . . .	2·9

FURTHER OBSERVATIONS ON THE STOMACH IN THE CETACEA. By PROFESSOR TURNER.

SINCE the publication of my contribution to the anatomy of the Pilot Whale in this Journal, November 1867, I have made some additional observations on the Cetacean stomach.

Amongst the specimens recently purchased by the University of Edinburgh for the Anatomical Museum, from the collection of the late Professor Goodsir, is an inflated and dried stomach, which, though unmarked, is obviously from its size that of an adult Cetacean, and presents the same type of arrangement of its compartments as I have already described in the young Globio-cephalus. The collection also contains a fœtus 13 inches long, which from the form of the head and body evidently belongs to the genus Globio-cephalus.

In the adult stomach the diameter of the lower end of the esophagus was 5 inches. The 1st compartment or paunch was 31 inches long, its greatest transverse circumference 42 inches. In the fœtus the length was only $\frac{8}{10}$ths of an inch. In the adult the length of the 2nd or globular compartment was 19 inches, its greatest circumference 38 inches. In the fœtus the same compartment measured $\frac{9}{10}$ths of an inch long, and its capacity about equalled that of the paunch. In the young pilot whale described in my former paper, the 2nd compartment was somewhat more capacious than the 1st; but in the adult stomach, as the above measurements show, the paunch greatly surpassed in its capacity the globular compartment. Hence in the Cetacea possessing this type of stomach the paunch undergoes a great increase of size when the animal acquires its food independent of the mother. In the adult stomach I was enabled to re-examine the relations of the esophagus to the openings into the 1st and 2nd compartments. The hand could be freely passed down the esophagus into the paunch, as well as into the orifice of the globular compartment, the opening into the former being about one-third larger than into the latter, which agrees with what I had previously seen in the adult Globio-cephalus shown me by Dr Murie. Separating the mouth of the 2nd compartment from the paunch was a strong fold of mucous membrane, projecting for 3 inches and terminating in a free crescentic border. This fold marks, I believe, the bottom of the esophagus and the upper orifice of the paunch, and the arrangement bears out the description I gave of my former specimen, that the 1st and 2nd compartments both open directly into the bottom of the esophagus. Since then M. P. Fischer[1] has described a similar arrangement in the stomach of Grampus griseus. A strong fold of mucous membrane extended

---

[1] *Annales des Sciences Naturelles*, VIII. p. 363, 1867.

round the greater part of the mouth of the 2nd compartment, and was in series with the mucous folds which projected into its cavity.

The 3rd compartment in the adult was $6\frac{1}{2}$ inches long.   Its greatest diameter at its middle was $3\frac{1}{2}$ inches, that of each of its two orifices 1 inch.   Its aperture of inlet was situated not at its upper end, but nearly 2 inches below, an arrangement, which, along with its median dilatation, strongly supports the view I have already advocated, that this is a true compartment of the stomach, and not a mere tubular passage.   In the fœtal stomach the 3rd compartment is so small that it is with diffi- culty recognizable.   The 4th compartment in the adult was 14 inches in circumference: in the fœtus about the size of a small pea.   The 5th or sigmoid stomach was 18 inches long in the adult, and its greatest transverse circumference was 14 inches: in the fœtus its length was 1·1 inch.   The dilatation imme- diately preceding the cylindrical duodenum was 12 inches long in the adult, and its greatest transverse circumference was 15 inches; a constriction externally, and a projecting fold of mu- cous membrane internally in series with the valvulæ conni- ventes, marked the commencement of the cylindrical gut.

The comparison of the adult stomach with the fœtal organ and that of the young animal previously described proves that in the Cetacea, as in the Ruminantia just before birth, the compartment which serves as the true digestive chamber is relatively larger than the pouch in the immature than in the mature condition.   It would require a more extended examina- tion of this organ in embryos of different ages to see if in the fœtal cetacean, as Mr Gedge showed in our last number, p. 323, Pl. VII. to be the case in the fœtal ruminant, the paunch ever possesses at any period of intra-uterine life a greater relative development.

In another fœtal Cetacean 15 inches long, with an elongated beak and apparently the young of a Delphinus, the stomach was arranged as in Globio-cephalus, and its compartments were of the same size as those in the fœtus just described.   Thus in Globio-cephalus, Delphinus, and, as M. Fischer has recently shown, in Grampus the same type of stomach prevails.

ON THE ALBUMINOUS SUBSTANCES OF THE BLOOD-SERUM. By A. Heynsius, *Phil. Nat. D. and M.D., Prof. of Physiology at the University of Leiden, Holland.*

It is generally admitted that in the blood-serum there are three albuminous substances: serum-albumin, globulin, and albuminate of soda.

The serum-albumin, which forms the chief part, differs, as it is known, in chemical character from the albumin of the egg. To obtain it pure it must of course be separated from the two other albuminous substances.

Globulin is precipitated from the diluted serum by weak acids, as Panum has showed. Generally it is separated from the diluted serum by carbonic acid. Schmidt discovered its important fibrino-plastic properties; and chiefly for that reason a particular place was assigned to the globulin among the albuminous substances.

After the removal of the globulin by carbonic acid, by the addition of diluted acetic acid another albuminous substance, although in smaller quantity, is precipitated. This substance possesses no fibrino-plastic properties, and is generally derived from the albuminate of soda in the serum, that could be decomposed only by acetic acid.

Brücke suspects that the globulin in itself has no fibrino-plastic effect, but is simply precipitated mechanically with the globulin. If this opinion be confirmed, no difference at all between globulin and albuminate of soda would exist. For albuminate of potassa or soda is not precipitated by acetic acid only, but also by carbonic acid, and, besides the fibrino-plastic effect, the properties of this precipitate quite agree with those of globulin. It is true that, if, as we said, by carbonic acid globulin is precipitated, by acetic acid another precipitate is produced, but that depends on the presence of phosphoric salts. Rollett has shown that albuminate of soda or potassa is not precipitated by carbonic acid, if phosphate of soda is present in sufficient quantity, as for instance in milk.

If globulin and albuminate of soda are separated in this manner, pure serum-albumin would remain in the fluid. This opinion is, as I found, incorrect. If blood serum be treated with carbonic and acetic acid, no pure serum-albumin is obtained. There is then a peculiar albuminous substance in the serum still present, which is insoluble in a concentrated solution of chloride of sodium, and by the addition of this salt can be precipitated.

I pass over for the present its origin and its connection with the substances just mentioned: albuminate of soda is, as it is known, precipitated in like manner by a concentrated solution of salt. I will simply remark here that much more albumin is obtained by the addition of chloride of sodium than by successive treatment with carbonic and acetic acid, and that in this respect the blood-serum of various animals exhibits a remarkable difference.

Blood-serum contents in 100 parts[1]:

Animal.	Dry residue.	Albumin precipitated by Carb. acid.	Albumin precipitated by Cl Na.	Together.
Cow	10·72	0·740	1·735	2·475
	10·66	0·745	1·715	2·460
Calf	7·24	0·220	0·185	0·405
	7·38	0·210	0·220	0·430
Calf (newly born)	6·92	0·115	0·400	0·515
	6·93	0·120	0·405	0·525
Pig	10·76	0·170	0·455	0·625
	10·60	0·180	0·480	0·660
Rabbit (old)	8·87	0·240	0·800	1·040
	8·95	0·240	0·840	1·080
Rabbit (young)	8·15	0·260	0·860	1·120
	8·05	0·260	0·900	1·160
Chicken	6·45	1·05	1·200	2·250
	6·65			
,,	7·34	1·680	1·920	3·600
	7·34	1·720	1·880	3·600
,,		1·5	2·6	4·100
Frog	2·65	0·425	0·250	0·675
	2·70	0·400	0·225	0·625

[1] The blood-serum in these analyses was always collected as pure as possible. The dry residue was after mixture of the serum with purified sand found by

Especially in the cases of the cow and the calf the difference is very great. So great even that by the dropping of the blood-serum into a concentrated solution of chloride of sodium it immediately becomes evident whether the serum of the cow or of the calf is the subject of observation. This difference is the more remarkable, because calf-serum is never so free from red blood-corpuscles as cow-serum, for which reason the amount of the precipitate obtained by carbonic acid and salt in the calf-serum is even larger than it would be if calf-serum were separated as colourless as cow-serum.

Also in the case of the chicken and frog (the serum was here as colourless as cow-serum), if the amount of the dry residue be kept in view the quantity is large, whereas in the case of the pig, the dry residue being here precisely equal to that of the cow, only the fourth part of this substance is found.

This substance is insoluble in water, but soluble even in attenuated solutions of salt. In diluted acetic and muriatic acid it is easily soluble. It approaches also myosine of the muscles, but is more soluble. Besides it naturally possesses all the characteristic properties of albuminous substances.

FIBRIN, A CONSTITUENT OF THE STROMA OF THE RED BLOOD-CORPUSCLES. By A. HEYNSIUS, *Professor of Physiology at the University of Leiden.*

NOTWITHSTANDING the excellent microscopic aid of the present time, it is well known that controversy still exists concerning the structure of the red blood-corpuscles. Although the opinion

---

evaporation at 120°. To find the amount of globulin, the serum was mixed with 10 vol. of water and treated with abundant carbonic acid. The precipitate formed was separated by means of fine Berzelius-paper, and once washed with distilled water. Generally the filtrated fluid was clear. Then it was saturated with purified chloride of sodium. The albuminous substance precipitated was collected on a filtrum with the adherent salt and dried at 120°. Then the filtrum was washed with distilled water till all the salt was eliminated, again dried at 120°, and weighed.

is generally gaining ground that they are solid bodies, without membrane, and in man as well as in most of the mammalia without nucleus, nevertheless there are not a few who even now dispute that opinion.

With regard to their chemical constituents the state of our knowledge does not fare much better. We know now that hæmoglobin is a constant constituent in the blood-corpuscles. This discovery did away with the former opinion, that globulin was the principal constituent of them, it being proved that this was produced by decomposition of hæmoglobin[1]. Of the other constituents we know only that most probably lecithin is one. That fatty substances containing phosphorus exist in them was already known to BERZELIUS. LEHMANN also found a considerable quantity of phosphoric acid in the ashes of the blood-corpuscles, and on that fact founded the opinion that glycerin-phosphoric acid might be among the constituents of the stroma.

When now LIEBREICH separated a substance containing phosphorus, protagon, from the brain, the opinion came generally into vogue that the phosphoric acid, found in the ashes of organic matter, proved the existence of a greater or less amount of protagon. HOPPE-SEYLER and HERMANN both have tried to separate this substance from the blood-corpuscles, and the results of their researches seemed to establish the fact. But subsequent investigations in the Laboratory at Tübingen showed that the protagon, prepared by LIEBREICH, was a mixture. Protagon was proved to be a crystalline body free from phosphorus, soluble in heated alcohol and ether, which by boiling with baryt is precipitated, and by treatment with sulphuric acid yields sugar, whereas the apparent presence of phosphorus was dependent on adulteration with lecithin, which

---

[1] This decomposition of hæmoglobin in hæmatin and an albuminous substance is effected by many chemical agents. Among them one of my pupils, Dr A. J. MUNNICH, found the effect of weak acids, especially of carbonic acid, particularly important. By the action of this acid on diluted blood or hæmoglobin the band of acid-hæmatin quickly appears in the spectrum; by prolonged contact it gradually increases, and at last the bands of hæmoglobin disappear all together. Then even the bands of hæmoglobin can be reproduced. If treated with STOKES's reducing fluid the band of reduced hæmatin comes to view, if the hæmoglobin was plainly decomposed, and by shaking with air the bands of oxyhæmoglobin under these circumstances reappear with full intensity.

in 100 parts contains 3·8 phosphorus. The great amount of phosphoric acid in the ashes of the ethereal extract of the blood-corpuscles was now, of course, attributed to the presence of lecithin.

HOPPE-SEYLER hints that perhaps this substance in the stroma, just as in the yolk of eggs, is combined with an albuminous one[1], and thus directs the attention again to the albuminous substances of the stroma, which had lately been lost sight of. On account of their energetic fibrino-plastic properties only some admitted, according to SCHMIDT'S hypothesis on the cause of coagulation of fibrino-genetic fluids, that it should contain a large quantity of globulin. Nevertheless DENIS had even in 1842, and afterwards repeatedly[2], mentioned that in some sorts of blood an albuminous constituent can be easily separated from the stroma of the blood-corpuscles. He recommends for this purpose to divide the human blood, obtained by a venesection, after the elimination of the fibrin into an equal volume of "eau salée au tiers" (a mixture of one part of a concentrated solution of common salt and two parts of water). The fluid then soon becomes glutinous, and this viscous mass being introduced into a large quantity of water, the hæmoglobin is dissolved, but another part of the stroma is separated in solid, but fragile threads. With the blood of birds DENIS found this experiment still more successful.

One of my pupils, DR S. VAN DER HORST, has lately investigated this point with me more closely. We mixed chicken-blood with "eau salée au tiers" and, when it had become glutinous, we let it drop into distilled water. Each drop immediately coagulates in the water and sinks to the bottom of the vessel, or forms a bag, just as KÜHNE says of myosin. If the

---

[1] *Med-chem. Untersuchungen*, Heft 2, 1867.

[2] When the French Academy, in the year 1843, had accorded to him the Monthyon prize for his "Etudes chimiques, physiologiques et médicales, faites de 1835 à 1840 sur les matières albumineuses," he continued his researches and communicated the results of them in a treatise of the year 1856, " Nouvelles, études chimiques," etc.; and at last in another of the year 1859, entitled "Mémoire sur le Sang." On the title-page of his contribution of 1856 he calls his inquiry: "Etudes faites en suivant la méthode d'expérimentation par les sels, la seule, qui dans l'état actuel de la science semble pouvoir être appliquée avec fruit à de recherches sur ces substances." An opinion the truth of which has in later times become more and more evident.

fluid is brought with a pipette to the bottom of the vessel, then it rises in the distilled water in the form of a staff and quickly becomes nearly colourless.

But the blood-corpuscles of the chicken are nucleated, and therefore we wished to prepare this substance also with blood-corpuscles without nucleus. No human blood was at our disposal, but with dog's blood the experiment succeeds very well. The other sorts of blood which we examined, such as that of the calf, horse, pig, rabbit, and guinea-pig, yielded the same membranes, but in a less degree.

Serum does not show a similar phenomenon, and blood-corpuscles freed from serum exhibit the phenomenon as plainly as the blood itself.

Immediately after its precipitation in water it is soluble in a solution of common salt of 5 to 10 per cent.; remaining in contact with water it gradually loses its solubility.

Dropped into muriatic acid of $\frac{1}{1000}$ the glutinous mass coagulates at first, but gradually redissolves. In diluted potash it is also soluble, and by introducing carbonic acid in this solution the substance is precipitated.

Moreover it possesses all the properties of albuminous substances. Heated on silver with potash, it exhibits the reaction of sulphur. Treated with MILLON's reagent, it shows the well-known colouring, &c. By alcohol and ether but a small portion of it is dissolved.

Not only, however, by treatment with a concentrated solution of salt, but also by introducing the blood into distilled water this albuminous constituent of the stroma is isolated. If chicken-blood be beaten during 10 minutes and the defibrinated blood is then mixed with a large quantity of water, glutinous flakes are separated, which rise to the surface and there form a viscous, slightly-coloured layer, whereas a smaller portion frequently sinks to the bottom of the vessel. This glutinous substance is evidently the same as that separated by salt. It has the same properties. It may be obtained quite colourless, but of course with a great loss of matter.

It possesses all the general properties of albuminous substances. By combustion of the substance, dried at 120°, with a mixture of carbonate of soda and nitrate of potash, I found in 100 parts the amount of sulphur:

1·17
1·00
1·01

The quantity of this substance that is obtained is in many cases proportionally large, in others smaller. This difference depends, as it appears, on the larger or smaller quantity of water used, and on the time in which the water is mixed with it. The largest quantity I obtained was when the defibrinated blood was gradually diluted with ± 25 volumes of water.

The blood-corpuscles themselves, isolated by a diluted solution of common salt, show the same phenomenon. Thus, without doubt, the substance must be derived from the stroma of the blood-corpuscles. Its origin is not to be sought for in the hæmoglobin, since by spectral-analysis no trace of decomposed hæmoglobin can be perceived.

It is of course difficult to prove, if the substance thus isolated is a simple, pure albuminous one (adulterated only with a small portion of hæmoglobin, as the pink colour shows). Mucosin, which the viscous appearance suggests, is at least not mixed with it in a considerable quantity, since acetic acid does not produce a similar decomposition in the blood. The large quantity of sulphur that we found tends to confirm that opinion.

The substance approaches myosin in many respects, but differs as being less soluble. Its character does not agree with vitellin, since it is completely insoluble in water. It most resembles fibrin, of which the solubility likewise, under different circumstances, exhibits a great variety. On the hyperoxide of hydrogen it has the same effect as fibrin.

The properties described have been traced on the substance separated from the blood-corpuscles of the chicken, since the quantity of fibrin in them is much greater, but I have lately succeeded in isolating this substance by the same process from dog's blood as well.

THE EFFECTS OF ROWING ON THE CIRCULATION, AS SHOWN BY EXAMINATION WITH THE SPHYGMOGRAPH. By Thomas R. Fraser, M.D., F.R.S.E., M.R.C.P.E., *Assistant to the Professor of Materia Medica in the University of Edinburgh.*

During the summer of the present year, I took advantage of an opportunity for making a number of observations on the effects of rowing on the circulation. These were recorded with the exactitude that the sphygmograph has now made possible; and, apart from any intrinsic importance, they may prove of some interest in relation to recent discussions on the possibly injurious effects of rowing-exercise.

The observations were made on the crew of one of our University four-oar boats, and they extended over two-thirds of the period of training immediately antecedent to the races. The members of the crew were men in robust health, their ages varied from twenty-one to twenty-eight years, and they were, at the time, living in the quiet and regular manner—with prescribed diet and exercise—which is usually considered necessary on such occasions.

The instrument employed was the well-known Sphygmograph of Marey; and in the absence of any arrangement to ensure uniformity and definiteness of pressure on the artery —the importance of which has been ably pointed out by Drs Anstie, Sanderson, B. Foster, and others—great care was always observed in obtaining such pressure as was necessary to produce the highest systolic ascent. Tracings were made immediately before the crew left the boat-house, and, on the same member or members, a few minutes after their return. In this interval a row of from two-and-a-half to three miles had been taken, of which the final mile consisted of a 'spurt,' during which the boat is impelled at the greatest possible speed. I thus obtained tracings immediately before and after violent rowing exercise. The changes that were produced were of an extremely uniform character, not only on the different

occasions, but also with the different members of the crew.
The examination of one set of tracings is, therefore, sufficient
to show what changes are produced.   I have selected for
illustration those taken from the 'stroke' of the boat, who, as
all the initiated are aware, has the greatest share of the labour
during rowing.

Figure 1 represents a tracing of the pulsations of the
right radial artery, obtained immediately before the crew left
the boat-house.

Fig. 1. D. T., aged 21. Right radial artery, before rowing.

The general appearance of this tracing is such as is very
usually obtained in normal health.   The lowest and highest
points of the repeated pulsations are nearly on the same plane ;
the lines of ascent are short and oblique ; and the lines of
descent are oblique and somewhat convex, and they are interrupted, in all cases, by a well-marked dicrotic wave, and, occasionally, by several slight undulations.   The rate of pulsation
was sixty-eight in the minute.

Figure 2 represents a tracing from the same artery, five
minutes after the return to the boat-house.   The tracing that
was taken *immediately* after the return exhibits several irregularities, that were not produced by the condition of the
circulation but by unsteadiness of the arm, which it is well
known is caused by exercise even when much less severe
than that of rowing.   It will be observed that in this tracing

Fig. 2. D. T. Right radial artery, after rowing.

a portion of the unsteadiness still remains, the irregularities in the lines of descent of the last three pulsations being due to it.

The general appearance of this tracing is strikingly different from that of Figure 1. The lowest and highest points of the repeated pulsations are not on the same plane; the lines of ascent are long and vertical; the summits are however, generally, rounded like those of Figure 1; the lines of descent are concave and much less oblique; and the dicrotism consists more of an interruption to the line of descent than of an additional wave. The rate of pulsation was ninety in the minute, and the space occupied by each pulsation is, therefore, shorter than in Figure 1.

The tracing depicted in Figure 2 differs most obviously from that in Figure 1, in the unequal levels of the lowest and highest points of systolic ascent (forming the *lignes d'ensemble*) and in the greater length and more vertical direction of the line of ascent. The curve of the *lignes d'ensemble* is caused by an increase in the respiratory efforts, which rowing, in common with other forms of physical exercise, produces. The effect of respiration in varying blood-tension is thus exaggerated.

The great length of the systolic line of ascent indicates a general diminution, at the moment of ventricular contraction, in the arterial tension, the result, principally, of dilatation of blood-vessels; and the vertical direction of this line shews that the contraction of the ventricles is performed quickly and sharply, or with *suddenness*. This line is continued for a short distance, before its descent, in a somewhat curved horizontal direction. This is a character of considerable importance, as it at once distinguishes the tracing from one where the long vertical line is the result of diminished blood-tension only, in which case the line of descent forms an acute angle with the line of ascent. The line of descent is oblique, and it is interrupted by a dicrotic curve, which does not assume the proportions of a distinct wave. This latter character, viewed in connection with the rounded summit, proves that the heart propels a large stream of blood during each ventricular contraction, so as to fully distend the arterial system, notwithstanding its dilated condition. Further, it is important to note that there is no evidence that the amount of blood propelled into the arteries during each ventricular contraction is greater than can freely pass into the veins.

I met, on one occasion, with an unimportant modification in the form of the horizontal line. This is represented in

Figure 3. In place of being a continuous curve, a slight break occurs at the commencement of this line. It would seem to shew that a slight interruption had taken place towards the end of the ventricular systole. All the other tracings from this member of the crew have a form similar to that represented in Figure 2.

Fig. 3.

The tracings I have obtained, show therefore that an extremely large quantity of blood is being circulated with great rapidity— a condition of the circulation we should consider essential, on *à priori* grounds, for the continuance of prolonged and severe muscular exertion. It is obvious that in the great majority of functional and organic diseases of the vascular system such a condition could not possibly be maintained. The subjects of these diseases are, therefore, completely incapacitated from *violent* rowing-exercise, and cannot be in a position to be injured by it. It is possible that the presence of incipient forms of disease of the vascular system may not altogether prevent such exercise from being undertaken ; but, I believe, that all such diseases may be detected by the use of the sphygmograph in time to prevent further mischief, the examination being made immediately before the boat is entered, and a few minutes after a moderate *pull* has been indulged in.

The effects that rowing produces on the circulation seem to be similar to those that are produced by many other forms of muscular exercise.

ON THE DIFFERENCE IN THE MODE OF OSSIFICATION OF THE FIRST AND OTHER METACARPAL AND METATARSAL BONES. By ALLEN THOMSON, M.D., F.R.S., *Professor of Anatomy in the University of Glasgow.*

ALL anatomists who have given attention to the progress of ossification in childhood are aware of the fact that, at the age when the epiphyses of the long-shaped bones of the hand and foot are most obvious, viz. from ten to fifteen years, each meta-carpal and metatarsal bone, and each one of the digital phalanges usually consists of two ossified pieces united by intervening cartilage and separable by maceration; one of these pieces forming the shaft and main part of the bone and extending quite to one extremity, while the other smaller piece constitutes an epiphysis occupying the opposite extremity of the bone. The epiphysis occupies the proximal extremity in all the digital phalanges, while in the metacarpal and metatarsal bones the epiphysis is usually proximal in the first (or that of the thumb and great toe), and distal in the four remaining bones.

The fact in human anatomy now referred to has been very generally described in manuals and systematic works; and some authors have even regarded the difference between the first and remaining metacarpal and metatarsal bones as so constant and marked as to have founded upon it an argument for regarding the first of these bones as properly constituting one of the digital series of bones, that is, the first or proximal phalanx of the thumb or great toe[1].

[1] On this ground Humphry (*Treatise on the Human Skeleton*, Camb. 1858, p. 395), inclines to regard the bone which rests on the trapezium in the hand as intermediate between a digital phalanx and a metacarpal bone, though he considers it on the whole to be most correct to call it a metacarpal bone, and regards the second phalanx to be the missing segment in the thumb. On this and other grounds Prof. Struthers ("On Variation in the number of Fingers and Toes," &c., in *Edin. New Philos. Journ.* for 1863, Vol. XVIII. p. 111), regards as established "that the bone which is wanting in the human thumb and great toe, and in the internal digit of other five-toed Mammals, is the metacarpal and metatarsal, although custom and convenience lead us to apply these terms to the bone which homologically is a proximal phalanx."

The object of the present paper is to show that the difference in the mode of ossification in question is neither so constant nor typical as to warrant the hypothetical view above stated, and to point out the fact that there are deviations from the mode of ossification which has generally been regarded as the usual one, existing occasionally in man, and to be found in a more marked degree in some animals, which lead to the view that the separate ossification of pieces of these bones in epiphyses is subject to considerable variations, and that the process must be viewed in a wider range of observation before it can be taken as the sole groundwork of conclusions as to typical or homological form. The caution which is necessary in forming such conclusions on purely osteogenic grounds has, indeed, been well indicated by Huxley and Gegenbaur with respect to the bones of the head; and although it may be allowed that there is less reason for doubt in respect to the larger bones of the limbs, among which a very constant and regular correspondence has been observed in the development of certain epiphyses both in man and animals, yet the possible varieties in these have been heretofore too little studied by actual observation throughout the animal series, to admit of their being made with confidence the basis of fundamental characters.

Having been engaged some years ago in the examination of specimens illustrating the ossification of the hand and foot in the earlier period of the formation of the epiphyses, I observed in several examples of the first metacarpal and metatarsal bones such distinct indications of the separation of distal epiphyses as led me to inquire farther into the subject. I then observed not only very distinct epiphyses of the kind mentioned, but also in one or two instances fainter indications of the tendency to the separation of a proximal epiphysis in the second metacarpal bone of man; and on extending my observations to animals, I found that while in the greater number of five-toed mammifers the epiphyses have the same disposition as that commonly ascribed to those of man, there are other animals in which distal epiphyses exist more or less perfectly developed on the first metacarpal and metatarsal bones, and that other deviations from the more usual mode of ossification of the bones of the hand and foot exist, sufficient to disprove altogether the hitherto supposed uniformity of the process.

The existence of distal epiphyses on the first metacarpal and metatarsal bones of man was not however altogether unknown to anatomists. On the contrary, Albinus was well aware of the fact, and several others have referred to it. In his work entitled *Icones Ossium Foetus, Brevis Osteogeniae Historia*, published at Leyden in 1737, at p. 115, Albinus, in describing the ossification of the metatarsal bones, says, that they are each formed from a centre in the cartilage of the shaft, and that, this growing upwards and downwards, the bone at birth consists of an osseous body with two cartilaginous extremities. The anterior extremities (of all five) pass at last into epiphyses, which he found about the fifteenth year almost entirely united with the bodies in four metatarsal bones, and completely united in that of the great toe. The posterior extremities, except that of the great toe, are occupied by the advancing bone of the shaft, and as yet he had not seen them forming epiphyses. The posterior extremity of the metatarsal bone of the great toe, however, forms an epiphysis not long separated.

At p. 137 again he says, that the same description as before given of the metatarsus applies to the metacarpus. But the inferior (distal) epiphyses of the metacarpals he found still separable at the age of fifteen years, and long afterwards fissures remain where they are united to the shaft. The inferior epiphysis of the thumb unites sooner with the shaft than the superior[1].

Cruveilhier, in his *Treatise on Human Anatomy*, after describing the development of the metacarpal and metatarsal bones in the usual manner, and distinguishing the first by its proximal epiphysis, appends the following note to his descrip-

---

[1] Nesbitt, in his work on *Human Osteogeny*, published in 1736, the year before Albinus' work, describes the metacarpal and metatarsal bones as only four in number in each limb, and reckoning thus the first metacarpal and first metatarsal as phalanges of their respective digits, he describes them as having the same mode of ossification with the other phalanges, viz. each one from a principal centre and a proximal epiphysis. Nesbitt was therefore not aware of the occasional existence of distal epiphyses in these bones. Op. cit. pp. 125, 126.

E. H. Weber, in his *Hildebrandt's Anatomie*, Vol. II. p. 227, refers to Albinus' observations, but he does not appear to have himself confirmed them.

tion of the metatarsal bones (Vol. I. p. 304): "I ought however to remark here, that in some subjects there appeared to exist in the digital extremity (of the first metatarsal) an epiphysal point which is very thin and which unites early with the body."

On the other hand Meckel, who was probably aware of Albinus' view, states explicitly in his Descriptive Anatomy that he had never seen a distinct nucleus in the distal end of the first, nor in the proximal end of the other four metacarpal bones.

In his work on *Human Osteology* (2nd edition, 1857, p. 154), Mr Holden has given a description of the formation of the metacarpal bones, which is somewhat inconsistent in itself, and does not agree with that of other authors, or with the facts as observed in nature, but which may have been suggested by observations of the same kind with those of Albinus, and of the author of this paper. He says, " Like all the long bones, each metacarpal bone has a centre of ossification for the shaft, *and one for each of the articular ends*. In the first metacarpal the artery of the marrow runs towards the lower end, therefore the lower epiphysis unites sooner than the upper to the shaft. This is just the reverse of what takes place in all the other metacarpals, in which the artery of the marrow runs towards the upper end." Again, with reference to the metatarsal bones, he makes, at p. 204, the following statement : " Each metatarsal bone has two centres of ossification; one for the shaft, the other for the head. The first metatarsal, however, has its terminal epiphysis not at the head, but at the base, which is precisely the case with the metacarpal bone of the thumb."

Observations in the Human Subject.

It is not my intention to enter into the consideration of the whole progress of ossification in the bones of the hand and foot; but it may be proper for me to recall to the recollection of the reader in a few words the main facts as to the first appearance of ossific deposits in them.

The earliest steps of ossification of the metacarpal and metatarsal and digital bones are, on the whole, very similar to those of the larger bones of the limbs; the first ossific deposit occurring in the centre of the cartilaginous matrix of the shaft at an early period, which varies in the different bones, according to their position in the series, from the 8th or 9th to the 12th or 13th weeks. From this primary centre the ossification extends in the cartilage with the usual changes attendant on the formation of medullary spaces, and finally of a medullary canal, if such exists; and the greater part of the bone forming the shaft is completed by this process, and by the known superposition of the subperiosteal layers. At the period of birth in all of them a considerable mass of cartilage still remains at each extremity of the bone. In these cartilaginous masses the ossific nuclei of the epiphyses appear in those extremities in which bony epiphyses are to be formed; but the commencement of their deposition dates considerably later than the primary ossification, at a variable period between the third and fifth or sixth years; or even one or two years later.

In those ends of the bones where no epiphyses are to be formed, the original cartilaginous ossification of the shaft gradually extends itself into the terminal cartilage; but when a separate epiphysis occurs, although the main ossification also extends somewhat towards that extremity, it is met by that of the epiphysal nucleus, the two parts of bone being for a time divided by the remains of cartilage. There is therefore a marked distinction between the ossification of an epiphysis, which is almost entirely cartilaginous, and that proceeding from the original nucleus of the shaft, which internally is cartilaginous, but superficially is subperiosteal.

The general fact is well known in regard to the larger bones that the separate epiphyses which soonest become united by bone to the shaft are the latest in the commencement of their ossification; and we see this general fact well illustrated in the bones of the hand and foot, in connection either with the early consolidation or the entire absence of an epiphysis at one extremity.

In now proceeding to mention shortly the result of the observations I have made, I will refer to the figures of p. 144 to explain more fully the appearances described. In all cases which I have examined at a sufficiently early age, that is, about seven or eight years, and in some more advanced, I have found, in addition to the more distinct and constant proximal epiphyses of the first metacarpal and metatarsal bones, traces of a separate distal epiphysis. In figure 1 and figure 3, a view is given of the appearances presented by the first and second metacarpal and metatarsal bones with their corresponding digits in the macerated and dried condition at the age of eight years. The fissures indicated at d', though deep, are not here such as to separate completely the epiphyses from the shaft of the bones. Figures 2 and 4 show the state of the parts in recent wet specimens taken from a subject stated to be about a year younger than the first. The section of the bones has been carried longitudinally from the dorsal to the palmar surface; and it will be observed that in the first metatarsal bone the distal epiphysis, in which ossification has made considerable advance, is completely separated from the ossified shaft of the bone by a plate of cartilage; and that, though somewhat irregular, the form of the epiphysis is very similar to the more constant epiphysis of the second metatarsal bone. In the first metacarpal bone the separating plate of cartilage is not complete, leaving a space in the centre where the bone of the shaft is continuous with that of the end portion, but yet sufficient to indicate the form of an epiphysis.

In figure 2' I and figure 4' I are represented the appearances observed in another specimen in the wet state; and in these it will be seen that, while the ossification from the main shaft has run onwards in the greater and deeper part into that of the end of the bones, the surrounding parts are interrupted by the indentation of small angular pieces of cartilage which mark the commencements, as it were, or lowest stage in the separation of an epiphysis, and correspond in every respect to the outer part of the more complete dividing cartilage.

Such observations as these are necessarily limited from the difficulty of obtaining subjects at a suitable age : but from the circumstance that in all favourable instances which have come under my notice at ages between seven and fifteen years, traces of the separation of the distal epiphysis have been found in both the first metacarpal and metatarsal bones, I am inclined to look upon the disposition at least to the formation of such epiphyses as general ; while in a certain number of instances, the proportion of which I cannot at present determine, the separation by cartilage of a bony epiphysis is at one time complete.

The circumstance that this epiphysis (which may be called occasional) is united by ossification to the shaft of the bone several years earlier than the proximal epiphysis has probably caused it to be overlooked by most anatomists.

The existence of an occasional proximal epiphysis on any of the metacarpal or metatarsal bones is according to my experience much rarer than the distal variation already described as occurring in the first. The distinct traces of separation of such an epiphysis are limited, indeed, so far as I have yet seen, to the second metacarpal bone.

In the instance represented in figure 1, II, I observed a groove of considerable depth extending inwards, fully a third through the thickness of the bone from the radial side near its proximal extremity ; and in another similar specimen examined in the wet state and represented in figure 2', II, a short strip of cartilage was found to dip inwards into the bone from the radial side ; and from the position and shape of this piece of cartilage and the correspondence of its position with the distinct groove in the macerated specimen, I cannot doubt that it is an indication of epiphysal separation. I have only seen very faint indications in the third metacarpal bone of any similar epiphysal fissure ; and I have not detected anything of the kind in the proximal extremities of the metatarsal bones.

The fact is well known to anatomists, that in the long bones of the limbs there is a very constant relation between the direction in which the so-called nutritious foramen passes through the shaft of the bone and the order of ossific union of the terminal epiphyses ; the foramen being generally inclined towards that extremity at which the consolidation of the bone first occurs. In the passage previously quoted from Holden's work, that author refers to this peculiarity of the nutritious foramina as existing also in the metacarpal and metatarsal bones. My observations are in general confirmatory of his state-

ment. Thus, I have found the direction of the nutritious foramen to be almost always upwards, or towards the proximal end,
in the four metacarpal and four metatarsal bones, while in the
first metacarpal and metatarsal bones it is most frequently
directed downwards or towards the distal extremity.

In one of two examples presenting the fissures which indicate partial distal epiphyses, the downward direction was more
distinct than in the other; and it so happened that in that side
the distal epiphysis was least separated from the shaft of the
bone. At the same time I may remark, that although I admit
the coincidence of the phenomena above stated, I have no other
grounds for connecting them in the relation of cause and effect.

Observations in Animals. I regret that my opportunities of
examining the skeletons of young animals have as yet been too
limited to enable me to deduce any general laws which might
result from more extended observations of this kind. I may
state here however shortly the result of the observations I have
made.

In the majority of five-toed mammifers, the mode of ossification of the bones under consideration is the same as that
usually described in man. This is the case in several different
genera of the Simiae : but among these I notice exceptionally
in a young chimpansee some indications of the separation of a
distal epiphysis on the first metacarpal bone. In the Arctic bear,
the badger, and the otter, the distal epiphyses of the four metacarpals and metatarsals, and the proximal only of the first of
these bones are very distinct, and this is all the more marked
that the ossific union of the epiphyses in these three animals
seems to be comparatively tardy. As however the specimens
I have examined were well advanced in age, in fact nearly full
grown, I do not venture to affirm that other epiphyses may not
have existed at an earlier period. In a young specimen of
dasyurus the same appears to be the condition of the epiphyses.

In the walrus the final union of the epiphyses seems to be
tardy, as appears to be the case in all the aquatic as well as in
the largest mammifers. In a macerated skeleton of this animal,
which however is nearly full grown, I observed the epiphyses
presenting the same conditions as in the animals previously

mentioned. The same statement applies to the metacarpal bones of the cat and dog. In the hind feet of the same animals, and in both limbs of all animals having fewer than five digital elements, such as the hog, the ruminants, and the horse, the metacarpal and metatarsal bones have invariably only distal epiphyses.

But in some other animals I have found a different state of things. Thus in the fore-limb of the kangaroo, of which, however, I have only examined one specimen, and that far advanced in growth, I could distinguish a fissure separating a distal epiphysis from the first metacarpal bone, of exactly the same nature, but not so open or distinct as those of the four other metacarpals. In the koala likewise (phascolarctos) I find the same appearances as in the kangaroo; and this animal was also nearly full grown. In the fore-foot of an Asiatic elephant of large size showing the separate epiphyses very distinctly in other parts of the skeleton, there is a fissure separating a distal epiphysis from the inner or first metacarpal bone almost as distinct as those of the other four metacarpal bones.

In the ornithorhynchus, seal, and cetacea, I have observed greater peculiarities which merit a special description.

With regard to the first of these animals my statements are made with some hesitation, as in the only skeleton which I have had an opportunity of examining previous to the completion of ossification the process was far advanced, and the epiphyses had begun to be united to the rest of the bones. The usual epiphyses of the mammifer existed in the larger bones of the limbs. This fact is in itself interesting, when we take into account the similarity between some parts of the skeleton of the monotremata and that of birds and reptiles,—in which animals it would appear that the epiphyses of the limb bones are either entirely wanting, or are united to the rest of the bones at so early a period as to have escaped notice.

In the fore and hind feet of the ornithorhynchus there are found indications of distal epiphyses on all the five metacarpal and metatarsal bones including the first; and, what is still more exceptional, besides the usual proximal epiphyses of the first metacarpal and metatarsal, there are also grooves separating epiphyses on the proximal ends of the second and third bones of the series, and less obviously of the fourth and fifth bones. In the foot, however, I found the groove on the fifth metatarsal bone more distinct than that on the corresponding metacarpal.

In a skeleton of the echidna histrix in my possession, and which appears to be full grown, although there are still marks of epiphyses in the larger bones of the limbs, ossification has proceeded so far in the bones of the foot as to prevent me from determining the position of the epiphyses[1].

I have examined two skeletons of the common seal, one somewhat more advanced in growth than the other, but both young, and with the ossification proceeding in the shaft and extremities in such a way as to present appearances peculiarly favourable for distinct observation. One of these skeletons had been macerated and dried; the other was in the wet state. The state of the parts was essentially the same in both, and is represented in so far as it appeared unusual in figure 5, I and II, taken from the wet specimen.

In the fore-limbs the mode of ossification did not differ in any respect from that which is considered most usual in man, there being only distal epiphyses in four metacarpal bones, and only proximal epiphyses in the first metacarpal and in all the digital phalanges. But in the hind-foot it was very different; for there the first metatarsal bone, besides the usual proximal epiphysis as in the metacarpal bone, presented a large and distinct distal epiphysis, precisely similar to those of the four other metatarsal bones which had only distal and no proximal epiphyses. Further, all the phalanges of the hind-foot, except the terminal ones, presented, in addition to the usual proximal

---

[1] I may remark here that in small mammals, and in birds and reptiles, there is some risk of being misled as to the presence of epiphyses, from the fact that a small groove, sometimes accompanied on one side by a thin linear elevation of the bone, not unfrequently occurs at the place of junction of the laminar subperiosteal bone of the shaft, and that portion occupying the extremity, and which has been entirely formed from cartilage. From this line the ligaments generally take their attachment externally, and it is from the inner side of the corresponding place in other animals that, when an epiphysis is present, the plate of cartilage proceeds, which for a time separates the bony epiphysis from the end of the shaft. In all cases of doubt it is desirable to determine the existence of epiphyses by longitudinal sections through the bones.

epiphyses, very distinct separate centres of ossification in epiphysal cartilages occupying their distal ends. The terminal phalanges possessed the usual broad proximal epiphyses, and ossification had already passed into the ends of the ungual processes. In all the epiphyses now mentioned, ossification had radiated from the centre of the epiphysal cartilage, and had proceeded so far as to occupy in the wet specimen a considerable part of it; but a cartilaginous plate still intervened between the bone of the shaft and the ossific nodule of the epiphysis.

Among the cetacea I was in some measure prepared to find a departure from the usual mode of ossification of the bones of the anterior limb, both from the known retardation of the process in these animals, and from my having many years ago observed double epiphysal crusts on some of their bones.

Figure 6 gives a view of the progress of ossification in the right fin of a young porpoise preserved in the wet state. I have found exactly the same condition of the parts in two other dried specimens of the same animal, and also in the fins of two other larger toothed cetaceans, so that I have no doubt the process is very similar in the whole of the animals belonging to the order[1].

The first metacarpal bone with its radial digit are little developed, and there is as yet formed only one point of ossification in the proximal phalanx. In the two next or second and third members of the digital series, in which a remarkable multiplication of the phalanges takes place, amounting to seven in the case of the third or middle digit, it will be seen that both in the metacarpal bones and in the two nearest digital phalanges, besides the larger central nucleus of bone representing the shaft, there are both proximal and distal epiphyses or

[1] In placing the number I on the bone which occupies the place to the reader's left hand of Fig. 6, I have not intended to raise specially the question of the homology of this bone nor that of the presence or absence of a trapezium, which I am not in a position to determine. At the same time I may state, notwithstanding the view entertained by some that in the Cetacea the trapezium is absent and is replaced by the shortened first metacarpal, that my observations would lead me to believe that in the porpoise the rudiments at least of both bones are present; and that in the specimen represented in Fig. 6, ossification has commenced in the first metacarpal, but not yet in the shorter cartilaginous mass representing the trapezium.

distinct nuclei answering to these structures. In the three succeeding phalanges of the middle digit the central nuclei only
have yet become ossified, but it is obvious from the shape of
the cartilages occupying either end, that in them also there
would occur later epiphysal ossification. The two last phalanges are still entirely cartilaginous[1].

Thus then we find in the order of Mammifers in which
ossification is most tardy, and in which the subdivision of the
digital phalanges is greatest, the formation of both proximal,
and distal epiphyses on all the members of the series.

It is deserving also of being noted, that in some of the short
bones of the carpus, while the greater part of the bone is
formed from a central ossific nucleus, there is produced separately from this an ossific crust in the surrounding cartilage,
not unlike the upper and lower plates of the bodies of the
vertebræ.

Recapitulation. As the inquiry to which the foregoing observations relate is incomplete, I will not attempt to draw any
general conclusions from them, but will only recapitulate the
more important of the facts previously stated.

1st. The prevalence of a general uniformity in man and the
greater number of mammiferous animals in the mode of ossification of the bones of the fore and hind feet. The most frequent
states to be noted are the following, viz. (1) the absence of proximal and the presence of distal epiphyses in four of the metacarpal and metatarsal bones, and conversely the presence of a
proximal and the absence of a distal epiphysis in the first of
these bones: (2) the presence of proximal and the absence of
distal epiphyses in all the fourteen digital phalanges.

---

[1] I find that the occurrence of epiphyses at both extremities of each digital
phalanx has been noticed by Professor Struthers (see note at p. 111 of the paper
previously cited): and I am informed by my friend Dr Murie, of the Zoological
Society, that in a Memoir on the Osteology of the Cachalot, by Mr Flower,
recently published in the *Transactions of the Zoological Society*, but which I
have not myself seen, that author has described the epiphysal crust or case
surrounding the cartilaginous ossifying surface of the central nucleus of the
carpal bones in the same manner as I have stated it to occur in the toothed
Cetacea which have come under my observation; but which he looks upon as
peculiar to the Cachalot. Mr Flower did not observe any appearance of an epiphysis at either end of the digital phalanges of the Cachalot, a circumstance
which he regards as remarkable, "as in some of the toothed whales (globiocephalus) the metacarpals and phalanges are completed by very large epiphyses."

2nd. The occasional and variable deviation from this general plan in man, and probably in some other animals, by the presence of a more or less developed distal epiphysis on the first metacarpal and metatarsal bones; and the slighter indication of a tendency to the formation of a proximal epiphysis on one or more of the other metacarpal bones.

3rd. The more complete and regular formation of a distal epiphysis on the first metacarpal or metatarsal bones of some animals, such as the kangaroo, koala and elephant, constituting in them apparently the normal mode of ossification.

4th. The pecular condition observed in the seal, in the fore-foot of which animal the ossification follows the usual plan, while in the hind-foot distal epiphyses are fully developed on the first metatarsal bone and on all the phalanges, except the terminal ones.

5th. The tendency in the ornithorhynchus to the formation of both distal and proximal epiphyses in all the metacarpal and metatarsal bones.

6th. The fullest extension of these accessory points of ossification occurring in the cetacea, in which distinct proximal and distal epiphyses exist in the metacarpal bones, and in the phalanges of the more developed digital series[1].

[Professor Thomson's observations in the foregoing paper receive confirmation from specimens of sections of the hand and foot from a girl, æt. 10, which I placed some years ago in the Anatomical Museum of the University of Cambridge. These show distinct epiphyses at the phalangeal, or distal, as well as

---

[1] In a communication which I have received from Dr Murie since the foregoing was in print, he informs me that in examining young specimens of the Orang and Chimpansee he has found the state of the epiphyses of the first metacarpal and metatarsal bones the same as that which is most usual in man. In the forelimb of the Otaria jubata, however, he has observed that the first metacarpal bone (that of the pollex) has not only the usual proximal epiphysis of large size, but also a smaller distal one; and he has found the same to be the case in the metacarpal bone of the pollex in a Walrus considerably younger than the one I examined. But in both of these animals the first metatarsal bone presented only the usual proximal and no distal epiphysis.

These observations are interesting, when taken along with those I have recorded on the seal, as confirming the view of the inconstancy of the absence of a distal epiphysis in the first metacarpal or metatarsal bone, and in showing that we must distrust the position of the epiphysis to these bones as the ground of a homological distinction.

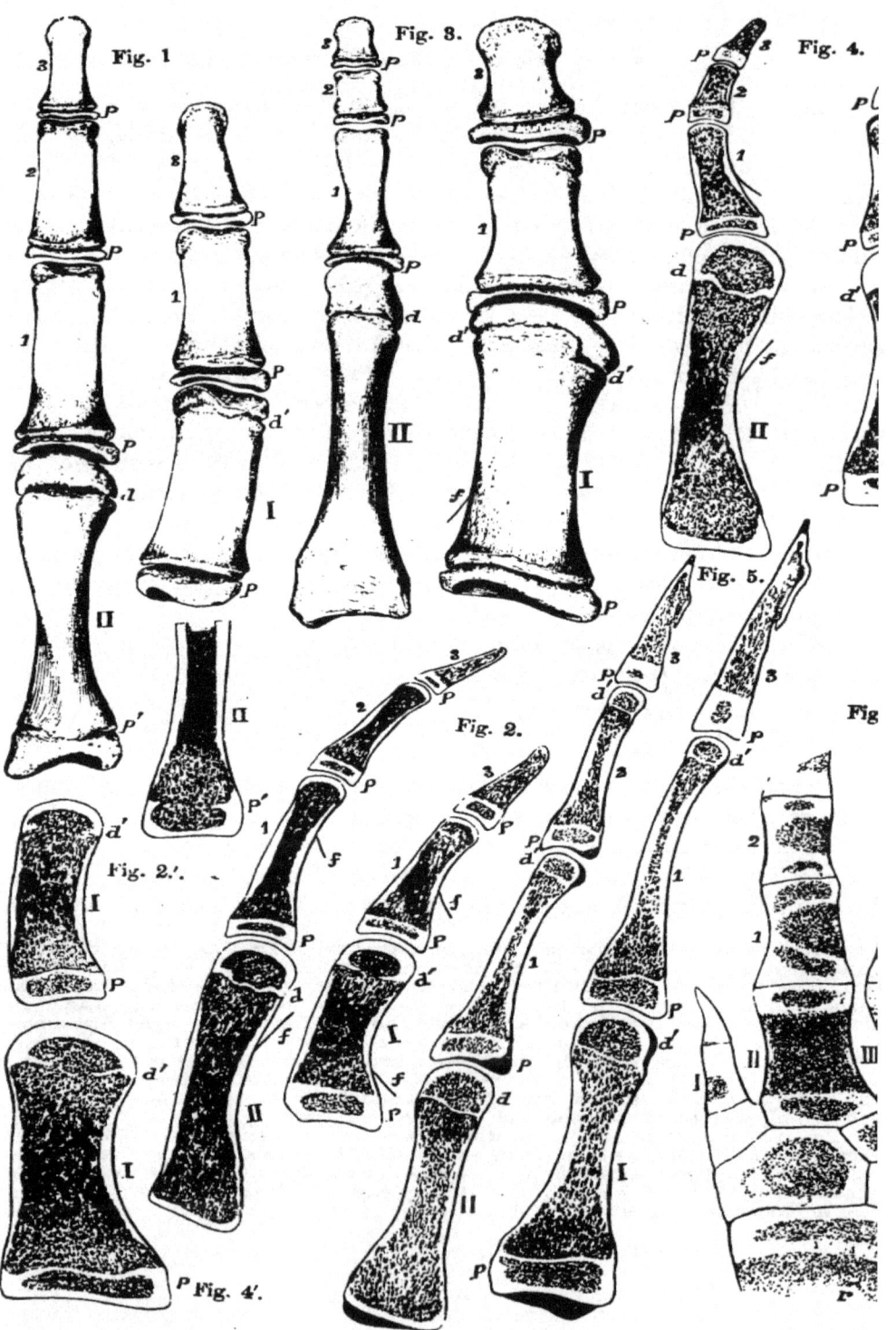

at the proximal, or carpal, ends of the metatarsal bones of the pollex and hallux. The cartilaginous lines separating the distal epiphyses from the shafts are quite visible; though they have been to some extent traversed by ossification near the centre. There is also an epiphysis at the proximal end of the second, or index, metacarpal, though the cartilaginous line separating it from the shaft is not quite so clear, especially towards the centre of the bone, as it is in the distal ends of the metacarpals of the pollex and hallux. There are no visible traces of epiphysial lines in the proximal ends of the other metacarpals or in the 5th metatarsal. The three middle metatarsals have not been cut; and the presence or absence of epiphysial lines cannot therefore be determined in them. G. M. HUMPHRY.]

DESCRIPTION OF THE PLATE.

In the several figures the numbers and letters indicate details as follows, viz. I, the first metacarpal or metatarsal bone. II, the second ditto.

1, 2, 3, the proximal, middle and terminal phalanges, in all excepting Fig. 6, in which there are seven phalanges marked in the middle digit.

p, the more common or usual proximal epiphyses; p', the less common and sometimes imperfect proximal epiphyses.

d, the more common or usual distal epiphyses; d', the less common and sometimes imperfect distal epiphyses.

In a number of the figures a slightly curved line marked f, represents the direction of a bristle introduced into the canal of the bones through the so-called nutritious foramen; that direction being in most instances towards the extremity which is soonest ossified, or in which an epiphysis is wanting.

Fig. 1. Dorsal view of the dried metacarpal and phalangeal bones of the first and second fingers (thumb and forefinger) from the left hand of a girl of eight years of age : d', the fissure separating a distal epiphysis on the first metacarpal bone; p', a small but deep fissure which indicates a partial proximal epiphysis on the second metacarpal bone.

Fig. 2. Antero-posterior longitudinal section of the first and second metacarpal bones and digital phalanges of the thumb and forefinger from the left hand of a child of seven years of age in the wet state: d', a strip of cartilage dipping inwards about a third through the thickness of the bone indicates the partial separation of a distal epiphysis.

Fig. 2'. I. A similar section of the first metacarpal bone from the hand of another child of nearly the same age, in which at d' a very slight degree of inward projection of the epiphysal cartilage exists.

Fig. 2'. II. Transverse section of the proximal half of the second metacarpal bone represented in Fig. 2, showing at p' a slight indentation of the cartilage on the inner side, indicating the tendency to the formation of a partial epiphysis.

Fig. 3. Dorsal view of the dried first and second metatarsal bones and the digital phalanges of the great and second toes from the left foot of the same subject as the hand represented in Fig. 1, of eight years of age: at d', d', deep fissures indicate the separation of a distal epiphysis.

Fig. 4. Antero-posterior longitudinal section of the first and second metatarsal bones and the digital phalanges of the great and second toes in the wet state, from the same child as the specimens represented in Fig. 2, of seven years of age: at d', a complete, but somewhat irregular plate of cartilage separates the distal epiphysis on the first metatarsal bone.

Fig. 4'. I. A similar section of the first metatarsal bone from the left foot of the same subject as the metacarpal bone represented in Fig. 2'. I, showing at d' an inward projection of the dividing plate cartilage which partially separates a distal epiphysis.

Fig. 5. Longitudinal and vertical sections of the first and second metatarsal bones and corresponding digital phalanges from the left hind-foot of a young seal in the wet state; three-fourths of the natural size; d' in the first metatarsal bone, and in the first phalanx of the first toe, and in the first and second phalanges of the second toe, indicates the distal epiphyses existing in this animal.

Fig. 6. Longitudinal and transverse section of a part of the right anterior limb of a young porpoise in the wet state: r, the lower end of the radius with its epiphysis; u, part of the ulna; I, II, III, the first, second, and third metacarpal bones; the second and third showing, in addition to the larger central ossified mass, both proximal and distal epiphyses; 1 to 7, the cartilaginous and partially ossified phalanges of the third digit, showing, in the first two, distal as well as proximal epiphyses; and in the third, fourth and fifth only the central nodule as yet ossified. In the first two phalanges of the second digit the same is shown as in the third.

REPRINT OF THE "IDEA OF A NEW ANATOMY OF
THE BRAIN; submitted for the observations of his friends;
by CHARLES BELL, F.R.S.E."

To which are added selections from LETTERS written by the Author
of the ESSAY to his brother, Professor George Joseph Bell,
between the years 1807 and 1821.

AT the meeting of the British Medical Association, held at Oxford
last August, a copy, in manuscript, of the Essay, of which the title
is given above, was brought under the notice of the Physiological
Section. Some members then expressed an opinion that, owing to
the well-known important character of the work, as containing the
first announcement of the principles on which the modern improvements in our knowledge of the nervous system are founded, and the
difficulty of procuring original copies on account of their scarceness,
it was desirable that a reprint should be made. When that wish
was communicated to the widow of Sir Charles Bell, she promptly
consented to its being reprinted in this Journal.

It was at the same time intimated to the Editors that, as the
main object of reproducing the Essay was to throw light on the
development in the author's mind of his views on the distinct functions of the nerves, certain unpublished documents, which would
add to the interest of the reprint, would be placed at their disposal.
These, were selected passages from letters which the author wrote
before composing the Essay, and when the "*Idea* of the New Anatomy of the Brain," had just flashed on his mind.

The letters were written to his brother George Joseph Bell;
who afterwards attained high eminence at the Scotch bar. Of him
it was said, by Lord Cockburn, in the "Memorials of his Times,"
that he was "Our greatest modern institutional writer." In another
part, speaking of the most elaborate of his works, the "Mercantile
Commentaries," he thus expresses himself: "Bell's is the greatest
work on Scotch jurisprudence that has ever appeared since the publication of Lord Stairs' 'Institute.' Its authority has helped to decide
probably eighty out of every hundred mercantile questions that have
been settled since it began to illuminate our courts; and it has done,
and will do, more for the fame of the law of Scotland in foreign

10—2

countries, than has been done by all our law-books put together."
To this brother, only a few years older, Charles was from earliest
youth warmly attached: and when separated, by the latter going
to London, they kept up a constant brotherly intercourse by letters. Fortunately those written by Charles were preserved; and,
at the death of George Joseph, which occurred after his brother's
decease, the letters, from which extracts are about to be given, came
into the possession of his daughter, Miss Bell. These were collected
and arranged by her, with the hope that, together with other materials, they might form a biographical memoir of both brothers. Her
death, however, impeded the publication; and those passages of the
correspondence only which relate to the early researches in the nervous system by Sir Charles are now offered to the profession; suffering, as it may be understood, in no slight degree, from being torn
from their contexts.

When Charles Bell, slenderly provided with money, and having
few friends, moved to the metropolis, it was an act of hardihood to
commence the career of Lecturer alone; the teachers in the several
great medical schools being then Cline and Cooper in the Borough,
Abernethy at St Bartholomew's, Sir Everard Home and Wilson in
the West. It is not without interest, that, in the very year (1807)
in which he founded his school, and delivered lectures to a class
of three pupils, he began to look upon the Nervous System as a
fertile field for cultivation.

The following are extracts from the letters up to the date of the
printing of the Essay :—

21st *May*, 1807.—"I am casting about for a subject to make
something new of. I have been thinking of the Brain—of Mind—
of Madness. Could I not put this subject in the form of queries,
as to the best way of prosecuting it, to be laid before Stewart[1], or
Jeffrey[2], &c.? I would not publish any thing but in Papers for these
many years."

26th *Nov.* 1807.—"I have done a more interesting *Nova Anato-
mia Cerebri* than it is possible to conceive. I lectured it yesterday.
I prosecuted it last night till one o'clock. And I am sure that it
will be well received."

31st *Nov.* 1807.—"My surgical books and lectures you will soon
see eclipsed by my character as an anatomist and physiologist. I
really think this new view of the Anatomy of the Brain will strike
more than the discovery of the lymphatics being absorbents."

[1] Professor Dugald Stewart of Edinburgh.
[2] Lord Jeffrey.

Dec. 5th, 1807.—" My New Anatomy of the Brain occupies my head almost entirely. I hinted to you that I was 'burning,' or, on the eve of a grand discovery. I consider the organs of the outward senses as forming a distinct class of nerves from the others. I take five tubercles within the brain as the internal senses. I trace the nerves of the nose, eye, ear, and tongue to these. Here I see established connection—there the great mass of the brain receives processes from the central tubercles. Again, the great masses of the cerebrum send down processes or crura, which give off all the common nerves of voluntary motion, &c. I establish thus a kind of circulation, as it were. In this inquiry I describe many new connections— the whole opens up a new and simple light, and the whole accords with the phenomena, with the pathology, and is supported by interesting views. My object is not to publish this, but to lecture it, to lecture it to my friends, to lecture it to Sir Joseph Banks' coterie of old women, to make the town ring with it, as it is really the only new thing that has appeared in anatomy since the days of Hunter; and, if I make it out, as interesting as the circulation, or the doctrine of absorption. But I must still have time : now is the end of a week and I will be at it again."

March 28th, 1808.—" I have been thinking of having a room five or six miles from town, and there pursuing my physiology of the Brain—that which is to make me, I am convinced."

8th July, 1808.—" I have your very kind letter beside me. The motives and views you give me are very consolatory. I am, or have been since you left me, a very idle fellow—taking extracts from Dante, and making appropriate sketches. But last night I sat late with my notes on the Brain; and I will send you my Introduction—which is a view of the whole System. It is this I would print; but the description of the Brain I will reserve for more labour of succeeding winters.

" I wish you would take a book of Anatomy, be it the *Encyclopedia*, or anything, to understand the received account; that you may know my *merits*—how different the view I take. I confess I like it the more I consider it : but this is common, you will say, in all hobbies."

15th July (*the letter continued*).—"The night ended with a guinea ; and the morning began with it.

" I have said that I have completed my view of the Brain. But it is only the Introduction to the strict anatomy, giving a view of my system. For I find that it embraces the whole Nervous System. As soon as John (Shaw) has transcribed it, I'll send it down to you. I expect you will correct it, and have it transcribed, and then give it to Jeffrey and Playfair[1] ; as I will here to Brougham[2] and some others.

" I think that to the profession at large it will prove most

[1] Professor Playfair of Edinburgh.
[2] Lord Brougham.

acceptable. And while some will adopt it I trust, the most captious will say it is ingenious. But read, and give me your opinion. Explain that I wish to have read before the Royal Society a series of Papers—this being the first; the second being more strictly anatomical; and the third being the subject treated pathologically. I'll write to Jeffrey about it. Or if it does not seem good to us to have it read before the Society, then perhaps to have it printed: or first read here, and then printed. But I wish to have it in some way agitated before the winter."

16th July (continuation of the same letter).—" I am writing my ' Dissections',' and, I trust, making it very good. And I have thought much, though I have done little in writing my ' Brain.' In truth, the writing must be short, and yet embracing much. I am delighted with it more and more; and I must very soon send you a précis of it, that we may talk it over in our letters."

5th Aug. 1808.—" I am much pleased with what you say of my MS. of the Brain. I hope Jeffrey will like it. How can you be anxious for its originality? Did I not tell you to read, before you got it? To tell you the truth, you cannot be more pleased with it than I am. I am sure that I am correct; and I think there will be a great proportion who will, as you say, acknowledge that it is ingenious, when they mean to say it is not true.

*   *   *   *   *   *   *   *   *

" I am really engaged so that my ' Surgery'' goes on slowly. You ask what Campbell² is doing. Between ourselves, he is palsied with fear. He dare not publish; and he has never gone further than you saw. If this delay were a test of genius I must be a mighty great one too:...Could you not get Dugald Stewart or Playfair to look at my MS. of the Brain?...(*Continuation of same letter*). I have just received your packet; and it is a little perplexing. I cannot distinguish Jeffrey from you. You have concealed from me the general impression upon Jeffrey. It is not meant to explain the anatomy of the Brain; but to state, to those who are supposed to know it, the ground and outline of a train of observations; to follow in Papers on the Anatomy and Pathology of the Brain; and to establish my claim to these discoveries, if I may yet term them so.

" Yet there may be good reason why I should address myself to the ignorant; though I know it will be construed into conceit and parade. But I will set earnestly to work to do it. Jeffrey is quite an unaccountable person; but I wish you had either told me his opinion, if he gave it, or given the MS. to somebody who would speak. For it is very unpleasant to be so long in the dark, writing to please oneself, without knowing how my system touches others. You seemed much pleased. And when you examine a subject I take

---

¹ Duodecimo edition.
² Operative surgery.
³ The Poet.

you for a better judge than Jeffrey. The points really the most interesting and novel in the ' Anatomy of Expression' never touched him; but, as now, he took to the manufacture of the thing only[1]. His observations, as you say, are admirable; and it will be my business to profit by them. To tell you the truth, what you got was my first penning of the subject; and I could never set about altering its arrangement. Jeffrey, I find, thinks that not important which is the very basis of the whole; he would like a beautiful Essay better than the most striking fact. Your questions on the margin show how far I have mistaken in not stating the present system of anatomy. But still, I say, if I do it in that way, instead of a short statement of what is new, you will find a long essay and controversy. A wise man, they say, should hear everything; but act according to his own sentiments. I'll try to do this."

4th Dec. 1809.—" I think I told you I was kept busy by having all my usual time of relaxation occupied by revising books for re-printing. But last night I took a long pull at the subject of my most anxious contemplation—the Brain; and so heated myself with it, that at half-past two I had no more disposition to sleep than now. All my patients are warlike—eight officers[2]...I shall be very bloody in this Brain of mine. I must make experiments; and that is what I hate to do."

26th Dec. 1809.—" Speaking of books, could you get a little tiny book printed for me, of the smallest 12mo.? For I must send you down the MS. of the Brain again, stated shortly, for my friends."

After anxiously attending John Shaw for scarlet fever, he himself had an abscess in one of the tonsils, from which he was for some time in much danger. Both repaired to Hampstead for change of air; and there he wrote :—

10th Jan. 1810.—" Precaution more than necessity takes me to the country; for before I lecture again I have much anatomical work to do; and that I won't do till quite in strength."

13th Jan. (the letter continued).—" I have even in my present sickness been intent on the idea of some great work. Sometimes I think of finishing my anatomy of the muscles; or of painting in great style. I have had thoughts of entering on a great work of Pathology. The Brain I wish still to resume, after giving out a short account of my view, as taken from my lectures. It was this I proposed to you to print in Edinburgh. In short, this inertia of the body has stirred up ambitious projects."

The extract which follows has a special interest, from marking

---

[1] Alluding to the review of that work in the *Edinburgh Review*, No. XVII. 1806.
[2] At that time he had published his " Dissertation on gun-shot wounds; founded principally on observations upon the wounded received into Haslar and York hospitals, from Corunna."

the date of the first series of experiments on the roots of the spinal nerves:—

2d March, 1810.—" I write to tell you that I really think I am going to establish my Anatomy of the Brain on facts the most important that have been discovered in the history of the science.

" You recollect that I have entertained the idea that the parts of the Brain were distinct in function; and that the cerebrum was in a particular manner the organ of mind; and this from other circumstances than what I am now to detail to you.

" It occurred to me that, as there were four grand divisions of the Brain, so were their four divisions of the spinal marrow: first, a lateral division, then a division into the back and forepart. Next, it occurred to me that all the spinal nerves had within the sheath of the spinal marrow two roots, one from the back part, another from before. Whenever this occurred to me I thought that I had obtained a method of inquiring into the function of the parts of the Brain.

" Exp. I. I opened the spine, and pricked and injured the posterior filaments of the nerves; no motion of the muscles followed. I then touched the anterior division; immediately the parts were convulsed.

" Exp. II. I now destroyed the posterior part of the spinal marrow by the point of a needle; no convulsive movement followed. I injured the anterior part, and the animal was convulsed.

" It is almost superfluous to say that the part of the spinal marrow having sensibility is what comes from the cerebrum; the posterior and insensible part belongs to the cerebellum.

" Taking these facts as they stand, is it not most curious that there should be thus established a distinction in the parts of a *nerve,* and that a nerve should be insensible? But then, as the foundation of a great system, if I can but sustain them by repeated experiments, I am made; and a real gratification ensured for a large portion of my existence."

25th May, 1810.—" I was at the play last night, Mrs Siddons in Constance. I go on with my old plan—taking her Commentaries on Shakespeare and the Passions [1].

" Indeed, I turn me more and more again to the Anatomy of Expression; and the more, that I have lately had the most severe disappointments in my experiments on the nerves. Confident that I was to make a system captivating as the circulation, and possessed powerfully by this idea of a decided superiority, at one brave bound, you may imagine my disappointment.

" I weary to see you, and weary for the country. The eternal din! O, for that silence in which I could distinctly hear myself speak. Solitary confinement is preferable to this incessant motion. Now, too, the foliage is cool and dark; the light breaks through the

---

[1] See *Life of Mrs Siddons,* by Campbell.

trees with silvery splendour, and the distance is bright and enticing. Of this the Park informs me. I shall go to Lynn's[1] cottage; but there is such studied negligence, such flower-pot gardening, it cramps and confines one's every thought."

9th June, 1810.—"I continue to paint. And my Brain will hold together still.

* * * * * * * * *

"I shall not forget to write to you of the paintings I occasionally see, but at this moment my mind is all agog about my Nervous System. It occupies me chiefly. Yet it is only in sitting ruminating, not in work."

About *Sept.* 1810.—"O! for time to write out my Brain. *It shall be good.* I won't publish though. Does this look like a man very unhappy?"

11*th Dec.* 1810.—"I should like to send my Brain (!) to the Edinburgh Society. It shall be my most pleasant work."

July, 1811.—"...But my serious study will be the small ornate account of the Anatomy of the Brain. On this I shall swell myself into importance, and make myself very happy..."

IDEA OF A NEW ANATOMY OF THE BRAIN; SUBMITTED *FOR THE OBSERVATIONS OF HIS FRIENDS.*
By CHARLES BELL, F.R.S.E.

NOTE.

THE want of any consistent history of the Brain and Nerves, and the dull unmeaning manner which is in use of demonstrating the brain, may authorize any novelty in the manner of treating the subject.

I have found some of my friends so mistaken in their conception of the object of the demonstrations which I have delivered in my lectures, that I wish to vindicate myself at all hazards. They would have it that I am in search of the seat of the soul; but I wish only to investigate the structure of the brain, as we examine the structure of the eye and ear.

It is not more presumptuous to follow the tracts of nervous matter in the brain, and to attempt to discover the course of sensation, than it is to trace the rays of light through the humours of the eye, and to say, that the retina is the seat of vision. Why are we to close the investigation with the discovery of the external organ?

---

[1] A distinguished Surgeon.

It would have been easy to have given this Essay an imposing splendour, by illustrations and engravings of the parts, but I submit it as a sketch to those who are well able to judge of it in this shape.

———————◆———————

THE prevailing doctrine of the anatomical schools is, that the whole brain is a common sensorium; that the extremities of the nerves are organized, so that each is fitted to receive a peculiar impression; or that they are distinguished from each other only by delicacy of structure, and by a corresponding delicacy of sensation, that the nerve of the eye, for example, differs from the nerves of touch only in the degree of its sensibility.

It is imagined that impressions, thus differing in kind, are carried along the nerves to the sensorium, and presented to the mind; and that the mind, by the same nerves which receive sensation, sends out the mandate of the will to the moving parts of the body.

It is further imagined, that there is a set of nerves, called vital nerves, which are less strictly connected with the sensorium, or which have upon them knots, cutting off the course of sensation, and thereby excluding the vital motions from the government of the will.

This appears sufficiently simple and consistent, until we begin to examine anatomically the structure of the brain, and the course of the nerves,—then all is confusion: the divisions and subdivisions of the brain, the circuitous course of nerves, their intricate connections, their separation and re-union, are puzzling in the last degree, and are indeed considered as things inscrutable. Thus it is, that he who knows the parts the best, is most in a maze, and he who knows least of anatomy, sees least inconsistency in the commonly received opinion.

In opposition to these opinions, I have to offer reasons for believing, That the cerebrum and cerebellum are different in function as in form; That the parts of the cerebrum have different functions; and that the nerves which we trace in the body are not single nerves possessing various powers, but bundles of different nerves, whose filaments are united for the convenience of distribution, but which are distinct in office, as they are in origin from the brain:

That the external organs of the senses have the matter of the nerves adapted to receive certain impressions, while the corresponding organs of the brain are put in activity by the external excitement: That the idea or perception is according to the part of the brain to which the nerve is attached, and that each organ has a certain limited number of changes to be wrought upon it by the external impression:

That the nerves of sense, the nerves of motion, and the vital nerves, are distinct through their whole course, though they seem sometimes united in one bundle; and that they depend for their attributes on the organs of the brain to which they are severally attached.

The view which I have to present, will serve to show why there are divisions, and many distinct parts in the brain : why some nerves are simple in their origin and distribution, and others intricate beyond description. It will explain the apparently accidental connection between the twigs of nerves. It will do away the difficulty of conceiving how sensation and volition should be the operation of the same nerve at the same moment. It will show how a nerve may lose one property, and retain another ; and it will give an interest to the labours of the anatomist in tracing the nerves.

IDEA &c.

WHEN in contemplating the structure of the eye we say, how admirably it is adapted to the laws of light ! we use language which implies a partial, and consequently an erroneous view. And the philosopher takes not a more enlarged survey of nature when he declares how curiously the laws of light are adapted to the constitution of the eye.

This creation, of which we are a part, has not been formed in parts. The organ of vision, and the matter or influence carried to the organ, and the qualities of bodies with which we are acquainted through it, are parts of a system great beyond our imperfect comprehension, formed as it should seem at once in wisdom ; not pieced together like the work of human ingenuity.

When this whole was created, (of which the remote planetary system, as well as our bodies, and the objects more familiar to our observation, are but parts), the mind was placed in a body not merely suited to its residence, but in circumstances to be moved by the materials around it ; and the capacities of the mind, and the powers of the organs, which are as a medium betwixt the mind and the external world, have an original constitution framed in relation to the qualities of things.

It is admitted that neither bodies nor the images of bodies enter the brain. It is indeed impossible to believe that colour can be conveyed along a nerve ; or the vibration in which we suppose sound to consist can be retained in the brain : but we can conceive, and have reason to believe, that an impression is made upon the organs of the outward senses when we see, or hear, or taste.

In this inquiry it is most essential to observe, that while each organ of sense is provided with a capacity of receiving certain changes to be played upon it, as it were, yet each is utterly incapable of receiving the impressions destined for another organ of sensation.

It is also very remarkable that an impression made on two different nerves of sense, though with the same instrument, will produce two distinct sensations; and the ideas resulting will only have relation to the organ affected.

As the announcing of these facts forms a natural introduction to the Anatomy of the Brain, which I am about to deliver, I shall state them more fully.

There are four kinds of Papillæ on the tongue, but with two of those only we have to do at present. Of these, the Papillæ of one kind form the seat of the sense of taste; the other Papillæ (more numerous and smaller) resemble the extremities of the nerves in the common skin, and are the organs of touch in the tongue. When I take a sharp steel point, and touch one of *these* Papillæ, I feel the sharpness. The sense of *touch* informs me of the shape of the instrument. When I touch a Papilla of taste, I have no sensation similar to the former. I do not know that a point touches the tongue, but I am sensible of a metallic taste, and the sensation passes backward on the tongue.

In the operation of couching the cataract, the pain of piercing the retina with a needle is not so great as that which proceeds from a grain of sand under the eyelid. And although the derangement of the stomach sometimes marks the injury of an organ so delicate, yet the pain is occasioned by piercing the outward coat, not by the affection of the expanded nerve of vision.

If the sensation of light were conveyed to us by the retina, the organ of vision, in consequence of that organ being as much more sensible than the surface of the body as the impression of light is more delicate than that pressure which gives us the sense of touch; what would be the feelings of a man subjected to an operation in which a needle were pushed through the nerve. Life could not bear so great a pain.

But there is an occurrence during this operation on the eye which will direct us to the truth: when the needle pierces the eye, the patient has the sensation of a spark of fire before the eye.

This fact is corroborated by experiments made on the eye. When the eye-ball is pressed on the side, we perceive various coloured light. Indeed the mere effect of a blow on the head might inform us, that sensation depends on the exercise of the organ affected, not on the impression conveyed to the external organ; for by the vibration caused by the blow, the ears ring, and the eye flashes light, while there is neither light nor sound present.

It may be said, that there is here no proof of the sensation being in the brain more than in the external organ of sense. But when the nerve of a stump is touched, the pain is as if in the amputated extremity. If it be still said that this is no proper example of a peculiar sense existing without its external organ, I offer the following example : Qŭando penis glandem exedat ŭlcŭs, et nihil nisi granulatio maneat, ad extremam tamen nervi pudicæ partem ubi terminatŭr sensus supersunt, et exquisitissima sensŭs gratificatio.

If light, pressure, galvanism, or eleĉtricity produce vision, we must conclude that the idea in the mind is the result of an aĉtion excited in the eye or in the brain, not of anything received, though caused by an impression from without. The operations of the mind are confined not by the limited nature of things created, but by the limited number of our organs of sense. By induĉtion we know that things exist which yet are not brought under the operation of the senses. When we have never known the operation of one of the organs of the five senses, we can never know the ideas pertaining to that sense ; and what would be the effeĉt on our minds, even constituted as they now are, with a superadded organ of sense, no man can distinĉtly imagine.

As we are parts of the creation, so God has bound us to the material world by this law of our nature, that it shall require excitement from without, and an operation produced by the aĉtion of things external to rouse our faculties : But that once brought into aĉtivity, the organs can be put in exercise by the mind, and be made to minister to the memory and imagination, and all the faculties of the soul.

I shall hereafter shew, that the opérations of the mind are seated in the great mass of the cerebrum, while the parts of the brain to which the nerves of sense tend, striĉtly form the seat of the sensation, being the internal organs of sense. These organs are operated upon in two direĉtions. They receive the impression from without, as from the eye and ear : and as their aĉtion influences the operations of the brain producing perception, so are they brought into aĉtion and suffer changes similar to that which they experience from external pressure by the operation of the will ; or, as I am now treating of the subjeĉt anatomically, by the operation of the great mass of the brain upon them.

In all regulated actions of the muscles we must acknowledge that they are influenced through the same nerves, by the same operation of the sensorium. Now the operations of the body are as nice and curious, and as perfectly regulated before Reason has sway, as they are at any time after, when the muscular frame might be supposed to be under the guidance of sense and reason. Instinctive motions are the operations of the same organs, the brain and nerves and muscles, which minister to reason and volition in our mature years. When the young of any animal turns to the nipple, directed by the sense of smelling, the same operations are performed, and through the same means, as afterwards when we make an effort to avoid what is noxious, or desire and move towards what is agreeable.

The operations of the brain may be said to be threefold : 1. The frame of the body is endowed with the characters of life, and the vital parts held together as one system through the operation of the brain and nerves; and the secret operations of the vital organs suffer the controul of the brain, though we are unconscious of the thousand delicate operations which are every instant going on in the body. 2. In the second place, the instinctive motions which precede the developement of the intellectual faculties are performed through the brain and nerves. 3. In the last place, the operation of the senses in rouzing the faculties of the mind, and the exercise of the mind over the moving parts of the body, is through the brain and nerves. The first of these is perfect in nature, and independent of the mind. The second is a prescribed and limited operation of the instrument of thought and agency. The last begins by imperceptible degrees, and has no limit in extent and variety. It is that to which all the rest is subservient, the end being the calling into activity and the sustaining of an intellectual being.

Thus we see that in as far as is necessary to the the great system, the operation of the brain, nerves, and muscles are perfect from the beginning; and we are naturally moved to ask, Might not the operations of the mind have been thus perfect and spontaneous from the beginning as well as slowly excited into action by outward impressions? Then man would have been an insulated being, not only cut off from the inanimate world around him, but from his fellows ; he would have been an individual, not a part of a whole. That he may have a motive and a spring to action, and suffer pain and pleasure, and become an intelligent being, answerable for his actions,—sensation is made to result from external impression, and reason and passion to come from the experience of good and evil; first as they are in reference to his corporeal frame, and finally as they belong to the intellectual privations and enjoyments.

----●----

THE brain is a mass of soft matter, in part of a white colour, and generally striated; in part of a grey or cineritious colour having no fibrous appearance. It has grand divisions and subdivisions : and as the forms exist before the solid bone incloses the brain; and as the distinctions of parts are equally observable in animals whose brain is surrounded with fluid, they evidently are not accidental, but are a consequence of internal structure; or in other words they have a correspondence with distinctions in the uses of the parts of the brain.

On examining the grand divisions of the brain we are forced to admit that there are four brains. For the brain is divided longitudinally by a deep fissure; and the line of distinction can even be traced where the sides are united in substance. Whatever we observe on one side has a corresponding part on the other; and an exact resemblance and symmetry is preserved in all the lateral divisions of the brain. And so, if we take the proof of anatomy, we must admit that as the nerves are double, and the organs of sense double, so is the brain double; and every sensation conveyed to the brain is conveyed to the two lateral parts; and the operations performed must be done in both lateral portions at the same moment.

I speak of the lateral divisions of the brain being distinct brains combined in function, in order the more strongly to mark the distinction betwixt the anterior and posterior grand divisions. Betwixt the lateral parts there is a strict resemblance in form and substance : each principal part is united by transverse tracts of medullary matter; and there is every provision for their acting with perfect sympathy. On the contrary, the *cerebrum*, the anterior grand division, and the *cerebellum* the posterior grand division, have slight and indirect connection. In form and division of parts, and arrangement of white and grey matter, there is no resemblance. There is here nothing of that symmetry and correspondence of parts which is so remarkable betwixt the right and left portions.

I have found evidence that the vascular system of the cerebellum may be affected independently of the vessels of the cerebrum. I have seen the whole surface of the cerebellum studded with spots of extravasated blood as small as pin heads, so as to be quite red, while no mark of disease was upon the surface of the cerebrum. The action of vessels it is needless to say is under the influence of the parts to which they go; and in this we have a proof of a distinct state of activity in the cerebrum and cerebellum.

From these facts, were there no others, we are entitled to conclude, that in the operations excited in the brain there cannot be such sympathy or corresponding movement in the cerebrum and cerebellum as there is betwixt the lateral portions of the cerebrum; that the anterior and posterior grand divisions of the brain perform distinct offices.

In examining this subject further, we find, when we compare the relative magnitude of the cerebrum to the other parts of the brain in man and in brutes, that in the latter the cerebrum is much smaller, having nothing of the relative magnitude and importance which in man it bears to the other parts of the nervous system; signifying that the cerebrum is the seat of those qualities of mind which distinguish man. We may observe also that the posterior grand division, or *cerebellum* remains more permanent in form : while the cerebrum changes in conformity to the organs of sense, or the endowments of the different classes of animals. In the inferior animals, for example, where there are two external organs of the same sense, there is to be found two distinct corresponding portions of cerebrum, while the cerebellum corresponds with the frame of the body.

In thinking of this subject, it is natural to expect that we should be able to put the matter to proof by experiment. But how is this to be accomplished, since any experiment direct upon the brain itself must be difficult, if not impossible ?—I took this view of the subject. The *medulla spinalis* has a central division, and also a distinction into anterior and posterior fasciculi, corresponding with the anterior and posterior portions of the brain. Further we can trace down the crura of the *cerebrum* into the anterior fasciculus of the spinal marrow, and the crura of the *cerebellum* into the posterior fasciculus. I thought that here I might have an opportunity of touching the *cerebellum*, as it were, through the posterior portion of the spinal marrow, and the cerebrum by the anterior portion. To this end I made experiments which, though they were not conclusive, encouraged me in the view I had taken.

I found that injury done to the anterior portion of the spinal marrow, convulsed the animal more certainly than injury done to the posterior portion; but I found it difficult to make the experiment without injuring both portions.

Next considering that the spinal nerves have a double root, and being of opinion that the properties of the nerves are derived from their connections with the parts of the brain, I thought that I had an opportunity of putting my opinion to the test of experiment, and of proving at the same time that nerves of different endowments were in the same cord, and held together by the same sheath.

On laying bare the roots of the spinal nerves, I found that I could cut across the posterior fasciculus of nerves, which took its origin from the posterior portion of the spinal marrow without convulsing the muscles of the back; but that on touching the anterior fasciculus with the point of the knife, the muscles of the back were immediately convulsed.

Such were my reasons for concluding that the cerebrum and the cerebellum were parts distinct in function, and that every nerve possessing a double function obtained that by having a double root. I now saw the meaning of the double connection of the nerves with the spinal marrow; and also the cause of that seeming intricacy in the connections of nerves throughout their course, which were not double at their origins.

The spinal nerves being double, and having their roots in the spinal marrow, of which a portion comes from the cerebrum and a portion from the cerebellum, they convey the attributes of both grand divisions of the brain to every part; and therefore the distribution of such nerves is simple, one nerve supplying its destined part. But the nerves which come directly from the brain, come from parts of the brain which vary in operation; and in order to bestow different qualities on the parts to which the nerves are distributed, two or more nerves must be united in their course or at their final destination. Hence it is that the 1st nerve must have branches of the 5th united with it: hence the *portio dura* of the 7th pervades everywhere the bones of the cranium to unite with the extended branches of the 5th: hence the union of the 3rd and 5th in the orbit: hence the 9th and 5th are both sent to the tongue: hence it is, in short, that no part is sufficiently supplied by one single nerve, unless that nerve be a nerve of the spinal marrow, and have a double root, a connection (however remotely) with both the cerebrum and cerebellum.

Such nerves as are single in their origin from the spinal marrow will be found either to unite in their course with some other nerve, or to be such as are acknowledged to be peculiar in their operation.

The 8th nerve is from the portion of the *medulla oblongata*[1] which belongs to the cerebellum: the 9th nerve comes from the portion which belongs to the cerebrum. The first is a nerve of the class called Vital nerves, controuling secretly the operation of the body; the last is the Motor nerve of the tongue, and is an instrument of volition. Now the connections formed by the 8th nerve in its course to the viscera are endless; it seems nowhere sufficient for the entire purpose of a nerve; for everywhere it is accompanied by others, and the 9th passes to the tongue, which is already profusely supplied by the 5th.

Understanding the origin of the nerves in the brain to be the source of their powers, we look upon the connections formed betwixt distant nerves, and upon the combination of nerves in their passage, with some interest; but without this the whole is an un-meaning tissue. Seeing the seeming irregularity in one subject, we say it is accident; but finding that the connections never vary, we say only that it is strange, until we come to understand the necessity of nerves being combined in order to bestow distinct qualities on the parts to which they are sent.

The *cerebellum* when compared with the *cerebrum* is simple in its form. It has no internal tubercles or masses of cineritious mat-ter in it. The medullary matter comes down from the cineritious cortex, and forms the *crus;* and the *crus* runs into union with the same process from the cerebrum; and they together form the *medulla spinalis*, and are continued down into the spinal marrow; and these crura or processes afford double origin to the double nerves of the spine. The nerves proceeding from the Crus Cere-belli go everywhere (in seeming union with those from the Crus Cerebri); they unite the body together, and controul the actions of the bodily frame; and especially govern the operation of the viscera necessary to the continuance of life.

In all animals having a nervous system, the *cerebellum* is ap-parent, even though there be no *cerebrum*. The cerebrum is seen in such tribes of animals as have organs of sense, and it is seen to be

---

[1] The *medulla oblongata* is only the commencement of the spinal marrow.

near the eyes, or principal organ of sense; and sometimes it is quite separate from the *cerebellum*.

The cerebrum I consider as the grand organ by which the mind is united to the body. Into it all the nerves from the external organs of the senses enter; and from it all the nerves which are agents of the will pass out.

If this be not at once obvious, it proceeds only from the circumstance that the nerves take their origin from the different parts of the brain; and while those nerves are considered as simple cords, this circumstance stands opposed to the conclusion which otherways would be drawn. A nerve having several roots, implies that it propagates its sensation to the brain generally. But when we find that the several roots are distinct in their endowments, and are in respect to office distinct nerves; then the conclusion is unavoidable, that the portions of the brain are distinct organs of different functions.

To arrive at any understanding of the internal parts of the cerebrum, we must keep in view the relation of the nerves, and must class and distinguish the nerves, and follow them into its substance. If all ideas originate in the mind from external impulse, how can we better investigate the structure of the brain than by following the nerves, which are the means of communication betwixt the brain and the outward organs of the senses?

The nerves of sense, the olfactory, the optic, the auditory, and the gustatory nerve, are traced backwards into certain tubercles or convex bodies in the base of the brain. And I may say, that the nerves of sense either form tubercles before entering the brain, or they enter into those convexities in the base of the *cerebrum*. These convexities are the constituent parts of the cerebrum, and are in all animals necessary parts of the organs of sense: for as certainly as we discover an animal to have an external organ of sense, we find also a medullary tubercle; whilst the superiority of animals in intelligence is shown by the greater magnitude of the hemispheres or upper part of the cerebrum.

The convex bodies which are seated in the lower part of the cerebrum, and into which the nerves of sense enter, have extensive connection with the hemispheres on their upper part. From the medullary matter of the hemispheres, again, there pass down, converging to the crura, Striæ, which is the medullary matter taking upon it the character of a nerve; for from the Crura

11—2

Cerebri, or its prolongation in the anterior Fasciculi of the spinal marrow, go off the nerves of motion.

But with these nerves of motion which are passing outward there are nerves going inwards; nerves from the surfaces of the body; nerves of touch; and nerves of peculiar sensibility, having their seat in the body or viscera. It is not improbable that the tracts of cineritious matter which we observe in the course of the medullary matter of the brain, are the seat of such peculiar sensibilities; the organs of certain powers which seem resident in the body.

As we proceed further in the investigation of the function of the brain, the discussion becomes more hypothetical. But surely physiologists have been mistaken in supposing it necessary to prove sensibility in those parts of the brain which they are to suppose the seat of the intellectual operations. We are not to expect the same phenomena to result from the cutting or tearing of the brain as from the injury to the nerves. The function of the one is to transmit sensation; the other has a higher operation. The nature of the organs of sense is different; the sensibilities of the parts of the body are very various. If the needle piercing the retina during the operation of couching gives no remarkable pain, except in touching the common coats of the eye, ought we to imagine that the seat of the higher operations of the mind should, when injured, exhibit the same effects with the irritation of a nerve? So far therefore from thinking the parts of the brain which are insensible, to be parts inferior (as every part has its use), I should even from this be led to imagine that they had a higher office. And if there be certain parts of the brain which are insensible, and other parts which being injured shake the animal with convulsions exhibiting phenomena similar to those of a wounded nerve, it seems to follow that the latter parts which are endowed with sensibility like the nerves are similar to them in function and use; while the parts of the brain which possess no such sensibility are different in function and organization from the nerves, and have a distinct and higher operation to perform.

If in examining the apparent structure of the brain, we find a part consisting of white medullary Striæ and fasciculated like a nerve, we should conclude that as the use of a nerve is to transmit sensation, not to perform any more peculiar function, such tracts of matter are media of communication, connecting the parts of the brain; rather than the brain itself performing the more peculiar functions. On the other hand, if masses are found in the brain unlike the matter of the nerve, and which yet occupy a place guarded as an organ of importance, we may presume that such parts have a use different from that of merely conveying sensation; we may rather look upon such parts as the seat of the higher powers.

Again, if those parts of the brain which are directly connected with the nerves, and which resemble them in structure, give pain when injured, and occasion convulsion to the animal as the nerves do when they are injured; and if on the contrary such parts as are more remote from the nerves, and of a different structure, produce no such effect when injured, we may conclude, that the office of the latter parts is more allied to the intellectual operations, less to mere sensation.

I have found at different times all the internal parts of the brain diseased without loss of sense; but I have never seen disease general on the surfaces of the hemispheres without derangement or oppression of the mind during the patient's life. In the case of derangement of mind, falling into lethargy and stupidity, I have constantly found the surface of the hemispheres dry and preternaturally firm, the membrane separating from it with unusual facility.

If I be correct in this view of the subject, then the experiments which have been made upon the brain tend to confirm the conclusions which I should be inclined to draw from strict anatomy; viz. that the cineritious and superficial parts of the brain are the seat of the intellectual functions. For it is found that the surface of the brain is totally insensible, but that the deep and medullary part being wounded the animal is convulsed and pained.

At first it is difficult to comprehend, how the part to which every sensation is referred, and by means of which we become acquainted with the various sensations, can itself be insensible; but the consideration of the wide difference of function betwixt a part destined to receive impressions, and a part which is the seat of intellect, reconciles us to the phenomenon. It would be rather strange to find, that there were no distinction exhibited in experiments on parts evidently so different in function as the organs of the senses, the nerves, and the brain. Whether there be a difference in the matter of the nervous system, or a distinction in organization, is of little importance to our enquiries, when it is proved that their essential properties are different, though their union and co-operation be necessary to the completion of their function—the developement of the faculties by impulse from external matter.

All ideas originate in the brain : the operation producing them is the remote effect of an agitation or impression on the extremities of the nerves of sense ; directly they are consequences of a change or operation in the proper organ of the sense which constitutes a part of the brain, and over these organs, once brought into action by external impulse, the mind has influence. It is provided, that the extremities of the nerves of the senses shall be susceptible each of certain qualities in matter ; and betwixt the impression of the outward sense, as it may be called, and the exercise of the internal organ, there is established a connection by which the ideas excited have a permanent correspondence with the qualities of bodies which surround us.

From the cineritious matter, which is chiefly external, and forming the surface of the cerebrum ; and from the grand center of medullary matter of the cerebrum, what are called the *crura* descend. These are fasciculated processes of the cerebrum, from which go off the nerves of motion, the nerves governing the muscular frame. Through the nerves of sense, the *sensorium* receives impressions, but the will is expressed through the medium of the nerves of motion. The secret operations of the bodily frame, and the connections which unite the parts of the body into a system, are through the cerebellum and nerves proceeding from it.

THE END [1].

The most distinguishing feature of the Essay—that which constitutes its originality, and justifies the title—" Idea of a New Anatomy

[1] The Essay by a singular oversight was brought out without a date, either on the title-page or elsewhere. Other means of ascertaining the date having failed, application was made to Messrs Spottiswoode, successors of the printers, for information ; and the following letter was received. NEW STREET SQUARE, *Feb.* 27, 1829. SIR, I have at length discovered that 100 copies were printed of the "Idea of the Anatomy of the Brain," at the end of August, 1811. I remain, &c. THOS. C. SHAW. *To* Mr (A.) SHAW, *Soho-Square.*

The Essay was first noticed publicly in April 1822, by Mr John Shaw, when he referred to it in his Paper, read before the Medico-Chirurgical Society, entitled, "On Partial Paralysis." The date he then gave was 1809. The mistake probably arose from his recollection of having, in 1808, transcribed the Essay, of the Brain," and which, it may be added, ought always to be kept in mind in estimating its value,—is the announcement in it of an entirely new principle of investigating the functions of the Nervous System.

The method of research formerly followed, was to take the nerves, as they might be found passing along any part of the body remote from the brain or spinal cord, say, in the upper or lower extremity, and cutting them across, to observe the effects. By such means, and noticing the phenomena attending wounds of nerves in accidents, physiologists were brought to conclude, that to every nerve belonged the double functions of bestowing motor power and sensation, with perhaps, other undefined properties. A certain number may have rejected the view: but they had no facts to bring against it; and they were obliged to put up with it. "Scholastici fingunt," says Sauvages, only twelve years before the principle enunciated in the Essay was conceived, "ad convulsiones explicandas, alios nervos esse tantum motorios, et sensus expertes : quod cum *millenis vivisectionibus* falsum evincatur admittendum non est: nulla enim in corpore est fibra nervea quin sentiat." (*Nosol. Method.*, Tom. III. p. 17, A.D. 1795.)

The "Idea," which formed both the title and theme of the Essay, seems at first view, quite simple; indeed, it bears on its face so much the semblance of truth, that it surprises us it should not have been thought of long before. It consists essentially in supposing,— that the divisions of the brain from which the various nerves proceed may have distinct endowments; and that the nerves connected with each division will partake the same endowments.

To prosecute the subject according to this theory, it is obvious that the mode of research must differ essentially from what had been followed before. Instead of going to the nerves in distant regions of the body, where they have contracted connections with others proceeding from many distinct parts,—the proper method will be to take the nerves near their origins in the brain and spinal cord, where they are perfectly simple in structure—where they are close, as it were, to the fountain head, and to make observations or experiments upon them there, at their roots. Through a knowledge of the functions of the roots of the nerves, it may be expected to

when it was in an early stage of preparation. See extract, 8th July, 1808. No competitor for the originality of the discoveries had appeared when his Paper was published.

learn what are the special endowments of the particular divisions of the Brain with which they are connected.

It was doubtless from being exalted with the thought that, in this new method of investigation, he had discovered a guide for penetrating into the arcana of the Brain, that the author expressed himself—with the confidence of one brother writing to another—in the sanguine tone of the Letters.

The Essay being professedly tentative, it is not fair to scan its contents too critically. Yet it will be allowed, even at this date, that the arguments in favour of the theory derived from the consideration of the essentially distinct nature of the impressions which are conveyed to the sensorium by each of the special nerves of the senses respectively, are full of interest in connection with the physiology of the brain.

The part of the Essay that will probably be read with chief interest, and canvassed with least favour, is the account at p. 14, of the experiments on the roots of the spinal nerves. In systematic works of physiology, principally foreign, it has become a custom, when treating of the originality of the discovery of the distinct functions of the nerves, to represent the experiments described in this Essay, as the only ones ever performed by the author,—to note their imperfections—and to assign to another physiologist the merit of having ascertained the true functions of the roots. An opportunity will occur before the close of this communication, to rectify this misconception. It is enough to say, at present, of the experiments related in the Essay, that the account is correct so far as it goes; that nothing is affirmed but what must have been actually observed. One positive statement alone is made, and it is this:—that on stimulating the anterior columns and roots, muscular contractions were excited: the remaining statement is negative—that on stimulating the posterior column and roots, no contraction of the muscles ensued. The accuracy of these observations cannot be questioned. And admitting their imperfections, the results were of essential service in confirming the theory: because they incontestably proved that the functions of nerves differ; and that the difference exists not only in the roots, but in the columns of the spinal cord with which the roots are connected.

By studying the context, and by that alone, it is made out that the author ascribed not only motor power (of which he had experimental evidence), but sensation (of which he had no experimental evidence) to the anterior roots. Here, then, was a palpable and indisputable error. But when it is considered how that mistake arose—from mere general speculations on the endowments of the cerebrum as contrasted with the cerebellum, and defective knowledge of the true origins of the roots, a candid person will allow that it was not of a nature to cling to the author's mind with obstinate tenacity, or to be cast off with difficulty. In none of his published works can we discern any trace of the error[1].

But in ascribing both motor power and sensation to one set of roots, it may be thought that the author contravened the fundamental principle which it was the object of the Essay to propound. From the general tenour of the Essay, however, it cannot be doubted that the author conceived that the anterior roots consisted of two distinct sets of fibrils. At p. 8, he adverts to the unreasonableness of imagining, "that impressions thus differing in kind are carried along the nerves to the sensorium, and presented to the mind; and that the mind by the same nerves which receive sensation, sends out the mandate of the will to the moving parts of the body." Again, at p. 9, he anticipates as one of the results of the establishment of his views that they will "do away the difficulty of conceiving how sensation and volition should be the operation of the same nerve at the same moment."

The following are extracts from the Letters between the date of the circulation of the Essay and the publication of the author's paper read before the Royal Society.

29th Sept. 1811.—"My Idea of the Brain seems to be very well taken by all with whom I have conversed. Has anybody read it with you?"

(*About the same date as the above*).—"Has nobody seen my Brain? If I am not flattered, it takes here[2]."

---

[1] At a later period (1834) the author proved by dissection that the column of the spinal cord into which the posterior roots, those of sensation, enter—the lateral column—is continued up into the cerebrum; thus confirming his original idea, that sensation, in common with the other senses, has its seat in the cerebrum, not in the cerebellum.

[2] The following is copied from a list in Charles Bell's own handwriting, found in a journal, or common-place book, containing miscellaneous entries, the earliest of which is dated 1808. It is headed—"Names to whom copies of the Idea of the Anatomy of the Brain have been addressed."

Dr Renwick, Dr Brandreth [Liverpool], Dr Gartshore, Mr Leighton, Newc. [Newcastle], Mr Abernethy, Mr Pearson, Mr Lawrence [Sir Wm. Lawrence], Mr Wilson [Great Windmill Street School], Dr Maton, Dr Wollaston, Mr Young [Dr Thomas Young], Dr Mayo, Dr Sutherland, Portsmouth (3 copies), Dr Gartshore (4 copies), Lord Meadowbank [Scotch Judge], Dr Buchan, Dr Jeffray [Glasgow], Mr Playfair [Professor, Edinburgh], — Roscoe [Liverpool], Mr Ing-

22 Nov. 1811.—" Send one of my Brains to Sandford'. He entreated me once to write something on this subject to convert the young men at College: and if this answers his idea, he may take the credit to himself. If you can at any time pick up an opinion on this subject, note it for me. I wish to know people's opinion."

(*Same letter continued*).—" I gave an animated and good lecture to-day: I lectured on the Physiology of the Brain."

(*Same letter continued*).—" I went out yesterday with the intent of paying twelve guineas for one book! Gall, on the Brain; but luckily found there was no copy left in town."

Dec. 1811.—" I am now lecturing on the Nerves: and I see in this subject a great field for a man of genius and industry."

12th Nov. 1812 (*First Course of Lectures in Great Windmill Street*).—" I have been giving lectures on the Brain and Nerves, yesterday and to-day. Good, they say; certainly very different from what they have been accustomed to. I proceed gaining more interest in the subject of the nerves, &c."

10th Nov. 1813.—" I gave a lecture to-day, to a large class, upon the Brain. Yesterday, I gave one on the same subject, of an hour and three quarters, with only a green cloth before me. This will give you an idea of my improvement in talking."

10th April, 1814.—" Spurzheim gives us a lecture on Dr Gall. This will just suit me—give me the whole nonsense, and excite me."

30th July, 1814 (*To his wife, then in Scotland*).—" This morning after consulting with the surgeon of Tring about another gentleman, who had been thrown from the stage coach, I went off alone, distanced those I saw toiling after me, and had three delightful hours among the woods. Some ideas intruded into my mind that will make a very pleasing and consolatory conclusion to my views of the operations of the mind, vide ' Physiology of the Brain.' I also took a sketch."

19th Nov. 1814.—" I have been strangely engaged, without being able to say that I have been busy. To-day I finished my lectures on the Brain. My demonstration of the Brain brought a great concourse."

ham [Newcastle], Mr Horn [Newcastle], Mr Cooper [Sir Astley Cooper], Dr Dick [Madras Medical Service], Dr Winthrop, Mr Frampton, Dr Adams, Mr Davy [Sir H. Davy], Mr Brydon, Mr Baylie, Stowm^kt., Mr Allen [Holland House], Dr Baillie [Dr Matthew Baillie], Dr Gower, Dr Burrowe, Philadelph., Mr Knight (Taste) [author of Essay on Taste], Edinburgh (20 copies), Vose [Liverpool], Joberns [Middlesex Hospital], Cartwright [Middlesex Hospital]. Smiles [Newcastle], Dr Pearson, Mr Thomson [Dr A. Tod Thomson], Dr Roget, Dr Curry [Guy's Hospital], Mr Chevalier, Young Cline [Henry Cline, Junior], Mr Park, Lpool., Dr Bostock, Jo. Brandreth, Dr Harness, Mr Brande, Soho Sq. [Chemist], F. Horner [Francis Horner, M.P.], Dr Gibson [America], Leo. Horner, Mr Bennell [Vicar of Kensington].

         [1] Bishop of Edinburgh.

(*About same date as the above*).—"My Anatomy of the Brain is ripening in my head. In concluding my lectures on the Nervous System, I shall this year lay open a fine system."

2nd Dec. 1814.—"Wilson is lecturing just now, and I am chiefly employed about these nerves. I am making experiments through the galvanic apparatus, to try how far the action of nerves and muscles will agree with the division of nerves which I have made by dissection. The apparatus I use is very simple. I have a zinc probe and a silver probe; by placing them in contact with the nerve and the muscle, and bringing their ends together, the parts are convulsed. Now you know what I hope to prove is that there are two great classes of nerves, distinguishable in function—the one sensible, and the other insensible! I shall tell you of these experiments as I proceed."

Dec. 1815.—"To-day I finished my lectures on the Nervous System, on the Senses, and I can perceive that my more copious and earnest manner, and the notions I have got, become more and more attractive. I have been well attended, and left a full class to-day."

2 March, 1818.—"I wish to enter upon the Comparative anatomy of the Nervous System, which I can make a thing surprising."

5th Aug. 1819.—"When you left us, I told you I was to sit down to my notes on the Nervous System. Believe me this is quite an extraordinary business. I think the observations I have been able to make furnish the materials of a grand system, which is to revolutionize all we know of this part of Anatomy, more than the discovery of the Circulation of the Blood. I have a good deal still to do. How I am to bring it forward I do not know. I think my lectures in the first place: then by a little Essay explaining the outline of a new system; and finally by magnificent engravings of the whole Nervous System."

17th August, 1819.—"I continue to make little sketches of *cuddies* (Anglice, donkeys) the moment I get out of London. In the mean time, I am making gigantic drawings of the Nervous System for my class."

Feb. 1820.—"That over" (his annual lecture on Expression), we shall lecture humdrum for a fortnight, and then commence my System of Nerves, which is making as great a change as radicalism itself. But, dear George, we must keep these sentiments in our own breasts, there they mellow."

20th March, 1820.—"I have two noble subjects awaiting my leisure—a *Revolution* in Anatomy, and the subject of Expression—addressed to the better part of society."

14th June, 1820.—"My occupations are humdrumish. When I have time, I dissect the Nervous System of the lower animals: and I think I have made some observations which will ornament my system and enrich my lectures. The only thing that interests me, and drags me to it, are my observations on the Nervous System. I have made some discoveries that must revolutionize this part of anatomy. But having succeeded, I find it dull work to prepare my observations in any way for the public. Lectures are pleasant and effectual, as far as they go. But the party of listeners is circumscribed: and others on whom the subject should be forced, stand squinting and jealous, and close their ears. You are a happy fellow to have such a good opinion of your profession."

22nd September, 1820.—" I have been so much taken up with finishing my illustrations of surgery—this MS. of John[1], and my experiments on the Nerves—that I am particularly deficient in preparation for my lectures this season, which will entail on me a season of discomfort."

March, 1821.—" This business of Nerves will be long of coming forward exactly as it should. But my own ambition has a rest in this—that I have made a greater discovery than ever was made by any one man in anatomy: and the best of it is I am not done yet."

April, 1821.—" I have just finished my Paper on the Nerves of the Face for the Royal Society. I put it into Jeffrey's hands this morning: but he is very busy....I do not know what he may think of it; he is no man of science[2]."

13th July, 1821.—" Last night my Paper was read before the Royal Society."

7th Aug. 1821.—" I think I told you my Paper was printing for the Royal Society: and I have been engaged yesterday and to-day in making a drawing for engraving in illustration of it."

30th August, 1821.—" My Paper is printing, and my drawing is under the engraver's hands, so that my lucubrations are in a fair way of being fairly before the public. John (Shaw) is off to Paris, and Richardson[3] comes to dine toe to toe to me."

The last series of extracts show that, during the ten years that intervened between the printing of the Essay, and the communication of his first Paper on the Nerves to the Royal Society, the author had not relaxed his efforts to advance the subject; on the contrary, many expressions point to his having then achieved, as he thought, several great successes. But before describing these, a word may be said about the reception which the Essay met with.

---

[1] John Bell's *Observations on Italy*.

[2] The paper eventually read to the Royal Society has the date 12th July, 1821. A rough copy, corrected by his own and other hands, is preserved, with the date 6th April. It is probably to the latter that the extract refers.

[3] A warmly cherished friend. See Notice of his Life, by the Lord Advocate Moncrieff, in the *North British Review*.

In the history of science, one may read of an example like this :—a man, of original genius, has had his mind illuminated by a bright insight of a comprehensive principle, pregnant with important results: from that moment, he will be afflicted with an aching dread lest some fellow labourer should hit upon the same idea, and by publishing anticipate him : not to be cut off from the expected honour of becoming a distinguished discoverer, what does the man of genius do ?   He forthwith writes out a declaration of the novel principle in cipher ; seals the precious document, and locks it in the iron safe of a learned society, to be forthcoming when wanted.   The author of the " Idea of a New Anatomy of the Brain," followed a course neither so ingenious, nor selfish.   Yet he has stated that no competitor for the discoveries molested him, at that period, by trying to take them out of his hands.   Of the distinguished anatomists and physiologists to whom copies were sent, not a single individual favoured him with observations, as solicited on the title page; far less showed any disposition to prosecute the enquiries independently.

Considering how critical was the position, as concerned his scientific reputation, in which the author had left the researches when he printed and circulated the Essay, it was fortunate that on returning to them, he should have found even a small fraction of the discoveries unappropriated and remaining to his share.   Look for example, how closely he had approached to declaring the true functions of the roots of the spinal nerves, and yet how he had missed doing so.   Is it not surprising that some clever man, or even intelligent pupil, did not detect the error in his interpretation of the experiments, and by presenting the correct one, secure high honour for his name ?

But here a question of some moment—as to the value of experiments within the narrow area of the vertebral canal, meets us. It is quite a different thing proving to which root of the spinal nerves motor power belongs, from proving to which root sensation belongs by direct experiments.   In the first, the evidence is indubitable.   In the second, it is apt to be fallacious.   When the spinal sheath is opened, and the anterior roots are taken hold of and pinched, there is instant contraction and quivering of the muscles subject to the nerves of the part; and the motion follows the stimulation so rapidly and constantly, that it is impossible to doubt the cause.   The only way in which we can recognize the existence of sensation, is by the animal's exhibiting, at particular manipulations, signs, interpreted as signs of pain. Yet these are but uncertain indications, and are frequently deceptive. What are they? They are cries, of different degrees of intensity; struggles of the limbs, more or less vigorous: mayhap, the use of the claws or teeth on the experimenter's fingers. Had the animal a mind, and articulate language, the evidence might perhaps be trustworthy: but as that mind would probably be clouded by the extensive wound in the back, together with the unavoidable concussion of the spine from the forcible breaking up of the vertebræ, doubts may be excusable on that head. At least, it will be admitted that the evidence as regards the root of sensation is not to be relied on with the same certainty, as that concerning the root of motion. And the remark is verified by the subsequent history of the enquiry. Soon after the promulgation of the discoveries, the experiments on the spinal nerves were often repeated. Those by M. Magendie became the most celebrated on account of their supposed exactness. In his first memoir he did give a correct view of the functions of each root, coinciding with that previously announced as held by the author. But in his second memoir, shortly following, he gave forth views directly at variance with those in the first. He alleged that sensation did not belong exclusively to either root. He asserted that the anterior root possessed sensation, as well as motor power; and he even assigned to the posterior roots a certain power of controlling the muscles. Out of these statements arose a grand controversy, prolonged into many years; the question being—on which of the roots, if on either, does sensation exclusively depend.

As none of the friends of the author complied with the invitation of the Essay, to be associated with the enquiries, he continued to prosecute them alone; eventually having the zealous assistance of his relative and early pupil, Mr John Shaw.

At this period, was conclusively solved the important problem of the distinction between the nerves of Motion and Sensation.

The mode in which that high feat in physiology was achieved may be briefly stated. It was mainly by observing with particular attention the differences in the anatomical characters of the roots of the cerebral nerves—comparing them with the nerves of the spine—and applying the principle of the researches announced in the Essay to the elucidation of their respective functions.

On taking a survey of the nerves of the encephalon with especial regard to their *roots*, it is apparent that, in the majority, their distinguishing feature is, that they come off, unlike the spinal nerves, by single roots. Now according to the principle so often quoted, it might be inferred that these single-rooted nerves—as the Portio-dura, Third, Sixth, and Ninth, would be capable of conferring only one property. Next, the author observed that in the midst of those simple nerves, there was situated one of large dimensions, bearing resemblance to the spinal nerves in arising by two distinct roots; yet with the remarkable peculiarity—that the size of one root was about five times greater than that of the other. In accordance with the principle, it might therefore be inferred that this large double nerve, the Fifth, would possess double functions, each commensurate with the size of the respective roots.

Here, then, was a positive invitation for the author to institute experiments; first, upon one or more of the nerves which arise by single roots; secondly, on the nerve which arises by two roots, of unequal size.

In regard to the first, for facility of operating, he selected the Portio-dura. Near its exit from the stylo-mastoid foramen, he cut the nerve across in a living animal; and the result was so clear that it admitted of no question. The muscles of the face to which the Portio-dura is sent, were immediately paralysed. And that was the only effect. Sensation in the face was not in the slightest degree impaired. The proof therefore was complete, that the Portio-dura was exclusively a motor nerve.

The nerve which was next submitted to experiment, in contrast with the Portio-dura, was the Fifth: and the branches selected were those which, emerging upon the face, are distributed to parts also supplied by the Portio-dura. Upon each branch separately being cut across, in a living animal, sensation was instantly destroyed. Hence, no doubt could be entertained that these branches bestowed sensation on parts for which a different nerve was provided for giving motor power, namely, the Portio-dura. Here, then, was a decided proof that a nerve of motion may be distinct from a nerve of sensation.

But it has just been stated that owing to the Fifth nerve arising by two roots, it might be expected to possess double functions. Now here it must be admitted that the experimental proofs which the author brought forward in his first Paper to the Royal Society, to show that besides sensation, the nerve could bestow motor power, failed. And as the history of the failure throws light on his mode of investigation, as contrasted with that of professed experimentalists, a few details in explanation may be pardoned.

One of the extracts (4th Dec. 1809) shows how averse the author was to making experiments. The only one by which he attempted to confirm the view—that the Fifth bestows motor power, in a limited degree, proportioned to the distribution of one of its roots, besides sensation generally, was made on the infraorbitary branches which supply the upper lip. And it cannot be doubted that he selected these branches, because he believed that part of both roots entered into their composition. But an anatomist of the present day does not require to be told that he was in error. However, before passing a severe judgment, the same anatomist ought to remember that, until a prominent interest in the anatomy of the roots of the nerves had been imparted by the author's own researches, a correct knowledge of the course and connections of those of the Fifth was not general. After carefully searching through all the standard books on Anatomy published in this country before the experiments in question were devised, I have not found a single work in which it is even stated that the Fifth arises by two roots. The author, accordingly, set about his experiments on the infraorbitary branches with the impression that he was about to show what would ensue from cutting across a nerve composed of fibrils coming from two distinct roots. And the results tallied in such a remarkable manner with what he had obviously looked for, that he concluded he had demonstrated the proposition accurately. When food was laid before the animal, an ass, it saw the oats, pressed its lips against the bowl containing them, and by moving the lips (through the Portiodura) mumbled the oats, yet did not catch them, or convey them into the mouth. Witnessing these effects, the author interpreted them wrongly. He conceived that the muscles of the lips had been deprived of their power of acting in association with the muscles of mastication generally. He, therefore, supposed that he had proved experimentally the possession by the Fifth of motor power, in addition to sensation. And in his first published account of the nerve, he termed it the "nerve of sensation and mastication." No long time, however, elapsed before the error was observed. Two different physiologists, one abroad, and the other at home, drew attention to it. The former[1] merely said that he could not observe any

---

[1] M. Magendie: October, 1821.

defect of motion in the lips, produced by cutting the infraorbitary branch. The other[1] stated, in addition, what was certainly correct, that the circumstance of the ass being unable to direct food into its mouth, proved nothing more than that sensation had been destroyed: for if the animal could not feel the oats, it could not regulate the action of the lips so as to retain hold of them and pass them onward into the mouth. Thus it fell out that the only proof of an experimental kind on which the author relied for demonstrating that this double rooted nerve, the Fifth, besides sensation, could give motor power, was defeated. At the time the last physiologist referred to published his criticism, the author was absent from London, taking an annual holiday; and Mr John Shaw was the first to become acquainted with it. Being thoroughly master of the views for which the experiments had been instituted, he was aware of the jeopardy into which the discoveries were brought by the correction—when unaccompanied with any reference to the anatomical structure of the infraorbitary branches in relation to the roots: for neither of the two gentlemen who pointed out the error even alluded to the roots. He saw that, as all the experiments then made on the Fifth agreed in showing that it bestowed sensation only, the conclusion of all unprejudiced persons, and especially of all experimentalists, would be, that, albeit the nerve arose by double roots, it was simply a nerve of sensation. To counteract the injurious effect, he lost no time, therefore, in performing new experiments; which set the question at rest. Having procured an ass, he selected for his proceedings those branches of the third division of the Fifth, situated in the spheno-palatine fissure, where the two roots are conjoined. First, he cut both trunks across; whereupon the muscles which move the lower jaw were paralysed, and the teeth fell apart. After the animal had expired, the trunks were next pinched with forceps: I was at the time early in my pupilage, and assisted my brother in the experiment: having been instructed to keep the jaws separate, I was obeying when as soon as the forceps closed on the nerve, the teeth came together with a snap, and inflicted a smart bite on my fingers.

Thus no doubt could remain as to the view which the author originally gave of the functions of the Fifth being essentially correct. But it is evident that when he ascribed to it motor power and designated it the nerve of " sensation and *mastication*," he had no sound

[1] Mr Mayo: August, 1822.

experiment to prove that it conferred more than sensation. Hence the conclusion is unavoidable that he obtained a true insight of the functions of the nerve by reasoning and observation on the origin and distribution of the roots, guided by the fundamental principle of the researches—and not by experiment.

Next, let it be considered how directly the discovery of the functions of the nerves of the brain contributed to throw light on the functions of the roots of the spinal nerves. Taking, first, the Ninth nerve of the brain: the fact of its plunging into the muscles of the tongue, and going to them, to the exclusion of the surfaces, is sufficient proof that the name by which it was commonly known, Motor Linguæ, had been correctly applied,—that it is a nerve of motion, in contrast to a nerve of sensation: and when the anatomist looks to its origin at the top of the spinal cord, he cannot fail to recognize the perfect resemblance between its root and the anterior roots of the spinal nerves. Again, off the same tract from which the Ninth arises, there come in succession two other nerves that are undoubtedly motor; namely, the Sixth, and the Third. Passing to the Fifth; preceding anatomists had perceived the likeness it bears in the structure of its roots to the spinal nerves: when it had been shown, therefore, that the lesser root, which resembles the anterior spinal roots, in having no ganglion, bestows motor power alone; and that all the other known motor nerves (Portio-dura, Ninth, Sixth, Third) are devoid of ganglions, the conclusion was obvious, that the anterior roots of the spinal nerves give motor power. Further, when it was ascertained that the large root of the Fifth, on which a ganglion is formed, bestows sensation, the inference could be legitimately drawn, that the posterior roots of the spinal nerves which have ganglions, likewise confer sensation. It was while his mind was charged with those observations, that the author recurred to the experiments on the roots of the spinal nerves, described before in the Essay. And he performed them afresh. The results confirmed the truth of the deductions which he had been led to draw concerning the functions of each, from examining the anatomy and functions of the cerebral nerves. Ceasing to entertain the former view, that both motor power and sensation were united in one root, he saw that motor power alone belonged to the anterior, and that sensation belonged to the posterior roots.

But in addition to these experiments on the lower animals,

the author had valuable assistance in verifying his conclusions, from observing the effects of injuries or diseases of the nerves, in man. Thus many cases of affections of the Portio-dura presented themselves: and the same effects were observed in all: the muscles of the features lost their power: but the skin in the same parts retained sensation perfectly. Examples in the Fifth were more rare; but it was always found when those branches which emerge on the face were injured or diseased, that sensation was abolished, but the muscles preserved their power. The charge of publishing those cases fell to Mr John Shaw: in whose valuable paper, entitled on "Partial Paralysis[1]," besides the reports of cases illustrating local palsy from morbid affections of the nerves of the face, was contained the following pathological problem, and its solution:—"*Why sensation should remain entire in a limb when all voluntary power over the action of the muscles is lost; or why muscular power should remain when feeling is gone*[2]?" The answer, now so obvious as not to require repetition, was given correctly, and nearly as fully and satisfactorily as could be done at the present day.

It thus appears that, unaided by any but Mr John Shaw, the author had succeeded in discovering the great physiological truth,—that the nerves of Motion are distinct from the nerves of Sensation. Furthermore, he had specified those particular roots, or nerves, of the brain, and of the spinal cord, to which Motor power, or Sensation respectively belonged.

But before the author presented those observations formally to the public, or did more than lecture upon them, he had conceived a theory, upon the basis of which he had also constructed a general Classification of the nerves.

The starting-point of this theory was, from observing the remarkable anomalies which are exhibited in the distribution of the Fifth nerve, and the Portio-dura. The Fifth nerve alone of all the nerves of the brain, had been ascertained to resemble the spinal nerves. Like them it arises by two roots, one being a motor, the other a sensitive root. But a striking dissimilarity exists between it and the spinal nerves, in the relative size of their roots. In all the spinal nerves, the two roots are approximately equal; but in the Fifth, the root which bestows motor power is only about one-fifth

---

[1] Read to the Medico-Chirurgical Society, April 30, 1822.
[2] Italics in the original.

the size of the root which bestows sensation. Furthermore—and this is a point of special interest as regards the theory—the only muscles in the head over which the Fifth has power, are the group which perform the actions of *mastication*. Turning next to the Portio-dura, this had been ascertained to be a motor nerve. Yet it was observed, that it was allotted to one particular set of muscles of the head. In a part of its course, the nerve lies close to the muscles of the jaws, but it does not give even a single small twig to one of them; several of its large branches are spread upon the temporal and masseter muscles, but they skip these muscles entirely; and they squander themselves on a thoroughly different set, the muscles of the *features*.

Here, then, looking from this stand-point alone, the question is suggested, Why should there be that appointment of distinct motor nerves to distinct groups or classes of muscles, which are situated so near each other that it might be thought one would serve?

The author endeavoured to solve this problem as follows. He first took a general survey of the members of the body which are placed under the charge of the large series of spinal nerves, together with the Fifth, their representative in the head. It then occurred to him that those members were; first, the *locomotive* organs,—or in man, the inferior extremities: secondly, the *prehensile* organs,—or, in man, the superior extremities: and thirdly, the *masticatory* organs,—or, in man, the apparatus of jaws. In the next place, he took a general view of the *features*, the motions of which are presided over by the Portio-dura. It then occurred to him that the parts of the face so called, being chiefly connected with the lips and nostrils, are particularly connected with the organ of respiration, as that organ is framed in *man*, in contrast with the lower animals.

Reverting to the first series, he thought that the members embraced in it were required in all animals, even the lowest in structure. But to comprehend the nature, or number, of such members, the question must be asked—What are the broad and main distinctions between vegetablism and animalism? The predominant character of a vegetable, is that, having all essential organs for sustaining life, it is comparatively *motionless;* it is fixed to the ground, and being supplied with nourishment through its roots, it need not shift its quarters. But the leading character of an animal is, that being, like the vegetable, endowed with the necessary organs for sustaining life, it is *vagabond;* to obtain food for preserving life, it must go forth to forage. Hence the necessity in the animal of a nervous system, for sense and motion. And in order to enable the animal to move and change its hunting ground, it must have *locomotive* organs; to enable it to seize and secure its food, it must have *prehensile* instruments; and, lastly, to enable it to reduce the food to a fit state for passing along the gullet, it must have grinding or *masticatory* organs. And so it may be seen that the most originally bestowed gifts to an animal, are those very members over which the spinal nerves, and Fifth, in man, exercise control. From arguments such as these the author designated that class, the " Original system."

Again, as to the muscles of the features, subject to the Portio-dura, what did the author mean by connecting them with the organ of respiration, as presented in *man?* The qualifying expression implies that the organ of respiration developed in man, possesses an exalted character which places it above the same organ in the lower animals. It is to be regretted that a fitter term for the class of nerves in which the Portio-dura was included could not be found than *respiratory:* for this reason, that the organ of breathing, particularly in man, performs two sets of offices, very different in character from each other. In the lowest animals, it has only one function, that of purifying the blood: in man, it continues to purify the blood; but at the same time it becomes, in connection with his Mind, the instrument of Voice, Speech, and Expression.

The changes in the structure of the organ of respiration throughout the animal kingdom are, indeed, manifold and vast. At first, the apparatus differs little from what is found in plants; it is situated on the exterior of the body, without provision, of course, for the air being collected, or expelled, to produce sound. By degrees, the purifying of the blood is effected by air being introduced into the interior, and permeating tubes, or even entering sacs: but communication is not yet established with a single outlet, or windpipe, to allow sound to be produced. In no member of the great division of Invertebrata does the air of respiration either enter, or escape, by the mouth. The first discernible trace of a tube, like windpipe, or of a sac, like lungs, is met with in the lowest of the Vertebrata, fishes: in them, for the first time, the mouth becomes a common orifice for food and breath. In all the subsequent acts of building up the organ to make it available for the double purposes of purifying the blood, and propelling the air outwardly with force, to produce sonorous vibrations, what are chiefly observed, are increased compactness in the walls of the chest, and provisions in the wind-pipe for greater concentration, within narrow straits, of the volumes of expired air.   But these adaptations for Voice affect not only the structures engaged in deglutition, but the circulation of the blood, chiefly the venous.   And thus it may be perceived that, to meet these new exigencies, modifications in the arrangements of the nerves and brain-centres must be introduced.   To that class of nerves, including the Portio-dura, the author applied the name "Super-added," in reference to the "Original System:" or "Respiratory," from their connection with the organ of respiration.

Adding the special nerves of the senses, and the nerves of the appendages of these organs, to the "Original" class, these and the "Respiratory" together, embrace the whole nerves of the cerebro-spinal axis.   There remain the "Sympathetic" nerves.   These gan-glionic nerves were supposed to preside over the organic processes in the economy; such as nutrition, growth, reproduction, secretion, absorption, &c. which are common to vegetable and animal life: and they were classed separately.   In the extract of 17th August, 1819, the author says that he was preparing "gigantic drawings of the nervous system for his class."   These were three diagrams, on ele-phant-paper: one representing the "Original;" another the "Respi-ratory;" and the last, the "Sympathetic" system.

ALEXANDER SHAW.

REVIEWS AND NOTICES OF BOOKS.

Untersuchungen über die erste Anlage des Wirbethierleibes von WILHELM HIS. *Die erste entwickelung des Hünchens im Ei.* Leipzig, verlag von F. Vogel.

THIS laboriously accurate and truly philosophical account of the early stages of the development of the vertebrate body is a worthy sequence of the writings of that great embryologist (V. Baer) to whom it is dedicated, and of that careful observer (Rathke), whose first lectures on development, delivered in Berlin to only two or three students, it was the privilege of the present professor at Basel to attend.' The volume contains 237 pages 4to, is illustrated by a great number of well-executed drawings in twelve large plates representing the several stages of development from, and including, the unimpregnated condition.

The main point upon which the author insists is the presence of two germinal elements, the principal or primary germ (Hauptkeim), and the subordinate or secondary germ (Nebenkeim). From the former of these proceed all the more important, essential, function-exercising tissues, which he calls 'archiblastic,' viz. the nervous, muscular, and epithelial. From the latter proceed the more passive 'parablastic' tissues, which perform the subordinate purpose of ministering to the archiblastic, and which are the vascular, areolar or connecting, fibrous, serous, cartilaginous, osseous, the fibrous basis of the skin, &c. Though soon intimately and inseparably interwoven and interdependent, these two are at first distinct and have very different developmental as well as functional endowments. Both are wrought out through the medium of cells; but the archiblastic cells do not pass through any indifferent period, that is to say each is, from the first, destined to its particular tissue—nerve, muscle, or epithelium—whereas in the case of the parablastic cells there is a period when they are indifferent, and during which it depends upon accidental circumstances whether cartilage, bone, vascular or fibrous tissue, is to be the resultant of the further development of any given cells. The development and disposition of these parablastic tissues is also shown (s. 201) to be dependent, to a considerable extent, upon external or mechanical influences such as pressure, the contraction of the muscles, &c.

The primary germ early divides into two archiblastic layers—an outer 'animal' and an inner or deeper 'vegetative' layer. From the superficial stratum of the former are developed, in the median line, the nervous axis and, more laterally, the epithelial and glandular tissue of the skin; and from the deeper stratum the striped muscular system is formed. From the inner or 'vegetative' layer of the germ are developed, internally, the epithelial stratum of the alimentary canal and its appended glands, and, externally, the unstriped muscular system. Thus the two muscular systems are formed respectively in the inner and outer, that is the apposed, strata of the animal and vegetative layers; and the visceral cavities are formed between them.

In the process of separation of these several layers, and in the development of their elements into tissue, spaces or vacancies are left, at first, of irregular shape and intercommunicating. Into these spaces processes of the secondary or 'parablastic' germ find their way and become developed into vascular, connecting, fibrous, or cartilaginous tissue according to circumstances, and under the influence of the first formed 'archiblastic' products. Even the heart originates in a space of this kind, and the canals for the aortæ, cavæ, and other vessels, are formed in like manner.

The first evidences of the secondary or 'parablastic' germ are found at the circumference of the 'archiblastic.' Here are observed 'blood-specks' or 'islands' which coalesce, the spaces and communicating channels are lined with an endothelium, and a circumferential vascular system is formed. Processes from this find their way towards the centre, first and chiefly, between the epithelial and muscular strata of the vegetative layer; and they reach the cardiac and aortic interstices at the axis of the embryo. The innermost cells of these sprouting insinuating processes become converted into blood-carrying tubes or vessels, and lined with an endothelium; while the outer cells become converted into various paraplastic elements, and acquire close union with the archiblastic structures. A difficulty obviously arises with regard to the derivation of the muscular elements of the heart and vascular system, forasmuch as those of the heart are striped, whereas those of the arteries and veins are unstriped. The muscular wall of the heart, as well as that of the pharynx, he finds to proceed from the inner division of the striped or animal muscular stratum of the embryo; whereas the muscular fibres of the aorta and vessels supplying the vegetative system proceed from the unstriped muscular stratum of this system. He supposes (s. 204) that the pale unstriped muscular fibres of the rest of the vascular system extend along the branches from the aortæ and venæ cavæ; and judges that the muscular tissue of the skin and of the interior of the eye proceeds, in like manner, from the same source. It may be observed that the aorta is at first (as it is in some animals permanently) muscular, but in course of development elastic tissue is, to a great extent, substituted for muscular.

It will be perceived, therefore, that in each tissue the preliminary to a vascular system is the formation of clefts or spaces in the fabric of the tissue, through which currents of the blood-fluid, or lymph, transuding through the adjacent vessels may circulate. These spaces have, at first, no endothelial lining; and this rudimentary kind of circulation in 'lymph-spaces,' probably, is the only one in some of the lower animals; and it exists permanently in certain parts of the human body, as the retina and parts of the nervous centres. In such situations the nervous elements themselves constitute the boundary walls of the circulatory channels. In a further stage of organisation these spaces become lined by endothelium prolonged from the adjacent blood-vessels into them; and thus they constitute the regular 'peri-vascular lymph-spaces' which have been described by the author of this work, and by others, as existing in the pia mater and other parts.

Professor His treats at much length, and with much ability, on the mechanical influences which are in operation during development and the effect which they have, as secondary agencies, in combination with the primary force—growth—in determining the form and disposition of the parts of the body. Thus the unequal rate of growth of different parts and the resistance to extension of some parts as compared with others, lead to flexures and foldings or plaitings of the early germ; and these exert a powerful mechanical influence upon the further growth and form of the several parts of the embryo. The formation of the primitive axial groove with its rising margins enclosing the neural chord, the division between the head and the trunk, and the outgrowth of the limbs are attributed, partly, to causes of this kind. The persistence of adhesion between the two layers of the primary, or archiblastic, germ, i. e. between the intestinal epithelial and the neural strata, at their anterior extremity, after they have become separated in the rest of their length by the chorda dorsalis and other structures forming between them, causes that which was originally the anterior extremity of the neural axis to be fixed in its position and prevents its being carried forward, as it would otherwise have been, by the greater rate of growth of the cerebral, as compared with that of the alimentary tube in this region. The consequence is that the upper part of the cerebrum is driven forward over its fixed anterior extremity, and the latter becomes a transverse ridge upon the *under* surface of the brain. The middle of this ridge—the part most closely connected with the alimentary tube—is elongated into the infundibulum; the hypophysis, or pituitary gland is developed between it and the alimentary tube; and the projecting lateral processes of the ridge become developed into the optic vesicles. The shifting of the heart backward, which takes place to so great an extent in the higher vertebrates, is attributed, partly, to the pressure of blood in the vessels caused by the contraction of the heart. These contractions are rhythmical from the first, when the organ is a mere pouch, which the author believes to be dependent then, as subsequently, upon the presence of nerve-cells; though it is not easy to distinguish these for certain.

Many other instances are pointed out of mechanical influences induced by inequality in the rate of growth of different parts, and co-operating with growth or modifying it in the formation of the embryo. The causes which determine the varying rate of growth of different parts, and of the preponderance of the animal, the vegetative, or the nervous system in the several classes of animals are dis-

cussed; and the attempt is made, in a suggestive and not presumptuous and, so far, in a satisfactory manner, to bring the facts of
embryology within the range of scientific explanation; but we must
not attempt to follow our author along this devious and difficult,
though highly interesting path.

The greater part of the work is devoted to a detailed account of
the changes which follow impregnation and of the early stages of development of the several organs; and on most of these points some
new light is thrown in addition to that already shed by the researches of V. Baer, Rathke, Reichart, Coste, Allen Thomson, and
others. Thus the lungs and liver, as the labours of these embryolo-
gists have shown, are developed from the alimentary tube. Prof.
His, with greater accuracy than his predecessors, describes the formation of a ridge or furrow upon the under surface of the fore part
of the intestinal tube which is single in front and divided behind.
The margins of the furrow coalesce, shutting it off from the alimentary canal. The divided or bifid part of the tube grows out
into the lungs, the part anterior to this forms the trachea and larynx,
and the foremost part is the palatine region of the pharynx. The
coalescence of the furrow commences behind, but is not completed
in front. Hence although the lungs and trachea are separated from
the alimentary canal, the larynx and palatine portion of the pharynx
remain open into it. From a continuance of the same furrow backwards is formed the liver which, therefore, at an early period is
connected by a groove with the lungs. The coalescence of the margins of the furrow here, as in the case of the respiratory tract, separates the liver from the intestinal tube, with the exception of one
part which remains open and constitutes the bile duct. The pancreas and spleen are not produced from this furrow but as distinct
outgrowths.

One is induced to compare the formation of the allantois, or
breathing organ of the embryo at the posterior part of the alimentary
canal with that of the lungs and trachea at the fore part; though the
process does not seem to be quite the same, the allantois being developed rather from a flexure than from a furrow; and Prof. His does
not himself make this comparison. He does however make some comparisons between the two ends of the embryo, suggesting that the
perineal folds are analogous with the maxillary processes, the part
immediately in front of the alimentary tube with inferior maxillary
processes, and the organ of copulation with the tongue.

We have said enough to prove that this is a work of no ordinary
kind, but full of information and interest in all the questions of
embryology, opening up fresh branches of enquiry, and which will
repay well a careful study of its contents.

Die Membrana fenestrata der Retina von W. KRAUSE, Professor in Göttingen, 8vo. pp. 59, Leipzig, verlag von W. Engelmann, 1868.

THE 'Membrana fenestrata,' which it is the chief object of this treatise to point out, is described as situated between the two granular layers of the retina, and as consisting of a stratum of multipolar, flat cells united into a sheet by their branches in such a manner as to leave apertures, fenestræ, into and through which the cells of the deeper granular layer project. It is present throughout the retina of all vertebrates. Externally, it is connected with the fibres of the cones and bacilli which terminate in conical expansions directly continuous with the cells or united with them by short intervening processes. Internally, it is connected with the 'membrana limitans interna' by the 'radiating fibres' which traverse the internal granular layer. It seems therefore to cut off the cones and bacilli from the deeper strata of the retina, and prevents any direct communication between them and the nerve-fibres and nerve-cells which occupy the internal or deepest strata; and he finds accordingly that the fatty degeneration, which affects the nerve-fibres and nerve-cells after section of the optic nerve, does not extend to the cones or bacilli. He differs from Max Schultze in several particulars relating to the detail of the structure of the retina, and in asserting the presence of the cones in night-roaming birds and mammals. The real peculiarity in these animals consists, he says, in the preponderating length of the outer parts of the cones and bacilli, especially of the latter, which obscure the cones till they are brought into view by the use of certain reagents.

Essai sur la structure microscopique du Rein, par CH. F. GROSS, M.D., Strasbourg. Treuttel et Wurtz, 1868.

THE author subjects the views of the many writers on the kidney to the test of a careful anatomical examination of the organ which he finds generally confirmative of the statements of Bowman and Henle. He particularly describes the looped tubes in the medullary parts of the kidney first pointed out by the latter author, and finds that they communicate on the one hand with the malpighian capsules, and on the other with the open uriniferous tubes—'the tubes of Bellini'—and undergo in their course differences in size and in the character of the epithelial lining. The complex disposition of the tubes is thus described. Traced from a malpighian capsule, each forms a 'winding tube' with well developed polyhedral epithelium. This contracts into a narrow tube with fine tesselated epithelium which descends into the medulla and forms the 'loop' of Henle. Ascending it enlarges, acquires a granular epithelium, and constitutes a 'canal of communication' which combines with other similar tubes to form a 'tube of Bellini'. This great length and varied structure of the uriniferous tube in its different parts inclines

Dr Gross to the view proposed by M. Küs that serum usually transudes through the malpighian plexuses, and that the albuminous elements are resolved by means of the epithelium of the uriniferous tubes. In the Batrachian kidney Dr Gross finds a narrow portion of the uriniferous tube with delicate tesselated epithelium ('a canal of communication') intervening between the wider parts of the tube above and below. The part above, expanding into the malpighian vesicle and lined with granular cuboidal epithelium, is called the 'secretory' tract, and that below opening into the ureter is called the 'excretory' tract.

Der Bau des menschlichen Körpers mit besonderer Rücksicht auf seine morphologische und physiologische Bedeutung ; ein Lehrbuch der Anatomie fur Ärzte und Studirende von CHR. AEBY, Professor der Anatomie in Bern, Leipzig, verlag von F. Vogel, 1868.

THIS *treatise on the human body*, as its title imports, is not a mere work of descriptive anatomy. That ground is already sufficiently occupied in Germany by the works of Henle and others. It enters, in addition, into considerations relating to morphology and physiology, in which respect it is a great improvement on its predecessors; for if we have a fault to find with the admirable anatomical treatises which have issued from the German press, it is that they are somewhat too special, describing structure accurately enough, but too little with reference to physiology, and sacrificing thereby much of that interest which attaches to the elucidation of plan and purpose in construction. It is, we grant, rare to find in the same person the qualities requisite for accuracy in description and comprehensiveness of view. Nevertheless we think more might be done without sacrificing correctness of detail in anatomical teaching and anatomical works, to connect the facts with their causes and their purposes, to blend, that is, physiology and morphology with descriptive anatomy. We, accordingly, welcome Professor Aeby's treatise as an attempt of this kind, and are glad to find that he has succeeded so well. We recommend all students of anatomy who are familiar with German to obtain and read this Lehrbuch. It is written in an easy style, contains much information which is not to be found elsewhere, presents some new view at almost every turn, and gives a glow of interest to the whole.

The first part, which has just appeared, gives an account of the tissues and of the skeleton. We will not, however, give extracts but the advice to read the book.

Tenth Report of the Medical Officer of the Privy Council, with Appendix, 1868.

FEW persons are aware of the grand scientific work which is going on under the direction of Mr Simon, and being published at the public expense. The Medical Officer's Report occupies about 24 pages, while the "Appendix," which is a vast mass of original research, adds 274 pages to the work. Dr Buchanan returns to the subject of the "Distribution of Phthisis as affected by Dampness of Soil," and works it out with a geological map of Surrey, Kent, and Sussex, counties which, from the disposition of the sands, clays, and cretaceous deposits, are peculiarly adapted for the enquiry. Dr Buchanan finds that wetness of the soil is undoubtedly one of the causes of Phthisis. Another point which comes out is that sea-atmosphere alone does not appear to influence the prevalence of Phthisis.

This is followed by Dr Sanderson's Report on the Communicability of Tubercle by Inoculation, which gives the author's researches on 53 guinea pigs, and treats of the whole subject in detail. The most important fact arrived at is that traumatic suppuration is alone sufficient to produce lesions characteristically tuberculous, in other words, that the production of tubercle after inoculation is not due to any peculiar property of the inoculated material; in fact, tubercle is not inoculable. The "Appendix" concludes with a paper by Dr Thudichum on "Researches intended to promote an improved Chemical Identification of Diseases." It is with an intense feeling of admiration that we turn over the 142 pages of laborious research which make up this paper, modestly styled by the author as "chiefly introductory."

After galloping over the whole subject of Physiological and Pathological Chemistry in a few pages, the author proceeds to extend our knowledge of substances already known, and also to add not a few to the number. Under the head of 'Chemolysis of Albumen,' he makes the somewhat sensational announcement of "six well-defined new and highly interesting chemical compounds." The paper is profusely illustrated. (See further notice in the Physiological report by Dr Gamgee.)

Among the figures there are 65 diagrams of spectra of organic substance, as well as a series of beautifully coloured plates which alone are worth more than the price of the volume. The report contains several other valuable communications.

Grundriss der Physiologie des Menschen, by Dr L. HERMANN. 8vo. pp. 479. Second Edition. Hirschwald, Berlin, 1867.

THIS is one of the best text books of physiology with which we are acquainted. It is a valuable work, not only because it is written by an excellent physiologist, but also because it is the only work of the kind which for many years has emanated from the Berlin School. Much thought has been spent on the arrangement of the work; and what is of no little importance to the English reader, the book is characterized throughout by a clearness and simplicity of expression rarely found in the scientific writings of the Germans. The work is concise yet comprehensive, and its perusal is calculated to give a highly philosophical conception of the nature of many physiological problems.

The Chemical section is well done, though we would rather that Hermann had used other graphic formulæ than the somewhat clumsy and by no means very intelligible ones devised by Kekulé. The only part of the work which we think too short is that which treats of the functions of the cranial nerves. Nevertheless we can most cordially recommend the book for perusal by all physiologists.

Die Lebensbedingungen der Nerven nach Untersuchungen aus dem Laboratorium des Reisingerianum's in München. Herausgegeben von Dr JOHANNES RANKE. Leipzig, 1868, p. 181.

No reader of the contemporaneous medical literature of Germany can have failed to observe with admiration the remarkable progress which has lately been made in the department of physiological chemistry. As long as the study continued to be the favourite pursuit of some chemists who were unacquainted with physiology, and of a few medical men who knew little of physiology and less of chemistry, little was to be expected, and little was in truth gained, from the researches which were carried on, and their chief result was to occasion distrust in the minds of physiologists with regard to the capability of chemistry to throw light upon vital phenomena, and to cause them to look upon the time as very far distant when chemistry should claim her rightful position as one of the chief bases of physiology. The physiologists of Germany have, however, appreciated the fact that chemistry is likely to throw the greatest light upon physiology, and have given us remarkable proofs of this in the researches which they have, thanks to a profound knowledge both of chemistry and physiology, been enabled to conduct. The names of Hoppe-Seyler, Pflüger, Kühne, Ranke and Hermann stand out prominently amongst those of the physiologists who by their work have of late almost completely altered the aspect of chemical physiology.

The book under notice cannot but excite the admiration of all who read it; it contains the results of a variety of researches on the conditions of the vitality of nerves by Dr Johannes Ranke and several of his pupils, and, quite apart from the profound and able speculations which it contains, the large body of facts which have been collected, throw a new light upon the physiology of nerve action.

The first division of the book treats of the processes of tissue-change going on in nervous organs; and the first chapter of this division deals with the chemical reaction of nerves.

The chemical reaction of the organs of the nervous system is, during life and in a state of rest, weakly alkaline, inclining to neutrality. In the process of dying the reaction of the nerve-substance changes, becoming faintly acid, and the same effect is induced by exposure to heat of from 45° C. to 55° C. With the occurrence of acidity there is observed an increase in the consistence of the nerve-substance; we may therefore speak of a rigor of nerves (nerven-starre) just as we speak of the rigor of muscles. A similar process of acidification and of increase of firmness occurs at death in the case of glands, so that we may speak of a rigor of glands. In continuous tetanus of the whole body, induced by strychnia or by electrical irritation, the weak alkaline reaction of the living nervous system is replaced by a weak acid reaction, which appears to be dependent on the presence of fixed acid. Nerves separated from the body become acid when subjected to electrical excitation.

In the second chapter the author pleads for a true respiration on the part of muscle and nerve, upholding the accuracy of George Liebig's statements, which have of late been rather placed in doubt by Hermann's investigation. He shows that muscular substance and nerve substance really do absorb oxygen and exhale carbonic acid when separated from the body and placed in contact with air.

The third and closing chapter of the first section treats of the physiological proportion of water in the central organs of the nervous system. Amongst other very interesting results, the author has found that, during the prolonged action of nerves, there is a marked diminution in the amount of water contained within them; under these circumstances water apparently passes from the nervous tissue in action to the blood, whilst solid matters pass from the latter to the former.

The second division of the book comprehends four chapters, and treats of the relation between variations in the excitability of nerves and the nerve-tissue change. This division of the book includes special researches on the variation in the amount of water in nerves, on the varying reaction of nerves, and on the quantity of potash salts contained in them; the neutral potash salts are shown to belong to the substances which are to be considered the proximate causes of nervous fatigue. The action of various gases and vapours on the nervous excitability is also examined. It would be quite impossible to do more than give a few of the more general conclusions to which the author has been led by the researches contained in this part of the book.

The nerve, according to Ranke, contains within itself a store of substance at whose cost it maintains its excitability, the duration of the excitability being proportionate to the amount of substance stored up. The substance consists of oxidizable and oxidizing constituents; their presence within the nerve renders it for a certain time independent of all external nourishment, although of course for its continued life it requires external supplies of oxidizable matter and oxygen. The nerve is capable, by means of chemical processes going on within it, to modify its excitability. Such changes occur during the continuance of nervous work, and result in a rise of excitability above, or a fall below, the normal, and coincidently we notice a change from a neutral or a weakly alkaline to a progressively in-

creasing acid reaction.   The appearance of the acid bodies is the
cause of the variations in nerve excitability, which can be artificially
imitated by acidifying living nerves, the first action of acids being to
increase, and the ultimate action to diminish, nerve excitability.
The acids which during nervous work, induce the changes in excitability are to be reckoned amongst the causes of nervous fatigue (er-
müdende substanzen für den nerven).   The chemical processes which
occur during the normal fatigue of nerves occur on the death of
nerves, which, like nervous activity, is connected with an acid-forma-
tion in the nerve substance.   During its vitality the nerve exhales
carbonic acid; as this gas possesses in high degree the power of diminishing the excitability of nerves, it probably may, under certain
circumstances, be one of the causes of nervous fatigue.

The third division of the book, which includes three chapters,
treats of animal electricity and electrical nerve irritation in their
relation to chemical tissue changes.

In the eighth chapter the changes in the chemical reaction of nerves
during the passage of a constant current are investigated.   When a
constant current is passed by means of metallic electrodes through
the ischiatic nerve of a frog, a strong acid reaction is developed at
the anode, and the normal alkaline reaction is increased at the cathode.
This change occurs even when very weak currents act upon nerves.

The author shows experimentally that the alterations in the excitability of nerves which occur under the influence of a constant
current may be explained on the hypothesis that they are due to the
electrolytic products which the constant current sets up, and can be
imitated by the action of acids and alkalies.

In the ninth chapter we find very interesting preliminary observations on a chemical theory of muscle and nerve currents.   We
may, as in Du Bois Reymond's physical hypothesis, suppose muscle
in a state of rest to be composed of rows of molecules in a state of
electrical polarity, such as would be imitated by an arrangement in
which a chain of small zinc and copper elements was immersed in a
conducting fluid.

In the electrical muscle molecule a weak acid may represent the
copper, and an alkaline substance the zinc element of the molecules
in Du Bois Reymond's arrangement, which are separated from one
another by layers of an alkaline medium.   Let us suppose that an
evolution of acid takes place along a line of these molecules : the
acid, as soon as generated, can be fully neutralized, and in the process of neutralization potential energy becomes actual.   The muscle
at rest, in which the production of acid is small, can therefore generate continuously electromotive force.   It is otherwise, however,
when the production of acid reaches a very high point, for then the
acid reaction is not confined to the point where it is generated, but
seizing the alkaline medium between the molecules, causes the alkaline reaction to disappear, and leads to the acidification of the muscular juice.   With the abolition in the difference of reaction of the
elementary molecules we have their action, as sources of electromo-

tive force, gradually weakened or abolished; in neutralization of the acid, or its withdrawal from the muscle, the electrical activity of the molecules is, however, restored.

The tenth and concluding chapter will certainly attract the attention, and secure the interest, of histologists.

In a weak ammoniacal solution of carmine we have, according to Ranke, a delicate reagent, which enables us to point out with a beautiful accuracy the differences in chemical reaction of the tissues. Beale had, as Ranke clearly and fairly points out, advanced the supposition that the staining of those portions of tissue, which he designated germinal matter, might be due to their acid reaction. The truth of this supposition is, we think, now proved, beyond dispute, by Ranke. We thus have it easily demonstrated to us, that whilst the axis cylinder of nerves is intensely acid, the reaction of the white substance of Schwann is decidedly alkaline; similarly in other tissues endowed with electromotive power, we have demonstrated to us regular differences in chemical reaction, or regular arrangements of acid and alkaline constituents. The author thinks that he is justified in considering the regular chemical differences in the tissues as the source of their regular electromotive properties.

The author concludes this remarkable book with the following sentences. "Through the researches which have been communicated, the physical properties of the vitality of nerves are, in part, brought within the category of ascertained, demonstrable, processes.

The newly obtained results urge us to follow, with renewed zeal, the hitherto embarrassed path, whose end it must be to mould the results of the physical and chemical investigations of physiology into a harmonious picture of life."

Die Anatomie der Menschlichen Gehirn-Nerven von Dr Rüdinger. Münich, 1868.

Dr Rüdinger of Munich, to whose beautiful series of photographic representations of the organ of hearing and of the nervous system we directed the attention of our readers in the first number of this Journal, has now published in a cheaper form an atlas of engravings in illustration of the distribution of the cranial nerves. The engravings are clear, and the nerves distinctly brought out. The book will be found useful both to the student and practitioner.

Dr Rüdinger also makes a valuable contribution to muscular anatomy—*Die Muskeln der vorderen extremitäten der Reptilien und Vögel* which is a prize essay published in the natural sciences transactions of the Dutch Society of Sciences (naturkundige verhandelingen de Hollandsche Maatschappij der Wetenschappen te Haarlem 1868).

Archives de Physiologie normale et pathologique. Edited by MM. Brown Sequard, Charcot and Vulpian. Paris, 1868. *Archiv für die gesammte Physiologie des Menschen und der Thiere* Edited by Prof. Pflüger. Bonn, 1868.

Our French and German scientific *confrères* have shewn their activity in physiological work by adding this year two new periodicals to the numerous list previously existing. The four numbers of the French *Journal* and the three numbers of the German *Archiv*, which have up to this time appeared, contain various interesting articles, notices of the more important of which appear in our physiological report.

The Anatomical Memoirs of John Goodsir, F.R.S., Professor of Anatomy in the University of Edinburgh. Edited by WM. TURNER, M.B., with a Biographical Memoir by Henry Lonsdale, M.D., 2 vols. with portrait and illustrations. Edinburgh, 1868.

These two volumes contain not only the various anatomical memoirs published during his lifetime by the late Professor Goodsir in Journals, or in the Transactions and Proceedings of Societies, but a number of lectures and essays on subjects of interest met with amongst his manuscript papers. In the first volume will be found a series of Lectures on the dignity of the human body, in which the author bases the distinction between man and animals both on psychological and anatomical grounds. He agrees with those anthropologists who do not place man in the animal kingdom. An animal he regards as a mere organism in which the physiological structure is conditioned by an immaterial element of a merely psychical character. In man again the combined physiological and psychical element is co-ordinate with and subject to the control of a spiritual element. He adduces a number of facts and observations to prove that whilst human structure is absolutely complete, animal structure is merely relatively complete. He argues that "*if it be a sound zoological doctrine that all the conditions of life in an animal ought to be taken into account in ascertaining its position in the zoological scale; so in like manner ought the spiritual economy of man to be taken into the consideration of the question as to his relative place in the animal series.*"

The first volume also contains a number of papers on Comparative Anatomy including one on the structure and economy of Tethea, and one on a new mollusc from the Firth of Forth not previously published.

In the second volume are collected his well known memoirs on the teeth, and on the morphology of the cranium and upper limb, together with the essays on anatomy, physiology, and pathology, originally published in 1845, as 'Anatomical and Pathological Observations.' His paper on 'Sarcina Ventriculi,' a series of papers on the mechanism of the joints, in which he developes his views as to the spiral curvature of the articular surfaces, and a number of shorter essays complete this volume. His friend Dr Lonsdale has contributed an interesting Biographical Memoir, and the work is illustrated with a portrait, and wood and copper engravings.

REPORT ON THE PROGRESS OF ANATOMY. By PROFESSOR TURNER [1].

OSTEOLOGY.—Chr. Aeby records a case (*Reichert u. Du Bois Reymond's Archiv*, 1868, p. 68) of ABNORMALITY OF THE RIBS. The right first and second were blended at their anterior ends, the cartilage of the first rib was rudimentary and attached to its osseous part by a fibrous band.——Prof. W. Gruber (*Bul. de l'Acad. des Sc. de St Petersb.* XII. p. 448) describes 5 examples of PROC. SUPRACONDY-LOIDEUS INTERNUS HUMERI observed in four subjects since Jan. 1865, additional to the forty-two cases observed by him prior to that date.—— The investigations of J. F. Larcher into the OSSIFICATION OF THE STERNUM (*Robin's Journal*, No. 4, 1868) agree in the main with conclusions previously arrived at.——An abstract of the researches of G. W. Callender into the FORMATION AND EARLY GROWTH OF THE BONES OF THE HUMAN FACE is in *Proc. R.S.L.* June 18, 1868. He states that the inferior maxilla grows from four centres, (1) by the cartilage which tips the condyloid end; (2) by the layer of membrane in front of Meckel's cartilage; (3) by the ossification of the anterior end of Meckel's cartilage; (4) by deposits of bone in the perichon-drium of the anterior and middle thirds of the same cartilage, from which proceeds the plate of bone which forms the base of the dental canal.——Jeffries Wyman communicates (*Proc. Boston Soc. Nat. Hist.* April 15, 1868) OBSERVATIONS ON CRANIA. He shows that the foramen magnum does not occupy the same relative position to the occipital protuberance in all the races of men. Assuming the long diameter of the head as 100, the distance of its anterior edge from that process in the white races is 45·6 parts of that diameter: in the Negro 44·4: in S. Sea Islanders 41·8: in Hindoos 41·4: in N. American Indians 40·9. In adult gorillas it is 22·7: in an adult chimpanzee 21: whilst in the young chimpanzee it is 35·3: and in the young gorilla 40. He gives measurements of 21 crania from the island of Kauai, one of the Hawaiian group, and of 5 Tsuktshian skulls from the Asiatic side of Behring's straits, and concludes with some observations on synostotic crania.——Ludwig Meyer describes by the name of CRANIA PROGENAEA a form of skull which is distinguished by the projecting character of the chin (*Separat abdruck aus Griesinger's Archiv für Psychiatrie*). His observations were made on the heads of the insane, and his paper contains a number of measurements and a comparison of the progenaetic with the normal cranium. ——Paolo Gaddi (*Giornale del. Accad. di Med. Turin*, No. 10, 1868), gives an account of the SKULL AND BRAIN of an Idiot.——G. Canes-

---

[1] To assist in making this Report more complete, Professor Turner will be glad to receive separate copies of original memoirs, or other contributions to Anatomy.

trini describes (*Modena*, 1868) some ANCIENT CRANIA discovered in
Venetia and the district of Trent.——A. Ecker makes some observations (*Archiv für Anthropologie*) on the REMAINS OF SKELETONS found
in ancient graves at Hinkelstein and Oberingelheim.——A. Garbi-
glietti gives a description of the observations of T. Zaaijer ON THE
PELVIS of the women of Java (*Giornale della Accad. di Med. Turin*,
No. 5, 1868).——Dr H. Allen describes (*Proc. Acad. Nat. Sc. Phila-
delphia*, No. 4, p. 137, 1867) ten crania from the Morton Collection
in which a TERTIARY OCCIPITAL CONDYLE was present on the anterior
border of the foramen magnum. He thinks that it had articulated
with the summit of the odontoid process of the axis. In the first
number of the Proc. of the same Academy, p. 11, Allen shows that
of 1100 human skulls he has examined, 23 possessed an articulation
between the temporal and frontal bones owing to the alisphenoid and
parietal not joining—12 of these crania were Negro, and one was
found in each of the following races: Anglo-Saxon, Pelasgic, Swede,
Chinese, Hindu, Bengalese, Mandar, Seminole Indian, Blackfoot
Indian, Iroquois, and Esquimaux. His results confirm the conclusion
previously arrived at by the Reporter (*Proc. R. S. Edin.* Jan. 16,
1865) that the temporo-frontal articulation is merely an individual
peculiarity in certain human crania.

MYOLOGY.—The literature of VARIATIONS in the ARRANGEMENTS OF
MUSCLES has received numerous additions since our last report. Prof.
Dursy (*Henle u. Pfeufer's Zeitsch.* XXXIII. p. 45) describes a specimen
of the *supinator longus* (brachio-radialis) as inserted into the base of
the third metacarpal bone: a separation of the *flexor sublimis* into
an upper and lower fleshy belly by a tendinous *inscription: a biceps
brachii* where the two bellies ended in distinct tendons, but were connected by an intermediate fleshy mass: a *diaphragm* with two
supplementary musculo-tendinous bundles on its under surface: a
supplementary pair of *inferior oblique* muscles connected above to the
mastoid processes.——At p. 49 of the same *Vol.* G. Bahnsen describes
a hip where the *pyriformis* tendon was blended not only with the
obturator internus and gemelli, but with the gluteus medius: a
special *flexor of the 2nd toe* arising along with the flexor communis:
modifications in the tendinous arrangements on the dorsum of the
foot, and a supplementary *tibialis anticus* inserted into the ligamentum
cruciatum.——Pye-Smith (*Virchow's Archiv*, XLIII. p. 142) has recorded an additional example of *m. supracostalis* to those referred to
in our last report. It was attached above to the 1st rib, and below
to the 4th rib and its cartilage. It was covered by the greater and
lesser pectorals, and existed only on the right side.——Wenzel Gruber
(*Bul. de l'Acad. des Sc. de St Petersb.* XII. p. 259) describes variations
in the arrangement of the *brachialis anticus:* at p. 277, variations in
the *supinator longus:* at p. 329, a list of the mammalia in which the
epitrochleo-anconeus muscle (See our report, Nov. 1867, p. 166) has been
found: at p. 335 variations in the arrangement of an occasional muscle, which he names *radialis internus brevis*, and forms of which he

had in 1859 described as radio-carpeus and radio-carpo-metacarpeus. This muscle has also been described as *m. flexor carpi radialis brevis* by John Wood (*Proc. R. S. Lond.* June, 1866).   To the *Memoirs* of the same Academy, Jan. 23, 1868, XI., Gruber contributes an elaborate essay on variations in the *palmaris longus.* His observations comprise cases of absence of the muscle and of the existence of substitutes : of duplicity and triplicity : of variations in its origin and insertion : of accessory portions lying in a deeper plane, and of the relations of many of these varieties to normal arrangements in the mammalia.——In the same *Vol.* Oct. 3, 1867, he gives an account of the arrangement of that part of the *cervical fascia* which lies above the sternum, of the sheaths of the sternomastoids and of the sacs which lie behind those muscles.——Th. Gies (*Reichert u. Du Bois Reymond's Archiv,* 1868, p. 231, describes some variations in the *flexor communis digitorum pedis.*—— Alex. Macalister records (*Proc. Royal Irish Acad.* Dec. 9, 1867, and *Annals Nat. Hist.* May, 1868) additional myological observations with remarks on *muscular homologies.* He sums up as follows: (1) the muscular structure of the vertebrate animal is constructed on a definite basis, or after a definite type; (2) this type is of a corresponding nature in all the regions of the body, with varying degrees of alterations. These repetitions are easily recognizable in the fish but much more obscure in higher animals; (3) the definite type of muscular arrangement consists of a series of fibres connecting the component arches of the vertebral segments of the body; (4) these segments are united by five typical muscle layers most regularly developed in the thoracic walls ; *a.* exo-interneurapophysial or hæmapophysial type; *b.* ento-interneurapophysial type; *c.* spino-neurapophysial; *d.* basio-neurapophysial ; *e.* interspinal; (5) these segments are most regular in the regions in which the bony skeleton is most typically developed, and vary in the direct ratio of their specialization of function ; (6) the muscles of the vertebrate limb are arranged as modification of a type, which is not completely represented in either of the human limbs ; (7) perfect or imperfect assumption of the function of one muscle by another is accompanied by suppression, diminution or coalescence of that muscle. The same anatomist expresses in our May number his views on the *homologies of the flexor muscles in the vertebrate limb.*——Dr Rüdinger of Munich communicates an elaborate memoir (*Haarlem verhandelingen,* XXV. 1868) on the *muscles of the anterior extremities* of reptiles and birds, and compares them analogically and homologically with those of man and mammalia.——S. M. Bradley (*British Med. Jal.* May 16, 1868) describes variations in the *pectoralis major, pronator teres, coracobrachialis, lumbricales, pyriformis* and *hamstrings :* a *costo-transversalis* extending from 2nd, 3rd, and 4th cervical transverse processes to angles of 1st and 2nd ribs, and a muscle from tip of styloid process to back of inter-articular fibro-cartilage of lower jaw.——John Wood (*Proc. R. S. Lond.* June 18, 1868) communicates a *fifth series of observations* on variations in the human muscular system. They extend over 18 male and 18 female subjects, and comprise 558 variations, of which 20 occurred in the head and neck, 390 in the upper limbs, and 148 in the lower limbs. The males presented the greatest number of variations, one subject having as many as 25. As a rule the muscles of the arms were more variable than those of the lower limbs. Enumerating together the variations observed in the last three years, 981 examples have been seen in 102 subjects, 623 in 68 males and 358 in 34 females : of which 623 occurred on both sides, 414 in males, 209 in females : 176 on the right side only, 108 in males and 68 in females : 182 on the left side only, 101 in males and 81 in females, in all 358 one-sided specimens. For the details of the particular variations the paper itself must be consulted.

Luschka (*Henle u. Pfeufer's Zeitsch.* xxxi. p. 364) gives a detailed description of the *Superior constrictor of the pharynx;* and in *Virchow's Archiv,* xlii. p. 480, of the *palato-pharyngeus.* He divides the latter muscle into a thyreo-palatine and pharyngo-palatine portion. At p. 473 he describes a case of *fusiform dilatation of the esophagus* met with in a woman æt. 50. The specimen presents a great resemblance to a preparation in the Anatomical Museum of the University of Edinburgh.——In *Reichert u. Du Bois Reymond's Archiv,* 1868, p. 224, he describes and figures a *m. hyo-epiglotticus* in the ox ; and a *m. genio-epiglotticus* in man, which consists of fibres of the genioglossi muscles that do not end in the tongue, but pass backwards to the middle glosso-epiglottic ligament.——P. Lesshaft describes in detail (*Reichert u. Du Bois Reymond's Archiv,* 1868, p. 265) the *m. orbicularis orbitæ* and its subdivisions. He considers the lachrymal muscle of Horner as an independent muscle arising from the inner surface of the lachrymal bone and attaching itself to the lachrymal sac and both lachrymal canals.

NEUROLOGY.——The TERMINAL BODIES connected with the endings of the nerves which Krause has especially described in the glans penis and clitoris have been examined by W. Bense (*Henle u. Pfeufer's Zeitsch.* xxxiii. p. 1) in a number of the mammalia and in birds. ——From observations made into the STRUCTURE OF NERVE FIBRES immersed when perfectly fresh into solution of nitrate of silver, Dr Grandry concludes (*Bul. de l'Acad. roy. de Belgique,* xxv. p. 304, 1868) that the axial cylinder is composed of two substances of different physical and chemical properties, which present a regular disposition. It probably consists of transversely arranged discs, separated from each other by a substance which possesses different properties from the discs themselves, a resemblance therefore may be traced between its structure and that of striped muscle. He concludes also that two different substances exist within the NERVE CELL, which appear to possess as in the axial cylinder a disc-like arrangement.——W. Turner (*P. R. S. Lond.* June 1868) describes an additional example of VARIATION IN THE LONG BUCCAL NERVE to that recorded in this Journal Nov. 1866. On the left side it arose, as in the previous case, from the superior maxillary trunk ; whilst on the right side, the part of the nerve, which pierced the buccinator muscle to supply the mucous membrane on its inner surface, arose from the inferior maxillary trunk, and the branches which were distributed superficial to that muscle arose from the superior maxillary nerve in the spheno-maxillary fossa. This case gives additional evidence of the sensory nature of the long buccal nerve and illustrates the importance of studying varieties in structure not merely from their practical or morphological relations, but from the teleological point of view.——L. Letzerich investigates the MODE OF TERMINATION OF NERVES in the TESTICLE of man and mammalia (*Virchow's Archiv*, March 1868). He states that the nerve-fibres pierce the membrana propria of the tubuli seminiferi and end in a more or less irregular pyramidal mass of protoplasm in which lie clear elliptic nuclei. The ends of the fibres lie therefore in close relation to the outer layer of secreting cells.——Lockhart Clarke details a second series of observations on the THE INTIMATE STRUCTURE OF THE BRAIN (*Phil. Trans.* Part I. 1868). His researches comprise not only an enquiry into the course of the fibres of the medulla oblongata, but into the relations of the nuclei to the roots of the nerves which arise from the medulla, and the structure and connections of the olivary and superior olivary bodies.——Ludwig Stieda communicates (*Siebold u. Kölliker's Zeitsch.* XVIII. 1) an account of the CENTRAL NERVOUS SYSTEM IN THE OSSEOUS FISHES, in which he not only describes the minute structure but reviews the general morphology of the subdivisions of the encephalon.

From an extended series of observations into the STRUCTURE OF THE SPINAL GANGLIA (*Schultze's Archiv*, IV. p. 45) G. Schwalbe concludes that in mammals, birds, reptiles and amphibia the cells within these ganglia are unipolar. In fishes again bipolar cells occur. Schwalbe has only seen twice in the mammalia, once in the sheep, once in the Gasserian ganglion of the calf, cells with two processes. He considers that the axial cylinder of the nerve fibre passes directly into the ganglion cell and becomes continuous with its substance. He supports the opinion that the cells of the sympathetic ganglia in the mammalia are distinguished from those of the spinal by their multipolarity.——G. Courvoisier (*ibid.* p. 125) from an examination of the SPINAL GANGLIA in the frog comes to the same conclusion as to the unipolarity of the nerve cells. He sometimes could trace the axial cylinder into the cell up to the nucleus, but whether it ended or not in the nucleus he could not determine. He recognizes the following points of difference between the sympathetic and spinal ganglion cells. The sympathetic cells have at least two processes which are very fine, and out of the nucleolus delicate rigid threads extend into the cell substance; the spiral fibres connected with these cells contain peculiar nuclei and the cells themselves have a ball-like form. The spinal ganglion cells are pear-shaped, they contain no rigid threads, possess only a single pole, and the fibre connected with that pole is double contoured.

ORGANS OF SENSE.——W. Steinlin criticises (*Schultze's Archiv*, IV. 10) the statements of Max Schultze respecting the rods and cones of the retina.——J. W. Hulke (*Proc. R. S. L.* June 18, 1868) describes the BLOOD VESSELS OF THE RETINA of the hedge-hog as situated on the inner surface of the memb. limitans interna in intimate relation with the memb. hyaloidea, while capillaries only traverse the m. limitans and penetrate the inner layers of the retina. The retina in the hedge-hog connects the non vascular retina of fish, amphibia, reptiles and birds with the vascular retinæ of most mammals.——Ch. Lovén, p. 96, and G. Schwalbe, p. 154, communicate to the same *Vol.* lengthy memoirs on the structure of the papillæ of the tongue.——M. Alix contributes (*Ann. des Sc. Nat.* VIII. 1867) the first part of a memoir on the DISPOSITION OF THE CUTANEOUS PAPILLÆ in the hand and foot of man, apes and other mammalia.

BLOOD-VESSELS AND HEART.——Prof. Eckhard (*Henle und Pfeufer's Zeitschrift*, 31, p. 408, 1868) records the ABSENCE OF THE LEFT INTERNAL ILIAC artery in a man. The abdominal aorta bifurcated opposite the 2nd lumbar vertebra. The iliac artery therefore was very long and formed a loop over the ileo-pectineal line, from which arose the obturator artery; a branch common to the sciatic and pudic; the glutæal, and a small artery, probably a vesical. The deep circumflex ilii arose immediately above Poupart's ligament. but no mention is made either of the deep epigastric, the ilio-lumbar, or the lateral sacral.——W. Gruber (*Bul. de l'Acad. des Sc. de St Petersb.* XII. p. 247) describes VARIATIONS IN THE EXTERNAL JUGULAR VEIN, more especially a case in which it passed superficial to the clavicle through a hole in the pectoralis major and opened into the subclavian.—— Ch. Legros notes (*Robin's Journal*, No. 3, 1868) the existence of an EPITHELIAL LINING TO THE BLOOD-VESSELS not only in the arteries and veins, but in the capillaries.——Max Lehnert gives an account (*Schultze's Archiv*, IV. 26) of those fibres, named after their discoverer, FIBRES OF PURKINGE, which form a network directly beneath the endocardium in the hearts of some mammalia, although they have not been recognized in the human heart. These fibres consist of threads of muscle in which the arrangement in bundles has quite disappeared, and the fibrillæ separated from each other cross in various directions, enclosing in their meshes numerous muscle-nuclei, pigment granules, and fat drops.——O. Lannelongue and A. le Dentu designate by the name of COSTO-PERICARDIAC LIGAMENT (*Archives de Physiologie*, No. 3, 1868) a band of fibrous membrane attached to the anterior surface of the pericardium, which passes upwards superficial to the great vessels, as far as the first rib behind the costo-clavicular joint. It seems to be the sheath of the thymus gland modified by age.——Bochdalek Jun. (*Reichert u. du Bois Reymond's Archiv*, 1868, p. 302) describes the so-called PARS MEMBRANACEA SEPTI VENTRICULORUM as having nothing more to do with the ventricular septum than that it is placed upon the posterior upper border. His observations on the FORAMINA THEBESII have satisfied him that these orifices are the mouths of small veins and not mere blind depressions in the wall of the heart.—— An important contribution to the DEVELOPMENT OF THE SEMILUNAR VALVES of the Aorta and Pulmonary Artery, and of the origin of these vessels from the truncus arteriosus by Dr Morris Tonge is in

P. R. S. Lond. April 30, 1868. In the chick at the 106th hour an oblique septum forked at its lower margin begins to grow at the branchial end of the truncus horizontally downwards into the vessel from the wall between the openings of the 4th and 5th pair of branchial arches. The channel in front of the septum becomes the aorta, that behind the pulmonary artery. As the division of the truncus proceeds the right limb of the forked septum winds to the left, the left limb to the right, so as to throw the root of origin of the aorta behind the pulmonary artery. The ventricular septum forms at the same time and joins the lower border of the forked arterial septum. The semilunar valves first appear on the interior of the truncus near the branchial arteries and at a considerable distance from the heart, and the anterior and inner valves of each artery appear before the arterial septum has descended to that part of the truncus in which these valves originate. All the semilunar valves are at first solid and appear as thickenings of the interior of the vessel, their further development consists in a hollowing out of the solid substance above and near the wall of the vessel while they grow in other directions. The pocketing commences when the bases of the valves have descended to the level of the bases of the ventricles. Tonge supports von Baer's view of the origin of the right and left pulmonary arteries.

LYMPHATIC SYSTEM.—In our Report, Nov. 1866, p. 148, we noticed Chrzonszczewsky's Observations on the ORIGIN OF THE MINUTE LYMPHATIC VESSELS from the corpuscles of the connective tissue. One of his pupils, N. Afonassiew (*Virchow's Archiv*, July, 1868), by employing the method of physiological injection introduced by his teacher (Report, Vol. I. p. 146) has arrived at similar results, which may be stated as follows: the connective tissue corpuscles are independent cells, and form through the union of their processes, a system of anastomosing nutritive canals, from which the finest lymphatic capillaries, possessing independent walls, arise. This view is not in accordance with the opinion entertained by certain anatomists of the Vienna school, who consider that the lymphatics arise from mere spaces in the connective tissue. Afonassiew has also enquired into the very curious observations made by Recklinghausen, Ludwig, Dybkowski and Schweigger-Seidel into the existence of minute pores between the epithelium cells forming the free surface of the serous membranes, and through which orifices the serous cavities communicate with the lymph-vessels, but he thinks it doubtful if such openings exist. Dombrowsky, in the same *Archiv,* admitting Recklinghausen's view of the presence of a system of nutritive canals beneath the serous investment of the diaphragm, considers that this system is in continuous connection with the lymph vessels, regards it as affording origin to them, and as acting like an intermediate system during the process of nutrition between the blood and the lymph. ——T. Wharton Jones (*P. R. S. Lond.* April 30, 1868) argues that the phenomena attending the propulsion of lymph from the anterior LYMPHATIC HEARTS OF THE FROG into the veins at their posterior bor-

der, with which they communicate by a valvular opening, essentially
resemble those attending the propulsion of lymph from the caudal
heart of the eel into the caudal vein—(Report, May 1868, p. 405).
He describes (May 8) the muscular fibres of the caudal heart of the
eel as not transversely striped, but possessing a granular aspect and
consisting of a fasciculus of fibrils $\frac{1}{10,000}$th inch broad, contained in
a delicate structureless sheath; they resemble the fibrils of the muscular coat of the veins of the bat's wing and of the lymphatic heart
of the eel, and with them may be grouped together as unstriped
rhythmically contractile muscular fibrils.

SECRETING GLANDS AND EPITHELIUM.—A contribution to the
STRUCTURE OF THE KIDNEY IN BIRDS by H. Lindgren appears in
Henle u. Pfeufer's Zeitschr. XXXIII. p. 15.——M. Gross investigates
the structure of THE KIDNEY in bats and children (*Robin's Journal*,
No. 4, 1868) by the method of isolating the tubes by the action of
hydrochloric acid. The straight tubes of the medulla pass towards
the surface of the cortical substance, where they branch, the branches
then bend backwards into the medulla, form the looped tubes of
Henle, which again pass into the convoluted tubes and capsules of
Malpighi.——Franz Boll relates (*Schultze's Archiv*, IV. p. 146) his
observations on the structure of the COMPOUND RACEMOSE GLANDS
(lachrymal, parotid, submaxillary). The epithelial cells usually
possess a pointed process. Numerous crescentic or multipolar
cells connected together so as to form a network, in the meshes of
which the secreting cells lie, were recognized. He confirms the
opinion of Pflüger that the nerve fibres enter the alveoli of the gland
so as to come into close connection with the secreting epithelium.——
Theodor Eimer communicates a long article on the GOBLET-CELLS OF
THE INTESTINAL MUCOUS MEMBRANE (*Virchow's Archiv*, March, 1868).
He reviews the previously published papers on this subject (See our
Report, p. 173, Nov. 1867). He adduces numerous observations and
arguments in opposition to Sachs and others in favour of the view
that the goblet cells (Becher zellen) are definite structures and not
artificial productions. He describes and figures the mouths (stomata) of
these cells opening between the free ends of the cylindrical epithelium,
and points out that from their deeper ends, as well as from the
narrow extremity of the cylindrical cells processes pass off into the
subjacent mucous membrane.——Rabl. Rückhard makes some remarks (*Reichert u. Du Bois Reymond's Archiv*, Part I., 1868) on the
GOBLET CELLS AND CILIATED EPITHELIUM in the mollusca. He regards
the striated appearance of the intestinal epithelium as due to folds in
the cell membrane. In Buccinum undatum he recognizes goblet
shaped cells, like those described in the vertebrata, situated between
the ordinary cylindrical epithelium.

TEETH.—Franz Boll investigates the STRUCTURE OF THE TOOTH
PULP (*Schultze's Archiv*, IV. p. 73) with reference 1st to the mode of
termination of the nerves in it: 2nd to the mode of origin of the
dentine from it. He finds in the pulp not only numerous double-

contoured nerve-fibres, but an enormous quantity of extremely fine shining fibres, which he regards as nerve-fibres without any medulla. They form a network and near the surface of the pulp free ends may be seen, which he thinks may enter the dentine tubes though he could not demonstrate it. In his enquiry into the development of the dentine he agrees in the main with the previous researches of Waldeyer, that the superficial dentine cells are calcified into the hard ivory, except one or more axial portions, which remain as the delicate soft threads which Tomes first precisely pointed out as occupying the interior of the dentine tubes.

PLACENTA.—P. Jassinsky (*Virchow's Archiv*, XL. p. 341) comes to the following conclusions : the large villi are uterine glands modified during pregnancy, and both in the human and other females the villi of the chorion grow into the glands of the uterus (Sharpey, Bischoff). Two kinds of villi occur in the placenta: free chorionic villi, and complex villi, *i. e.* such as are situated in the glands. The free villi consist of a simple layer of pavement epithelium and a simple structureless membrana propria, the complex villi of two structureless membranes and two epithelial layers, the outer of which is formed of a cylinder, the inner of a pavement epithelium (Goodsir, van der Kolk). The complex villi are not so numerous as the simple, and some of the uterine glands do not contain chorionic villi. In a mature placenta all the glands show fatty degeneration. The tissue of the maternal placenta belongs to the epithelioid texture.

MALFORMATION.—Thos. Bryant (*Guy's Hospital Reports*, XIII. p. 419) records several cases of MALPOSITION OF TESTIS, HYPOSPADIAS and EPISPADIAS. In one case the epispadias was confined to the urethra, in others was complicated with eversio vesicæ.——B. S. Schultze of Jena relates a case of HERMAPHRODITISM (*Virchow's Archiv*, May, 1868).——Max Barte's (*Reichert u. Du Bois Reymond's Archiv*, 1868, p. 137) gives an account of the literature of VESICO-ABDOMINAL FISSURE, and relates two additional cases.——At p. 456 of the same *Vol.* Messrs. Hicks and Bankart describe dissections of two ACEPHALOUS MONSTERS in which the head, heart, lungs and liver were absent.——Von Thaden (*Henle u. Pfeufer's Zeitschr.* XXXIII. p. 58) records a curious case of MALFORMATION OF THE LEFT VENTRICLE OF THE HEART in a male infant which lived five months. A long finger-like hollow process continuous with the apex of the left ventricle passed through an opening in the diaphragm into the abdomen, and could be felt pulsating during life behind the linea alba. The process terminated below in a bulbous dilatation. Its cavity communicated with the ventricle and its inner wall gave origin to carneæ columnæ, one of which became continuous with a musculus papillaris. The infant had an umbilical hernia and the bulbous end of the process formed a part of its contents.——Julius Arnold describes a case of MALFORMATION OF THE HEART (*Virchow's Archiv*, March, 1868, p. 449) where there was only one ventricle into which both auricles opened. The aorta arose from it, but the pulmonary artery was closed at its origin. The pulmonary veins communicated with the portal vein and the spleen was absent.———O. Fraentzel (*Virchow's Archiv*, May, 1868, p. 420) relates a case in which the AORTA COMMUNICATED WITH THE PULMONARY ARTERY by a circular opening one-fourth of an inch above the aortic valves. The woman lived to the age of 25.———B. G. Wilder discusses the subject of POLYDACTYLISM (*Proc. Massachusetts Med. Soc.* II.); he tabulates 152 cases, and finds that males are more frequently affected than females, that the right and left sides are almost equally the seat of extra digits, but that the hands are much more frequently affected than the feet. When two extra digits occur in the same individual the repetition is more likely to occur in the opposite sides, than at the opposite ends of the body.

COMPARATIVE ANATOMY AND MORPHOLOGY.—W. H. Flower contributes a series of memoirs on the anatomy of the Cetacea. In *Trans. Zool. Soc.* VI. Part III. p. 87, he describes the SKELETON of INIA GEOFFRENSIS and the SKULL of PONTOPORIA BLAINVILLII. He subdivides the cetacea into two suborders, Balænoidea (mystacoceti) and Delphinoidea (odontoceti). The former consists of two families, balænidæ and balænopteridæ; the latter of three, physeteridæ, platanistidæ and delphinidæ. The physeteridæ consist of the subfamilies physeterinæ and ziphiinæ; the delphinidæ of the beluginæ and delphininæ and the platanistidæ of the platanistinæ and iniinæ, to which latter subfamily Inia and Pontoporia(?) belong.———In the same *Transactions*, VI. p. 309, Mr Flower gives the most detailed description of the OSTEOLOGY of PHYSETER MACROCEPHALUS which has yet appeared; and in the *Proceedings* of the Society March 12, 1868, he notes the probable identity of the fin-whale termed Balænoptera carolinæ by Malm, with the Physalus sibbaldii of Gray.———J. Reinhardt (*Vidensk. Meddelelser fra den natur hist. Forening*, 1867) makes observations on the cetacean called STEYPIREYDR by the Icelanders.———Drs M'Carte and Macalister (*Phil. Trans.* Part I. 1868) communicate a detailed account of the ANATOMY OF BALÆNOPTERA ROSTRATA of Gray, the piked-whale of Pennant.———M. Fischer details OBSERVATIONS ON A GRAMPUS GRISEUS (*Ann. des Sc. Nat.* 1867, p. 363) cast ashore on the coast of France.———J. H. Thomson states (*Proc. Zool. Soc.* March, 1867) that the deformities of the LOWER JAW OF THE CACHALOT, described by Murie and Fischer (see our last Report, p. 402) are not uncommon, and are attributable to the fighting propensities of the young bull-whales.———Claudius (*Mem. de l'Acad. imp. de St Petersb.* XI. 1867) gives an account of the ORGAN OF HEARING IN RHYTINA STELLERI and in the same *Vol.* Owsjannikow and Kowalevsky describe the ORGAN OF HEARING and central nervous system of the CEPHALOPODA. In the *Bulletin* of the same *Academy*, XII. p. 287, Owsjannikow describes the CENTRAL, and at p. 297 the PERIPHERAL NERVOUS SYSTEM OF AMPHIOXUS LANCEOLATUS. He considers the anterior end of the nervous axis as a rudimentary brain, which gives origin to nerves of sense. In it is a ventricle, corresponding to the 4th and lined with epithelial cells, and into which the canal of the spinal marrow opens. In front of this ventricle is a rudimentary eye, consisting of pigment granules. The spinal cord has no enlargement and ends posteriorly in a hollow thread. The nerves arise unsymmetrically from its sides, their fibres are continuous within the cord with the processes of the multipolar nerve cells. The peripheral nerves partly end in peculiar vesicular 'end-organen,' but more especially in epithelium cells.——Kowalevsky (*Mem. de l'Acad. imp. de St Petersb.* XI. 1867) traces the DEVELOPMENT OF AMPHIOXUS LANCEOLATUS from the earliest changes which occur in the ovum. He describes and figures the formation of cilia on the outer surface of the embryo, which at this stage corresponds with the embryo of *phoronis, limnæus, ophiura*, &c., and at the 24th hour, whilst the cilia are yet visible, the central nervous axis, and intestinal tube, with the chorda dorsalis situated between them, begin to be differentiated. At the 30th hour the anterior end of the embryo becomes pointed, the opening of the mouth is formed, the small cilia disappear and are replaced by a long cilium projecting from each epithelium cell, whilst two small warts with two tactile threads project from the under surface of the embryo, not far from the mouth. Near these warts he recognized the small glands already described by Pagenstecher, Leuckart and Max Schultze. He describes the formation of the peculiar disk-like particles, which J. Goodsir showed composed the substance of the chorda. The nervous axis originally consists of a simple tube, the wall of which is formed of a simple row of cells : anteriorly it widens and the lumen of the tube is filled with distinct nucleated cells. The 1st branchial cleft appears soon after the formation of the mouth. The cavity into which the branchial clefts open is formed in the same way as the corresponding cavity in other fishes.——To Vol. x. Kowalevsky contributes an important Memoir on the DEVELOPMENT OF THE SIMPLE ASCIDIÆ. He describes an axial cylinder in the tail of the ascidian larva which possesses almost the same structure as the chorda dorsalis of amphioxus, only in the ascidia it is not quite so much subdivided into discs, and of a softer consistency. This discovery is important in its bearings on the affinities of the vertebrate and invertebrate subkingdoms.——An elaborate essay on the MECHANISM OF FLIGHT, by J. B. Pettigrew, appears in *Trans. Lin. Soc.* XXVI. p. 197. His observations are made, not only on birds and insects, but embrace an enquiry into the progression of fish, aquatic and land mammalia. His general conclusion is that the wing acts as a helix or screw. All wings are twisted on themselves naturally and they twist during action, so that their movement is essentially spiral.——W. H. Flower (*Proc. Zool. Soc. Lond.* June 11, 1868) from observations made on young specimens of the nine-banded Armadillo (*Tatusia peba*) concludes that in the DEVELOPMENT AND SUCCESSION OF THEIR TEETH, the Armadillos are not mono-phyodonts : that seven milk-teeth exist on each side of each jaw, whilst the eighth tooth only appears to have no predecessor. He confirms and adds to the observations of Professor Gervais.—— J. C. Schrödte (*Annals of Nat. Hist.* May, 1868) enquires into the POSITION OF THE EYE IN THE PLEURONECTIDÆ. He has examined young specimens of Rhombus barbatus, Pleuronectes platessa and Hippoglossus pinguis, and concludes " that the eye of the blind-side does not only glide over from its own to the eye-side of the fish, but when arrived there it recedes a little along the dorsal fin. Hence the eye moves round the anterior end of the dorsal fin, not the fin that prolongs itself past the eye." The change of position of the eye is a slow process, preparation for which is made in the fœtus.——P. Harting gives a zoological and anatomical description of ORTHRAGORISCUS OZODURA (*Verhand. der Konink. Akad. Amsterdam*, 1868). He thinks it possible that under the collective name of O. mola several different species (O. ozodura, Blochii, Retzii and Mola nasus) are united. He describes the skin, mouth, alimentary canal, liver, heart, blood, branchial apparatus, brain, eye, ear, ovary, skeleton. His account of the structure of the skeleton is elaborate and he enquires into the process of osteo-genesis in the Teliostiens generally. He reviews the previous observations made on this genus by Cuvier, Wellenberg, Arsaky, Goodsir, Bellingeri, Cleland and Turner. He describes and figures three semicircular canals in the ear, one of which had been overlooked by Cleland in his original memoir, but which that anatomist, in a letter to the *Reporter*, states that he has since observed in a more recent dissection of this fish.——Fr. Wahlgren (*Acta Universit. Lundensis*, 1867) also makes, under the name of Mola nasus, zoological and anatomical observations on Orthragoriscus. ——W. H. Flower makes notes on the VISCERAL ANATOMY OF HYOMOSCHUS AQUATICUS (*Proc. Zool. Soc.* Dec. 12, 1867). He points out an extraordinary development of the thyroid cartilage, but in other respects its internal anatomy closely corresponds with that of the allied genus, Tragulus.——At the Royal Institution, Feb. 7, 1868 (*Proceedings*), T. H. Huxley discoursed, on the ANIMALS INTERMEDIATE BETWEEN BIRDS AND REPTILES. He inclines to the hypothesis that the *phylum* of the class Aves has its root in the extinct Dinosaurian reptiles: that out of these, passing through a series of such modifications as are exhibited in one of their phases by *Compsognathus*, the *Ratitæ* have been evolved, while the *Carinatæ* are still further modifications and differentiations of these last.——C. Gegenbaur criticises (*Jenaische Zeitschrift*, IV. 50) the memoir of M. Martins on TORSION OF THE HUMERUS as an element to be considered in the comparison of the upper and lower limbs. He recognizes the value of M. Martins' theory and communicates many additional measurements of the humerus in adults, children, mammalia, birds and reptiles.——W. Peters (*Monats Berlin Akad.* Nov. 21, Dec. 5, 1867 ; *An. Nat. Hist.* May, 1868) considers the HOMOLOGY OF THE QUADRATE BONE. He doubts the morphological identity of the incus and os quadratum. From the examination of young monotremata, he finds that a bone composed of two or more pieces presents the same articular connexions as the os quadratum in birds, that by these pieces, through the os tympanicum, is effected the union with the os pterygoideum and the inner angular process of the lower jaw, whilst that with the squama temporalis is effected by the malleus and incus or by the incus alone.

REPORT ON THE PROGRESS OF PHYSIOLOGY, from 1st March to 1st August, 1868. By ARTHUR GAMGEE, M.D., THOMAS R. FRASER, M.D., and WILLIAM RUTHERFORD, M.D., *Edinburgh*[1].

Dr RUTHERFORD'S REPORT.

Vascular System.

HEART.—CAUSE OF FIRST SOUND.—Dogiel and Ludwig (*Sächs. Acad. Sitzungsbericht, Math.-phys.* Cl. 1868, p. 89—96. *Ludwig's Arbeiten,* 1868. Abstract by Hermann in *Centralblatt,* No. 31, 1868), from recent experiments regarding the causes of the first cardiac sound, conclude that it is chiefly due to contraction of the muscular fibres of the ventricles assisted by closure of the auriculo-ventricular valves.

In dogs poisoned with curara and kept alive by artificial respiration they exposed the heart, and passed a ligature round each of the vessels connected with it. The ligatures were *tightened* on the vessels in the following order, descending and ascending venæ cavæ, pulmonary artery, pulmonary veins, finally the aorta after gentle pressure had been made on the heart. The almost bloodless heart was removed and suspended in a funnel-shaped glass filled with defibrinated blood, care being taken to prevent the heart from coming in contact with the wall of the vessel. The glass vessel was closed below by a thin plate of caoutchouc and the latter surrounded by a caoutchouc tube to which a stethoscope was fitted by means of a small glass tube. As long as the heart continued to contract regularly the systolic sound could be distinctly heard, which only differed from the same sound heard previous to removal of the heart in its being of feebler intensity.

In another series of observations they examined the heart *in situ.* After having emptied the heart of its blood in the above-mentioned way, they placed a stethoscope directly on the heart. Stethoscopes of different materials were used. In every case the systolic sound was heard, somewhat weakened, together with feebler sounds whose character varied with the kind of stethoscope used.

CIRCULATION IN THE WALLS OF THE HEART.—For an excellent abstract of a paper by Dr Lannelongue on this subject (*Archives de Physiologie,* No. i. p. 22, 1868), see Mr Power's "Chronicle of Physiology," *Brit. and For. Med. Chr. Review,* July 1868.

---

[1] In order to assist in making this Report as complete as possible the Authors will be glad to receive copies of original memoirs and other contributions to Physiology.

INFLUENCE OF THE THYROID GLAND UPON FLOW OF BLOOD THROUGH THE CAROTIDS.—Guyon (Note sur l'arrêt de la Circulation carotidienne pendant l'effort prolongé; *Archives de Physiologie*, p. 56) has observed that during powerful muscular effort especially during the act of expelling the child, the pulse in the temporal and facial arteries cannot be felt, while it still continues in the radial. He supposes this to be due to compression of the carotids by swelling of the Thyroid Gland through venous engorgement of it. He supposes that this mechanism is an important one for partially checking the arterial supply to the brain so as thereby to prevent congestion of it during prolonged muscular effort.

SPHYGMOGRAPH.—For an excellent description of recent improvements in the sphygmograph, by Mr Berkeley Hill, Dr Burdon Sanderson and Dr Anstie, see a paper by the last-mentioned gentleman in the *Lancet*, June 20th, 1868.

Nervous System.

BRAIN.—PHYSIOLOGY OF LANGUAGE.—Dr Hughlings Jackson does not attempt to localise the seat of the faculty of language in the brain. He considers that it resides *nowhere* because it resides *everywhere*. Dr Jackson's theory regarding the function of the brain is briefly this,—that in most people the left half of the brain is the leading side—the side of the so called " will" while the right half is the *automatic* side. Our space will not permit of a resumé of the arguments by which Dr Jackson has been led to this conclusion—but we subjoin a list of his writings on the subject kindly furnished to us by Dr Jackson himself—which will doubtless prove useful to many. *London Hospital Reports*, Vol. I.—*Med. Times and Gazette*, June 23, 1866. Dec. 14 and 21, 1867. Aug. 15 and 22, and Sept. 26, 1868.—*Lancet*, Nov. 26, 1864. Feb. 17 and Dec. 1, 1866.— *Brit. Med. Jour.* Vol. I. 1866.—*London Opthal. Hospital Reports*, Dec. 1866, and a Paper read at Norwich, August 1868, published as a Pamphlet.

CRUS CEREBELLI.—Curschmann, in an inaugural dissertation (*Beiträge zur Physiologie der Kleinhirnschenkel*, 8vo. pp. 35, Giessen, 1868, gives the results of a number of experiments upon the Crura Cerebelli of rabbits, The author, working under the direction of Professor Eckhard, has taken great care to ascertain the exact position and extent of the lesion which he inflicted.

The excellent resumé which he gives of all that previous observers had done, serves to show how much such precision is needed. He gives an exact description of his mode of operating, which will prove of not a little service to those who may wish to perform experiments, whether for the purpose of research or demonstration.

In his experiments on the " tract of the Crus Cerebelli, formed by the anterior and posterior crus," he found that very much the same effects followed a variety of injuries to the tract comprehending punctures to the depth of one—usually two, millimètres—some in its middle, some on its outer, others on its inner side. Irregular but not violent contractions followed these injuries. Voluntary movement was slightly disturbed. Some animals showed a tendency to lie upon the injured side. The position of the eyes was normal. He never saw any forward or backward movements of the animal, such as Flourens observed when the anterior and posterior Crura Cerebelli were injured (movements forward followed injury of the anterior—backward movements followed injury of the posterior Crus Cerebelli). His injuries however were not inflicted on either crus, but on the tract formed by the union of both. . He cannot explain why his injuries inflicted on various parts of this tract should never have called forth the movements produced by injury of either crus of which it is composed.

In a second series of researches he studied the effect of complete division of this tract. The section was followed by irregular convulsive contractions of varying intensity, extending throughout the entire body. These movements were not peculiar either as regards their character or site. Voluntary movement seemed to be almost entirely abolished. The animal lay upon the injured side and fell always into this position when it was placed in any other. Some animals were observed in this state for three or four hours; others died from the hæmorrhage which the operation for exposure of the brain had occasioned. In all the experiments of this series the dissection shewed that the tract composed of the anterior and posterior crus had been completely divided without injury having been inflicted on any neighbouring part.

In four cases he partially divided the Crus Cerebelli ad Pontem, but in only one case did he produce the rotatory movements said by many to follow such injury; in his experiment there were only six to eight rotatory movements towards the injured side. This animal, together with the other three, presented the same features as those in which the tract composed of the anterior and posterior crus only was divided. He found however when he produced a trocar through the Tuberculum Acusticum into the brain substance lying immediately below it, that the animal always manifested the most energetic rotatory movements upon its longitudinal axis towards the injured side. The eye on the injured side was always rotated downwards; the eye on the other side upward. In none of these cases was there the slightest injury of the Crus Cerebelli ad Pontem found on dissection. He, in conclusion, suggests the possibility that other experimenters may have injured the part of the brain he mentions in addition to the Crus Cerebelli ad Pontem, when they got well marked rotatory movements following injury of the latter, and says that none of the experimenters describe exactly the depth of the lesions inflicted by them.

SPINAL CORD.—Vulpian (Influence de l'Abolition des Fonctions des Nerfs sur la région de la Moelle Epinière que leur donne origine, *Brown-Sequard's Archives de Physiologie*, 1868, p. 443) has examined the spinal cord in two cases where one leg had been amputated

many years previous to death.   The nerves destined for the amputated limb, the roots of these nerves and the spinal cord were not in
a state of fatty degeneration ; there was however a diminution in the
volume of the grey and white substance of that portion of the cord
which gave origin to these nerves, but that it was a simple diminution
in volume and not the lesion Lockhart Clarke has described in cases of
progressive muscular atrophy.   He concludes that the lesion of the
spinal cord observed in muscular atrophy is not the *result* of the
atrophy.   Moreover, Vulpian has injured the grey matter of the
cord in mammals and birds and has not been able to find atrophy of
the muscles supplied by nerves from the injured portions of the cord.
He therefore infers that traumatic lesions of the cord do not without complication produce muscular atrophy.   He concludes " that
if, as appears probable, there is a close connection between the causation of lesion of the cord and that of the muscles in progressive muscular atrophy and in infantile atrophy, it must be presumed that the
influence of the cord on the muscles belongs to the irritative nature
peculiar to this lesion, and it must be admitted that experimental
traumatism cannot devolop in the cord this pathological energy, which
raises up certain morbid alterations."

Dr Sigmund Mayer (Über die Unempfindlichkeit der vorderen
Kückenmarkstränge für die elecktrische Reizung, *Pflüger's Archives
der Physiologie*, 1868, p. 166) from researches on the spinal cord of
frogs, concludes that Engelken was mistaken when he denied the
accuracy of Van Deen's statement that in frogs the anterior and
posterior columns of the spinal cord cannot be excited by either electrical, mechanical, or chemical irritants.   Guttmann and Funke had
previously confirmed Van Deen's observation.   And Schiff and
Brown-Sequard have made the same observation on higher animals.

Dr H. Sanders-Ezn has a curious paper giving the results of a
" preliminary enquiry for the investigation of the reflex mechanism
of the lumbar portion of the spinal cord of the frog" (*Ludwig's
Arbeiten*, 1868, pp. 1—30). He describes the movements which occur
in the various joints of the lower extremity of the frog, and gives a
large number of drawings of the various postures—some of which are
most peculiar—assumed by the legs when certain cutaneous terri-
tories are irritated.

VAGUS AND RESPIRATION.—As is well known, Rosenthal found
that when the superior laryngeal nerve is irritated by means of electricity, the number of the respirations is diminished, and if the irritation be powerful enough the respiration is completely arrested,
owing to spasmodic contraction of the diaphragm.   R. Burkart (*Pflüger's Archives der Physiologie*, Erstes Heft, 1868, p. 107) at the suggestion of Pflüger has investigated the influence of irritation of the
recurrent laryngeal nerve and of the trunk of the vagus below the
superior laryngeal on the respiratory movements.   He finds that in
the trunk of the recurrent laryngeal sensitive fibres are to be found,
slight irritation of which diminishes the number of the respiratory

movements. Under favourable conditions strong irritation arrests the respiratory movement in the stage of expiration (diaphragm in a state of rest). These changes in the respiration did not ensue when previous to the irritation of the nerve the trunk of the vagus on the same side was divided in the neck. When the trunk of the vagus containing the filaments of the recurrent laryngeal was divided in the middle of the neck, and the central end of the vagus irritated by electrical currents, sometimes increase, at other times diminution, in the number of the respiratory movements ensued (facts observed by many experimenters). When the frequency of the respirations was diminished in this case, it was due to lengthening of the expiratory movement or of the pause which follows expiration. It appears that the expiratory phenomena ensue upon feebler irritation of the central end of the vagus of one side, if the vagus on the other have been previously divided.

SPLANCHNIC NERVES.—An elaborate research has been carried out in Ludwig's Laboratory, by Dr Asp, on the nervous supply of vessels, chiefly bearing on the influence of division and irritation of the splanchnic nerves (Beobachtungen über Gefässnerven, *Ludwig's Arbeiten*, 1868, p. 131. Abstract by Hermann in *Centralblatt*, No. 22. 1868).

He cut down upon the splanchnics in dogs and rabbits from behind and divided them without opening the peritoneum. After section of both great splanchnics the blood pressure fell greatly while the rapidity of the pulse increased. The higher the blood pressure before—the more did it fall after division of the nerves. Strange to say, in some animals which survived the operation, when the blood pressure was again observed after some days' interval it was found to have attained a degree as high as it had been before division of the nerves, and this notwithstanding the fact that the breach in the continuity of the nerves had remained unhealed.

On irritating the peripheral end of the divided splanchnicus major or the central ends of any of its roots, the blood-pressure *always* rose, and with few exceptions slowing of the pulse resulted. The latter was much less marked when the vagi had been previously divided.

Although the slight slowing of the pulse which usually followed increase of the pressure after division of the vagi would seem to favour Marey's view regarding the effect of blood pressure on cardiac rapidity, viz. that if the former be increased the latter must necessarily be diminished owing to the increased resistance to the heart's action, Dr Asp does not accept this interpretation, for he has found that the slowing of the pulse does not regularly follow increase of pressure, and thinks that were Marey's view correct, there ought to be no exceptions. Asp ascribes the slowing to irritation of the cardiac terminations of the Vagus.

Irritation of the central end of the divided nerve or its branches slowed the pulse (as Bernstein had previously shown in the frog and rabbit) and increased the blood pressure. Although the same results appear to follow irritation of both the central and peripheral ends of the divided nerve, yet there are essential points of difference. During irritation of the former, the rise in pressure is more and the slowing of the pulse is less marked than during irritation of the latter, although an irritant of the same strength be used in both cases.

By a number of experiments he satisfied himself that in both cases the slowing of the pulse is due to the action of the increased blood pressure on the roots of the vagus in the medulla oblongata. And he supposes that the slighter slowing of the pulse which follows the rise in pressure on irritating the central end of the splanchnic, is probably due to a reflex contraction of vessels in the great nervous centres which oppose the influences of the increased blood pressure on the vagus.

To show how complicated is the question regarding the influence of blood pressure on cardiac rapidity we may cite the following results obtained by Asp, which when viewed in connection with those given above, show that we are yet far from an explanation of them.

When he increased the blood pressure in the thorax and head, &c., by compressing the thoracic aorta, and afterwards irritated the distal extremity of the divided splanchnic nerve, the blood pressure rose (blood had reached the mesenteric vessels by collateral circulation). While the blood pressure was *increased* in this way, the rapidity of the pulse was sometimes diminished, sometimes it remained unaltered, but *most frequently it was increased.* (The italics are ours.)

RADIAL NERVE.—Mr Savory (*Lancet*, Aug. 1, 1868) relates a case in which he removed several inches of the musculo-spiral nerve. Although the muscles supplied by it were paralyzed, there was however but slight impairment of the sensibility of the skin supplied by the radial nerve. His explanation is the following : " We know that in the forearm, just above the wrist, some small branches of the external cutaneous nerve communicate with the radial, and it may be that at this junction the radial receives filaments from the external cutaneous which pass down to be distributed with the filaments of the radial, even to the skin of the hand. This seems to be the most probable view of the matter, indeed the only feasible one."

INHIBITION OF CONVULSIONS.—Brown-Sequard (*Archives de Physiologie*, 1868, p. 157) gives an account of seven cases in which irritation of sensory nerves was found to allay tetanic spasm and convulsion. The irritation of sensory nerves was effected by violent flexion of the great toe. He considers that this is an instance of the same kind of action that we have in the stoppage of the heart by irritation of the vagus. He also thinks that the arrest (*Archives*, p. 317) of an epileptic fit by irritating centripetal nerves, is due to an action similar to the foregoing. Application of a ligature to a limb affected with an aura is a mode of producing such irritation; the ligature does not arrest the propagation of the irritation towards the brain, but it creates another irritation which neutralizes the effect of the first.

ELECTROTONIC STATE IN HUMAN NERVES.—Erb (*Deutsches Archiv für Klin. Med.* III. p. 514. Abstract in *Centralblatt*, No. 9, 1868) confirms Eulenburg's conclusion regarding the influence of a galvanic current on human nerves, that is, the + pole lowers while the − pole increases the excitability, just as Pflüger found to be the case with the moter nerves of the frog.

RAPIDITY OF NERVOUS TRANSMISSION IN HUMAN NERVES.—For a good abstract of a paper by von Wittich (*Henle und Pfeufer's Zeitsch.* (3) XXXI. pp. 87—125) on this subject, see Power's Chronicle of Physiology, *Brit. and For. Med. Chir. Rev.* July, 1868.

Digestive System.

SALIVARY GLANDS. PAROTID.—Under the direction of Eckhard, Brettel (*Die Parotidensecretion des Schäfes im Vergleich zur Nierensecretion*, Inaugural Dissertation, Giessen, 1868, p. 21) has instituted some experiments on the secretion of the parotid gland with a view to compare its secreting powers with those of the kidney. The following are his conclusions :

1. The parotid secretion of the sheep is within very wide limits independent of the state of the circulation. (Goll and Hermann had previously found that the renal secretion is greatly influenced by the condition of the circulation. Brettel altered the circulation by section and irritation of the vagi, and by venesection.)

2. The parotid secretion of the sheep is not inferior in quantity to that of the kidneys, although the kidney is from four to five times heavier than the parotid. (In one experiment he found that, in spite of the unequal weights of the parotid and kidney, the amount of secretion was the same in both cases, viz. 0·5 cubic centimetre in five minutes.)

3. Ferrocyanide of potassium and lactate of iron—perhaps *all* salts of iron—do not pass into the saliva when these are injected into the blood ; when iodide of iron is injected the iodine appears in the saliva, but never the iron. (The two first-mentioned salts are excreted by the kidneys.)

4. The parotid secretion in the sheep continues for at least a quarter of an hour after death. He believes, with Eckhard, that the parotid like the kidney secretes continuously.

SUBMAXILLARY AND SUBLINGUAL GLANDS.—A number of most important contributions to our knowledge of the salivary secretion, and of the structure of the sub-maxillary and sub-lingual glands have recently been made by Heidenhain. (*Beiträge zur Lehre von der Speichelabsonderung*, p. 121. *Studien des Physiologischen Insti-*

tuts zu Breslau, 1868, Heft 4.) An excellent abstract of this valuable monograph has already been given by Mr Power (Chronicle of Physiology, *Brit. and For. Med. Ch. Rev.* July, 1868).

RESULTS FOLLOWING DIVISION OF INTESTINAL NERVES.—Moreau (*Centralblatt*, No. 14, 1868) has found that after division of intestinal nerves in dogs a large secretion of watery fluid into the intestine results. In a large healthy dog, which had fasted for twenty-four hours, he exposed a knuckle of bowel, and put four ligatures round it; these were separated from each other, so that three portions of intestine, each about fifteen centimetres in length, were included within the ligatures. He carefully isolated and divided the nerves, supplying the middle ligatured portion, taking care to avoid injury of the vessels. He closed the wound in the abdominal wall, and allowed the animal to remain at rest. After some time he found a quantity of fluid in the portion of intestine whose nerves had been divided, while the two other portions were quite empty. In one dog a hundred grammes of fluid were found in the intestine three hours after the operation, and in another dog, killed eighteen hours after, two hundred and twenty-five grammes were present. The fluid did not contain coloured blood-corpuscles. On standing, mucus corpuscles and "leucocytes" separated from it. The filtered fluid was clear and of a yellowish tinge. Specific gravity 1008, strongly alkaline. It contained alkaline carbonates and bicarbonates. The organic constituents of the filtered fluid amounted to 0·35 or 0·45°/$_0$. He intends investigating the nature of the fluid more closely. The experiments were performed in Bernard's laboratory.

LIVER.—R. Heidenhain (Weitere Beobachtungen, betreffend die Gallen secretion, *Studien des physiolog. Instituts zu Breslau*, 1868, Heft 4) has continued the observations, begun under his direction, by Lichtheim and Max Heidenhain (see *Journal of Anatomy and Physiology*, II. 414). He found that when he irritated the spinal cord in rabbits—in which all voluntary movement was suspended by means of curara—that the flow of the bile through a canula inserted in the gall-bladder was increased for a short period after the irritation of the cord was begun, but was soon afterwards diminished. (Passage of the bile into the intestine was prevented by ligature of the common bile duct.) He ascribes the increased biliary flow to contraction of the bile ducts occasioned by the irritation, and the diminished biliary flow he attributes to diminished secretion, occasioned by contraction of the hepatic vessels. According to him the interlobular bile ducts, undoubtedly, contain non-striped muscular fibres. They form a circular layer immediately outside the epithelium. The fibres may be coloured yellow by chloride of palladium (see Schultze's *Archives*, III. p. 480), and isolated by dissection after the ducts are macerated in dilute acetic acid (10°/$_0$).

In the course of his investigations he had occasion to study absorption from the bile ducts. He connected to the canula in the biliary fistula a tube containing a column of a blue fluid (solution of indigo-carmine), the pressure of which was sufficient to overcome the pressure of the bile. He found that this fluid readily passes from the bile ducts into the blood. He found, however, that while the interlobular bile ducts were injected with the blue fluid it had not entered the intralobular ducts. He infers from this fact that "in the liver absorption and secretion take place in different localities, the former between, the latter within the lobules." He supposes that when the bile is absorbed in icterus the absorption likewise takes place from the interlobular ducts.

Respiratory System.

INFLUENCE OF RESPIRATION UPON ANIMAL HEAT.—Dr Lombard of Harvard (United States) gives the following as the results of his experiments on the influence of respiration upon animal heat (Recherches expérimentales sur quelques influences non étudiées jusqu'ici de la Respiration sur la Température du Corps Humain." *Archives de Physiologie*, pp. 479—497, 1868).

1. Increase in the frequency and extent of the respiratory movements during ten minutes is capable of producing a fall of temperature over the radial artery to the extent of 1·11° centigrade.

2. When the respiration is suspended at the close of an ordinary or full inspiration, the temperature over the radial artery falls from ·001 to ·01° centigrade in a minute or a minute and a half. The fall usually begins some seconds after the suspension of the respiration.

3. The temperature of parts of the forearm other than those over the radial artery are not at all, or only very slightly, influenced by suspension of the respiration after an inspiration.

4. The cause of the fall of temperature when the respirations are increased in number and extent is to be found in an alteration of the circulation. The use of the sphygmograph in these cases shows that frequency of the pulse is increased while its tension and force are diminished. It is not improbable that these changes in the circulation are, up to a certain point, the result of causes purely mechanical; but they appear, at least in part, to result from a direct action on the heart by nervous influence.

5. Change in the circulation is also the cause of the fall of temperature when the respiration is suspended. By the sphygmograph it may be shown that in such a case while the tension and frequency of the pulse are augmented its force is diminished. The increase of tension is due to an obstruction in the thorax to the flow of the blood through the right side of the circulatory apparatus. Venous congestion in the system generally is the result of this. The venous congestion produces an analogous state in the arteries pari passu with the increase of tension—the quantity of blood received in a given time by a part is diminished, although there is an increase in the absolute quantity of blood. The fall of temperature (over the radial

artery) is due to the passage of a smaller quantity of blood through the radial artery.

6. The temperature of parts of the forearm—not near the radial artery—*rises* in the above cases: this is due to the fact, that these parts depend for their temperature on the state of the veins and capillaries, and these vessels being very dilatable become engorged with blood when an obstruction exists in the venous side of the circulatory apparatus, and the total quantity of blood can more than compensate for the diminution in the quantity of arterial blood supplied to the part in a given time.

7. All the above results have been obtained when the inspired air was saturated with moisture, and had a temperature of 50° Fahr. or 130° Fahr. (Therefore the lowering of temperature in the radial artery in one of the above cases could not be due to cooling of the air by the increased respiration. Bernard's researches appeared to have shown that the blood is cooled as it passes through the lungs; but Savory, some years ago, showed that this conclusion resulted from the imperfect method employed by Bernard in performing the experiments.)

In his experiments, Dr Lombard used a thermo-electric pile invented by him, which is capable of showing $\frac{1}{2000}$ th of a degree centigrade; this ingenious apparatus is figured and described by him. (*l. c.* page 498—506.)

SPIROGRAPH.—Mr David C. M'Vail (*Lancet*, March 7, 1868) describes, under this title, an instrument for recording the respiratory movements. The instrument consists of two revolving cylinders, on which is placed the paper to receive the tracing. A pen, consisting of a glass tube drawn to a point, is moved vertically by a rod resting on the surface of the chest. He says that this instrument may be made of a size about that of a "fair sized snuff-box."

Cutaneous System.

CAUSE OF DEATH WHEN THE SKIN IS COVERED WITH VARNISH. —Some have supposed that when an animal dies from the effects of having its skin covered with varnish, its death must be ascribed to the retention of deleterious matters given off by the skin. Edenhuizen thought that the noxious matter is volatile alkali. Gerlach and others thought that death was due to suppression of the respiratory function of the skin; while Valentin had on the other hand shown that the morbid symptoms manifested by a varnished animal disappear if the animal be placed in a higher temperature, thereby leading to the notion that death in such a case results from increased loss of heat.

Laschkewitsch of St Petersburg (*Reichert's Archives*, 1868, pp. 61 —67) has by recent researches confirmed the truth of the last-mentioned theory. A varnished animal, when surrounded by cotton wadding, suffered no harm though it died when the wadding was removed. He found the blood-vessels much dilated below the varnish; he supposes that the dilatation of cutaneous vessels favours the loss of heat by the skin. He has found that the volatile alkali spoken of by Edenhuizen results from the decomposition of hair and epidermis. He further disproved Gerlach's view that asphyxia is the cause of death, by placing an animal in an atmosphere of hydrogen, taking care to cover the animal's mouth with an elastic funnel communicating with the external atmosphere; the animal lived in this medium for six hours without suffering any deleterious effects.

Muscular System.

GALVANIC IRRITATION OF STRIATED MUSCLE.—Von Bezold believed that when a muscle is thrown into action by a galvanic current, irritation takes place only at the negative pole on closing the current, and only at the positive pole on opening it. Pflüger had previously shown that this holds true for the irritation of a nerve by means of a galvanic current. Aeby opposed Von Bezold's conclusion, maintaining that both on closing and opening the current irritation of the muscle takes place at both the + and − poles, although unequally. Engelmann (see Dr Moore's translation of his paper, *Jl. of Anatomy and Physiology*, II. 435) by a new experiment maintained that Von Bezold's conclusion is correct. Aeby (*Reichert's Archives*, 1867, p. 688) has reinvestigated the matter, and maintains, in opposition to Von Bezold and Engelmann, that he is in the right. He says, however, that when *weak* currents are used the irritation may be unipolar.

FORCE PRODUCED BY FROG'S MUSCLES.—E. Weber long ago showed that the height to which a muscle can raise a weight depends on the *length* of its fibres, while its power depends on the *number* of its fibres. The power of a muscle may be represented by the weight which is just sufficient to prevent shortening of the muscle when it is irritated. E. Weber estimated this at 600 grammes per square centimetre of muscle in the frog.

Rosenthal of Berlin (*Comptes Rendus*, Juin 3, 1867) has re-examined the question by means of an apparatus which, in his opinion, prevents the possibility of error due to fatigue of the muscle more completely than that employed by Weber. He has found that in the adductor magnus and semimembranosus of the frog, the force of the contraction of each square centimetre is equal to from 2·8 to 3 kilogrammes. He says, " the absolute force of the gastrocnemius of a frog of average size varies between 1000 and 1200 grammes; this enormous figure is explained when we remember that the transverse section of the muscle is very great in proportion to its entire volume. From this we see that muscles are machines which in proportion to their weight generate a much greater quantity of force than machines constructed by human industry."

INFLUENCE OF HEAT ON MUSCLE.—Schmulewitsch (*Robin's Journal*, 1868, p. 27 ; *Med. Jahrb. d. Ges. d. Aertze Zu. Wien*, xv. 3. Abstract in *Centralblatt*, No. 11, 1868) found that when a frog's muscle is gradually heated to 30° or 33° centigrade the work performed by it when irritated by inducted currents increases. If however the temperature be raised above 33°, the muscle quickly grows. weaker, and on increasing the temperature a point is soon reached, when the muscle no longer contracts. The greater the weight to be raised by the muscle the sooner does this apparent death supervene. The muscle is not dead however, for if the temperature be lowered, the muscle again becomes contractile. Rosenthal found that a similar result is reproduced by temperature in nerves (*Centralblatt*, p. 276, 1866). The oftener the experiment was repeated with a muscle the lower became the degree of temperature at which the muscular power became weakened. Schmulewitsch further found that muscle, like caoutchouc, has its elasticity increased by a high temperature. This fact he considers of great importance, for, according to Wertheim, the elasticity of metals is diminished by heat. He thinks that the difference in the deportment of elasticity of muscle and metal under the influence of heat, may greatly assist in the comprehension of the nature of elasticity. He moreover regards this alteration of muscular elasticity by heat as furnishing fresh proof of Weber's view, that muscular contraction is nothing more than the play of elastic forces. In his opinion the mechanical work performed by a muscle increases on raising the temperature because the elasticity increases. He believes that his experiments serve to explain the greater muscular energy and rapidity of exhaustion in the case of those who inhabit warm climates, and why it is, that in summer the inhabitants of temperate regions are not so able to sustain prolonged muscular exertion as they are in winter.

Organs of Special Sense.

EYE.—Coccius (*Der Mechanisums der Accomodation des menschlichen Auges nach Beobachtungen im Leben*. 8vo. p. 153, Leipsic, 1868) has made a number of observations on the mechanism of accommodation in the human eye by examining during life the eyes of those who had had iridectomy performed upon them. He observed that when the accommodation of the eye is altered from that for a distant, to that for a near object, the ciliary processes advance and become somewhat larger ; the zonule becomes broader ; and the dark band which represents the border of the lens becomes broader and darker. Atropin occasions a decided retraction, Calabar Bean, a decided advance of the ciliary processes. He thinks that the cause of these changes can only be found in the action of the ciliary muscle. He thinks that the ciliary muscle cannot have a fixed point anywhere but anteriorly near the canal of Schlemm, else the ciliary processes could not be drawn forward. He thinks that the lateral swelling of these is due to compression of their veins by the contracting muscle. The increased curvature of the lens during positive accommodation (accommodation for near objects) is according to him not only due to the traction exercised by the ciliary muscle, but also to pressure.

Helmholtz's theory is that during negative accommodation the lens is kept flat by the elasticity of the zonule, and that during positive accommodation the ciliary muscle counteracts the action of the zonule, and the lens becomes more · convex by the action of its own elasticity. In opposition to this, Coccius adduces the fact that the transition from accommodation for distant to that for near objects, takes place more rapidly than the inverse movement does. He thinks that this fact does not favour the idea that the elasticity of the zonule is greater than that of the lens, but that the lens returns to its somewhat flattened form during negative accommodation by reason of its own elasticity. (From an abstract in the *Centralblatt*, Nos. 31 and 32, 1868.)

On the other hand Hensen and Völckers (*Experimental untersuchung über den Mechanismus der Accomodation*. 8vo. pp. 56, Kiel, 1868), from numerous experiments on the eyes of dogs and pigs, support Helmholtz's theory of accommodation.

These authors made also some interesting observations on the movements of the iris in the dog. They found that after removal of the ciliary ganglion, the pupil is of medium size and insensible to the action of light. Nevertheless irritation of the cervical sympathetic produced dilatation as before removal of the ganglion, showing thereby that the sympathetic fibres do not pass through the ganglion : they form fine fibres which lie either upon the optic nerve, or in the surrounding tissue : irritation of the peripheral ends of these after they have been divided dilates the pupil, while irritation of the central portions occasions pain. Irritation of the ciliary nerves caused extreme contraction of the pupil. Irritation of the four chief ciliary nerves occasioned a pear-shaped contraction of the pupil. Dilatation of the pupil followed the use of atropin after, just as before removal of the ganglion.

After laying bare the ciliary muscle by removal of a portion of the sclerotic, it was seen to sink when the ciliary nerves were irritated, the portion of the choroid lying behind became arched forwards synchronously with the sinking of the muscle. (From an abstract in the *Centralblatt*, 1868, Nos. 29 and 30.)

EAR.—According to Helmholtz (Über die Mechanik der Gehör, Knöchelchen, *Verhand. d. Natur. Med. Ver. Heidelberg*, IV. p. 153—161 ; *Pflüger's Archives*, p. 1, Erstes Heft, 1868), by the transference of the vibrations of the tympanum to the much smaller membrane of the oval fenestra mechanical power is thereby gained for throwing the somewhat immoveable fluid of the labyrinth into vibration. The apparently loose connections of the tympanic ossicles would seem to be unfavourable to the transmission of fine vibrations, but Helmholtz shows that the firmness of the bony chain is much greater than has hitherto been supposed.

Among other things he points out that the articular surfaces of the Malleus and Incus are furnished on their inferior aspects with little processes or teeth (Sperrzähnen), which are so placed that when the Malleus moves outwards the articular surfaces easily separate as far as the somewhat loose capsule will allow, when however, the Malleus moves inwards it embraces the Malleus with great firmness. The consequence of this is, that when air is blown into the tympanic cavity, the Membrana Tympani can move outwards without dragging the Stapes out of the Fenestra Oralis.

Helmholtz also shows that the curvature of the Membrana Tympani, while it diminishes the amplitude of the vibrations increases their force.   (From an abstract in the *Centralblatt*, No. 15, 1868.)

Miscellanea.

IMPERMEABILITY OF THE VESICAL EPITHELIUM.—Susini ("Recherches sur l'imperméabilité de l'épithélium vésical," *Jl. de l'Anatomie,* 1868, p. 144—166) has performed a number of experiments which lead him to believe that the absorptive power which some authors have attributed to the epithelium lining the bladder does not in all probability exist.   Through a catheter introduced into his own bladder, he injected solutions of Iodide and Ferrocyanide of Potassium, and extract of Belladonna : but he could obtain no evidence of the absorption of these substances.

A like negative result followed the injection of Curara into the bladder of a dog in the hands of Bernard.   Susini has performed a number of other experiments which support his conclusion.

ON FORCE IN THE ANIMAL BODY.—Dr B. W. Richardson gives a number of ingenious propositions in the *Medical Times and Gazette,* March 21, 1868, on this subject.   His propositions chiefly bear on the physiology of the nervous system.

DR. FRASER'S REPORT.

Physiological Action of Medicinal and Poisonous Substances.

TARTAR EMETIC.—Dr Alfred Nobiling (*Zeitschrift für Biologie,* IV. Band. 1 Hft. ; and *Practitioner*, No. II. 1868) has made some researches into the effects of tartar emetic in small doses. He believes that this drug has a compound action, the antimonial being distinct from the potash effects.   The latter produce cardiac depression, while the former influence the alimentary canal.   The principal portion of this paper is, however, occupied with questions of a purely Therapeutical bearing.

BROMIDE OF POTASSIUM.—In addition to the numerous investigations into the physiological action of this salt, which we have referred to on previous occasions, we have now to mention, one of considerable importance by Dr. J. H. Bill, Director of the U. S. Army Laboratory (*American Journal Med. Sc.*, July, 1868). The experiments were made on man, and extended over a long period of time, and they entailed a vast amount of labour on the investigator. Dr. Bill found that the quantity of urine passed in the twenty-four hours was increased by the bromide, and that this was not due to any increase in the quantity of fluid drunk, for thirst was not caused, even with the largest doses. The acidity of the urine was usually increased; the colouring matters were invariably increased; while the urea was not affected. The phosphoric acid varied; but small doses always increased it. The chlorides were greatly increased except with poisonous doses; and this increase was due to chloride of potassium. Even after poisonous doses, bromides were but scantily present in the urine, but they were readily found in the fæces, in the pharyngeal mucus, and in the pulmonary fluid. Uric acid was increased by both bromide of potassium and of sodium; but mostly by the former. The excretion of carbonic acid by the lungs was decidedly decreased, but this decrease was followed in the days succeeding the use of the drug by increase above the normal quantity. It was also found that the weight of the fæces was diminished. Dr. Bill expresses a decided opinion that the effects of bromide of potassium are not due to any separate or special action of either bromine or potassium, but to the combined *salt*. The author's views as to the action on the nervous system may be thus summarized: it is "an anæsthetic to the nerves of the mucous membranes, and a depressor of their action. Its hypnotic effects are secondary."—At the conclusion of a valuable paper on the therapeutic uses of this substance, Dr Russell Reynolds (*Practitioner*, July, 1868) expresses his opinion that its specific action is exercised on the vaso-motor nerves, and that it acts on these as a "sedative," reducing such morbid activity as would lead to the spasmodic narrowing of vessels, and consequent irregularity in the supply of blood. Dr Reynolds also advances the following among other negations—1st, Bromide of potassium does not lessen the force or frequency of the normal pulse. 2ndly, It does not, in therapeutic doses, affect notably any of the secretions. Occasionally the amount of urinary water appears to be augmented, but this result is not invariable. 3rdly, It does not interfere with the reproductive functions of either sex.

BROMATES.—Dr Rabuteau (*Centralblatt*, 1868, p. 448; and *Gaz. Hebd.* 1868, No. 17) has made some researches with bromic acid and the bromates of potash, soda, lead, and quinia, to determine if bromates are reduced in the system. He found that small doses are converted in the organism into bromides. When large doses are given, a part is rapidly eliminated (in about twenty minutes) unchanged, while the remainder afterwards escapes as bromide.

PHOSPHORUS.—M. Ranveir has examined the local action of phosphorus, and his results, originally communicated to the Société de Biologie, have been recently published (*Arch. Gén. de Médecine*, Juillet, 1868). This substance is usually regarded as an irritant, but this opinion is opposed by M. Ranvir. He placed fragments of phosphorus under the skin and in the muscles of frogs, and found that they died in two or three weeks with the usual characteristic appearances, the liver and kidneys having undergone fatty degeneration. The fragments of phosphorus were but slightly diminished in volume and retained their transparent appearance, while the tissues with which they had been in contact did not exhibit inflammatory changes, such as exudation, suppuration, or even thickening of the connective tissue. In dogs and guinea-pigs, poisoning was not produced by the introduction of phosphorus under the skin. The animals were killed on the tenth or fifteenth day of the experiment, and were found to be perfectly healthy; but the fragments of phosphorus were enclosed in slight circumscribed swellings of connective tissue. These experiments appear to show that in place of being a local stimulant, phosphorus is a *contra-stimulant* to the tissues. The author supposes that it is in virtue of this action that phosphorus produces fatty degeneration, when acting through the blood.———— Mialhe, in a note on the absorption of phosphorus (*Centralblatt*, No. 33, 1868, p. 527; and *Union Méd.* 1868), discards his former view that it is absorbed by the action of alkalies, in favour of the view that the absorption is effected by the fat in the bowels. He adduces as evidence in support of this, the observation that persons recovering after phosphorus-poisoning have relapses when they take food. According to him, phosphorus acts as such and not in chemical combination (see Dybkowsky, *Journ. of Anat. and Phys.*, Nov. 1867, p. 183), for phosphuretted-hydrogen would be decomposed in the blood into phosphorus and water.——In order to discover if the icterus in phosphorus-poisoning is catarrhal, by the plugging of the intestinal portion of the biliary duct, Wyss (*Centralblatt*, No. 46, 1868, p. 736) made biliary fistulæ in dogs, and injected phosphorus-oil into the rectum. These dogs became jaundiced, biliary acids were found in their urine, and bile and mucus, in place of bile only, escaped from the fistula. The last sometimes completely plugged the opening of the fistula. Wyss concludes that the icterus in phosphorus poisoning is catarrhal, but that the catarrh is not limited to the opening of the biliary duct.——The first portion of an elaborate research by Dr Lecorché is published in the *Archives de Physiologie* (No. 4, 1868), but we defer our abstract until the remainder has been published.

PRUSSIC ACID.——M. Preyer's name is already intimately associated with the present condition of our knowledge of the physiological action of prussic acid. In a recent publication (*Die Blausäure. Physiologisch Untersucht.* 1868), he adds many important and interesting facts, among which are the following. In *small* or *moderate* fatal doses, prussic acid acts by suddenly depriving the blood of its oxygen. In these circumstances, resaturation of the blood with oxygen, if quickly accomplished, will restore the animal to life, without any secondary evils. When, however, prussic acid is given in *large* fatal doses, paralysis of the heart is produced in addition to the above effect. Oxygenation of the blood is, in the latter circumstances, of no avail; indeed, the cases are probably quite beyond our power of treatment. Preyer believes that where apnoea without cardiac paralysis exists—after small or moderate doses—the chances of successful treatment are extremely encouraging. He considers that the usual methods of producing blood-oxygenation, such as insufflation of the lungs with oxygen and artificial respiration, are too slow in their operation, and recommends sulphate of atropia as a true physiological antidote to prussic acid. This substance paralyses the peripheral terminations of the vagi in the heart and lungs, and, at the same time, stimulates the nerve-centres in such a manner as to produce rapid respiration. Preyer makes the very important announcement that after the administration of small, or moderate, fatal doses of prussic acid to rabbits and guinea-pigs, fatal consequences have been prevented by the exhibition of sulphate of atropia in minute doses.

IODIDE OF PHOSPHETHYLL.—M. Vulpian (*Archives de Physiologie*, No. 3, 1868, p. 472) had occasion to employ various preparations of phosphorus in diseases of the spinal cord, among which was iodide of phosphethyll. He found that this substance appeared to have no effect on man in doses of one grain and a half, and that only nausea and vomiting were caused when fifteen grains was introduced into a dog's stomach. On the other hand, it proved to be a violent poison to frogs. Vulpian describes an experiment in which he introduced a minute quantity under the skin of a frog. In eight or ten minutes a condition of general paralysis was present, during which he found that the motor nerve conductivity was destroyed, while ideo-muscular irritability was retained and the cardiac contractions continued. He concludes that iodide of phosphethyll resembles those poisons that cause, at a certain period in the development of their effects, the same action as curare on the functions of the motor nerves.

PAPAVERINE.—The physiological action of papaverine on man has been studied by Dr Leidesdorf (*Wochenblatt der Zeitschrift der k. k. Gesellschaft der Aertze in Wien*, 1868, No. 14). He examined the hydrochlorate and phosphate, but found the latter objectionable as it caused considerable inflammation when subcutaneously administered. Papaverine acts as a narcotic and soporific, and produces muscular relaxation. It reduces the frequency of the pulse without any unpleasant secondary action; and appears to relax the bowels slightly. Its effects are manifested in about three hours, and continue for from twenty-four to forty-eight hours. Continued use does not seem to induce tolerance. Leidesdorf recommends doses of from half a grain to one grain for internal use, and from three to five drops of a solution of six grains of hydrochlorate of papaverine to sixty drops of water, for subcutaneous injection.

CAFFEINE.—The action of this substance on man and the lower animals has been studied with great care by Dr M. Leven (*Archives de Physiologie*, No. 1, 1868, p. 179). The author asserts that the principal effects of coffee are due to this active principle, of which coffee contains 17 per cent.; and that each individual absorbs about twenty grains of caffeine daily (in France? F.). Leven's most important conclusions are :—1. Caffeine excites the heart directly. At first, the circulation and the respirations are accelerated ; the pulse is more rapid and softer ; and the secretions are augmented. 2. The central nervous system, and the nerves are irritated (?). 3. The voluntary and involuntary muscles contract with increased energy. The voluntary muscles are affected with tremulous or with general contractions ; the fibres of the stomach, intestines, and bladder contract equally. 4. In the second period, the heart's contractions are weakened ; the frequency and tension of the pulse is diminished ; and the activity of the muscles and nerves is lowered, without being destroyed. 5. Caffeine does not completely abolish the reflex function, nor does it destroy the conductivity of the nerves or the irritability of the muscles. 6. The frog's heart continues to beat after death. 7. Caffeine and Coffee possess, in common with alcohol, the power of diminishing the excretion of urea, and of retarding tissue-waste. 8. The fatal dose of caffeine for frogs is $\frac{1}{15}$th of a grain, for guinea-pigs from one and a half to two grains, for rabbits from five to eight grains, but it may be given to man in doses of upwards of thirty grains without any bad effects.

THEINE.—Dr Leven has also published an important investigation into the action of theine (*Archives de Physiologie*, No. 3, 1868, p. 470). He believes that although this active principle is said to be chemically the same as caffeine, physiology proves it to be distinct. He thus summarizes his results :—1. The toxic (fatal) dose of theine is greater than that of caffeine—that of the latter being about one half of the former. 2. Theine produces convulsive movements in the limbs, wherein it differs from caffeine. 3. It agrees with caffeine in directly exciting the heart and the respiratory movements, in increasing the arterial tension, and, by exciting the circulation, in stimulating the central nervous system, without destroying its functions or those of the nerves. 4. The tetanic state induced by theine (as well as by caffeine) is caused by excitation of the spinal cord. 5. Theine does not abolish the properties of muscle ; and the heart's contractions do not cease immediately after death.

CHINOVIC ACID.—This is a resinous acid contained in all cinchona barks. Its physiological effects have been partially examined by Dr G. Kerner, in a paper treating mainly of its therapeutic value (*Wiener Med. Wochensch.*, 43 ; and *Practitioner*, No. 2, 1868, p. 127). He finds that it adds greatly to the tonic effects of bark, and that it is not liable, like quinia, to cause "cerebral congestion."

CYNOGLOSSUM OFFICINALE.—Dr J. Setschenow was informed by Dr Diedülin of St Petersburgh, that the alcoholic extract prepared from the fresh plant acts on vertebrates like curare. Dr S. made a few experiments on frogs (*Centralblatt*, No. 14, 1868, p. 211) with this extract, which were confirmatory of Dr Diedülin's observation. In eight or ten minutes after poisoning with a minute portion of the extract, the frogs were completely paralysed; and the condition of the muscular and nerve systems and of the heart was the same as after the administration of curare.

BELLADONA.—Dr Meuriot has published a most important and elaborate research on the physiological action of belladona (*Bulletin Génér. de Thérapeutique*, Tome LXXV., 1868, pp. 5 and 49). We can allude to only a few of his conclusions. 1. The local application of sulphate of atropia to the frog's web produces contraction of the arteries, a marked activity of the circulation, and then, if the quantity applied be large, a stasis in the veins, which frequently appears, afterwards, in the arteries also. Hence, the tissues are, first, pale and, subsequently, congested. The same general effects are produced on the blood-vessels by internal administration. 2. Atropia invariably accelerates the heart's action; but if a poisonous dose be given, this acceleration is succeeded by slowing. 3. With a small dose, the arterial tension is increased and the cardiac contractions rendered more frequent; the former effect being due to contraction of the blood-vessels, and the latter to paralysis of the terminations of the vagi. 4. In small doses, atropia always increases the number of the respiratory movements, even after section of the vagi; and in large doses, it first increases and then diminishes or paralyses them. These effects are accounted for by the excitability of the medulla being increased by small doses, while the pulmonary branches of the vagi are paralysed by large ones. It follows from this that it is necessary to give large doses in order to influence the pulmonary branches of these nerves. Ignorance of these facts is, according to Meuriot, the reason why belladona so often fails in asthma, when other drugs, in very small doses, have a beneficial effect. 5. Experiments on frogs show that atropia first destroys sensibility, and then destroys the excitability of motor nerves; but it does not abolish the irritability of muscles unless very large doses are given. In man, loss of sensibility has been found to occur in only very grave cases of poisoning. Still, in therapeutic doses it possesses the property of diminishing pain, but this effect is only a topical one. 6. Atropia invariably increases the reflex power of the cord—an assertion which is in opposition to the opinion of the majority of writers on this subject. 7. Belladona cannot be regarded as a hypnotic, but it is, perhaps, a stupifying narcotic. Small, or therapeutic doses cause agitation and sleeplessness, somewhat larger doses cause various disturbances of the organs of sense, vertigo, hallucinations, uneasiness, general trembling, and, at times, a strange sense of fear, fantastic dreams, and gay delirium; and poisonous doses cause noisy delirium, interrupted by exacerbations of a furious character, and followed by trismus, loquacity, continual agitation, helplessness, and coma, often accompanied with convulsions and clonic contractions. The effects on the brain are due to disturbances of the circulation, and not to any elective action on the cerebrum. This opinion is supported by the observations of Schroff, who found that delirium occurred only when the frequency of the pulse was increased; and by the enormous congestion of the encephalic vessels, which is seen in animals killed with this poison. 8. The temperature is increased in man by some tenths of a degree, from 0·5 to 1·1. In the lower animals, small doses increase and large doses diminish the temperature; an increase of from 2 to 3 degrees and a diminution of from 4 to 5 having been sometimes observed. These effects on the temperature are supposed to result from changes in the circulation. 9. Atropia seems to diminish all the secretions with the exception, in certain circumstances, of the urine, which is, however, more properly an excretion. The modifications in the effects on the urine are due to differences in the circulation : small doses augment the blood-pressure and, thus, have a diuretic action; poisonous doses diminish the blood-tension and, therefore, either diminish or altogether prevent this excretion. Dr Meuriot concludes this valuable paper by stating that belladona should no longer be regarded as a narcotic or even as a narcotico-acid; that it has a special action on the blood-vessels and on the innervation of the heart, in virtue of which all its other physiological effects are produced; and that it should therefore be placed in the class of the *vasculo-cardiacs* of M. Sée.

DIGITALIS.—Dr Constantin Paul, the able editor of the last edition of Trousseau's *Traité de Thérapeutique*, has published a research on the influence of digitalis on the pulse (*Bulletin Général de Thérapeutique*, Tome LXXIV., 1868, p. 193), in which his principal results were obtained by the use of the sphygmograph. He thus states his conclusions:—Digitalis, in small doses, generally diminishes the frequency of the pulse; in large doses, it increases it. When digitalis is exhibited in such doses as to produce its hyposthenic effects, it lowers the arterial tension; and the contrary effect may, possibly, be produced by very small doses, as some investigators have asserted. Finally, it is probable that digitalis raises the arterial tension when it diminishes the frequency of the pulse, and that it lowers this tension when it increases the number of the pulsations.

CYCLAMINE.—In 1860, Dr Vulpian had observed that Cyclamine (an active principle of Cyclamen Europæum) causes in frogs a rapid decomposition of the fluids with which it is brought in contact, and the appearance in them, before the death of the animal, of numerous vibriones. Since then he has further investigated this interesting fact (*Archives de Physiologie*, No. 3, 1868, p. 466). These vibriones may be developed in the blood of frogs not only when Cyclamine is introduced under the skin, but also when it is placed in the œsophagus. After the latter operation, the frog remains in apparently good health for two or three days, but soon after dies. If the blood or blood serum be examined before death, but during symptoms, small granulations in active movement and several vibriones will be always discovered. Blood taken from the heart, even before death, will also be found to contain these bodies. Vulpian has also discovered that the blood thus affected may, by inoculation, cause in other frogs this same diseased condition; and that this condition is indefinitely transmissible from diseased to healthy frogs. The presence of these vibriones in the blood produces, after a time, an alteration of the plasma, sufficient to render life impossible. Thus, the symptoms appear only after a certain interval, and are then progressive. When death occurs, usually about two days after the vibriones may be discovered in the blood, this fluid is generally blackish in colour, and does not redden on exposure to the air. A microscopic examination of this blood shows that the red and white corpuscles retain their normal characters. Nevertheless, several of the red corpuscles have been found to contain vibriones in their interior, but more commonly, the vibriones connected with these corpuscles are simply adherent to their surfaces. Vibriones may also be seen in several of the white corpuscles.

CHEMISTRY AND PHYSIOLOGY.—In an ingenious, though mainly theoretical, paper, Dr W. H. Broadbent makes "an attempt to apply chemical principles in explanation of the action of poisons" (*Proceedings of the Royal Society*, Lond. Vol. XVI., 1868, p. 465). The author introduces his subject by stating the two following postulates:—1. "That there must be some relation between the substance administered and the animal organism, on which the effects depend. 2. That, so far as the substance is concerned, the basis of the relation can only be its chemical properties, using the term in its widest sense." From these he derives three corollaries, the second of which —that the action of food, remedies, and poisons, must be capable of explanation on the same principles—is taken as the guide in his inquiry. The paper is chiefly occupied with the effects of organic poisons, whose action is principally exerted on the nervous system. He asserts that the source of nerve-force is oxidation, and the seat of this the nerve-structures. Various data lead him to conclude that the constituent of the nerve-structures, by whose oxidation force is yielded, possesses "chemical tension." All the poisons that powerfully affect the nervous system contain nitrogen, and possess chemical tension. Nitrogen cannot be the poisonous element; but it is the pivot on which this influence turns. Its affinity for H_1O_1 and C is but feeble. "When, therefore, in a molecule containing C_1H_1 and N_1 or C_1H_1N and O_1, the elements are not so arranged that the mutual affinities of C_1H_1 and O co-operate to maintain the integrity of the molecule; there may be a more or less powerful tendency on the part of C_1H_1 and O to rearrange themselves without regard to the N_1 or to combine with O or H_2O if present." To this the author applies the term chemical tension[1]. The manifestations of nerve-force are asserted to depend on the varying degrees and directions of this tension in the substances introduced into the blood. The author then proceeds to apply his theory in explanation of the action of prussic acid. This poison is carried by the blood to the nerve-centres; "under the influence of the affinities thus brought to bear upon it (affinities that normally determine the oxidation by which nerve-force is evolved), its elements are dislocated from each other, and C and H liberated in the latent condition, appropriate the O destined for the evolution of nerve-force, which is thus arrested." The author concludes his paper by referring to, and attempting to explain, several of the objections against the theory he propounds; but we shall not dwell on these, as the present paper does not contain a full discussion of his explanations.—Bearing on this interesting subject of the relation of chemistry to physiology, is an investigation by MM. F. Jolyet and A. Cahours on some of the substitution compounds of aniline (*Comptes Rendus*, Tome LXVI., 1868, p. 1131). It is well known that an equivalent hydrogen may be substituted in various compounds by an organic radical without chemically changing the fundamental properties of the original compound. The French investigators have for their object the solution of the question:—Does such a substitution modify the physiological properties of the compound? For this purpose they compared the action of aniline with that of ethylaniline, of methylaniline, and of amylaniline. The physiological action of these aniline-derivatives was found to be perfectly different from that of aniline itself; the most prominent action of the former being the abolition of the functions of the cerebro-spinal centres, that of the latter, excitation of these centres and the consequent production of convulsions. The authors, therefore, give an affirmative answer to their question.

DR GAMGEE'S REPORT.
Physiological Chemistry.
DIGESTION.

ACTION OF THE PANCREAS.—Senator (*Virchow's Archiv*, XLIII. 358—367) finds that the pancreas exerts a similar action upon albuminates as it was shewn by Kühne to exert upon fibrin. In one experiment a solution of albuminate containing 34·4 grammes of dry substance in two litres of water, was digested with 36·5 grammes of pancreas. At the end of five hours little action had taken place. After 14 hours 16·71 parts of the albuminate (calculated dry) remained undissolved. From the solution 0·99 grammes of albumen, 1·75 grammes of peptone, besides 4·5 grammes of leucine and 7 grammes of tyrosine were separated. In a second experiment at the end of twenty hours 73·5 per cent. of albuminate had been dissolved. In an experiment of Kühne's nearly 87 parts of the quantity of

[1] By "chemical tension" the author appears to mean the *unexhausted potential energy of the compound.* F.

fibrin placed in contact with the pancreas were dissolved in the course of 4½ hours, so that although the action of the pancreatic ferment appears to be substantially the same on fibrin and alkaline albuminates, with the former the process proceeds with greater energy than with the latter.

DIGESTIVE ACTION OF INTESTINAL JUICE.—Schiff (*Fl. Morgagni*, 1867, No. 9, *Centralblatt*, 1868, No. 23) has made many observations on dogs with duodenal and jejunal fistulæ. When the fistula had been perfectly established and the mucous membrane of the intestine appeared pale, he found that it became red on mechanical irritation, as well as through the influence of drastic or saline substances (Aloes, Jalap, Sulphate of Sodium). In the case of the first of these drugs the secretion was decidedly, of the second slightly, and of the third not at all increased. Little pieces of albumen, fresh casein, fibrin, cooked and fresh muscle, were dissolved when introduced into the fistula. Starch was very rapidly converted into sugar.

Dr W. Leube (*Centralblatt*, 1868, No. 19) has also examined the digestive action of the intestinal juice.

1. Raw fibrin is dissolved by intestinal juice and the peptone which results possesses the following properties. It is not precipitated by boiling; when treated with solution of mercurous nitrate it gives Millon's reaction. It is precipitated by solutions of tannic acid and corrosive sublimate. The peptone possesses the property of diffusing through parchment paper.

2. Intestinal juice converts cane sugar into glucose.

INFLUENCE OF DIET ON THE EXHALATION OF MARSH GAS.—Reiset (*Comptes Rendus*, LXVI. 172—177) states that calves fed on grass expire considerable quantities of marsh gas; this does not occur when they are fed on milk.

BLOOD.

ON CARBONIC ACID IN BLOOD CORPUSCLES.—Alexander Schmidt (*Arbeiten aus des Phys. Inst. zu Leipzig*, Mitgetheilt durch C. Ludwig, Leipzig, 1868, p. 30—57) has attempted to ascertain whether the blood corpuscles contain carbonic acid. He allowed blood to flow from the blood-vessels of a living animal simultaneously into two tubes filled with mercury. The tubes were so arranged that their contents might easily, and without risk of air getting access to them, be transferred to the receiver of a mercurial pump. One of the tubes was allowed to remain undisturbed so as to permit the serum to separate, whilst the other was defibrinated. Determinations were made simultaneously of the gases in the serum and defibrinated blood. In one experiment (No. I.) 100 vols. of blood yielded 30·50 vols. of CO_2, whilst 100 vols. of serum contained 31·95 vols. In another (VI.) experiment 100 vols. of blood yielded 33·88 vols. of CO_2, whilst 100 volumes of serum gave 42·33 vols. of CO_2.

From his researches the author arrives at the following conclusions.

1.   The corpuscles of normal blood always contain CO_2.   The amount is, however, very variable, rising occasionally to the proportion present in the serum ; more commonly it amounts only to a few per cents. of the volume of the corpuscles.

2.   The amount of CO_2 which the corpuscles contain is affected by bringing the blood in contact with CO_2; the amount always undergoes variations under these circumstances, sometimes being increased, and at others diminished.   When the amount of CO_2 only amounts to 40 per cent. of the volume of blood with which it is brought into contact, CO_2 continues to diffuse out of the corpuscles; this diffusion goes on until the relative proportion of the gas in the serum and the corpuscles is such that the quotient obtained by dividing the amount of CO_2 present in the serum by that present in the whole blood sinks to 0·77—0·87.

If this great facility for the diffusion of carbonic acid out of the corpuscles did not exist, the amount of the gas within them would be always on the increase.   When the blood is however saturated with CO_2 the amount in the corpuscles rises so that it nearly equals that present in the serum.

As the amount of CO_2 in the serum is confessedly larger than can be retained by simple absorption, we must in the case of the corpuscles, as in that of the serum, admit the existence of a substance capable of combining with CO_2.   The substance present in the corpuscles which has the power of fixing the CO_2, can only do so as long as the pressure of the carbonic acid in the medium around them does not fall below a certain figure.

In a supplement to his paper the author states that he has proved experimentally that when blood is agitated with oxygen so as fully to saturate the corpuscles with that gas, a certain amount of carbonic acid is still retained by them.

The paper on Respiration within the blood, by A. Schmidt, of which an abstract (taken from the *Centralblatt*) was published in the last No. of the *Journal of Anatomy*, will be found at page 98 of Ludwig's *Arbeiten*, 1868.

Dr E. Sertoli (*Centralblatt*, No. 10, 1868), gives a preliminary notice of the results of experiments intended to elucidate the state of combination in which carbonic acid exists in the blood.   Amongst other facts referred to the author mentions that if globulin, obtained from the crystalline lens, be diffused in water and added to serum of ox's blood, which has been deprived of its gases by boiling in vacuo, a fresh and not insignificant quantity of carbonic acid is evolved.   If air be introduced into the cavity of the peritoneum, and allowed to remain within it for one hour, it is found to contain 6 per cent. of carbonic acid.

CHANGES IN THE BLOOD CIRCULATING THROUGH THE MUSCLES OF CARNIVORA.—*C. Ludwig* and *A. Schmidt* (*Centralblatt*, 1868, No.

32) have made an investigation on the changes which the blood undergoes when circulating through the muscles of carnivora. Defibrinated blood was caused to circulate through muscles. The authors found that arterial blood preserves in a high degree the irritability of muscles and nerves, and restores the irritability when it has been lost; yet after twenty hours the irritability of muscles, through which a current of arterialized blood has been kept up, is lost. The muscle removes O from the blood circulating through it. Blood which contains little oxygen may give it up entirely to the muscle. As a rule muscles in action were found to remove more oxygen from the blood than muscles at rest. The amount of CO_2 formed by the muscle was greater than corresponded to the amount of oxygen absorbed by it.

AMMONIA IN BLOOD.—Brücke (*Centralblatt*, 1868, No. 14) states that ammonia is exhaled by healthy blood at a temperature of 18°— 20° C. The method employed consisted in placing the vessel containing the blood under a bell jar; under which was also a vessel containing dilute sulphuric acid. After a short time the acid yields, when tested with Nessler's reagent, a perceptible ammonia reaction. Under the same circumstances ammonia was obtained from sputum and healthy tears, from fresh egg-albumen, and from urine, even when the latter had an acid reaction.

COMPOUNDS OF NITRITES WITH HÆMOGLOBIN.—Dr Gamgee (*Phil. Trans.* 1868) pursuing his investigation on the action of nitrites on blood has arrived at the following conclusions. 1. When a solution of any nitrite acts upon blood, peculiar changes occur in the colour, and simultaneously in the absorption-spectrum. 2. These changes are due to the formation of compounds presenting the same crystalline form, colour, and spectrum, whatever the nitrite which has been employed in their preparation. 3. These bodies appear to be compounds of the nitrite used with oxidized hæmoglobin. 4. The substances formed by this process of chemical addition, although isomorphous with hæmoglobin, differ from it in many of those remarkable properties upon which its functions in the economy of the body depend. By this process of addition the blood-colouring-matter appears to have lost its power of absorbing oxygen. 5. The addition of nitrites to hæmoglobin appears to result in the locking up of the loosely combined oxygen, so as to make it irremoveable by CO, or by a vacuum.

CRYSTALLINE HÆMATINE.—Dr Thudicum (*Tenth Report of the Medical Officer of the Privy Council*, pp. 224—226) describes and figures the different spectra of Hæmatine, and states that he has succeeded in obtaining this substance in a crystalline condition. He finds, in fact, that hæmine crystals consist of pure hæmatine, and not of its hydrochlorate, as has been generally supposed.

CRUENTINE.—Dr Thudicum also describes, under the name of Cruentine, a substance obtained by boiling hæmoglobin or hæmatine with sulphuric acid. "When human or animal hæmatocrystalline is boiled with sulphuric acid it becomes chemolysed (*sic*), the albumen dissolves and yields its particular products, a portion of the hæmatine also dissolves and colours the fluid ruby red, while a brownish red grumous matter remains suspended in the fluid in an insoluble state. This is a mixture of neutral cruentine with its sulphate. By washing with water this matter loses sulphuric acid, and becomes ultimately free from it. Treated with sulphuric acid it dissolves completely, and is now sulphate of cruentine[1]."

ACTION OF TINCTURE OF GUIACUM AND H_2O_2 ON BLOOD.—Dr Day of Geelong, in a paper on Allotropic Oxygen (*Australian Med. Jl.* May 1867), of which the reporter has only seen a notice in the *British Med. Journ.*, Sept. 5, 1868, describes a modification of the Guiacum test for blood. If to an exceedingly dilute solution of blood, a drop or two of tincture of guiacum be added, a precipitate of the uncoloured resin takes place. On the addition to the fluid of a small quantity of ether containing in solution peroxide of hydrogen, a bright blue colour is developed. The test is one of extreme delicacy, and the suggestion of its application to medico-legal purposes is valuable. The facts upon which it is founded have, however, long since been made out by Schmidt's investigations.

MUSCLES AND NERVES.

ON THE ORIGIN OF MUSCULAR FORCE.—In one of the Physiological Reports published in this Journal (Nov. 1867, p. 179) some allusion was made to the researches of Hermann (*Untersuchungen über den Stoffwechsel der Muskeln*). Owing to the work having appeared only a short time before, the sketch of Hermann's views then published was not sufficiently complete. Considering the importance of the subject it may be right to give an epitome of Hermann's researches and theory, as these are developed in his recently published work on Physiology; this course is rendered almost necessary in order that the reader should be enabled to follow our account of Hermann's still more recent work on the physiology of muscles and nerves.

Having drawn attention to the chief chemical processes which have in his opinion been made out with certainty as taking place when muscles are in a state of activity, and referred to the numerous less positively ascertained phenomena, Hermann shews that the

[1] The term *chemolysis* is applied by Dr Thudicum to "the artificial and mostly rapid decomposition of animal matters into proximate nuclei by means of chemical agents, which do not themselves undergo any change, but only combine for a time with some of the products, and may ultimately be removed entirely." Usually, however, Dr Thudicum seems to use boiling sulphuric acid (!) to induce *chemolysis*. There will probably not be much difference of opinion amongst chemists as to the kind of value to be attached to the characters of bodies procured by boiling blood or urine with strong sulphuric acid.—A. G.

following facts may be regarded as proved with respect to the nature of the chemical processes going on during muscular work. The chemical processes going on during muscular action are identical with the processes attending rigor mortis; for

1. A separated muscle produces the same total quantity of CO_2, be it directly made to pass into rigor, or previously caused to generate CO_2 by muscular contraction; the more CO_2 is formed during contraction, the less can be generated on the muscle passing into a state of rigor (Hermann).

2. The same is true in the case of sarco-lactic acid. On the occurrence of rigor least acid is produced by muscles which have previously been in a state of activity.

3. Both muscular contraction and rigor mortis are independent of the supply of oxygen; even in vacuo and in indifferent gases the muscle can contract and become rigid; these are, therefore, not processes of oxidation but of decomposition (Spaltungsprocesse), which lead to the saturation of strong affinities, through which a certain amount of potential energy becomes actual.

4. A restoration of the muscle which has lost its irritability, either through continued activity or through commencing rigor mortis, may be brought about by causing blood to circulate through it.

5. The muscle can pass directly from the condition of activity into that of complete rigor.

The simplest explanation of the chemical processes occurring during rigidity and the active condition is probably the following; the muscle contains constantly a store of a complicated nitrogenous substance (Inogene substance) which is capable of splitting up and developing energy; the products of the reaction are, besides others, carbonic acid, sarco-lactic acid and an albuminoid body, which separates at first in a gelatinous, but afterwards in a strongly contracted form (Myosin). The decomposition takes place very slowly in a state of rest, more rapidly the higher the temperature; it is suddenly increased by excitation, this sudden increase constituting the essential nature of the active condition. If the substance is used up no more muscular work is possible. As the *inogene* substance is necessary to muscular activity it is essential for the continued activity of a muscle that it should receive a continual supply of, or be the seat of a new formation of the substance. The restitution of a muscle is brought about by the blood (as has been already said) as well in the case of muscle exhausted by rigor as in that of muscle exhausted by work.

The restorative action of blood does not merely consist in supplying to the muscle a fresh store of Inogene substance, but also in removing the products of decomposition, which are themselves injurious to muscle. The blood removes carbonic acid and probably lactic acid, and gives up oxygen to the muscle. It is clear, however, that in addition to the latter it must convey to the muscle organic material rich in carbon and hydrogen, to make up for what has been thrown off in the shape of carbonic and lactic acids.

Whilst, on the one hand, the whole of the products of decomposition of the *Inogene substance* do not leave the muscle, (Myosin remaining in the muscle seeing that the nitrogen excretion is not increased during work), on the other, it is only the constituents of, and not the ready made substance, which are conveyed to the muscle; it is highly probable that the restitution of muscle, besides being attended by the removal of the products of muscular waste, consists in a synthesis of *Inogene*, in which Myosin takes a part, and to which blood contributes oxygen and a not yet separated organic substance free from nitrogen. Myosin would thus appear to take part in a kind of chemical circulation which goes on in muscle.

CHEMICAL EXPLANATION OF ELECTRO-MOTIVE PROPERTIES OF MUSCLE AND NERVE.—Proceeding from his supposition that both muscular action and muscular rigidity are dependent upon the same process of chemical decomposition (Spaltungsprocess) the author (Further remarks on the Physiology of muscles and nerves by L. Hermann. Berlin, Hirschwald, 1867. *Centralblatt*, 9th Nov. 1867, No. 48) tries to explain the electro-motive properties of muscle by supposing that the substance engaged in the decomposition behaves itself negatively in respect to those substances in contact with it, which are decomposing slowly or not at all. In support of this opinion the author adduces the fact that when cheese is placed in contact with a solution of milk sugar, if the conditions favourable to the lactic fermentation exist, the cheese behaves itself negatively to the sugar solution. The author sees a close analogy between the decomposition of sugar with the production of lactic acid, and the decomposition going on in muscle, and points out that the substances engaged in the more rapid transformations must act as ferments toward the neighbouring substances; a similar action must, in his opinion, go on, when artificial transverse sections become rigid, and in the process of propagation of muscular action.

The author points out:—1. That the negative relation of artificial transverse sections towards the longitudinal section is due to the layers near the point of section dying much more readily than the others[1].

2. The negativity of those points in the longitudinal section of a muscle which are close to a transverse section, in respect to the points more near to the equator of the section, is to be explained on the hypothesis that the more removed the layers are from the transverse section, the slower they are to die, and consequently less rapid is the process of chemical decomposition.

3. The fact that, in oblique sections of a muscle, the points situated near the acute angles are negative in relation to those lying near the oblique angles, is explicable on the supposition that owing to

[1] Of course the term dying must be in this case looked upon as synonymous with occurrence of rigor mortis, which as Hermann's previous researches have shewn, is necessarily connected with the decomposition of *Inogene*, and the evolution of *energy*.

the greater area of muscular substance which is exposed, death is more rapid in the former than in the latter.

The author attributes the current in uninjured muscles to inequalities in the rapidity of the decomposition going on within them; the currents which are observed immediately after the skin covering the muscles has been removed, are directed from the thinner muscles, and portions of muscle, towards the thicker; cold weakens these currents, by making the decomposition more slow, and can like scalding or radiant heat, which destroy the muscular substance, even reverse the direction of the currents, if it happens to act most energetically upon those portions of the muscle which were previously negative.

The reversal of the current in tetanus is attributed (simultaneous action of the entire muscle being presupposed) to the normal difference in the rate of decomposition being disturbed; the rate being suddenly increased, and especially in those parts which were previously less active. At the moment of the passage of a *wave of action* along a muscle, the author thinks that oscillations in the current must occur in consequence of the rate of decomposition being interfered with unequally at various points.

The preceding explanation is applied by the author also to the case of nerves in which, he thinks, there must, as in muscle, exist a substance which splits up during action and in the process of dying.

Electrotonus may be looked upon as due to an acceleration of decomposition at the cathode and a retardation of decomposition at the anode. As the action of the electrodes on the excitability of the nerve, according to Pflüger, is in harmony with the above supposition as to the decomposition, the author is inclined to consider excitability and rate of decomposition as being identical, and further that the disappearance of anelectrotonus and the commencement of cathelectrotonus, which according to Pflüger, are connected with excitability, indicate a sudden acceleration in the rate of decomposition and lead to the conclusion that whilst *excitability* on the one hand consists in sudden increase of decomposition, *conduction*, on the other consists in the propagation of a sudden increase of decomposition.

The only result of the splitting up of the hypothetical substance supposed by the author to exist in nerve, consists in the transmission of a similar chemical action to the particles around, and indeed throughout the continuity of the nerve; this transmitted chemical decomposition constitutes *conduction*. In the case of nerve the products of the chemical operation supposed to go on, have no function assigned to them; in muscle, on the other hand, one of the products of the reaction—Myosin—is the agent whereby the shortening of the fibre is effected, both in the process of muscular contraction, and in that of rigor mortis.

Without entering into a criticism of Hermann's views it may be well to point out that, according to Ranke's most recent researches, an increased oxygen consumption during work does occur in muscles separated from the organism (ausgeschnittenen Muskeln);

indeed this author considers that he has satisfactorily made out the respiration of muscles and nerves.

In connection with Hermann's researches it is here only necessary to remark that, since their appearance, Johannes Ranke has published an account of investigations on the conditions of the vitality of nerves and muscles which have led him to propose a very probable and much less hypothetical chemical theory of the muscle and nerve current. The reader is referred to the complete abstract of Ranke's book which appears in the present number of this Journal. Heidenhain (*Studien der Phys. Inst. zu Breslau*, Heft IV.) published lately, before the appearance of Ranke's book, a short paper in which he affirmed that he had never been able to discover an acid reaction in nerves which had been in a state of activity. His observations were entirely carried out on the sciatic nerve, of which the reaction very rarely, according to Ranke, becomes actually acid.

PRODUCTION OF HEAT DURING RIGOR MORTIS.—Drs Dybkowsky and Fick (*Centralblatt*, 1868, No. 13) confirm previous observers with regard to the evolution of heat during rigor mortis, shewing that the development of heat exactly coincides with the shortening of the muscular fibre. Their observations were made with thermometers made by Geissler as well as with thermo-electric arrangements.

DR THUDICUM ON THE CHEMISTRY OF MUSCLES.—It is almost hopeless to attempt to mention all the new bodies which Dr Thudicum has obtained by acting upon muscle and nerves with strong sulphuric acid, and of which he has as yet published little more than a catalogue (*Tenth Report of the Medical Officer of Health*, 1868). "I instituted an extensive research," says Dr Thudicum, "on the chemolysis of fibrin, albumen, caseine, blood, and almost every tissue and organ of the human body, the main features and results of which will be described in Chapter V.; and I obtained not only products which had been obtained by former observers since Braconnot and by my own former researches, but I was also fortunate enough to isolate six compounds, a portion of which were quite unknown hitherto, and another portion, though known, not having been hitherto discovered in the course of this process" (p. 186). The following are the six bodies referred to: 1st. A new alkaloid, to which, from its most striking power of fluorescence, Dr Thudicum gave the name of *Fluorescentine*. "The phenomena of fluorescence," says Dr Thudicum, "will in future yield important means of diagnosis in animal chemistry. When speaking of urochrome, I shall have to describe two of its products, which yield absorption and fluorescence phenomena in the spectrum and condensed sunlight. Possibly fluorescentine may be the chemolytic form of that particular part of the nucleus of albumen, which in the course of biolysis leads to urochrome, and by the chemolysis of the latter to omicholine and omicholic acid," (p. 238). 2nd. *Parafluine*, a substance accompanying fluorescentine, which is red, amorphous, readily soluble in alcohol and ether, but insoluble in water and dilute sulphuric acid. 3rd. A matter having a powerful odour, causing great irritation of the nose and eyes and in a concentrated state spasms of the muscles of the eyes and lacrymation. Its odour and action are like those of a mixture of mustard and garlic oil. Very curiously Dr Thudicum does not appear to have considered *this* substance worthy of a name! 4th. By the same process another product, *Fluopittine*, is obtained. Fluopittine is insoluble in dilute sulphuric acid and in ether, but is easily soluble in alcohol. 5th. A crystalline substance, called *Thiotherine*, containing sulphur, was obtained from albumen. "As the process is at present, only small quantities are obtainable, 70 pounds of acid and 50 pounds of hair having yielded me only a few grains." 6th. "*Fluorescentic acid*, which seems to be the basis of all albuminous substances" (!!)

DR THUDICUM ON THE CHEMISTRY OF BRAIN.—Having become satisfied of the unsatisfactory nature of all previous researches, Dr Thudicum has undertaken the task of examining the constitution of brain matter. "I found, however," says Dr Thudicum, "that none of these observers had even touched the question of the constitution of brain matter ; and that there was in this latter a nucleus of power holding together a molecule of immense size which could not be separated by any of the reagents employed by former observers. I therefore proceeded to split up this molecule by the process of chemolysis." "These researches," remarks the author further on, "left me the impression that the constitution of brain matter possesses some analogy to the constitution of the blood corpuscles, in this respect, that its basis is a body which contains phosphorus, nitrogen, carbon, hydrogen, and oxygen, and may be transformed into or appear in the shape of cerebric acid; that this body possesses originally the properties of a polydynamic alcohol, which is combined with a number of molecules of albumen corresponding to the number of its dynamicities" (!!)

MILK.

E. Klebs (*Centralblatt*, 1868, No. 27) in a paper entitled "Die pyrogeue Substanz," following up his observations which shewed that both pus and milk possess the power of blueing intensely guiacum tincture, has attempted to isolate the principles upon which this property depends. The following are his interesting results. (1) Casein precipitated from cow's milk by Hoppe-Seyler's method gives the reaction intensely. (2) Casein exposed for two or three days to the air ceases to give the reaction. (3) Some varieties of milk (e. g. mare's milk) do not cause the blueing of tincture of guiacum. (4) The "ozone-carrier" of casein is soluble in dilute hydrochloric acid of 1 per mille. The solution may be evaporated at low temperatures, and when dissolved again still gives the reaction. (5) From fresh pus a substance may by a similar treatment be obtained, which blues guiacum. (6) This substance introduced into the living body produces, like fresh pus, a rise in temperature; the author therefore gives to it the temporary name of *pyrogenous substance*.

A SOLUTION OF CASEIN OBTAINED BY DIALYSIS.—A. Müller (*Journ. f. Pract. Chem.* CIII. 49—51) by dialyzing solutions of casein in caustic soda obtained a neutral solution of casein which contained 2·15 per cent. of solid matter, and 0·11 per cent. of salts. The solution was not precipitated by heat, but fully precipitated by acids.

BILE.

BILE AND URINE PIGMENT.—Dr Max. Jaffé (*Centralblatt,* 1868, No. 16) has carefully studied the changes in the spectrum which attend the well-known colour reaction produced when impure nitric acid acts upon bile. As soon as the colour of the solution approaches a blue tint a broad dark absorption band between C and D, but nearer D, makes its appearance. On dilution this band is resolved into two, a and β, separated by a small space. These bands persist until the red tint appears in the fluid. Shortly after a and β, a third band is seen between b and F, designated γ, which attains its greatest intensity towards the end of the reaction, and then fades. By dissolving biliverdin in fuming HNO_3, and then cautiously neutralizing the excess of acid with NH_3, a stage is reached where the colour is nearly blue and the bands a and β are seen. On agitating the solution with water and chloroform, the latter dissolves out a dark violet body, insoluble in water, but easily soluble in alcohol, ether and chloroform; the slightest trace of acid causes it to assume a splendid blue colour. The acid solution shews the bands a and β, and slightly γ. The neutral and alkaline solutions possess no absorption bands. This pigment is soluble in strong sulphuric acid, and water precipitates green flakes from the solution. These flakes when treated with nitric acid develope the same tints as are produced by the action of the acid upon bile. The blue body described by Jaffé is obviously identical with Thudicum's previously described Cholocyanine, and the green flakes with Thudicum's Cholothalline to which he ascribed the formula $C_9H_{11}NO_3$. There is considerable discrepancy between Jaffé's and Thudicum's description of the spectrum of Cholocyanine.

On treating dog's bile with concentrated hydrochloric acid a red filtrate is obtained, shewing a band coincident with the previously described band γ, but darker and sharper. On rendering the solution alkaline by means of soda, the colour becomes yellow; the first band disappears and a new one (δ) is seen between b and F, but nearer to b. On acidifying, the first spectrum is obtained. On agitating with chloroform a part of the pigment is dissolved, and on evaporation the solution leaves a red residue soluble in water, alcohol and chloroform, precipitated from its aqueous solution by means of normal and basic acetates of lead. This pigment agrees so closely with normal urine pigment as to lead Jaffé to suspect their identity. (See Urine.)

ON PETTENKOFER'S REACTION.—Koschlakoff and Bogomoloff (*Centralblatt,* 1868, No. 33) have examined the spectrum of the intense red fluid developed by the action of sugar and sulphuric acid in the bile acids.

After developing the reaction the authors diluted the fluid with acetic acid and then examined the spectrum. With a medium concentration four absorption bands are seen; the widest and most intense near E; another at F, a third between D and E but nearer to D, and a fourth beyond D. When the fluid is less dilute the band at E is seen sharply, the one between D and E much less distinctly, and those at D and F very indistinctly. When sufficiently diluted with acetic acid the fluid exhibits dichroism. The authors point out that these characters enable us to distinguish the red fluid produced with bile acids from that generated by the action of sulphuric acid and sugar on albumen. The latter possesses a single absorption band between E and F.

Thudicum (*Op. cit.*) has also described the spectrum of Pettenkofer's reaction, but his description differs entirely from that of the authors quoted above. He has only noticed a single absorption band in the yellow.

Protagon when treated with sugar and sulphuric acid gives, according to Thudicum, the same colour as the bile acids, and possesses a very similar spectrum. The reading in the case of the band developed in Pettenkofer's reaction was

$$142^\circ - 141^\circ \, . \, 24' = 0 \cdot 36',$$

in the case of the Protagon reaction

$$141^\circ \, . \, 30' - 141^\circ = 0 \cdot 30'.$$

ACTION OF SULPHATE OF QUININE ON BILE.—Malinin (*Centralblatt*, 1868, No. 24) proves that when bile is treated with sulphate of quinine, glycocholate of quinine separates out as a crystalline mass.

URINE.

URINE PIGMENT.—Dr Jaffé (*Op. cit.*) states that, without any treatment, human urine shews, when a stratum 3—6 cubic cents. thick is examined with the aid of a very brilliant light, an absorption band at the border between the green and blue. This band corresponds with band γ developed by the action of HCl upon bile. By treating urine with lead acetate and decomposing the precipitate by means of sulphuric or oxalic acids the pigment is set free. It is soluble in chloroform, which removes it on agitation. The concentrated urine of fever is admirably suited for making the above observations. Urine pigment is, according to Jaffé, by no means an easily decomposed body, remaining unchanged in urine which has been exposed for some weeks.

ON THE ORIGIN OF THE URIC ACID OF THE URINE OF BIRDS.— G. Meissner (*Henle und Pfeufer's Zeitschrift* 13, XXXL 144—223) in opposition to the statement of Zalesky (*Centralbl.* 1865, 202) states that uric acid can be found in the blood of birds, if sufficient quantities be examined: for this purpose Meissner used the blood of 10—18 hens. He opposes the view that uric acid is formed by the kidneys and considers the liver to be the chief seat of the formation of uric acid in the animal body. This organ always contains large quantities of uric acid, 500 grammes of liver yielding $0 \cdot 31$ grammes of uric acid.

Meissner's other observations on the urine of birds are of great interest.

ORIGIN OF UREA IN THE URINE OF CARNIVORA.—As his researches on the formation of uric acid in birds had led Meissner to the conclusion that uric acid is almost entirely formed in the liver, he was led to enquire whether the urea in the urine of the carnivora (whose formation by the kidney he denies) is likewise, wholly or in part, produced by the liver.

Already Heynsius and Stokvis had, although not in a perfectly conclusive manner, proved the presence of urea in the liver. Meissner now finds considerable quantities as well in the liver of carnivorous as herbivorous animals. 474 grammes of dog's liver yielded 0·09 grms. of urea, and 347 grms. of rabbit's liver yielded 0·025 grms. of urea. For a description of the process which he employed in the separation of urea from liver Meissner's paper must be referred to.

As urea has been hitherto not detected, with certainty, in any organ but the liver—not even in the muscles—Meissner concludes that the urea of the urine is in great part derived from the liver.

In support of this opinion we have the facts that Frerichs and Städeler did not find urea in the urine of acute atrophy of the liver, nor Harley in that of chronic atrophy, whilst Alfred Vogel found it diminished in cases of cancer of the liver.

Meissner has also made interesting observations, although not of so novel and startling a character as those above reported, on the excretion of creatine, creatinine and other nitrogenous products, in the dog.

C. Voit (*Zeitschrift f. Biologie,* IV. 77—162; *Centralblatt,* 1868, No. 30) has with the help of his pupils Oertel, Zantl, F. Hofman, F. Halenke and Riederer, made observations of great interest on many of the subjects investigated by Meissner.

He has carefully estimated the amount of creatine in muscles of different animals under different circumstances. He confirms the observation of Nauroski that tetanized muscles are not richer in creatine than muscles at rest. The heart contains less creatine than other muscles. The blood contains, according to Voit, creatine but not creatinine, whilst the urine usually contains the latter and not the former substance. In discussing the question of the origin of urea in the animal body the author opposes the view that it is formed in the kidneys. Whilst he opposes this view he also disputes its origin in the blood, seeing that it is not proved that the organs do not form urea.

THEORY OF URAEMIA.—Voit looks upon uraemia as a true poisoning by the urinary constituents, not merely by urea. He attaches, for instance, importance to the action of the potash salts. He rejects Traube's hypothesis, as after extirpation of the kidney the blood is not watery, but on the contrary tenacious and thick.

ALBUMINURIA.—Stokvis (*Recherches expérimentales sur les conditions pathogéniques de l'albuminurie*. Mémoire Couronnée Bruxelles 1867. Abstracted at length in *Centralbl.* 1868, No. 14 and No. 15) has investigated many of the most interesting points in connection with Bright's disease, and we regret that for want of space we cannot give the chief results. One alone may be mentioned. The author does not admit that mere chemical alterations on the blood *can* produce pathological albuminuria.

URINE IN LEUKAEMIA.—Dr H. Jacubasch (*Virchow's Archiv*, May 1868, p. 196) publishes his observations on the conditions of the urine in two cases of splenic leukaemia.

His analyses shew that in leukaemia a marked diminution in the urinary solids occurs; lactic acid, acetic acid, and hypoxanthin occur as regular ingredients.

URINE OF DIABETES INSIPIDUS.—Prof. Mosler of Griesswald (*Virchow's Archiv*, May 1868, p. 229) gives the results of the examination of the urine in a case of this disease, which he calls *Inosuria with hydruria*. The results were as follows—presence of inosite, absence of grape sugar, presence of traces of albumen, great increase of urinary water, diminished urea excretion (23·8 grammes in 24 hours).

DECOMPOSITION OF URIC ACID.—Strecker has shewn (*Comptes Rendus*, LXVI. 538—539) that when uric acid is heated in sealed tubes with HCl or HI at from 160°—170° C., it splits up entirely into glycocine, carbonic acid, and ammonia thus;

$$C_5H_4N_4O_3 + 5H_2O = C_2H_5NO_2 + 3CO_2 + 3NH_3.$$

The author thinks that just as hippuric acid may be looked upon as glycobenzoic acid, so may uric acid be considered glycocyanuric acid,

$$C_7H_6O_3 + C_2H_5NO_2 - H_2O = C_9H_9NO_3$$
$$C_3H_3N_3O_3 + C_2H_5NO_2 - 2H_2O = C_5H_4N_4O_3.$$

CONSTITUTION OF LECITHIN. (*Centralblatt*, No. 28, 1868).—Diaconow states facts which confirm ·his previously published views on the constitution of this substance, viz. that it consisted of a compound of distearyl glyceryl-phosphoric acid with neurin = an acid salt of a substituted glycero-phosphoric acid. Further remarks have shewn that when an ethereal solution of Lecithin is shaken with dilute sulphuric acid, the watery solution which afterwards separates contains sulphate of neurin and the ethereal solution distearyl glyceryl-phosphoric acid. On neutralizing with potash a crystalline substance separates—Potassium Lecithin.

$$\left.\begin{array}{l}(C_{18}H_{35}O)_2 \\ C_3H_5 \\ PO \\ K_2\end{array}\right\} \begin{array}{l}O_2, \\ O, \\ O_2.\end{array}$$

NOTICES OF RECENT DUTCH AND SCANDINAVIAN CONTRIBUTIONS TO ANATOMICAL AND PHYSIOLOGICAL SCIENCE. By W. D. MOORE, M.D. Dub. et Cantab., M.R.I.A., &c. &c.

1. *Bidrag till kännedomen om tungans smakpapiller, af Christian Lovén, Prosector vid Carolinska Institutet.* A contribution to our knowledge of the gustatory papillæ of the tongue, by Christian Lovén, Prosector in the Carolinean Institute. *Medicinskt Archiv,* Stockholm, 1867, Tredje Bandet, Tredje Häftet.

Hr Lovén has carried on similar investigations to those of Engelmann on the Frog (Vol. II. 433, of this Journal). He comes to the conclusion that in the papillæ circumvallatæ in the calf and in man, the gustatory nerves, after losing the medullary sheath in the outer layer of the mucous membrane, are continued up into the gustatory bulbs as naked axis-cylinders, and so divide into a number of branches, which pass directly into the gustatory cells.

On comparing his researches with those of Axel Key upon the tongue of the frog, Hr Lovén remarks, that while in the frog the axis-cylinders are resolved, after they have emerged from their medullary sheaths, into a great number of the "most minute varicose filaments," which at their extremities bear the gustatory cells; in the calf, on the contrary, the connexion between the nerves and the gustatory cells is effected through somewhat thicker, only sparingly and irregularly varicose filaments, having the same appearance as isolated axis-cylinders. In the fungiform papillæ too, in the calf, gustatory bulbs and gustatory cells occur, though much more sparingly. The arrangement of these bulbs and cells is, however, different, for, while in the papillæ circumvallatæ they occupy a certain well-defined zone, namely, the sides of the papilla, in the fungiform they are met with scattered without order between the small papillæ on the upper surface.

2. *Fall af Encephalitis corticalis et Hydrocephalus acutus.* Dr Oedmansson records, in the same Journal, as a contribution to Physiology, and specially to the functional topography of the brain, a case of cortical encephalitis and acute hydrocephalus. The symptoms were at first those of intermittent fever, but soon delirium, loss of memory and stupidity supervened. To questions the patient gave incoherent and lengthy replies, speaking at first in Swedish, but afterwards in an articulate but perfectly incomprehensible gibberish, delivered with much declamation. Rather more than three weeks later, on the 28th February, 1865, the right angle of the mouth was drawn somewhat upwards, the tongue deviated to the left, the left arm and leg were paralysed. The patient died on the 11th of

March. *Dissection.* On the anterior and middle lateral portions of the right hemisphere, the soft membranes projected here and there in the form of cysts as large as nuts, and filled with serum. On cutting through the right hemisphere on a level with the corpus callosum, a spot was met with somewhat behind the middle of the hemisphere, and near the surface of the brain, about two inches long, one inch broad, and three quarters of an inch in depth, where the white substance was softened. The corresponding cortical substance on the small convolution behind the gyrus ascendens posterior was much thinner than is normally the case, it had a yellowish grey colour, a dry granular surface of section, and a brittle consistence. In the lower part of the gyrus ascendens posterior, as well as in the whole lower lateral portion of the frontal lobe, to within half an inch or an inch of the summit, the grey substance was more or less altered. The lateral ventricles were somewhat distended with a flocculent, turbid, greyish-red fluid. In the posterior cornu was a loose, yellowish-green, pus-like mass, that on the right side filling the apex of the cornu like a plug. The ependyma over the corpora striata and septum was studded with fine shining granulations. The fornix was pale and softened.

3. *Om Trikinernas naturliga förekommande,* af Axel Key, Professor i Pathol. Anat. vid Karolinska Institutet. Professor Key contributes a paper on the natural occurrence of *Trichinæ,* his object being, by pointing out the mode in which the pig becomes affected, to facilitate the prevention of the diffusion of the disease.

It would appear that the trichina spiralis never occurs in birds, fishes, amphibious or invertebrate animals, and that these cannot even be experimentally infected. On the other hand, all the mammalia are, with more or less difficulty, capable of being infected. Nevertheless, trichinæ are fortunately not so widely diffused in nature as might be expected from this fact, many animals being protected from trichinosis, not only by the difficulty of infecting them, but also by the nature of their food. It is quite certain that trichinæ are not conveyed to animals in any kind of vegetable food. In addition to men and swine, the animals which have been found *spontaneously* affected with trichinæ are rats, cats, foxes, polecats, martens and hedgehogs. There is no doubt, however, that these dangerous parasites occur also in other carnivorous animals, not yet fully examined. The ruminants seem to be scarcely susceptible of trichinous infection. Professor Sjöstedt succeeded, nevertheless, in infecting a goat and a sheep. He thinks it important that to these animals the infected food should be given in a fluid form, or cut up in small portions in water, so as to avoid rumination, which probably prevents infection. The author believes that the chief source of the infection of the pig is the rat, in which latter animal the trichina is very common. He says it is ascertained that pigs eat rats, whether they find them dead or catch them living, and he shows that it is precisely the animal infected with and lamed by the disease, that will most easily be caught.

Hence he infers that the extirpation of the rat, and its exclusion from the pigsty, will be the most efficacious prophylactic means.

4. The same Journal contains a valuable paper (*Studier öfver lifmodrens byggnad hos menniskan*) by Hjalmar Lindgren, Licentiate in Medicine, upon the structure of the human uterus. Hr Lindgren's primary object was to study the more minute structure of the mucous membrane of the uterus, especially of its cervical portion and of the os; he has however, extended his observations to the structure of the organ in its integrity. He gives very accurate measurements of the several parts of the virgin womb, taking the mean of those made by himself, and by Guyon and Hennig (*Der Katarrh der inneren weiblichen Geschlechtstheile*, Leipzig, 1862), all of which agree pretty closely with one another. The principal difference between the virgin uterus and that of a "nullipara deflorata," depending on the fact that the body and its cavity increase through frequent coitus in the longitudinal direction, is, that while the cavity of the body in a virgin is less by 2 or 3 mm. than the cervical canal, in a nullipara deflorata it becomes as long or longer. The vaginal portion becomes enlarged, and the os externum and the cervical canal are dilated. The author's measurements of the several parts in a child aged $10\frac{1}{2}$ years, and in a new-born infant, show that the changes which the state of the uterus undergoes after birth in its several periods of development have their seat principally in the body, while the cervical portion from the very beginning presents its permanent character very well marked.

The author has examined microscopical sections of the walls of the uterus, taken in different places and in various directions. These sections are illustrated in very beautifully executed plates, some of them being coloured. A sagittal [vertical?] section from the wall of the body of the uterus shows that a division of the muscular structure into three layers is here admissible, although the transition between them is rather diffuse and the lamination is in some preparations more decided than in others. Only in sections lying near the median plane, and not always in these do we observe, close to the peritoneum, a thin layer of vertical fibres. Within these is a stronger layer of transversely cut muscular bundles. The fasciculi are very small and are nearly uniformly divided, surrounded by a scanty connective tissue, in which vessels, chiefly veins, occur. The middle layer presents an interwoven net-work of filaments in all directions, especially alternately transverse and longitudinal filaments, characterised by large vessels and rather coarse fasciculi. This layer occupies about one half of the thickness of the muscular structure.

The inner layer occupies about the remaining third of the whole muscular structure, and exhibits transversely and obliquely cut oval fasciculi, for the most part coarser than in the foregoing layers. The connective tissue becomes in the neighbourhood of the mucous membrane more abundant and more highly nucleated, and some of the muscular fasciculi here resolve themselves into filaments, radiating in the mucous membrane itself.

The arrangement of the muscular structure in the gravid and unimpregnated uterus is found to be, on the whole, very similar. A dissimilarity is, however, met with in the relative thickness of the several layers, as in the former they are, according to Hélie, about equally powerful, while in the latter the middle layer measures on section as much as the other two together.

The mucous membrane of the uterus in the fundus and body is of a very different character from that in the cervix and vaginal portion. The several divisions agree however, in this, that the membrane is everywhere firm and incapable of being displaced, united as it is, without the intervention of any submucous layer, with the subjacent muscular structure, which sends into it radiating fasciculi.

The author enters into a detailed description of the mucous membrane of the body, of the cervical canal, and of the os uteri or vaginal portion of the uterus. It would be impossible, in the limited space allotted to these "Contributions," to follow him satisfactorily through this description, and on many points he is only confirming the results obtained by previous investigators. With reference to papillæ on the mucous membrane of the cervix he says :

"My experience is that papillæ, far from occurring constantly on the cervical mucous membrane, are, as a rule, absent in perfectly healthy virgin uteri, and that they occur in development and number in proportion as the uterus has been exposed to any kind of irritation, and therefore particularly in elderly women. In such persons I have not unfrequently met with free papillæ of the character above described, with very varying dimensions. We must however, be careful not to mistake transversely cut small folds, or connecting ridges between them, for papillæ ; these may in fact present about the same form." p. 28.

In the mucous membrane from the vaginal portion in young children the author has never met with either elastic filaments or masses of protoplasm. This division of the membrane, containing in great abundance small cells and nuclei, has its vessels arranged as those of the adult uterus, and like the latter, has papillæ and a multilamellar epithelium, differently developed in different individuals.

The remainder of Hr. Lindgren's essay is devoted to descriptions of the lymphatics and of the nerves of the uterus. The five plates with which his work is fully illustrated, after drawings by Professor Axel Key and a German draughtsman named Kreutz, are beautiful specimens of lithography and chromolithography.

5. The *Nederlandsch Archief voor Genees- en Natuurkunde* III, 3ᵉ Afl. 1868, contains an elaborate paper by Professor Donders, founded upon numerous experiments, upon the Innervation of the Heart, in connection with that of the Respiratory Movements. At the conclusion of this essay, which occupies 47 pages, the author states that the object of his investigation, the explanation of the

connexion between the respiratory movements and the duration of the cardiac periods, has been in no part obtained, but that, however, among others, the following facts, not unimportant in reference to the nerve-mechanism of respiration and of the circulation of the blood, have been established :

" 1º. In dyspnœa a strongly increasing stimulation of the retarding nerves of the heart is associated with each inspiration. 2º. In the course of the nervus vagus run centripetally acting nerve-fibres, which depress the activity of the central organ of the retarding nerves of the heart."

6. We have also a paper, by W. Koster, on the exudation of the colourless blood-cells through the walls of vessels, and the morbid processes resulting therefrom.   This paper affords an exemplification, in addition to others already given in this series, of the close alliance existing between physiology and pathology.   It consists chiefly of illustrations drawn from pathology, of the fact originally observed by Cohnheim of Berlin (*Virchow's Archiv*, xi. 1), that :

" By a simple and easily repeated experiment with the mesentery of a frog, we can satisfy ourselves that in the commencement of an inflammatory process, while the red blood-cells are still carried along with great rapidity through the axis of the vessel, the colourless blood-cells remain firmly adherent to the inner surface of the minute veins and capillary vessels.   We speedily see, particularly in the minute veins, the colourless blood-cells penetrate *into* and soon *through* the wall, and gradually diffuse themselves in the intervening tissue.   At the same time they now and then, like amoebæ, alter their form, acquire one or more pointed outrunners, in a word distinctly manifest their contractility."

From the foregoing the following corollaries are deducible : the analogy between pus-cells and colourless blood-cells ; the impossibility of distinguishing the two in the blood ; the morphological agreement between a recent exudation (as in pneumonia or pleuritis) and the product of purulent softening of the same, on microscopical examination, &c.

7.   Dr Engelmann and Dr Place investigate a method of preventing unipolar currents in irritation of the nerves.   On this subject Professor Donders made the following communication at the meeting of the Royal Academy of Sciences, on the 29th February, 1868.   " If we bring an electrode under a nerve-trunk, which is not divided, and is therefore on both sides in connexion with the animal, the latter forms an approximate connexion, through which a current constantly passes: consequently the nerve must always be divided, which moreover presents the advantage that the phenomena dependent on centripetal and centrifugal conduction, are separately obtained.   But also on irritation after division the interpolar portion of the nerve forms, on account of its great resistance, only an imperfect closure, which does not guard against unipolar discharge.

Only with the most perfect insulation of everything in connexion with the nerve, can we produce tolerably strong induction-strokes, without diversion beyond the interpolar piece. This appeared in the experiments performed by Dr Place in the physiological laboratory respecting the contraction-wave of muscles (*Ned. Archief*, III. bl. 177). The object was, among other things, to compare the wave on irritation of the nerve and on irritation of the muscle itself: this latter must therefore be carefully avoided in irritating the nerve. In order to produce complete insulation, the apparatuses are placed on a large cylindrical flask filled with nearly boiling water and hermetically closed, on which for hours no vapour had externally settled, and this seemed then to be sufficient for the experiments with a separate muscle (the ordinary frog-preparation). But if the muscle remained in connexion with the animal, in order to keep up the circulation, unavoidable practical difficulties presented themselves in the flowing of the blood, &c.

This now suggested the idea of conducting the electricity streaming along the nerve, directly to the ground. In doing this Dr Place was for starting from the nerve, Dr Engelmann from the inferior electrode, and the result at once showed that the object was attainable in both ways. For various reasons it is, however, better to derive from the electrode, and this method was more accurately investigated by both gentlemen. The derivation was made to the gas-pipes. It was the more efficacious the closer to the nerve it started from the electrode. Currents, much stronger than were necessary to obtain the maximum of contraction by an induction-stroke, now acted exclusively on the interpolar piece : the usual time for the nerve conduction and the latent irritation in the muscle elapsed regularly, before the setting in of contraction, and no trace of contraction occurred when the nerve was divided and the two portions were only laid against each other. On now discontinuing the derivation, contraction of the muscle at once ensued, just as on intentional irritation of the muscle itself, and as fully in the divided nerve with the portions in apposition as in the uninjured nerve....With very strong shocks it was however, even with diversion of the inferior electrode, still desirable to insulate the part tolerably well.

The explanation is evident: the electricity of the inferior electrode passes in fact directly into the gas-pipes, without irritating the nerve; that of the superior passes through the interpolar piece, in order, when arrived at the inferior electrode, to pass into it, and also to be lost along the gas-pipes. Now it is remarkable, as experiments with feeble currents proved, that in diversion of the inferior electrode to the gas-pipes the stimulating action of the current on the nerve, apparent from the amount of shortening of the muscle, remains unaltered.

If the diversion took place from the superior electrode, the effect was precisely the reverse: much more electricity flowed along the nerve, and the unipolar discharge in the animal was much stronger, than without diversion. Of this too the cause is easily understood:

the electricity of the superior electrode now flows directly away; but that of the inferior spreads more readily over the nerve to the muscle, because in the interpolar portion no opposite electricity any longer meets it. Moreover, as inversion of the induction current showed, the contracting effect is in general greater in the descending current through the nerve, than in the ascending.

The current in the diversion to the gas-pipes was demonstrable by laying the nerve of a frog-preparation on the wire, whereby the muscle lying on a glass plate at once contracted, when it was connected by contact with the ground, not without this contact. If the diverting wire was cut through and the nerve joined in the current, a strong contraction was always obtained by its irritation. Although by this joining in of the nerve, the resistance in the derivation to the gas-pipes was very much increased, it nevertheless was a complete security against unipolar currents, flowing along the nerve in the animal, if the animal was only tolerably well insulated.

8. N. J. A. C. Stemberg, Med. Cand. contributes a paper based upon the observation recently made, independently of each other, by Cohnheim and Recklinghausen with Hoffman, that cells from the lymphatic vessels find their way into the irritated cornea. Professor Donders thought it important to ascertain whether the pus-cells in syndesmitis mucipara are likewise derived directly from the vessels, which a priori appeared to him not improbable. He wished also to investigate the remarkable influence of nitrate of silver, which usually rapidly produces an ordinary syndesmitis mucipara with increase of mucus, and, when applied to healthy connective tissue, is followed by temporary production of muco-purulent matter.

The action of the nitrate of silver was investigated first on the vessels of the mesentery of the frog, in solutions of various strengths. All produced dilatation of the vessels, lasting only some moments, and followed by strong contraction. After some hours the latter again gave place to dilatation. The changes affected chiefly the arteries. As an immediate result of the contraction, the exudation of the blood-corpuscles was diminished, if not entirely prevented.

A second point investigated was the origin of the mucus-globules in inflammation of the conjunctiva. On touching the membrana nictitans of the frog with nitrate of silver in substance, numerous pus-cells were found collected, a couple of hours later, between the cornea and the membrana nictitans. The latter, cut off and brought under the microscope, exhibited a mass of colourless blood-corpuscles with some red ones, scattered in the tissue, but especially along the vessels. Here and there the blood-corpuscles were seen also situated between the epithelial cells.

On dropping into the eye of a rabbit one part of nitrate of silver in 480 of water, many colourless corpuscles were usually found, after the lapse of half an hour, in the plica conjunctivæ. On trying whether, without previous irritation, such corpuscles occur on the conjunctiva, a positive result was obtained : in the rabbit, and particularly in man, they are not entirely absent, and it is therefore not improbable, that in the normal condition also colourless blood-corpuscles penetrate to this mucous membrane.

9. & 10. I have received from Sweden two works by Dr M. V. Odenius, Prosector in Lund. Of these one, on the Epithelium of the Macula Acoustica in Man, was published in German, and has been already noticed in this Journal (II. 170). The other, on the form and situation of the sacs of the vestibule in the human ear, is in Swedish, and was read before the Physiographical Society of Lund on the 13th March, 1867. Having given a sketch of the parts in the vestibule specially connected with his subject, the author proceeds to describe the *Utriculus* (*Sacculus Oblongus s. Hemiellipticus*), its form, situation and attachment. This is pear-shaped, with the thicker end forward. It occupies not merely the proper recessus ellipticus, but the whole upper arch of the vestibule, and is consequently curved in the longitudinal direction downwards and backwards, so that the anterior part stands about horizontally, the posterior nearly vertically. Two walls can be distinguished, a superior, turned upwards towards the arch of the vestibule, and moulded to it, and an inferior flat wall turned downwards and forwards. The length of the utriculus not unfrequently amounts to from 4 to 4·5 mm. Its inferior free wall is attached internally to the median wall of the vestibule. At the side it is attached from the pyramid of the vestibule along the line running parallel with the upper boundary of the fenestra to the posterior extremity of the latter. The whole anterior part of its inferior wall with its macula acoustica is thus kept constantly tense, and it is so firm, that the preparation can be roughly handled without anything being loosened.

Sacculus (*rotundus*) has two walls, one inner and nerve-bearing, adherent to the recess, the other outer and for the most part free. The *inner* wall, which is completely sunk in the recessus sphæricus and is everywhere attached to it, is pulpy and in its middle attains a thickness of 0·42 mm. The *outer* free wall is much thinner, brittle and difficult to examine. The author has not as yet succeeded in preparing the sacculus of an adult entirely uninjured and in connexion with the utriculus.

Dr Odenius concludes with a description of the *perilympha space*, which is divided by the inferior wall of the utriculus and its attachment to the vestibule into two communicating, but otherwise quite dissimilar parts, a superior and an inferior.

11. Pt. 1 of Vol. IV. of the Dutch Archives of Medical and Physical Science (*Nederlandsch Archief*, 1868) contains an elaborate paper, extending to 91 pages, by Dr Th. W. Engelmann, on *Ciliary Motion*. In a previous number of the same Journal the author communicated the results of some investigations upon this phenomenon, especially with reference to the influence exercised thereupon by different gases, acids and alkalies. He has now continued his re-

searches, and studied the influence upon it of water, of chloride of sodium in different degrees of concentration, of ether, alcohol, chloroform, poisons, heat and electricity. He proposes, in a third article, to treat of the modifications produced by different agents on the movements of the ciliæ of invertebrate animals, and on those of the spermatozoids, in order to ascertain what more general conclusions respecting the nature and conditions of this remarkable form of contraction may be deduced from the assemblage of facts when complete. As it would be quite impossible to give a satisfactory analysis of Dr Engelmann's present important essay in the space assigned to these "Contributions," it will probably be better to defer any further notice of his interesting researches, until I am in a position to bring the general conclusions thus promised before the readers of this Journal.

12.   To the same Journal (p. 117) Professor Donders contributes the first part of an essay on the *Rapidity of Psychical Processes.* Previous researches of the author on this subject have been alluded to in Vol. II. of this Journal, p. 198.   Professor Donders had already calculated that the *physiological time,* or that elapsing between stimulus and signal, was for the three senses of feeling, hearing, and sight, respectively about $\frac{1}{7}$, $\frac{1}{6}$ and $\frac{1}{5}$ of a second.   But in this physiological time many occurrences take place, as 1. action on the percipient elements of the senses ; 2. communication to the peripheral ganglionic cells and the increase required for discharge (the 'Schwelle' of Fechner); 3. conduction in the sensory nerves to the ganglionic cells of the medulla ; 4. increasing action in these ganglionic cells ; 5. conduction to the nerve-cells of the organ of imagination ; 6. increasing action in these nerve-cells ; 7. increasing action of the nerve-cells of the organ of volition ; 8. conduction to the motor nerve-cells ; 9. increasing action in these cells ; 10. conduction in the motor nerves to the muscle ; 11. latent action in the muscle ; 12. increasing action to overcome the resistance of the signal.   How much then of the physiological time belongs to the proper psychical process of imagination and volition ?   To obtain some clue to the solution of this question, it occurred to Professor Donders to introduce new periods of psychical action into the process.   By ascertaining how much the physiological time was thereby prolonged, the duration of the period introduced would, he imagined, become known. The experiments were now made in two modes: *a.* it being known to the person operated on, on which foot, for example, a stimulus would act, the signal to be given with the hand of the same side ; *b.* similar conditions, but the person to be kept in ignorance which foot would be acted on.   *b* required on an average $\frac{1''}{15}$ more than *a*, which therefore represented the time necessary to form the idea which side was irritated, and, in connexion with this idea, to determine the action of the will to the right or left side.   This was the first determination of the duration of a well-defined psychical process, involving the solution of a dilemma and an operation of the will corresponding to that solution.   The same method of investiga-

tion was applied in the action of stimuli upon the senses of sight and hearing.

13. I have received from Upsala, Vol. II. Nos. 7 and 8, and Vol. III. Nos. 1, 2, 3, 4, of the Transactions of the Medical Society of Upsala (*Upsala Läkareförenings Förhandlingar*) a work which contains many important papers on subjects connected with physiological science. One of these, an interesting and elaborate, though rather diffuse essay, by Frithiof Holmgren, " Physiological Investigations on the Stomachs of the Pigeon," I have translated *in extenso*. The author details numerous original experiments. He comes to the conclusion that Retzius' opinion is correct, when he considers the glandular and muscular stomachs as a whole, corresponding to the stomach of man, the former representing the fundus, the latter the pyloric region. In some carnivorous birds, especially such as live on fish, where the walls of the muscular stomach are relatively thin, the boundary between the two stomachs is also imperceptible, and we have, from the outward form, no reason to consider them otherwise than as a single stomach. In a subsequent paper the author details the results of a number of experiments on the influence of diet on the stomach, and exhibits in a plate the changes produced in that organ by keeping pigeons exclusively on animal food during periods of four and six months.

14. Dr Christian Lovén has published, in the *Hygiea* (Stockholm) for March and April, 1868, a very valuable *résumé* of " Recent Contributions to the theory of the innervation of the heart and blood-vessels." Of this important paper a translation *in extenso* has appeared in the *Medical Press and Circular* for August 12, September 23, and October 7, 1868.

ON THE VARIOUS FORMS OF THE SO-CALLED "CELTIC" CRANIUM. By Professor Rolleston, M.D. F.R.S. Oxford.

Professor Nilsson, 18 years ago, declared that he considered nothing more vague and uncertain than the form of the Celtic cranium[1]; and Professor Ecker[2] has expressed himself in much the same language as to the Roman cranium: the latter of these two authors, however, has done much towards removing some of the uncertainty of which he complains. Upon these two points I should wish here to make a few remarks. Under the head of pre-Roman skulls, found in Britain, most writers would be agreed that three distinct types may be classed under the three distinct types of the "River-bed" type of Professor Huxley, of the brachycephalic type of Dr Thurnam, and the dolicho-cephalic "pre-Celtic" type of the same author. I have to say that a dolicho-cephalic cranium, distinct from the dolicho-cephalic Celtic cranium found in the long barrows, exists in addition to these three types, with the latter of which, I believe, it is sometimes confounded. Representatives of this type of crania may be found in a cast in the easily accessible Museum of the London College of Surgeons, and in another cast, made by Dr Thurnam, and now widely circulated, of a cranium procured by me, through the kindness of J. C. Athorpe, Esq., from a barrow near Dinnington, in South Yorkshire; and, finally, in no less than thirty-two crania or calvaria, which the inexhaustible civility of William Aldworth, Esq. has enabled me to procure from an all but equally inexhaustible cemetery on his estate at Frilford. First, of the cast in the College of Surgeons; in the Catalogue of the Osteological Series it may be found described thus at No. 5709: "A plaster cast of the cranium of an ancient aboriginal of Scandinavia regarded as the Celt. The cranium is long in proportion to its breadth, and resembles in size and shape the Gentoo skull, No. 5553. This is the type of a class of skulls, called dolicho-cephalic by the donor, Professor Retzius." Secondly, of the Dinnington cranium, I would remark that Professor Ecker, in *Archiv für Anthropologie*, Bd. I. Hft. 2, p. 283, has remarked of it, that it is exceedingly like the Frankish skulls obtained by him from his grave-row cemeteries. And Dr Barnard Davis, in his *Thesaurus Craniorum*, p. 10, speaks of it as "a very large, even enormous, subscapho-cephalic skull." Of the thirty-two crania obtained by me from Frilford, which from archæological evidence detailed by me in a paper to be published by the Society of Antiquarians have been shown to belong to pre-Saxon times, I may say, firstly, that they resemble very closely the two casts already mentioned; and secondly, that they differ from the dolicho-cephalic crania ordinarily obtained from long barrows, and notably from such crania obtained for me, by the agency of the Rev. David Royce, from a long barrow at Netherswell, near Stow-on-the-Wold, as much as any two sets of dolicho-cephalic crania can differ. Their frontal region though not loftier is yet fuller and wider; and much the same description may apply to every other part of the calvarium, which in no point corresponds to the description given by His and Rutimeyer to their Hohberg type of skull, except that occasionally in male skulls, though by no means always, it has the mesial vertical carina, developed in male specimens (cf. Professor Ecker, *Archiv für Anthropologie*, Bd. I. Hft. 1, p. 84). The skulls

[1] *Crania Britannica*, Letter to Dr Thurnam, p. 17.
[2] *Archiv für Anthropologie*, Bd. II. Hft. 1. 110.

themselves, whether belonging to young or old, present signs of culture in the softness and even rounding of their outlines, to which the retention of verticality by the forehead presents an exception in subordination to the rule or reason of the absence of angles elsewhere, but if the skulls themselves differ their owners seem to me to have differed much more. Of all differences which relate to life there is no one more important than difference as to its duration, and in this the British crania of Frilford differs most essentially and to great advantage from the dolicho-cephalic individuals described by Dr Thurnam, in *Memoirs of Anthropological Society of London*, Vol. I. as found by him in dolicho-taphic barrows. Eleven, or more than half of twenty-one, male crania, obtained by me from Frilford, I have classed as aged; it is needless to say that this very high average of senility is as characteristic of a state of civilization as the surroundings of the tenants of long barrows are of barbarism; secondly, the average height of these individuals was 5 ft. 8·3 in., whereas the average height of the dolicho-cephalic Britons from long barrows is given as 5 ft. 6 in. Firstly, the dolicho-cephalic Celt, whose distinctness I am advocating, survives to the present day, and I am a little doubtful whether as much can be said for his rougher dolicho-cephalic representative. I am aware that there are points of resemblance, as well as points of difference, between these two types; and I am also aware, and indeed would suggest, that the points of difference may be referable to differences of culture. But within the limits of any one species, whether vegetable or animal, brute or human, differences produced by culture seem to me as great as any other. It is in favour, certainly of their kinship, that they appear, both of them together, in the same cemetery, as at Dinnington; whereas neither of them has ever been found by me so interred as to make it seem probable that their owners ever occupied one area simultaneously and in peace with the brachycephalic British Celt. There are several explanations for this fact, if fact it be; I leave them to what the German would call the *Willkühr* of the historian. I will just remark that anthropologists, in whom the tendency I have just mentioned is little less marked, have observed that a certain furrow or *rainure*, which Von Baer has noted in the Aleutians (see *Crania Selecta*, p. 265 (25)), and I have seen in Eskimos, is, according to their *Willkühr*, sometimes characteristic and sometimes not (*Pruner Bey. Bull. Soc. Anth.* Paris, 1863, and M. Bonté, *Bull. Soc. Anth.* Paris, 1864, Vol. v.). I can only say that it sometimes is and sometimes is not found in these crania, and that its presence or absence seems to me to depend simply upon the necessity which the posterior parts of the parietal bones may or not be under, to accommodate themselves to the requirements of a growing or not growing brain, whilst under no circumstances are their apposed portions, underlaid by the longitudinal sinus, under any obligation so to accommodate themselves. It is, I apprehend, in a somewhat similar way that the presence of a transverse, wide, and shallow furrow, a little way posteriorly to the coronal suture, is to be explained, as it very often is, in well-developed skulls (*Med. Chir. Review*, April, 1863, p. 508). In well-developed human brains the posterior parts of the upper frontal[1] convolutions, as also the lobule of the second ascending parietal convolutions, are largely developed; whilst the first ascending convolution and the fissure of Rolando (Thurnam, *Nat. Hist. Rev.* 1865, p. 267) remain as lines of indifference between them, along which no stimulus is propagated to the outer pericranium, and no absorption of the tabula vitrea inside excited. Both the posterior coronal furrow and the furrow at right angles to it in the posterior portion of the sagittal suture are present, though but faintly indicated, in the Dinnington cast I have spoken of.

[1] See Marshall, *Phil. Trans.* 1863, p. 513.

It is not beside the purpose to add here that Retzius (*Ethnologische Schriften*, p. 108, 1864) distinguished these two varieties of Celtic crania from such other as emphatically as I have striven to do. After describing a long narrow and laterally compressed skull, which he says, is specially found in England and France, and which obviously corresponds to the ordinary Long Barrow or Hohberg Type, he says, "nevertheless this is not the common Celtic form, which is ordinarily somewhat broader and not so compressed, whilst the "Cimbric" Celtic form, which is here and there found in South Sweden, and Denmark, is somewhat broader still. This form is very like the Scandinavian Gothic." Both these forms of crania seem to me to be different from the Roman form of cranium which may be seen figured from Maggiorani in V. Baer's paper on the Rhætians in the *Bull. Acad. Imp. Sci. St Petersburgh*, 1860, p. 58. This form of cranium however I am enabled to say, a specimen from the Towyn y Capel Tumulus, having been presented to the University Museum by the Hon. W. O. Stanley, co-existed with the River Bed Type in this island just as this latter co-existed and apparently peacefully with Retzius' "common Celtic" form in the Frilford cemetery, and with the "Brachycephalic Celtic" form of Dr Thurnam, in a barrow at Crawley. Finally the platycephalic Roman form as figured and described by Maggiorani and Sandifort (Ecker, *Crania Germaniæ*, p. 86) is very precisely and abundantly represented in the series obtained by me from the barrow at Dinnington, where it coexisted with both the longer forms of Celtic crania. Of this barrow, as it is now so frequently referred to, it may be well to put here on record such notes as I have been able to gather from the report of persons present at the removal of the stones of which the barrow was made up, and from personal observations made upon the spot where it had been, after its removal.

Dinnington is a small village about two miles south of Laughton-en-le-Morthen (in the Moorland) in South Yorkshire. A little to the south of Dinnington and on the left hand of the road leading from Dinnington to Anston, and some little way short of the quarries from which the stone for the new Houses of Parliament was taken, there was on the estate of J. C. Athorpe, Esq. a heap of stones about 134 paces in circumference, 42 long, and 35 or a little less in breadth, and 7 or 8 feet in height. The stone was the light porous sandstone common in the neighbourhood; the individual pieces were of nearly equal size throughout; and there was no protecting lean-to nor cist anywhere in the tumulus. Up to the end of 1862 the tumulus was covered with turf, had thorn shrubs growing upon it, and had rabbit burrows in it. In the autumn of 1862 Mr Athorpe began to dig away the turf, and stub up the thorn-bushes, and finally to cart away the stones for wall-building. It was in doing this that the workmen came upon the skeletons, of which there were in all as many as 22, 12 lying in the centre of the cairn, near to each other, but not piled one upon the other, and without any orientations, ornaments, weapons, flints or pottery. Some of the skeletons were at as great a depth as 12 feet, one skeleton however was no deeper than 2½ feet. The workmen said, "the skulls lay between the legs;" "the thigh-bones were at the back of the neck;" and I suppose consequently that the bodies had been buried in a sitting posture. Only one skeleton was extended, and its head lay at the north-west. The barrow itself had its long diameter, which however was only the longer by a very few yards, and may have become so by virtue of the paring to which it may have been subject in agricultural processes, lying east and west. At its east end a skeleton was placed far apart from the rest, a point of importance to be noted, as Sir R. C. Hoare (cit. *Crania Britannica*, I. p. 230) has put on record that the deposit in the long barrows he excavated was usually at the east, which was also the broader end. A considerable proportion of these skeletons had belonged to aged individuals, and from this as from other circumstances detailed above, the hypothesis of a battle will not account for the facts of these burials. Many of the skulls possess the subquadrate general outline combined with smoothly swelling and elegantly rounded individual contours which are described as characteristic of the Roman cranium ; and the locality renders the admixture of Roman soldiers by no means an impossible supposition. I am not acquainted, though professed archæologists may be, with any account of a cemetery exactly resembling this in Great Britain; but the following account which Wienhold gives (*Sitzungsberichte Kaiser. Akad. Wien. Phil. Hist. Class.* 1858, Bd. 29, Hft. 1, p. 166) of a variety of grave mounds found in Germany and containing unburnt bodies may be compared advantageously with the imperfect account I have given above of the Dinnington Tumulus. His words are, " Manchmal vermisst man an den aufgedeckten Gerippen die gewohnliche sorgfaltige Behandlung der Todten ; sie scheinen nur nachlassig hingelegt oder hingeworfen. (Keller, *Grabhugel in Burghölzli bei Zürich ;* ebd. *Helvet. Heidengräber und Todten hügel.* p. 16). Wenn die Gebeine völlig über einem Haufen liegen, wie in einem Tumulus bei Biewer in Luxembourg und einem Heidenbuck bei Ossingen in Thurgau wird man annehmen mussen dass der Todte sitzend bestattet würde ; in beiden Fallen zeigt das Grab nicht die mindeste Spur einer späteren Störung. (*Publicat Soc. Hist. Luxembourg,* VII. 106. Keller, *Helvet. Heidengraber.* 18).

The skeletons after the removal of the stones which had covered them were reinterred in the earth, and it was only after the second disinterment that, through the kindness of the owner of the soil, they came into my hands.

ON THE ACTION OF THE THYRO-HYOID MUSCLE. By GEORGE BUCHANAN, A.M., M.D. *Lecturer on Anatomy in Anderson's University, Glasgow, &c.*

In explaining to my Students the complicated agencies which are brought into play during vocalisation and deglutition I am in the habit of saying that though in almost every action of the larynx there are involved several muscles, yet in order to understand their action it is necessary to study the effect of each muscle singly, as we could conceive it to act if it alone were present. Thus each muscle of the larynx has a primary action on the position of the cartilages, and a secondary result on the tension of the vocal cords and on the shape of the rima glottidis.

It has often struck me that the thyro-hyoid muscle has had a subsidiary place assigned to it and that its true meaning is not properly brought out. It is grouped as a depressor of the hyoid bone and often (as a prolongation of the sterno-thyroid) is considered in a general way to be one of the agents in depressing the larynx after deglutition. Its nerve-supply, by a special twig of the hypoglossal, instead of a branch from the loop between the descendens noni and communicans noni, does not seem to have led to a search for a special function.

From the study of a number of dissections I have made with a view to determine this point, I am satisfied that the use of the thyro-hyoid is to elevate the thyroid cartilage close to the hyoid bone during deglutition so as to cause or permit the folding back of the epiglottis over the upper orifice of the larynx. I am quite aware that other agencies effect the same object—that of closing the larynx against the entrance of food during the act of swallowing—but that the principal office of the epiglottis is to do this there is no doubt. In order to shew the part taken in this by the thyro-hyoid muscle let a larynx be prepared as follows. Let the mucous membrane and muscles be entirely dissected off, leaving the membranes and ligaments alone. It will then be seen that the epiglottis has two *strong* attachments. By one the foot-stalk of the leaf-like cartilage is fixed to the angle of the thyroid cartilage. The other ligament extends from the anterior surface of the epiglottis in a semilunar curve to the posterior edge of the body of the os-hyoides. Let the preparation be held up by the hyoid bone held horizontally. It will be seen that the tension of the hyo-epiglottic ligament retains the epiglottis in an upright position. Let the thyroid cartilage be now pushed up within the larger curve of the hyoid bone and the epiglottis will be seen to fall back, and at the end of the movement to be pushed back by the tension of the same ligament acting in a reverse way. To perform this movement of the thyroid cartilage is the special function of the thyro-hyoid muscle.

CAMBRIDGE: PRINTED AT THE UNIVERSITY PRESS.

Journal of Anatomy and Physiology.

ON IRREGULARITIES IN THE ARTERIES AND MUSCLES OF AN IDIOT. By E. CARVER, M.A. M.B. F.R.C.S. *Demonstrator of Anatomy in the University of Cambridge.*

THE following peculiarities in the disposition of the arteries and muscles observed in an Idiot subject in our dissecting room last winter seem to me worthy of being related. The number of varieties occurring in one person, and that an idiot nearly, if not quite, from birth, is remarkable; and I am not aware of any other instance in which the dissection of an idiot has been recorded.

ARTERIES.—The left *vertebral* arose from the arch of the aorta and entered the foramen of the sixth cervical vertebra as usual. The *inferior thyroid,* on the right side, was given off from the common carotid about an inch from the division of the innominate; it was large and had the usual distribution.

The right *axillary,* in the second part of its course, gave off a large branch which coursed down on the outer side of the median nerve and joined the radial at the bend of the elbow; it gave no branches. The *brachial* divided at the bend of the elbow into the *ulnar* and a small *radial;* the latter was joined almost immediately by the branch from the axillary just mentioned. Before that junction it gave off its *recurrent* branch, which passed upwards and outwards behind the tendon of the biceps muscle to the space between the brachialis anticus and supinator longus, anastomosing with the superior profunda.

The trunk resulting from the junction of the radial with the axillary branch preserved the usual course of the radial passing between the metacarpals of the thumb and index finger and forming the deep palmar arch, and after turning round the end of the radius, gave off a large branch which passed beneath the tendons of the extensores carpi radiales, along the second dorsal interosseous muscle, to the cleft between the index and middle fingers—there it dipped towards the palm dividing into two branches which supplied the opposed sides of these fingers. Just before the division it received a palmar branch from the superficial arch. The *princeps pollicis* gave off the radialis indicis. The *superficialis volæ*, derived from the radial as usual, ended in the muscles of the thumb and did not communicate with the superficial palmar arch. The ulnar artery was disposed as usual except that its superficial palmar arch joined the princeps pollicis instead of the superficialis volæ.

ON THE LEFT SIDE the *posterior circumflex* gave a large branch which accompanied the musculo-spiral nerve to the outer side of the arm in the place of the terminal branch of the superior profunda. The *superior profunda* arose from the upper part of the brachial as usual, but was small; it passed with the musculo-spiral nerve to the back of the arm, but was lost in the triceps muscle. The *brachial*, one inch below the tendon of the latissimus dorsi, gave off a large branch which descended on the inner side of the biceps muscle and upon (superficially with regard to) the median nerve to a little above the bend of the elbow, at which point it crossed the tendon of the biceps to take up the ordinary position of the radial in the forearm. The *brachial* itself descended in the usual course crossing behind the median nerve. At the bend of the elbow it gave off (in the usual position for the radial) a branch which joined the radial trunk descending from below the latissimus dorsi. From this communicating vessel came off two branches, (1) ascending as the *radial recurrent,* which was disposed as usual and anastomosed with the branch descending from the posterior circumflex in the place of the superior profunda : and (2) a branch which descended upon the supinator brevis and inosculated with a branch from the posterior interosseous, the resulting vessel being distributed to the extensores pollicis, and anastomosing with branches from the anterior interosseous; there was no anterior ulnar recurrent. The *ulnar* and *interosseous* arteries were regular, except that the *posterior interosseous recurrent* passed upwards in front of the elbow where it anastomosed with branches of the radial recurrent. The posterior interosseous supplied the extensor digitorum communis and the extensor indicis and the special extensor of the middle finger, the extensores pollicis being supplied as already mentioned. The *superficial palmar arch* ended in the princeps pollicis as on the right side. The *deep palmar arch* gave off the *princeps pollicis;* a large branch derived from it was joined at the cleft between the index and middle fingers by a branch from the superficial arch which passed between the flexor tendons, the vessel formed by this union dividing for the supply of the adjacent sides of the index and middle fingers. This was the more remarkable because these fingers received their usual trunk from the superficial arch.

The *sacra media* was larger than usual and supplied the fifth lumbar arteries on the two sides. These were very small.

The *sciatic* on the right side, much smaller than usual, was given off from the glutæal within the pelvis. It passed through the substance of the pyriformis muscle behind the greater sciatic nerve, supplying only the coccygeus muscle and the sciatic nerve. A large branch from the glutæal supplemented the sciatic artery by giving branches to the external rotators of the thigh as well as the branches anastomosing with the internal circumflex.

The *sciatic,* on the left side, had a similar origin and distribution. It passed however in front of the great sciatic nerve.

The internal circumflex and *superior perforating* arteries on both sides came off by a common trunk from the profunda at the usual site of the superior perforating artery. The *circumflex* passed to the back of the thigh through the substances of the adductor magnus muscle.

On the left side the *peroneal* artery was absent. The *posterior tibial* in descending inclined outwards, entering the substances of the flexor longus pollicis about its middle. Having perforated that muscle it passed behind its tendon (between it and the tendo achillis) and appeared at inner ankle. This

17—2

relation was preserved as it passed on into the sole of the foot. A little above the ankle it gave off (1) a large branch which was distributed about the inner malleolus; and (2) another which, taking the place occupied by the terminal branch of the peroneal, passed through the interosseous membrane to the front of the leg, supplying branches to the outer side of ankle and foot, and one, of considerable size, which communicated with the anterior tibial.

On the right side the distribution of the arteries in the leg and foot was normal.

MUSCLES. In the right forearm the *palmaris longus* was absent. The *lumbricales* formed a large fleshy muscle arising from the front and sides of the tendons of the flexor profundus digitorum, completely concealing them. This ended in five tendons, four of which had the ordinary distribution terminating in the extensor tendons of the four fingers; whereas the fifth joined the radial side of the tendon of the flexor sublimis of the ring finger. The *extensor ossis metacarpi pollicis* and the *extensor primi internodii pollicis* formed a single muscle, the tendon of which, at the wrist, divided into three slips. Of these one, very slender, passed to the terminal phalanx of the thumb; another passed to the base of the first phalanx of the thumb; and the third passed to the scaphoid bone. The middle finger as well as the index had a special extensor. It arose from the ulna, a little to the ulnar side of the indicator muscle, and passed through the posterior annular ligament with the common extensor of the fingers and joined the ulnar side of the extensor tendon of the middle finger.

In the left forearm the *palmaris longus* was merely a thin muscular slip from the flexor sublimis. Its narrow tendon, spreading out at the wrist, ended by a few scattered fibres in the palmar fascia. Beneath the flexor sublimis there was a small muscle which derived its origin partly from the flexor sublimis and partly from the flexor profundus; its muscular fibres ended in a fine tendon which became free at the middle third of the arm and, just above the anterior angular ligament, divided into two; one part joined the tendon of the flexor pollicis, the other became blended with the deep flexor tendon of the index finger. The *lumbricales* were very large and fleshy as on the right side, but there was not any tendon joining the flexor of the ring finger. The *extensors of the thumb* had the same arrangement as on the right side. The *extensores carpi radiales* arose as one muscle dividing below into three tendons. Two of these were inserted into the radial border of the base of the metacarpal bone of the index finger ; the third was inserted into the contiguous sides of the second and third metacarpal bones.

There were also certain peculiarities in the skull, such as a wormian bone, on either side, between the lesser alæ of the sphenoid bone and the orbital plate of the frontal bone : an unusual thickness of the walls : unevenness of the internal surface : the edges of the sutures both internally and externally were thick, raised and rounded : the oblique diameter from the left side of the occipital bone to the right side of the frontal bone was long, at the expense of the opposite diameter. I forbear saying more respecting the skull, as it may form the subject of a future communication by another person.

REMARKS ON THE HOMOLOGIES AND NOTATION OF THE TEETH OF THE MAMMALIA[1]. Read at the Meeting of the British Association for the Advancement of Science, at Norwich, Aug. 20, 1868. By WILLIAM HENRY FLOWER, F.R.S.

THE object of the present communication is to review the recent advances, the present state of our knowledge, and the direction which future inquiry might advantageously take in reference to certain points connected with the dentition of the Mammalia. I must premise that the observations I shall make, will be, partly from limits of time, but chiefly from imperfection of knowledge, extremely incomplete. I would willingly have waited for the further researches of many years, with more ample materials than are at present available, before venturing to treat generally of so large a subject; but perhaps the interests of science may best be served by bringing together some scattered fragments of exact and certain knowledge, and by shewing their incompleteness, give a stimulus to the exertions of other workers in the same field.

Among the modern advances in the science of comparative anatomy, few are more captivating and impress the mind more forcibly with the harmony and beauty of the organic creation, than the application of the doctrine of homologies. At a meeting of this association, exactly twenty years ago, Professor Owen concluded a paper upon the same subject as that which I have now ventured to bring before the meeting, by stating his conviction "that nothing would influence more the rapid and successful progress of the knowledge of the structure of animal bodies than the determination of the nature of the parts by tracing their homologies and

[1] As this paper is printed almost verbatim as read at the Meeting, no reference is made in it to the subsequently published observations "On the nomenclature of Mammalian teeth, &c." by H. N. Moseley and C. R. Lankester, in the last number of this Journal, or to the third volume of Prof. Owen's *Anatomy of Vertebrates*. The latter contains no material deviation from the author's previous enunciations on the points referred to in the present communication.

the condensation of the propositions respecting them by attaching to the parts so determined symbols, or at least single substantive names distinctly defined[1]."

This object was carried out with remarkable success in connection with the dental organs of, at least some portion of, the Mammalia, and Professor Owen's observations in this field, spread over a long series of years, and embracing a vast number of individual objects, threw so much light upon our knowledge of these organs, previously in a very confused condition, that no follower in the same course of study, can fail to recognise them gratefully. Indeed to many it has seemed, that the system propounded was so symmetrically perfect and the generalizations embraced by it so complete, that nothing further remained to be done, except here and there to fill up a small hiatus, which it was confidently believed would only add further to the harmony and symmetry of the whole.

But are these generalizations to escape the fate of all others which have taken their place as recognised portions of the creed of science? That is, shall they not pass through the ordeal of criticism, and be tried at every point to see whether they are proof against all objections? It is one of the main uses of theories, that they provoke criticism, and so lead to further investigation of facts; and the endeavour either to maintain or subvert them, if honestly conducted, necessarily adds to the common stock of actual knowledge. I shall have occasion therefore, in the course of the present enquiry to endeavour to ascertain how much of the generally adopted system of the homologies of the teeth, both of the deciduous and permanent set, does stand the test of renewed investigation, how much seems doubtful and requires further examination before it can receive unqualified credence, and how much (if any) is at actual variance with well ascertained phenomena. This will be done, I trust, in no spirit either of partiality or hostility to the theories examined, but simply with an endeavour to follow where the facts seem to lead; and as before mentioned, the present remarks must be considered in many

---

[1] *British Association Report*, 1848, p. 93.

cases rather as tentative or suggestive than as affording any approach to a complete solution of the difficulties with which the subject is often involved.

One of the most important of the generalizations above alluded to is the division of the animals of the class Mammalia in regard to the times of formation and the succession of their teeth into two groups ; the *Monophyodonts* or those that generate a single set of teeth ; and the *Diphyodonts* or those that generate two sets of teeth. The *Monophyodonts* including the Orders *Monotremata, Edentata* and *Cetacea ;* all the rest of the class being *Diphyodonts*. " The teeth of the former group are more simple and uniform in character, not distinctly divisible into the sets to which the terms incisor, canine, premolar or molar have been applied and follow no known numerical law." " In the Armadillos, Megatheroids, and Sloths " it is said " the want of germinating power, as it may be called, in the matrix is compensated by the persistence of the matrix, and by the uninterrupted growth of the teeth." "On the other hand in the mammalian orders with two sets of teeth, these organs acquire fixed individual characters, receive special denominations and can be determined from species to species." " They follow a definite numerical law, and vary in any given animal only by the suppression of some particular members of the series, which can in every case be exactly indicated[1]."

Now it will be observed that these two divisions of the Mammalia exactly correspond in extent with the sections to which the terms *Homodont* and *Heterodont* (meaning animals with equal or one kind of teeth, and animals with different or several kinds of teeth) have been applied by other authors, sections the significance of which is very easily appreciated by any one conversant with the characters of mammalian teeth, though not perfectly easy to define with rigid precision.

Let us first consider the question whether all the mammals of the first group, the Homodonts, including the orders Cetacea and Edentata (for the Monotremata, having no true teeth, may be left out of the question), are really monophyodont.

As far as the Cetacea are concerned, no trace of a vertical succession in the teeth has yet been observed. The rudimen-

[1] *Cyclopædia of Anatomy and Physiology*, Art. Teeth.

tary denticles met with in the fœtal Whalebone-whales, are, according to a view to be developed further on, the representatives of the permanent teeth of the grampuses and other Odontoceti, and therefore of the remainder of the mammalian class.

With regard to the Edentata, the case is quite otherwise. In his *Histoire Naturelle des Mammifères* (1855, Vol. II. p. 252), Professor Gervais figured and described the teeth of a nearly adult nine-banded Armadillo (*Tatusia peba*, Desm.) in the process of change. This remained an isolated observation, and notwithstanding its great importance received very little if any notice from subsequent writers, until recently I had the good fortune to be able to verify it, and trace in greater detail some of the earlier stages of the dentition of the same species of Armadillo[1]. To these observations I can now add another from a specimen exhibited in the "Orfila" Museum at Paris, in which the change is advanced still further than in that figured by Gervais, many of the milk teeth having their roots almost completely absorbed, and being apparently on the point of falling out. In this stage they are generally divided into two distinct fragments, between which the permanent tooth thrusts itself forwards.

The result of these various observations proves unquestionably that of the eight teeth habitually found in each side of the mouth of the nine-banded Armadillo, both in maxilla and mandible, all except the most posterior in each set are preceded by well-developed functional milk-teeth, which closely resemble the permanent teeth in form, and nearly equal them in size, and are not shed until the animal has almost attained its full development.

Here then is an animal, a true Homodont and yet a Diphyodont; and though so complete a Diphyodont, not answering to any of the other characters assigned to the group. The

---

[1] "On the Development and Succession of the Teeth of the Armadillos (*Dasypodidæ*)," *Proc. Zool. Soc.* 1868, p. 378. Since this paper was published, my attention has been called by friends to the mention of milk teeth in *Tatusia peba*, by Rapp in the 2nd edition of his well-known Monograph on the Edentata (1852), p. 69, and in *T. Kappleri*, by Professor Krauss of Stuttgardt (*Archiv für Naturgeschichte*, 1862, p. 19), but in neither case with any allusion to the importance of the observation in reference to the generally admitted doctrine of the monophyodont nature of the Edentata.

teeth have acquired no fixed individual characters, follow no known numerical law, and can not be homologically determined with those of other Diphyodonts.

As this is but one of numerous species of Armadillos, it would be very interesting to know the condition of the succession of the teeth among allied forms, for we can scarcely believe that it should stand alone in so remarkable a peculiarity. Unfortunately we have as yet no information of any value upon the subject; owing to the absence of requisite materials in our museums all statements regarding the succession of the teeth of the other Armadillos rest on no solid basis of observation.

With regard to the Sloths, I think there can be little doubt but that they are truly Monophyodonts, for in examining a large number of young specimens of various ages, both of *Bradypus* and *Cholœpus*, I have not been able to find any appearance of a change. Still it must be remembered that these are only negative observations.

We next turn to the remainder of the Mammals, the Heterodonts, and enquire whether they all correspond to the definition of the Diphyodonts? We know of course that it is not intended by this term to imply that all the teeth are changed; the fact is so well known that it may be taken as understood that a certain number of the hindermost teeth in each series are never changed. "Diphyodont" then implies that a certain number of the anterior teeth are changed in the course of the animal's life; but it is most important to observe, and until very recently it has not been fully recognised, that the number of those teeth that are changed, and their position in the series vary greatly; also there are important differences in the period at which the change takes place, and the amount of development to which one of the sets may attain, so that among the Heterodonts there is almost every intermediate condition between the true typical *Diphyodont*, and the *Monophyodont* dentition, and indeed there are cases in which no change occurs, at all events cases in which no change has yet been proved.

Some of the examples to which I refer, are the *Sirenia*, placed by Professor Owen among the Diphyodonts, though their claim to this position is a very slender one. The large upper incisors of the Dugong appear to have milk predecessors, unless the small and early deciduous anterior incisors should prove to be abortive rudiments of teeth of the permanent set, as the small, concealed lower incisors probably are. In the Manatee no change has yet been shown and the characters of the teeth completely set at nought all the definitions; the molars considerably exceed the regulation number for the *Diphyodonts*, yet in their complex characters, with many fangs and cuspidate crowns, they entirely differ from those of the ordinary Monophyodonts.

The Elephants, at least the recent species, show no vertical succession except in the incisors, while in the Rodents on the other hand, the incisors appear not to be changed.

I now come to the group which presents the most singular condition of dental succession, the Marsupials. These animals are true Heterodonts, their teeth are as distinctly divisible into incisors, canines, premolars and molars as those of any other of the Mammalia, and until very lately they have always been considered as true diphyodonts; nay, more than one anatomist of note has described the characters and shedding of the milk-teeth, as if precisely resembling that of the rest of the class, the only difference observed relating to the number of the molar teeth that were replaced. I believe, however, that it may now be considered as absolutely proved, that no marsupial ever has milk-incisors (at least so far developed as to reach the calcified stage) or canines, or more than one milk-molar on each side in each jaw[1]. Or, as it may still be an open question whether the persistent, but non-replacing teeth of the marsupials represent the milk or the permanent set of the Placental Mammals, I may state the case as originally put in the paper referred to below. "The teeth of Marsupials do not vertically displace and succeed other teeth, with the exception of a single tooth on each side of each jaw. The tooth in which a vertical succession takes place is always the corresponding or homologous tooth, being the hindermost of the premolar series, which is preceded by a tooth having the characters, more or less strongly expressed, of a true molar." Here I must however observe, there is still a gradation in the character of the succession even within so apparently narrow a

[1] See "On the Development and Succession of the Teeth in the Marsupialia," *Phil. Trans.* 1867, p. 631.

Fig. 1.   Upper milk and permanent dentition of Opossum (*Didelphys Virgi-niana*) nat. size.   This and all the other figures are from specimens in the Museum of the Royal College of Surgeons.

compass.   In certain forms of Marsupials the milk-molar is a well-developed functional tooth, retained until the other teeth are nearly all in use, and the animal has attained a considerable portion of its growth.   Such is the case with the Macropodidæ, especially *Hypsiprymnus* and the Phalangers, Perameles and Opossums (fig. 1).   On the other hand, the milk-molar in *Thylacinus* is exceedingly small as compared with its successor and all the other teeth, and quite functionless, being shed at a very early age, even before any of the other teeth have come into use.   I believe now that some Marsupials present a still further anomaly in not having even this rudimentary tooth developed, and being really monophyodonts.   At least I have not been able to detect it in the youngest Koalas (*Phascolarctos*) that I have had an opportunity of examining, and I am inclined to think it doubtful in the Dasyures, but want of materials prevents me speaking positively on this point.   If it should turn out to be true, the above quoted generalization will require a slight modification, such as "when any vertical displacement and succession takes place in the teeth of Marsupials it is always limited to a single tooth on each side of each jaw," &c.

The above cited cases are clearly examples of one kind of transition from the full diphyodont to monophyodont dentition; the number of the teeth that are changed being reduced to as few as possible.   I will now take an example of another mode in which a similar transition is effected.   Professor Huxley in his Hunterian lectures at the Royal College of Surgeons a few years since, in discussing the relations of the Cetacea to the rest of the Mammalia, sketched out a line of affinities, leading from the true terrestrial carnivora through the seals, and the extinct Zeuglodonts to the carnivorous Cetacea. As this line always appeared to me a very natural one, I have endeavoured to ascertain how far the dental characters bore it out. Unfortunately the materials available for the purpose are very incomplete, but an outline of the results, such as they are, may be elucidated by aid of these diagrams (figs. 2 to 5).

In the more typical terrestrial carnivora, such as the Dog (fig. 2), the milk-teeth, as is well known, form a distinct, well-grown and functional set, with characters generally resembling those of the permanent teeth, being of a fair proportional size, and not discarded until the animal has attained to half or two-thirds of its full growth, although perhaps not retained quite so long as in some of the herbivora. In the Bears, which of all the terrestrial carnivora most nearly approach the Seals, the milk-teeth are much smaller in proportion to the permanent set than in the Dog, and are shed at a much earlier age; in fact it is quite rare to find in museums, any specimens of Bears' skulls, however young, in which the permanent set of teeth are not in place[1].

In the ordinary Seals (fig. 3), the milk-teeth are extremely rudimentary in size and form, and perfectly functionless. The majority of them never cut the gums and are absorbed actually before birth, and certainly within a week after birth scarcely a trace of any of them remains, as I lately had an opportunity of verifying in a specimen which was born and died in the Zoological Society's Gardens.

It is very interesting to note that in the Eared Seals (genus *Otaria*), which more nearly approach the terrestrial carnivora in many points in their structure as well as habits, the milk-teeth are less rudimentary and evanescent than in the true seals, the canines especially being of moderate size and retained for several weeks.

The Seal which appears to me most removed from these

---

[1] In a skeleton of a young *Ursus arctos* in the Leyden Museum, which measures but 14″ high at the shoulder and not 2′ in length (skull, 6½″ long), the canines are the only milk teeth remaining. All the permanent incisors are in place, except the outer one of the mandible, which is just appearing. The permanent molar teeth are *in situ* except the most posterior in either jaw, and of these the upper one has the surface of its crown fully formed, calcified and uncovered by bone, though still below the level of the alveolar border. The second small premolar is very backward, only just appearing while the first is fully in place.

Fig. 2.

Fig. 3.

Fig. 4.

Fig. 5.

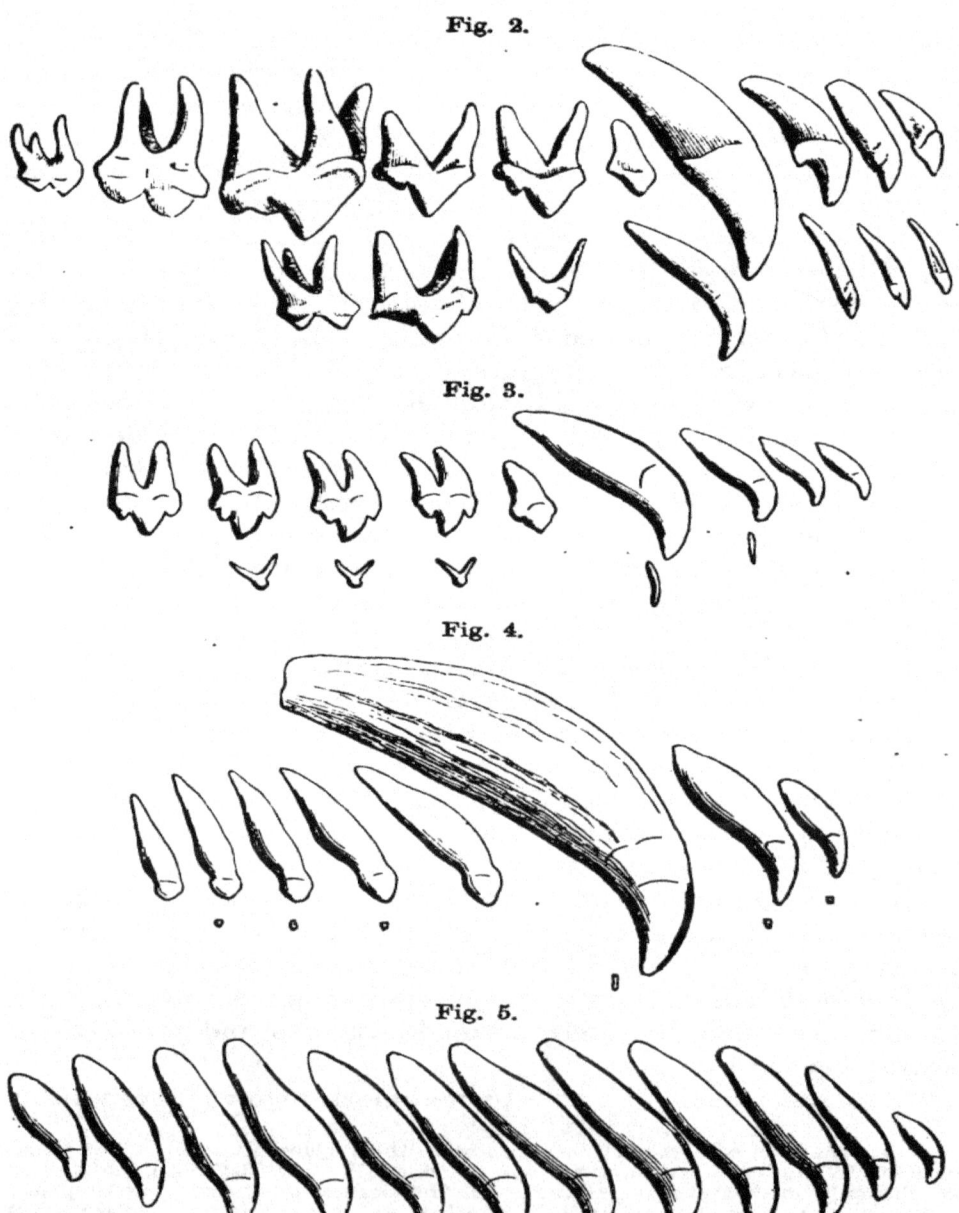

Upper permanent and milk dentition. Fig. 2. Dog, nat. size. Fig. 3. Seal (*Phoca grænlandica*), nat. size. The anterior milk incisors were already absorbed in the specimen figured. Fig. 4. Elephant Seal (*Morunga proboscidea*), ½ nat. size. Fig. 5. Grampus (*Orca capensis*), ¼ nat. size.

last, and really to offer an approach towards the Cetacea in some points in the structure of the skull, in the simple character of the teeth, and in the absence or rudimentary condition of the claws, is the great Proboscis or Elephant Seal of the South Seas (*Morunga proboscidea*, Fig. 4), and hence an examination of its milk-teeth would be of great interest. In the stores of the museum of the Royal College of Surgeons are two small fœtuses, whence obtained, I am not able to say, but which I believe, from their characters to belong to this species. The specimen most particularly examined was 11″ long, without any hair except the whiskers and tufts over the eyes. The jaws contained a complete set of very minute teeth, viz. $i. \frac{2}{1}$, $c. \frac{1}{1}$, $m. \frac{3}{3}$, on each side, all of the simplest character. The incisors and canines were cylindrical, and open at the base. The upper canine, which was the largest tooth, and of which the whole of the crown and greater part of the root were calcified, measured in length 0·1″ and in greatest thickness 0.04″. The second upper incisor was about half this size, and the first still smaller. The molars consisted only of a rounded crown, about the size of a small pin's head, the roots were not calcified.

As the crowns of teeth once calcified never enlarge in diameter, we may presume that these rudimentary teeth had attained their full dimensions, except perhaps as to the length of the root in some of them. It will be extremely important, when opportunity serves, to confirm this observation and trace the further progress of the milk-teeth, their relation to the permanent set, and the period at which they disappear.

From such a dentition as this to that of the completely monophyodont predaceous Cetacean, as the grampus (*Orca capensis*) fig. 5, is no great step.

After following such a series of gradations, can we hesitate as to which set of teeth of the diphyodont Carnivora, the deciduous or the permanent, is represented by the only set of the Cetacea?

This question naturally leads to the consideration of the nature of those non-successional teeth which frequently occur among the diphyodonts, often in a rudimentary and transient condition, and which occasion great difficulties in attempting

a satisfactory notation.   As an illustration I will take the case
of an animal belonging to the group lately spoken of, though
remarkably aberrant in its dentition.   The diagram (fig. 6)
shows all that has yet been ascertained regarding the numbers
and succession of the teeth of the Walrus.   It is founded on
many observations that I have made myself on young animals,
aided by those of others, especially Professor Malmgren.   Al-

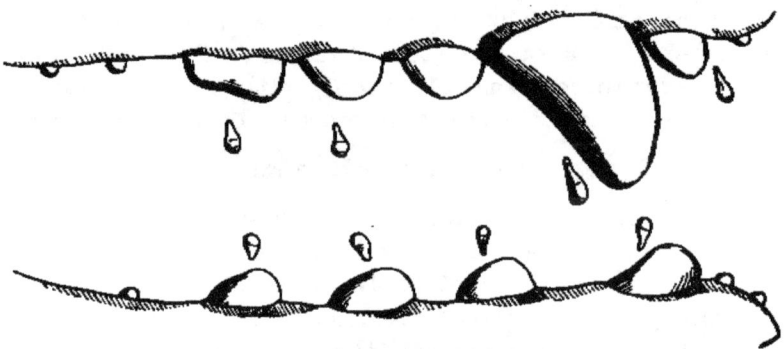

Fig. 6.   Diagram of dentition of Walrus (*Trichecus rosmarus*). It is probable
that an anterior rudimentary incisor is developed in the upper if not in the
lower jaw, but as I have never met with it, it is not introduced in the figure.
The denticles placed apart from the others are milk-teeth, and disappear soon
after birth.   The small teeth in connection with the jaws are often persistent
throughout life.

though still imperfect, as sufficient individuals, especially at
early periods, as about the middle of fœtal life, have not been
examined, it will suffice for the present purpose.

I believe that the rudimentary milk-teeth never cut the
gum, and are absorbed rather than shed.   This process commences before birth.   In the young animal, supposed to be
about eight months old, which died last autumn in the Zoological Gardens, not a trace of any of the milk-teeth, that is, of
teeth which had preceded others, remained.   The rudimentary
teeth, however, in front of and behind the large teeth were present, and these teeth are not unfrequently persistent to extreme
old age, although commonly lost in macerated skulls.

These rudimentary teeth are usually described as "milk-
teeth;" even the posterior ones are sometimes so called[1], but it
appears to me an open question whether they do not rather
represent permanent teeth in a rudimentary or aborted condi-

[1] Peters, *Monatsbericht, Berlin Akad.* 1864, p. 685.

tion. Supposing the present dentition of the Walrus to have been brought about by the gradual modification of the more normal dentition of some kindred form, we must consider that any one of these rudimentary teeth occupies the place, or is the homologue of, either one of two things—the minute transient milk-tooth, or the large persistent functional true tooth. When we contrast the condition and circumstances of this related pair of organs, we can scarcely doubt which of the two is the more likely, when the process of disappearance is taking place, to linger awhile on the scene, and leave the most enduring traces of its former presence.

The dentition of the Hippopotamus throws some light on this question. The first premolar in both jaws is a simple conical single-rooted tooth; it appears at the same time with the milk-teeth; as far as I have been able to ascertain it has no predecessor, and it generally (in the common species of existing Hippopotamus) disappears before middle life, often leaving no trace of its presence in the alveolus. Is this to be reckoned as a milk-tooth or a permanent tooth? A knowledge of its history in the species above mentioned alone, might lead to the idea, that it is an example of a well formed milk-tooth, without a successor; but it is interesting to observe that in the nearly allied extinct animal, the Asiatic *Hexaprotodon*, this tooth is retained throughout life, and the same appears to be the case with the diminutive Liberian Hippopotamus, for in the skeleton of a rather aged animal of this rare species in the Paris museum, all the four premolars are in place. Such a tooth can scarcely be called a milk-tooth, but may safely be regarded as of the same nature as the first premolar of the hog, and many carnivores which, although a permanent tooth, has no predecessor. If the transient or deciduous premolar of the common Hippopotamus, is to be regarded as the representative of one of the permanent set, so also may the rudimentary or almost suppressed teeth in the Walrus. In the same manner the rudimentary and generally deciduous first premolar of the Horse is the representative of a permanent tooth in *Hipparion*.

To speak of deciduous permanent teeth may seem to involve a contradiction, yet there are many cases of teeth undoubtedly corresponding to those of the permanent set in other animals, as for instance, the premolars and first and second true molars of *Phacochœrus*, which are habitually shed before the natural termination of the animal's life. Some new method of terminology is clearly required, though I do not at present see the way to proposing a satisfactory one. The conditions under which the teeth of mammalia occur may however be formularized as follows:

Teeth are either,

(1) Milk-teeth = preceding teeth. Teeth which precede or are replaced by other teeth.

(2) True teeth. Teeth never succeeded or replaced by others. These may be

A. Permanent ; lasting through the lifetime of the animal.

B. Deciduous ; falling out before the termination of the ordinary lifetime of the animal.

They are also,

a. Succeeding teeth ; replacing milk-teeth.

β. Primary teeth ; not replacing milk-teeth[1].

I think that the various facts brought forward above serve to show that the terms *monophyodont* and *diphyodont*, though useful additions to our language, as means of indicating briefly certain physiological conditions, have not, as applied to the mammalian class, precisely the same significance, that their author originally attributed to them. I will now discuss certain questions regarding the classification, nomenclature and homologies of the permanent teeth of the Heterodont mammals.

In endeavouring to determine the teeth which in one animal correspond to, or are homologous with those of another, the difficulties (as in all similar cases) increase as the animals recede from each other in relationship ; and these difficulties often arise, I believe, not only from our want of ability in discerning obscure indications, but often because we may after all be striving to grasp at shadows and not realities. By the operation of variation and natural selection parts may be gradually developed in some groups of animals, which have no direct homologues in others. The teeth of reptiles and

---

[1] A case lately under my close observation shows that the development of a true tooth may be quite independent of that of its usual milk predecessor. A boy had his milk set completely formed except the lower left canine, which was never developed. A gap remained in its place, until the second set of teeth began to appear, when it was filled by a well-formed permanent canine.

those of mammals taken as a whole are certainly corresponding portions of the system, but no one has succeeded in tracing any special homologies between individual members of the series. In the same way little progress has been made in showing any special correspondence between the individual teeth of the Homodonts and the Heterodonts, or with the teeth of the former group, one among another.

It is among the latter, with their comparatively restricted number, and strongly individualized characters, that a rigid adherence to a typical system has been most strongly advocated; and undoubtedly, a very large number of cases do agree with the general dental formulæ now usually adopted in this country, and as I said before, originally propounded at a meeting of this association twenty years ago.

First among the generalizations regarding Diphyodont (or it would be safer to say Heterodont) dentition, is that the teeth (except for the increased number of incisors in some Marsupials) never exceed 44 altogether, divided in the following way, viz. in each jaw on each side, 3 incisors, 1 canine and 7 molars; this therefore is regarded as the typical number, and cases of deviation from it result always from suppression of some particular members of the series, which ought in every case to be capable of being exactly determined. After excluding the aberrent Manatee, no instances are yet known of normal or habitual variation from these numbers by excess, except the well known ones of the African Long-Eared Fox (*Otocyon*) which has one, and in some instances two additional true molars in each series, making altogether 48 or 52, and the singular genus *Myrmecobius* among the Marsupials. The generalization may therefore be received as good, the exceptions being always noted.

To proceed to the nomenclature of the individual teeth. The upper incisors are readily defined as "the teeth implanted in the premaxillary bones." The lower ones are by no means so clearly indicated as "those implanted in the corresponding part of the lower jaw." There is however seldom much practical difficulty in deciding upon which shall be called lower incisors, though the distinction between them and the canine is in some cases, as in the Lemurs and Ruminants, rather arbitrary and artificial. In the homological system of notation " the incisors are counted from the median line, commonly the fore-most part of both upper and lower jaws, outwards and back-wards." When their number falls short of the typical number, it is assumed that the absent ones are missing from the outer or posterior end of the series. Thus, when but one incisor is present it is I. 1, when two they are I. 1, and I. 2. This is, I think, open to great doubt. In many cases the homology is quite obscure; in others, among nearly allied animals it can be shown, that sometimes the third (as in *Babirussa*—compared with *Sus*) is suppressed, and in other cases it is the first which disappears as in the Labiate Bear, Sea Otter, Walrus, &c. Moreover the single incisor of the Camels, *Rhynchocyon*, and *Dasypus sexcinctus,* more resembles in position the third than the first of the typical mammals.

"The tooth in the maxillary bone, which is situated at or near to, the suture with the premaxillary, is the 'canine,' as is also that tooth in the lower jaw which in opposing it, passes in front of its crown, when the mouth is closed." This defini-tion is anything but satisfactory, but all others derived from the shape or function of the tooth are even less so, consequently some zoologists have thought of abolishing the distinction between the canine and premolars, treating the former only as the first of the premolar series. However the special modifica-tion that the tooth presents in certain orders, especially the Carnivora, makes the retention of the name essential for the purposes of descriptive zoology.

We come next to the molar series of teeth, divided into pre-molars and true molars according as they have or have not predecessors in the milk set. This division is an improvement upon the former ones founded merely on the configuration of the crowns of the teeth, although it has the practical inconve-nience of requiring a knowledge of the condition of the organs in a young state before it can be applied.

The definition of " premolars " as " the teeth which displace and succeed deciduous molars vertically," requires modification, as it has been shown that in many cases one or more of the permanent premolars have no predecessors in the first set. These are however always at the anterior part of the series, and as the last premolar is almost invariably a replacing tooth, there is rarely any doubt (when the succession is known) as to the point where the premolars terminate and the true molars begin. The generalization, the annunciation of which is due to Professor Owen, that among the placental Heterodonts the complete number of premolars is four, and of true molars three, while among the Marsupials these numbers are reversed, appears fully established.

The rule of notation generally adopted with reference to these teeth is founded on the following dictum: "When the premolars and the molars are below their typical number, the absent teeth are missing from the fore-part of the premolar series, and from the back part of the molar series."

If this were invariably so, the labours of those who have to describe teeth would be greatly simplified, but it appears that a far more rigid investigation is required before the assumption can be universally admitted. There are many cases among the premolars in which, judging by the gradual diminution in size and ultimate disappearance of a tooth in allied forms of animals, it appears pretty evident that the reduction of number is not due to the loss of the first. Professor Peters has proved in this way[1] that in certain bats, the *Phyllostomata* and *Rhinolophi*, the diminution of the number of premolars arises from want of development of a middle tooth.

In the Bears, as Professor Owen has himself pointed out, it is the second premolar which is least constant and disappears earliest. I will add another and very striking case, which occurs among the Marsupials. In the family *Dasyuridæ*, the animals of the genus *Dasyurus* are distinguished from those of *Phascogale*, by possessing but two premolars on each side above and below, instead of three, the typical number among the Marsupials, and a careful comparison of the teeth of various members of the last named genus, leaves little doubt but that the two present in *Dasyurus* are the first and second of the more typical form, the third or hindermost being absent. In some species of *Phascogale* all three premolars are well developed, the third being as large, or even larger than the others. In other species (as *P. melas*) the third is the smallest, both in the

---

[1] *Abhand. Konj. Akad. der Wissenschaft*, Berlin, 1866, p. 87.

upper and lower jaw, but especially in the lower, where it may be called rudimentary. The transition is completed in a species lately made known by Mr Krefft under the name of *Chæto-cercus cristicauda*[1], in which the third upper premolar is described as being "very diminutive," and the lower one entirely absent, the number being reduced to two as in *Dasyurus*. If, as these facts seem to show, the homologue of the posterior premolar of other Marsupials is absent in *Dasyurus*, it will be very interesting to ascertain whether the milk-molar is transferred to the antecedent tooth, or as I rather suspect, is absent altogether. At present I have been unable to meet with specimens at the right age to determine this point.

It will be seen from these rather fragmentary observations, that we are still far from having attained to a perfect and satisfactory system of notation of teeth. It is possible that the nature of the subject will never allow of one which is equally applicable to all the different groups of the Mammalia. In the meantime, the varying mode of succession and development of the teeth in the different orders and families offers a fruitful field for research, and one which will become yearly more practicable, if the awakening interest in zoological science expends some of its energies in urging forward the growth of anatomical museums. The lack of sufficient materials at command will then be no longer, as at present, the bane of the would-be observer.

[1] *Proc. Zool. Soc.* 1866, p. 435.

ON SOME POINTS IN THE ANATOMY OF STENTOR AND ON ITS MODE OF DIVISION. By W. Moxon, M.D., F.R.C.P., *Assistant Physician and Pathologist to Guy's Hospital.* (Pl. v. and vi.)

IN this paper I wish to relate the results of some of my observations on Infusoria and especially on Stentor Cæruleus, and to discuss certain questions concerning the anatomy of Infusoria which those observations concern. Also I shall shew the real nature of that "Lateral crest" which is described by authors as present in some species of Stentor.

One of the most interesting structures in the animal creation is the Infusorial "contractile vesicle." This, as is well known, is a cavity which has a constant and characteristic position in the several kinds, and which is endowed with a power of rhythmical contraction. Its constancy of occurrence in the Infusoria, its regularity of position in the kind concerned, and its rhythmical beat, mark it as an organ of importance, and one that serves some essential function in their œconomy. But it is not yet settled what that function is, some observers regarding the vesicle as a heart belonging to a minute vascular system which they conclude is present, and others regarding it rather as an excretory organ. A full account of the position of the question is found in Mr Pritchard's work on Infusoria. That author himself judges that the former conclusion is the correct one. He supports his opinion by long extracts from Lieberkühn's *Observations on Bursaria and Ophryoglena.* Lieberkühn came to the conclusion that he perceived canals ramifying minutely in the wall of the creature's cyst-like body, thirty such ramifying vessels he describes as opening into the contractile vesicle of a Bursaria, and in such Bursariæ as had two vesicles he concluded to perceive two sets of the vessels. He describes minutely the contraction and dilatation of the vesicles, the process being essentially as follows: viz. as the systole progresses the stellate rays which stretch from the vesicle enlarge somewhat, but the vesicle is entirely obliterated, contracting

itself to a point at which the rays then meet.   He affirms that
the vessels run out over the whole body at the time of contraction, but are only seen as short processes during the filling
of the vesicle.

These observations it is necessary to remark were made
on specimens so fixed that they were not able to move, or
could move but very little; that is, on specimens compressed,
for only by compression can they be fixed, as any one knows
who has experience of their locomotive propensities. Lieberkühn
goes on to remark that under somewhat more compression of
the animal peculiar phenomena present themselves not only
in the contractile vesicle but also in the vessels.   Shortly these
are they.   The vesicle divides into two vesicles each pulsating
for itself in its own time; and the same phenomena which
satisfied him of the existence of finely ramified vessels are
repeated in the case of each of these new vesicles.   The vessels
exhibit the same play as if there were but one uninjured vesicle.
The vesicles may re-unite and work as if nothing had happened.
Siebold also describes the subdivision of one vesicle into two.
Lieberkühn could never find a lining membrane to his vessels
nor any cilia within them.

In enquiring concerning the functions of this system he
supports Claperede who in his paper on Actinophrys regards
the vesicles as organs of circulation, from having been unable
to see any external opening to the vesicle in that creature,
in which the vesicle during its diastole rises off the surface
of the animalcule by $\frac{3}{8}$ of its whole surface; and he opposes
Oscar Schmidt's view who believed that he saw openings to
the vesicles of Bursaria and Paramæcium, he admits that he
saw an orifice in the body of a Bursaria exactly at the spot
which the vesicle contracts upon.   But from having seen the
discharge of fœcal matter through it he concludes that it is
really the anus of the creature and only by chance in the
neighbourhood of the contractile vesicle.   He concludes that
Schmidt saw in the Paramæcium a canal run towards the
surface and did not see that the canal then turned and ran under
the surface.   Stein also strongly questions the existence of an
external opening in Vorticella.   Lieberkühn then considers
it certain that the vessels carry liquid *to* the vesicle during its

diastole, and in difficulty as to the channel of exit of the liquid from the vesicle during its systole, he gives an observation on Vorticella Bursaria in which he believed himself to see a vessel run on either side full of clear liquid during the diastole of the vesicle. These vessels emptied during the systole. He was, in short, quite unable to find any special canals by which the fluid is seen to flow back into the body during the systole of the vesicle.

I have thus fully given these statements because it is important to clearly apprehend the reasons of fact on which the dispute concerning the nature and office of the Infusorian contractile vesicle is founded. It appears to me that the truth may be best approached by separating the two means of enquiry which these observers use undistinguished, namely analogy and observation. On the ground of *analogy* it is plainly supposed by those who believe the contractile vesicle to be a circulating organ, that a circulating system such as exists in the higher animals may and should exist in these minute beings also. Now I wish to join issue with this assumption on *a priori* grounds. For one general truth seems to have very commonly eluded consideration, and that is the absolute relation to size, which is shewn in the magnitude of all capillary meshes in all animals. It is a remarkable thing that whether we take the limb of a water-louse or of an elephant the capillary network is of about the same dimensions. In the little articulate there will be a single mesh in a limb, while in the incomparably greater vertebrate there are myriads of the meshes; but the meshes in the huge vertebrate are no larger than those in the tiny articulate notwithstanding the vast disproportion of bulk between them. Be it noted also that the general plan of construction of the two creatures contrasted is wholly unlike. As this constancy of size of capillary meshes is, within very narrow limits, maintained in all beings, whatever their size and type of construction, may we not draw from it such a conclusion as follows; namely, that the Living tissue, within the area of the capillary mesh, has an attractive power strong enough to enable it to draw its nutrition from a distance equal to one half of the diameter of the mesh, as the tissue at the centre of the mesh must get its nourishment from such a

distance out of the nearest vessel. This conclusion is I suppose
the natural and easy consequence of the facts offered. The
only escape from the conclusion that living tissue is so endowed
with power to draw its nourishment from a certain distance
is by the supposition of minute canals in the textures within
the mesh through which a stream of nourishment is urged by
circulatory power. Such a system of excessively minute canals
with such a power is however quite unknown in vertebrates
(one of Virchow's connective tissue cells is nearly as great
as the *whole body* of an infusorium); so that the assumption of
their existence would be a gratuitous hypothesis; and as to
the small Invertebrata we are able to go further and say that
direct observation proves their non-existence. The accompanying drawing (fig. 10) represents the vascular system in a joint
of a leg of a small *oniscus*. The vessels are seen running along
at *a*, and at *b b* are nuclei upon them such and so placed that
the vessel corresponds as exactly with the capillary of a vertebrate as the muscles of the oniscus correspond in their histology
with the muscles of a vertebrate. At *c c* are seen " blood"-
corpuscles which are very few in these larvæ. These can be
seen moving in the track indicated by the arrows, passing down
the vessel *a* through its open mouth *d* and then becoming quite
free in the space about the muscles *e f.* Their freedom would
be matter of doubt if the creature were dead ; the conditions
would then offer the same difficulty of observation as is found in
the case of the tissues of Vertebrates where the slender pellucid
substance does not offer sufficiently precise outlines for one to follow the tracks of minute vessels without injection or other artificial
means more or less destructive of the integrity of the parts.
In the living limb, however, it is quite otherwise, the corpuscles
can be seen to shoot out of the vessel, if one may so speak, and
turn about in an irregular way: one of them will move one
way, its follower another way, others will oscillate backwards
and forwards; and the motions, so free, prove the absence of
any containing vessel after the exit of the corpuscle from the
capillary orifice. Only a general tendency to move towards
the heart is seen which determines them each and all onwards
into the venous channels. This instance is one of very many;
for the like facts are well known to be true not only of low

articulata, but also of Molluscs and Radiates, indeed, of any Invertebrates which from their small size and the clearness of their tissues allow an observer to witness the course of the capillary circulation in their bodies.

Assuming that in Vertebrates and articulate animals the living tissue is able to draw food across a space not less than $\frac{1}{120}$th of an inch, why should not the living tissue of Infusoria be equally able to attract food through the same distance? Their vital activity is not less but rather, perhaps, much greater than that of "higher" beings, forasmuch as their consumption of food is more constant and their rate of multiplication more rapid. The supposition of a circulation of nutritious liquid on such an excessively minute scale as that supposed by Lieberkühn involves the assumption that the vital activity of the component tissue of the creature's body is feeble in the same proportion as the vascular ramifications are minute. If the tissue of a Paramæcium or Bursaria requires to have its nourishment circulated to every $\frac{1}{30000}$th of an inch in its frame then the vital activity of its tissue must be most excessively low.

Now this is an assumption that will raise up against itself a great measure of doubt, because of the very general scope of the law that fixes a limit to the smallness of capillary meshwork. Thus analogy, so far from being in favour of a belief in the existence of circulatory channels in these minute beings, is strongly against such a belief; and an exception to a law so general as that of the size of capillary meshes should be substantiated by very exact and undoubtable facts. But in examining the foundations in fact of the view which affirms the existence of circulatory channels in Infusoria, that view is found to rest on these two facts only: *first*, that the contractile vesicle of Paramæcium becomes stellate in contraction, and, *secondly*, that the eye of many observers fails to perceive an outlet to the vesicle.

In reference to the first fact it should be noted that the observations on stellate rays from the contractile vesicle have only been made in specimens subjected to compression; and the observer goes on to say that when the pressure was so severe as to part the vesicle into two portions, each of these portions had the same stellate rays as those given off by the undivided vesicle. This instantaneous formation of vessels and rearrangement of them around a heart in the moment when the creature was being squeezed to death does not surely need serious notice. The only point of importance in the whole statement is the fact that the secondary groups of vessels were like the first. Reversing this statement and regarding the first as like the second, we shall probably arrive at a true conclusion respecting them, viz. they were fissures produced in the creature's body by the violent compression, and were indeed the commencement of the final breaking up and dispersion of its tissues. I have repeatedly made the observation and have seen what so far corresponded with the description given above, that I could not doubt that the phænomena were identical with those seen by Lieberkühn, yet from the irregularity of the little fissures that extended from the contractile vesicle, and from the fact that by increasing the pressure yet more the body of the infusorium parted along these fissures in breaking up, there could be no doubt that they were only lines of separation in the compressed body of the animal.

Another point which is regarded as evidencing the presence of vessels into which the contractile vesicle throws a circulating liquid, is the fact that the stellate rays of the vesicle of paramæcium swell out during the vesicle's contraction. The true explanation of this fact, which I can indeed verify, is, I believe, the following : The paramæcium when observed with such care as is required in order to see the distension of the stellate rays has to be kept quiet by compression, and he is so compressed that the orifice of the vesicle is against one of the glasses between which he is squeezed (otherwise the front view required for the observation would not be obtained). But there cannot be so close a compression without the orifice of the vesicle being obstructed by the close pressure of the glass against it. Now with the little hole in the vesicle wall so stopped up, the vesicle would throw the liquid it contained at the time of contraction in some other directions, probably back along the way it came into fissures among the soft "sarcode" of which the interior of the body is composed.

It is however plain that one is not obliged to substantiate

this denial of a plexus of minute canals in order to support my foregoing argument against the existence of a nutritive vascular system, for such canals might exist and have some other function than that of conveying a nutritive current. At the same time the ground I have taken up in reference to the connexion between organization on the one hand, and a constant size on the other militates, so far as it is of force, against the probability of finding any system in one class of beings excessively out of proportion to the general size of corresponding system in all creatures. I hold that a very great burden of proof is undertaken by any who will strive to shew that any system whatever is laid out on the excessively minute scale supposed in the above-quoted description of Bursaria. It is unsupported by any analogy, and runs counter to all.

No one will doubt that what is true of the Infusorian contractile vesicle in any one instance is true also in all other Infusoria. The general plan of construction is nowhere else so harmonious in all creation. Various as are their shape, the constitution of their simple frames is wonderfully constant, the tegument with lines of cilia, the mouth with short ciliated œsophagus, the nucleus, and the contractile vesicle. If then any instance can be found which offers evidence of an external opening of the canal system, it will be rendered certain that such is the general condition in all others. This evidence I offer in the case of Stentor Cæruleus, and I offer it confidently. To make the observation wants not much patience and no great magnifying power. The species in question offers an advantage which renders it very suitable for the observation, that is its blue skin. The colour of this is very strong and is uniform, any pale spot on it is at once seen. The coat of this Stentor is apparently composed of rather broad blue bands separated by fine colourless lines which run from the narrow to the wide end of the trumpet-shaped body of the animal. The cilia with which the surface is furnished are all arranged on the colourless lines (fig. 8) and none on the blue bands. These bands are narrow at the narrow end, and widen with the widening towards the expanded end of the creature. Some fail to extend all the way, ceasing in points between their neighbours, just as some of the papillary ridges on the tip of one's fingers may be seen to cease. Indeed the striped appearance of the creature's coat is very like that of the tip of a finger, but when seen with a ¼th inch objective, it is on a much larger scale of appearance. The rim which bounds the mouth of the trumpet, which the creature so curiously resembles, is not entire, but starts rather abruptly, and running round $\frac{9}{10}$ths of the border turns in with a graceful curve and assumes a spiral course as it passes down into the body of the animal forming its œsophagus, or rather forming a strong line of support in the wall of its spiral œsophagus. The contractile vesicle, about as wide as three of the blue bands, is placed a little below the rim, and at a short distance from the point at which the rim turns in to make its spiral curve. Now if one looks carefully at the part of the blue tegument over the contractile vesicle, one sees in the band that crosses its middle two or sometimes three small pale spots (fig. 2, fig. 6); they can easily be seen because of the prevailing uniform deep blue colour of the tegument, there are no other such spots. These spots having been found, the eye must be fixed steadily on them, and the time of the contraction of the vesicle awaited, and then there will be no mistake about its opening. At the moment of commencing contraction one of the small pale spots before mentioned widens out into a large sharp bordered hole, and the vesicle contracts down to this hole in the creature's tegument (fig. 6'). I have seen this many times, and always with increasing interest, the whole process is so beautifully simple, and plain and easy to observe. It only requires that one patiently waits the contraction, and that the creature be quietly rooted to some spot. The contractions take place at pretty long intervals, and the body of the Stentor is apt to be constantly rolling slowly round; but if we patiently wait until the favourable opportunity comes, the evidence of the external opening of the contractile vesicle is quite decisive. After contraction it fills again slowly; no branches could I distinguish in connection with it.

In another Animalcule I have discovered a contractile space which has hitherto escaped notice, and which gives very convincing proof of its external opening. This animalcule is Spirostomum ambiguum (fig. 11). The body of this creature consists of a long flexible cylinder, furnished externally with the usual lines of cilia and with a crest of long cilia, which starts from one end and runs ⅘ths of the length of the body, then gives a spiral turn, and at the same time enters the interior as part of the œsophagus. At the end of the animal which is opposite to the commencement of this crest, there is an irregular space nearer one side than the other, and reaching quite to the creature's extremity (fig. 11. c). In some specimens this space is larger, in some smaller. In some it is not seen. If it be watched patiently, it will be found that these different appearances of the space are due to the fact that it contracts and dilates. It dilates however very slowly, and contracts at long intervals. When fully dilated its size is very striking. It bulges indeed in some specimens. The act of contraction begins at the end farthest from the tail, and passes towards the tail. Obviously the space empties itself outwards. The quantity of liquid contained by it is so great that if it were thrown into the body of the animal its passage must easily be seen. This space is very interesting as it is, I believe, the only instance of an infusorian contractile vesicle of unsymmetrical form. In all other Infusoria I believe the vesicle is globular.

Not far from the opening of the contractile vesicle in Stentor is the point of surface which gives exit to the solid residues of the creature's food. This point can be seen usually very easily. Its place is marked, not by any pore or opening, but by an irregularity or break in the course of one or two of the longitudinal blue bands before described. It is curious to watch the process of extension. The mass to be thrown out is brought to the surface and simply forced through it, sometimes carrying with it a thread of the glairy contents of the saccular body of the animal (fig. 7). Indeed it was such a glairy thread, projecting from a stentor's body, that first drew my attention to the site and the mode of defœcation. I afterwards watched the process on several occasions[1]. After having

[1] The supple pliancy of the tegument of the stentor was well seen in a curious accident that happened to a stentor under my observation. A little oxyuris came with its usual incessant wriggling motion against a stentor, and without further trouble wriggled into its inside. The oxyuris kicked about for some time very violently, lashing about in the soft contents of the stentor's body in such a way that any delicate vessels must have been torn to shreds; nevertheless the stentor did not appear to suffer in the least, it remained extended with its cilium-wreath in full activity, feeding actively. The figure

watched the habits and studied the structure of Stentor for some time, it was with much surprise that I found in systematic authors on Infusoria, that a certain longitudinal ciliated line, or "lateral crest" as it is called, is included among the characters which are distinctive of the different species or genera of the family.

Thus, for instance, the Lateral crest is said to be indistinct in S. Mülleri, to be continuous with the Frontal wreath in S. Cæruleus, to be absent in S. Igneus, and so forth.

My surprise at this was great, because I had seen that the "Lateral crest" is nothing else than the "Frontal wreath" of the caudal or proximal segment of the *dividing* stentor. By a curious process it becomes curved round, and forms the new trumpet-edge of the caudal half of the dividing stentor, while a new tail is developed for the old trumpet-shaped head.

In order to render clear the description of the process, I must use some terms to distinguish the several parts of the body which are concerned in it.

The narrow pointed end of the stentor I will call the caudal end, and the wide end, where the mouth is situated, the oral end. The disc which fills in the part corresponding to the mouth of the trumpet, which the creature resembles, I will call the oral disc. The wreath of long cilia which surrounds the margin of the trumpet I will call the oral crest, the lateral line of long cilia the lateral crest, and will speak of the end of this nearer the caudal extremity of the stentor as the caudal end, and the opposite as the oral end.

When a stentor is about to divide, this lateral crest is seen running along its side in the same longitudinal course as that of the blue bands, so that it has the appearance of being parallel to these, which it is for the most part, although however early I made the examination, I always found that some of the blue bands join the lateral crest at its caudal end, the caudal end curving to receive them. Now in the caudal segment of the divided stentor, this lateral crest (which becomes its oral crest)

represents the appearance just at the moment of the oxyuris' escape, which it effected by piercing the stentor's tegument. The yielding consistency of the coat is well seen in the extent to which it is carried out by the pressure of the pointed end of the oxyuris. I may add, that watching the oxyuris for some time, he did not seem to be affected in health by his Jonah-like stay within the monster.

runs at right angles to the same blue bands to which it was parallel when it first appeared. It is an interesting question how this change of relation of the lateral crest to the longitudinal bands is effected.

The dotted line on figure 2 shews the plane in which the division is virtually effected. The line of division starting from the caudal end of the "lateral crest" passes spirally round the body of the creature, and meets the oral end of the lateral crest, then runs up that crest to where it started. In the process of self-division, the caudal half so cut off will have to make to itself a part corresponding to the oral half, and the oral half will have to make to itself a part corresponding to the caudal half. The process is thus really one of division, and not strictly of simple budding, because there is no complete new zooid formed as a bud from an old, but half of each of the new zooids is old. Yet owing to the lateral projection of the new head of the caudal zooid, the appearance of budding is almost perfect. Indeed the whole process has to be watched throughout before one can be quite sure that a bud is not thrown out from the creature's side, perfected, and detached. This process may be chosen as an excellent example to prove the likeness of the two processes of budding and division, for the head of the caudal stentor can be seen to grow out of the side of the dividing stentor *as a bud*. The lateral crest is the part which first draws attention. On it are developed the long cilia characteristic of the oral crest. The crest and cilia appear to grow together. They probably are to each other as parts of the same machine, the motor power of the cilia lying in the thick substance of the crest. The lateral crest is then lifted away from the side of the creature by the formation of new matter on either side of it; meantime its ends curve towards each other so as to give the crest a concave form; this concavity has the same direction as the concavity of the old oral crest. The caudal end of the crest appears to dip into the animal's body; a mass of formative substance collects there, and a depression appears in the concavity of the crest just at its end. This concavity deepens, and, as it deepens, becomes spiral, the crest itself being prolonged as a rib in the wall of the spiral concavity. So the œsophagus is formed.

But I never could see any dividing stentor in which the concavity of the new œsophagus was commenced, but in that stentor the new contractile vesicle was already apparent. Indeed, I never saw any stentor with the lateral crest developed, but the contractile vesicle was to be seen, so that it appears to me that the contractile vesicle is the part first formed, the oral wreath (as lateral crest) next, the œsophagus last.

The new matter which grows in the concavity of the lateral crest forms the disc that closes the trumpet-mouth-like oral end of the caudal zooid. As it forms, it pushes away those of the old blue bands that lie on that side of the crest, while in it appear new blue bands, which run nearly parallel with the crest, many of those near the crest joining it, however, at acute angles towards either end of it, while those more distant turn in at the mouth to form the œsophagus, joining in it that produced end of the crest that has been described as dipping in and strengthening the spiral œsophagus. At first, these blue bands are narrow and close set. They widen afterwards, and so the disc enlarges; in other words, they develope first, and afterwards they grow.

While all this is taking place in the concavity of the lateral crest, other changes are taking place on its convexity. This convex crest, lying as it does generally parallel to the blue bands of the original stentor, must cut across some of these where its ends turn; it cuts many more at the caudal bend of the crest than at the oral bend. The oral bend only divides about five, which run from it to the old oral wreath (see fig. 2); while the caudal bend cuts a very great number, which run from it to the tail. As the developement of the new head proceeds, the number divided by the caudal bend greatly increases until nearly all are divided by it, and run from it to the tail; while, on the other hand, the number divided by the oral bend diminishes until, at last, none run from the lateral crest to the old crest, but all run from the lateral crest to the tail. I have had great difficulty in making out any describable steps in this wonderful process. It appears that new soft matter grows on the convexity of the curve of the lateral crest, and the softness of this matter enables the crest actually to change its position with reference to the bands formerly parallel to it or running to its bends. The blue bands disappear for a time along a line corresponding to the line in fig. 2, their loss being due to a production of formative matter along that line of separation, and while they are absent the oral end of the lateral crest comes down, detaching from its old connexions as before described; and when the blue bands across that line re-appear, they are found to grow to the convexity of the lateral crest nearly at right angles to it; in other words, formative matter is produced beside the crest and also in the line of separation, and this softens the parts along the crest and along that line, so that the lateral crest *moves* into the line and so may be said by its convex side to cut across the original stentor's blue bands, joining their caudal ends at right angles. Meantime, the newly-developed oral disc on the concave side of the lateral crest pushes away the oral ends of the divided bands to continue in union with the old oral crest of the original stentor, and, by prolongation downwards, to form a new tail for the oral zooid.

And so the developement of the new oral disc, in the fashion of a bud, is the means whereby the old head is separated from the old tail. This bud is seen to cut the old bands of the body in two, and while making union with one set of the segments of bands to push away the other set. The budding disc may perhaps, however, be rather the more obvious instrument in the division; for, of course, in the meantime the new tail for the original head is growing: the formation of this latter is a very simple process, consisting in the elongation of the distal ends of the divided blue bands, which grow narrower as they lengthen and as their connexion with the caudal stentor is rendered smaller and smaller by the successive cutting of the longitudinal bands. As the uncut bands are at the distal end of the new crest, and these uncut bands form the connexion between the two zooids, it will be seen that the last part divided will be situated at the distal end of the new crest (fig. 4).

I have traced this process thus in detail because, from the beautiful distinctness of the creature's blue stripes, one can follow on its body the curious process of division with an exactness and completeness that can perhaps not be equalled in the case of any other creature which undergoes self-division; certainly cannot be equalled in the case of any other of the interesting group of Infusoria.

19—2

One point worthy of note was the probable effect of the oral crest of the original stentor in causing the new oral wreath to move across and cut the bands of the original stentor. The motion of the stentor when going from place to place is rotatory, and the same rotation is produced by the action of the oral crest of cilia when the creature is fixed. Now when the two new zooids are very nearly separate, there is an obvious spiral twisting of the narrow connexion between the two, from the caudal zooid not partaking in the motion of the oral zooid; and it occurred to me that, as the caudal end of the distal zooid is attached to that end of the oral wreath which moves across to make a union with the divided end of the bands, the motion may be caused by the effort at rotation of the distal zooid by means of its oral wreath. If this is so, it is an interesting instance of the use of a creature's locomotive apparatus in giving form to its offspring, and shews a way in which practically external agencies may aid in causing the specific forms of developing animals.

In Mr Pritchard's work on Infusoria, the stentor is said to "increase by self-division, which is either longitudinal or oblique." The latter stages of the process I have just described no doubt correspond to the oblique division. What I shew is, that the so-called "lateral crest" is the first stage of this process, which may be called oblique division. I have never seen any longitudinal division in stentor. I have seen two animalcules joined together longitudinally (fig. 9) in such a way that the idea of longitudinal division is suggested; but in such cases I have always found the animals perfect, and applied mouth to mouth in the manner described by Balbiani as an act of copulation, such as is witnessed in Paramæcium, Euplotes and other genera, and I believe that his view of the process is correct. This act of copulation has probably been mistaken for a longitudinal division.

In studying the structure of the integument of stentor, I have not been able to detect any division of it into external and internal layers. There is but one tunic, and that is marked by blue bands, separated by fine white lines, as I have before described. The white lines carry on them the cilia, and no cilia are on the coloured parts. These white lines differ in consistency from the blue lines. When a stentor was crushed, I saw the former bend into zigzags (fig. 8′), and appear as highly refractile lines persisting after the blue bands had almost dispersed. In these blue bands, the colour is not quite uniform, but is granular. When the creature contracts its body, the bands assume a transversely striated appearance, looking like muscular fibres stained blue. In crushing up stentors, I have sometimes detached the large cilia from the thick marginal band to which they are attached. I have never seen them move after being so detached. They bend permanently, as if flaccid, not rigid. On the other hand, I have seen the fleshy marginal band from which they were detached move in a vermicular manner, tremulous waves passing along it after patches of the cilia were detached; the cilia remaining attached vibrated at the time of the passing of the vermicular wave. On one occasion, a slender oxyuris ran into the mass of the crushed stentor, and began to feed, whipping about the remains of the stentor in its usual restless motion. The consistency of the tegument of the creature then proved itself to be considerable; and, after a deal of thrashing from the tail of the worm, the white lines which bear the cilia were still visible. The whole of these creatures' textures are, however, very perishable; if crushed, the shaper parts are all disintegrated in an hour, nothing remains but a few crooked relics of cilia attached to fragments of the thick rim which gave them motion.

DESCRIPTION OF PLATES IV AND V.

Fig. 1. Stentor cæruleus.
  „ 2. Stentor cæruleus, or lateral crest.
  „ 3. The crest developing into the head of the caudal zooid.
  „ 4. The process of division nearly complete.
  „ 5. The act of separation.
  „ 6. The orifices of the contractile vesicle. 6′. The same widely open during contraction of the vesicle.
  „ 7. Escape of some of the sarcode during defœcation.
  „ 8. Sectional view of tegument, shewing limitation of cilia to the pale lines. 8′. The same crushed, shewing the lines in zigzag stiffish rods.
  „ 9. Copulation of stentors.
  „ 10. Joint of leg of Oniscus, shewing—*a.* Capillary vessel; *b.* Nuclei on it; *c.* Blood corpuscle; *d.* Open mouth of the capillary; *e.* Muscle.
  „ 11. Spirostomum Ambiguum; *c.* Its large irregular contractile space.

THE MYOLOGY OF THE LIMBS OF PTEROPUS. By Professor Humphry (Pl. VI. & VII.)

THE muscles of the limbs of Cheiroptera present so many features of interest that I think it worth while, although they have been described by others, to give an accurate description of them as recently dissected by me in two specimens of Pteropus Edwardsii, a male and a female.

The peculiar features of interest are, *first*, the modifications by which the muscles of the fore limb are adapted for flying, leading us to observe by what slight deviations from the ordinary mammalian type the end has been attained. The large pectorals springing from a keeled sternum, and the *tensores plicœ alaris* constitute some approach to the peculiarities of the bird. The latter muscles, however, do not spring, as in the bird, from the shoulder girdle, but are obviously prolongations of the *platysma*, and no part of them passes to the forearm; nor does the deeper stratum of the pectorals (*pect. min.* and *subclavius*) show any special avian characters. Moreover the resistance to the pull of the pectoral muscle upon the shoulder is afforded not by the presence of a coracoid bone or by the union of the clavicles, but the manner in which the broad flat surfaces of the strong clavicles are jointed with corresponding articular surfaces on the sternum. The *biceps* has, in one of the specimens, a slight muscular slip from the humerus; but this is not uncommon in mammals or indeed in man, and it is rather a detachment from the brachialis anticus than a distinct origin of the muscle, as it is in the bird, from the upper end of the humerus; and unlike the same in the bird, the main (coracoid) portion of the muscle is in two parts, and these are unusually distinct. The *supinator longus* stops short at the upper third of the radius, acting simply as a flexor of the forearm ; and the radial flexors and extensors of the carpus are inserted as in mammals, none of these muscles being attached, as their two representatives in birds are, to the foremost metacarpal.

The *flexor carpi ulnaris* arises as usual. It does not, as in the bird, arise behind the inner condyle and pass beneath it, playing under it as under a pulley. This provision in the bird for harmonising flexion of the carpus with flexion of the elbow, like the provisions in the supinator longus (its connection with the tensor plicæ alaris above and with the metatarsus below) for harmonising extension of the carpus with extension of the elbow, is wanting in Pteropus.

In these and in the other myological differences from birds we recognise an inferiority in the adaptation of the animal for flight which is more strongly evinced in the want of concentration and simplification of the osseous and muscular structures characterizing the distal segment of the bird's wing, and which is most of all shown in the dermal extension as a substitute for feathers, whereby the hinder limbs are involved in the work of aerial movement and are unfitted for any other mode of locomotion[1]. Thus, while we admire the manner in which this order (Cheiropterous) is specialized for flight from a class (Mammalian) which is not constructed for such movement, we are conscious of the great superiority of the mechanism attained in the several members of that class which is throughout, or in great measure, constructed for flight, and in which the hind limbs are left free to subserve to terrestrial locomotion, while better motor power in air is obtained by the more perfect adaptation of the fore limbs and of the body generally. A similar illustration of the same principle is found in the fact that the mammalian inhabitants of the deep show their adaptation to the watery medium to be inferior to that of the fish, by the necessity which compels them to come to the surface for the purpose of breathing air.

Secondly. It is interesting to find that though the hind limbs are unfitted for the performance of the locomotory functions, they, nevertheless, retain in the main the structural composition and disposition of parts usual in those limbs. The functions of the hind limb in Cheiroptera are almost exclusively those ordinarily assigned to the fore limb; yet they are effected by a modification of the ordinary structure of the hind limb rather than by a substitution of that of the fore limb. The

---

[1] The reduction of the number of the phalanges in the fore limb to two in each of the three ulnar digits has relation no doubt to their great length and attenuation, which is incompatible with the additional source of weakness that would have been entailed by the usual series of bones and joints.

peculiarities, that is to say, of the hind limb, or most of them, are retained. The femur is jointed with one leg bone, although the rotary movement of the leg upon the thigh is lost. The tarsus is articulated with the tibia, by one bone—the astragalus—; the scaphoid intervenes between that bone and the distal row of tarsals, and the os calcis stands up towards the middle of the flexor aspect of the limb to receive the tendo Achillis. Some approximation, however, to the osseous conformation of the fore limb is found in the fact that the os calcis is situated chiefly on the fibular side of the ankle, rises to a level with the astragalus, and subtends the lower end of the fibula, reminding us of the relations of the cuneiform to the scapho-lunar and to the ulna. Moreover the small size of the tarsus in relation to that of the metatarsus and phalanges are reminders of the ordinary relations of the carpus to the metacarpus and digits; and the foot is in the same plane with the leg. With regard to the muscles, the gastrocnemius is derived from both the condyles, and the peroneus longus, in spite of the absence of the upper part of the fibula, is present, and takes its usual course; and the various muscles of the foot and leg present the usual characters of the hind limb, except that the flexors of the leg run all together to its middle instead of passing, in two divisions, to its more lateral aspects.

Thirdly. There is, however, an assumption by the hind limb of one character of the fore limbs, which renders the anatomy of these animals peculiarly instructive and valuable in instituting a homological comparison between the two limbs. I mean the direction of the flexor and extensor surfaces of the limb, which, instead of being, as it usually is, in the thigh and leg at any rate, the reverse of that in the fore limb, is, in Cheiroptera, very nearly the same with that of the fore limb. Thus, the extensor surface of the thigh and leg and the prominence of the knee, like the extensor surface of the arm and forearm, and the prominence of the elbow, are directed backwards, and the hallux and tibial line, like the pollex and radial line, are on the outer side.

In another place (*Essay on the Limbs of Vertebrate Animals*) I have shown that the fore and hind limbs, in their primary transitory condition in the fœtus and in their persistent con-

dition in some of the lower animals, are, in this respect, alike—
are both, that is, directed in the same manner. They are both
projected at right angles and nearly straight, from the trunk
with the dorsal or extensor surfaces superior, and the pollex
and hallux with the respective radial and tibial margins anterior; and the flexion at the elbow and knee, in both, takes
place upwards, away, that is, from the abdominal aspect of the
embryo. Thus far the correspondence between the two limbs
is pretty exact; and if things remained in this position there
would be little difficulty in pointing out the serial homological relations of the several parts. But, while the flexion at the elbow
and knee takes place, a rotation is going on in the two limbs and
in opposite directions. The elbow with the superior or extensor
surface of the fore limb becomes turned backwards, and the
knee with the superior or extensor surface of the hind limb is
turned forwards. · This causes the hallux, tibia, tibial condyle
and side of the femur, that is, the line of the hind limb which
was originally anterior, to be directed *in*wards, and the pollex,
radius, radial condyle and side of the humerus, that is, the line
of fore limb which was also originally anterior, to be directed
*out*wards. Rather, I should say, with regard to the fore limb,
this would have been the effect, but that a rotation in an opposite direction to that in the rest of the member takes place
in the middle and distal segments (the forearm and hand).
This causes the pollex and lower part of the radius to be
directed inwards while the upper part of the radius and the
radial line of the upper part of the limb retain the direction
outwards which I have indicated. This opposite rotation of
the two limbs has, I need not say, proved a source of much
perplexity in their comparison and led to many errors.

In Cheiroptera the rotation of the hind limbs differs from
that which usually takes place in those limbs, and corresponds
with that which takes place in the fore limbs. The convexity
of the knee and the extensor surface of the limb are directed
backwards; and the hallux, tibia, and tibial line of the femur
are directed outwards : they afford us, therefore, a peculiarly
favourable opportunity for comparing the muscles in the two
limbs, and for settling some of the disputed points. They show,
for instance, unmistakeably, that the extensor muscles (*triceps*)

on the arm correspond with the extensor muscles (*quadriceps*) on the thigh, and that the flexors in the two limbs are in similar corresponding relation. They give additional support to the view that the inner, or tibial, condyle of the femur corresponds with the outer, or radial, condyle of the humerus, that the tibial (usually inner, in these outer) trochanter of the femur and the muscles passing to it are homologous with the radial (outer) tubercle of the humerus and its muscles, and consequently, that the muscles on the outer surface of the scapula are, to some extent, homologous with those on the inner surface of the ilium. Still, the rotation of the hind limb being the reverse of that which is usual, has so far altered the parts from their ordinary disposition that it is not, in every instance, easy to refer a given muscle to its correspondent in the hind limb of other animals. It is scarcely necessary to add that caution is, therefore, needed in drawing inferences with regard to serial homologies with the fore limb.

These animals show that the direction of the rotation in each limb has no close relation to the particular structure of the limb; for in them, the rotation of a fore limb is associated with the ordinary structure of a hind limb. We must, therefore, look to some other agency as the determining cause of the direction of the rotation. At present I can discern no other cause than that mysterious agency in development, whatever it is, which determines the general conformation and the detailed structure of a limb in accordance with the part it will have to play in the economy of the animal.

Nor do I see that the illustrations thus furnished of the modification of one order in a class to suit, to some extent, the habits of another class and the modification of one pair of limbs to fulfil, to some extent, the ordinary functions of the other pair, aid us much in the elucidation of the great questions of the mode of derivation of species. In each instance the change seems to be wrought out suddenly and completely, per saltum as it were. At least the known connecting links between these aerial and the ordinary terrestrial mammals are too few to enable us to draw any definite inferences from them.

Some of the points of interest which suggest themselves I will refer to in the course of the description.

CUTANEOUS MUSCLES

are disposed as follows. They are remarkable for their extent, their disposition, and their osseous connections.

The *Platysma* portion consists of four muscular bands (1, 2, 3, 4 in Pl. VI.),

(1) arising from the side of the lower jaw, where some of the fibres are blended with those of the muscles of the angle of the mouth[1], and from the side of the head behind the lower jaw. It is the 'cervico-facien' of Cuvier and Laurillard[2].

(2) from the hinder part of the parietal crest, from the occipital crest, and slightly from the middle line beneath the latter covering, in part, the space usually occupied by the cervical portion of the trapezius. It is the 'dorso-occipitien' of Cuvier, who regards this as the main portion, the other three being accessories.

(3) from the middle line of the lower part of the neck, in front of the trachea, where it is confluent with the corresponding muscle of the opposite side.

(4) from the fore part of the keel of the sternum, superficial to the pectoralis major. These several bands, distinct from one another at their origins, converge to the free edge of the humero-radial expansion of skin, along which they run, forming a narrow band (5) (corresponding with the tensor plicæ alaris in the bird[3]) as far as the pollex into the side of the phalanges of which it is inserted. In the middle of the edge of the wing-fold the muscular fibres are supplanted by a thin band of highly elastic tissue. This again, one-third from the pollex, gives way to muscular fibres which, after about an inch, terminate in common tendon. Thus there is first muscle, then elastic tissue, then muscle, and, lastly, tendon.

The muscle thus disposed serves to give tension to the fold of the wing, bends the forearm upon the arm and the pollex upon the forearm, also abducts the pollex and so may aid in separating the digits and expanding the wing, besides exerting some influence upon the humerus.

---

[1] This reminds us of the corresponding part of the muscle in Orycteropus (Vol. II. of *this Journal*, p. 293) which passes from the depressor anguli oris upon the arm and forearm.

[2] *Anatomie Comparée*, Planches.

[3] This muscle in the bird is derived from the deltoid or pectoral or both.

Another cutaneous muscle (*cutaneo-pubic*) arises from the fore part of the pelvis and radiates over the abdomen, the front of the pectoral muscle, and the shoulder. A lateral band, taking a direction different from the rest of the muscle, passes into the wing on the outer side of the thigh and leg, and runs quite to the edge of the wing. A third muscle (Pl. VI. *F. C., femoro-cutaneous*) arises from the lower part of the tibial (or outer) side of the shaft of the femur and passes forwards radiating over the back.

A fourth (*I. C., ischio-cutaneous*) runs from the ischium, across the ischio-pedal fold of skin and the supplementary calcaneal bone, upon the dorsum of the foot.

A fifth (*C. C., coraco-cutaneous*) arises from the coracoid in company with the biceps muscle, leaves the latter in the upper third of the arm, and runs through the brachio-crural flap of the wing to its lower edge[1]. Neither of these are mentioned or represented by C. and L.

Other similar bands of muscle, parallel with this last, descend, at nearly regular intervals, through the brachio-crural wing-flap to its lower edge from near the arm and forearm, though they do not appear to have any direct connection with the arm or forearm; and there is a broad thin muscular sheet extending from the back of the thorax and abdomen, near the spine, into this flap, and sending off bands which radiate in various directions in the folds of the skin.

MUSCLES OF THE FORE LIMB.

Pectoral in three portions :

(1) Sternal portion (*Pect.*), of great size and thickness, arises from the side of the keel of the sternum and the sternal ends of the sternal ribs, slightly from the lateral portion of the

---

[1] In Echidna setosa and in the Jerboa a thick band of muscular fibres arises from the anterior tubercle of the humerus, close to insertion of the pectoral muscle, and runs into the pannicle on the side of the abdomen. Part of the pannicle is also connected, in the Echidna, with the edge of the ulna; and in the Jerboa it is, as in Pteropus, attached to the face and side and back of the head, and by a distinct slip to the sternum. In it, as well as in Pteropus, the latissimus dorsi is nearly covered by this part of the pannicle, and is, as it were, stunted by it, being very small. In the Mole and the Rat, also, the pannicle is connected with the sternum, the humerus and the ulna. It is rarely, however, attached to the coracoid.

manubrium sterni but not at all from the clavicle, to the ridge on the outer side of the bicipital groove of the humerus.

(2)   Clavicular portion, from the deeper part of the inner third of the clavicle, lies beneath the preceding, and beneath the deltoid, and might perhaps be regarded as belonging to either.   It is inserted into the upper part of the same ridge in close relation to the fibres of the pectoral and of the deltoid. It is the 'petit pectoral' of C. and L., but may, probably, be more correctly regarded as a part of the pect. major.   It does not arise, in either of my specimens, as represented by Cuvier, from the rib, but is connected only with the clavicle.   It has not the ordinary characters of the clavicular part of the pectoralis major; for this usually lies more superficially, and crosses in front of the rest of the muscle to a lower part of the pectoral crest of the humerus.

(3)   Abdominal portion arises from the pubes in company with the rectus abdominis, forming the outer part of the compound muscle, separates from it as it ascends to the ribs, passes beneath the sternal portion of the pectoral, between it and the biceps, to the upper and inner margin of the same ridge just beneath the preceding.

It is called 'portion ventrale' by C. and L.   It might be said that the rectus divides as it ascends and thus forms its outer detachment.   In many animals (Fawn, Pig, Calf) a portion of the pectoralis arises from the sheath of the rectus or the linea alba. In Batrachians it is, as in this instance, blended with the muscle itself.   The relation of this portion (which may probably be regarded as the representative of the Pectoralis minor), and of the subclavius in Pteropus as well as of the scaleni, in some animals, to the rectus suggest these may all belong to one series or one muscular plane commencing at the pubes, terminating in the cervical vertebræ and diverging to the shoulder, sometimes continuous, but more commonly interrupted by one or more ribs[1].

---

[1] The *Pyramidalis* is large, has a broad origin from the front of the pubes, and covers a considerable portion of the lower and fore part of the abdomen. The fibres ascend with an inclination inwards, and are chiefly inserted into the linea alba.   Some however run on to the sternum and adjacent cartilages of the ribs.

In the female Pteropus, the Pyramidalis arises from the pubes on the side of the pubic gap, just in front of the rectus.   The fibres pass obliquely inwards to the linea alba.   The lowest are almost transverse, parallel with and quite close to the symphysial ligament, so as completely to cover all the part above the ligament in the interval between the recti.   The upper fibres are more oblique.

Rectus is attached above to the ribs wide of the sternum, as high as the first rib,

Meckel's (*Vergleich. Anat.* iii. 454) description of the relation of the pectoral with the rectus in Vespertilio corresponds with the above. This anatomist believes that in cases where the pectoralis minor appears to be absent it is really blended with the scalenus (s. 490) and says the same is also occasionally the case with the subclavius (s. 416).

Subclavius (*Subcl.*) is large. It passes from the under surface and anterior edge of the broad sternal portion of the first rib (the rectus abdominis is inserted into the posterior edge), along the lower surface of the clavicle, to be inserted beneath its outer part. It is inserted exclusively into the clavicle.

Serratus magnus anticus is in two portions, as Meckel describes. The upper, thick and muscular, arises from the first rib behind the subclavius and beneath the tendinous insertion of the scalenus and also slightly from the second rib, and is inserted into the upper part of the hinder margin of the scapula, internal to the insertion of the levator scapulæ, but not extending so far down the scapula as it does. It is quite distinct from the levator scapulæ in its whole extent. The lower portion is broader, arises from the eight ribs below the first and is inserted into the inferior margin of the scapula between the teres major and the subscapularis.

It is nearly the same in the two-toed Anteater, but the lower portion is in it attached more to the angle and hinder margin of the scapula than in Pteropus and does not advance so far forward between the teres and subscapularis. This muscle undergoes subdivision in Birds, Reptiles and Amphibia, especially in the Frog, with varieties of insertion. Rüdinger, *Die Muskeln der vorderen Extremitäten der Reptilien und Vögel.*

is joined near its upper part by the pectoral as above stated, and descends behind the pyramidalis to the pubes. There are no tendinous intersections in it or in the pyramidalis. In the female the recti separate as they descend to the pubic bones, leaving the lower part of the abdomen uncovered by them.

Obliquus Externus, indigitating above with serratus, forms a thin expansion, covering the rectus and pyramidalis. Below, in the male Pteropus, it has a free edge some distance above the pubes; and beneath this edge the large spermatic cord escapes, carrying with it some fibres of the muscle beneath, the obliquus externus, which form a *cremaster* and are disposed nearly transversely upon the cord.

In the female, where the pubic bones are widely apart and connected by a fibrous band passing across in front of the vagina, the lower margin of the obl. ext. is less defined. Its expanded tendon passes to the pubes and to the symphysial band.

The *obliquus internus* passes entirely behind the rectus, no part of its tendon going in front. At the lowest part of the abdomen it is very thin.

Biceps (*B.*) has two distinct heads, one from the summit of the long coracoid process, the other, larger, from the retiring angle at the root of that process and the ridge between the coracoid and the margin of the glenoid surface. It cannot, therefore, be said to arise from the glenoid part of the scapula at all. Neither does it pass through the shoulder-joint, but lies in a bursal canal, separate from and over the joint. It then traverses the bicipital groove. The two heads come into contact in the middle of the arm still preserving their distinctness, though the smaller portion (that from the extremity of the coracoid) derives some fibres from the other larger and longer portion. They are inserted on the inner or ulnar side of the radius, the smaller portion a little in front of the other. A bursa intervenes between their tendons and the bone.

The smaller, or shorter, or coracoid portion of the biceps is not unfrequently inserted in front of the other. It is so in man and in a Green Monkey now before me. It is the part also chiefly connected with the fascia of the forearm in man.

Brachialis Anticus (*Br. a.*) small, arises by muscular fibres from the inner side of the shaft of the humerus just beneath the coraco-brachialis. Its tendon, which is long and thin, travels, in company with those of the biceps, to the internal lateral ligament[1]. There it separates from them, passing on the inner side of the ligament to the fore part of the ulna where it is inserted. In the female some fibres of this muscle— not a distinct muscle, but fibres arising in common with the brachialis anticus—join the smaller portion of the biceps.

The distinctness of these three flexors and particularly of the two portions of the biceps is remarkable, especially as the latter arise so near together. The small size of the brachialis anticus has relation to the small size of the ulna. Meckel describes the biceps as arising in the Bat from the humerus and the coracoid. So far as my observation has gone in the human subject portions of the brachialis anticus which join the biceps join its coracoid portion and terminate chiefly, if not entirely, in its fascial expansion.

Coraco-brachialis (*C. b.*), from the extremity of the coracoid process and the upper part of the tendon of the biceps, which

[1] This ligament is long and very strong. It passes from the lower and fore part of the internal condyle, between the tendons of the biceps and the brachialis anticus, to the ulnar side of the radius, a little below the joint.

arises from the same point, to along the inner side of the humerus between the lesser tubercle and the origin of the brachialis anticus. The portion arising from the tendon of the biceps can easily be separated from the remainder, there being a stratum of areolar tissue between them; and it is inserted higher than the remainder of the muscle. A few fibres of the brachialis anticus arise from the lowermost part of its tendon of insertion in front.

Trapezius (*Trap.*). The cervical and occipital portions are absent[1]. The upper edge is very defined, and extends across between the shoulders. The remainder of its origin is as usual. It is attached to the back of the acromion and the outer fifth of the clavicle.

Cervico-humeral (*C. h.*) (omo- ou acromio-trachélien), from the second and third transverse cervical spines to about a fifth of the clavicle immediately internal to the trapezius. In its origin this muscle is a continuation of the levator scapulæ in its insertion of the trapezius. I am disposed to agree with Meckel (*l. c.* 481) in assigning it to the latter muscle rather than to the levator scapulæ.

Levator scapulæ (*Lev. sc.*) is large from the cervical transverse spines, beneath the cervico-humeral, to the edge of the scapula between the spine and the superior angle.

Rhomboideus, one strong muscle from the upper dorsal spines to the spine and edge beneath it of the scapula. There is no cervical or occipital portion.

Latissimus dorsi (*Lat. d.*) is narrow, having no attachment to the ribs. It arises from two or three anterior lumbar and three hinder dorsal spines, beneath the trapezius, overlaps, but has no attachment to, the angle of the scapula[2], and is inserted by a narrow tendon into the inner tubercle of the humerus.

Deltoid (*D.*), from the outer half of the clavicle, extending, that is, for some distance internal to the region of attachment of the trapezius and cervico-humeral, and from the acromion. The fibres of the clavicular portion take nearly the same direction as those of the clavicular portion of the pectoral muscle,

---

[1] Cuvier suggests that the deficient cervical and occipital portions may be represented by the ' dorso-occipitien.' *Vide supra.*
[2] The angle (*A. sc.*) of the scapula in Pl. VII. has been raised up from beneath the cover of the trapezius.

and are partly blended with them at their insertion[1]. The acromial portion, on the contrary, which is separate from the clavicular, meets the pectoral muscle and is inserted, opposite to it, into the same ridge. The fibres of the deltoid are inserted into the same length of the bicipital ridge with the pectoral. The hindmost fibres of the deltoid, arising from the outer part of the acromion, join the outer part of the triceps and become blended with it.

Teres Major as usual. It has a broad musculo-tendinous termination, which can scarcely be said to be inserted with the latissimus dorsi, but into the inner bicipital ridge beneath it.

Teres Minor (*T. m.*), large, from a considerable part of the hinder edge of the spine as well as from the lower costa of the scapula to the outer part of the great tubercle of the humerus. It nearly covers the *Infra-spinatus* (*Inf. sp.*), which is small.

It is represented by Cuvier as a part of the deltoid; and certainly it has the usual origin of part of the deltoid. Yet it is quite distinct from the deltoid and crosses it nearly at a right angle, running beneath it to the tubercle of the humerus. Meckel considers that it is wanting, and, I conclude, takes it for the infra-spinatus which he says is large. But that muscle is distinct, lying beneath the teres, and of rather small size.

Supra-spinatus is situated as usual.

Subscapularis presents nothing peculiar. It is thick, and arises from the whole of the under surface of the scapula, passes over the shoulder-joint quite free from the capsule, and is inserted into the inner tubercle of the humerus.

Triceps (*Tr.*). The long head has a broad musculo-tendinous origin from the scapula behind the glenoid cavity. The remainder of the muscle arises from the posterior surface of the upper half of the humerus quite up to the shoulder-joint, deriving, on the outer side, fibres arising with those of the deltoid from the hindmost part of the acromion; and, internally, its fibres arise from the posterior surface of the tendon of insertion of the coraco-brachialis. The long, strong, well-defined tendon includes a sesamoid bone (*s*), the homologue of the patella, as it passes over the trochlea to the projecting edge of the ulna.

Pronator teres (*Pr. t.*) has no connection with the ulna. Arising from the inner condyle in conjunction with the four

[1] Meckel finds it difficult to decide whether this clavicular portion belongs to the pectoral or the deltoid.

following muscles, it passes across to the oblique line on the palmar surface of the upper third of the radius [1].

Flexor carpi radialis (*Fl. c. r.*) from the inner condyle to the ulnar side of the base of the metacarpal of index.

Flexor carpi ulnaris (*Fl. c. u.*) from the ulna as well as from the inner condyle to the distal margin of the transverse process of the os magnum [2], opposite the interval between the third and fourth metacarpals.

Flexor digitorum sublimis (*Fl. d. s.*) [3] from the condyle and the upper part of the radius. As it passes through a tendinous sheath in front of the carpus it divides into two tendons, of which one passes to the sesamoid bone on the ulnar side of the metacarpo-phalangeal joint of the pollex, and the other, having a slight attachment to the metacarpal bone of index, passes on to be attached to the base of the second phalanx of index.

Flexor digitorum profundus (*Fl. d. p.*) arises from the inner condyle together with the preceding, but soon becomes distinct from it, and situated beneath and to the ulnar side of it. It arises, in addition, from the anterior surface of the ulna and from the contiguous margin of the surface of the radius, passes over the carpus in a pulley beneath the preceding and beneath the process of the os magnum, and divides into two tendons. Of these, one passes between the bellies of the short flexor pollicis and the sesamoid bones to the ungual phalanx of pollex. The other again divides into two, which pass to the terminal phalanges of the index and middle digits. These slender tendons are accompanied, just below the carpus, by some muscular fibres, like lumbricales, which seem to terminate in as well as to arise from the tendons. In the female Pteropus the tendon to the third digit is quite interrupted by the mus-

---

[1] Cuvier says there is an absence of all pronators and supinators. Meckel finds a long pronator and a short supinator. I find in addition the long supinator very distinct, but no short pronator.

[2] The *os magnum* is the largest in the distal row of carpal bones; and its palmar surface is expanded into a broad process extending tranversely across the bases of metacarpals II, III, IV, and reaching partly across metacarpal I. There is no distinct hooklike process to the *unciform* bone. The *trapezoid* and *trapezium* are of moderate size. The proximal part of the carpus is formed almost entirely by the thick transversely elongated *scapho-lunar* bone, in which a slight oblique groove on the palmar surface indicates the distinction between its component parts. The *cuneiform* is very small and articulated with the distal surface of the lunar. I do not find any *pisiform*.

[3] Meckel describes one flexor muscle in the bat dividing to each of the fingers as well as to the thumb.

cular belly. That to the second digit retains its continuity, the muscular fibres being superadded.

Interossei are well marked and regular, two at least for each digit passing in pairs along each metacarpal and attached to the bases of the several first phalanges constituting 'interosseal flexors.' In the case of digit v, they arise from the transverse process of the os magnum; and, in addition to the two interosseal flexors (*Fl. b.*), one, separate from and ulnad of them, becomes attached to the palmar surface of the metacarpal about one quarter from the carpus, and may represent an 'interosseal abductor' (*Abd.*), while a slip from the interosseal flexor on the radial side extends beyond the rest, passes along the radial side of the first phalanx and joins the extensor tendon, so that it may be regarded as an 'interosseal adductor.' The interossei of digits I, II, and IV. arise from the proximal ends of the metacarpals and the contiguous carpal bones, therefore on a plane deeper than those of digit v. The flexor tendons of digits II. and III. run between the interosseal tendons; all the interossei are free in the whole, or nearly the whole, of their length from the metacarpals, and are round muscular bellies like lumbricales. In the case of the pollex, a short, thick, muscular belly descends from the carpus, on either side of the metacarpal, to the sesamoid bones and the adjacent base of the first phalanx, constituting interosseal, or short, flexors, as in the case of the other digits; and an additional muscle arising from the os magnum terminates in a thin tendon, which passes along the ulnar side of the first phalanx to its dorsum, and is inserted into the back part of the terminal phalanx, constituting the 'interosseal adductor,' and proving the sole extensor of that phalanx.

The interossei constitute the only flexors of digits IV. and V, and extend only to their first phalanges; the flexion of the second or terminal phalanges being, apparently, effected to the required extent by the muscular tissue in the covering of the wing.

The above muscles, with the exception of the fl. c. u. and the interossei, have the effect, in addition to their other purposes, of flexing the metacarpals upon the carpus; and these are so articulated that they are at the same time inclined towards the ulnar side and approximated to one another, that is to say, they are folded together as they are bent upon the forearm. The metacarpals indeed are articulated to the carpus in such a manner as to permit the opposite

20—2

movements of flexion with inclination ulnad or folding together, and of extension with inclination radiad or separation from one another.

Supinator longus (*Sup. l.*), from the outer surface of the humerus above the condyle to the outer surface of the radius just external to the insertion of the pronator radii teres. Is a flexor of the forearm.

Supinator brevis (*Sup. br.*), from the outer condyle and the tendons of the extensors of the digits to the oblique ridge on the front of the radius to which the pronator teres is attached. Is an extensor of the forearm.

Extensores Carpi radiales longior et brevior (*Ex. c. r. l. et. br.*), from the outer condyle together. The *longior*, the anterior and rather the smaller, passes to the process on the back of the proximal end of the second metacarpal bone. The *brevior* passes to the process on the radial side of the end of the third metacarpal.

In the male Pteropus a slip passes from this tendon to the fourth and fifth metacarpals. I found a similar slip to the fourth metacarpal in the Chimpanzee.

These muscles extend and abduct the metacarpals on the carpus as well as extend the carpus.

Extensor Carpi ulnaris (*Ex. c. u.*), chiefly from the outer surface of the ulna and slightly from a fascia connected with the outer condyle to the ulnar surface of metacarpal v. just below the carpus.

Extensor digitorum (*Ex. dig.*), from the fascia connected with the outer condyle and the olecranon, and divides into three separate tendons, which pass to the terminal phalanges of the three ulnar digits. They lie on the ulnar sides of the metacarpals, pass over the dorsal surfaces of the metacarpo-phalangeal joints, expand there, become connected with the joints, and narrow slips pass on to the terminal phalanges. The tendon to digit v. runs in a separate sheath, and is joined by a slip from that to digit iv.

Extensor primus (*ossis metacarpi*) *pollicis* (*Ext. poll. pr.*), from the radius and ulna high up, runs over the edge of the lower end of radius above the base of the pollex, having here a small ossicle in it, to the radial extremity of the transverse process of the os magnum.

Secundus (*Ext. poll. sec.*), just beneath the preceding, through a groove on the ulnar side of the end of the radius, in company with the succeeding muscle to the base of the dorsum of the first phalanx of pollex. The 'interosseal adductor' is the extensor of the third or terminal bone of the pollex.

Extensor indicis, beneath preceding, and in company with it to the terminal phalanx of index [1].

Thus each of the terminal phalanges of the digits is supplied with an extensor, though those of iv. and v. are devoid of flexors.

The differences from the dorsal muscles of the human forearm and hand are in the insertion of the supinator and in the extensores pollicis.

MUSCLES OF THE HIND-LIMB.

Psoas parvus (*Ps. p.*), from the two or three lower dorsal and the three upper lumbar vertebræ, a small muscle. Its slender tendon is inserted into the outer extremity of the projecting spine of the pubes which overhangs the hip-joint [2]. Some of its fibres are continued on into the pectineus.

Psoas magnus (*Ps. m.*), from the bodies of all the lumbar vertebræ, lying external to the preceding, as well as from the front of the ilium and the adjacent surface of the sacrum, passes beneath the overhanging pubic spine, external to and behind the hip, to the outer or tibial trochanter.

Iliacus internus (*Il. i.*), from the outer surface of the ilium close to the crest, has no further connection with the ilium, is distinct from the psoas, and passes beneath it to the outer surface of the femur quite beneath the tibial trochanter. It crosses external to the extensor cruris.

Sartorius, not clearly distinguishable. Cuvier describes under this name some fibres passing from the ilium to the lateral part of the pannicle. Meckel says it is absent in cheiroptera.

Pectineus (*Pect.*), a round muscle in its upper part, arises by a strong well-defended tendon from the most projecting point of the pubic crest just beneath the insertion of the psoas parvus, and from the tendon of that muscle. Becoming wider and flatter it crosses anterior and external to the psoas and iliacus, and is inserted, beneath the latter muscle, into the

---

[1] Meckel does not mention this muscle, but describes the ext. dig. as passing to the four fingers.

[2] The mistake in the *Leçons* respecting the absence of this muscle as well as of the psoas magnus and the iliacus is rectified in the *Anatomie Comparée, Planches* of Cuvier and Laurillard.

middle of the outer (tibial) side of the femur. It is the 'pectineus' of Cuvier and Meckel; still it is a question whether it may not be the adductor longus of which there is no other representative; or it may be the representative of both these muscles.

Adductor brevis, from the outer surface of the pubes under cover of the gracilis, between it and the obturator externus, crosses the psoas to the fore and outer surface of the femur immediately in front of the insertion of the iliacus.

Adductor magnus. There is a considerable mass of muscle, consisting of three or more parts, arising from the outer surface of the pubes and ischium, appearing superficially between the gracilis and the semi-tendinosus and semi-membranosus, and extending beneath the latter muscles to the middle line. It is inserted along the fore part of the femur from the outer, or tibial, trochanter three fourths down the bone. An upper portion, easily separated, may represent the *Quadratus femoris,* and another portion, separated in great measure from the rest by the sciatic nerve and the origins of the semi-tendinosus and semi-membranosus and connected with its fellow in the middle line and inserted lower and rather more on the fibular aspect of the femur than the remainder of the muscle, may possibly represent the *Biceps* which, owing to the absence of the fibula in the upper part of the leg, may have stopped short in the thigh and acquired an attachment to the femur[1].

Glutæus Maximus (*Gl.*) arises, muscular, from the hinder margin of the crest of the ilium and from the sacral spines, and is inserted, tendinous, into the upper half of the inner, or fibular, side of the shaft of the femur between the adductor mass and the vastus externus which is here internal.

Glutæus Medius arises from the outer and hinder surface of the ilium, under cover of the glutæus maximus and iliacus, and is inserted, tendinous, into the summit of the inner, or fibular, trochanter. There is no *glutæus minimus* distinct from the medius.

Obturator Externus (*Obt. e.*) is a large muscle arising from the whole of the exterior of the obturator ligament and the

[1] Cuvier and Meckel mention only one adductor besides the pectineus and make no mention of a quadratus.

surrounding margin of bone. It passes immediately over the front of the hip-joint and is inserted into the outer part of the tibial trochanter and into the adjacent part of the capsule of the hip. It reminds one strongly of the supra-spinatus.

Gemelli. A small short muscle arises from the deeper part of the tuber ischii near to and in front of the acetabulum and immediately in front of the preceding muscle. It is inserted into the inner surface of the inner or fibular trochanter. This I conclude may be regarded as the representative of the ge-melli. None of its fibres entered into the pelvis.

There is no trace of a distinct *obturator internus* either in the interior or on the exterior of the pelvis.

Three flexor muscles of the knee pass from the fore and inner part of the pelvis to the middle of the plantar or anterior surface of the tibia, instead of being attached as usual to the sides of the leg bones; in this respect resembling the flexors of the forearm. They are the three following.

Gracilis (Gr.) from the edge of the spine of the pubes, in its whole length, also from the symphysis and from the rounded angle between the two. Its tendon joins that of the following muscle ;

Semi-tendinosus from almost the hindmost part of the is-chium (the back part of the tuber ischii). The tendons of these two are united in the lower third of the thigh, and are inserted into a projecting ridge in the middle of the back of the tibia, $\frac{1}{4}$th from the upper end, beneath therefore the space that would usually be occupied by the popliteus.

Semi-membranosus from the tuber ischii just in front of the preceding. Its tendon runs clear of the other two and above them to the same ridge a little higher up.

This accords with the description of the above three flexors by Cuvier and Meckel, neither of whom admit the presence of the *Biceps* in Cheiroptera. The tendons of all these three lie entirely on the tibial side of the gastrocnemius which indicates them to be tibial muscles. The insertion of these flexors into the middle of the front of the tibia, instead of on either side of the leg bones, accords with the fact that, owing to the transversely excavated or grooved con-dition of the upper surface of the tibia, no rotatory motion—no pro-nation and supination—of leg can be effected. These movements are limited to flexion and extension as in the case of the *two* bones of the forearm upon the humerus ; and the disposition of the flexor muscles is accordingly the same. It is also interesting to observe that there are no interarticular cartilages in the knee-joint.

Extensor cruris (*Ext. cr.*), not large, from the margin of the ilium, external to and behind the acetabulum; also from the upper half of the hinder surface of the femur, on one side being prolonged up to the tibial, or outer, and on the other up to the fibular, or inner, trochanter. The two portions—the iliac and the femoral portion—are quite distinct, though stated by Meckel not to be so in the Bat. Its tendon descends along the back of the thigh, over the projecting knee, to a ridge-like process on the middle of the posterior and upper edge of the tibia, which is not so large as that in the bird, but rises rather more directly upon the joint. There is no patella.

The absence of the patella may be associated with the circumstance that little or no weight is borne upon the hind limbs in these animals and that, consequently, the pressure of the extensor tendon upon the femoral condyles is proportionately small.

The view of parts obtained by a dissection of the outer region of the left thigh and haunch, given in Pl. vi. figs. 3 and 4 is highly instructive with reference to their comparison with corresponding parts in a fore-limb. The angle formed by the femur with the ilium resembles that of the humerus with the lower or hinder margin of the scapula. The *pubes* is directed inwards overhanging the joint like the *acromion*. The *ischium* is directed backwards and inwards from the joint. The *ligamentum teres* ascends, from the dimple on the outer and fore-part of the head of the femur, beneath the edge of the cotyloid ligament covering the notch between the pubes and ischium, to the edge of the acetabulum between these two bones, reminding us of the *gleno-humeral ligament*[1]. The *extensor* muscle (*Ext. cr.*) passes from behind the acetabulum, down the back of the thigh, over the projecting back of the knee, to the hinder edge of the tibia. The *flexors*, semi-tendinosus and semi-membranosus, pass from the ischium in front and on the inner side of the joint, over the front of the thigh, on the tibial side of the flexors of the foot, to the middle of the fore-part of the tibia. The *gracilis* passes from the outer and anterior projecting edge of the pubes—like part of the delto-pectoral group in the fore-limb from the clavicle and sternum—and joins the semitendinosus, just as the part of the *deltoid* in Orycteropus (Vol. ii. p. 299) joins the biceps and becomes a flexor or (which is more appropriate for comparison) as the clavicular or the upper sternal part of the *pectoral* not unfrequently extends to the forearm or the elbow. The *pectineus, adductor brevis*, and *adductor magnus* pass from the crest of the pubes to the outer surface of the femur, just as several parts of the *deltoid* pass from the acromion and clavicle to the

[1] See my *Treatise on the Human Skeleton*, p. 411.

outer surface of the humerus. The *obturator externus* passes from the obturator ligament, between the pubes and ischium, over the front of the hip, to the capsular ligament covering the interval between the trochanters and to the inner or fibular trochanter, reminding us forcibly of the *supraspinatus* which passes from between the acromion and the coracoid, over the front of the shoulder, to the capsule between the tubercles. The difference is that this muscle inclines to the outer or radial tubercle and extends beyond the interval between the acromion and coracoid to the dorsum of the scapula; whereas the obturator inclines to the fibular trochanter and is limited by the obturator ligament. The *psoas magnus* and *iliacus internus*, passing from the anterior and outer surface of the ilium, beneath the pectineus and gracilis, to the outer trochanter, remind us of the *infraspinatus* and *teres minor* passing from the outer surface of the scapula beneath the deltoid, to the outer tubercle of the humerus. The *glutæus* passing from the spines of the sacrum, on the inner side of the extensor muscle, to the inner side of the femur beneath the inner trochanter, is the reminder of the *latissimus dorsi*, which takes a nearly similar direction and has a similar attachment in the fore-limb.

Gastrocnemius, a delicate muscle, arises from the condyles of the femur in the usual manner, except that it is attached only to the fibular side of the outer or tibial condyle. The inner head (from the fibular condyle) is tendinous; the outer head (from the tibial condyle) is muscular. There is a minute ossicle in the outer head; I cannot find one in the inner head. Both these heads lie on the inner, or fibular, side of the flexores curis. They unite and terminate in a thin tendon, which runs down to be inserted into the os calcis. A little above its insertion the base of the styliform bone (*St. b.*) is closely connected with it. The bone takes its curved course inwards towards the opposite limb in the connecting cutaneous fold, having no direct bony connection. A slip of muscular fibres (*S. m.* styliform muscle) passes from the proximal end of the fifth metacarpal and radiates out to be inserted along the lower margin of this bone.

I do not find any representative of the *Solæus* or of the *Popliteus*. The absence of the latter accords with the want of pronatory and supinatory movement mentioned above (Meckel notes the absence of this muscle in the bat). Neither do I find any *Plantaris*.

Tibialis posticus (*Tib. p.*), small, from the lower half of the nner (fibular) surface of the back of the tibia and from the adjacent surface of the fibula to the tarsal bone supporting the second metatarsal.   Meckel thinks it is absent in the bat.

Flexores digitorum longi, two long and large muscles from the two sides of the leg and the leg bones, separated above by the flexores cruris.   One, *Tibialis* (*Fl. d. tib.*), arises by a large muscular belly from the outer or tibial condyle of the femur, external to and encroaching upon the space usually occupied by the gastrocnemius, from the posterior and outer surface of the tibia, and by a muscular slip from the tendon of the semi-tendinosus.   A muscular slip also is derived from the back of the tibia above the flexor tendons in the position usually occupied by the popliteus.   This extends to the inner (fibular) articular surface of the tibia, but does not pass over the joint to the condyle of the femur.   The other, *fibularis* (*Fl. d. fib.*), corresponding with the Fl. l. h. of man, arises tendinous from the tubercular projection on the fibular side of the head of the tibia, and muscular from the tibia beneath it and from the upper half of the fibula[1].   Their strong tendons pass through distinct sheaths in front of the ankle; the tibial flexor sends a tendon to the ungual phalanx of the hallux; the fibular flexor sends one to the ungual phalanx of digit V; and the tendons of the two muscles combine to send tendons to the ungual phalanges of the three middle digits.   The tibial lies, in the sole, superficial to the fibular; but their three middle tendons are intimately blended.

By this blending of the tendons from the two flexor muscles and the non-division of the extensor tendon till it has neared the phalanges, synchronism in the movements of the digits is insured, any one not being moveable alone.   The greater individuality in the movement of the digits, especially in the hand, which is so marked in man, is in him provided for by the greater separation of the flexor and extensor tendons passing to the fingers and toes.

The origin of the tibial flexor of the toes from the condyle of the femur[2] and from the flexor tendon of the leg is interesting.   It has the effect of associating flexion of the toes with that of the leg[3], and

---

[1]   The fibula, though deficient above, is pretty well developed in the lower part of the leg, and has a broad surface at the lower end which is jointed with the os calcis.

[2]   It is worthy of remark that in birds the flexors of the toes derive origins from the condyles of the femur.

[3]   Just as, in the bird, the insertion of part of the tensor plicæ alaris, from the clavicle, into the supinator longus, which is inserted into the metacarpal of

it has the further effect of causing the forced extension of the leg
when the animal is hanging by its curved pedal claws, to give tension
to the flexor muscle of the toes, and so increases the grasp of the
claws.   In short the weight of the animal is thus made to conduce
to the firmness of the hold by which the weight is maintained.   This
connection of the flexors of the digits with the femur is very rarely
met with in mammals.

Lumbricales are eight in all, and large.   One from the tibial
or superficial flexor tendon going to digit I. is inserted into the
fibular side of that digit ; one from the tendon of the fibular
or deep flexor going to digit V. is inserted into the tibial side of
that digit ; the others, arising apparently from the combined
tendons of the tibial and the fibular flexors, are inserted one on
the tibial and one on the fibular side of each of the other digits.
They are inserted, not into the extensor tendons, but into the
sides of the shafts of the first phalanges about the middle.

The imperfect complement of lumbricales in digits I. and V. shown
by the absence of the marginal or distal ones, whereas two are present
in each of the other digits, may be regarded as among the many evidences, of which small size is the most obvious, of the incompleteness
of these lateral and least constant, last segmented and, as it were,
least cared for elements of the terminal part of the limb.   The less
complete blending of the tibial and fibular components of the flexor
muscle in the tendons passing to these digits as compared with those
passing to the other digits, as well as the absence of the flexor brevis
on the fibular side of digit V. and its total absence in digit I, and the
absence of a long extensor in digit I, are features of similar import.

Accessorius I do not find.

Flexor brevis digitorum arises from the os calcis and the
lower part of the tendo Achillis on its tibial side—that is, in
the situation usually occupied by the plantaris tendon which,
as I have said, is absent.   It passes to the second phalanges of
digits II, III, and IV, splitting to permit the long flexors to pass
just as the corresponding tendons do in man, and reuniting
above them.   It passes also to digit V, but only to its fibular
side.

Interossei constitute a pair of muscles on the plantar surface
of each of the metatarsals, arising also from the tarsals, ten in
all.   One is on the tibial and one on the fibular side of each

the pollex, serves to associate extension of the carpus and digits with that of
the forearm.

metatarsal. They pass to the tibial and fibular sides of the palmar surface of the first phalanges of their respective digits a little beyond their proximal ends. I could not trace them to the extensor tendons. They act chiefly as flexors of the first joints of the digits[1].

Abductor minimi digiti, a short, thick muscle extending from the os calcis, near the insertion of the tendo Achillis, to the fibular side of the fifth metatarsal.

Transversus pedis (*Tr.*) is a distinct muscle arising from the inner cuneiform bone, from the fibular side of the proximal end of the first phalanx of the hallux, and from a tendinous arch between these two points, beneath which passes the fibular interosseous of the hallux. From this broad origin the fibres converge to the tibial side of the first phalanx of the fifth digit, where they are blended with the interosseous of that side. It corresponds, apparently, with the 'adducteur transverse' of Cuvier, who does not mention its presence in this animal.

The metatarsals admit of a certain amount of lateral movement, abduction and adduction, which is effected by the alternate action of this transversus and the tibialis anticus and the peroneus brevis aided somewhat by the lateral interossei. The peroneus longus not passing to the metatarsal of hallux and playing little or no part in adduction may be a reason for the presence of this transversus. Moreover the interossei are more parallel than usual, and those to the lateral digits (I. and IV.) do not extend across so as to serve as adductors, which is an additional reason for the presence of a distinct and well developed transverse muscle. It will be observed that the separators of the metatarsals—tibialis anticus and peroneus brevis —are on the dorsal or extensor aspect of the limb, and the approximator of them—the transversus—is on the plantar or flexor aspect. With regard to this association of abduction with extension and of adduction with flexion, see preceding Vol. p. 306.

Tibialis anticus (*Tib. a.*) descends as usual from the fibular surface of the tibia, over the tibial side of the tarsus, and is inserted into the tibial side of the first metatarsal, abducting it and turning the foot outwards.

Extensor digitorum (*Ext. dig.*), from the fore part and the fibular side of the head of the tibia. Its long tendon passes over the tarsus and metatarsus and, near the phalanges, radiates into four slips to the four small toes. It is a delicate muscle.

---

[1] See remarks on the arrangement of the interossei in preceding Vol. p. 305.

Extensor brevis, comparatively strong, arises from the front of the os calcis and the back of the metatarsals.   It passes as usual to the four, in this instance, outer digits (I, II, III, IV.), being the only extensor of the hallux.   Its four divisions are distinct, each lying along its metatarsal bone.   The two middle, to digits II. and III, present a longitudinal separation, somewhat reminding us of the interossei on the plantar aspect.   These divisions join the long extensor tendons, one portion of each joining the fibular and the other the tibial edge of a tendon. The division to digit IV. is developed, or well developed, only along the fibular side of the metacarpal, and joins only the fibular side of the extensor longus tendon, which is the usual disposition of the extensor brevis in the case of all the digits in other animals.   The division to digit I. is large, is inserted partly into the back of the first phalanx, and sends a delicate tendon along the back of this phalanx to the base of the second phalanx.

The distribution of the extensor brevis to the two sides of the extensor tendons of digits II. and III. is interesting in connection with the anatomy of the lumbricales.   Usually the tendons of the extensor brevis lie only on the fibular sides of those of the extensor longus ; and to balance them, as it were, the lumbricales pass to the tibial sides of the tendons of the extensor longus.   But in this instance there is a greater completeness and separation of the extensor brevis and the lumbricales : the tendons of the former pass to both sides of the tendons of the extensor longus and the lumbricales have no connection with the extensor tendons, pass on both sides of the phalanges, and are inserted into them.

Peroneus longus, from the fibular side of the head of the tibia and the septum between the extensor and the flexor digitorum descends, in front of the lower end of the fibula, through a groove on the outer side of the tarsus, to the under part of the proximal end of the second metatarsal bone.   I cannot trace it to the metatarsal of hallux.

Peroneus tertius, rather large, from front of fibula, beneath and internal to extensor digitorum, to metatarsal bone of digit V. In the male it sends a tendon to join the extensor tendon of this digit ; and there is also a small slip to this digit from the extensor brevis.   In the female this slip is wanting ; but the peroneal tendons to the extensor and to the metatarsal are from

distinct muscles.   Thus the extensor tendon of digit v. is supplied from two or three sources, whereas that to hallux is derived
only from the Ext. br.   No other peroneus present.   Meckel
finds only one peroneus in Cheiroptera.

PLATE VI.

Fig. 1.   Muscles on the abdominal aspect of male Pteropus.
The right hind-limb has been partially and the left has been much
turned or rotated from the natural position for the purpose of showing the muscles on the two surfaces.

1. 2. 3. 4.   The facial, occipital, cervical and sternal portions of
platysma uniting to form 5 the tensor plicæ alaris, which is elastic
from near the convergence of the muscular bundles to a, between a
and b is again muscular, and between b and its insertion is tendinous.

St. h., sterno-hyoid.   *Digr.*, Digastric.   *Tr. m.*, trachelo-mastoid.
St. cl. m., sterno-cleido-mastoid, from the anterior extremity of the
keel, from the upper edge of the keel (this is rather in shade) and
from the clavicle.   *Subcl.*, subclavius.   *C. h.*, cervico-humeral.   *R. a.*,
rectus-abdominis. The sternal portion of the first rib is seen between
this and the subclavius.

RIGHT FORE-LIMB. *Pect.*, sternal portion of pectoralis major divided
and reflected from its origin. *Pect. a.*, abdominal portion of pectoral.
The clavicular portion has been removed to show subclavius.   *B.*,
biceps.   *C. b.*, coraco-brachialis.   *Br. a.*, brachialis anticus.   *Ext. c. r.*,
extensor carpi radialis.   *Sup. l.*, supinator longus.   *Pr. t.*, pronator
teres.   *Fl. c. r.*, flexor carpi radialis.   *Fl. d. s.*, flexor digitorum
sublimis.   *Fl. c. u.*, flexor carpi ulnaris.

RIGHT HIND-LIMB. *Ps. p.*, psoas parvus. *Ps.*, psoas magnus. *Il. i.*,
iliacus internus.   *P.*, pectineus.   *Gr.*, gracilis.   *F. c.*, femoro cutaneous.
Fl. d., flexor dig. long.   *P. l.*, peroneus longus.   *Ext. d.*, extensor
digitorum.   *P. 3*, peroneus tertius.   *Tib. a.*, tibialis anticus.

LEFT HIND-LIMB. *Gr.*, gracilis.   *Ad.*, adductor muscles.   *S. m.*,
semi-membranosus.   *S. t.*, semi-tendinosus.   *I. c.*, ischio-cutaneous.
St. m., styliform muscle.   *St. b.*, styliform bone.   *T. Ach.*, tendo
Achillis. *Fl. d. fib.*, flexor digitorum fibularis. *Tib. p.*, tibialis posticus.
Fl. d. tib., flexor digitorum tibialis.

LEFT FORE-LIMB.   *Fl. br.*, flexor brevis, 'interosseal flexors' of
digit v.   *Abd.*, abductor of digit v.   *Fl. c. r.*, flexor carpi radialis.
Fl. d. pr., flexor digitorum profundus.   *Fl. d. s.*, flexor digitorum
sublimis. *Fl. c. u.*, flexor carpi ulnaris. *Pr. t.*, pronator teres. *Sup. l.*,
supinator longus.

Fig. 2.   The right side of pelvis femur and upper part of tibia,
of male Pteropus.   *Il.*, upper part or crest of ilium.   *C.*, crest of pubes
where psoas parvus and pectineus are attached.   *S.*, symphysis pubis.
Isch., ischium.

Fig. 3. View of superficial muscles on the outer side of the right hip in female Pteropus the bones being in the same position as in preceding figure. *S. t.*, semi-tendinosus. *S. m.*, semimembranosus. *P.*, pectineus. *Gr.*, gracilis. *Ad. br.*, adductor brevis. *Ps. p.*, psoas parvus. *Ps.*, psoas magnus. *Il. i.*, iliacus internus. *Gl.*, glutæus maximus. *Ext. cr.*, extensor cruris. *F. c.*, origin of femoro-cutaneous.

Fig. 4. View of deep muscles about right hip of the same animal. *Gr.*, gracilis divided and reflected upwards and downwards. *S. t.* and *S. m.*, semi-tendinosus and semi-membranosus. *P.*, pectineus divided and reflected upwards and downwards. *Ad. m.*, adductor magnus divided and upper part reflected upwards. *Ad. br.*, adductor brevis reflected upwards and downwards. *L. t.*, ligamentum teres. *Obt. e.*, obturator externus. *Ps. p.*, psoas parvus. *Ps.*, psoas magnus. *Il. i.*, iliacus internus.

Fig. 5. Dissection of foot showing the transversalis muscle (*Tr.*). *Fl. br.*, flexor brevis divided and reflected to the os calcis. *Inteross.*, the interossei of hallux and digit v. *S. m.*, muscle from metacarpal v. to styliform bone.

PLATE VII.

Fig. 6. Muscles on the dorsal aspect of male Pteropus.
Fore-limbs. *Ex. c. u.*, extensor carpi ulnaris. *Ex. dig.*, extensor digitorum. *Ex. p. sec.*, extensor pollicis secundus. *Ex. i.*, extensor indicis. *Ex. p. pr.*, extensor pollicis primus. *Ex. c. r. br.*, extensor carpi radialis brevior. *Ex. c. r. l.*, extensor carpi radialis longior. *Sup. l.*, supinator longus. *Sup. br.*, supinator brevis. *B.*, biceps. *D.*, deltoid. *Trap.*, trapezius. *C. h.*, cervico-humeral. *S.*, sesamoid bone in tendon of (*Tr.*) triceps. *A. sc.*, angle of scapula projected from beneath (*Lat. d.*) latissimus dorsi. *H.*, humerus. *Lev. sc.*, levator scapulæ. *S. sp.*, supra-spinatus. *I. sp.*, infra-spinatus. *T. min.*, teres minor. *T.*, teres major.
Hind-limbs. *Il. i.*, iliacus internus. *Gl. med.*, glutæus medius. *Ext. c.*, extensor cruris. *S. m.*, semi-membranosus. *S. t.* and *Gr.*, semi-tendinosus and gracilis. *Ad.*, adductors. *Gl.*, glutæus maximus. *Q. l.* quadratus lumborum.

Fig. 7. Side view of muscles of shoulder and hip for purpose of comparison. *D'.*, portion of deltoid passing to humerus. *D".*, portion of deltoid continued into outer part of triceps. *Pect.*, pectoralis major. *B.*, biceps. *Br. a.*, brachialis anticus. *Gr.*, gracilis. *P.*, pectineus. *Ad.* adductor. *S. m.*, semi-membranosus. *S. t.* semi-tendinosus. *Ext. cr.*, quadriceps extensor cruris. *Il. i.*, iliacus internus. *Ps.*, psoas magnus. *Ps. p.*, psoas parvus.

ON THE DISPOSITION AND HOMOLOGIES OF THE EXTENSOR AND FLEXOR MUSCLES OF THE LEG AND FOREARM. By PROFESSOR HUMPHRY.

THE peculiar disposition of the extensor and flexor muscles of the leg in Cheiroptera and their similarity, in many respects, to those of the arm have led me to reflect further upon the disposition of these muscles in man and other animals, and to offer the following remarks upon them.

In the *first* place I must assume as scarcely admitting of question that the extensors and flexors of the leg and forearm are respectively homologous, i.e. that the extensors of the leg are serially homologous with the extensors of the forearm, and the flexors of the leg are serially homologous with those of the forearm (p. 296). *Secondly*, there is such good reason to consider the pollex line of the fore limb (including the radius, the outer condyle, and the outer, or larger, tubercle of the humerus) to correspond with the hallux line of the hind limb (including the tibia, the inner condyle, and the inner, or lesser, trochanter of the femur) that I shall take this also for granted. *Thirdly*, the coracoid portion of the scapula is by most anatomists, apparently with good reason, regarded to correspond with the ischial portion of the pelvis.

The two joints concerned—the knee and elbow—are in the main similar, ginglymoid, two bones in each revolving in about the same range upon a third. The movements are accordingly similar; and we may expect to find the muscles effecting them, also, similar. Further, the movement of flexion being in the same plane and similar to that of extension, we may expect the muscles engaged in these two movements to be similar. In other words, we should expect a correspondence in the muscles in each of the four instances—extensors and flexors of the leg and extensors and flexors of the arm—, that the same general plan would be observable in all, modified of course to meet the peculiarities of the individual requirements, and that this plan would correspond with that usually employed in those other parts of the body in which the movements are of a similar kind.

As a general rule in a hinge-joint the muscles on each side (flexors and extensors) are in three divisions, one in the middle and one on either side; and it is not uncommon for one or more of the three to take origin from a more distant point than the segment above the joint and to extend beyond it, so passing over two or more joints. Thus, at the ankle there is the *extensor digitorum* arising often from the femur, with its laterals—the *tibialis anticus* and the *peroneus tertius*—on one side, and the *flexor digitorum*, with its laterals—the *tibialis posticus* and the *gastrocnemius*—on the other side. At the wrist are the *extensor* and the *flexor digitorum* with their radial and ulnar laterals on the two sides; and in the case of the digits, in both limbs, a somewhat similar arrangement of tendons to the phalanges is traceable.

In the extensor muscles of the leg and forearm this arrangement is well marked. The long median portion arises from the edge of the ilium, or from the subglenoid edge of the scapula, and extending over the thigh or the arm is inserted, through the patella, into the tibia or into the olecranon, the similarity between the two being increased (as in Pteropus) by the occasional substitution of a sesamoid for the olecranon, and a projecting process of bone for the patella; and the lateral portions —the vasti or the humeral origins of the triceps—arise from the sides of the femur or of the humerus, and pass over the sides of the knee or at the sides of the olecranon. In consequence of there being one bone only above the joint, in each case, these lateral portions are close together and coalesce, forming in the thigh what is sometimes described as the cruræus, that is, a fourth or deep median portion.

The correspondence of these muscles in the two limbs and the serial homology of their respective parts is so obvious as quite to outweigh the objection to such a view furnished by the insertion of the triceps into the olecranon and the quadriceps into the tibia. This difference in the mode of insertion is only one of the ever-recurring instances in which precise homological arrangement, that is, exact general plan, is departed from to meet particular requirements; and though such deviation may be less frequently observed at the insertion than at the origin of a muscle, yet its occurrence there need be no matter for surprise when a sufficient teleological ground can be shown, which may be easily done in this instance. The hind limb having for its chief purpose to propel the body onwards, before it, the one bone (the tibia), which is articulated with the ankle is, for greater strength, expanded to be articulated with both condyles of the femur, and the extensor muscle is accordingly attached to it. The fore limb, on the other hand, being constructed for the purpose of drawing the body after it, as well as of seizing, holding, &c., a hook-like process of one of the bones is thrown up behind the trochlea; and it, at the same time, affords a favourable point of attachment for the extensor muscles. This hook-like process is derived from the ulna, because in the fore limb it is necessary, for the purpose of permitting greater movement of the distal segment, to leave the bone (the radius) which chiefly carries that segment more free to rotate upon the condyle of the humerus.

The difference in the disposition of the bones, in accordance with the difference of function in the two limbs, as well as the more varied duties of the flexor muscles, is also the cause of those muscles deviating from the simple pattern of the extensors and presenting greater differences in their modifications in the two limbs than do the extensors. The extensors have, in each instance, the one simple duty of straightening the joint; but the flexors in addition to bending the joint have the further work of rotating the part to which they are attached; and this is effected in a different manner in the two limbs. In the hind limb the fibula is necessarily carried with the expanded tibia; and the flexor muscles pass to the two sides of the leg in order to give it a rotatory movement. Hence they diverge as they descend the thigh and embrace the muscles arising from the condyles of the femur. In the fore limb, the radius alone revolving and carrying the distal segment with it while the ulna remains stationary, the flexors converge towards the middle and become blended together as they descend; and they pass between the muscles arising from the condyles of the humerus which are extended laterally to give those muscles better action upon the carpus and digits. The differences in construction between the shoulder and the pelvis necessitate further differences between the flexors in the two limbs; and these two features of difference between the limbs, added to the difference in the direction of their rotation (p. 297), are sources of much perplexity in the comparison of the flexor muscles. The difficulty of comparing the flexors with the extensors is further increased by the fact that, for greater efficiency, the flexors derive their origin more from the pelvis and shoulder girdle and less from the femur and humerus than do the extensors. Still the evidences of homological resemblance between the elements of the flexor groups in two limbs and of their similarity to the extensors may be traced with sufficient clearness.

The femoral and humeral portions of the extensors are evidently represented in the flexors, in part at least, by the *femoral origin* of the *biceps cruris*, the fibres of which, or most of them, are by dissection traceable to the fibula and which may therefore be named 'femoro-fibular,' and by the *brachialis anticus* which passes from the humerus to the ulna and may be named 'humero-ulnar.'

There can be little doubt that these two elements of the flexors are serially homologous. Their disposition assures us of this, and there is nothing to contra-indicate it in the animal series. The one—the femoro-fibular—it is true is generally absent, whereas the other—the brachialis anticus—is always present. This is merely a carrying out in the hind limb, to a greater extent than in the fore limb, of the principle of throwing back the origin of the flexors to the distant point for the purpose of obtaining better purchase. The varieties are very few. The *femoro-fibular* now and then, as in the two-toed Anteater, is inserted near the lower part of the fibula. The *brachialis anticus* commonly consists of one part only. Sometimes however it shows a greater resemblance to the deep portion of the extensors by more or less division. Thus in Man it has somewhat of a bifid tendency above, ascending a little on either side of the deltoid; and a more extensive division has sometimes been observed. In the crested Agouti and the Rabbit it consists, in its whole length, of two parts which arise from the humerus and are inserted into the ulna[1]. In tailed

[1] Mivart and Murie, *Proc. Zool. Soc.* June 26, 1866.

Batrachians and Chelonians it shows still greater tendency to duality by passing to the radius as well as to the ulna. In other Reptiles and Birds it is usually disposed as in Mammals; but in the Penguin it is said by Meckel to be inserted into the radius only, taking the place of the biceps which is absent.

The remaining parts of the flexors pass from the pelvis, or the shoulder girdle, to the tibia and the fascia of the leg, or to the radius and fascia of the forearm. In the hind limb they are three, the *semimembranosus* arising from the ischium above the tuber and inserted into the back of the tibia near to the inner side of the joint, the *semitendinosus* arising from the most projecting point of the ischium and inserted into the inner side of the tibia lower down, and the *biceps* arising from the ischium with the semitendinosus and inserted into the fascia on the outer or fibular side of the leg.

In the fore limb there is what appears at first sight to be one muscle only—the *biceps brachii*—having two points of origin, to correspond with the three flexors of the leg just named. This muscle is, however, easily resolvable into two, a 'glenoid[1]' and a 'coracoid'; for although these two come into contact in the middle of the arm and are united by muscular fibres and terminate in one chief tendon which is inserted into the radius, yet, they are really more separate than such an account or than the usual description of the muscle would imply. Nearly to the elbow a delicate, white, tendinous line of demarcation may, in most instances of the human subject, be distinguished between them, into which the approximated muscular fibres of the two bellies, or some of them, are inserted. This longitudinal inscription is more evident on the anterior surface of the muscle than behind, being in the latter situation obscured by the muscular fibres of the glenoid passing across to the coracoid portion of the muscle. The two portions continue their course to the radius so closely connected as to form what is usually regarded as one tendon. A little dissection however shows that the glenoid portion of the muscle

[1] I have previously (Vol. II. of this Journal, p. 300) intimated that both these origins really belong to the coracoid part of the scapula. When I speak, therefore, of the 'glenoid' as distinguished from the 'coracoid' part of the biceps, I mean that portion of the muscle which arises from the coracoid bone where it enters into the formation of the glenoid cup.

terminates chiefly in the upper part of that tendon and is inserted nearer to the joint; whereas the tendon resulting from the coracoid portion is inserted a little lower down. Moreover the coracoid portion, as it passes the elbow, sends off a fascial expansion which constitutes the chief part of the semilunar fascia and is disposed upon the ulnar side of the forearm. We may therefore say that the biceps muscle is resolvable into three elements:—(1) A '*gleno-radial*,' passing from the glenoid part of the coracoid and inserted into the radius near the joint. This appears to correspond to the *semimembranosus*.—(2) A '*coraco-radial*,' passing from the most projecting part of the coracoid and inserted into the radius a little lower down. This appears to correspond with the *semitendinosus*.—(3) A '*coraco-fascial*,' arising and passing in close union with the preceding, but expanding into the ulnar side of the forearm[1]. This appears to correspond with the 'ischio-fascial' part of the *biceps cruris* which arises and passes for some distance in close union with the semitendinosus and expands into the fascia upon the fibular side of the leg.

These three flexor elements, it is true, are not so fully separated or segmented in the fore limb as in the hind. They are united by fibres passing from the belly of the glenoid portion to that of the coracoid and by a few passing in the opposite direction. They are united also by fibres passing from the glenoid portion to the fascia on its superficial and its deep aspects[2]; and the two coracoid portions are in close union in nearly their whole length. This I apprehend is due chiefly to the convergence of these elements in the fore limb as contrasted with their divergence in the hind limb; and even in the latter

[1] Mr Macalister (*Proc. Irish Acad.* Dec. 1867) mentions an instance in which this part was separate in its whole length. It arose from the coracoid process in common with the short head of the biceps, from which it soon separated and formed the entire of the semilunar fascia.

[2] These may correspond with the detachment of the semimembranosus to the fascia of the leg. There is nothing in the fore limb to correspond distinctly with the detachment from the semimembranosus to the back of the knee, called the 'ligament of Winslow.' The free movement of the radius upon the ulna forbids the presence of any corresponding connexion of the gleno-radial with the ligaments of the elbow, and the absence of any forced extension here with superincumbent weight, such as there is in the case of the knee, renders unnecessary the support of a musculo-ligamentous adjunct like that of the ligament of Winslow.

some trace of imperfect segmentation remains in the union of the biceps and semitendinosus at and below their origin.

An additional humeral adjunct to the flexors of the forearm in the form of the 'humeral origin' of the biceps is so frequent a variety in Man and so usual in the Bird as to demand consideration. It answers clearly, like the brachialis internus, to a part of the humeral division of the extensor[1]. It arises most frequently from the ulnar side of the humerus, is very often an offset from the brachialis internus, and, so far as I have had an opportunity of observing, is traceable chiefly into the semilunar fascia. It would seem, therefore, to be homologous with those fibres of the femoro-fibular part of the biceps cruris which join the ischio-fascial part and are distributed with it upon the fibular side of the leg. It has been supposed to represent a portion—that below the tendinous intersection—of the semitendinosus; but its origin usually from the ulnar side of the humerus and its insertion into the ulnar side of the fascia seem to militate against that view.

This transverse tendinous intersection generally, if not always, present in the semitendinosus in man is a remarkable feature. Whether it is peculiar to man I am not sure. I have invariably found it in him, but have not met with it in any other animal, though I have often looked for it. I am not aware of a similar feature in any other of the muscles of the limbs and I scarcely know what importance to attach to it. Guided by the intersections in the trapezo-deltoid of animals which are devoid of clavicle and in the digastric of some animals, as the Rabbit, in which the muscle runs straight from the occiput to the jaw and consists of one portion with an intersection, we should infer that it is an indication of a segmentation which has its more complete fulfilment in some other animal; but that has not, so far as I am aware, been found in any instance. If we are to seek for its explanation by reference to the fore limb such may possibly be afforded in the manner just mentioned, or by the fact that fibres from the gleno-radial (the homologue of the semimembranosus) pass into

---

[1] Not unfrequently there are more than one of these humeral adjuncts. Henle met with three muscular bands arising from near the points of insertion of the pectoralis, the coraco-brachialis, and the deltoid.

and contribute to the formation of the coraco-radial (the homologue of the semimembranosus) in the lower part of the arm. If we suppose that in the hind limb the homologues of these fibres, instead of being continued upwards with the semimembranosus, run along with the semitendinosus and become implanted into it, the line of such union might be inscribed by a tendinous intersection.

The close connexions of the *coraco-brachialis*, at its origin, with the *biceps*, resembling that of the *semitendinosus* with the *biceps cruris*, has suggested that it may appertain to the flexor group; and the further connexion shown by variations in man—portions occasionally being found to pass into the brachialis internus or into the biceps[1]—are in favour of such a view. It seems not improbable that it may contain some elements which are homologous with certain ingredients in the flexors of the hind limb—with parts of the biceps cruris or of the semitendinosus or both—but which stop short at the humerus instead of running on to their more distant destination. In accordance with such a view I have thrown out the hint that one of the muscles passing from the ischium to the femur in Pteropus (p. 310) may be a part of a flexor of the leg which has thus stopped short in the thigh. Taking into consideration, however, the very regular attachment of the coraco-brachialis to the humerus we must, I think, regard it as belonging essentially to the adductors. True, it is attached to the ulnar side of the humerus, whereas the adductors of the thigh are, in man at least, attached to the tibial side of the linea aspera of the femur. In other animals, however, the adductors, especially the adductor magnus, not unfrequently extend to the fibular side; and in the two-toed Anteater I find one of them, arising from the tuber ischii conjointly with the biceps tendon and related to it as intimately as the semitendinosus usually is, or more so, and as intimately as the coraco-brachialis is usually related to the biceps brachii. In the Jerboa the adductor magnus is, in its whole length, scarcely separable from the semimembranosus, a tendinous arch over the knee connecting them even at their insertion. The

[1] On the variations in the coraco-brachialis see Wood in Vol. I. of this Journal.

close relation, thus, often observed between the adductors and the flexors in the thigh, and the occasional passage in man of some fibres of the coraco-brachialis into one or other of the portions of the biceps or into the brachialis internus, are arguments in favour of the view I have taken, that the coraco-brachialis may contain mixed flexor and adductor elements, the latter preponderating. In many animals, and occasionally in man, it breaks up into two or more portions, a division indicated in normal human anatomy by the passage of the external cutaneous nerve through its substance. These divisions are probably homologous with the divisions of the adductors in the thigh; and the relations of the external cutaneous nerve to this muscle or set of muscles and to the radial side of the fore limb are similar to those of the obturator nerve to the adductor muscles and to the tibial side of the hind limb. The brachial artery has also been observed by Mr Wood and others[1] to pass from behind forwards, between or through the divisions of the coraco-brachialis when it extended far down the humerus, much as the femoral artery passes from before backwards between or through the divisions of the adductor of the thigh. I may observe however that in all the animals I have dissected in which the muscle extended to the inner condyle the artery and nerve travelled, as they usually do, not through it but internal to it.

The *popliteus* can scarcely be numbered among the flexors of the leg. I may however observe with regard to it that its origin from the fibular condyle of the femur and its insertion into the hallux edge of the tibia and an oblique line descending thereto indicate clearly that it is the homologue of the *pronator teres* which arises from the ulnar condyle of the humerus, and is inserted into the pollex edge of the radius and an oblique line descending thereto. An occasional partial or complete[1] origin from the fibula may square with the occasional partial origin of the pronator from the ulna. The difference in the relation of the two muscles to the great blood-vessels and nerves

[1] Henle, *Handbuch der Anatomie*, I. 178.
[2] In Paracyon I found a distinct tolerably strong origin from the head of the fibula in addition to a strong tendon from the outer condyle, and can confirm Mr Mivart's statement, that in Echidna it arises from the process at the summit of the fibula instead of from the condyle of the femur. In the Jerboa the

is accounted for by the fact that a more superficial position of the pronator is required for its effective action in rolling the radius upon the ulna; and hence any vessels or nerves traversing its surface would, during its contraction, be thrown into relief and subjected to injurious pressure and disturbance. Whereas the contraction of the popliteus, which rotates the whole leg upon the thigh, causes no difference in the relation of the tibia to the fibula; and hence there is no prominence of the muscle and no interference with the vessels and nerves which lie upon its surface.

The foregoing remarks upon the flexor muscles are based chiefly upon considerations drawn from their disposition in man; because the several parts, in the fore limb at least, acquire their greatest individuality and expression in him, and furnish, therefore, the best opportunity for comparison. Even in him, as we have seen, the flexor elements are in the fore limb blended in a perplexing manner, the segmentation is imperfect, but it is much less so than in many of the lower animals. The principle of division of labour and specialization of function, so well exemplified in his upper and lower limbs, is carried out in a proportionate manner in his muscles, and is attended with greater independence and individualization, and, therefore, greater perfection in their action and greater variety in the movements they effect than is to be found among the lower animals.

That this specialization and individualization of parts is commonly attended with complication of structure and such departure from simple pattern as increases the difficulty of homological comparison there can be no doubt; and the great advances in this branch of science are, accordingly, for the most part, made or proved by reference to the simpler forms of animal life, and by tracing from them the changes which are developed in the ascending scale. Still, paradoxical as it may seem, complexity may be involved in simplicity, that is to say, the unevolved elements of the complex form may, and probably

popliteus is large and has a sesamoid in its tendon where it passes by the fibula; and a delicate tendon from the head of the fibula descends with it and gives origin to the lowest fibres of the muscle. In tailless Amphibians (Meckel, *Vergleich Anat.* III. 254) it is large, arising from the fibula and extending all down the leg.

often do, lie hid in the simple structure, giving to it a homological significance which we learn only by the study of those examples in which developement has proceeded to a higher grade. This is the case in the instance before us. It is only in the most fully segmented condition of the biceps brachii, such as it is in man, that we are able at all to trace the true composition of the muscle, and to show how its elements may be compared with the flexor muscles of the leg. Even here it can be done only with difficulty and some uncertainty.

This difficulty is increased rather than diminished by reference to comparative anatomy; forasmuch as the varieties which the biceps undergoes in different animals are very great, greater, perhaps, than occur in any other muscle, a circumstance which may be viewed in connexion with its composite nature in man. On the whole, however, I think, the disposition of the muscles in animals will be found to be confirmatory of the view I have based upon their anatomy in man.

In mammals that which we call the 'glenoid' part is always, or nearly always, present; and not unfrequently it is the only part, all the elements being combined in it. It descends to the forearm, the radius (Seal), the ulna (Jerboa), or both (two-toed Anteater), being selected for its insertion according as either or both afford the best provision for its action upon the limb. It is rarely inserted into the ulna only. Commonly it shows a tendency to segmentation by sending a slip from its fore part to the radius; and when it is inserted, as it more generally is, into the radius, it often detaches a slip from its hinder part to the ulna which enters into more or less close relations with the brachialis anticus, ensheathing it or blending with it. Sometimes, as in the Cat, Lamb, and Jerboa, it sends an expansion into the fascia; thus completing the evidence of its tripartite nature. On the whole it indicates a radial rather than an ulnar affinity; but it presents a good illustration of variability in the place of insertion and in the degree of segmentation, warning us to caution in reliance upon either of these as trusty guides to homological arrangement. Above, it is often, to all appearance, quite single. This is when the coracoid process is short. Even then sometimes (in the Dog and Lamb, but not invariably in them) a more or less distinct groove indicates an incipient segmentation which becomes more manifest, and passes into complete division when the coracoid process is more projecting.   When the coracoid portion of the muscle is distinct it may usually be traced by a little dissection to the radius below the point of insertion of the glenoid portion[1].

In those animals in which the coracoid bone remains separate the upper end of the biceps arises from it, is commonly single, and seems, at first sight, to correspond with what we call the 'coracoid' portion in mammals.   It is clear, however, from the mode of termination of the muscle below, in the radius, ulna or fascia or in two or more of these, that it, as just remarked of what we call the 'glenoid' in mammals when it exists alone, contains all the elements appertaining to the biceps or some of the factors which go to make up each of the elements.   Thus the 'coracoid' origin of ovipara and monotremes and the 'glenoid' origin of mammals, when either exists alone[2], are to this extent, identical.   The difference being that the shortening and closer union of the coracoid bone with the scapula in mammals throws the origin of the biceps near to the glenoid cup and, apparently, upon the scapular part of it.   In the tailless Batrachians, the origin of the biceps extends upon the sternum as well as the coracoid bone; and in the tailed Batrachians, though commonly supposed to be absent, it is represented by a narrow tendon passing from the coracoid bone to the radius[3].

With the exception of the femoro-fibular part of the biceps to which I have already referred, the several flexors of the leg are very constant in their presence and do not present many irregularities in their disposition.   The most remarkable deviations in mammals from the ordinary plan with which I am acquainted are those in Pteropus (p. 311) where the *biceps* is absent, unless indeed its undeveloped elements, or some of them, are blended with the semitendinosus or inserted into

---

[1] In Pteropus (p. 303), as in man, where the glenoid part is inserted into the radius, the coracoid passes in front of it, and derives fibres from it.   In the Rat, where the glenoid is inserted chiefly into the ulna, the coracoid crosses behind it and contributes fibres to it.

[2] In Saurians and Emys (according to Rüdinger, *die Muskelen der vorderen Extremitäten der Reptilien und der Vögel*, s. 50 and 71), the biceps arises by two heads from the coracoid bone, and in addition to the attachment to the radius and ulna, a fasciculus is sent to the fascia of the forearm.

[3] Rüdinger, *loc. cit.* s. 95.

the femur (see page 310). Not unfrequently the origin of the *biceps* is extended to the sacrum through the medium of fibres of the sacro-sciatic ligament, as in man, or by a distinct muscular band which may constitute the sole origin of the muscle, as in Orycteropus (Vol. II. of this *Journal*, p. 312). In Phoca (same Vol. and page) this band, crossing beneath the ischiatic portion of the biceps, reaches to the foot and expands there upon the extensor tendons. The ischiatic portion of the muscle also often reaches to the heel. An extension upwards to the sacrum or ilium is sometimes gained by the other flexors[1], but they do not often reach so far down the leg as does the biceps. The arrangement in the lower animals is much the same as in Mammals; but in Saurians and Amphibians the segmentation of the flexors from the adductors and abductors is commonly less complete, and the muscles passing to the leg derive more extensive origin from the pelvis.

The relations of the *gracilis* to the flexors, especially in Pteropus (p. 311) where it descends to the middle of the back of the tibia in company with the semitendinosus, might seem to claim a place for it in the flexor group. It has however a different origin from them; and there are many reasons for attaching it rather to the adductor group, and regarding it as furnishing an additional illustration of the close connexion of the adductors with the flexors—in other words of their imperfect segmentation from them—to which I have already alluded when speaking of the coraco-brachialis. It probably represents a part of the pectoral portion of the adductor group in the forelimb, some of the fibres of which often extend along the radial side of the flexors of the forearm, and even upon the forearm itself nearly to the wrist.

It may be further remarked that the relations of the *gracilis* to the tibial side of the flexors resemble that of the *glutæus* and *tensor vaginæ femoris* (which are members of the abductor group) to the fibular side of the extensors; and taking the view,

---

[1] I find it so in the case of the semitendinosus in the Jerboa. Both the semitendinosus and the biceps have an origin from the sacrum in the Hyrax and Crested Agouti described by Mivart; and in Birds and Reptiles the semimembranosus also, not unfrequently, arises from the sacrum or ilium. A more distinct homologue of this sacral origin of the biceps than the continuity of fibres with the sacro-sciatic ligament has been described as a variety in man by Wood, *Proc. R. S.* xv. 541.

which many considerations favour, that the *glutæus* is the homologue of the *latissimus dorsi*[1], the connexion of the glutæus with the fibular side of the extensor cruris will represent that, so common among other animals though rarely present in man, of the latissimus dorsi with the ulnar side of the extensor antibrachii. This detachment from the lat. d. sometimes (Mole and two toed-Anteater) extends, over the side of the ulna, to the carpus just as (Rat and others) does the prolongation of the glutæus extending downwards over the side of the fibula, reach to the ankle. The glutæus is, moreover, not unfrequently (Jerboa), connected inseparably with the biceps. Indeed, the segmentation of the flexors and extensors from the abductors and adductors, which is so imperfect in Amphibians, is in many mammals much less complete than it is in man; and this imperfect segmentation of the flexors from the abductors and adductors in the hind limb, like the very imperfect segmentation of the flexors from one another in the fore limb, renders the lower animals less favourable than man for the comparison of these muscles in the two limbs.

Thus, starting with the comparatively simple hinge-pattern of the extensor muscles of the leg and forearm, I have endeavoured to show the relations of the flexors with this pattern, and to trace their correspondence in the two limbs. I am quite aware that the result is far from complete, and that the views expressed may require correction. I cannot hope altogether to succeed where so many others have tried and failed. Still it must be the desire of every philosophical anatomist to acquire and to give some rational exposition of the construction of the animal body, and of the varieties which he sees in it, to indicate in what manner the simple form of one animal, or one part, is modified to perform the more complicated functions of another, to show how homology and functional requirement are blended and modify one another, and, as far as he can, to trace uniformity of plan through variety of detail.

The views which I entertain may be thus briefly summarized.

---

[1] In this and many other points, my views of the serial homology of the muscles of the limbs are in accordance with those expressed by Prof. Rolleston in his valuable and comprehensive paper ' On the Homologies of certain muscles connected with the shoulder-joint.' *Trans. of Linnæan Society*, xxvi. 609.

1. The plan of disposition of the extensor and flexor muscles is most simply portrayed in the extensors, and consists of a long median portion—represented by the *rectus* in the thigh, and the *scapular part* of the *triceps* in the arm—and a short deeper portion extending more laterally, and represented by the *vasti* and *cruræus* in the thigh, and by the *humeral part* of the *triceps* in the arm.

2. The *femoro-fibular* part of the *biceps cruris* and the *brachialis anticus* are serially homologous, and correspond antithetically to the deep—femoral or humeral—portions of the extensors.

3. The *gleno-radial*, the *coraco-radial*, and the *coraco-fascial*—the three parts into which the *biceps brachii* is resolvable—are severally homologous with the *semimembranosus*, the *semitendinosus* and the *ischio-fascial* part of the *biceps cruris;* and these three elements in each limb correspond anthithetically with the long—pelvic or scapular—portions of the extensors.

A reference to Dr Macalister's able and instructive paper on the Homologies of the Flexor Muscles of the Vertebrate Limb in the preceding Vol. of this *Journal* will show that my views differ in several respects from those given by him. One fundamental source of difference consists in the fact that he regards the inner and outer sides of the two limbs to be homologous; whereas I take the inner side of the fore limb, in its humeral part at any rate, to be homologous with the outer side of the hind limb. A want of agreement on this point must entail numerous discrepancies on other points. Indeed the attempt to arrive at satisfactory conclusions respecting the serial homologies of the several parts of the limbs is obviously hopeless until the question of the correspondence of the respective antero-posterior and lateral aspects of the limbs is determined. To do that with more certainty and give a more secure starting-point for further investigation is a leading object with me in this and the preceding paper.

ON THE ARRANGEMENT OF THE PRONATOR MUSCLES IN THE LIMBS OF VERTEBRATE ANIMALS. By Alexander Macalister, *Demonstrator of Anatomy, Royal College of Surgeons, Ireland.*

In most vertebrate limbs a group of muscles exists, for the production of motion between the two parallel bones composing that limb segment which is the second from the shoulder-girdle; and as the pectoral extremities of animals are usually more perfect than the pelvic in point of development, being often more or less subordinated to the use of the head, this group of muscles consequently, as a rule, preserves a more perfect individuality in the fore limb than in the hinder.

For obvious reasons, many animals are incapable of the actions of pronation and supination, but it does not necessarily follow that in such these muscles should become completely suppressed, for in many instances of the kind subordinate functions assume the preponderance, and action changes accordingly.

The group of muscles under consideration consists of two series—pronators and supinators. To the former of these we will limit our attention at present. When fully developed, the pronators are two—first, a long pronator (epitrochlo-radial); and secondly, a short transverse muscle (ulno-radial).

1st. The long pronator or pronator radii teres is one of the most regular and invariable of limb muscles. In *man* its origin is from the inner condyle of the humerus, on a plane superficial to that of the other flexors; (its second head is of a different nature, as shall be seen hereafter). In all the Quadrumana its origin is similar, but its difference of plane is less marked. Among the Carnivora, Insectivora, Cheiroptera and Rodentia I have found it to be similar in origin in the *seal, dog, dingo, wolf, fox, brown* and *Virginian bears, otter, lion, tiger, cat, hyena, paradoxure, weasel, marten, hedgehog, bats* (both *Vespertilio* and *Pteropus*), *rabbit, hare, rat;* among Edentata, it is regular in the *six-banded Armadillo,* the *three-toed sloth,* the *anteater* and

Orycteropus (Humphry); among Marsupials, it is likewise similar in *Macropus major* and *Vallabiense, Dasyurus, Phascolomys,
Phalangista* and *Virginian Opossum;* in *Echidna* and *Ornithorhynchus* it is large, and seems to act as a powerful flexor.
Among Pachyderms, it is present in rudiment in the *elephant,
hyrax, pig* and *peccary;* and among Ruminants, traces of it are
present in the *camel* and *dromedary;* and, according to Meckel,
in the *roebuck.* It is absent in Cetacea, Solipeda, the *rhinoceros,
sheep, goat, nylghaie, Tragulus napu, sambur, axis* and *cariacus.*
Cuvier says, but incorrectly, that it is absent in *bats.*

Among birds, it has often an accessory head from the medial
ligament of the elbow-joint, which remains separate for its
entire extent from the condyloid head. This portion, however,
is not homologous with the human coronoid head, for in the
latter case the median nerve is between the two muscles, in the
former the nerve is underneath both muscles. This double condition occurs in the *golden eagle,* the *falcon, vulture, owl, stork,
Weka rail, grebe, jabiru* and *crane.* I have not been able to
trace this separation in the *ostrich, rhea, emu,* or *cassowary.*
In the *penguin,* according to Schoepss, this muscle is modified
into two parallel tendinous bands (Schoepss quoted by Rüdinger
*über die Muskeln der Vordern Extremitäten der Reptilien und
Vögeln,* Tab. xii. Fig. 23, No. 9).

Among reptiles, the origin of the round pronator is normal,
and its presence is tolerably constant in those possessing limbs.
It is present in the *Chelonia imbricata, caretta,* and *mydas,
Testudo europœa, Emys geographica, Lacerta viridis, Chamœleon,
Iguana tuberculata* (Mivart), *crocodile* and *alligator.* In all
these its origin is regular, its action is mainly that of a flexor,
and it attains its reptilian maximum in the *alligator.*

Among Amphibia it is tolerably constant, as in Reptilia, and
it exists in *Rana temporaria, mugiens, esculenta,* in *Bufo cinereus*
and *vulgaris,* in *triton,* the *maculated salamander, siredon, proteus*
and others. In many of these its origin is extensive, as in *R.
mugiens,* and occupies the entire of the medial process of the
lower end of the humerus. In these animals it is large, and
acts as a flexor of the elbow, and as such was named by Ecker
"flexor antibrachii medialis."

The insertion of this muscle is subject to little variation, being usually inserted into the radius for a variable extent ; its attachment is to a central part of the bone, about the middle-third in the Primates in general, as in most of the Quadrumana, and many of the Carnivora and others. It is attached to the ulnar side of the middle-third of the radius in many of the Amphibia, which is contrary to its usual habit, and indicates its assumption of a flexor action. It stretches to the lower half of the radius in the *three-toed sloth*, in which its insertion is split into two parts—a lower, extending to the front of the carpal end of the radius, and to the anterior ligament of the wrist joint ; and an upper, which is attached to the lower half or sometimes two-thirds of the radius. It is attached nearly to the upper half of the radius for a variable extent in the *kangaroo* and *wallaby*, but to the middle third in *Perameles, Didelphys,* and *Phalangista*. It occupies more than two-thirds of the radius in *Iguana* (Mivart, *P. Z. S.*, 1867, p. 783); and in the *alligator* and *crocodile* it is attached nearly to the entire length of the radius, as is likewise the case in the *green lizard;* while in the *Greek tortoise* it is attached to the lower third of the radius only.

The second pronator normally developed is the short, nearly transverse ulno-radial muscle ; the pronator quadratus, which, when perfectly developed, occupies the entire anterior surface of these bones from elbow to wrist joint. This muscle is most largely developed in the *dog,* in which it occupies the entire interosseous space from the elbow to the wrist, and a similar development occurs in the allied forms the *dingo, fox, wolf, and hyena,* also in the *wallaby* and *Perameles* among Marsupials. Rarely, however, is this muscle developed as an unbroken, continuous sheet, but it is much more commonly the subject of either of two modifications—either becoming diminished from above downwards, and shrinking to smaller dimensions, or else being parted into two in the centre, and remaining in the form of upper and lower separate muscles ; the former of these varieties occurs in by far the largest number of animals—thus, in the *giant kangaroo*, it shrinks to the lower two-thirds of the forearm ; in the *tiger, lion, cat, opossum, porcupine,* and *civet cat* it occupies about one-half ; in the *Virginian bear, racoon, agouti* and *marmot* it extends for about one-third ; in *man,* most *monkeys, apes* and *lemurs*, the *coati*, *paradoxure*, the *brown bear*, the *otter*, and *marten* it occupies about one-fourth; it is very small and rudimentary in the *three-toed sloth*, the *Orycterope*[1] and the *seal*, occupying in these from one-fifth to one-sixth of the forearm bones. In the last-named animal, Carus and Duvernoy mention it as non-existent. Prof. Haughton does not refer to it, and twice I have looked for it in vain. Meckel and Humphry, however, describe it as present, and I found it in a third seal.

The second and more interesting variety of this muscle is the form found in man and reptilia, in which the short pronator becomes deficient in the centre, leaving its upper and lower ends persistent. This condition is most perfectly to be traced in saurian reptiles, where a short upper pronator underlies the median nerve; in some cases, as in the *green lizard*, closely connected to the true quadrate pronator. This muscle is sometimes, in origin, promoted above the ulna to the inner ligament of the elbow, as in the *chamœleon*, or to the inner condyle, as in the *Iguana tuberculata*, in which it forms the pronator accessorius so accurately described by Mr Mivart. In its insertion, this muscle usually seeks the radius above the pronator teres, but in all the fore-mentioned cases, its radial attachment is extended to touch or even to overlap the pronator quadratus; the cause of separation in these instances seems to be the necessity for an ulnar origin for the flexor of the digits. A further divergence from the type occurs in *Gongylus ocellatus*, in which this pronator accessorius is connected to the pronator teres, and separated from it by the median nerve, a state which directly conducts us to the arrangement of the two-headed pronator teres of *man* (for further observations on which, see Vol. L. N. S. of this Journal, p. 8, *et seq.*). This muscle is entirely obsolete in Solipeda, Proboscidea Ruminantia, Cheiroptera, Cetacea, the *hyrax, hare, rabbit, armadillo*, &c.

There are some interesting varieties of arrangement, in the human subject, of these muscles. Among the most striking of these is the form of pronator quadratus, in which the lower fibres arose from the lower seventh of the ulna and formed a round belly, whose tendon passed across the lower end of the radius

---

[1] Mr Galton, *T. L. S.*, Vol. xxvi. p. 5, describes this muscle as larger in Orycterope than I have mentioned above.

to be lost in the aponeurotic structures over the scaphoid, trape-zium and trapezoid bones (*Proc. Royal Irish Acad.* 1867). In a fine Bengal *tiger* dissected in Febuary, 1869, the lower fibres passed over the inferior extremity of the radius to be inserted into the tendon of the extensor ossis metacarpi pollicis.

In some animals, as the *chamæleon*, the segmentation of the superficial pronator teres is almost complete, and its fibres form two nearly separate bellies. This throws light upon the fission in the avian pronator, as the co-existence of a split superficial pro-nator over the median nerve with the pronator accessorius shows that the deep avian muscle is not necessarily of a different type from its superficial neighbour, both lying over the median nerve. The homotypes of these muscles are by no means clearly de-fined. Meckel and Huxley regard the popliteus as representing the pronator teres; and it has likewise been surmised that the tibial head of the solæus represents the quadrate pronator. The former of these homologies is by no means unobjectionable, for, leaving out of account the question of direction, or of the interpretation of the upper parts of the tibia and fibula, there are the following objections to the hypothesis—the origin of popliteus is from the outer condyle, that of pronator teres from the inner; the former arises by a long tendon, the latter, as far as I am aware, never does; the former lies deeply seated in contact with the joint, the latter lies the most superficial of the ento-condyloid group of muscles; the former lies beneath the popliteal nerve, the latter lies superficial to the median nerve; the former crosses above the point of perforation of the anterior tibial artery, the latter crosses on a plane below the origin of the posterior interosseous artery. These considerations seem to abnegate the hypothesis of Meckel, and lead us to look else-where for a muscle fulfilling the required conditions. As pro-nation is the normal and unalterable position of the lower or pelvic limb, we can easily understand why this muscle is not developed as a pronator. Not being a pronator in function, we need not expect to find its typical insertion preserved, for when-ever a muscle loses its usual action and assumes another function, its insertion must be the part to become varied, as that is one of the two essential conditions determining action (the other being direction). In the prone position likewise, for an obvious reason, a pronator runs more longitudinally and less obliquely than in the supine state, hence, on *à priori* grounds, we may expect to find the homotype of the pronator teres as a longitudinally directed muscle, not necessarily preserving its typical insertion, but probably arising superficially from the flexor side of the inner condyle, over the other flexor muscles, over the great flexor nerve, over the artery whose branch perforates the interosseous membrane (ulnar or popliteal, giving off posterior interosseous or anterior tibial), and forming probably an inner boundary to the space in which the limb artery lies (anticubital or popliteal). Now all these conditions are fulfilled by the inner head of the gastrocnemius muscle, a part perfectly separate in its nature from the outer head, as they are quite distinct in the early embryo, but which, by coalescing with other muscles, can utilize its power, which is perfectly useless for its own special purposes. This muscle is liable to very little variation, and is constantly present in the animal series.

Of the short or quadrate pronator, the traces in the pelvic limb are scant. I have, on a former occasion, given some reasons for believing that the inner head of solæus represents the upper part of this muscle (see Vol. II. of this Journal, p. 8), and also that the peroneus sextus (quartus, Otto) or peroneo-calcanian muscle might represent pronator quadratus proper; certainly this muscle is the close parallel of the anomaly of pronator quadratus quoted above, and is very similar to the arrangement of this muscle in the *pig* (called by Gurlt Abductor pollicis longus), or to the lower attachment of it in the *tiger* quoted above. The only instance in which a true pronator quadratus has been found in the hinder limb, as far as I am aware, was in a fine Alligator which died in the Dublin Zoological Gardens, February, 1869, in whose hind limb a distinct transverse fasciculus of fibres crossed from tibia to fibula perfectly differentiated from all the other muscles in this locality.

THE EUSTACHIAN TUBE, WHEN AND HOW IS IT OPENED? (A Commentary on Professor CLELAND's paper in the preceding number of this Journal.) By JAMES JAGO, M.D. *Oxon.*, A.B. *Cantab.*, *Physician to the Cornwall General Infirmary.*

IN treating in the preceding number of this Journal "On the Question whether the Eustachian Tube is Opened or Closed in Swallowing," Professor Cleland proposes to refute the latter view, which he speaks of as the prevalent one, and as originating with Toynbee in a communication to the Royal Society in 1853, and as repeated in another to the British Association in 1861, from which latter as it appeared in their Report he makes his sole quotations. He leaves unnoticed his work on the Diseases of the Ear, and several later occasional writings of his which recur to the subject at issue.

Had these writings been looked into, and three papers of mine published a little after Toynbee's first communication in 1853 to 1858, or a more recent essay of mine on the "Functions of the Tympanum," being one of the "Original Articles" in the January and February numbers of the *British and Foreign Medico-Chirurgical Review* for 1847, in which these papers and those writings are cited, it would have been seen that Toynbee's views had in his later years undergone material modifications :—that the last of his reasons, as extracted from the Report, for closure of the tube, except in deglutition, viz. lest "the sounds from the fauces also enter the tympanum," he acknowledges to have derived from me, though it is but a meagre statement of my proposition; and that finally he had abandoned the whole of his fanciful notions as to the acoustical advantages of a perfectly-closed chamber, and adopted my explanation for the closure just alluded to, which had been published in 1853. Moreover, that he had finally accepted a correction of mine of the date of 1858, to the effect that when we swallow with stopped nostrils, the air in the drum is not condensed[1], as he taught, but on the contrary rarefied.

It being understood that he did not cease to use his illustra-

---

[1] The physical cause assigned by him for the feeling of tension in the ears then experienced, which Pr. Cleland deals with as if Toynbee had assigned no such cause, but merely spoken of as "the sensation produced in the ears."

tion, that in descending in a diving-bell the denser air is admitted into the drum by swallowing, and others (and these were not entirely his own), which show that in this way the equilibrium between the pressure of the air in the drum and that in the meatus may be restored, whether the former happen to be less or greater than the latter, it may be affirmed that of *his own* propositions cited by Pr. Cleland he ultimately adhered but to the two following :—

"Firstly, that the faucial orifice of the Eustachian tube is always closed, except momentarily during the act of deglutition, or when air is forcibly blown through it ; secondly, that the Eustachian tube is opened by the muscles of the palate, the *tensor* and *levator palati*."

The first of these statements is wanting in precision, inasmuch as swallowing cannot strictly be defined as an act. It consists of a continuous series of acts. I had aimed at being more definite, and I will now venture upon putting my propositions to the test of Professor Cleland's investigations.

Having a rare opportunity of comparing in the same individual the phenomena furnished on the one hand by an open Eustachian tube with those furnished on the other by a shut one, I was enabled to announce that it is of utter indifference to hearing, provided that the aërial pressure on the two surfaces of the membrana tympani be equal, whether the tube be closed or open, and thus to anticipate like observations made by Dr Cleland on his patient Browne's manifestly patent tube.

I ascertained, moreover, that in the case of the unclosed tube, the noises from breathing through the nostrils, from vocal utterances, sneezing, coughing, &c., enter the drum directly through the tube, producing a grievous annoyance by their loudness, and disagreeable shocks upon the membrana tympani, and that the intrusion of aërial currents into the ear, in this way, on the occurrence of violent explosive expirations, even threatens the integrity of the membrane and of the ossicular chain. I thus convinced myself and ultimately Toynbee, that the tube is ordinarily closed as a provision against such accidents.

In the case of Browne, there is no mention of corresponding inquiries. Dr Cleland's ideas evidently ran at the outset in an opposite direction, and he must have been unacquainted with the above statements. The fact of Browne's having an orifice in the velum palati just in front of the orifice of the tube, would render him somewhat less liable to have expiratory currents turned into the drum by the impediment offered by a pendulous palate to their escape through the mouth, but I do not doubt that he might have been found to be a victim to them nevertheless. Moreover, I suspect that in spite of the morbidly thickened condition of his velum, it might have been ascertained that his other Eustachian tube was not commonly open.

To return to my own observations, my earliest conclusion was that the glottis and Eustachian tubes must never be open at the same time, and thus to agree that the latter is shut in swallowing.

Subsequently, however, I remarked that bubbles of gas ascending from the stomach, if allowed to escape through the nostrils, were apt to pass into the tympanum through the Eustachian tubes, and that this did not seem to me to be effected by the superiority in elasticity of such air to that in the drums, but by the liability of the tubes to be opened by muscular action at the moment of transit. In this event the larynx and pharynx are raised, and the soft palate *depressed*, much as happens in swallowing, so that upon the whole, in an effort after greater accuracy, my most recent definition ran thus:—

"The correlation between the glottis and Eustachian tubes should be thus expressed :—*The Eustachian tubes are shut whenever the glottis is open, but whatever act shuts the latter opens the former.* I should anticipate that the muscles that drag up the rima under the tongue, that is towards the tubes, must have some share in preserving this correlation[1]."

The hint in the concluding sentence I must further unfold before I can compare my conception of the process of swallowing with that of Professor Cleland.

I had demonstrated by visible deep depressions of the lachrymal sacs, and also of the alæ nasi when we swallow with closed nostrils, that there is an instant in the process in which the naso-pharyngeal cavity, cut off from the larynx, becomes en-

---

[1] Op. cit. p. 312. I quote *verbatim*, but the word glottis had better have been repeated than rima introduced. The italics are in the original.

larged, so that the air within it has its elasticity reduced below that of the surrounding atmosphere, and that this corresponds to the very instant in swallowing when the Eustachian tubes open to communicate with the throat. Now as the tongue, unraised at its root, can reach little further than just to lick the vault of the palate, at the commencement of deglutition the lips and cheeks are squeezed against the teeth, and then the tongue by their help manages to get the bolus of food or liquid to be passed on towards the stomach, as far as to the end of the bony palate. But once thus far, it has to be transmitted thence to the isthmus by the sole moveable structures connecting these limits, that is, the tongue and the velum palati; and these must be brought together from before backwards in order to effect the object. That is to say, that the root of the tongue is lifted and the soft palate depressed. If we are attentive, it is easy to feel this depression of the velum when we swallow saliva, and it is this forcible depression of the velum that augments the capacity of the naso-pharyngeal chamber and occasions the partial vacuum above described at the instant that the tubes open; when, owing to the diminution in the wonted air-pressure on the faucial structures, they all swell, so that as the tongue cleaves to the palate, the sides of each Eustachian tube stick together. Thus it is apparent that at the instant, *par excellence*, in which the glottis is closed, the soft palate is not "jerked up," as Pr. Cleland assumes, but *forcibly pulled down*.

Of the many muscles which participate in the complicated acts, or successive acts, of swallowing, it may suffice for my purpose to refer to a few. At the critical instant, it is clearly indispensable that each palato-glossus or constrictor isthmi faucium must strenuously contract, it being the muscle that immediately brings the root of the tongue and velum in contact. Each palato-pharyngeus, I presume, exerts sufficient force to keep well back the free edge of the velum, and the pulley-like action of the tensor palati probably helps to regulate the stages by which the palate is lowered from before backwards, and to keep the velum tense enough transversely to prevent its being converted by preponderating action of the constrictors into a pouch to detain the bolus. It is possible that the levator palati may also exert some moderating action on the shape of the palate which facilitates swallowing; but, at all events, if in action at the same time it is not strong enough to disconcert the combined actions of the muscles just noticed.

In any case the velum having become a fixed point of insertion for certain fibres of the levator, if these should be inserted at the other ends into a yielding portion of the wall of the Eustachian tube, they would tend to draw it downwards. Indeed it would not convey an idea wide of the mark, if for the study of the mechanism in question, the levator and constrictor on each side were regarded as one muscle directly connecting the orifices of the Eustachian tube and larynx, so that it cannot contract without, in its effort to bring those orifices towards each other, closing one and opening the other :—the velum being looked upon as a more or less muscular structure uniting such imagined lateral muscles. The tensors may produce any effect of which they are capable on the walls of the tubes by acting against each other round their pulleys.

I do not not deem it incumbent on me to pursue the acts of swallowing beyond the isthmus; but it results from what has just been said that it is only for the constrictors to relax, whether the associated muscles of the palate delay to do so or not, and the larynx will be on the descent, and the palate ascend, and any yielding under-portion of the Eustachian tube ascend also.

If the foregoing description is in accordance with the actual occurrences in deglutition, it will be perceived that a patient cannot be trained to swallow with his mouth open so that the conduct of his Eustachian tube may be watched through a hole in the soft palate. The observations in Browne's case were made after the critical act had been performed by the depressed velum and when it was again rising. It being observed "that the lower margin of the orifice of the tube, instead of being pulled down as Toynbee believed, was spasmodically twitched up," as the velum was "jerked up," affords no evidence against the supposition that the tube is closed in swallowing, but tends to confirm it. For it would seem as if the tube gaping for want of normal contractility, or from the strain occasioned by its connection with an injured palate, had nevertheless been made to open wider still at the critical instant, and that it was reco-

vering its usual calibre when observed. Nor may it be amiss
to mention here, that there was something wrong with the
palate in the case that led me to pay attention to the phenomena of open and shut Eustachian tubes. The uvula having
become exceedingly relaxed, was partially amputated, and subsequently its trunk hung coiled towards the side which there-
after became affected with irregular patency of the Eustachian
tube, while the other tube retained its normal condition. Though
Browne's palate, unlike this one, was stiffened with the effects
of secondary syphilis, yet the two examples taken together
indicate the probability that a shortening or tension of certain
parts of the palate may cause such an affection of the tube.

Debarred from the privileges of a dissecting-room, I am
incompetent to discuss the questions on the minute anatomy of
the guttural portions of the Eustachian tubes that have been
raised by Professor Cleland ; and it may be long before some
appropriate case of post-mortem may offer me a chance of
attempting to see for myself how the mechanism of opening the
tube is contrived. In the meanwhile I remain convinced that
that careful anatomist has quite mistaken the physiological
actions that he has investigated.

I have heretofore, unless I deceive myself, recorded such a
variety of observations and arguments in favour of my exposition of the question at issue as to amount to a demonstration.
Moreover, in doing so, I have by anticipation *directly* refuted
every physiological objection now advanced by Pr. Cleland. I
have, for instance, shewn as a matter of fact that a permeable
Eustachian tube is traversed by air from every respiratory current that passes it to or fro. Besides, it is an error in physics
to imagine that any "moisture" so free from viscidity as to be
transmissible by "the cilia of the epithelial lining," would in a
tube never so small, accumulate so as to appreciably obstruct
the passage of air through it, more than if it previously only
contained air ; as any one may satisfy himself by experimenting
on a little fluid in the fine nozzle of a syringe for subcutaneous
injection ; and I have already pointed out that the sole mode of
causing the sides of such a tube to cohere is to withdraw from
it some of the air that usually supports them. And, as to the
capping objection, that it is a circumstance " fatal to the Toynbee

theory," that air blown into the tympanum, "if it be allowed to remain, or if swallowing is ineffectual to remove it, will often after a little suddenly disappear with a slight noise when no act of swallowing is being performed," I must remark, that if by a rare chance swallowing did not remove the excess of air in the drum, the air which had been blown into it was of a lower temperature than that previously therein, and had become of greater elasticity on becoming heated; and, if allowed to remain, it was in the predicament of being confined in a chamber supported without by air of less density than itself, and therefore had a tendency to effect a road of escape by rupturing the wall at the weakest point (here the guttural orifice of the tube), and it gets out, for precisely the same reason that it got in, by its extra pressure becoming stronger than the power of resistance of the tissues that hold the tubes shut.

NOTE.—I may be expected to notice an instrument, named a tympano-manometer, which has lately been devised by Herr Politzer. It consists *essentially* of a few inches of fine glass tube, so bent as, when in position, to have two equal upright limbs; one of which is turned off a little horizontally and tipped round with india-rubber, that it may fit in an air-tight manner into the cartilaginous throat of the external auditory meatus. It is open to the air at both ends, whilst the limbs are partially filled with a coloured fluid. Thus any change in the volume of that portion of the meatus lying between the membrana tympani and the perforated india-rubber stopper will be indicated by a displacement of the column of fluid. If it undergo diminution, the air within it will force the fluid to rise in the distal limb, if augmentation, the air without will depress it in that limb. In this way, it has been assumed, the occurrence and direction of every current of air that passes through the Eustachian Tube, may, through the to-and-fro movements of the membrane, be ascertained.

Were the aural end of the instrument so constructed as to be introducible into the entirely bony portion of the meatus, so as to pass loosely through the cartilaginous entrance, and to accurately fit only at the terminal unyielding wall, the assumption just mentioned might have been well founded. In the two most generally approved types of the manometer which I have seen it was not constructed in this manner. It would probably have proved impracticable to so construct it had it been thought desirable to do so. As now in use it is obnoxious to the following strictures.

The slightest extra pressure of the manometer into the meatus causes the fluid to ascend, and the slightest diminution of pressure causes it to descend. Thus any unintentional relative approximation or sundering of the hand that holds the instrument and the head (ear) may lead to an erroneous inference.

The condyle of the lower jaw as it works in the glenoid depression actually presses against the cartilaginous meatus.   The jaw not only rotates up and down, but rotates and slides from side to side, causing, thus, one condyle to advance and the other retire alternately.   Besides it may be carried forwards and backwards bodily without rotation.   Every one of these acts affects the capacity of the meatus through the direct operation of the condyle, so that the said manometrical column of fluid rises whenever this retreats, and sinks whenever it advances.   As examples, if with jaws parted just as is usual in quiet breathing through the mouth, the chin be pulled backwards, the fluid rises, and if it be thrust forwards, it drops.   In ordinary swallowing the under-jaw glides backwards as it is brought up to force the bolus or draught through the fauces, and then, on that object being effected, forwards again;   and thus whether we swallow with stopped or unstopped nostrils, the fluid momentarily rises.   Nevertheless, if in performing this act we forcibly protrude the under teeth in front of the upper, the fluid will make a contrary oscillation.

In an extreme rotation of the jaw, as in deep yawning, the capacity of the meatus is altered in a somewhat different mode.   If whilst the under jaw is lowered, especially if at the same time the upper be, so to speak, raised by the actions of the sterno-mastoid and digastric muscles, the meatus, being pulled upon directly or indirectly by various muscles, becomes elongated somewhat vertically, and its volume diminished, and an ascent of the fluid ensues.   In very many persons the meatus becomes thus perfectly closed in severe yawning, so that they are momentarily deaf.

Now, in the presence of such phenomena, it requires a great deal of caution to verify by aid of the manometer even the greatest movement of which the drumhead is capable, as when for instance, immediately after exhausting (as far as possible) the drum of air we forcibly inflate it.   My experiments on my own and other persons ears convince me that it is vain to attempt to discern minor displacements of the membrane in this way.   And when I perceive that other observers ascribe to movements of the membrane oscillations of the manometrical fluid precisely like those that I find to be occasioned by movements of the under jaw that take place in the several experiments they describe, I am persuaded I have met with no worse success than they.

If the jaw be kept steady the tongue may be protruded or gathered back into the throat, the palate may be raised and breathing carried on through the mouth alone, or the palate be depressed and it be carried on through the nose alone.   Or it may be allowed free passage through both channels, and the said fluid remain uninfluenced.   Thus my conclusion is, that the manometer in its present form is worthless for the purpose of studying the movements of the drumhead, and the passage of air-currents into and out of the drum, whilst no one at all accustomed to aural experiments can fail to be immediately sensible of such phenomena in his own person.

NOTE ON THE MEDIASTINUM THORACIS. By JOHN STRUTHERS, M.D., *Professor of Anatomy in the University of Aberdeen.*

IN his interesting paper "On the Topographical Relations of the Arch of the Aorta," &c., in the last number of this Journal, Mr John Wood makes suggestions in regard to the definition of the several regions of the mediastinum. Mr Wood mentions that he is in the habit of calling the upper portion the "superior" or "cervico-thoracic" region or "root of the neck," and of distinguishing a middle as well as an anterior and a posterior mediastinum in the lower four-fifths. The more usual modes of dividing the mediastinal space, and the nomenclature of the divisions, have long appeared to me to be insufficient and vague. I had been taught when a pupil to speak of a middle as well as of an anterior and a posterior mediastinum; the middle, however, and the upper limit of the posterior, being very vaguely defined. Besides endeavouring to give more precise definitions of these, I have for many years been in the habit of describing a "superior mediastinum"—the space between the three upper dorsal vertebræ and the manubrium sterni, undivided from before backwards. As the mediastinum contains parts of great importance anatomically and to the physician, the position of which it is therefore of importance to be able to indicate accurately and easily, it would be well if anatomists could agree on more precise definitions and terms.

The mediastinum is to be considered both longitudinally and antero-posteriorly as a general median interpleural space, much larger in the fœtus when the heart and thymus are large and, with the other contents, fully block up the middle of the chest, causing the formation of two separate pleural sacs. Considered developmentally, the parts which are strictly *posterior* in the general mediastinal space are the dorsal blood-vessels—the descending aorta and the vena azygos. The heart is anterior, pushing forwards and downwards towards the sternum; while the food and air channels (œsophagus and thoracic duct, and the trachea) are middle in position, passing down through the aortic ring, which, antero-posteriorly or obliquely, connects the heart to the dorsal aorta. Thus the trachea and bronchi, and their accompanying vessels in the root of the lung, belong to the *middle* system. From this point of view, therefore, of the parts essentially present in the mediastinum, the heart would be in the anterior region, the dorsal aorta and vena azygos in the posterior, while in the middle there would be the aortic arch, pulmonary artery and veins, trachea and bronchi and root of lung generally, the food channels, and the phrenic, vagi, and recurrent nerves—the air and food channels and recurrent nerve being within, the phrenic and vagi nerve trunks without the aortic ring. Although the thoracic duct appears to lie quite posterior with the aorta and vena azygos, while the œsophagus is anterior to the three, this is due to the small size of the duct enabling it to sink in by the side of the large aorta, where it also receives the intercostal lymphatics and is protected by the pleura, while the great size and variable condition of the œsophagus and the necessity of its more anterior perforation of the diaphragm enable and require it to maintain its position, and loosely, in front of the blood-vessels.

But as the object of regional subdivision is preciseness in indicating the position of the developed structures, a method founded on the above considerations would not satisfy. The thymus, pushed in between the pericardium and sternum, causes a space anterior to the heart, to which the term anterior is assigned naturally and by long usage; while the œsophagus and thoracic duct, partly from the disappearance or opening up of the right side of the aortic ring, partly from their posterior position, are naturally placed in the posterior mediastinum. Besides, the œsophagus, duct, aorta and vena azygos are related not only anatomically but physiologically, as the four primary nutritive canals—the œsophagus taking the food down, the thoracic duct (ascending œsophagus) bringing it up; the aorta taking it down again farther elaborated as arterial blood, the vena azygos again bringing it up as venous blood. Although the vena cava has become the largest, the vena azygos was the cardinal vein, and remains along the thoracic part of the vertebral column as the typical dorsal vein, having its arch over the root of the right lung as the aorta has over the root of the left.

I would, therefore, place these four canals (with the vagi nerves, now on the œsophagus) in the posterior mediastinum, limiting its contents at the same time to them, the upper limit of the space being the fourth dorsal vertebra, where the arch of the aorta enters the posterior from the middle mediastinum. The aorta is (pathologically) its most important content, and the extent of the posterior mediastinum may be indicated by calling it also the region of the dorsal aorta. This is the usual definition if we exclude the parts in front of the three upper dorsal vertebræ; nor is there occasion to alter the usual definition of the anterior mediastinum, as the space between the sternum and part of the left costal cartilages in front, and the pericardium behind,—in the fœtus wide and occupied by the thymus, in the adult vacant.

The discrepancy or vagueness in the books in regard to the mediastinum in which the parts contained between the three upper dorsal vertebræ and the manubrium sterni are placed, is unavoidable from the arrangement of the parts; some are anterior, some middle, some posterior, without regional division or distinct stratification, and the lateral pleural boundaries of the space pass from sternum to spine without interruption. I have, therefore, been in the habit of giving a distinct name to this region—the "superior mediastinum," a term with which my pupils have been long familiar. I define it as bounded behind by the three upper dorsal vertebræ, in front by the manubrium sterni, on each side by the uninterrupted pleura; as reaching above to the superior aperture of the thorax, below to the top of the aortic arch. Its contents are—first, the venous layer, the left and right innominate veins; next the arteries, the innominate, left carotid, and left subclavian; the phrenic, vagi, cardiac, and left recurrent nerves; the trachea, the œsophagus and the thoracic duct.

These might be described in layers or strata—the venous; the arterial, with the nerves; the air passage, and, behind, the food channels; and were we to endeavour to group them and to subdivide the space in correspondence to and as if in prolongation of the three mediastina below, we might recognise—the anterior, containing the thymus or vacant ; the middle, containing the vascular layers, venous and arterial, and the nerves; the posterior, containing the œsophagus and duct ; the trachea being in the middle (as I would place it), or in the posterior, according to our definition of the middle mediastinum below. But the absence of actual stratification, or antero-posterior subdivision, together with the very different levels of the arteries in relation to the trachea—the innominate being anterior, the left subclavian soon quite posterior—renders any such attempted subdivision useless for the purpose for which regional subdivision is made. As the anterior mediastinum is usually held to reach to the top of the sternum, if this definition be continued the part opposite the manubrium will be at the same time the anterior part of the superior mediastinum. But the disadvantage of this is greatly outweighed by the advantage of using the term superior mediastinum.

The definition of the *middle* mediastinum now becomes clear by exclusion. It is the part of the general mediastinal space not included in the above definitions of the superior, anterior, and posterior mediastina. I subdivide it into two parts—the lower or *cardiac* part, containing the heart (with thoracic stage of lower cava), surrounding pericardium and phrenic nerves, bounded on each side by the pericardial pleura; and the upper or *aortic* part, containing the upper part of the pericardium, the aortic arch, superior cava and arch of the vena azygos, pulmonary artery and its divisions, pulmonary veins, the bifurcation of the trachea and the bronchi, including all the parts which form the root of the lung. It includes, also, its stage of the phrenic and vagi and left recurrent nerves. It may be termed aortic, after (pathologically) its most important content, or aortic and bronchial to express its depth, or the region of the great vessels. It is the region of the great vessels both systemic and pulmonic, and their first branching, of the assembling from opposite directions of the great vessels and tubes before they pass laterally into the pulmonic mass, which may be said to lie as it were in a lateral expansion from the middle mediastinum, of which the root of the lung is the pedicle.

A more simple definition of the middle mediastinum and its contents might have been the pericardium and the parts contained within it; but this would leave out the bronchi, and thus divide the root of the lung unnaturally. The nearest short definition would be the pericardium and its contents, and the parts which form the root of the lung. In naming the great vessel part "aortic," or arch-aortic, I sometimes, by way of contrast, apply the term "supra-aortic" to the superior mediastinum. The arch, in passing behind the root of the lung, makes its transition from the middle to the posterior mediastinum.

Mr Wood proposes to place in the posterior mediastinum " the descending portion of the aortic arch, and all the parts usually described therein, with the addition of the bifurcation of the trachea, including the bronchi and hinder part of the root of the lung and the recurrent laryngeal nerve of the left side," being all the parts in the dorsal incurvature of the spine, from the fourth to the twelfth dorsal vertebra, as marked off by a perpendicular plane passing through the centre of the first dorsal and second lumbar vertebræ, in the line of gravity of the head and trunk in the upright posture. I may be influenced by partiality, but it has seemed to me that the subdivisions of the mediastinum as I have defined them would be the most useful to the anatomist and pathologist; that they correspond to the natural grouping of the parts; that particularly the superior mediastinum deserves a special recognition and name in topographical anatomy.

It may be observed in regard to the use of the mediastinum, that the apparently most prevalent view, that it is for the purpose of giving two distinct pleural sacs, is not satisfactory. As the advantages of having two distinct pleural sacs have reference chiefly to the results of wound or disease, it is doubtful how far it would be correct to assign them in explanation of a natural structure. The teleology becomes questionable when the attributed advantages are to the patient, not to the healthy person. Whether for the renewal of air or for fixing the chest, there does not appear to be any advantage in each lung having its own pleural sac. We may regard the reflection of the pleuræ at the mediastinum as having reference rather to the mediastinal contents, as caused by their presence there, and as performing functions which may be enumerated thus :—(1) Containing or conducting function. (2) Retentive or ligamentous function; inwardly, retaining the contained structures in their places, outwardly, keeping the lung in its place. (3) Diaphragmatic or septal function; giving two distinct pleural sacs; a fortunate result in disease or accident, but doubtful as an explanation of a natural structure.

CASE OF ADDITIONAL BONE IN THE HUMAN CARPUS. By JOHN STRUTHERS, M.D., Professor of Anatomy in the University of Aberdeen.

THIS variety occurred in a muscular male subject, aged 29, dissected in the University rooms during the present winter session. The additional bone occurs in both wrists, at the same place. It ranges with the second row, which has five bones, of which it is the middle; placed between the os magnum, trapezoid, and the second and third metacarpals. It is of an irregularly quadrate form. Above and to the outside, it articulates with the magnum, encroaching on it and occupying the space which usually belongs to the lower and inner part of the magnum; above and internally, it articulates with the trapezoid. Below, it presents a large facet for the middle metacarpal, supporting nearly half the breadth of the base of that bone; and, internally and below, a smaller but distinct facet for the outer angle of the second metacarpal. This is on the dorsum. The bone does not show itself on the palmar aspect, but is seen on opening up the articulations to penetrate about one-third of the distance, where it ends as the apex of a blunt four-sided pyramid, pushed in among the four bones with which it articulates. At the dorsal surface it measures, transversely, one-third of an inch; longitudinally, one-fourth; and from base to apex, one-fifth. Although, on comparing the two sides, there are minute differences in the proportions by which it articulates with the four surrounding bones, the arrangement may be described as quite symmetrical. The os magnum is chiefly affected by the additional bone. It is both narrowed and somewhat pushed outwards; is excluded from its usual contact with the second metacarpal; its terminal facet for the middle metacarpal is narrowed; and its angular facet for the fourth metacarpal is rather broader than usual. But on the palmar aspect it presents its usual angular facet for the second metacarpal. The middle metacarpal is blunt when it usually sends up a styloid projection between the trapezoid and magnum.

In the few cases in which an additional bone has been found in the human carpus, it appears to have been variously placed. The situations of greatest interest would be in that of the intermediate bone of Vrolik, which occurs normally in the carpus of the orang and of certain other quadrumana, though not in the chimpanzee or gorilla; or in the situation of part of the unciform, which supports two digits. In the case above related there are five bones in the second carpal row, the full typical number, and each articulates with the numerically corresponding metacarpal, but still the unciform supports most of the fourth and the magnum most of the third.

In this case, a small single radial sesamoid is present at the metacarpo-phalangeal joint of both fore-fingers, and the phalanges are broad and muscular, though the metacarpals are small and the whole hand short (only six and a half inches), but a sesamoid at the root of one of the human fingers, or at the distal joint of the thumb, is not uncommon; and if we understand by a sesamoid a bone playing in connection with a tendon, or with the ligament of a joint, the additional bone in this case cannot be so regarded, as it has no such relation to the soft parts. It is held to the four bones with which it articulates only by the necessary dorsal ligaments; and the tendon of the extensor carpi radialis brevior, with which if with any tendon it would have been connected, is seen to pass by on the radial side, quite free from it, to reach the middle metacarpal bone. Contrast this, for example, with the conditions of the ossicle which occurs on the radial side of the carpus of the quadrumana. On dissection, that ossicle is seen to lie loosely connected on the edge of the carpus, its two articular slopes playing by a synovial bursa in the depression between the scaphoid and trapezium, and to belong to the tendon of the extensor ossis metacarpi pollicis, which uses it as a sesamoid both for its longitudinal

23—2

portion, which passes to the trapezium and metacarpal bone, and more especially for its transverse palmar portion. But even these conditions are not necessarily to determine a bone to be only a sesamoid, for then it might be held that especially the human pisiform is but a sesamoid.

The non-penetration to the palm of the additional bone in this case suggests progress towards the normal form of its more developed neighbour the trapezoid, which is so large on the dorsum and so small on the palmar aspect, this having reference to maintaining the dorsal convexity of the carpus. There is no disease to account for ossific deposit, the carpal and all the other bones being healthy. The foot, like the hand, was short, but its bones were normal. In order to preserve the evidence of locality and connection, the bones have not been macerated but cleaned, leaving the ligaments; and both hands, showing the additional bone *in situ*, may be seen in the anatomical museum of the University.

AN INVESTIGATION INTO SOME PREVIOUSLY UN-DESCRIBED TETANIC SYMPTOMS PRODUCED BY ATROPIA IN COLD-BLOODED ANIMALS; WITH A COMPARISON OF THE PARALYTIC AND CONVULSANT SYMPTOMS PRODUCED BY ATROPIA IN FROGS AND IN VARIOUS MAMMALS. By THOMAS R. FRASER, M.D., F.R.S.E., *Assistant to the Professor of Materia Medica in the University of Edinburgh.*

(Abstract of a Paper communicated to the Royal Society of Edinburgh, 21st December, 1868.)

AUTHORITIES on the action of medicinal substances agree in including convulsions among the effects on man of belladonna and of its active principle, atropia. Similar effects are described as occurring when large doses of this substance are administered to dogs, rabbits, and other mammals, and to various birds. The recent progress in our knowledge of the exact and intimate physiological action of many medicinal substances is greatly due to investigations that have been made on animals of a lower type of organization, and, accordingly, numerous observers have instituted experiments on such animals, and, especially, on frogs. Hitherto, however, convulsions and tetanus have not been described among the effects of atropia in cold-blooded animals[1].

While making a series of experiments, in April 1868, to determine the minimum fatal dose of atropia for frogs, I was somewhat surprised to find that increased reflex excitability, convulsions and tetanus occurred, occasionally, at a certain stage in the poisoning. Believing that a careful examination of these symptoms might probably serve to throw some light on the causation of several of the complicated effects of a sub-

---

[1] Since this was written, I have communicated with Dr John Harley of London (the author of several important papers on the physiological action and therapeutical employment of belladonna), and have had the pleasure of learning that he also has observed tetanus and other symptoms of abnormal reflex activity in frogs, during protracted atropia-poisoning.

stance that has long occupied an important position as a therapeutic agent, I have made a number of experiments to determine, accurately, the characters of these convulsive effects; to ascertain the dose necessary for their production; to differentiate, as far as possible, the structures on whose affection they depend; and to harmonize these symptoms with analogous effects in warm-blooded animals, and explain their appearance in special circumstances only, in both frogs and mammals. This investigation is limited to these objects; only those effects of atropia that are directly connected with the convulsive symptoms will, therefore, be considered.

Soon after a small fatal dose, or one rather less than fatal, of a salt of atropia is administered to a frog, a slight degree of weakness occurs in the anterior extremities; the respiratory movements of the chest cease, those of the throat continuing; and the motor power becomes gradually more and more impaired, until, at length, no voluntary nor respiratory movements occur, and the animal lies on the abdomen and chest in a perfectly flaccid state. If the condition of the heart be now examined, it will be observed that the cardiac impulse is scarcely perceptible, and that the contractions are reduced to a very few in the minute. At this time, the application of various stimuli shows that the functions of the afferent and efferent nerves are retained, though in a greatly impaired condition.

Several hours afterwards, it may be not until the following day, the action of the poison is still further advanced; for the afferent and efferent nerves are completely paralysed, while but an occasional and scarcely perceptible cardiac impulse can be discovered : the only signs of vitality being this imperfect cardiac action and the retained irritability of the striped muscles. This condition may last for many hours or for several days. Previous observers have apparently mistaken it for one of death, and have, therefore, failed to observe the symptoms that subsequently appear, and to which, more particularly, I wish to draw attention.

The first of these symptoms is usually caused by a change that occurs in the flaccid condition of the animal; the anterior extremities becoming flexed, and, gradually, more and more arched until they assume a state of rigid and continuous contraction, with the webs pressed either against each other or against the opposite elbows—tonic spasm of the chest-muscles assisting to retain the anterior extremities in this position. At this time, a touch of any portion of the skin increases the spasm of the anterior extremities and of the chest-muscles, and causes some slight spasmodic movements in the posterior extremities. After varying intervals, the respiratory movements reappear, the cardiac action improves greatly in strength and in frequency, and the posterior extremities assume an extended position with the webs more or less stretched. If the skin be now touched, a violent attack of tetanus occurs (usually opisthotonic, at this time), which may last for from two to fifteen seconds, and is succeeded by a series of clonic spasms. During the first attacks of tetanus, the posterior extremities are often more or less abducted; and immediately after each attack they become flaccid, but the anterior extremities almost always remain rigidly flexed.

At a somewhat later period, tetanus of a still more violent character and of longer duration may be excited, and the attacks are now almost invariably emprosthotonic. During them the posterior extremities are rigidly extended, while at their conclusion not only do the anterior extremities remain rigidly arched, but the head continues bent downwards by tonic spasm of the muscles of the abdomen, chest and neck.

A series of such attacks may be produced by repeated touches of the skin; but after a number have been excited in quick succession, the subsequent convulsions become shorter and rather less violent, though they reacquire all their former violence after a period of rest.

During the convulsive stage, and especially at its latter portion, the animal may execute various movements; but from the difficulty with which these are performed, even when they do not themselves excite spasms and tetanus, it is apparent that the power of voluntary movement is still considerably impaired.

The period during which this tetanic state remains was found to vary greatly in different experiments, and, as might have been anticipated, the larger within certain limits the dose of atropia administered the longer the continuance of this condition. It has been observed to continue in some experiments for only a few hours, in others for several days, and in one experiment for so long as seventeen days.

The following experiment illustrates the usual characters and duration of the symptoms with such a dose of atropia as produces convulsions.

A solution of 0·4 grain of sulphate of atropia in four minims of distilled water was injected under the skin at the left flank of a frog, weighing three hundred and eighty-six grains. As usual after such a dose, in the course of an hour, the frog was flaccid and unable to perform any voluntary movement.

On the following day—eighteen hours after the administration—the frog was lying motionless on the abdomen and chest. It was ascertained by galvanic stimulation, that the conductivity of the sciatic nerves was suspended, while the contractility of the muscles was apparently unaffected. At twenty-two hours after the administration, however, a weak stimulus produced feeble reflex movements. The heart's impulse was now barely perceptible, and contractions occurred but eight times in the minute.

On the third day—fifty hours after the administration—the frog was still lying on the abdomen, but the chest and head were slightly raised by flexion of the anterior extremities. The reflex function was in a more active state, for a slight stimulus applied to the skin of the head caused an increase in the flexion of the anterior extremities—by which the head was still further raised—and a sudden extreme abduction of the two posterior extremities. Irregular respiratory movements of the throat were now observed.

On the fourth day—sixty-three hours after the administration—a faint touch of the skin of the head was followed by an attack of opisthotonic tetanus, lasting for four seconds; during which the anterior extremities were rigidly arched, while the posterior were extended backwards in a straight line. When the stimulus was applied to any other region, the only effect was an increase in the tonic spasm of the anterior extremities, and a sudden and somewhat spasmodic flexion of the posterior.

On the fifth day—ninety-five hours after the administration—the frog was lying on the back with the anterior extremities rigidly flexed and having the webs pressed against each other, and with the posterior extremities stiffly extended. A slight touch of the skin of any region was immediately followed by a sudden and violent attack of emprosthotonic tetanus. These convulsions were general for about ten seconds, but the tetanus continued for several seconds longer in the anterior extremities than elsewhere. The respiratory movements had now become more frequent and regular.

During the two following days the frog remained in this condition.

On the eighth day—one hundred and sixty-four hours after the administration—it was more difficult to excite general tetanus; somewhat irregular convulsions occurring, most frequently. When the skin of an ankle was touched, tetanus occurred in that limb and in the two anterior extremities, and continued for five seconds; but merely spasms, without extension, occurred in the opposite posterior extremity. General tetanus could be excited only when the irritation was applied to the head. The cardiac impulse had now greatly improved in character, while the rate of the contractions had increased to twenty-two beats in the minute.

After this, a daily improvement was apparent. On the twelfth day, the frog had resumed a normal sitting posture, the anterior extremities being, however, still slightly arched; and on the sixteenth day the tonic spasm of the chest muscles and of the anterior extremities had completely disappeared: but during all this time it was possible to excite a short attack of general tetanus, though severe or frequently repeated stimulation had to be employed.

On the seventeenth day—three hundred and eighty-two hours after the administration—stimulation, even when severe, excited mere stiff reflex movements of the posterior extremities, and comparatively slight and short tetanus of the anterior.

The complete disappearance of the exaggerated activity of the reflex function was but slowly effected, and did not occur until the twenty-fourth day after the administration. For several days after this, the frog was in a somewhat torpid state, moving about very sluggishly and obviously preferring to remain quiet; but, ultimately, it recovered perfectly.

In several of the experiments, the functions of the cerebro-spinal nervous system were not observed to be completely suspended in the stage of the poisoning antecedent to the appearance of tetanus. Only impairment of these functions was observed, but as the state of flaccidity often lasts for several days, it is obviously impossible to make observations so continuously during this period as to authorize the assertion that total suspension did not occur. There is, at the same time, no reason for supposing that complete paralysis is a necessary antecedent to tetanus.

It is almost superfluous to allude to the resemblance in frogs between the tetanic symptoms of atropia and those of strychnia. There are, however, certain peculiarities connected with the tetanus which atropia causes, apart from the remarkable circumstance of this tetanus being preceded by more or less complete paralysis. After poisoning by atropia, the symptoms of exaggerated reflex excitability are, as has been shown, extremely slight on their first appearance, and they acquire their greatest violence only after a considerable time. When the motor-stimulant effects have become fully developed, the state of the animal is one of nearly constant spasm—this tonic spasm being rarely general but almost always restricted to certain regions—so that the attacks of tetanus are rather of the nature of exacerbations of existing spasm than of successive and independent convulsions. Strychnia tetanus, on the other hand, becomes fully developed with great rapidity; and during the stage of remission the animal is usually in a perfectly flaccid state. Further, in atropia-poisoning, the attacks of tetanus can seldom be excited by the very slight stimuli that are sufficient to do so in strychnia-poisoning.

A large number of experiments have been made with both the sulphate and acetate of atropia, and it was found that nearly the same doses of both salts were required to produce these remarkable convulsive phenomena. Tetanus, or at least a state of greatly exaggerated reflex activity, may be looked for with considerable confidence when a dose equivalent to about the $\frac{1}{1000}$th of the weight of the frog is administered by injection either under the skin or into the abdominal cavity. It is also pretty constantly produced by doses somewhat greater or less than the above; indeed, in the experiments that were made, it was produced by the majority of the doses included between the $\frac{1}{715}$th and the $\frac{1}{1350}$th of the frog's weight. The larger doses usually cause the most violent tetanus, and they may be given to very small frogs, and to those that have been kept in a laboratory for several months. The smaller doses seem best adapted for large frogs, and for those that have been recently obtained from their natural *habitats*. It is of some importance to dissolve the atropia-salt in only a few minims of water—from four to eight is quite a sufficient quantity.

It is by no means an easy matter to ascertain what structures are concerned in the production of these convulsant effects, for the protracted intervals that often elapse between the administration of the poison and the appearance of tetanus, and the differences in the severity of the tetanic symptoms that follow even the most carefully calculated doses, frequently necessitate a patient repetition of the experiments. In the first series of experiments, the blood-vessels of one or of both posterior extremities were tied before atropia was given, and, by frequently modifying the dose, tetanus was on several occasions produced sufficiently soon to give results that were not materially influenced by the previous ligature of the blood-vessels. The following experiment shows the nature of the evidence that was thus obtained.

The left sciatic artery and veins were ligatured in a frog, weighing two-hundred-and-eleven grains, and, immediately afterwards, a solution of 0·2 grain of sulphate of atropia in four minims of distilled water was injected under the skin of the right flank.

On the second day, general tetanic convulsions could be readily excited by touching the skin in any region; *and both posterior extremities—poisoned as well as non-poisoned—were equally involved in these convulsions.*

On the third day, the left (non-poisoned) posterior extremity was somewhat rigid and took no part in the convulsions.

In this experiment, as well as in many others of a similar kind, tetanus occurred in the limb to which the access of the poison had been prevented. It was thus demonstrated that the tetanus does not depend on an action on motor or sensory nerves, nor on muscles; and it is, therefore, apparent that it must depend on an action on the central nerve-organs.

The predominance of cerebral symptoms during atropia-poisoning, in animals of a higher developement, suggested the possibility of these tetanic symptoms being caused in frogs by an influence originating in the cerebral lobes, or, more probably, in the ganglia at the summit of the medulla. Accordingly, on several occasions, the spinal cord of a frog in the stage of tetanus was divided immediately below the brachiál enlargement. After this operation, however, the tetanic condition of both the anterior and posterior segments remained. Violent tetanus could be readily excited in either segment; and this condition sometimes lasted for several days.

The most satisfactory evidence has, therefore, been obtained to prove that these tetanic symptoms are caused by an action of atropia on the spinal cord.

An attempt will now be made to show that the paralytic and tetanic symptoms that have been described in frogs are represented among the symptoms of atropia-poisoning in rabbits, dogs, and other mammals; and that, in both cases, the special characters of these symptoms, as well as the peculiarities of their occurrence, are the results of exactly the same actions.

There can be little doubt that in many cases the convulsions that appear during poisoning by atropia in man, dogs, rabbits, and other mammals, are partly due to asphyxia, caused by impairment of the functions of the cerebro-spinal nervous system. Frequently however, they are chiefly due to a special and primary stimulant action of atropia on the spinal cord and medulla oblongata. The latter method of production has been recognised by observers who were fully alive to the possibility of such symptoms being caused by asphyxia alone[1]. Several experiments on dogs have satisfied me that this is the case; for after the administration of doses that were about the minimum fatal, I have, on several occasions, observed a condition of partial

---

[1] Meuriot, *De la Méthode Physiologique en Thérapeutique et de ses applications à l'Étude de la Belladone*, Paris, 1868, p. 98, &c.; Brown-Séquard, *Lectures on the Diagnosis and Treatment of Functional Nervous Affections*, 1868, p. 66. Both of these authors account for the increased excitability of the spinal cord by dilatation of blood-vessels,—a method of causation which, I believe, cannot be established by any evidence that we at present possess.

paralysis and exaggerated reflex activity continue for longer than twenty-four hours, while during a considerable portion of this time the respirations were of fair character.

The remarkable position which the convulsive symptoms occupy in frogs—occurring subsequently to either a partial and short or a complete and protracted paralysis of the cerebro-spinal nervous system—at first sight appears to lend but little support to the assertions that atropia has a primary spinal-stimulant action in mammals, and that atropia-convulsions are caused by the same action in both frogs and mammals. It is, however, necessary to remember that *in atropia the amount of spinal-stimulant is less than the amount of paralysing action, while paralysis is more readily produced by atropia in frogs than in mammals.*

The first of these propositions is founded on the fact that the principal symptoms produced by an aggregate of various doses are those of paralysis. Thus, in frogs, the smallest doses that affect motricity cause slight paralysis without any obvious symptom of spinal-stimulation; somewhat larger doses cause more decided paralysis with slight symptoms of spinal-stimulation; still larger doses cause complete paralysis and violent symptoms of spinal stimulation; and doses so large as to rapidly produce death cause complete paralysis without any manifestation of a spinal-stimulant action. In mammals, the symptoms are alike confirmatory of this proposition; paralytic symptoms being alone present after small doses, and paralytic and convulsant coexisting after large doses.

The second proposition may likewise be established by an appeal to observation. Complete paralysis (and, therefore, absolute suspension of reflex excitability) may be caused in frogs by doses of atropia considerably below the minimum fatal. On the other hand, it is well known that in mammals even fatal doses do not completely suspend reflex excitability before death. Indeed, it is not to be expected that they should do so, for an amount of paralysis considerably short of complete suspension of reflex activity would undoubtedly cause such an embarrassment of respiration as to produce death by asphyxia[1]. Hence,

---

[1] It is scarcely necessary to state that this difficulty in causing complete paralysis does not occur with frogs, because they are endowed with the function

it is necessary to employ artificial respiration in order to produce complete paralysis of motor nerves with even so powerful a paralysing agent as curara (Wourali)[1]. It has been shown, in the first experiment, that atropia completely suspends the conductivity of motor nerves[2]. This one method, among several, by which it produces paralysis is, therefore, sufficient to account for the greater readiness with which paralysis is produced in frogs than in mammals.

These two propositions explain why atropia paralyses frogs more readily and rapidly than mammals, and also why in both frogs and mammals spinal-stimulant effects are manifested only when atropia is administered in doses that are near the minimum fatal—that is, in doses which contain the largest amount of spinal-stimulant action consistent with the production of a prolonged duration of symptoms.

Paralysis co-existing with spinal-stimulation forms the leading characteristic of the action of large doses of atropia on the spinal nervous system, and unless this combination be taken into account—which it has not hitherto been—the symptoms that are produced by such doses cannot be rationally explained. In the antecedent portion of this paper, this combined action has been demonstrated by a process of physiological *analysis*; and I now propose to add some confirmatory proof derived from a process of what may be termed physiological *synthesis*. This process, which is not a strict synthetical one, consists in imitating these effects of atropia by a combination of a substance that produces paralysis with one that produces spinal stimulation. The two substances I have selected are sulphate of methyl-strychnium[3] and strychnia. It will been seen, from the following

of cutaneous respiration. In this animal, reflex activity may be so far impaired by the action of a poison that pulmonary respiration is rendered impossible, but still, as the circulation continues, the poison is allowed a sufficient time to act on the living nerve structures, in order to produce on them its complete physiological effects.

[1] Vulpian, *Leçons sur la Physiologie générale et comparée du Système Nerveux*, Paris, 1866, p. 196.

[2] This action has been already demonstrated by Botkin, Virchow's *Archiv*, Bd. xxiv. 1862, p. 84; by Von Bezold and Bloebaum, *Untersuchungen aus dem Physiologischen Laboratorium in Würzburg*, 1867, p. 13; and by Meuriot, *op. cit.* p. 90. The last author attempts to prove that it is the result of a local action on the nerves by imbibition, and not of poisoning through the blood; but his arguments seem insufficient to establish this view.

[3] The paralysing action of sulphate of methyl-strychnium on motor nerves has been demonstrated by Dr A. Crum Brown and the author, in a paper pub-

experiment, how closely the symptoms of atropia are imitated by this combination.

One minim of a mixture of two minims of *liquor strychniæ* (B. P.) in eighteen minims of distilled water (equivalent to 0·00083 grain of strychnia) was added to three minims of a solution of 0·1 grain of sulphate of methyl-strychnium in ten minims of distilled water (equivalent to 0·03 grain of sulphate of methyl-strychnium), and the four minims of solution thus obtained were injected under the skin at the right flank of a male frog, weighing three hundred and fifty-five grains. Paralysis and flaccidity were rapidly caused. The reflex activity was frequently tested; at the commencement of the experiment, it was perfectly normal, and as the symptoms advanced, its activity gradually diminished, but there was never the faintest reflex exaggeration or other strychnic symptom. At forty minutes, the conductivity of the motor nerves was completely suspended.

On the second day, the frog was lying on the abdomen with the thorax raised and supported by the anterior extremities, *which were rigidly arched.* A slight touch of the skin caused a violent attack of emprosthotonic tetanus, lasting for seven seconds, during which the posterior extremities were extended stiffly with their webs stretched, while the anterior were rigidly arched.

During the third, fourth, and fifth days, the frog remained in this state; except that on the fifth day the convulsions were less powerful and prolonged.

On the sixth, seventh, and eighth days, excitation caused sudden spasmodic movements merely; but the anterior extremities were still rigidly flexed.

The symptoms entirely disappeared a few days afterwards.

By combining a paralysing with a convulsant substance it is therefore possible to produce in frogs paralytic and tetanic effects, which in their general characters are indistinguishable from the paralytic and tetanic effects of atropia.

The next step was to administer to a mammal a mixture of these substances in the relative proportions employed in

lished in the *Transactions of the Royal Society of Edinburgh*, Vol. xxv. Part i. pp. 151—203, and (in abstract) in the last number of this Journal. I prefer this substance to curara because of its strength being constant; and on this ground I would recommend it to physiologists and physicians.

the last experiment. Again, the effects of atropia were imitated; for paralysis and convulsions occurred together, and formed the most obvious symptoms during the poisoning.

It was thus clearly demonstrated that such a combination of a paralysing with a spinal-stimulant substance as produces in frogs paralysis followed by convulsions, will produce in mammals paralysis co-existing with convulsions and impeding their manifestation. So that by a process of what may be termed *physiological synthesis* further evidence has been obtained in support of the conclusions, that the effects of large doses of atropia on the cerebro-spinal nervous system (excluding the mental phenomena) are due to the combined paralysing and spinal-stimulant actions of that substance, and that the difference in the relations of these effects to each other that are seen in different animals may be explained by this combination acting on special varieties of organization. Atropia, therefore, forms no exception to the general law, that poisons affect the same structures in the same way in whatever animal these structures occur.

It is generally admitted that atropia produces both paralytic and convulsant effects in mammals, but no satisfactory attempt has hitherto been made to harmonize these effects with each other, or to explain why certain doses should cause one of them to appear more prominently than the other. This investigation has shown in what manner the paralysing is related to the convulsant action; and, also, it has accounted for the special prominence in the symptoms of one or other of these actions after certain doses of atropia. It may, without presumption, be asserted that it throws a new light on the causation of some of the symptoms not only of atropia, but also of many other active substances.

The principal results that have been obtained may be thus summarized :—

1. Atropia produces in frogs well-marked convulsant and tetanic symptoms, which when present in an extreme degree form a separate stage in the poisoning succeeding that of paralysis.

2. Tetanic symptoms follow the subcutaneous administration of a dose of sulphate or acetate of atropia, equivalent to

the $\frac{1}{1000}$th of the weight of the frog, and of doses a little greater and less than this.

3.   These symptoms are due to a direct action of atropia on the *medulla oblongata* and *spinalis*.

4.   The differences in the paralysing and convulsant symptoms that occur in frogs and in various mammals may be explained by the greater susceptibility of the former to the action of a paralysing agent, and by the amount of paralysing being greater than the amount of spinal-stimulant action in atropia.

5.   The different symptoms that are produced by different doses of atropia in animals of the same species may be explained by its paralysing being greater than its convulsant action.

6.   The paralysing and convulsant actions of atropia can be imitated in both frogs and mammals by a combination of a paralysing with a convulsant substance.

ON THE ACTION OF THE HORSE. By Joseph Gamgee Senr., *Veterinary Surgeon, Edinburgh.*

Almost any work published in this century which treats in any way on the locomotive powers of the horse, would supply me with a quotable passage to shew the requirement of more being said on the matter. I trust, however, to the facts which I hope to establish, and the importance of the subject, as affording the best reasons I can give for breaking in somewhat abruptly upon this question.

In the *Times* of 16th February, 1869, an anonymous correspondent wrote under the heading, "The Turf and breed of horses," and said, "In our day a horse is considered strong if he clears 15 or 16 feet in his first bound. If he covers a greater space, he is considered to be of superior strength. But Flying Childers cleared at each bound 25 feet, and as from his compact form those wonderful strides would follow each other in quick succession, the laws of motion lead us to conclude that no horse of this day could live with him."

Here the writer displays mistakes, not entirely of his own making, but which have been handed down to our generation, and that of our fathers, for the last 80 years.

The doctrine that horses bound, or spring through space in their fast actions, is a delusion which originated, as far as I have been able to trace it, with "Sainbel," and bequeathed to us in his *Essay on the proportions of Eclipse*, in which he says, (illustrating the text with a profusion of figures and diagrams), "that the gallop consists of a repetition of bounds, or leaps, more or less high, and more or less extended, in proportion to the strength and lightness of the animal;" further, he says, that "Eclipse covered 25 feet at each action." And thus was the wisdom of three thousand years, as it came down through Xenophon and Borelli, set aside.

I have had to deplore the transmission of this false teaching to us, because it has vitiated the theoretical and practical knowledge of horsemen, professional and amateurs, on questions the most important to be rightly understood. For at least half of the forty-five years that have passed since I entered on the practice of the Veterinary art, I was under the thraldom of that dogma, the influence of which in its extensions perplexed physiologists of the highest rank, who, regarding the horse as the typical exponent of animal locomotion, refer to it comparatively in the belief that what is accepted by all, has been established on sound premises. Finding at length that the prevalent theory of the action of the horse was unintelligible, that it did not accord with practical observations, and that it was absurd, I had recourse to experiments and systematic observation, to the aid of which I brought my anatomical knowledge, and made efforts to improve and increase it.

During several years horses of different breeds were examined under varying conditions, as well as dogs, of which some belonged to the less fleet varieties, whilst others were greyhounds of coursing notoriety; and the results which I obtained by observations on these quadrupeds were checked, and extended by others on the walking, running, and jumping of man. I arrived at the conclusion that the horse does not bound off the ground in the gallop, nor in any other pace, and that the bound or leap is altogether a distinct action, only occurring for the purpose of accomplishing what the regular paces cannot possibly effect. In the fast paces, as in the slowest movement, the horse has never less than two of his feet acting on the ground; and further, when the animal is in action no two of the four feet are in similar positions, or acted on in like manner, at the same instant. In the leap or bound the gallop is interrupted and a new order of movements set up, which as they require a great concentration and expenditure of power, and are only designed for emergencies, cannot be frequently repeated.

The results of my enquiries on the gallop will be better comprehended by referring to the annexed illustration, the 3rd in particular, which was appended to one of my papers on the subject, published in the Journal of the Royal Agricultural Society for 1863 (On the breeding of Hunters and Roadsters,— Prize Essay). This diagram exhibits five positions on the ground, drawn to a scale of the feet of a two year old colt in

MR GAMGEE.

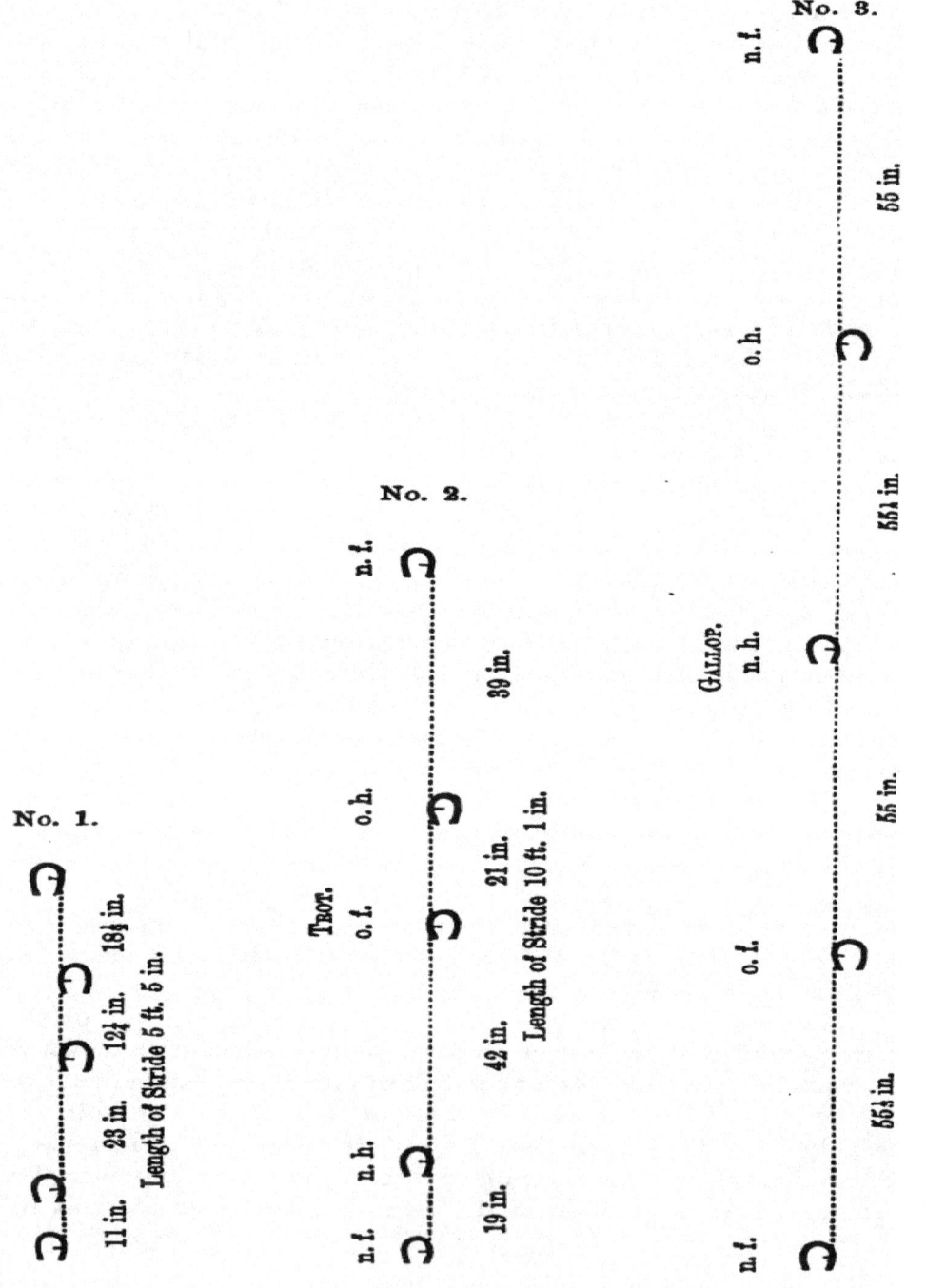

No. 1.

n.f.   o.h.   n.f.
o.f.
n.f. n.h.

11 in.   28 in.   12½ in.   18½ in.

Length of Stride 5 ft. 5 in.

No. 2.

Trot.

n.f.
o.h.   o.f.

n.h.

n.f.

39 in.   21 in.
42 in.
19 in.

Length of Stride 10 ft. 1 in.

No. 3.

n.f.
o.h.
Gallop.
n.h.
o.f.
n.f.

55 in.   55½ in.   55 in.   55¾ in.

training, which had been galloped over the ground for the purpose. My object was to find out the exact distance through which each foot was carried from the place where it was lifted to that where it alighted.

Looking at such a diagram we find that the marks of the four feet appear simply in a continuous line. If we measure the distance between two successive impressions produced, say of the near fore foot, we find it to be eighteen feet one inch and half. Midway between these two impressions is the mark of the near hind foot, which therefore subdivides the space into nine feet and six eights of an inch, but each of these is again subdivided into two halves by the impressions produced by the off fore and off hind feet. It is thus seen that the horse's body instead of being propelled through the air by bounds or leaps even when going at the highest attainable speed, acts on a system of levers, the mean distance between the points of resistance of which is four feet six inches. When the ground has been galloped over, an ordinary observer will barely distinguish between the line of imprints made by the feet of the near from those of the off side, so nearly do these appear to lie in the same straight line; indeed a tape may be so stretched that it will cut for an indefinite distance the inner sections of the foot marks of both sides of the body. The exact length of stride, of course only applies to that of the particular horse observed, and the rate of speed at which he was going. In the case of any one animal, the greater the speed the longer is the individual stride. In progression, the body moves before a limb is raised from the ground, as is most readily seen when the horse is beginning its slowest action: an opportunity for testing this fact may be found at most railway stations, where powerful horses are kept for drawing heavily laden trucks.

When one of these horses is attached to the carriages he walks to the extent his traces admit, and applies his shoulder to the collar; no effect following, the noble animal prepares for the required ordeal by planting his feet in position, flexing his limbs, and then plying his vast force equally upon all four feet, keeping up the strain until the resistance is overcome; when, both body and burden moving, the feet are shifted, first one fore, then its diagonal hind, and thirdly the opposite fore and its diagonal hind, and thus, if the load follows, the walk is established.

Mistakes have been made in attributing undue range and effect to the extension of the limbs, in determining the length of stride. To prove this question no other animal is so well suited, or so controllable for the test, as man himself. If we observe a person starting into a walk, it is found that the first foot raised moves over a distance of two to three feet, and that the opposite one, moving secondly, passes over double that distance, and if the pace be kept up and the person be a fairly good walker, six feet will be the average length of each stride, and the half that, the measure of every step; and if the pace be changed from the walk to a fast run, these distances of stride and step respectively, will be found to be about ten feet and five. A proof of the limit of extension may be obtained as follows:—let a man stand, keeping his body and head erect, and his feet in parallel positions, and request him to extend one foot, the utmost extent will only reach about twenty inches, before the vertical line of the body; and now requesting that the foot be set on the ground no other change of position being made, it will be found that *that* foot will come back to almost a parallel position with the other, and that no extension of the limb, tending to progression, has happened, or is compatible with inaction of the body; thus proving that the limbs are carried from the one position to the other with the body, and not extended away from it.

In the movements of the horse, comprised in three natural paces, calling respectively for different degrees of energy, and accomplishing relative degrees of speed, we find, according to observations taken, that in the walk five feet five inches are covered by each foot in their respective movements, in order; ten feet one inch, in the trot; and eighteen feet one inch and half in the gallop.

In the first of these paces, three feet are in constant action on the ground in the slowest move; but in the free walk, as represented, in which the hind foot passes the position from which the parallel fore moves, there is a fraction of time when only two feet are upon the ground, but the interval is too short for the eye to measure it. The proportion of time therefore during which the feet are acted on upon the ground, to that occupied in their removal to new positions is as three to one in the slow and a fraction less in the fast walk. In the fast gallop these proportions are as five to three. In all the paces the power of the horse is being exerted mainly upon a fore and hind limb with the feet implanted in diagonal positions, at a distance apart in this fast action of one step, *i.e.* four and half feet. There is also a constant parallel line of positions kept up by a fore and hind foot, alternating sides in each successive move. The fore foot begins and the hind terminates the action by its toe with extended limb becoming the fulcrum, at a distance from its parallel fore of less than nine feet; and as the hind is set free when the vertical line from the hip-joint is passed, the fore foot ready in position becomes the new stay[1].

These relative positions are renewed and maintained thus. Each fore limb assumes, as it alights, the advanced position parallel with the hind just released and moving; the hind feet move by turns, in sequence to their diagonal fore and in priority to their parallel fellows, which following they maintain for nearly half their course, when the fore in its turn is raised and carried to its destined place, the hind alighting midway as stated. All the feet passing over equal distance and keeping the same time, no interference of one with another occurs, and each successive hind foot as it is implanted forms a new diagonal with the opposite fore, the latter forming the front of the parallel in one instant, and one of the diagonal positions in the next; while in the case of the hind, they assume the dia-

[1] It must be borne in mind that in contemplating length of strides, with reference to the fulcra, allowance has to be made for the length of the feet, which is to be deducted from that of the strides, because the apex, or toe of the horse's hind foot forms the fulcrum in one instant, and the heel of the fore foot in the next, and *vice versa*. This phenomenon is very obvious in the action of the human foot, and is remarkable also for the range of leverage thus afforded in some of the fleetest quadrupeds, of different species. In the hare for instance, between the point of its hock and the termination of its extended digits, there is a space of upwards of six inches of extent of leverage and variation of fulcrum, and in the fore limb from the *carpus* to the toe-nails (whose function in progression is not to be underrated) upwards of three inches of leverage are found, being about ten inches for each lateral biped, and the double of that for the action of all four feet. Viewed in this way the stride is not really as long as would be supposed if merely estimated from the space between the footprints.

gonal on alighting, and become the terminators of the parallel in the last part of their action.

Many interesting remarks might be made on the length of the stride of various animals; the full movement of the greyhound is, for instance, upwards of sixteen feet; that of the hare at least equal; whilst that of a Newfoundland dog is a little over nine feet.

Power to carry weight and fleetness of action are, to a great extent, distinct and incompatible phenomena in horses, determined chiefly by their construction, muscular energy determining the extent of speed within the possible limits; the speed acquired determines the length of stride, and therefore length of stride is the effect and evidence of speed, and not the cause of it.

NOTE ON THE TEMPERATURE IN DIABETES. By
BALTHAZAR W. FOSTER, M.D., *Professor of Medicine in
Queen's College, Birmingham*, &c.

IN this note I wish to call attention to some peculiarities in
the temperature of the body in cases of Diabetes. Considering
the intimate connection which has been supposed to exist between the process of oxidation in the body and the presence of
sugar in the urine, it is somewhat remarkable that so little attention has been paid to the temperature of Diabetics. The
admission of four such patients, recently, under my care at the
Birmingham General Hospital afforded me an opportunity of
confirming and extending observations I had previously made
on the subject. Some of the principal results I state below,
reserving for future comment the many interesting points suggested by them. The temperatures were carefully taken twice
daily, and during the observations no special treatment was
adopted.

The conclusions to which I am led by my investigations
are—

1. That the temperature is always below the normal standard, the depression generally varying from one half to three
degrees (F.). In cases of recent origin the temperature ranges
mostly between 96·5° and 97·5° (F.), never mounting to, or
beyond, the normal standard, except from some disturbing
cause. In more advanced cases the temperature is nearly always below 97°, and occasionally falls as low as 94·5°.

2. That the temperature in the evening is (generally one
half to $\frac{8}{10}$ths of a degree) higher than in the morning of the
same day. No exception to the evening elevation has been
observed in cases of recent origin, but in a case of long standing
the temperature has been occasionally noticed to fall in the
evening.

3. That the variation in the quantity of sugar passed in
the 24 hours is not proportional to the rise or fall of the temperature of the body. The same temperature has been observed in the same cases to coincide with widely different
quantities of sugar.

4. That the daily range of temperature bears no proportion to the quantity of sugar passed in the 24 hours, as seen in the following table.

	CASE I.			CASE II.	
No. of Observation.	Daily range of temperature.	Quantity of Sugar in 24 hours.	No. of Observation.	Daily range of temperature.	Quantity of Sugar in 24 hours.
1	$\frac{6}{10}°$	990 grs.	1	$\frac{4}{10}°$	1856 grs.
2	$\frac{8}{10}°$	2310 grs.	2	$1\frac{2}{10}°$	660 grs.
3	$\frac{2}{16}°$	3640 grs.	3	$\frac{6}{10}°$	792 grs.
4	$1\frac{2}{10}°$	2730 grs.	4	$1°$	1320 grs.

In one case observations were made in the following manner:—the bladder was emptied one hour before the Thermometer was used, and emptied again about half an hour after the temperature had been recorded. The quantity of sugar per oz. in the urine thus procured, was compared with the temperature with the results recorded below.

Observation.	Temperature.	Sugar per oz.
1	97.4	32 grs.
2	96.8	19 grs.
3	97.2	$23\frac{1}{4}$ grs.
4	96.5	33 grs.
5	96.7	24 grs.

In two cases the administration of mixed diet for a few days was followed in each instance by a slight ($\frac{1}{2}°$) elevation of temperature and a diminished daily range: the morning temperature ceasing to fall as much as usual. The sugar was much increased by the change of diet.

5. That the occurrence of Pulmonary and other complications produces an elevation of temperature but to a very limited extent. In one case in which well marked Phthisis with local pleurisy existed the temperature was seldom higher than 99°, and only once did it reach 99·4°. In another case, a bad whitlow only raised the temperature to 98·8°.

ON THE MECHANISM OF PERCHING IN BIRDS.[1]

By Morrison Watson, M.D., *Demonstrator of Anatomy, University of Edinburgh.*

The peculiar mode of action of the muscles of the bird's leg, so far as relates to their condition during the act of perching, has long been a subject of interest to Anatomists and Physiologists.

It is well known that even during stormy weather, or when asleep, birds easily maintain their position on the branches of trees. The *rationale* of this had been a puzzle till towards the end of the eighteenth century, when Borelli, in his work *De motu animalium*, stated his opinion that the solution of the difficulty was to be found in the peculiar arrangement of that muscle which Meckel has since described under the name of the Rectus femoris. This muscle arises from the pelvis, immediately in front of the acetabulum, passes obliquely across the convexity of the knee joint and finally, uniting with the flexor perforatus digitorum, is continued through the medium of that muscle to the toes.

This idea seems to have prevailed since that time, for Dr Macartney, the writer of the article "Birds," in *Rees' Cyclopædia*, agrees with Borelli as to the function of that muscle; and Professor Owen, in the *Cyclopædia of Anatomy*, writes as follows :—"The disposition of the former muscle (*i.e.*, Rectus femoris) is such (passing, viz., first over the convexity of the knee joint, and afterwards over the projection of the heel) that from its connection with the flexor of the toes, these must necessarily be bent simultaneously with every inflection of the knee and ankle. As these inflections naturally take place when the lower extremities yield to the superincumbent weight of the body, birds are thus enabled to grasp the twigs on which they rest while sleeping without making any muscular exertion." A passage to the same effect occurs in the same author's recent work on the *Anatomy of the Vertebrates*. Meckel, in his *Anatomie Comparée*, appears also to sanction the above explanation, for, after describing the muscle, he goes on to say

[1] This paper formed a part of a graduation Thesis, "On the Myology of the Hind Limb in Birds," submitted to the Medical Faculty of the University of Edinburgh, March, 1867, for which a gold medal was awarded to the author.

that he has been unable to find it in the Crested Grebe, the Guillemot, and the Cormorant; and adds, "This remark is so much the more curious, that its action on the flexion of the toes is not necessary in these birds."

Since I began to examine into this matter, it has seemed to me that too much stress has been laid upon the peculiar action of this muscle in accounting for the maintenance of the bird securely on its perch without muscular exertion. For the small size of the muscle itself and the mode of its transmission through the medium of the flexor digitorum to the toes, appeared inadequate to account for the effects produced. Dissatisfied, therefore, with the theory, and determined to submit the matter to the test of experiment, I cut down along the inner side of the thigh of a domestic fowl, and securing the tendon of the Rectus, divided it. Two days afterwards I operated in like manner on the muscle of the opposite side. After each operation there was noticed only slight inversion of the foot—the bird walked, ran, and perched as well as before the operations. It was then suggested to me that the experiment was not satisfactory, inasmuch as the cut ends of the tendon might have again united, and thus in reality have left the bird in the same condition as it was previous to the section. Accordingly I operated on a second fowl in like manner, taking, however, the additional precaution to pull upward the tendon of the Rectus, so as to be able to cut away about half an inch of it on each side. As in the first experiment, a slight inversion of the toes was observed, but otherwise the bird conducted itself much as it did before the operation, perching as usual along with its companions.

A third individual was subjected to a similar ordeal, and was examined by Professor Turner, who was satisfied that its powers of perching were in no way interfered with. The bird being killed, the ends of the tendons were found separated by about half an inch, neither having in any way united nor contracted adhesions to neighbouring parts. In all the above experiments, the birds were allowed to have access only to a slender perch, and care was taken to exclude all fallacies as regards their powers of perching.

These experiments, taken in connection with the facts I

shall now communicate as to the absence of this muscle in certain birds, seems perfectly to prove the incorrectness of the theory under review. In the course of an examination of the muscles of the hind limb in a number of birds, I ascertained that the muscle was absent in four birds of this country which habitually perch—viz., the blackbird, magpie, thrush, and starling, —while it was present in several which never under any circumstances perch, such as the swan, black scoter and black headed gull.

The only other theory as to the function of this muscle with which I am acquainted is that advanced by the Rev. Samuel Haughton, of Dublin, in the *Proceed. Roy. Irish Academy*, 1865, Vol. IX., who considers it only with reference to the ostrich. He states that it is an arrangement whereby dislocation of the leg is prevented in this bird during the sudden and violent extension of the joints which occurs when the creature is in rapid motion. This theory, however ingenious, is, I am afraid, hardly tenable, for the reason that the Rectus is quite as well developed in proportion to the size of the bird in the diving sea ducks, such as the black scoter, and in the true swimmers, such as the swan, as it is in the ostrich. In these birds, no such violent extension of the leg takes place as would necessitate such an arrangement in order to prevent dislocation, supposing for the time being that it were effective in this respect, which is doubtful. In the ostrich, moreover, the arrangement and enormous strength of the ligaments is such as would effectually prevent any dislocation even during the most violent movements of the animal.

The true explanation of the act of perching is, I believe, to be found in the peculiar arrangement of certain muscles of the limb in birds—viz., the Biceps, Flexor perforatus digitorum, Flexor longus pollicis, and Tibialis anticus. Of these muscles the three latter have their origins carried up to the femur, which so far as I can ascertain, occurs in no other class of vertebrate animals except that of birds[1], whilst the tendon of the biceps passes through a fibrous pulley attached to the lower end of the femur before it is inserted into the head of the fibula. It will be observed that each of these muscles passes

---

[1] Professor Humphry has since informed me that he finds in Pteropus the flexor of the toes continued up to the femur (see p. 314).

over at least two joints, and they are so arranged that when the limb is fully flexed as it is in the act of perching, they shall, each and all of them, be passively stretched. In no other position of the limb does this occur.

Bearing these facts in mind, let us observe what takes place when a bird settles upon a branch. In the first place, the muscles which act directly as flexors of the hip-joint, more especially the Gluteus medius and minimus (Meckel), come into play. Or it may be that the bird, abstaining from all muscular exertion, the weight of the body is sufficient to accomplish the flexion of this joint. This flexion of the hip-joint, however, necessitates a corresponding flexion of the knee, as the hamstrings, and more especially the Biceps from the peculiar arrangement of its tendon of insertion, are not sufficiently long to admit of flexion of the one joint without that of the other. And here I would point out that, were it not for the fibrous pulley through which the tendon of insertion of the Biceps passes, the different functions of that muscle could not be efficiently performed. For were the muscle attached directly to the fibula, without passing in the first place through this fibrous loop, either it would be too short to admit of the requisite extension of the knee-joint, or were it sufficiently long to allow of this, it would not fulfil the conditions necessary to secure the bird firmly in its position without loss of muscular exertion. In other words, it could not then be passively stretched. Furnished with this pulley, however, the Biceps is enabled to fulfil both conditions, as it is evident that, by so much as the knee and hip-joints are flexed, by so much is the pulley drawn forwards, and the Biceps correspondingly put upon the stretch ; whilst, when the limb is extended, the muscle acts much as if no pulley were present and, therefore, retains the requisite length.

The knee-joint being flexed, it will be observed that the point of insertion of the Sartorius into the front of the tibia will be removed farther from its point of origin at the pelvis than during extension of the joint, and as its tendon of insertion is at the same time compelled to pass in front of the convexity of the knee, it is evident that the entire muscle must be passively extended. We have therefore the body of the bird secured both in front of and behind the hip-joint—in the former direction by the Sartorius, in the latter by the Biceps. Simultaneously, moreover with the flexion of the knee, the point of origin of the Tibialis anticus from the front of the external condyle of the femur, being rotated upwards, is removed to a greater distance from its insertion into the front of the tarso-metatarsal bone, and it will follow that, in order to avoid rupture of the muscle, the latter point must be approximated to the former, and this can only be accomplished by flexion of the ankle-joint. In the act of flexing this joint, the heel being thrown backwards, the long flexors of the toes are necessarily drawn tense ; and as the tendons passing to the toes in front are closely connected with that one passing to the posterior toe, they are consequently put upon the stretch at the same moment, and thus compel the toes to grasp firmly the branch on which the bird is situated.

Here it may be asked, Why should the origin of the flexor muscles of the toes be transferred to the femur? Simply, I believe, to procure consentaneous flexion of all the joints from the knee to the toes, as it is evident that when this muscle flexes the toes, it must also flex the knee in this portion of the bird. Doubtless it may be said that the Gastrocnemius is sufficient to effect this latter movement, when the Flexor digitorum has its usual origin from the tibia, yet it is evident that there cannot be the same security in this respect when *several* muscles pass over the separate joints as when *one* muscle, as the Flexor digitorum, passes over all of them. It will thus be seen that by means of the mechanism just described, the bird is enabled to perch securely, and that the arrangement of the muscles is such, that by simple flexion of the limb, those passing in front of as well as those passing behind the various joints are necessarily drawn tense, and thus as it were brace the bird to its perch without any exertion of muscular action on its part. That the Rectus femoris may assist those birds in which it is present to perch, I do not deny ; but that it is the principal, or even an essential agent in effecting this, is, I think, sufficiently disproved by the facts mentioned in the first part of this paper.

The ease with which the Grallatorial birds, as well as some belonging to other orders, poise themselves when asleep upon one leg, has also been referred by some to the action of the Rectus femoris. In this case, as in the former, the statement appears to me to rest upon insufficient data. I have ascertained, in the course of my dissections, that not only in the Flamingo and Curlew is this muscle more slightly developed than in the generality of birds ; but that in the Heron, which also habitually assumes this position, the muscle is entirely absent. The true explanation of this action is, as it seems to me, to be referred to the arrangement of the Tibialis anticus before mentioned. It will be observed that when the hip and knee joints are flexed to the utmost, as they always are in such cases, that the Biceps and Sartorius will co-operate in balancing the bird precisely as in the act of perching. The Tibialis anticus being drawn tense when the knee is flexed, the foot at the same time being fixed, this muscle will, by virtue of the annular ligament which confines its tendon at the lower end of the tibia, produce extension of the ankle-joint. The body will accordingly be balanced in this position, without loss of muscular exertion, if the leg be brought sufficiently under the centre of the body to counteract *lateral* displacement. This explanation receives confirmation from the fact that on dividing the femoral head of origin of the Tibialis anticus on both sides, the bird, when placed on the perch, had the utmost difficulty in balancing itself, except when *all* the joints were completely flexed.

With reference to this question it is of interest to remark that in those Grallatorial birds which I have had an opportunity of examining, the Biceps, in addition to its usual origin, is connected to the posterior border of the Gluteus maximus (Meckel), which arises from the pelvis *above* the acetabulum. Hence at the same time that the Biceps is passively extended, it will tend to bring the median plane, and consequently the centre of gravity of such birds more directly over the single limb on which it is poised.

That the muscles, to the consideration of which this paper has been devoted, have other and more important functions to perform is evident from the fact that they are present in many birds which never assume either of the positions I have referred to. I submit, however, that the special arrangements I have noted afford a rational explanation of the facts when they do occur, and at the same time it is to be observed that the *majority* of birds do habitually occupy one or other of the positions I have been considering.

OBSERVATIONS ON SOME NEGRO CRANIA FROM OLD CALABAR, WEST AFRICA[1]. By JOHN ALEXANDER SMITH, M.D., and Professor TURNER.

ABOUT a year ago, we received from the Rev. Alex. Robb, D.D. of Old Calabar, eight negro crania, the most important characters of which we propose to describe in the following communication. Dr Robb informs us that the crania of the people of Old Calabar are difficult to obtain, as the dead are carefully buried, and the exact site of their graves is usually kept secret. The skulls which he procured for us were picked up, as opportunity offered, from skeletons found lying in the forest. They are those of the slaves of the Calabar people, whose dead bodies are thrown into the bush, where they rapidly putrefy, and serve as food for wild animals. These slaves are drawn partly from the people of the delta of the Niger or Quorra, lying chiefly to the west of the Cross river, or main stream of the Calabar river, and partly from the east of Old Calabar. To the west of the Cross river the Ibos, or Eboes, dwell, and eastwards those negroes, who in the West Indies are generally designated by the name of Mocos. Dr Robb thinks that whilst it is probable that these crania are mostly those of Ibos, yet that some may belong to the tribes lying more in an easterly direction.

With one exception, that of a youth about eight years old, the crania are those of adults, four being males, and four females. In the following remarks, the crania are designated by the letters A to H.

The skulls A and B are those of adult males, and have a strong resemblance to each other. The form of the cranium in both is an elongated oval, with flattened sides. The forehead is somewhat receding, and the supra-orbital ridges and glabella are well, but not excessively marked. The upper frontal and anterior parietal regions are roof-shaped. The muscular ridges and processes are well marked. Nasal bones elevated medially into a ridge. Facial outline prognathic. Lower jaws strong, with decided angles and well-marked chins.

[1] Read before the Royal Physical Society, Edinburgh, March 24, 1869. The crania are deposited in the Anatomical Museum of the University.

Palate of A deeper and more rounded in front than that of B. Teeth in both crania well worn.   B is an older skull than A, as the cranial sutures are ossified, and in part obliterated.

F is probably a young male eight or ten years old.   The permanent incisors and first true molars are erupted, but the milk molars are still *in situ*.   The bones of the face and cranial vault have not yet reached their full growth, and the muscular ridges are feeble.   The centres of ossification are prominent, so that the oval outline of the skull is not so decided as in A and B.   The capacity is 87 Cubic Inches, 3 C. I. more than the adult male A, showing that in the negro, as in the European, the cavity of the skull attains its full size and dimensions at a comparatively early period of life.

H is an adult, but not aged male.   The skull is unsymmetrical; forehead very receding; glabella prominent; posterior part of skull projecting much behind the foramen magnum. The right parieto-occipital region flattened.   The skull looks as if it had been artificially distorted by pressure applied in early infancy, partly in the frontal, partly in the parieto-occipital region.   Sutures unossified.   Teeth but little worn.   Prognathism decided.

Male Crania.	A	B	F	H
Extreme length......................	7	7.1	6.8	7.1
,, breadth	5.1	5	5.3	5.3
,, height	5.3	5.6	5	5.3
Horizontal circumference.........	20	20	19.2	20.1
Capacity in cubic inches	84	87	87	93
Proportion of breadth to length	73	70	78	75
,, height ,,	76	79	73	75

A and B are well marked dolico-cephalic crania.   F has not yet reached its adult form, and the breadth bears a much greater relative proportion to the length, partly on account of the greater relative size of the parietal eminences and partly from the absence of a glabella and of supra-orbital ridges. The want of symmetry in H necessarily affects the ratio between length, breadth and height.

The crania C, D, E and G are evidently those of adult females.

C, D and G are oval in form, and present the same general conformation as the male skulls A and B. To all appearance they belong to the same race. The foreheads are smooth and non-receding above the orbits. D has a slight flattening in the right parieto-occipital region, such as might have resulted from pressure applied during nursing.

The skull E differs from the other female crania in possessing much greater frontal and parietal dimensions, so that its cubic capacity is large, and the oval form of the cranium is not so well marked. The frontal and parietal eminences are prominent, and the skull resembles in form that of the young male F. The palate is broad and rounded, the teeth are much worn, and the prognathism is strongly pronounced.

Female Crania.	C	D	E	G
Extreme length	6.7	6.3	6.9	6.8
„ breadth	4.7	4.6	5.4	4.9
„ height	5.1	4.8	5.2	5.0
Horizontal circumference	19.0	18	20	19
Capacity in cubic inches	68	65	87	73
Proportion of breadth to length	70	73	78	72
„ height „	76	76	75	73

C, D and G are well marked dolico-cephalic crania. E is sub-brachy-cephalic, and must be regarded, both from its form and proportions, as of a different race from the other female crania and the male skulls A and B. Apparently it and the young skull F belong to the same people.

In the whole series of male and female crania, the denticulations of the sutures are comparatively simple, as is indeed the rule in the skulls of savage races. In A and C, more especially in the latter, Wormian bones occur in the lambdoidal suture, and in H in the squamoso-parietal suture. All the crania have the great wing of the sphenoid bone articulating with the parietal, although in C the extent of this articulation is very small. In each skull both nasal bones are fairly marked, although in C and E the right preponderates in size over the left. The nasal region is not so flattened as one sometimes sees in negro crania. Owing to the rounding of the lower lateral angles of the anterior nares in A, C, D and F, the aperture is not so triangular as in the European skull.   In all, the anterior nasal spines are present.   In none does the os planum of the ethmoid possess a triangular form, as has been observed in some degraded forms of Australian skulls.   In none is there any diastema in the dental series.   In B, C and H, the parietal foramina are large.   The variation in the prognathism exhibited by these crania may be gathered from the following table, in which the radii are measured, according to Mr Busk's plan, from the external auditory meatus to the most projecting part of the superior alveolar arch, and to the fronto-nasal suture.

Crania.	A	B	C	D	E	F	H
Maxillary radius.........	4.3	4.2	3.8	3.8	4.2	3.5	4.1
Fronto-nasal do.	3.8	3.9	3.4	3.5	3.6	3.4	3.7

The skull E therefore, which, in its cubic capacity and general dimensions, is the largest of the female crania, is at the same time the most prognathic.   The young skull F, on account of the incomplete development of the upper jaw, shows scarcely any alveolar projection.   In G the upper jaw was broken away.

The breadth of the face in the different skulls is shown by the following table :—

Crania.	A	B	C	D	E	F	H
Zygomatic breadth......	4.9	5.4	4.5	4.6	4.9	4.3	5.3

The crania possess a considerable range of variation in the amount of internal capacity, greater indeed than might have been expected in a rude negro people.   Amongst the male skulls, H, which seems to have been artificially deformed, is as high as 93 C. I., whilst A is not more than 84.   The mean capacity of the four male crania is 87.7 C. I.   E, the largest female skull, is 87 C. I., whilst D is only 65.   The mean capacity of the four female crania is 73.2.   The mean capacity of the eight crania is 80.5. The female skulls C and D are amongst the smallest normal human crania which have yet been measured. They are both well proportioned crania. Dr Meigs, in his catalogue of the Morton Collection, states that the smallest native African skull in that series is 65 C. I. Dr Barnard Davis, in his recently published *Thesaurus Craniorum*, p. 361, gives the capacity of one of the Guanche crania in his possession as 66.8, and amongst the Gaboon negroes he found one as low as 69.9; but the smallest of four Eboe skulls in his collection had the capacity of 79 C. I. All these were the skulls of females. On the other hand, he possesses the skull of a Gaboon negro which has a capacity of 103.3 C. I.; but his largest Eboe skull, said to be that of a female, is not more than 85.1. The average of his four Eboe crania is 82 C. I.

Mr W. F. Daniell has given[1] an account of the natives of Old Calabar. He regards them as of Eboe race, but presenting some physical deviations, which serve to distinguish them from other tribes of a similar derivation. He thinks that the climate of the healthier, more elevated sandstone region of Old Calabar has improved the race beyond the natives of the same origin living in the swamps and low-lying ground of the Bonny and adjoining rivers. The average male stature of the Old Calabar people varies from 5 ft. 6 in. to 5 ft. 10 in., that of the females from 5 ft. to 5 ft. 4 in. Although they possess in a more or less modified form the thick and massive cranium, narrow convex forehead, and compressed lateral parietes of the skull, the projecting jaw and oblique contour of the visage, yet they partially lose the thick lips, flat nose, large protuberant eyes, high facial bones and other facial peculiarities of the Krooman—the most pronounced type of the negro.

These statements of Mr Daniell as to the cranial characters of these people are substantially confirmed by the examination of the skulls we have just described.

· The Rev. Dr Robb, who has long been a resident missionary in Old Calabar, states that the mental and physical degradation of these delta negroes is due to their paganism, and that they possess, like other men, the capability of being elevated to a higher platform of intelligence.

[1] *Journal of Ethnological Society of London,* 1848.

ON THE CAUSE OF THE DIASTOLÉ OF THE VENTRICLES OF THE HEART. By A. H. GARROD, *St John's College, Cambridge.*

THE existence of an active diastolé of the ventricles of the heart following each systolé has been long recognized by physiologists, and there have been several explanations given of the phenomenon ; but they are all subject to grave objections, and fresh methods of research have overthrown them one after another.

The object of the present article is to shew that this active diastolé is mainly dependent on the turgescence of the walls of the heart, consequent on the flow of blood into the coronary arteries immediately after the systolé.

The experiments of Vaust in 1821, together with the known anatomical arrangement of the commencement of the aorta, strongly favour the supposition that during the ventricular systolé the circulation in the walls of the heart ceases on account of the close relation between the segments of the aortic valve and the orifices of the coronary arteries.

Immediately the aortic valve is closed the impediment to the flow of blood into the coronary vessels is removed, and the sudden repletion thus caused, directly after the closure of the valve, produces an equally sudden turgescence of the walls of the ventricles, the auricles from their thinness not being similarly affected. This turgescence of the tissue of the heart produces an active opening out of the cavities of the ventricles, and in a very short time they reach their maximum size.

The following experiment supports this theory ;—take . a sheep's heart which has at least two inches of the aorta left on ; attach the cut end of the aorta to a pint syringe full of water and inject ; the first effect of this operation is the closure of the aortic valve, immediately after which water enters the coronary arteries, the ventricular walls swell and the cavities of the ventricles open out to their full extent. It will be then found that the heart is tough and not easily compressible, and if it be cut in two between the apex and base, the halves shew the cavities fully dilated, and they remain so until the water has escaped from the cut orifices of the vessels. The shortness of the coronary arteries and the sudden way in which they break up into minute ramifications favours the rapid turgescence of the heart walls.

If this theory be correct it follows that there must be an absorptive force exercised in both the ventricles immediately after the closure of the aortic valve, and Marey found that to be the case when he placed in either ventricle an ampoule registering negative pressures only.

The relation between the cardiograph traces from the ventricles and aorta throw so much light on the point under consideration that a detailed description of them will not be out of place.

The diagram is taken from Marey's work *De la circulation du Sang*, p. 189.

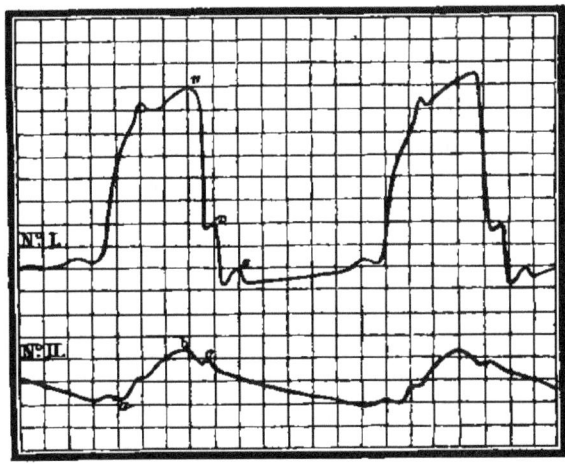

No. I. is the trace from the left ventricle.
No. II. is from the aorta.

Simultaneous events are recorded in the same longitudinal line, and the traces by their rise and fall indicate alterations of pressure in the ventricle and aorta respectively.

No more reference will be here made to the systolic than is necessary to explain the diastolic movements.

Towards the end of the cardiac systolé, the pressure which continues to increase in the ventricles (v) dimininishes in the aorta (b), because then the latter receives less blood from the heart than it transmits to the capillaries.

After this; it is considered by Marey that the undulation x in the upper trace corresponds with c in the lower, and that they are both caused by the closure of the aortic valve; he also thinks the fall between x and z in the upper trace to be due to the relaxation of the ventricle, and, without explaining why, states that at that moment the pressure falls ordinarily below zero.   But on carefully looking at his own diagram, as copied above, it is clearly seen that the undulation c in the aortic slightly precedes x in the ventricular trace, and this together with the results obtained by Chauveau, by means of his combined haemadromometer and sphygmoscope, and confirmed by Lortet, leads me to doubt the correctness of Marey's explanation and to advance the following.

During the main ventricular descent the aortic pressure increases (c), probably from the rise of the base of the heart after its contraction, just as at the commencement of the systolé it falls (a) from the opposite cause.

When all contraction has ceased, the only impediment to regurgitation from the arteries, is the passive resistance of the ventricular walls, which is comparatively slight; so that blood flows back to the heart, compressing the ampoule in the ventricle and causing the elevation x in the upper trace, while it necessarily produces a similar depression in the lower one.

When the reflux of blood has become sufficiently rapid, the aortic valve closes, and in so doing puts an abrupt stop to the ventricular rise x.   Immediately after this the coronary repletion and consequent turgescence commences, as shewn above, and by opening out the cavities of the ventricles, diminishes the pressure on the contained ampoule, and so depresses the trace below zero.

This tendency to the formation of a vacuum, together with the associated raising of the base of the heart, causes so great a rush of blood from the auricles, which as Mr Bryant has shewn, are then quite full, that a slight undulation is produced in the ventricular trace z.

The increase in bulk of the ventricular walls, consequent on the coronary repletion, takes place in all directions, and by expanding the whole conical heart, pushes the base up into the cavity previously occupied by the full auricles, which it simultaneously empties by the absorptive force.

This theory being true, the heart is a machine in which simplicity of action and economy of force are most marked. The systolic movements fill the reservoirs which are to feed the cavities they empty; and all the diastolic forces are expended in active preparation for the succeeding systolé; the circulation in its walls, besides its primary object, even aiding its mechanical function.

The observations of Professor Lister on the LIGATURE OF ARTERIES ON THE ANTISEPTIC SYSTEM (*Lancet*, April 3rd, 1869) are important, not only in their application to the practice of surgery, but from the light they throw on certain physiological and pathological processes. He has found that a portion of dead tissue is not necessarily thrown off by suppuration, but unless altered by putrefaction, or artificially imbued with stimulating salts, serves as pabulum for the surrounding living parts, which remove it by a sure process of absorption. Silk ligatures, impregnated with a solution of carbolic acid, tied round an artery, the wound being dressed on the antiseptic system, were found, after the lapse of time, to be resolved into minute fragments of silk fibre, which were eroded by the absorbing action of the surrounding living tissue. Animal ligatures formed of cat-gut, impregnated with carbolic acid, and used in wounds treated antiseptically, become surrounded by a ring of living tissue; the ligature having served as a mould for the formation of new tissue, the growing elements of which had replaced the materials absorbed, so as to constitute a living solid of the same form. The animal ligatures were transformed into bands of living tissue. The tissue, formed at the expense of one ligature, consisted of fibro-plastic structure, the coarse fibres which mainly constituted it being composed of very large elongated cells, often containing several nuclei, whilst that produced at the expense of a second smaller ligature of cat-gut consisted of comparatively well-developed fibrous tissue.

ON SOME POINTS OF THE EPITHELIUM OF THE FROG'S THROAT. By MICHAEL FOSTER, M.D. (Pl. VIII.)

WITHIN the last two or three years a very considerable controversy has arisen concerning the so-called "goblet cells" (*becherzellen*). In that controversy I have no desire to take a formal part; but, having had occasion to examine for another purpose, with some care, the mucous membrane of the pharynx and œsophagus of the frog, where these goblet cells are peculiarly abundant and obvious, I have been incidentally led to make a few observations upon them.

The epithelium of this region occurs in two forms only: the common ciliate cells and the goblet cells. At least I have been unable to satisfy myself of the existence of any other type. And the characters of these two forms are so different that they throw out in strong relief each other's qualities.

The ciliate cells (Figs. 1 and 2) are pyramidal in form, three-, or more commonly, four-sided, with rounded angles. The ciliate base is typically rhomboidal in outline, its surface being gently convex outwards. The homogeneous, thick, highly refractive, so-called cuticular crust, in which the cilia are set, is well marked.

The cell-substance occupying the interval between the crust and the nucleus is not only (from the pyramidal form of the cell) thicker and therefore more opaque, and more highly coloured by carmine, osmic acid and other reagents, than elsewhere, but has also a peculiar finely granular appearance, most marked immediately under the crust, and gradually disappearing towards the nucleus. It is not unfrequently beset with other granules of larger but variable size.

The *nucleus* is an ellipsoid in form, apparently a solid mass of colloid material, normally homogeneous and transparent, though occasionally disfigured by a few granules or vacuoles. Under the action of most reagents except osmic acid it becomes coagulated and corrugated into a granular mulberry-like heap. It is invariably so situate that more of it appears in the upper than in the lower half of the cell, with the long diameter of which its long axis more or less completely coincides. During life the nucleus touches on all sides the cell-substance in which it is imbedded. After death, and especially after the use of reagents, it shrinks; and a space is consequently developed between it and its matrix. Occasionally either from its own unequal shrinking, or from the formation of vacuoles immediately around it, the nucleus assumes an irregular form, being sometimes stellate.

In the centre of the nucleus is a conspicuous highly refractive but transparent and homogeneous *nucleolus*, either spherical, oval, rod-shaped, or hour-glass shaped. The last two forms probably indicate approaching cleavage; but the nucleolus, like the nucleus, may be deformed by reagents. Occasionally two nucleoli are visible (then situate at the foci of the nucleus); but I have never seen either two nuclei in one cell, or a nucleus at any stage of cleavage.

Below the nucleus the cell-substance, limited by anything but a bold outline, gradually tapers away, being sometimes bifurcate or even branched. It is confessedly a difficult thing to be sure of the natural form (supposing that they have a constant shape) of any epithelium cell which cannot be seen as a transparent object *in situ* and in a living state; but I am inclined to think that (in the frog's throat) the tapering long form is the true form, and that the apex of the pyramid is always continuous with the protoplasmic matrix of the layer next underneath, and that all the truncated pyramids are artificial products. When the cells are killed *in situ* by immersion in some one of the preservative fluids, the pyramidal (or in section triangular) forms are abundant. But if a few living cells be scraped off the membrane and allowed to die slowly in a medium (sodic chloride half per cent.) which allows isolated cells to move about by means of their own cilia for some considerable time, very many of the cells will be found upon examination to have contracted into almost a spherical form, the upper hemisphere being covered with cilia, and the nucleus often placed transversely.

Very different in all respects are the goblets cells, of which however there are many varieties. The most common, perhaps the typical form, is that of a globe or of an oval flask with its neck broken off short (Fig. 2). The lower pole of the globe is occupied by a mass of somewhat refractive cell-substance, in the midst of which may with difficulty be detected a shrunken nucleus, often a third less in size than the nucleus of the ciliate cells, with an inconspicuous nucleolus. The ordinary cell-substance around the nucleus varies somewhat in amount, and also in form. Not unfrequently, like the corresponding end of the ciliate cell, it is continued into delicate branching processes. It is always more or less vacuolated. As the eye moves from the nucleus towards the upper pole of the globe the vacuoles are seen increasing in size, and then suddenly, a very little way farther on, the whole of the cell appears to have become converted into one large cavity whose walls very speedily unite with the outline of the cell itself (Fig. 7).

The cavity thus occupying at least four-fifths of the total area of the cell is crowded with refractive spherules of variable size, the most abundant being those about as large as the nucleolus of the ciliate cell. Sometimes these spherules are absent; then the walls of the cavity are seen to be marked with a net-work of fine lines, giving to one's mind the impression of a stroma in which the spherules had previously been imbedded. The cavity is not however empty in the absence of the spherules; it is filled with mucus, i.e. with viscid, obscurely filamentous mucin, in which are still entangled a few irregular granules.

At the upper pole of the globe is a well defined, clean cut, more or less regularly circular, opening called by the Germans the *stoma*. (They similarly call the spherule-holding cavity the *theca*.) In their natural position these goblet cells are scattered among the ciliate cells (in variable proportion) in such a way that the stoma is situate between the converging angles of three or more ciliate cells (Fig. 12) at the junction, that is to say of the shallow furrows which run between the ciliate cells. The stoma of the goblet cell is consequently below the level of the highest points of the ciliate surface, while its nucleus is on a level, or even below, the apex of the ciliate pyramids (Fig. 2).

These stomata are not artificial products. They are most readily seen in osmic acid preparations, that is in pieces of epithelium scraped from a membrane which has been immersed for 24 hours in a 1 per cent. solution of osmic acid; but when the eye has become accustomed to their appearance they may be easily seen with careful focussing in perfectly fresh living specimens.

Other forms (Figs. 3 to 9) besides the globular are also common, such as that of a miller's sack. Sometimes a distinct neck is observed at the summit of which is the stoma. Some cells are cylindrical, others almost hour-glass shaped; and they vary in size as well as in shape. Sometimes the spherule-cavity or theca is separated from the nucleus by a long stretch of vacuolated cell-substance (Fig. 13).

But all these forms may readily be thrown into two classes.

In all cases the nuclei lie at the bottom of the cells; this alone distinguishes the goblet cells at once from their ciliate fellows. But in one class the nucleus is small, shrunken, and obscure. When this is the case the form is nearly always globular or at least of the broad type, and the stoma is well defined and unmistakeable. In the other class the nucleus is large, easily seen, well formed, with a conspicuous nucleolus, in fact quite like the nucleus of the ciliate cell. When this is the case the form is nearly always cylindrical or at least of the narrow type, and the upper end is either entire and unbroken, or the orifice which it bears is ill-defined, ragged, and irregular, being evidently, to a large extent at least, an artificial product.

To the first class evidently belong what may be called the adult forms; the members of the second class are apparently cells on the way to become globular and to receive stomata.

The spherules when seen in a cell where they are abundant and close packed, very curiously resemble the vitelline spherules of many invertebrate ova. And at first I was inclined to entertain an opinion which has been adopted by Eimer, that they arose by means of a species of cleavage. But I have since satisfied myself that that is not their mode of origin. These spherules are worthy of notice; they are proteid in nature (not fatty), and the larger ones seem not to be homogeneous but to contain other smaller spherules or a spherule within them; in fact they in many ways resemble the smaller globules of the white yolk of the hen's egg.

Their mode of origin I take to be as follows. The first stage of a goblet cell, as of other cells, is a nucleus surrounded by a mass of protoplasmic cell-substance, situate in the "mucous layer" of the membrane, in the line in fact of indifferent growth. The cell substance increases in size and takes on the form of a cylinder growing most rapidly towards the free surface of the membrane. Soon the protoplasm of the cell-substance becomes vacuolated; the fluid contents of each vacuole suffer a chemical differentiation by which the central portion becomes a solid spherule, the outer more fluid mucin. The portion of cell-substance which undergoes this change is the oldest, that is to say the uppermost. Cells are often seen in which, working from above downwards, first a region of spherules, then a district of vacuolated protoplasm, and then a fair well-proportioned nucleus surrounded by new unchanged cell-substance are met with. Sometimes it would seem as if after a certain number of spherules had been formed, the process had been suddenly arrested. The portion containing spherules continuing its changes, the whole mass of its protoplasm becomes converted into spherules, mucin and the cellulose-like stroma, all gathered together in a distinct cavity, while the rest of the cell-substance immediately surrounding the nucleus appears to be resting awhile before commencing a new formation of spherules, and meanwhile becomes parted by a constriction of the cell from the upper spherule-holding cavity (Fig. 13). But under ordinary circumstances, the protoplasm as it gathers round the nucleus from below is gradually converted into spherules and mucin, the whole cell thus rising higher and higher until at last its upper pole reaches the free surface and the stoma is formed.

By this time it has most probably worn itself out; the shrunk nucleus indicates the failure of its powers; though it might possibly continue for some time to secrete mucin, it is not very likely that having once discharged its brood of spherules it would a second or third time become pregnant with them; it is natural to suppose that it would be shed or absorbed. I have never seen anything that could be called a collapsed form (the goodly nucleus of the cylindrical or narrow forms proves that they are not collapsed specimens), and am therefore inclined to think that they are shed.

In reference to a continued secretion of mucin, it is well known that when this membrane of the frog's throat is employed in experiments on ciliary action, a very considerable secretion of mucus takes place. This mucus though very rich in mucin, is remarkably poor in spherules or corpuscles especially after any experiment has been going on for some time; and if, after any prolonged use, the membrane be examined it will be found that its goblet cells but rarely contain spherules though all are filled with mucin. The quantity of mucus secreted under such circumstances appears to be in direct proportion to the energy of the ciliary movement, as might be expected; for there is no reason to think that the goblet cells are emptied by any other means than the *vis a tergo* of secretion and the *vis a fronte* of the ciliary current across their mouths.

The characters I have given above are of themselves, I venture to think, sufficient to remove any *a priori* probability from the idea that worn out ciliate cells might be further utilized by remission to the lower grade of goblet cells. Never having seen a worn out ciliate cell, I do not know what it is like; but I have never seen either so much as any trace of cilia on any goblet cell, or anything like an intermediate grade between a ciliate cell and a goblet one.

Into the probable future of these spherules and their relation to the various cellular constituents of mucus I cannot now enter; and I would repeat that these observations are entirely confined to the epithelium of the frog's throat, though of course goblet cells are abundant elsewhere. Their mucus-secreting function is well illustrated by their remarkable development in the skin of the slug[1].

1. Ciliate cell from pharynx of frog.

2. Ciliate cell and goblet cell side by side: *st.* stoma; *th.* theca; *sr.* stroma; *n.* nucleus.

3—9. Various forms of goblet cells. Fig. 7 shews vacuolation of cell-substance.

10. Fragment of theca containing a few spherules.

11. Lower end of broken goblet cell; theca still contains some mucin.

[1] BOLL (Max Schulze's *Archiv.* Supplement, 1869).

12. Bird's eye view of epithelium : *st.* stomata of goblet cells; *t.* ciliate surface of ciliate cells ; *r.* junction of ciliate cells.

13. Goblet cell with cell-substance constricted and nucleus far apart from theca. Theca broken off short.

14, 15, 16. Young forms of goblet cells.

All the above are from osmic acid preparations.

NOTE ON THE ACTION OF THE INTERRUPTED CURRENT ON THE VENTRICLE OF THE FROG'S HEART. By MICHAEL FOSTER, M.D.

IT is well known that if the ventricle of the frog's heart be divided transversely (into an upper fourth and lower three-fourths for instance) the upper fragment will often continue beating spontaneously for some time while the lower fragment will never beat spontaneously at all. The explanation usually given is that the ganglia of the heart are centres whence rhythmic stimuli proceed, and that the upper portion of the ventricle being still connected with Bidder's ventricular ganglia is still subject to those stimuli, whereas the lower fragment being disconnected with those ganglia and not being connected with any other ganglia is not so subject.

The following observation made a long time ago, but which I have not seen recorded anywhere, has led me to doubt the validity of this explanation.

If the lower portion of the ventricle, devoid of spontaneous energy, be submitted to the influence of the interrupted current (with a single small cell, and the cylinders barely overlapping each other, the current being hardly more than susceptible to the lips), the piece of cardiac muscle will not, as would a piece of ordinary muscle, be thrown into tetanus, but will give a series of beats separated from each other by distinct intervals of complete rest. Care must be taken of course that no fallacy creeps in through removal of the muscle from the electrodes during the act of contraction.

The fig. beneath is an exact copy (magnified) of a tracing taken from a portion of ventricle so treated, the defects of tracing being also rendered.

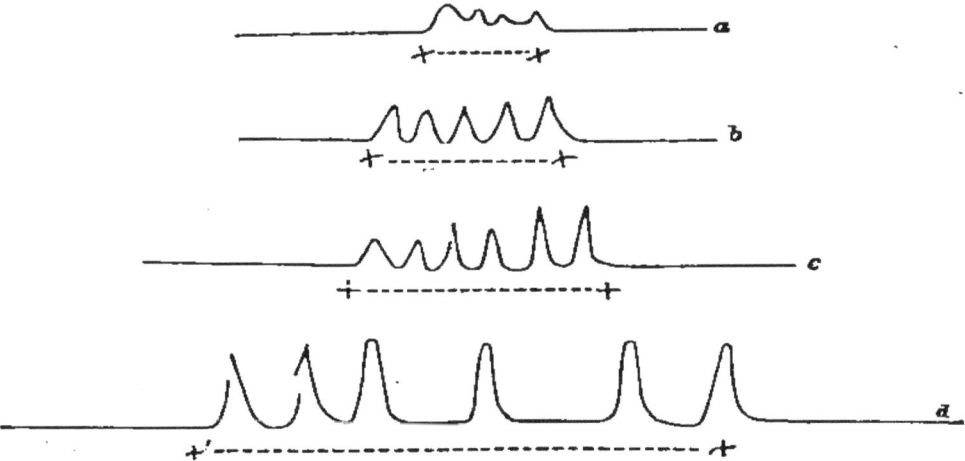

It will be seen that, when the current was first applied (*a*), while the heart was as yet under the influence of shock, an irregular tetanus was produced, but that afterwards (*b, c, d*) as the fragment recovered from shock and besides began to enjoy the beneficial effects of reaction after moderate exercise (so constantly observed in the heart) the rhythm (totally unconnected with the interruptions of the current) became more evident, and each stroke more decided and forcible.

It is well known that it is very difficult to throw the heart into tetanus by any use of the galvanic current. In the case of the small hearts of invertebrata it may be done; but with regard to all the large hearts of invertebrata, we may say with Eckhard, "the heart knows no tetanus."

Putting this and the above facts together we may infer that the cardiac muscular tissue itself differs for some reason or other from ordinary muscular tissue in a disposition towards rhythmic rather than continuous contraction; and that the influence of the ganglia is probably not rhythmic but continuous, whatever the exact nature of that influence be. Other arguments drawn from various sources might be brought forward in support of this view.

INFLUENCE OF THE VAGUS UPON THE VASCULAR SYSTEM. By WILLIAM RUTHERFORD, M.D. F.R.S.E. *Demonstrator of Practical Physiology in the University of Edinburgh*[1].

THE innervation of the vascular system is a subject which has engrossed the attention of physiologists ever since the days of Galen.   Yet, notwithstanding the number of distinguished observers who have advanced our knowledge regarding it, there are still many points of importance which are enveloped in obscurity, and not a few regarding which opinion is most conflicting.

During the past three years I have been more or less engaged in experiments, which have been chiefly directed to the influence which the pneumogastric nerve exercises over the vascular system.   In order that their bearing may be more clearly comprehended, I shall give a brief sketch of what is at present known regarding the innervation of the heart and blood-vessels.

INNERVATION OF THE HEART.

That the heart possesses within itself the conditions necessary for its rhythmical movement is a theory which was advanced by Galen, and is now believed by all physiologists.

The peculiar nervous arrangements essential for the rhythmical movement are as Remak pointed out, ganglia situated in various parts of the organ.

It is moreover admitted by all that the movements of the heart may be influenced by certain nerves connecting it with the cerebro-spinal axis.   These are branches of the sympathetic and vagi.   The sympathetic filaments take origin in the brain and medulla oblongata, pass through the cervical portion of the

[1] Abstract of a paper to be read before the Royal Society of Edinburgh on 3rd May, 1869. *All* references will be given and the experiments fully detailed elsewhere.

spinal cord, the last cervical and first dorsal ganglia, (M. and E. Cyon, Reichert's *Archiv*, 1867, p. 389), and from thence to the heart. These nerves convey to the cardiac organ influences which accelerate its action. Von Bezold thought that they do so continually, but Ludwig and the brothers Cyon have conclusively shown that there is no ground for such a supposition. That cardiac motor filaments are also to be found in the trunk of the *cervical* sympathetic was maintained by Von Bezold, but has been denied by Ludwig. Regarding this point, I have performed three experiments on rabbits. I never observed any effect on the heart follow irritation of this nerve, provided that the electrical currents were prevented from reaching the inferior cervical ganglion and thereby from affecting the cardiac branch derived from the spinal cord. Only when this ganglion was implicated did acceleration of the heart ensue. These observations lead me to conclude with Ludwig that the trunk of the cervical sympathetic nerve is not a cardiac nerve at all.

The heart is connected with the trunk of the vagus in the neck by a superior and an inferior branch. The former in the rabbit leaves the vagus with the superior laryngeal branch, courses down the neck in close proximity to the sympathetic, joins one or two branches of the inferior cervical ganglion with which it proceeds to the heart where its terminations have not yet been minutely traced. According to Cyon and Ludwig (*Journal de l'Anatomie*, Nov. 5, 1867) when this nerve is divided and its cranial end irritated, the blood pressure falls owing to dilatation of abdominal blood-vessels effected through the medulla oblongata and spinal cord. Because of the remarkable power which it possesses of lowering the blood-pressure, they have termed it the "depressor" nerve. They suppose that it is thrown into action when the heart is overloaded with blood, in order that by dilatation of blood-vessels the resistance to its contractions may be diminished. In six of my experiments on rabbits I took occasion to examine the influence of stimulation of this nerve upon the blood-pressure, and can bear testimony to the accuracy of Cyon and Ludwig's observation.

The inferior cardiac branch of the vagus arises with the inferior laryngeal nerve, and according to Bidder terminates in the cardiac ganglia. The nature of the influence exerted by it upon the heart has been much disputed. According to Willis, Lower, Valsalva, Schiff, Moleschott, Lister and others it is a *motor* nerve of the heart, while in the opinion of the brothers Weber, Volkmann, Pflüger, Von Bezold and others, its function is to inhibit or restrain the heart's movements, so as to diminish their frequency and even to bring the organ for a time into a state of complete rest.

For the purpose of ascertaining which of these theories is correct, or whether there be not some truth in both, I have performed a number of experiments the results of which will presently be given.

In this as in the case of other nerves, we must study the effect of division and of irritation. Owing to the difficulty of dividing the inferior cardiac branch of the vagus, and the almost impossibility of irritating it without implicating other cardiac nerves if the thorax be not opened, most of my experiments like those of previous observers, have been performed on the trunk of the vagus in the neck. It will be convenient for us to consider the result of irritation previous to that of division.

EFFECT UPON THE HEART OF IRRITATING THE LOWER END OF THE VAGUS AFTER IT HAS BEEN DIVIDED IN THE NECK.

In 1845 the brothers Weber (Müller's *Archiv*, 1846, p. 497) discovered that on irritating the vagi or those portions of the central nervous system from which they spring, the heart beats more slowly and may even come to rest in a state of relaxation. From this observation they concluded that the vagus exerts an inhibitory or controlling power over the heart's action. No one has called in question the accuracy of their experiment, but their interpretation, though it receives the support of many physiologists, is at the same time energetically opposed by Schiff, Moleschott, Lister and others. These observers, while admitting that *powerful* irritation of the cardiac end of the vagus arrests the heart's action, maintain that *gentle* stimulation *quickens* it, and they thinking that the slowing or arrest of the heart's action is due to exhaustion of the nerve or the cardiac ganglia, therefore conclude that the vagus (inferior cardiac branch) is a motor nerve of the heart. As the quickening of the heart by *gentle* stimulation of the nerve is the fundamental observation upon which they base this theory, it is of great importance to ascertain whether or not it be true. Pflüger and Von Bezold, deny that such is the case, but Schiff and Moleschott have simply replied that these observers have not performed their experiments with sufficient care. In most of the experiments the nerve was stimulated by inducted currents, and according to Schiff it is so difficult to hit upon the proper degree of strength which the current must possess in order to quicken the heart, that unless the greatest care be taken to apply the electrodes properly to the nerve and to prevent the latter from becoming exhausted, the experiment will fail.

In 1866—67 I performed a number of experiments in a manner which is, I imagine, less open to objection than the methods adopted by previous experimenters. In all the experiments I opened the larynx anteriorly in order that movement of the arytenoid cartilages might be perceived. On applying the electrodes to the lower end of the vagus divided in the neck, I invariably watched the arytenoid cartilage of the same side to see whether or not it was moved. In this way I was able to compare the effects of the stimulant upon the laryngeal muscles and the heart, and thereby to give a degree of precision to my experiments which, but for this test, they could not have possessed.

After having divided both vagi in the middle of the neck, I stimulated the lower end of one by means of Faradic currents, obtained from Du Bois Reymond's induction apparatus. In this machine the strength of the currents can be varied with great nicety by altering the distance between the primary and secondary coils. The secondary is pushed to or from the primary coil along a grooved board having a millimetre scale attached to it which serves to indicate the distance between the two coils, and in that way to give an idea of the comparative strength of the currents employed. I always began the observations on the influence of excitation of the nerve, by ascertaining the weakest current necessary to stimulate the filaments of the recurrent laryngeal nerve in the trunk of the vagus. Having determined this, I made the current still weaker and proceeded to stimulate the lower end of the vagus at intervals. The strength of the current was very gradually

The following will serve as an example of 17 experiments, 1 upon a dog, 4 upon frogs and 12 upon rabbits.

STRONG RABBIT. *Trachea and Larynx opened. Both vagi divided in the neck.* One Daniell's element employed.

Time.	Distance in millimetres of primary from secondary coil of induction machine.	Cardiac beats in 10 seconds.		State of arytenoid muscles.
		Before irritation of vagus.	During irritation of vagus.	
			Cardiac end of left vagus.	
4·22	740	—	—	Contraction.
4·23	800	51	50	Rest.
4·24	800—750	52	52	,,
4·25	750—730	52, 52	52, 52, 52	Contraction.
4·26	730—700	51, 52	52	,,
4·27	700—670	51	51	,,
4·28	670—640	52, 52	52, 52	,,
4·30	640—620	51, 52	52, 51	,,
4·31	620—630	51, 50, 51	51, 50, 50	,,
4·33	630—640	50, 51	51, 50	,,
4·38	640—600	52, 51	50, 51	,,
4·40	600—550	51, 50	51, 51	,,
4·41	550—500	50, 50	51, 50	,,
4·44	500—450	50	50	,,
4·45	450—400	50	49	,,
4·48	400—350	52, 50	50	,,
4·52	350—300	50, 50	50, 48, 49	,,
4·54	300—250	48, 49, 50	49, 50	,,
4·59	250	50, 49	49, 49	,,
5·1	250—230	48, 50	33, 29	,,
5·5	250	48, 48, 48	48, 48	,,
5·8	240	48, 48, 49	19, 19	,,
			Right vagus.	
5·15	240	47, 48	47, 48	,,
5·17	230	46, 47	47, 47	,,
5·18	230—225	42, 45, 46	45, 44	,,
			Left vagus.	
5·23	225	45, 45	38, 37	,,
			Right vagus.	
5·27	210	42, 41	38, 37	,,
5·29	200	42, 42	35, 34	,,
5·32	190	43, 43	34, 34	,,
5·35	160	42	32, 33	,,
5·38	140	40	30	,,
5·40	100	41	Stoppage	,,

increased in order that the influence of weak currents might have a fair trial, and in order that currents of every intensity might be used, they were always strengthened by drawing the secondary towards the primary coil while the nerve was being irritated and the effect upon the heart observed. The cardiac pulsations were counted with the aid of a stethoscope immediately before and during each irritation of the nerve.

In the above experiment the heart was usually counted for two or more successive periods of ten seconds in order that any variation in its rapidity might be detected. With weak currents the stimulation of the nerve was usually continued for about half a minute.

The foregoing results show no acceleration of the heart. They thereby indicate the general result of my experiments. It must be mentioned, however, that the observations made on the heart, while the animal exhibited signs of uneasiness, have not been recorded. *These generally showed quickening of the heart's action,* unless the irritant was powerful enough to slow the heart in spite of the excitement. Whenever the animal struggled I invariably repeated the observation and I found that if there was no struggling there was no quickening of the heart. The same results followed irritation of the inferior cardiac branch of the vagus; but it was observed that during its stimulation the animal much less frequently struggled, unless the heart was arrested. The experiment also very clearly shows that a much more powerful stimulus was required to slow the heart than was necessary to throw the laryngeal muscles into action. This seems at first glance to lend support to the idea that the slowing results from exhaustion of the cardiac ganglia produced by a too powerful excitement. It must however be remembered that the case of the laryngeal muscles is very different from that of the heart. In the former, there is no opposition to the muscles being thrown into contraction, while in the heart there are influences at work which cause movement, and these must be overcome by a stronger influence ere the heart can be brought to rest. As it is, however, none of the so-called "too powerful" currents are in ordinary cases able to completely arrest the heart's action for more than a few seconds: the influences which prompt the heart to contract become so strong that stimulation of the vagus, be it ever so powerful, fails to prevent it.

The theory, that the inhibitory influence of the vagus upon the heart is due to exhaustion of the cardiac ganglia produced by over-stimulation seems to me irreconcilable with the following fact which I have repeatedly observed and demonstrated. If any irritating vapour, such as that of chloroform, ether, alcohol, acetic acid, &c. be brought before the nose of a rabbit, it instantly closes its nostrils and ceases to breathe— often for 30—40 seconds. Within three seconds after the cessation of respiration the heart comes almost to a stand-still, and continues to beat very slowly until respiration be re-established. This arrest of the heart is due to stimulation of the inferior cardiac branch of the vagus by the asphyxiated condition of the blood, for the slowing of the heart does not set in until death approach, if the vagi have been previously divided. The perfect calmness with which a rabbit will often sit with its heart almost stopped seems to forbid the idea that in such a case the vagi are over-stimulated.

Wundt has said (*Verhandlungen des naturhistorisch-medizinischen Vereins, Heidelberg,* 1860) that curara produces such an influence upon the vagus that its irritation no longer slows but quickens the heart. As shown by Von Bezold, this substance, and also atropia, paralyse the inferior cardiac branch of the vagus; that is to say—they so affect the nerve that its stimulation however powerful does not retard the heart's action. In a rabbit I divided both vagi in the neck and stimulated the lower end of one of the nerves with a powerful current. (Secondary 40 mm. distant from primary coil. One Daniell.) The heart's action was arrested. I then injected $\frac{1}{60}$th grain sulphate of atropia into the jugular vein. When two minutes had elapsed I stimulated the same nerve with a current of the same strength. The heart's action instead of being arrested as before was quickened. This acceleration took place when the animal exhibited no signs of excitement, and it seemed to indicate that in the inferior cardiac branch of the vagus there are cardiac *motor* fibres which are not paralysed by sulphate of atropia; but another experiment proved that a different explanation is necessary. In a rabbit I divided the *inferior cardiac branch of the right vagus* after having cut the *trunk* of the nerve on the *left* side of the neck. I then severed the *trunk* of the *right vagus* in the neck and irritated its lower end. The heart was quickened, as in the former case; and this, although the electricity was carefully localised, and thereby prevented from reaching the inferior cervical ganglion and its cardiac nerves. I observed that the laryngeal muscles, œsophagus, stomach, and intestines, were thrown into violent movement by the irritation ; and it occurred to me that possibly the excitement of these organs might produce an influence on the cerebrum or medulla oblongata sufficient to excite the cardiac motor nerves. The quickening could not be ascribed to increased blood pressure, for irritation of the lower end of the vagus produces scarcely any effect thereon. This experiment seems to me to give the finishing blow to the notion that the vagus is a motor nerve of the heart.

The foregoing experiments lead me to regard the inferior cardiac branch of the vagus as an inhibitory nerve of the heart, and also to think that it cannot, in any sense, be looked upon as one of its motor nerves. I can only account for the discrepancy between my results and those obtained by Lister, Schiff, and others, by supposing that they frequently regarded the effect of general excitement upon the heart's movement as the direct result of irritating the vagus, or as Eckhard has hinted (*Experimental Physiologie*, 1867, p. 201) that the currents which they employed were not sufficiently localised in the vagus, and thereby prevented from reaching the sympathetic (motor) nerves of the heart.

The arrest of the evolution of energy in the cardiac ganglia seems to be owing to a direct action of the nerve upon the ganglionic cells. It has been shown that the nerve ends in the cells. Brown-Séquard and Traube suppose that it is a vasomotor nerve for the coronary vessels, and that the arrest of the heart during its stimulation is due to spasm of these. This theory seems to be irreconcilable with the fact observed long ago by Erichsen, and confirmed by Von Bezold, that closure of the conorary arteries produces no immediate change on the heart's movements. Irritation of the vagus usually arrests the heart within a second or two. Moreover, after the heart has been for some time stopped by excitation of its inhibitory nerves it again begins to beat, and notwithstanding the continuance of the irritation it often attains its former speed. This seems to be due to increased blood pressure in its right cavities, exciting the incident nerves of the ganglia so powerfully that the inhibitory influence is no longer able to prevent the evolution of energy from taking place within them.

Effect upon the Vascular System of Division of the Vagi in the Neck.

(a) *Effect on the Rate of Cardiac Action.*

The majority of observers agree that after division of both vagi in the neck the heart usually beats with increased rapidity. On the other hand, Lister (*Proc. R. S.* IX. 374) divided the vagi four times in rabbits and once in a calf, and found that in no case was the heart accelerated. According to Von Bezold it is quite exceptional for division not to be followed by increase in the heart's speed. He considers that this only occurs when the heart is acting with unwonted frequency previous to the section, thereby indicating that the vagi are exercising no restraint upon it. My experiments show that non-acceleration of the heart is by no means uncommon after such an operation. The probable cause of this will presently be explained.

Cause of the Increased Rapidity.

Dr John Reid ascribed the quickened cardiac action to "the struggles and terror of the animal produced by division of the nerves." (*Physiological Researches*, 1848, p. 132). Undoubtedly this is to some extent true, but I have frequently noticed that the quickening took place when all struggling was prevented by a small dose of curara.

Moleschott (*Jl. de la Physiologie,* v. 131) believes that irritation of the inferior cardiac nerve produced by its section is the cause of the acceleration. But even were this a motor nerve of the heart, it would be difficult to believe that the irritation due to an incision could produce a change in the heart's speed lasting for hours.

Brown-Séquard (*Jl. de la Physiologie*, v. 656) believes that it is owing to the stimulating influence upon the cardiac motor nerves of an excess of carbonic acid in the blood. This theory is plausible, for it is well known that after division of both vagi the respirations usually become much slower. But I have observed the acceleration in cases where in order to prevent asphyxia I maintained a thoroughly hyperoxygenated condition of the blood by artifical respiration both before and after division of the nerves. Further, recent researches by Voit and Rauber (*Centralblatt*, 1868, No. 47) show that until the pulmonary textures undergo inflammation the increased *depth* of the respirations after division of the vagi entirely compensates for their diminished frequency, so that the amount of oxygen and carbonic acid in the blood undergoes no change.

These facts therefore seem to me to show that an asphyxiated state of the blood cannot be regarded as the cause of the acceleration of the heart.

Von Bezold (*Untersuch. über die Innervation des Herzens*, 1ᵗᵉ Abtheilung 1863, p. 84) thought that the cardiac inhibitory filaments of the vagi are in *constant* action, and to freedom from their restraint he ascribed the acceleration of the heart which follows their division. At the present moment this theory is generally believed. Its importance is such that it demands a most careful examination of the data upon which it rests. The only fact advanced is that section of the vagi is generally followed by accelerated cardiac action. It occurred to me, that if this be only due to loss of the inhibitory power of the inferior cardiac branches of the vagi, no acceleration of the heart's action ought to follow division of the vagi, if these have been previously paralysed by Sulphate of Atropia (vide supra). Accordingly in 9 dogs and 4 rabbits I paralysed the cardiac inhibitory branches of the vagi by sulphate of atropia, and found that in 5 dogs and 1 rabbit, division of the vagi in the neck was followed by increased speed of the heart. The following experiment is also of great importance. In a rabbit I divided the trunk of the left vagus and the cardiac inhibitory branch of that on the right side. No change in the heart's speed ensued, but when the *trunk of the latter nerve* was divided in the neck *decided acceleration was the result.* It is therefore certain that the increased activity of the heart which follows section of the vagi may be due to division of other filaments than those which retard the heart's action.

The consideration of this will be resumed when we have attended to another effect of the section, viz.

(b) *Effect on the Arterial Blood-pressure.*

Bernard, Volkmann, Jacobson, Ludwig, Traube, Von Bezold, and others have observed that section of the vagi is generally followed by a rise in the arterial blood-pressure. So far as I can make out every one has ascribed this change to the accelerated action of the heart, but I have repeatedly observed that the heart's speed may undergo very considerable variation without producing any change in the blood-pressure ; for example, in a rabbit the heart beat 228 times in a minute, and very shortly afterwards the number was only 180, yet the mean pressure remained constant. In another rabbit the mean pressure was the same, although at one time the heart gave 204 and at another only 156 pulsations in a minute. Moreover in another instance I found on dividing the vagi of a rabbit that although the arterial pressure rose to the extent of half an inch the rapidity of cardiac action remained the same. It is therefore evident that the rise in the blood-pressure which follows division of the vagi must in general be ascribed to another cause than the heart. By a number of experiments I have proved that this is to be found in the state of the abdominal blood-vessels, chiefly those of the stomach. If the vagi be divided during digestion the blood-pressure rises, while if the animal be fasting it usually undergoes no change. This remarkable fact will however be more clearly comprehended after a brief account has been given of what is known regarding the

INNERVATION OF BLOOD-VESSELS.

By the investigations of Bernard and Brown-Séquard, it has been established beyond a doubt that the contractile elements of the blood-vessels are supplied by motor nerve filaments derived from the sympathetic. Diminution in the calibre of blood-vessels is produced by the action of these nerves. According to Ludwig and Thiry the most general centre for the vasomotor nerves is situated in the medulla oblongata. Lister (*Phil. Trans.* 1859, p. 625) supposes that it exists throughout the whole spinal cord and in the posterior part of the brain in frogs at any rate; and further, his observations on the changes which the vessels of the frog's web undergo after division of the sciatic nerve lead him to suppose that there exists in the *limbs* of that animal "a local co-ordinating apparatus—probably ganglionic—capable of independent action, although, under ordinary circumstances, in strict subordination to the spinal system."

The existence of these ganglia in the limbs has not as yet, however, been demonstrated.

The cerebro-spinal vasomotor centre is in a more or less constant state of activity whereby vessels are usually maintained in a state of semi-contraction. The amount of contraction may be increased or diminished *reflexly*, that is, by the action of incident nerves upon the cells of the vasomotor nerve centre. Bernard was the first to show by experiment that vessels may be dilated by the irritation of certain nerves. He found that this takes place in the sub-maxillary gland when the chorda tympani, and in the parotid when the auriculo-temporal nerve is stimulated. He also discovered that dilatation of the vessels of the ear in rabbits follows irritation of the central end of the auricular nerve. The dilatation in this case is preceded by slight contraction. Lovén (Ludwig's *Arbeiten*, 1866, p. 1) has confirmed this observation of Bernard's, and has shown that dilatation of vessels in the leg of the rabbit succeeds irritation of its afferent (sensory?) nerves; in short, that dilatation of the vessels of a part may be produced by reflex action. Like Bernard, he found that transient contraction of the vessels generally precedes the dilatation so induced.

Eckhard (*Beiträge*, Giessen, 1863) and Lovén (*Lib. Cit.* p. 18) have shown that irritation of the nervi erigentes in the dog produces erection of the penis by causing dilatation of vessels.

Dreschfeld (Bezold's *Untersuchungen*, 1867, p. 326) found that the blood pressure is lowered owing to dilatation of blood-vessels when the cranial end of the vagus is irritated in the neck. But the most remarkable instance of a nerve capable of producing vascular dilatation was discovered by Cyon and Ludwig (*Sächs. Acad. Bericht*, 1866, p. 307; *Jl. de l'Anat.* 1867) to be the superior cardiac branch of the vagus. When the cranial end of this nerve is stimulated, dilatation of abdominal vessels takes place without any previous contraction.

These facts seem conclusively to show that the contractile elements of the blood-vessels are like those of the heart presided over by two systems of nerves, one motor, the other inhibitory. The dilatation effected by the inhibitory nerves is passive, and is simply due to the elasticity and blood-pressure being no longer opposed by the contraction of the vessel. The inhibitory nerves, whether they convey influences to the medulla oblongata, salivary glands, heart, or penis, seem always to end in ganglia; in short, they appear to end in vasomotor nerve cells whose evolution of energy they are capable of diminishing. Perhaps these vaso-inhibitory nerves form a system distinct from those which convey influences to produce reflex *action* or sensation.

The facts observed by Bernard and Lovén admit, as the latter has shown of the general statement, that the vessels of a part may be *dilated* by nervous action. A similar idea however has long since been entertained regarding the congestion in inflamed parts. But although facts already ascertained render this idea extremely probable, its truth has not hitherto been demonstrated; for no one has succeeded in actually showing that these vaso-inhibitory nerves *are* in action during congestion of a part which is the seat of active nutritive change.

In numerous experiments upon dogs and rabbits, I have found that if the vagi be divided *during* digestion, the blood-vessels of the stomach, which are then in a state of dilatation contract. The blanching which takes place is usually quite perceptible to the naked eye. There is no evident change however when the division of the nerves is made during fasting; the blood-vessels being then already in a semi-contracted state. This fact shows that during digestion, influences pass through the vagi to keep the vessels of the stomach dilated. These travel *from* the stomach *to* the medulla oblongata, and not in the contrary direction, because, when the vagus is cut across and the gastric portion excited, no change in the vessels ensues; while if the cranial end be irritated, these although they are often contracted are also sometimes dilated[1]. The influences which pass to the medulla appear to inhibit the splanchnic nerve filaments supplying the gastric vessels, because section of the vagi produces no change in the blood-vessels of the stomach, if the cervical portion of the spinal cord, or the splanchnic nerves have been previously divided. The conclusion at which I have arrived is—that whatever be the action of the vis à fronté in producing congestion of a part—its chief cause is the action of the tissues upon their vaso-inhibitory nerves whereby the vessels are partially or completely paralysed.

As I have already said, it is the state of the gastric blood-vessels which in general determines whether or not the blood-pressure will rise on section of the vagi. In 3 dogs and 4 rabbits I divided the vagi *during digestion.* In all, the blood-pressure rose. I divided the nerves *during fasting* in 3 dogs and 6 rabbits. In 2 of the former and 5 of the latter the blood-pressure underwent no alteration, while in the third dog it was slightly increased, and in the sixth rabbit it was diminished. In many of these experiments I guarded against the possibility of increased cardiac speed or struggling after division of the nerves—being the cause of the increased pressure, by paralysing the inferior cardiac branches of the vagi by sulphate of atropia, and the voluntary nerves by curara.

The increased speed of the heart which follows division of the vagi seems in general to be *owing to the increased blood-pressure.* I have come to this conclusion from finding that in 6 dogs and 2 rabbits, whose *inferior cardiac nerves were paralysed by sulphate of atropia,* division of the vagi was followed by increased blood-pressure and cardiac rapidity. Like other observers I have found that increased blood-pressure is not always followed by increased cardiac action (vagi being divided); in 1 dog and 1 rabbit the rapidity was unaltered, while in 1 dog

---

[1] This seems to be owing to the fact that the vagus like most afferent nerves contains filaments which produce vascular contraction, as well as those which bring about dilatation. As regards the gastric vessels the result of dividing the vagi is more satisfactory than that of irritating the upper ends of the nerves.

and 1 rabbit it was slightly diminished although the pressure was increased.

In a fuller account of my experiments I will detail a number of other points of less importance than the foregoing which this research has brought to light. I will now briefly sum up the *chief* results of 120 experiments which I have performed with reference to this question.

1. The inferior cardiac branches of the vagi are inhibitory nerves of the heart, and their function cannot in any sense be regarded as motor.

2. There is no evidence that they are in constant action as Von Bezold and others have supposed: indeed a state of activity seems to be the exception.

3. The increased rapidity of cardiac movement which often follows division of the vagi in the neck may be owing to increase of the blood-pressure merely.

4. The increased blood-pressure which often results from section of the vagi is not in general due to increased rapidity of the heart's action, but to contraction of the gastric blood-vessels.

5. Additional support is given to the theory that the contractile elements of the entire vascular system are presided over by two kinds of nerves, one motor, the other inhibitory. The former brings about contraction, the latter throws the motor nerves and contractile elements into a state of rest.

6. The vessels of the stomach are dilated during digestion chiefly by the vaso-inhibitory action of incident filaments of the vagi upon the splanchnic nerves.

NOTE ON THE FINE ANATOMY OF THE SKIN OF LIZARDS. (Pl. IX.). By J. W. HULKE.

THE following note embodies the results of a microscopic examination of the skins of several lizards (most of them from Bahia) which has lately occupied some of my leisure moments. My attention was drawn to the subject in the early part of last summer, and finding very scanty information respecting it in the common text-books it appeared to me that a short memorandum might not be unwelcome to the readers of this journal.

The epidermis and the cutis vera together compose the SCALES which distinguish this class of Reptiles, so that after the epidermis has been artificially separated the cutis still bears a scaly pattern. In the epidermis a superficial, horny stratum, and a deeper stratum mucosum are recognizable (Fig. 1. *a*). The horny layer consists of large, flattened scalelike cells many of which are nucleated where the epidermis is thin and delicate ; while in situations where the epidermis is thick, as at the free edges of imbricated scales, and also in the flexible membranous tegument which holds the scales together, the nucleus is usually absent. The cells of the stratum mucosum are small, and always nucleated ; those of the deepest tier are subcolumnar, and placed vertically on the outer surface of the cutis (Fig. 1. *b*).

The cutis vera consists principally of connective tissue (unmixed with elastic fibre) with connective-tissue corpuscles, pigment, blood-vessels, nerves and glands, and sometimes delicate plates of bone. The connective tissue occurs in the form of strong fibres crossing one another in planes more or less parallel to the surfaces of the cutis, an arrangement which gives to vertical sections of this division of that skin a laminated appearance. The horizontal fibres are crossed vertically by other fibres passing between the inner and outer surfaces near which they break up into fibrillæ that bend away from the vertical direction and lose themselves between the horizontal lamellæ.

Connective-tissue corpuscles occur throughout the cutis in the interstices of the fibrous tissue, but they abound at the outer and inner surfaces, and are only sparingly present in the middle of the cutis where they mostly accompany the blood-vessels and nerves. The pigment which by its quantity, diffusion or aggregation, and the manner of its distribution, produces the manifold colours of the skin is contained in these corpuscles. In some lizards I have found it most abundant at the outer surface, in others at the inner surface of the cutis.

The cutis is connected with the underlying parts by a loose areolar tissue largely composed of curling elastic fibres. This contains vascular and nervous plexuses from which minute arterial and nervous twigs pass off nearly at right angles and traverse the cutis with little diminution of their size nearly to the outer surface under which they break up into fine terminal nets.

Bone, so far as my observation extends, when present, is always in the cutis. I speak only of true ossifications—these I formerly supposed were always metamorphosed fibrous tissues, membrane bones ; but this was a mistake, for some miniature scutes are cartilage bones. The skin of the Spanish Gecko furnishes a beautiful example of this latter kind of bone. This little lizard's skin is armed with small imbricated scales, in cutting which a distinct grittiness is perceptible. After the epidermis has been detached the cutis exhibits under a low magnifying power an exquisitely beautiful rectangular pattern suggestive of vegetable rather than of animal structure (Fig. 2). With quarter-inch objective in these minute rectangles corpuscles are recognizable which cannot be distinguished from bone lacunæ (Fig. 3). The addition of acetic acid causes effervescence, and it makes the little rectangles swell up and become globular, rendering it evident that each corresponds to a primary cartilage cell or capsule the nucleus of which has endogenously multiplied (Fig. 4). The other cell contents calcifying the brood of nuclei is transmuted into bone corpuscles, around which traces of the secondary cell-membranes are often plainly discernible, while the persistent primary capsule forms the boundary of the minute rectangular bony plate.

The much stronger bony plates of the snake-like lizard Ophiurus striatus (Fig. 5) afford us a good example of the other mode of bone formation which is identical with the ordinary ossification of fibrous tissue and therefore does not require particular description. The only things worthy of notice in these scales are the irregular medullary spaces in the sunken half of the scale and the canals which run from the centre towards the free margin.

The tegumental GLANDS are of two kinds, large composite tubular glands restricted to certain regions, as the femoral glands ; and small, simple follicles scattered over the surface. The former open externally by slightly raised orifices, easily recognizable by the unaided eye, *e. g.* the well-known femoral pores, which are encircled by scales of a peculiar shape (Fig. 6). These pores open into a short wide tube which in the cutis vera, or at its inner surface, breaks up into a number of tubuli most of which are simple and undivided, while a few divide once dichotomously. They are filled with a large variety of pavement epithelium which exudes through the pore when the gland is squeezed. When the skin is stripped off these glands are seen in the form of small rounded knots upon its inner surface. The simple glands (Fig. 7) are microscopic and not discernible by the unassisted eye. Their external orifices are circular. In the Iguana tuberculata a single pore pierces one margin of each of the smaller scales, while in another lizard I found the edge of the scale perforated by several minute pores. In the larger scales the pores are not restricted to the margin but they occur throughout their area. The epithelium lining the follicles is smaller and more spheroidal (Fig. 8) than that of the composite glands.

EXPLANATION OF PLATE IX. ILLUSTRATING THE FINE ANATOMY OF THE SKIN OF LIZARDS.

Fig. 1. A vertical section of the skin of Iguana tuberculata. *a.* Epidermis. *b.* Cutis vera. x. 220.
 „ 2. Cutis vera of Spanish Gecko after separation of Epidermis. x. 20.
 „ 3. A more highly magnified view of the same. x. 220.
 „ 4. The same after addition of Acetic acid. x. 220.
 „ 5. Bony scale of Ophiurus Striatus. x. 20.
 „ 6. Femoral pore of Arneiva Guttata. x. 20.
 „ 7. Gland-pores perforating scales, in Iguana tuberculata. x. 20.
 „ 8. One of these pores more highly magnified. x. 350.

ON CILIARY MOTION. By Dr Th. W. Engelmann, Assistant in the Physiological Laboratory of the University of Utrecht. Translated and abbreviated from the *Nederlandsch Archief voor Genees- en Natuurkunde*, III., 304-356 ; and IV., 26-116 and 275-339 ; Utrecht 1867 68. By William Daniel Moore, M.D., Dub. et Cantab. ; M.R.I.A., &c.

Before proceeding to lay before the reader the general views deduced by Dr Engelmann from his very elaborate essay on the above subject, which, from the great length of his communications, is all that can be here attempted, it will be necessary to give a brief statement of the object of his investigation, and a description of the gas-chamber used by him. This I shall do in his own words, by translating the opening pages of his essay. I shall then merely enumerate the agents he has employed in his researches, and in conclusion, I shall endeavour to reproduce the essential part of the whole essay by giving the "General Considerations" in which he himself sums up the results of his labours.

The conditions under which ciliary motion takes place, and the changes which it undergoes in modifications of these conditions, are only partially known. Valentin and Purkinje investigated the influence which different organic and inorganic matters exercise upon ciliary motion; and they endeavoured, as Calliburces and Kistiakowsky subsequently did, to ascertain the influence of temperature and of electricity; Virchow discovered the effect of alkalies, and Kühne recently investigated the influence of gases.

It appeared however that we were not yet in a position to bring together numerous facts contributed by these and other investigators under a common point of view. Scarcely anywhere do we recognise an effort accurately to define the changes on which the effects of the several agents depend. Thus many facts continue to stand alone as interesting phenomena. Perhaps some points will be found in the following experiments which may serve as a foundation for a tolerably complete idea of the elementary conditions of ciliary motion.

What first gave rise to the investigation now communicated was the establishment of a fact, which was not reconcileable with the previous state of our knowledge. Thus I found that cilia which were taken from the mucous membrane of the mouth of a recently killed frog, and were brought to rest in fresh serum of frog's blood by means of hydrogen, on the addition of simple carbonic acid entered into active vibration. This observation surprised me the more, as according to Kühne's statements, carbonic acid is said under all circumstances to have a destructive action upon the ciliary motion, and not even to be capable of removing a quiescent state caused by alkalies. Now in order to understand the modus operandi of carbonic acid it was necessary, so far as possible, to ascertain the conditions under which the ciliary motion is maintained or altered. With this object the experiments now communicated were undertaken.

In the majority of these experiments I required an apparatus which should admit of the action of gases on the object placed in the field of the microscope. For this purpose I had a gas-chamber prepared, so adjusted that it may be used both alone and in connexion with the object disc arranged for heating, and at the same time permitting electrical irritation under the most different circumstances. With this apparatus the most powerful object glasses may be used, and it can, as it is so small, without the least preparation, be used with any microscope. The gas-chamber in fact consists of a flat little box, 80mm. long, 42mm. in breadth, and 8mm. in height. The side walls are of brass, the floor consists of a glass plate hermetically inserted into them by means of a very infusible cement. The cover of the box rests on a projecting ledge of the side walls and can be taken off. When it is used the edges are smeared with a little fat and firmly pressed down, and, if necessary, fastened with two brass screws. I use different covers, all of the same measurements: their length is 77.5mm., their breadth 36mm., their thickness 1.5mm. If I do not wish to use electrical irritation, or to make determinations of temperature on the object plate adapted for warming, I employ a brass cover, in the middle of which is an annular opening of 15mm. in diameter. This opening is closed by a covering glass fastened to the inside of the cover, in the same manner as the floor, and varying in thickness as may be desired. The object is placed in a drop at the side of the covering glass, which on applying the cover is turned towards the inside of the gas-chamber. The distance between the object and the surface of the object disc amounts then to about five or six mm. It is true that the clearness of the field is thus somewhat lessened, but to so slight a degree that it is not necessary to raise the mirror, and that with moderate illumination even narrow diaphragms may be used in the object disc. If it be wished however, to use the gas-chamber on the object disc of Schultze arranged for warming, which transmits only a slender bundle of rays, it is desirable, although in most cases not absolutely necessary, to bring the object closer to the mirror. For this purpose a covering with a wider opening is used, to the inside of which a glass ring 2.5mm. in height is cemented, which is closed from beneath by the covering glass. The distance from the object floating in the drop, on the under surface of the covering glass to the upper surface of the object disc amounts then to only from 2.5 to 3 mm. If it be desired to observe with only a low magnifying power, the drop with the object may be brought also on the glass plate, which forms the floor of the gas-chamber. We might also, although this is less practical, omit the glass-ring and the covering glass, apply a moist chamber according to Recklinghausen's construction to the tube of the microscope, and place this externally on the cover of the gas-chamber. The object comes then on the floor of the gas-chamber. In this case the objective apparatus is situated in a space communicating with the gas-chamber, and can at choice be let down therein through the opening in the cover. Nevertheless through the greater diameter of the opening in the cover we have, even when the objective is brought very far down, satisfactory lateral excursions. With objective apparatus, with not too broad boxes it is sufficient, when the diameter of the opening in the cover amounts to 20mm.

In order to be able to employ galvanic irritation in the gas-chamber, I make use of a glass cover, of the measurements indicated above, in the middle of which is a round opening 15mm. in width, closed inferiorly by a covering glass. On both sides of this opening the cover is perforated by the conducting wires, which in this manner reach the interior of the gas-chamber. Of the arrangement of the electrodes I shall speak on another occasion. The object is now in a drop on the under surface of the covering glass. If we irritate on the object-plate arranged for warming, it is better to use a glass cover with a wider opening, and we can, as above, bring the covering glass lower by means of a glass ring, or employ a Recklinghausen's chamber, and place the object on the floor of the gas-chamber.

In order to conduct the gases through the apparatus, a brass tube of 5mm. in thickness and 3mm. in calibre is screwed into the middle of the two shorter brass sidewalls, over which an indian-rubber tube is drawn. If it be used with the object-plate arranged for warming, it is desirable, on account of the warming of the elastic tube, that the extremities of the brass tubes should project over the edge of the object-plate : a length of 35mm. is sufficient for this purpose. Of course we can, if the longer tubes should be inconvenient, for ordinary use screw on shorter ones.

We may, as has already been seen, also use the gas-chamber as an ordinary vapour-chamber, by, for example, applying to the appended brass tubes small indian-rubber tubes closed with glass stoppers. A few drops of water or a piece of moistened bibulous paper placed on the floor of the gas-chamber, keep the space damp. We have thus this advantage over Recklinghausen's vapour-chamber, that the microscope and the object are not firmly connected with each other. We can at any moment, without the investigation being thereby disturbed, remove the vapour-chamber, and use the microscope for other purposes.

The experiments were for the most part made with cilia, taken from the mucous membrane of the mouth of a living or recently killed frog (Rana temporaria et esculenta). In general a piece of about 0.5mm. in breadth, and 2mm. in length was cut out from the mucous membrane and placed in a drop of the desired fluid. It is unnecessary in doing this to isolate the epithelium : at the edges of the piece of the mucous membrane we can very well observe the ciliary motion, and moreover there are always loose groups of ciliary cells in the preparation. It is of great importance to use carefully cleaned instruments in making the preparation. The slightest trace of alkaline or acid fluid on the point of the scissors or forceps may reverse the result of the experiment.

I sometimes used also cilia from the pericardium of the same animal, and from the mucous membrane of the air-passages of the rabbit. The phenomena entirely agreed in all leading points.

Another series of experiments was undertaken with the ciliary epithelium of different salt water mollusca, and in particular with the epithelium covering the sensitive horns of Planorbis, and with ciliary Epithelium of Anodonta.

Finally the ciliary motion was occasionally observed in different infusoria, particularly in Paramæcium, Balantidium, Plagiotoma and Opalina. The motion of the spermatozoa, which under the same influences undergoes the same changes as that of the ordinary ciliary cells, has also been the subject of observation. Experiments on the peculiar Protoplasm-movements and their conditions follow.

Before passing to the study of the changes which the ciliary motion undergoes under the influence of different agents, it is necessary to premise some remarks on it, as it occurs under normal circumstances. Both its rapidity and its form seem to me to differ entirely from what is generally stated. Its rapidity has been often measured. Krause states as the frequency of the vibrations (in man?) 190-320 in the minute, while Valentin (*Handwörterbuch der Physiologie*, Art. Flimmerbewegung) found it to be only 100-150 in Anodonta.

I find in cilia under normal or nearly normal conditions, the movements at first innumerably rapid, and even the to and fro strokes to follow one another so quickly as to give a continuous visual impression. Distinct vibrations are therefore not at all distinguishable. Seen in profile, the row of cilia appears as a light streak of shade, everywhere of equal height, extending over the outer surface of the epithelial cells. It seems even to be perfectly quiescent, and betrays its motion only by the current it excites in the surrounding fluid. The retardation of the motion is perceptible first from little shadows, which exhibit themselves from time to time with the rapidity of lightning in the apparently homogeneous row. At first these occur but seldom and only in some places, gradually however they follow one another more rapidly and occur more numerously, and finally the greater part of the ciliary row presents the vibrating fluctuation peculiar to ciliary motion. The several cilia are however still far from being distinguishable, much less can their vibrations be reckoned. Only the at first apparently persistent visual impression has now evidently become intermittent. Soon however the vibrations become slower and slower, and after some time it is possible to reckon them. I cannot do this with certainty until the number of vibrations in the second is reduced to 8. Much as this number exceeds that of the above-named investigators, it obtains, as appears from what I have already said, only for a motion already considerably slackened. I must therefore even look upon the motion as already retarded, when the impression of vibration in general arises, to which the phenomenon owes its name. It is in many cases very difficult to observe the degree of rapidity which gives a persistent visual impression, especially when the ciliary cells cannot be investigated in the living animal. The observation succeeds however, very well in little larvæ of Batrachia or in snails, examined alive and whole in the water in which they occur. Infusoria are also very good objects, especially the adoral ciliary spirals of the adherent species, Vorticellina (Epistylis, Carchesium, Vorticella, &c.). In these the row of cilia in full motion gives the impression of a quiescent shadow, in which no ciliary motion whatever is visible. I have, however, sometimes succeeded in finding the motion so accelerated in ciliary cells of a frog, examined fresh in serum and at a somewhat elevated temperature (77°-86° F.), that it no longer gave the impression of vibration.

It would be important to inquire how great the number of vibrations is, which a cilium makes in a second during its maximum motion; the question is, whether this number is different or the same in cilia of different organs and organisms, or whether a deviation from this number of known properties of cilia is demonstrable. On this point I am as yet unable to state anything with certainty. I think, nevertheless, that this number is greater than 12.

After remarks on the form of the motion of the cilium, the author passes to an enumeration of the numerous agents, the influence of which upon ciliary cells in the frog and other vertebrate animals, he has investigated; among these are: hydrogen gas, oxygen gas, and carbonic acid gas; of the latter he says, "The influence of carbonic acid on ciliary motion is therefore duplex. Small quantities of this agent not only prevent the occurrence of the quiescent state, but they also redevelop movements which had ceased in oxygen, atmospheric air, or hydrogen. In larger quantity carbonic acid produces a state of quiescence, combined with the formation of a coagulum in the interior of the cells. Displacement of the carbonic acid by oxygen or hydrogen removes the state of quiescence, while the coagulum is dissolved." A similar series of experiments was carried out upon spermatozoa, at the close of his report of which the author appends the following

General Considerations.

From the investigation above detailed we see what are the external conditions, under which the motion of the cilia and spermatozoa may arise and continue, and what changes it undergoes when these external conditions vary. The question now is, whether it is possible, from the results obtained, in connexion with the other known facts, to draw conclusions as to the essence of ciliary motion, as to the nature of the processes on which it depends.

In order to answer this question it will be advisable, first to glance at the development, structure and chemical composition of the ciliary organs, and to inquire, what analogy in reference to these points exists between the different vibratory apparatus. *All vibratory apparatus, cilia as well as undulating membranes, are developed*, as it appears, *directly from protoplasm.* Two cases may here be distinguished: in the one the vibratory organ is formed from a portion of the most superficial layer, the cortical layer, of the protoplasm; in the second, from the innermost parts of the protoplasm. The latter case seems to be exemplified in the development of the spermatozoa.[1] Often even in this instance, according to Schweigger

---

[1] Only Kölliker still adheres to his former opinion, according to which the spermatozoa are developed solely from the nucleus of the sperm-cells. Conf. Kölliker, *Gewebelehre*, 5 Aufl. 1867, p. 530.

Seidel[1] and v. la Valette St George[2], the whole mass of the protoplasm of the mother cell is used in the formation of the vibrating filament. The first case is very common, and may be very easily studied, especially in the infusoria. In ciliary epithelial cells the formation of the cilia from the protoplasm has not yet been accurately investigated, but it takes place most probably in the same manner as on the surface of the body of the infusoria[3].

The process here commences with the formation of a vitreous, homogeneous elevation on the cortical layer of the body. From the commencement this elevation exhibits undulating movements. The part of the protoplasm of the body situated immediately beneath the newly forming elevation meantime maintains entirely its normal appearance, and no movements are visible in it. It is not clearly distinguishable from the adjoining parts of the cortical layer. Accordingly as one or more cilia are to be developed from the primitive elevation, does the form and further development of this elevation differ. If it serves for the formation of a single cilium, it soon assumes the globular form and extends with rhythmical movements, recurring mostly in irregular, short periods, gradually into a cilium. But if a row of cilia is to be produced from this elevation, the latter acquires immediately a longitudinal ridge form. This ridge becomes, with the progress of its growth, higher and higher, and soon appears as an undulating membrane. When this has attained a certain magnitude, it divides gradually into parallel pieces, which by further division separate into distinct cilia. The division may be perfect or imperfect[4]. The new formation of persistent undulating membranes takes place precisely in the same manner from the cortical layer of the protoplasm, only it does not in this instance proceed to separation into cilia[5]. Never do cilia seem to arise as prolongations or outgrowths of true preformed cell membranes. Formerly, when in every mass of protoplasm an enveloping membrane internally acutely defined was assumed, the cilia were tolerably generally looked upon as prolongations of the cell-membrane. Now however we have no reason for such a view; for as yet the presence of a genuine cell membrane has not been demonstrated in any ciliary cell, or it is only rendered probable that the most superficial layer of each ciliary cell is something else than protoplasm.

[1] "Ueber die Samenkörperchen und ihre Entwickelung," *Arch. f. mikr. Anat.* i. 1865, pp. 309 et sqq.

[2] "Ueber die Genese der Samenkörper," *Arch. f. mikr. Anat.* i. 1865 and iii. 1867.

[3] The most superficial layer of the body of the infusoria must, from its physical and chemical properties, be at once recognised as a denser layer of protoplasm. Only exceptionally does it advance to the formation of true membranes; then however cilia are wanting.

[4] The whole process, which we have here sketched, can with the most desirable distinctness be observed in vorticellæ, which divide, or, better still, in large species of Epistylis (Epist. plicatilis for example) and Opercularia, which on the point of freeing themselves from their stem, form, on that side, a fringe of new cilia. Stylonychiæ and oxytrichæ during the act of division are also very favourable objects.

[5] The development of permanently undulating membranes is easily observed in all oxytrichæ during the act of subdivision.

In some cases the protoplasm itself possesses, even before the cilia are developed from it, a spontaneous mobility, as for example in the mother cells of the seminal corpuscles of many vertebrate animals, according to v. la Valette St George[1]. We do not, however, attach any great importance to this fact, for it is quite established, among other things by observations on infusoria, that both from motionless and persistently immovable protoplasm, movable cilia may be directly developed.

Just as in the mode of development, so also in the structure of the different kinds of ciliary apparatus—so far as in the defective state of our knowledge we can give an opinion—some important points of analogy are exhibited. Of the form we cannot, however, say this; we find thin cylindrical, thick conical, broad undulating membranes, and all possible intervening forms[2]. The occurrence of ciliary motion in general is consequently not connected with any definite form. It is only for the special character of the motion that the form of the ciliary organ is of any importance.

Very analogous are the *optical properties* of cilia, seminal filaments[3] and undulating membranes. All consist of a transparent, tolerably strongly light-refracting, colourless substance, containing neither granules, nor vacuolæ, but being perfectly homogeneous[4]. How they react on polarised light, has not yet been accurately investigated. According to allusions of Valentin's[5], the seminal filaments should possess the property of double refraction. I did not succeed in finding anything of the kind in the cilia of the epithelium of the mouth of the frog. Perhaps the thick and large cilia of many infusoria would afford better results.

All vibrating organs, and especially those of the seminal corpuscles, possess, so far as is deducible from microscopical investigation, in the normal state a certain *firmness (cohesion)* and, of course only within very narrow limits, perfect *elasticity*.

Many possess a very great tendency to splitting[6] in the longitudinal direction, as seen in the large adherent cilia, with a broad base, of the epithelium of the gills of bivalves, but still more frequently and better in the cilia of many infusoria[7]. The division is

---

[1] "Ueber die Genese der Samenkörper," *Arch. f. mikr. Anat.* i. 1865, pp. 403, &c.

[2] All these different forms of ciliary organs are found together in many infusoria, for example, in every Stylonychia.

[3] The so-called tail of the spermatozoon.

[4] According to A. Stuart, with a very strong magnifying power and very favourable illumination, "elongated rows of oblong, quadrangular, rounded off muscular particles, imbedded in a faintly refracting, slightly granular protoplasm," are recognisable with the hairs of the "cirrhi-velum" of opisthobranchii. Conf. *Zeitschrift f. wiss. Zool.* xv. 1865, p. 99. I have not been able to perceive anything of the kind in any single sort of cilia, not even in the large cilia of infusoria.

[5] *Untersuchung der Planzen und Thiergewebe in polarisirtem Lichte*, 1861, p. 305.

[6] Nowhere is this so great as in the cells of the intestinal epithelium of the arthropods (Conf. also Leydig, *Lehrbuch der Histologie*, 1857, p. 832, fig. 177 and p. 835, fig. 181).

[7] Oxytrichinæ, Stylonychia, and Euplotinæ, they being furnished with great and powerful streamers.

in these easily effected by mechanical means, especially by pressure ; we see it however from time to time without being able to assign its cause. Often it affects only the point of the cilium, which then appears to be a bunch of fine capillary fibrillæ ; often too the cilium divides in its whole length from the point to the base, into two, three or several pieces, often of different thickness. Frequently, too, striæ alone are to be seen, without the occurrence of actual division. The cilium divided by splitting becomes actively movable. In cilia of infusoria even in general each fibrilla vibrates independently. Not unfrequently too it happens, that a split cilium by the union of the fibrillæ becomes a whole one, and as such continues to vibrate.

A general property of the ciliary substance, which is of great importance for the production and energy of the ciliary motion, is its power of imbibition. All vibrating organs readily take up water, with increase of their volume, and also, with diminution of the same, easily give off fluid. The capacity for taking up water, seems to be strongest in those cilia, which during life are surrounded by tolerably strongly concentrated saline solutions, above all therefore in the vibratory apparatus of marine animals. These are by the addition of pure water at once destroyed, becoming by swelling up a mucus-like, transparent mass. In the cilia of the mucous membranes of vertebrate animals the imbibition of water takes place somewhat less rapidly. When put into pure water these become paler and thicker. If they stand very closely together on a cell, the swelling will bring them into contact, and cause them to coalesce into a dense mass. These cilia do not appear to be capable of being totally destroyed by water. The same is the case with the spermatozoa. Especially those of amphibia and fishes swell up considerably in water. The cilia on the contrary, which during life are surrounded by fresh water, exhibit in distilled water no changes worth mentioning resembling swelling.

Caustic alkalies even in a state of strong concentration, produce much greater swelling than water; potash causing the greatest, ammonia the slightest. In neutral saline solutions there is a degree of concentration, varying for each salt, at which no swelling or shrinking takes place. Increase of the amount of salt causes shrinking, increase of the amount of water produces swelling, and this swelling is greater in proportion to the amount of water. In general the cells swell more rapidly in alkaline than in neutral saline solutions. Tolerably strongly concentrated solutions of neutral salts, which by themselves produce shrinking or at least are not attended with any swelling, may, when mixed with pure alkali (without water), cause great swelling. The imbibition coefficient of such saline solutions cannot in most cases be raised by acids. Only in the spermatozoa of amphibia and fishes is the opposite noted by Kölliker. I can confirm this for those of the frog. In the cilia of vibrating epithelial cells I have never observed distinct swelling as the result of the addition of acid, though I have observed distinct corrugation, which disappears again on neutralisation with alkali. It seems moreover, that to maintain the normal state of imbibition, oxygen is required. At least we can only on the assumption of this theory explain why cells, which lay in so far as possible indifferent fluids, in so many cases became corrugated sooner when they were brought into an atmosphere of hydrogen, than when they remained in atmospheric air.

Warming to a degree below 104° F. increases the rapidity of imbibition. Cilia from the mucous membrane of the mouth of the frog, for example, swell in water at 86° F. much more rapidly than in water at only 59° F., and in like manner in largely diluted warm saline solutions. This holds good also for the spermatozoa of the frog. Strong electrical currents have a similar effect; this is distinctly perceptible, for example, in cilia of the frog, which are beginning to swell in water.

It is not improbable that the phenomena of swelling, perceptible in cilia and seminal corpuscles, are dependent for the most part on the presence of a certain amount of protagon, which they are said to possess, and which has been demonstrated at least in the spermatozoa. Even Kölliker has expressed this conjecture. The differences between the several varieties of cilia, with reference to their power of imbibition, would then indicate a difference in their amount of protagon.

How important the power of imbibition of the ciliary substance is for the phenomenon of ciliary motion, both our investigations, and those of Kölliker on spermatozoa in particular, have in numerous instances shown. In imbibition lie the most important mechanical conditions on which the occurrence of the motion depends. A great part of the changes which ciliary motion undergoes through external agents, depend mainly on the modifications of the imbibition state of the cilia.

If the amount of fluid in the cilium falls, through shrinking, beneath the normal, the excursion range and the frequency diminish, in proportion to circumstances, to complete arrest and vice versa. This goes far to explain the action of water, alkalies, and many reagents.

If only the normal state of imbibition be maintained by the addition of water and of oxygen, the movement is maintained uninterruptedly, even for weeks after the death of the whole organism, and is first arrested by decomposition. In half decomposed, putrid mucous membranes, the movement is still found active after the addition of water. *No trace of rigidity therefore, corresponding to that of muscle, exists in the cilia.* The fact that the state of quiescence produced by heat usually occurs at the temperature at which myosin suddenly coagulates, we consider to be insufficient to justify the assumption of the existence of a *spontaneously* coagulating substance in the cilia.

In the action of acids, ether, alcohol and sulphuret of carbon the change in the imbibition-state seems in general to be of less importance, for it appears that both in greatly swollen and in shrivelled cilia these have first a reviving and then a retarding action. For the same reasons the retarding action of chloroform also does not depend on change in the amount of fluid in the cilia. At present it does not seem possible more accurately to assign the cause on which the exciting influence exercised in so many cases on ciliary motion by acids, ether, alcohol and sulphuret of carbon, depends. The facts already quoted are for the most part in favour of the view, that this influence is rather the result of a direct increase of the chemical changes on which the ciliary motion depends, than on improvement in the mechanical conditions or on diminution of the resistances in the cilium. At all events this influence is very remarkable also in those agents, which are distinguished by the magnitude of their mechanical action, as water, neutral saline solutions, alkalies, which is made probable especially by the changes in frequency. These two actions may oppose or support each other, and the total influence of an agent (excitation or retardation of the movement) will depend on the magnitude of each action, and on the direction in which each was exerted.

It can scarcely be matter of doubt, that elevation of temperature, and very probably also electrical currents, are indebted for their exciting influence principally to an increase of the physiological metamorphosis of matter in the cell, and only in a slight degree to the alterations of the mechanical conditions (greater swelling) directly caused thereby.

It appears not difficult to discover the reason of the retardation which follows the continued action of acids, ether, alcohol, chloroform and heat. The turbidity, distinctly perceptible with the microscope, mostly finely granular, which exhibits itself in the cells and cilia, on the action of ether, alcohol, chloroform, metallic salts, besides in the spermatozoa of amphibia and fishes, also on the action of acids, even of carbonic acid, and the occurrence of the same turbidity on heating to about 113° F., show that the cilia contain albuminous bodies coagulated by the agents above-mentioned. This coagulation may be looked upon as the cause of the cessation of the motion. That the state of quiescence, produced by these agents, is often present before an optical change of cells or cilia is perceptible, is not irreconcilable with this view, for we know that albuminous masses in the first stage of coagulation may still be perfectly transparent. The coagulated albumen, by which the cilia become firmer, must even on purely mechanical grounds be an impediment to the production of the movement. In fact by its resolution the movement may again be called into play: in fixed acids by alkalies; in carbonic acid by air or alkalies; in ether, alcohol and chloroform by air.

Of the solution of the fundamental question, *on what chemical processes the ciliary motion depends*, there of course exists, in the defective state of our knowledge even of the qualitative chemical composition of the ciliary substance, but very little prospect. Nevertheless from the existing material some general conclusions may be drawn with reference to the nature of the chemical processes on which the ciliary motion is founded, and respecting the chemical conditions whereupon the life of the cilia depends.

It indeed is at once evident, that not much is thus gained towards the explanation of the ciliary movement. For we arrive at the result, that the metamorphosis of matter of the cilia agrees in the main points with that of the muscles, according to the most recent statements of Ranke, as well as with that of the nerves, and perhaps also with that of many other tissues. In the first place this analogy is apparent in the fact, that *every sort of vibrating movement may exist and continue for a long time, while neither oxygen, nor any oxidisable substance is supplied to the cell.*

That the ciliary motion can exist independently of the absorption of oxygen from surrounding matters, is shown by the experiments with hydrogen and illuminating gas free from carbonic acid : we saw both the movements of the different ciliary cells and those of the spermatozoa continue for some time, even for hours, in a medium perfectly free from oxygen. The fact that completely isolated cells or groups of cells continue to vibrate in pure solutions of common salt of from 0.5°/₀ to 0.7°/₀, or in other as far as possible indifferent solutions of inorganic salts, proves that the motion is not directly dependent on the addition of organic, oxidisable material. And it appears even, that the ciliary cells can dispense with the supply of organic substance much longer than with that of oxygen, for the movement continues for days in the saline solutions, if only oxygen be supplied in sufficient quantity.

From the two fundamental facts, that all ciliary motion can continue for a time both without a supply of oxygen and without a supply of organic substance, it follows that in each ciliary cell, in each seminal corpuscle, a certain store of chemical energy is laid up, capable of providing, for a time, for the maintenance of its life and of its activity. But that oxygen is indispensable to the continuation of the movement, proves further, that in the chemical process with which the production of the latter is connected, the consumption of oxygen plays a part. Hence it follows that *each cell,* besides a supply of oxidisable substance, *must possess also a stock of oxygen stored up, which is consumed in the action of the cell.* This stock of oxygen can saturate only a very small part of the oxidisable material stored up in the cell. If it be consumed, the cilium can then, by taking up oxygen in the gaseous form from without, spare the surrounding parts. This appears from the revival of the motion from the state of hydrogen quiescence, and from the acceleration which a supply of oxygen develops in movements which had been retarded in the current of hydrogen.

But in the cases too, where there is no reason to assume that the oxygen contained in the cell is diminished, the cell readily takes up more oxygen and uses it in increasing its physiological activity. We must deduce this from the facts above mentioned, namely, that the movements of fresh ciliary cells which have been retarded by the short action of tolerably concentrated solutions of chloride of sodium, of pure water, or gradually in indifferent fluids, almost suddenly re-acquire greater activity through the influence of a stream of pure oxygen. Although therefore the occurrence of the ciliary motion is not necessarily connected with the taking up of oxygen from without, the *intensity* of the phenomenon is in great part determined by the amount of free oxygen in the surrounding medium. This is proved also by the experiments where the ciliary cells were placed in gaseous mixtures of hydrogen and different quantities of oxygen.

Hence we may now assume, that the extent of the physiological metamorphosis of matter in the ciliary cell, is determined by the

contemporaneous amount of oxygen in the surrounding medium.—
Whether the cell is also in a condition, to attract to itself disengaged
oxygen from the surrounding parts, and to use it for the maintenance
of its physiological activity, as Kühne, resting on experiments with
oxy-hæmaglobine, asserts, I leave undecided, though I think it not
improbable.

From these few results, I regret to say, no satisfactory idea of the
peculiar nature of the chemical process on which the ciliary motion
depends, is obtainable. We do not know the substances which con-
sume the oxygen present in the cell, with development of vital force ;
we know not what are the products of the metamorphosis of matter
in the living cell, whether carbonic acid, other acids, or, and if so,
what nitrogenous products of decomposition, are formed.

A single series of facts is in favour of the view, that the chemical
processes taking place in the cell in action, are connected with *acidification*. In the first place the addition of a little alkali promotes the arous-
ing of the ciliary cells out of the " heat rigidity (Wärmestarre)"—
other exciting means, as *acids*, water, ether, fail to produce this effect ;
2ndly, the retardation caused by excess of alkali, is not unfrequently
removed by rapid warming, and replaced by considerable acceleration—
on the other hand, a state of quiescence produced by acid or water
could never be removed by the application of warmth, nor the
retardation caused by acid or water be prevented[1].

By the establishment of all these facts relating to the metamorphosis of matter in the ciliary cells, important analogies between the
vital phenomena of the ciliary cells and those of the muscles and
nerves are indicated. These tissues also can live for a long time
without taking up oxygen or oxidisable material. They too develop
acid during their action. These analogies increase, moreover, when
we consider that the ciliary cells, as I have recently shown, have an
electromotor action. It is at least most probable, that the electromotor forces found by us in the mucous membrane of the mouth of
the frog, are to be sought in the ciliary cells, and not in the cup cells
(perhaps, however, in both).

In conclusion I shall mention some important inquiries relating
to the connexion between *cilia* and *protoplasm*. Very recently the
question of the anatomical connexion between the cilia and the
subjacent protoplasm has been repeatedly under discussion. Investigators have often thought that they could demonstrate the existence
of prolongations of the cilia into the deeper layers of the protoplasm ;
and the opinion has been expressed, that the ciliary motion was and ·

---

[1] A formation of acid can be directly proved neither in the cilia nor in the
whole mass of the ciliary cells, for it is impossible to obtain ciliary cells in
sufficient quantity, free from admixture with other histiological elements.

In passing I may here point out that the living *protoplasm* of amœbæ and
infusoria is feebly alkaline or neutral, but that it may also have a faintly acid
reaction. I tried this by feeding the organisms in question with granules of
litmus, which remain blue for hours. When a trace of carbonic acid was passed
over the preparation, the granules within the amœba were instantly coloured
red, without the protoplasm-movements ceasing.

must be excited through contractions in the protoplasm subjacent to the streamers.

In fact some observations certainly favour this kind of theory. Different observers (Valentin, Buhlmann, Friedreich, Eberth, Marchi) think they have distinctly seen that the cilia do not sit externally on the surface of the cell, but that they penetrate more deeply into the protoplasm. But especially A. Stuart[1] has communicated some observations, which, for one case at least, should make the correctness of the view in question probable. He saw the contents of the ciliary epithelium cells of the velum of young eolidinæ divided into a number of striæ running parallel to the longitudinal axis of the cell, and which appeared to be continued through the hyaline row or cover directly into the cilia. These protoplasm filaments exhibited in cells, whose cilia were active, brisk movements, by which the nucleus of the cell was pushed hither and thither. If the cilia were quiescent, the nucleus also was usually at rest ; if they began their movements, the displacement of the nucleus also recommenced[2]. According to Rabl-Rückhard[3], the so-called continuations of the cilia observed by Eberth and Marchi in the interior of the cell are ascribed to confusion with folds in the cell membrane. There are many liabilities to mistake, and no continuations of the cilia in the interior of the protoplasm are demonstrable. The cells are in most ciliary epithelium cells, simple appendices, outgrowths from the cortical layer of the protoplasm.

Moreover it is quite certain, that the protoplasm of most ciliary cells possesses no active mobility. Of this I have convinced myself by frequently repeated observations. And by this fact the theory is at once refuted, that the impulse to the ciliary motion proceeds from *contractions* in the protoplasm. Besides the incorrectness of this opinion is proved by observations on spermatozoa.

It is quite another question, whether it be a requisite for the production of the motion, that the cilia should still be in connexion with the cells. To this too belongs the inquiry, whether the stimulus for each movement of the cilium proceeds from the cell, or whether the impulse to motion is developed in the cilium itself.

The first opinion is tolerably generally received, and it is founded chiefly on the fact, that cilia, removed from the cell, no longer perform movements. Now, if we assume that the cause of the movement lies in the cilium and not in the cell, this result is not surprising, since the means, whereby the cilium is removed from the cell, are such that the vital capacity of both may be destroyed.

There are, however, other reasons in favour of the view, that the impulse to movement proceeds not from the cilium, but from the protoplasm in which it is planted. In the cilia of the infusoria,

---

[1] Stuart, *Ueber die Flimmerbewegung*, Inaug. Diss. Dorpat., 1867, p. 12. The accompanying drawing is unfortunately not calculated to inspire confidence.

[2] Stuart does not say whether the movements of the protoplasm filaments were regularly periodical and isochronous with those of the cilia, or how else.

[3] "Einiges ueber Flimmerepithel und Becherzellen," *Archiv f. Anat. und Physiologie*, 1868, p. 72.

which are under the control of the will, no other possibility is imaginable, than that the normal stimulus is given through the protoplasm. But beyond this, other facts remain, which throw weight into the scale. Above all the *isochronism* of the movements of all cilia implanted on one and the same cell shows, that the stimulus which gives rise to them proceeds from a common source, consequently from the ground on which all these cilia together rest. The significance of this fact is increased by an observation, of the correctness of which it is easy to satisfy one's self, namely that the frequency in two closely adjoining cells may be very different; sometimes the cilia on the one cell make scarcely one, while those on the next make five and more vibrations in the second. If the cilia are brought into a state of quiescence by the effect, for example, of alkalies or acid vapours, the cilia of one and the same cell are roused almost always simultaneously on the neutralisation of the injurious fluid, while this is very often not the case with two adjoining cells. These observations are in favour of the correctness of the above opinion, as is equally the fact that the movements of all cilia commence at the base, and are transmitted thence towards the point.

Nevertheless it might be doubted whether the impulse to movement proceeds actually from the proper protoplasm of the cell, or perhaps simply from the coverlike border which usually forms the common basis of all the cilia of a cell. We think this forms a question of a very subordinate kind, as looking at the chemical and physical properties of the outermost boundary layer of the protoplasm, we cannot admit the existence of an actual cell-membrane, but must consider this to be only a denser layer of protoplasm, such as we find on the free surfaces of almost all living protoplasm-like bodies, a denser layer, in fact, which, internally, gradually passes into protoplasm of less density.

It is certain, at all events, that a great part of the cell-protoplasm may be lost, without the movements ceasing or changing. Several times I have seen whole rows of cilia from the gills of oysters oscillate for minutes, after the greater part of the cell-protoplasm with the nuclei was cut off. In like manner we sometimes see seminal corpuscles, of mammalia for example, in motion, notwithstanding that the head is wanting, and that it is often doubtful whether a part of the middle portion is still in connection with the movable caudal extremity. Hence it appears, in any case, that the nucleus does not give the impulse to the motion, and that, if the protoplasm of the cell (corresponding to the middle portion of the seminal corpuscle) be really the source of the irritation, the part situated directly beneath the cilia is sufficient to keep up the rhythmical irritation.

With the question which at present engages our attention, some interesting facts, to which we shall here give a place, are closely connected. It appears that they afford a proof, not only that the impulse to the movement of the cilia proceeds, in the normal state, from the cell-body, but at the same time that the stimulus, in such ciliary epithelium at least, whose cells are still normally connected with one another, may be transmitted from cell to cell. If we look at an oscillating strip of epithelium, best a piece of the gills of a Mussel, we observe at once, that the oscillations of the cilia on adjoining cells, are not isochronous, but follow one another in a fixed order, and the wave always runs in the same direction[1]. This direction is usually rectilinear, but with reference to the surface of vibration of the cilia it is not in all places similar.

Another remarkable phenomenon I observed in the epithelium of the gills of bivalves. The movements were slightly retarded by rather concentrated solutions of chloride of sodium; in different places the movements were in long rows of cells completely extinguished. Suddenly in one or more of these rows the movements began anew, and indeed at once with great force and frequency. After from 15 to 20 seconds all was again quiet. After some time the movement suddenly began once more in the same manner, and this took place several times consecutively. Still more remarkable is a similar observation made by Purkinje and Valentin on the lateral gills of the mollusca, and of which I too have sometimes satisfied myself. It is very well described by Valentin in the following words: "After a row of cilia has for a time vibrated uniformly and in a definite direction, it turns suddenly with a jerk, and likewise uniformly, just as a wheeling column of soldiers, in the opposite direction, now vibrates in this direction, and not unfrequently turns with a fresh similar, uniform, but opposite jerk back again to its original direction. In general the column is sharply defined anteriorly and posteriorly, while cilia close to these continue more independently to vibrate undisturbed."

These observations indeed are most in favour of the view, that the impulse to the movement of the cilia arises not in the cilia themselves, but proceeds from the cells. Against this however, are some other facts, which might rather lead to the opinion, that also in the substance of the cilium itself, independently of the protoplasm of the cells, stimuli to movement, and indeed to rhythmical movement, may arise. The observation, which would solve all this at once, namely that of a completely isolated, vibrating cilium, has unfortunately not been made. However the filamentary spermatozoa of some lower animals (especially certain worms and arthropods) appear to afford examples of automatically excitable cilia. According to the investigations hitherto made these filaments are not divided into morphologically different parts (analogous to the head, middle portion and tail of other spermatozoa), but seem to consist throughout their whole length of the same substance[2]. It does not however, follow from this, that all cilia are automatically excitable: for it is also conceivable that in those cases where the cilium is connected with protoplasm, the stimulus should always proceed from the latter. But

---

[1] This phenomenon is also very apparent in parts of the body which are studded with cilia, but where a combination of cells is not perceptible. Thus in many of the lower organisms. The radiatæ are indebted to it for their name.

[2] I have myself no experience respecting the structure of these corpuscles. It is conceivable that on closer examination they also should reveal a complex structure.

the observations which are in some measure in favour of the view, that in the latter cases also automatic irritation is possible, are the following. Often only the points of the cilia move, while the parts situated more towards the base are completely at rest. This I have already mentioned, and among others in treating of the hydrogen-state of quiescence in the frog I have shown, that these vibrations take place rhythmically, but almost always are no longer isochronous in the different cilia of one and the same cell. Such a phenomenon is often observed in the cilia of infusoria (the terminal cilia, for example, of Euplotes) whose points are split into fibrillæ. The principal mass of the cilium, which otherwise remains in all parts perfectly moveable, is in this case often for a time quite still, while the fibrillæ at the point make active movements. These facts are to be explained only in two ways: we may assume that the ciliary substance is automatically excitable, or that it is excitable only through a process of irritation proceeding from the protoplasm, which may be transmitted through a part of the cilium, without producing motion in this part. Both solutions are defensible.

In conclusion let us here reflect on the results, remarkable, in so many points of view, which the investigation of the influence of electrical irritation has yielded. Above all I consider the observations of the action of a single current of vibration, of importance, because they so strikingly prove, how certain comparisons, which are so readily made between ciliary and muscular substance, are nevertheless not completely applicable. We saw that as the result of momentary electrical irritation, a simple phenomenon, comparable with the contraction of the muscle, never took place, but that the irritation manifests itself as an exaltation of, though under certain known circumstances also as a hindrance to, the periodico-rhythmical action of the cilium. This fact admits of two explanations: either the ciliary substance itself is not electrically excitable, and then the action of the stimulus depends on an exaltation of the periodico-rhythmical activity of the protoplasm, on which the cilia sit, probably accompanied by an alteration of the sensibility of the ciliary substance to the stimulus coming from the protoplasm; or the ciliary substance itself is excitable, and then the cause of the periodicity of the movements lies in its peculiar structure. Whichever of the two explanations is to be looked upon as the correct one, this fact at all events proves that there are fundamental differences between muscular and ciliary substance. It warns us, in connexion with the other results of our investigation, against the attempt, which has of late often been made, to establish an almost complete analogy between the phenomena observed in the muscular, and those seen in the ciliary apparatus. Nor do I think the study of the analogies existing between ciliary and protoplasm motion, promises much useful result, so long as the conditions giving rise to protoplasm-movement, and the changes it undergoes through the influence of different agents, under different circumstances, are not more thoroughly known. Perhaps we shall even soon find an opportunity of communicating something towards the supplying of this want.

28—2

REVIEWS AND NOTICES OF BOOKS.

ON THE ANATOMY OF VERTEBRATES. By RICHARD OWEN, F.R.S., &c. Vol. III. MAMMALS. London: Longmans, Green & Co.

THE volume before us is the concluding part of a work of very large design, in which the learned author has sought to give an outline of the organisation of the animal kingdom. Begun in the Lectures on the Comparative Anatomy and Physiology of the Invertebrate Animals published in 1843, this design has been continued after the lapse of many years in the Anatomy of Vertebrates of which this is the third, the largest, and concluding volume. We congratulate Professor Owen on the completion of his task, and we congratulate the public on the acquisition of a most useful summary of a large amount of work which has been done in the field of Vertebrate Anatomy, and particularly of what has been done by the illustrious professor himself. Professor Owen's contributions form a most important part of the anatomical literature of the last forty years, and we think it an advantage of this book that it makes copious reference to those contributions, and even that it puts prominently forward his claims to priority of discovery in matters in which he considers that the public voice has not done him justice; yet we are constrained to pronounce the perpetual *ego* a literary flaw, and to regret that Professor Owen cannot, as a great man ought, in patience abide the verdict of the future. History in adjudging him his place will form its opinion, not from the book which is now before us, nor from the angry polemics of the present day, but from his massive and beautiful monographs in palæontological and recent anatomy, and from his work in the Royal College of Surgeons and British Museums. It will judge of his philosophic speculations not by their shortcomings, but by what they added to our previous knowledge, and for the rest it will be content to say that Owen was pertinacious in his opinions, and averse to change them save when the initiative of the change had been taken by himself.

The Mammalian skeleton having been considered in Volume II. the present volume with the exception of the chapter entitled "General conclusions," is devoted entirely to the other systems of Mammals. Naturally, some chapters evince a greater amount of care and ability than others; thus, the chapter on the dental system is most elaborate; those on the alimentary canal, the generative system and the generative products are full of interest; and the chapter on the nervous system contains a great amount of valuable matter; but we venture to think that those on the muscular and the absorbent systems are susceptible of great improvement. The chapter on the muscular system begins philosophically with an account of the diaphragm, that being the muscle specially characteristic of mammals;

it then proceeds to give some account of the muscles in different natural orders, beginning with the monotremata. We admit that mammalian myology is a difficult subject to treat of in a compendious manner, but it might have been made more interesting than it is here; the facts might have been better selected and grouped, and in some instances might have been more accurately stated; also it is to be regretted that a comprehensive comparison has not been given of the muscles of the limbs in the various types of Mammalia. A number of pages are devoted, and very justly, to the myology of the horse. At page 30 is the following sentence:—

"The 'trapezius' consists of that part only which is called the ascending portion in the human subject, and which is inserted into the posterior margin of the spine of the scapula."

And doubtless it is so described in old veterinary books, including 'Perceval.' But it is not so in the horse; and hippotomists have long since recognised the mistake. The trapezius muscle of the horse consists of a cervical as well as a dorsal part; but it happens that these parts are separated by an aponeurosis stretching, without interruption by muscular fibres, to the commencement of the spine of the scapula; and this confused veterinarians, but ought not to have confused Professor Owen. The next sentence proceeds:—

"The 'sterno-mastoid' is present, but the 'levator anguli scapulæ,' the cleido-mastoid and the clavicular portions of the trapezius and deltoid are all replaced by the muscular expansion which, taking its origin from the paroccipital and from the transverse processes of some of the cervical vertebræ, passes downward in front of the head of the humerus and descends along the inner surface of the forearm, into which it is ultimately inserted."

But, at page 53, referring to the "*quadrumana* below the Apes," is the following statement:—

"In these the 'levator anguli scapulæ' is distinct from the 'serratus magnus'; but is the fore part of that muscle in Baboons."

Yet, the levator anguli scapulæ is described as represented in the horse in the manner quoted, and this, notwithstanding that an accurate account is given of the cervical as well as dorsal origin of the serratus magnus both in the horse and the ox, and in the latter instance a graphic description is added of the suspensory action of the muscle. Nothing could be more palpable than that the levator anguli scapulæ of man corresponds to the cervical part of the serratus magnus in all those animals in which a cervical part of that muscle is present.

The reader who expects, from the space given to the subject, to obtain from this book any conception of the remarkable arrangements in the lower parts of the horse's limbs, will we fear be rather disappointed. Even the lumbricales and interossei muscles, the presence of which must be a matter of wonder and interest to any thinking mind, are passed over in silence. A paragraph at page 35 is devoted to an enumeration of the ligaments of the fore limb, and the only reference made to a ligament which is so important that its weight is possibly greater than that of all the other ligaments of the limb put together, namely the suspensory ligament, is this:—"ligament from the inner splint bone (metacarpal II.) to the sesamoid behind the metacarpo-phalangial joint." Unfortunately it happens that in veterinary phraseology the great metacarpal bone is liable to be called the second, from being the second of the three which exist in the horse, and the ligament in question is a huge structure descending from the upper end of the great metacarpal bone.

Having exemplified the occurrence of the three kinds of lever in the body after the time-honoured fashion, our author proceeds to make the following generalization on the actions of joints.

"The joints in the mammalian skeleton are chiefly of two kinds, 'gingly-moid' or hinge-joints, and 'enarthrodial' or ball-and-socket joints. In man the former are less definitely fitted for motion on one plane than in most brutes. The arm and forearm move in concentric planes upon the elbow-joint; the knee-joint allows a certain rocking motion of the leg upon the thigh; the ankle-joint has a greater latitude of motion, and the foot may be directed out of the plane of the leg's motion."

We cannot see the joints maltreated in this way without protesting. Mammals have numerous joints which are neither gingly-moid nor enarthrodial; and the paths in which the articular surfaces move in man are in the instances mentioned perfectly definite. In neither knee-joint nor ankle-joint is there any rocking motion allowed; but in the knee, when it is bent and then only, a most definite description of rotation is permitted. There certainly are peculiarities in the joints of man distinguishing them from those of other animals, but the paragraph quoted does not do them justice.

The part of the chapter on the nervous system which will excite most attention is the description of the cerebral convolutions. Referring to his lectures on this subject delivered before the Royal College of Surgeons of England in 1842, as well as to his communication on the Cheetah in 1833, the learned author goes on to describe and compare the convolutions in different animals, and illustrates the subject very fully with sketches in which the fissures are marked with figures and the convolutions with letters. He proposes a nomenclature for the fissures, and another for the convolutions which he compares with the names proposed by Rolando, Leuret, and Gratiolet. A footnote (p. 146) is devoted to a complaint against "anthropotomists," because they "still describe the connections and course of the 'crura rhinencephali' as the origins of the olfactory nerve," and for some reason or other the weight of his displeasure falls on the editors of the 7th edition of Quain's Anatomy. This is curious enough, for on turning up that book we find, at the place to which Professor Owen directs us, and midway between a line which he quotes, and a passage which he professes to paraphrase, this statement—"The bulbous part is therefore rather to be regarded as an olfactory lobe of the cerebrum than as a part of a true nerve." Indeed, notwithstanding Professor Owen's gentle sneer, we must say that we have never met an "Anthropotomist" yet who was not quite aware of what is to be said in favour of that proposition. That our readers may judge for themselves whether there is any resemblance between a 'paraphrase' by Professor Owen and the passage paraphrased, we shall quote both, and leave them to make the comparison. Professor Owen writes :—

"Some even maintain the view by such remarks as the following : 'As it is known that in the first development of the ear, the peripheral part or vestibular expanse, as well as the rest of the acoustic nerve, is originally formed by the extension of a hollow vesicle from the first or hindmost fœtal encephalic compartment, so in the case of the crus cerebri, although the peripheral or distributed part (crus rhinencephali or olfactory nerve) is of separate origin from the hemispheric bulb, this latter part is comparable in its origin with the acoustic vesicle.' I have paraphrased the argument of the editors of the 7th edition of Quain's Anatomy (Vol. II. p. 584), to show that development, as a vesicle in connection with nervous centres, is no ground of homology or homotypy. Whenever a false homology has to be maintained, the earliest and obscurest phenomena of embryonal development are usually resorted to in support of such view."

On turning up the passage referred to in Quain's Anatomy we find the following :—

"The question whether the olfactory bulbs ought to be considered as nerves or cerebral lobes is, if testified by reference to the history of development, not so simple as might at first appear. It is in favour of their being regarded as lobes that in the lower vertebrate animals, the olfactory bulbs are generally recognised by comparative anatomists as additional encephalic lobes, and that in most mammals they are much larger proportionally than in man, and frequently contain a cavity or ventricle in their interior, and further that in their minute structure they nearly agree with the cerebrum; but as it is well known that in the first development of the eye, the peripheral part or retina as well as the rest of the optic nerve, is originally formed by the extension of a hollow vesicle from the first fœtal encephalic compartment, so in the case of the olfactory nerve, although the peripheral or distributed part is o separate origin from the olfactory bulb, the latter part is comparable in its origin with the optic vesicle."

There is no reference here to the acoustic nerve at all. We need only note further that no Anthropotomist has ever been so odd as to describe the olfactory bulb as the distributed part of the crus cerebri, and that there is abundant evidence that the editors of the 7th edition of Quain (see p. 768) are perfectly aware that the primary auditory vesicle is "produced solely by invagination of the integument, and has no original connection with the brain," and therefore is not comparable with either the retina or the olfactory bulb; so that altogether it would have been better for the learned professor to bear his mistakes on his own shoulders and not lay them on other people. Every scientific observer makes errors, but a man need not be scientific to be able to quote accurately.

It would have been well if our author, before making the strong statement which we have quoted with regard to the use of embryology in helping the elucidation of morphological points had made himself more thoroughly acquainted with the results of researches which have cleared away the obscurity from some of the phenomena of development. The paragraph which we have been considering is not the only evidence of weakness in embryology. At page 241, we are told that Meckel's cartilage has no "relation of a mould to the malleus."

"This ossicle, starting as a wart-like prominence from the wall of the tympanic cavity, is precociously developed on the inner side of Meckel's cartilage, early showing its long process above, and quite distinct from that cartilage or its capsule."

That both incus and malleus are derived from Meckel's cartilage is, notwithstanding this, most easily demonstrated and perfectly certain. True, it has been remarked that their ossification begins in the periosteum, so that at a certain period they exhibit a hollow within them filled with cartilage (Kölliker's *Entwicklungsgeschichte*, p. 216), and thus it happens that the long process which does not entirely surround the cartilage may be seen above it; but that is no justification of the statement quoted. Curiously enough, Rathke describes the origin of the long process of the malleus from Meckel's cartilage in a passage referred to by Professor Owen, a few lines further on. The narrative proceeds to give an account of the development of the stapes, in which it is never mentioned that it is the proximal part of the band within the second visceral process. Indeed this passage, the account of the cochlea and that of the brain, are all written as if Reichert had never lived; and we make bold to think that they all materially suffer by it.

It is admitted (p. 536) that the disposition of the branches of the arch of the aorta and their anomalies, especially the latter, are explicable by reference to modified or arrested stages of development. The number of embryonic arches, however, is not mentioned, but a footnote runs thus :—

"I have failed to find in any embryo of bird or mammal more than three pairs of primitive vascular arches, conveying the blood, in that form, from the heart to the dorsal aorta......But the notion of the human embryo having gills and gill-slits tickles the fancy......."

The answer to this is, that nobody supposes that the human embryo has gills; and that as to the number of the arches in birds and mammals, since Von Baer and Rathke first described five pairs, it has always been understood that they are never all present at one time, and that it is very seldom that more than three pairs co-exist.

A great deal of minute anatomy is professedly taught in this volume, but it is not particularly precise, and is rather behind the present state of science. Thus, following the course of the optic nerve into the eyeball, it is said that "on entering the cavity of the eyeball, the neurine forms a slight prominence before expanding into the sheet called 'retina;'" the yellow spot of Soemmerring "is a modification of the retina;" but no explanation is given of the properties of either optic pore or yellow spot. Jacob's membrane is described as a "delicate transparent membrane," and so on; but its bacillary structure is not even hinted at. "The cellular structure of the part of the hyaloid, at the circumference of the lens, when demonstrated by inflation or injection, produces the appearance, called by its describer Petit, 'Canal godronné,'" "If a small part of the spiral plate (of the cochlea) be magnified, the filaments are seen, as they diverge upon the osseous part, to subside or flatten on approaching the middle tract, and there to anastomose in loops ; the neurilemma being continued on to blend with the membranous part of the spiral plate." In the chapter on absorption, it is stated unhesitatingly that each columnar epithelial cell of the villi "becomes gradually filled with a clear globule of refractive fluid like oil ;" that "the oil-like globule undergoes changes which mainly consist in a sub-division or reduction of the globule to the granular state," and that "these granules or molecules escape by a rupture or solution of the cell wall." These short extracts will give some idea of how questions in minute anatomy are touched on. But the most interesting thing connected with histology in the volume is, that the author formally declares his abandonment of the theory of omnis cellula e cellulâ, and this change in general doctrine affects histological details. At page 499, the following statement is made:—

"In using the terms 'cell' and 'nucleated cell', I would not be understood as implying that such are progeny of previous cells, owing their origin to a genetic process, inherited from 'one primordial form into which life was first breathed.' The cell is one of the forms in which proteine matter in solution may be aggregated, with limitation of size and definition of shape, such forms differing from crystals in being rounded instead of angular, as shewn in the instructive experiments of Rainey."

In the description of epidermis these principles are applied thus:

"Upon the papillose surface of the derm, in the embryo, albuminoid atoms in the solution exuding therefrom formify as cells, and between the outermost of these, condensed and dried by exposure after birth, and the derm, formifaction continues, throughout life, to produce a precipitate of cells."

This sentence occurs as portion of a description of the epidermis, and not as an illustration of the mode of growth of texture ; but we have quoted it to illustrate how the newly espoused doctrine of formifaction operates on the author's mind in describing histological detail.

The same doctrine leads him now to regard the theory which he formerly put forward to explain the "parthenogenesis" of the aphides as "fundamentally erroneous." But at the same time that he abandons that theory, he claims for it that it is the same as Mr Darwin's pangenesis.

"It may be a defect of power, but I fail after every endeavour to appreciate the 'fundamental difference' between Mr Darwin's cell-hypothesis of 1868 and mine of 1849 " (p. 813).

Now one does not require to be a believer in Mr Darwin's hypothesis to see that it is something entirely different from Professor Owen's, and that the difference may be more fully expressed than has been done by Mr Darwin himself. Both theories assume certain hypothetical gemmules, but that is all their resemblance,

The gemmules assumed by Professor Owen are "progeny of the primary impregnated germ-cell," which, not being "required for the formation of the body," "remain unchanged, and become included in that body," and may subsequently produce a new animal. The gemmules assumed by Mr Darwin are supposed to be thrown off from the germinal matter of every cell throughout the body, and to become aggregated so as to transmit to the offspring of the whole animal the peculiarities of the individual parts. Thus the two theories differ completely, both in what they assume and in what they were framed to explain.

Professor Owen makes another claim to anticipation of Mr Darwin in advancing hypotheses; for in a long note in which he repels the supposition that he claims to have promulgated the theory of natural selection, he renews the assertion that he anticipated Mr Darwin in the basis of that theory, and founds it on a passage in which, in 1850, he pointed out that large animals are more liable than small ones to extinction by seasonal extremes, introduction of new enemies, &c., and that the small ones have the additional advantage over the large in being more prolific. This passage he considers, as pointing out "the preservation of favoured races in the struggle for life;" and so it does, but not in the sense which Mr Darwin explains: it does not point out how the weak individuals of one species are most likely to perish, nor how minute differences may give an advantage to individuals over others of the same species, nor the effect of these individuals being left to perpetuate the race. The facts of the case seem to be very simple, and it is a great pity to see scientific books defaced with personal disputes. Still more to be deplored are offensive allusions to men who are held in high and deserved estimation; and therefore it is impossible too much to regret that so great a scientific man as Professor Owen should have put on record the most unjust remarks which he has written (p. 802) concerning another man so great in science as is Sir Charles Lyell.

The chapter devoted to general conclusions opens with an interesting account of the impressions made on the author's mind in 1830 by the discussions between Cuvier and Geoffroy Saint-Hilaire, and how his opinions were subsequently modified with regard to morphology, and the succession of species. The author goes on to show proof that this succession has been due to "secondary causes," and to point out how "the guesses made by those who have given the rein to the imaginative faculty in attempts to explain the mode of operation of the derivative law have mainly proved repellant to its study," reviewing unfavourably the theories of Lamarck, St Hilaire and Darwin. He then states his own opinion.

"Being unable to accept the volitional hypothesis, or that of impulse from within, or the selected force exerted by outward circumstances, I deem an innate tendency to deviate from parental type, operating through periods of adequate duration, to be the most probable nature, or way of operation, of the secondary law, whereby species have been derived one from the other" (p. 807).

"Species owe as little to the accidental concurrence of environing circumstances, as Kosmos depends on a fortuitous concourse of atoms. A purposive route of development and change, of correlation and interdependence, manifesting intelligent Will, is as determinable in the succession of races as in the development and organisation of the individual. Generations do not vary accidentally, in any and every direction; but in preordained, definite, and correlated courses" (p. 808).

The question of germs is next taken up. The experiments of Pasteur and Pouchet are referred to, and the author, with characteristic decision, ranks himself on the side of Pouchet. To his mind, the following experiment of that observer appears to be conclusive.

"A glass tube containing a filtered infusion is placed in the middle of a glass dish containing the same infusion: this stands in a wider dish of water, in which a bell glass is placed, covering the vessels with the infusion. At the end of four or five days the tube-infusion has a thick film abounding with ciliate infusoria: the dish-infusion has a thin reticulate film containing only bacteriums and other non-ciliated 'microzoaires'. It is difficult to see how the germs of the one kind of creatures should have entered or become developed in the one vessel and entirely different kinds in the other."

We own that this, to our mind, carries no proof. For as Professor Owen seems himself to remark, the development in the one place and not in the other is part of the wonder. It is indeed the important matter. It is observed as a fact that development of certain animals takes place in the tube, and of others in the dish. To suppose that development will proceed without germs does not explain this fact; and to suppose that germs have been equally distributed does not make it more difficult to explain. Possibly it results from some operation of the struggle for existence.

Still plunging into deeper intricacies, the learned Professor ventures, with a prefatory apology, "the expression of belief on one or two points where proof is wanting." He elaborately seeks to trace a parallel between the phenomena of magnetism and life, and thinks that by doing so he gets rid of the necessity of supposing, as he imagines he must otherwise do, "a special miracle" for the manifestation of the higher phenomena of animal life. Passing on into the field of religious belief, he makes remarks which are hard to understand, but seems quite sure that the mind will never act without the body, and finishes the book with a claim on behalf of the physiologist and pathologist for gratitude from the Christian world for ending all dispute as to how the soul is to be disposed of until the resurrection of the body. He seems, like many others, to forget that while the phenomena of matter are entirely resolvable into manifestations of force, those of mind are not entirely so resolvable.

Although in criticising this volume it has been our duty to comment on various things not altogether right, we honestly repeat that we congratulate Professor Owen on the completion of his task; and we trust that, now freed from the distractions of angry polemics, he may long be spared to enjoy genial and peaceful labour in that noble repository of the records of Natural History over which he presides.

Handbuch der Lehre von den Geweben des Menschen und der Thiere. Herausgegeben von S. Stricker. Leipzig, 1868.

The first part of a new text-book on Microscopic Anatomy has just appeared, under the editorial superintendence of Dr Stricker, of Vienna. It contains an article by the editor, on the general method of microscopical research, and an account of the general doctrine of cells; a chapter on the connective tissue substances, by Dr Rollett; one on the nerve tissues, by Max Schultze; and chapters on the muscular tissue, by Julius Arnold, W. Kühne, and Professor Brücke. It is illustrated by woodcuts. Should the future numbers come up to the standard of this part, the work will contain an excellent abstract of the present condition of knowledge on the minute anatomy of the tissues and organs.

Der Schlund—Kopf des Menschen, von Hubert v. Luschka. Tübingen, 1868.

Prof. Luschka, to whose writings on the anatomy of the pharynx we have had occasion more than once to direct the attention of our readers in the half-yearly report on the progress of anatomy, has incorporated his investigations in a systematic treatise on the anatomy of the Pharynx, and Soft Palate.

The description of the arrangements of the various muscles, fasciæ, blood-vessels, nerves, and mucous membranes is precisely written. The work is illustrated by twelve well-executed lithographic plates.

Zur Entwicklungs-geschichte des Kopfes des Menschen und der höheren Wirbelthiere. Von Emil Dursy, Tübingen, 1869.

This systematic treatise on the development of the head in man and the higher vertebrata, illustrated by several woodcuts and an Atlas of nine large copper plates, has reached us too late to give time to prepare a proper abstract. It is obviously a work on which much time and labour have been expended.

Demonstrations of Anatomy, by GEORGE VINER ELLIS, Professor of Anatomy in University College, London. Sixth Edition. A most important addition has been made to the new edition of this valuable manual by introducing the action of the muscles, the movements of the joints, and the topographical anatomy of the convolutions of the cerebrum, illustrated from Prof. Turner's monograph on that subject. It is most desirable that the student should have his thoughts directed to the use of each part at the same time that he is learning its anatomy; structure should always be studied in relation to functions. Thus only can anatomy be regarded as a science.

The Forces which carry on the Circulation of the Blood, by ANDREW BUCHANAN, M.D., Professor of Physiology in the University of Glasgow. Pt. I. *The force of the Heart effective and absolute.* G. Richardson, 55 Glassford-street, Glasgow. A short pamphlet. The distinction between 'effective' and 'absolute' force is stated to be the same as that which is familiar in mechanical science between the weight to be raised and the power which raises it. The effective force of the heart, accordingly, is estimated from the quantity and velocity of the blood issuing from the left ventricle and the amount of resistance which opposes its movement. The quantity emitted at each contraction is taken at 2 oz., the velocity at 50 feet in a minute, and the resistance is found by the experiments of Hales and Poiseuille to equal a column of blood of 90 inches : and from this the effective force of the ventricle is calculated to equal 22 oz. The internal surface of the ventricle is equal to 15 square inches ; and when contraction commences every part of this surface, equal to the aortic orifice (·4187 of an inch), is pressed upon by a weight of 22 oz., which would give a total force of 49 lbs. The surface of the ventricle however diminishes during contraction, and the muscle power decreases according to a fixed law as the fibre becomes shorter ; and the calculation of the diminution from these two causes brings down the force actually exerted by the heart, *i.e.* the 'absolute force', to about 22 oz. The conclusion therefore is that there is no difference between the effective and the absolute force of the heart which " is in exact accordance with the general economy of nature displayed in the muscular system."

Das Hemmungsnervensystem des Herzens. Eine vergleichend physiologische Studie, by Dr ADOLPH BERNHARD MEYER. 8vo. pp. 93. Berlin, 1869. The first part of this memoir consists of a criticism of the views of those who are opposed to the theory that the vagus exercises an inhibitory influence upon the heart.

The second part is a " Comparative Physiological Study" of the inhibitory nerves of the heart.

With regard to the invertebrata, Carus, Brand and Eckhard have observed stoppage of the heart in diastole follow irritation of some of the cardiac nerves. Several observers have as yet failed to find ganglionic cells in the heart of the crab. Meyer specially investigated the heart of astacus fluviat., but though on one occasion he found structures resembling ganglionic cells, he never succeeded again.

In various kinds of fish, E. Weber, Valentin, Stannius, Wagner and Hoffmann have found that the heart is slowed by irritation of the vagus. Meyer has observed this also in Leuciscus rutilus and Anguilla vulgaris. In the latter he was able to arrest the heart's movements for sixteen minutes by irritating the sinus with an interrupted current. He sometimes also observed this in the frog. When he irritated a certain part of the sinus he could keep the heart perfectly at rest for an hour (the irritation being continued all the while). In several snakes he ascertained that the vagus inhibits the heart. In the common tortoise, Emys lutaria, curiously enough, the right vagus only inhibits the heart; the left has no influence on the cardiac rapidity. In other species of tortoise both vagi slow the heart. The influence of the vagus on the heart of the bird has been disputed. Wagner seldom, and Bernard never observed stoppage of the heart follow stimulation of the vagus. Einbrodt however ascertained that in the goose and fowl the vagi inhibit the heart, and Meyer has found the same in the case of Cypselus apus and Falco bubo. The acceleration of the heart which follows division of the vagi in birds is generally very slight; the author thinks that this is accounted for by the generally very high rate of cardiac action previous to the division. The author shows that it is a mistake to suppose that the nerves of warm- are more easily exhausted than those of cold-blooded animals. There are numerous other points of interest in this elaborate memoir, but our space will not permit a notice of them all; we cannot however refrain from expressing our admiration of the careful manner in which the author has analysed and classified the very extensive literature on the subject.

THE BELL MAGENDIE CONTROVERSY.—As additional contributions to the history of the discovery of the properties of the anterior and posterior roots of the spinal nerves, to that furnished by the reprint of Sir C. Bell's original memoir, and the commentary thereon by Mr Alexander Shaw, in the last number of this Journal, we may refer to a critical memoir by Dr Austin Flint, in the October number, 1868, of the *New York Journal of Psychological Medicine and Jurisprudence.* This memoir has been translated in Robin's *Journal de l'Anat. et de Phys.* IV. 520, 575, by Dr Clemenceau. In the *British Medical Journal,* Jan. 9, 1869, Mr Cæsar Hawkins, who had assisted Sir C. Bell and Mr John Shaw in many of their experiments on the spinal and facial nerves, discusses the relative claims of Bell and Magendie. The comments of Mr Alexander Shaw, in relation to the discovery of the functions of the roots of the spinal nerves, correspond in the main with Mr Hawkins's knowledge of the subject.

REPORT ON THE PROGRESS OF ANATOMY.

By PROFESSOR TURNER[1].

OSTEOLOGY.—Leonard Landois contributes a memoir (*Virchow's Archiv*, Nov. 1868) on the GROWTH OF THE DIAPHYSES OF THE LONG BONES during intra-uterine life. Up to the 9th and 10th weeks of fœtal life, the diaphyses are (irrespective of the ribs) absolutely the largest in those parts of the body in which they are the smallest in the perfect skeleton, and conversely (not including the bones of the hand and foot) they are absolutely the smallest in those in which they are the largest at birth. According to their absolute size they may be arranged as follows:

$$\text{mandible, clavicle,} \quad \left.\begin{array}{l} \text{humerus} \\ \text{radius} \\ \text{ulna} \end{array}\right\}, \quad \left.\begin{array}{l} \text{femur} \\ \text{tibia} \\ \text{fibula} \end{array}\right\}.$$

About this time their absolute size almost corresponds with their relative, so that the same bones are absolutely and relatively the larger. At the 6th month this relation alters, and the absolute size of the bones appears to be as in the skeleton of new-born children, femur, tibia, fibula, humerus, ulna, radius, mandible, clavicle, bones of hand and foot. The absolutely larger bones are also relatively the smaller. The long bones of the upper limbs are at all periods of fœtal life relatively larger and further developed than the long bones of the lower limbs. During the first half of the fœtal state they grow more than twice as much in a given period of time than during the latter half, in conformity with the more rapid growth in the first period of the entire body.——Messrs Bankart, Pye-Smith, and Phillips (*Guy's Hospital Reports*, XIV. 1869) record a SUPERNUMERARY TARSAL BONE, wedge-shaped, one-third of an inch long and deep, and half as wide, placed between the internal cuneiform and second metatarsal bones, with its broad surface on the dorsum of the foot. It had distinct articular cartilage and synovial membrane.—— Ludwig Stieda gives (*Reichert u. Du Bois Reymond's Archiv*, Feb. 1869) some examples of SECONDARY TARSAL BONES. 1st. A portion of the astragalus, where it is grooved for the tendon of the flexor longus hallucis, developed as a separate bone and united to the proper talus by connective tissue. On its lower surface was a facet which articulated with a corresponding facet on the upper surface of the os calcis. This variety Stieda saw once in 60 subjects, though Gruber has seen it once in 24 to 25 bodies. 2nd. The separation of the ento-cuneiform into secondary dorsal and plantar portions, such as Th. Smith had described in *Trans. Path. Soc.* 1867. 3rd. The sepa-

---

[1] To assist in making this Report more complete, Professor Turner will be glad to receive separate copies of original memoirs, or other contributions to Anatomy.

ration of the small articular facet on the upper surface of the anterior process of the os calcis. 4th. Neither Stieda nor Gruber have seen the subdivision of the cuboid bone which Blandin has described in his topographical anatomy.——W. Turner records here a case of DOUBLE ENTO-CUNEIFORM BONE in the right foot of a female. One subdivision of the bone was dorsal, the other plantar; the dorsal part articulated with the meso-cuneiform, first and second metatarsal, scaphoid, and plantar subdivision. The plantar part articulated with the dorsal part, the first metatarsal, scaphoid, and meso-cuneiform. The bones were of about the same size and together equalled the normal ento-cuneiform.——C. Hasse makes a preliminary communication on the TRANSVERSE PROCESSES OF THE VERTEBRÆ (*Henle u. Pfeufer's Zeitsch.* XXXIV. 253). He believes that he can recognise in the human cervical vertebræ the following points of similarity with the dorsal and lumbar:—in the tubercle at the tip of the posterior transverse process a *processus accessorius*, in a feeble tubercle at the tip of the superior oblique process of the higher cervical vertebræ a *processus mammillaris*, and a *processus costalis* in the bridge-like connection between the two subdivisions of the transverse process. ——A French translation, illustrated by several woodcuts, of C. Gegenbaur's memoir on TORSION OF THE HUMERUS, is in *Ann. des Sc. Nat.* x. 55, 1868. He follows Welcker's method of tracing on the same plane the head and condyloid end of the bone, and then measuring the angles between two lines drawn through them. In 36 human humeri the mean angle was 12°, the maximum 32°, the minimum 2°. Measurements of the corresponding angles in various mammalia are also given.

MYOLOGY AND ARTHROLOGY.——Messrs Bankart, Pye-Smith, and Phillips record the MUSCULAR ABNORMALITIES observed in the Guy's Hospital Dissecting-Room during the winters of 1866-7 and 1867-8 (*Guy's Hospital Reports*, XIV.). Amongst the most interesting of these varieties were an example of the *coraco-brachialis brevis* (J. Wood) passing from the coracoid process to the upper part of the humerus; three cases of an *extensor brevis digitorum manus*, in one of which it arose from the dorsal surface of the third metacarpal bone, and was inserted into the tendinous expansion on the back of the same digit, in two others it arose from the posterior annular ligament, and was inserted in one case into the tendon of the extensor indicis and that of the common extensor for the middle finger, and in the other case into the external abductor of the middle finger: in three cases the *psoas parvus* passed behind Poupart's ligament to the line leading from the small trochanter to the linea aspera.——Prof. Bochdalek (*Prag. Viertel Jahrschrift*, IV. 1868) describes ANOMALOUS MUSCLES IN THE ORBIT: a *m. gracillimus*, such as Albinus had previously described, and a *m. anomalus transversus*, which arises from the anterior and upper part of the os planum, passes outwards above the eyeball in close connection with the levator palpebræ to the outer wall of the orbit.——C. Hüter contributes (*Virchow's Archiv*, Feb. 1869) a paper on the ACTION OF MUSCLES PASSING OVER TWO OR MORE

JOINTS, in continuation of a previous notice in Vol. XXVIII. of the same *Archiv.* If a muscle passes over two joints its action on one will be made easier, if its fibres, through the position of the other joint, maintain the greatest possible extension. Thus plantar flexion of the foot by means of the gastrocnemius is easier if the knee is first extended, for if the knee is flexed a large part of the muscular contraction is expended in tightening the muscle before it can act on the foot. When the hand is in extreme palmar flexion the fingers cannot be fully flexed, and the power of the extensors is greatly increased, for their tendons are more fully stretched. In dorsi flexion of the wrist again the relative power of the flexors is increased and that of the extensors diminished.——W. Henke communicates his opinions on the ARTICULATIONS AND THE ACTION OF MUSCLES (*Henle u. Pfeufer's Zeitsch.* XXXIII. 108). They embrace the consideration of flexor and rotator muscles; the action of muscles on the hip-joint in standing and walking; the insufficiency in the length of many of the muscles when compared with the extent of movement of the joint on which they act; this insufficiency may be passive, as when a muscle can be no further elongated, and then becomes perfectly resistant, like a ligament: or it may be active, as when a muscle has reached the limit of its contraction and yet the movement of the joint, in the direction of that contraction, is not at an end. He considers also the absolute power of the muscles, and makes remarks on the arrangement of the muscles of the back. Neither Hüter nor Henke seem to be aware that the action of muscles passing over more than one joint had been discussed by J. Cleland in this *Journal,* Nov. 1866.——Observations on the MECHANISM OF THE KNEE AND HIP-JOINTS, and on the CURVATURES AND MOVEMENTS OF THE ACTING FACETS OF ARTICULAR SURFACES form chapters in the second volume of John Goodsir's *Anatomical Memoirs,* Edinburgh, 1868.——In his eleventh memoir on the MECHANISM OF THE HUMAN SKELETON (*Reichert u. du Bois Reymond's Archiv,* Feb. 1869) H. Meyer discusses the flexion of the knee in the hinder of the two lower limbs, and the pendulum movement of the limb as it is swung forward in the act of walking.——G. Schwalbe contributes (*Schultze's Archiv,* IV. 392) some observations on the STRUCTURE OF THE NON-STRIPED MUSCLE. He distinguishes in each fibre-cell one or two nuclei, surrounded by a mass of protoplasm and contractile material. He states that in the fresh fibre the nucleus is ellipsoidal, and regards its usually described rod-like form as the result of a *post-mortem* change. These fibres in the vertebrata have no sarcolemma, though it is probable that this membrane is present in the smooth fibres of the invertebrata. The outer part of the contractile substance of the smooth fibre in the vertebrata differs from the central part. Fine longitudinal streaks are often seen in it. In one case he saw in fibre from the dog's bladder a partial transverse striation.——W. Krause (*Henle u. Pfeufer's Zeitsch.* XXXIII. 265, XXXIV. 110), Hensen (*Arbeiten des Kieler phys. inst.* 1868), and C. L. Heppner (*Schultze's Archiv,* V. 1869) communicate observations on the STRUCTURE OF STRIPED MUSCULAR FIBRE. They recognise, in addition to the well-known alternating dark and clear transverse bands, a fine transverse line passing through each clear band and subdividing it into halves. They do not seem to be aware that this appearance had previously been described and figured by W. Sharpey, *Quain's Anatomy*, 7th ed. 1867.

NEUROLOGY.—Lockhart Clarke contributes to 2nd ed. of Maudsley's *Physiology and Pathology of the Mind* some important observations on the MINUTE STRUCTURE OF THE CEREBRAL CONVOLUTIONS. He recognises seven distinct and concentric layers of nerve substance, alternately paler and darker from circumference to centre. These laminæ are most distinct in the posterior lobe where the nerve cells are small in all the layers and of nearly uniform size, the inner layer only containing some that are a little larger. In front of the posterior lobe cells of a much larger kind are found; in one of the vertex convolutions large, triangular, oval, and pyramidal cells irregularly scattered between arciform fibres, which run transversely, obliquely, and longitudinally, from the central white axis of the convolution, and curve inwards from opposite sides to form arches along some of the grey layers. The bases of the pyramidal cells are quadrangular, directed towards the central white substance, and give off four or more processes which run partly towards the centre to be continuous with fibres radiating from the central white axis and partly parallel with the surface of the convolution to be continuous with arciform fibres. The opposite end, as in the pear-shaped cells described by Rudolph Arndt (*Report*, May 1868, p. 394), run directly towards the surface of the convolution. Many of these cells, as well as others of a triangular and oval shape, are as large as the cells in the anterior grey substance of the spinal cord. In the superior frontal gyrus pyramidal, triangular, and oval cells throng the three inner layers of grey substance. In the island of Reil the cells are somewhat larger than in the inner orbital convolution. Not only do modifications in structure occur in different convolutions, but in different parts of the same gyrus.——Rudolf Arndt continues (*Schultze's Archiv*, IV. 407) his observations on the STRUCTURE OF THE CEREBRAL CONVOLUTIONS. He commences his memoir by an elaborate criticism on an essay by Meynert on the same subject (*Vierteljahr-schrift für Psychiatrie* I.), and describes his method of preparing his specimens. He then proceeds to discuss the nature of the neuroglia, the ganglion bodies, and nerve-fibres, and concludes with observations on the cerebral blood-vessels. He considers that the ganglion bodies are not cells, but convolutions of fibres with central and peripheral processes. The peripheral processes may become continuous with nerve-fibres either directly or indirectly.——J. Henle and F. Merkel (*Henle und Pfeufer's Zeitsch.* XXXIV. 49) discuss the nature of the so-named CONNECTIVE TISSUE OF THE CENTRAL ORGANS OF THE NERVOUS SYSTEM. They regard the frame-work in which the nerve-fibres of the white substance of the spinal cord lie, not so much of the nature of connective tissue, as like the molecular material of which the outer cortical part of the cord is composed. They recognise in this molecular substance 'granules,' and a homogeneous material in which the 'granules' are contained. They describe and speculate as to the nature of the small globular bodies (Körner) which occur so abundantly in all parts of the grey and white substance of the central organs of the nervous system. Numerous figures illustrate the memoir.——From observations on the CHORDA TYMPANI NERVE A. Vulpian concludes (*Archives de Phys.* 1869, 209) that it is distributed to the submaxillary gland, and that no fibres pass from it to the tongue.—— Amongst the most interesting VARIATIONS IN THE DISTRIBUTION OF THE NERVES, reported by Messrs Bankart, Pye-Smith and Phillips (*Guy's Hospital Reports*, XIV.) are the following : a case in which on both sides the anterior belly of the digastric and the mylo-hyoid muscles were supplied by a branch of the glosso-pharyngeal : cases in which a branch of the external anterior thoracic nerve accompanied the cephalic vein, and in one instance was traced into the shoulder-joint : once the nerve of Wrisberg and one intercosto-humeral nerve were absent, and the internal cutaneous of the musculospiral supplied the skin over the inner head of the triceps as low as the elbow, whilst the ulnar gave a branch to the skin over the upper half of the fl. carpi ulnaris and was itself joined by a branch from the internal cutaneous.——J. Gerlach (*Henle u. Pfeufer's Zeitsch.* XXXIV. 1) describes a DECUSSATION of the fibres of the HYPOGLOSSAL NERVES across the mesial plane at their origin in the medulla oblongata.——Lockhart Clarke also in his 2nd MEMOIR ON THE MEDULLA OBLONGATA (*Phil. Trans.* I. 1868) figures and describes the arrangement of the fibres of the hypoglossal nerves at their origin.

Paul Michelson re-investigates (*Schultze's Archiv*, v. 145) the STRUCTURE OF THE PACINIAN BODIES.——Ludwig Letzerich describes THE TERMINAL BODIES in connection with THE NERVES OF TASTE (*Virchow's Archiv*, Nov. 1868). His observations were made on the tongues of kittens and oxen. The terminal apparatus consists of flattened vesicles which send processes both to the interior of the papillæ, and outwards to the surface of the mucous membrane. The former receive the nerves which, up to the place of junction, remain double-contoured. The axial cylinder branches in the vesicle, filled with a clear, watery, somewhat granular fluid, and then is attached to very short, stalked, glistening prismatic bodies, the terminal nerve structures. The processes of the vesicles which pass to the surface of the papilla between the epithelial cells are lost in the horny epithelium.——Lionel S. Beale reprints (*Quart. Micros. Jnl.* Jan. 1869), with some additions, his memoir on the ANATOMY OF THE PAPILLÆ OF THE FROG'S TONGUE, which originally appeared in the *Phil. Trans.* 1865.——R. L. Maddox contributes a paper on the same subject to the *Month. Micros. Jnl.* Jan. 1869. He employs the mode of investigation which has proved so useful in the hands of Dr Beale.—— Ch. Rouget (*Archives de Physiologie*, No. 5, 1868) investigates the TACTILE CORPUSCLES in the skin and mucous membranes. He considers that he has established a continuity between the double-contoured nerve fibres and the proper cortical fibres which are as it were rolled round and constitute the superficial part of the touch corpuscle. There the nerves lose their double contour, and it is difficult to follow them to their termination, but he considers that the fibres sink into a soft nucleated substance which constitutes the core of the corpuscle. B. Lœwenberg (*Robin's Journal*, IV. 626) concludes his memoir on the STRUCTURE OF THE SPIRAL LAMINA OF THE COCHLEA, and on the mode of termination of the auditory nerve.——— Paul Langerhans records some new observations on the NERVES OF THE HUMAN SKIN (*Virchow's Archiv*, Sept. 1868). He describes a fine network of nerve-fibres in the cutis, from the superficial part of which fine fibres deprived of the white substance of Schwann pass out of the cutis and enter the Malpighian layer of the epidermis. He saw in the epidermis also well marked cells, which gave off several processes towards the horny layer of the cuticle, and one long slender process which passed through the Malpighian layer into the cutis. He considers these cells to be nervous in their nature, and the peripheral processes which proceed from them to be the terminal parts of the nerves of the skin.

BLOOD VASCULAR SYSTEM.—Messrs. Bankart, Pye-Smith and Phillips record (*Guy's Hospital Reports*, XIV.) several VARIATIONS IN THE ARTERIAL SYSTEM. Twice the right subclavian arose from the back of the 3rd part of the aortic arch, in one of which it passed between the spine and oesophagus, and in this case both carotids arose from the highest part of the aortic arch by a short thick trunk less than half an inch long; in the other it went between the oesophagus and trachea, in its course to its normal position. The latter variety is the more uncommon, but Dr Bayford (*Mem. Med. Soc. London*, 1793) and Meckel (*Path. Anat.* II. 100) have recorded similar cases. In 50 cases specially examined, the internal maxillary passed over the external pterygoid muscle 23, under it 27 times. In 6 cases the left vertebral arose from the arch between the carotid and subclavian, once the right vertebral arose from the aorta, once from the common carotid. In 17 out of 31 cases the posterior scapular arose as a separate branch from the third part of the subclavian, and in two of these the supra-scapular also arose separately from the same part of the subclavian, and in one case from the first part of the axillary : in 4 cases there was no thyroid axis, and its branches arose independently from the first part of the subclavian, in 3 cases the internal mammary arose from the axis.

They have seen the obturator artery arise 15 times from the deep epigastric, and in only 4 of these did it pass to the inner side of the femoral rings, once it passed between the femoral artery and vein. Twice the deep epigastric artery arose from the profunda in the thigh, and twice an accessory pudic artery occurred. Variations in the arteries of the upper and lower limbs are also recorded.———W. Turner describes (*Proc. R. S. Edin.* Jan. 4, 1869) the heart of a male subject in which a VALVE occurred at the MOUTH OF THE SUPERIOR VENA CAVA. A membranous semilunar valve, formed by a reduplication of the endocardial lining membrane, lay across the anterior and inner border of

the auricular orifice of the superior vena cava, and hung pendulous in
the auricular cavity. It measured 1½ inch in its long or transverse
diameter, but was scarcely half an inch deep; so that when drawn
across the mouth of the vein, it did not cover over much more than

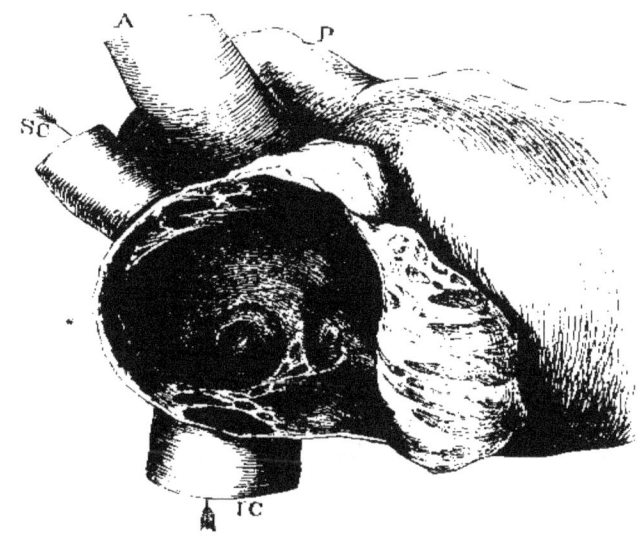

A. Aorta. P. Pulmonary artery. SC. Superior, and IC. Inferior cava. * The
fibrous cord connecting the two valves. C. Coronary sinus.—*From a drawing of
the specimen by Mr T. D. Nicholson in the Proc. of the Roy. Soc. Edinburgh.*

one-third of the orifice. Its free border was almost straight. The
attached border was semilunar in form, and connected to the wall
of the auricle, close to its line of junction with the anterior wall of
the vein, not by a continuous membrane, but by numerous slender
fibrous bands. Between these bands were apertures of various sizes,
one of which, larger than the rest, was situated at the upper and
inner part of the valve, which consequently had a fenestrated
appearance. From the outer (right) end of the valve, and continous
with its free border, a fibrous cord (*) arched downwards beneath the
lining membrane of the right wall of the auricle, and became continuous with the right border of the Eustachian valve. The inner (left)
end of the valve was connected to a short papillary muscle, which
was continuous with the muscular wall of the auricle. There did not
appear to be any deficiency in the thickness of the muscular coat of
the superior cava.

The Eustachian valve projected for upwards of an inch into the
auricular cavity, and presented in a remarkable degree the fenestrated
character which that valve occasionally exhibits in the adult heart.
At its left extremity it subdivided into two parts, one of which
passed in the usual way to the auricular septum, and became con-

tinuous with the annulus ovalis, whilst the other was blended with the valve at the mouth of the coronary sinus, which also exhibited a fenestrated appearance.

Owing to its fenestrated condition, and small size, when compared with the orifice of the superior cava, it is obvious that the valve situated at the mouth of that great vein could have had but little influence in preventing the regurgitation of blood during the contraction of the auricle in the adult heart. But it is probable that in the fœtal stage of this heart the backward flow into the vein would have been very considerably impeded by its presence; for there is reason to believe that the fenestrated state, not only of this, but of the other valves at the mouths of the great veins, is due to atrophy taking place after birth. As the muscular coat of the superior cava possessed its usual thickness, the valve was obviously not developed to compensate for any deficiency in that portion of the wall of the great vein.

As the Eustachian valve at the mouth of the inferior cava serves in the fœtus to direct the current of blood passing upwards along that vein through the foramen ovale, it is possible that the valve at the mouth of the superior cava may have exercised some directing effect on the blood which entered the auricle by the latter vessel. From its position it would, perhaps, have directed the blood of the superior cava away from the auricular septum, and thus have aided in preventing, during the fœtal condition, the mingling of the blood of the two cavæ in the auricular cavity.

The occurrence of such a valve is not, however, of interest merely in its physiological relations: it possesses also a morphological value. For it may be regarded as presenting in the human heart a rudimentary example of an arrangement which is met with in the heart of the bird. If the heart of a large bird, *e.g.*, the ostrich (*Struthio camelus*), be examined, it may be seen that the sinus, into which the venæ cavæ open, is separated from the auricle proper by a large double muscular valve. The right segment of this valve is related not only to the mouth of the right superior cava, but extends down the wall of the auricle to the mouth of the inferior cava, and is then prolonged as far as the mouth of the left superior cava, which may be regarded as representing in position the coronary vein in the human heart. Now, in this specimen the valve at the mouth of the superior cava was continued, through the intermediation of a fibrous cord (*), into the Eustachian valve, and the latter again was directly united with the valve at the mouth of the coronary sinus. Two other human hearts also are referred to in which a fibrous cord extended from the Eustachian valve, along the right posterior wall of the auricle, almost as far as the mouth of the superior cava.

Alex. Golubew describes (*Schultze's Archiv*, v. 60) peculiar spindle-formed structures in the WALLS OF THE CAPILLARIES OF THE FROG, which when stimulated alter their form, become thicker, more or less diminish the calibre of the vessel, so that the lumen may disappear in the smallest capillaries. He describes also the formation of new vessels by offshoots, and the subsequent hollowing out of these processes.——Lionel S. Beale describes (*Quart. Microscop. Journ.* April 1869) the NERVOUS MECHANISM IN THE AURICLE OF THE FROG'S HEART. The finest nerves form net-works amongst the muscular fibres, but do not penetrate the sarcolemma; neither end-organs nor end-plates can be detected. The only nerve cells in the cardiac ganglia are oval or pyriform, which may have from two to six fibres connected with them. He infers that the fibres leaving each cell are afferent and efferent, *i.e.* a fibre leaving a cell, after ramifying in the wall of the auricle, returns to the cell.——MM. Ranvier and Cornil contribute (*Archives de Physiologie*, 1868, 551) observations on the HISTOLOGY OF THE ENDOCARDIUM and inner coat of the arteries. ——In a paper on the STRUCTURE OF THE RED BLOOD-CORPUSCLE OF OVIPAROUS VERTEBRATA W. S. Savory (*Monthly Microscop. Journ.* April 1869 and *P. R. S. Lond.*) contends that the 'nucleus' is the result of changes which occur in the substance of the corpuscle after death, which are usually hastened and exaggerated by exposure and the disturbance to which the corpuscles are subjected in being mounted for the microscope.

EYEBALL.——In a paper on the NERVES OF THE CORNEA H. Petermöller states (*Henle u. Pfeufer's Zeitsch.* XXXIV. 101) that he has repeatedly seen, in the rabbit and guinea-pig, nerves pass out of the cornea into the epithelium on its anterior surface, assume there a varicose appearance, give off secondary branches, and course outwards to the free surface of the epithelium, where they came to a free end.——W. Flemming (*Schultze's Archiv*, IV. 353) relates his observations on the CILIARY MUSCLE in the DOMESTIC MAMMALS.——G. Gulliver (*Month. Microscop. Journal*, April 1869) describes the FIBRES OF THE CRYSTALLINE LENS IN PETROMYZONINI. They are in the lamprey long, flexible, smooth, of nearly equal breadth, commonly flattened, joined laterally by level and straight sutures, colourless and transparent. In diameter they range between $\frac{1}{1700}$th and $\frac{1}{5000}$th of an inch.——The first part of the 5th Vol. of *Schultze's Archiv* contains a beautifully illustrated memoir by Max Schultze on the RODS OF THE RETINA IN CEPHALOPODA AND HETEROPODA.

MISCELLANEOUS.——W. v. Nathusius (*Reichert u. du Bois Reymond's Archiv*, 1869, 69) gives an account of the MEDULLARY SUBSTANCE IN VARIOUS HORNY TISSUES, the development of cartilage in the horns of the roe-deer, with some general observations on cells. ——Hubert v. Luschka describes the ARRANGEMENT AND STRUCTURE OF THE MUCOUS MEMBRANE OF THE LARYNX (*Schultze's Archiv*, V. 126).——Researches on the GANGLION INTERCAROTICUM and the SUPRA-RENAL BODIES are recorded by Pförtner of Göttingen in *Henle u. Pfeufer's Zeitsch.* XXXIV. 240.——From observations on the PROSTATE GLAND in man, the hedge-hog, mole, mouse, rat, rabbit, and guinea-pig H. Reinert concludes (*Henle u. Pfeufer's Zeitsch.* XXXIV. 194) that this gland contains ganglion cells either in its substance or, in the case of man and the hedge-hog, the nerves, which pass to it, are provided with ganglion cells.

MALFORMATIONS.—N. Hickmann (*American Jour. Med. Sc.* Jan. 1868) relates a case of complete TRANSPOSITION of the THORACIC and ABDOMINAL VISCERA.——A similar-case in an old woman is recorded by Messrs. Bankart, Pye-Smith, and Phillips in *Guy's Hospital Reports*, XIV.——R. D. Powell (*Brit. Med. Jnl.* April 17, 1869) also relates a case in a boy, æt. 10, in which the visceral transposition was detected during life.——T. Annandale describes (*Edin. Med. Jnl.* Jan. 1869) a case of CONGENITAL MALFORMATION OF THE ŒSOPHAGUS in an infant in which the gullet terminated in a dilated *cul-de-sac* $\frac{1}{10}$ths of an inch above bifurcation of trachea. The gastric end of the gullet was normal, and opened into the posterior wall of the trachea a little to the left of the middle line, three-tenths of an inch above the bifurcation of the trachea, and the same distance below the œsophageal *cul-de-sac*. Between this opening and the *cul-de-sac* a few muscular fibres were the only representatives of the œsophagus. The preparation is now in the Anatomical Museum of the University of Edinburgh. The infant lived 48 hours.—— N. Friedreich discusses (*Virchow's Archiv*, Nov. 1868) the case of Katharina Hohmann, an HERMAPHRODITE, with well-developed testicles, secreting spermatozoa, and with a beard, masculine voice and figure, but who has a periodical menstrual flux from the sinus urogenitalis, which opens at the root of the penis.——Sir J. Y. Simpson gives an account of the SIAMESE TWINS (*British Medical Jnl.* Feb. 13, March 13, 1869). The band of union, about as thick as the forearm, extends from the ensiform cartilage down to the umbilicus, which is single, and can be felt on the middle of the lower surface of the band. On its upper surface the ensiform cartilages of the twins meet at their apices, whilst the band below is soft, thin, and elastic, and on coughing the intestine can be felt passing into its interior. When the middle of the band is touched both feel it, and each seems to be sensible of a prick half-an-inch on the opposite side of the middle of the band. The vascular connections across the band are extremely small. It is probable that a peritoneal canal is continued across the band which connects together the two abdominal cavities. ——Lawson Tait (*Dublin Quar. Med. Jnl.* Feb. 1869) records a case of CONGENITAL ABSENCE of the PERICARDIUM in a female, æt. 29. The parietal pleura on the left side was continued from the great vessels downwards to about an inch from the apex of the heart and forwards as far as the anterior coronary artery, thence to the cartilages. The right parietal pleura was in relation only with the right auricle. He also records two cases of CONGENITAL MALFORMATIONS of the folds of the PERITONEUM, which are of interest in connection with the cases recorded by Drs Chiene and Cleland in Vol. II. of this Journal.——Wenzel Gruber (*Virchow's Archiv*, Sept. 1868) communicates some additional cases of MALFORMATIONS of the MESENTERY and of internal mesogastric hernia.——E. Münchmeyer describes a case in which ARREST OF DEVELOPMENT OF THE URO-GENITAL SYSTEM had occurred (*Henle u. Pfeufer's Zeitsch.* XXXIII. 207). In a boy, æt. 12, the left kidney, ureter, vesicula seminalis, and ejaculatory duct were absent, whilst the testicle and supra-renal body were present. The left epididymis was represented by a lobulated organ, which consisted of connective tissue, fat cells, and blood-vessels. An elongated cord passed from this lobulated organ to the back of the bladder. About its middle it was hollowed into a canal lined by polygonal epithelium, but it did not communicate with the interior of the bladder. The author regards this cord as an early stage of the par-epididymis, and considers that the case supports Kupffer's view of the development of the uro-genital system, according to which the permanent urinary system is formed from a saccular dilatation of the posterior wall of the Wolffian duct. In this case the development of this duct had been arrested in its early stage, no dilatation had taken place, and consequently no formation of the urinary secreting arrangements.——T. A. G. Balfour records a case of CONGENITAL DIAPHRAGMATIC HERNIA (*Edin. Med. Jnl.* April, 1869), in which the stomach, spleen, pancreas, a part of the liver, the small intestine, the cœcum, appendix vermiformis, and parts of the colon were in the left pleural cavity. The left half of the diaphragm was undeveloped. An excellent commentary and bibliography is appended to the account of the case.——P. D. Handyside communicates (*Edin. Med. Jnl.* 1869) some observations on ARRESTED TWIN-DEVELOPMENT in the form of anterior duplicity in a female calf, in which the anterior and posterior extremities of a parasite twin-calf were connected at two separate parts with the ventral surface of the autosite. The points of attachment were the jugulary fossa of the sternum and the lower umbilical region. To the former the anterior limbs were connected by integument; whilst the tegumentary bond of union of the posterior limbs enclosed a rudimentary pelvic bone. He inclines to the belief that, when an imperfect twin ovum or embryo coalesces with a perfect autosite, the germ is abnormal from the first.—— C. Dareste refers (*Ann. des Sc. Nat.* x. 123, 1868) to a series of experimental RESEARCHES RELATIVE TO TERATOLOGY, which he has been pursuing for some years, with the view of substituting a scientific basis, for the hypothetical one, which has hitherto guided the study of teratology.

COMPARATIVE ANATOMY AND MORPHOLOGY.—Several important contributions to COMPARATIVE MYOLOGY have recently proceeded from the Oxford Anatomical School. Prof. Rolleston (*Trans. Linnæan Soc.* xxvi.) discusses the *homologies* of certain *muscles connected with the shoulder-joint*. He regards the pectoralis secundus, or levator humeri, in birds as the homologue of the subclavius in mammals, and of the epicoraco-humeral in the reptile and echidna, and not of the mammalian pectoralis minor. He bases his argument not only on the position, connections, origins, and insertions of the muscles, but on their mode of nervous supply. The subclavius of the mammal is supplied by a nerve homologous with that which supplies the pectoralis secundus, whilst the pectoralis minor is supplied by the nerve which is distributed to the great pectoral. He regards the pectoralis major in the bird as the equivalent of both pectorals in the mammal. He makes the following suggestions with reference to the homologies of various muscles in the upper and lower limbs: Pectoralis major in the mammal with "gracilis" of the Iguana; subclavius, inner head of pectineus; coraco-brachialis brevis, upper fascicles of obturator externus; coraco-brachialis medius and longus with rest of obturator ex. and adductors; deep parts of coraco-br. in monotremes, obturator internus; deltoid, outer part of pectineus; spinati, iliacus; teres minor, iliacus internus minor; scapulo-humeral, scansorius; teres major, tensor fasciæ femoris; iliac head of pyriformis, scapulo-humeral slip in macropus; sacral head, acromio-trachelian; hamstrings, mammalian muscle from postero-vertebral angle of scapula to olecranon.——J. C. Galton contributes a descriptive memoir (*Trans. Linnæan Soc.* XXVI.) on the *muscles of the Fore and Hind limbs of Dasypus sexcinctus*, and in the same volume a memoir on the *muscles of the anterior and posterior extremities of orycteropus capensis*, the latter of which furnishes, along with the essay by Prof. Humphry in our May number, 1868, a very complete account of the myology of this rare mammal.——Georges Pouchet (*Robin's Journal*, IV. 658) contributes a memoir on the BRAIN OF THE EDENTATA.——Julius Sander gives an account of the TRANSVERSE COMMISSURAL SYSTEM IN THE BRAIN OF THE MARSUPIALS (*Reichert u. du Bois Reymond's Archiv*, 711, 1868). He dissected the brains of Macropus giganteus and Didelphis Azarae, and agrees with the conclusions previously arrived at by W. H. Flower that a corpus callosum exists in the marsupials, but a large portion of the white part of the frontal lobe, which in the placental mammals is formed of fibres of the corpus callosum, is in Macropus formed of fibres of the anterior commissure. ——Hugo Magnus relates (*Reichert u. du Bois Reymond's Archiv*, 1868, 682) observations on the STERNUM OF BIRDS. He reduces the different forms of sterna to 5 types. 1st. That of the Cursores, in which the crest is small and the sternum is a rounded, shield-like, slightly excavated bone. 2nd. In birds, well adapted for flying (swallows, &c.), the sternum is long, broad, deeply concave, with a very strong crest, a flat posterior border with only small perforations. 3rd. In the Scansores the sternum is smaller, not so concave as in group 2, crest more feeble, posterior border with one or two deep excavations. 4th. In swimming birds the sternum is broad and long, rather concave, with a strong crest projecting forwards, posterior border with one or two excavations on each side. In *mergus*, however, the excavations are changed into perforations. 5th. In the Grallatores the sternum is long and narrow, crest strong, deep concavity, posterior border never without excavations. He gives numerous figures of the different kinds of sterna.——An abstract of W. Kitchen Parker's observations on the STRUCTURE AND DEVELOPMENT OF THE SKULL OF THE COMMON FOWL appears in *P. R. S. Lond.* Feb. 11, 1869.——Dr Waldeyer of Breslau communicates (*Henle u. Pfeufer's Zeitsch.* XXXIV. 159) remarks on the germinal layers and the primitive streak in the DEVELOPMENT OF THE CHICK.——F. Cramer (*Würzburg Verhand. N. F.* I. 1868) relates his observations on the DEVELOPMENT OF THE BIRD'S EGG, which substantially agree with those made by Gegenbaur (*Müller's Archiv*, 1861).——W. Peters contributes (*Monats.*

Berlin Akad. 19 Nov. 1868) observations on the development of the EAR BONES AND MECKEL'S CARTILAGE in the Crocodilia, which correspond in their general results very closely with those he had previously recorded (*Report*, Nov. 1868, p. 206). The want of the incus in birds and crocodiles forms a transitional stage to its atrophied condition in monotremata.——C. Kupffer relates (*Schultze's Archiv*, IV. 209) OBSERVATIONS ON THE DEVELOPMENT OF OSSEOUS FISHES. ——R. Salbey communicates (*Reichert u. du Bois Reymond's Archiv*, 729, 1868) an essay on the STRUCTURE AND GROWTH OF THE SCALES OF FISH.——W. C. M'Intosh notes (*Jnl. Linnæan Soc.* x. 251) observations on the DEVELOPMENT OF LOST PARTS IN NEMERTEANS, in one species of which, *Borlasia octoculata*, he has seen each of the fragments into which it breaks become a perfect animal.——A supplementary number of *Schultze's Archiv*, 1869, contains an elaborate memoir by Franz Boll on the COMPARATIVE HISTOLOGY OF THE MOLLUSCA.——Jules Kunckel (*Ann. des Sc. Nat.* x. 86, 1868) has satisfied himself of the existence of a SYSTEM OF CAPILLARY VESSELS IN INSECTS, connected with the arteries, which ramify not only in the muscles, but in other organs.

REPORT ON THE PROGRESS OF PHYSIOLOGY from 1st
August, 1868 to 1st April, 1869. By WILLIAM RUTHERFORD,
M.D., ARTHUR GAMGEE, M.D. and THOMAS R. FRASER, M.D.,
Edinburgh[1].

Dr RUTHERFORD'S REPORT.

Vascular System.

HEART. TEMPERATURE OF BLOOD. H. Jacobson and M. Bernhardt (*Centralblatt*, 1868, p. 643) ascertained that in only two out
of seventeen experiments on rabbits was the blood in the right side
of the same temperature as that in the left side of the heart : in the
other fifteen cases the blood in the left was from 0·12 to 0·42° Cent.
warmer than that in the right ventricle. Their measurements were
made by thermo-electric needles pushed through the thorax into the
ventricles.

PULSE IN CAPILLARIES AND VEINS. Dr H. Quincke (*Berliner
Klinische Wochenschrift*, 1868, No. 34) has observed that a capillary
pulse may be seen under the finger-nails of most persons. He says
that the white lunula of the nail becomes smaller at every systole of
the left ventricle. The phenomenon is best seen when the hand is
raised above the head so as to diminish the blood pressure in the
hand and thereby exaggerate the difference between the systolic congestion and diastolic anaemia which takes place in its vessels. This
capillary pulse is well marked in slight forms of anaemia and chlorosis
and also in cases of aortic insufficiency. Quincke observed a venous
pulse in the veins on the back of his hand when they were subjected
to a high temperature ; he also noticed it in the victims of aortic
insufficiency. It was present in the veins of the hand of a woman
who had slight hypertrophy of the left ventricle, and in a man who,
owing to fracture of the vertebra and injury of the spinal cord appeared to have palsy of vaso-motor nerves.

FORMATION OF BLOOD CORPUSCLES IN MARROW.—Prof. Neumann
(Preliminary Communication in *Centralblatt*, 1868, p. 689) says that
" in the so-called red marrow of the bones of man and the rabbit
there are, in addition to the well-known marrow-cells, certain elements not hitherto noticed, viz. nucleated red blood-cells in every
respect closely resembling the cells from which the red blood corpuscles are developed in the embryo.
In marrow which is rich in fat cells, these blood-cells are present
in small number." He believes that they have their origin in the
marrow cells (Markzellen).

[1] In order to assist in making this Report as complete as possible, the
Authors will be glad to receive copies of memoirs and other original contributions to Physiology.

G. Bizzozero (*Gazzetta Medica Italiana-Lombardia*, 1868, No. 46, and 1869, No. 2, Abstract in *Centralblatt*, 1868, p. 885, and 1869, p. 149) confirms Neumann's observation. Amongst other things he says that the condition of the marrow in the bones of frogs in winter as compared with summer furnishes an important argument in favour of the theory that marrow is a blood gland. In winter the white corpuscles in the blood of the frog are not half so numerous as they are in summer, and in winter the marrow consists almost entirely of fat cells whereas in summer it contains hardly anything but lymphoid cells. He examined the costal marrow and the spleen in five cases of death from typhus fever, and observed in both structures an enormous increase of cells containing blood-corpuscles.

Nervous System.

VAGUS. Meyer (*Das Hemmungsnervensystem des Herzens*, Berlin, 1869). See Abstract of this work at p. 445 of the present number.—Goltz (*Centralblatt*, 1868, p. 593) has made the curious observation that when a frog is repeatedly struck upon the abdomen, the heart is slowed, owing to inhibitory action of the vagi; but the heart is unaffected if simultaneously with the abdominal irritation there be an intense excitation of sensory nerves in the extremities. He supposes that the irritation of cutaneous nerves in the extremities throws the medulla oblongata into a somewhat paralysed condition, whereby the roots of the cardiac inhibitory filaments of the vagi remain unaffected by the mechanical irritation of the abdominal viscera.

Kowalewsky and Adamük (*Centralblatt*, 1868, p. 546) and E. Bernhardt (*Inaug. Dissert.* 8vo. pp. 32. Dorpat, 1868) have found that in the cat the depressor nerve (see *Jl. of Anatomy and Physiology*, No. 1, 1867, p. 190) is sometimes a separate branch of the vagus in the neck. When the cranial end of the nerve is irritated the blood pressure falls as Cyon and Ludwig have already shown in the case of the rabbit. In cases where the depressor was isolated from the vagus K. and A. found that irritation of the cranial end of the trunk of the vagus lowered the blood-pressure. This resulted without previous removal of the influence of the brain, a condition which Dreschfeld (see *Jl. of Anatomy and Physiology*, May 1868, p. 408) considered essential. (Aubert and Roever have found the same. Vide infra.)

Aubert and Roever ("Influence of the Vagus, Superior Laryngeal and Sympathetic Nerves upon the Blood-Pressure and Frequency of the Pulse." *Centralblatt*, 1868, p. 578) have divided the vagi and irritated the central ends in curarised dogs, cats, rabbits and lambs. They found that on irritating the central end of the vagus in rabbits the blood-pressure is usually lowered, sometimes however it is raised. Even in the same animal, one vagus sometimes lowers while the other raises the pressure. The administration of morphia to the animal does not affect the result (see Dreschfeld's paper quoted above). In cats a very marked lowering of the pressure frequently followed irritation of the central end of the vagus in those cases where the depressor nerve was a separate branch. In dogs, after forcible removal of the sympathetic nerve, stimulation of the cranial end of the vagus usually lowered the pressure to the extent of one third of the total pressure. Stimulation of the central end of the vago-sympathetic always raised the pressure. The results as regards the blood-pressure were the same, whether the vagus on both sides or on one side only were divided previous to the excitation of the cranial end of the nerve. This was not however the case with the frequency of the heart's contractions. When the vagus or vago-sympathetic of one side was divided and the cranial end irritated while that on the other side was intact, slowing of the heart was generally the result in rabbits, cats and dogs. This was especially marked in dogs. When both vagi were divided however irritation of the cranial end no longer slowed the heart, often indeed it quickened it; thus showing that a centripetal influence may pass from the central termination of the vagus on one side to that on the other and there affect the cardiac filaments so as to slow the heart. Stimulation of the central end of the cervical sympathetic nerve increased the blood-pressure in all the above-mentioned animals. In this case division of the vagi made no marked difference in the frequency of the pulse. Irritation of the central end of the superior laryngeal nerve generally increased the pressure.

According to E. Hering (*Wien. Acad. Sitzungsbericht*, Cl. 2. M. N. Abtheil. LVII. pp. 672—677) there are in the pulmonary branches of the vagi two kinds of fibres. One set is excited by inflation of the lungs. In consequence of the stimulation of these fibres inspiration is inhibited and expiration brought about. The other fibres are stimulated by the collapse of the lungs in expiration; they inhibit expiration and bring about inspiration. In this way respiration is regulated as long as the vagi are intact.

SPINAL CORD. S. Mayer ("On the Insensibility of the Anterior Columns of the Spinal Cord to Electrical Stimulation." Pflüger's *Archives*, I. pp. 166—173). While Van Deen, Schiff, and others, have said, that the substance of the spinal cord is not influenced by stimulants applied to it directly. Engelken (see *Jl. of Anatomy and Physiology*, 2nd Series, No. 1, p. 188) has from observations on the action of electricity upon the cord maintained the reverse. Wislocky has not been able to confirm Engelken's observations. He found that movement of the lower extremities followed irritation of the upper part of the spinal cord only when the electrical current escaped into the nerve roots of the latter. On the other hand, Mayer, like Engelken, observed combined movements of the posterior extremities follow careful irritation of the cervical portion of the spinal cord in frogs. In opposition to Engelken, however, he found that such movements followed stimulation of the posterior columns more readily than they did that of the anterior. This difference was most marked at the cervical enlargement of the cord. Engelken said he observed movements follow irritation of the cord after removal of the posterior columns, but Mayer could not confirm this. On the contrary, he found on splitting the cord into an anterior and a posterior half, leaving the two halves united at the origin of the ischiatic nerves, that irritation of the posterior half produced movement of the posterior extremities, while that of the anterior columns was without effect. These facts therefore indicate that the movements observed on irritating the cord directly are reflex, that is to say, they are due to irritation of the posterior roots. (From an abstract by Rosenthal in the *Centralblatt*, 1868, p. 759).

Digestive System.

INSALIVATION. Hallier, in his remarkable work on "Gährungs-serscheinungen," endeavoured to show that the Alcohol, Lactic and Butyric Acid fermentations and all the decompositions taking place in putrefaction have their essential cause in the presence of fungi. He stated that the conversion of starch into sugar by Saliva is not due to Ptyaline, but to the presence of the fungus Leptothrix Buccalis in the Saliva.

Dr Ferdinand Lösch of St Petersburg (*Beitrag zur Speichel-verdauung. Wurzburger Untersuchungen,* 1868, p. 67) has made a number of experiments on the action of the Saliva on Starch, which have led him to the conclusion that Ptyaline can transform starch into sugar in the absence of all fungi, and that the fungi contained in the buccal saliva contribute nothing to the transformation.

F. Nawrocki (*Studien des Physiol. Instituts. Breslau.* 4ter Heft. p. 125) has performed thirty-five experiments regarding the innervation of the salivary glands in the dog, cat, and rabbit. His conclusions essentially agree with Bernard's. The three salivary glands obtain their trophic nerves from the sympathetic and facial. The fibres derived from the facial pass to the sub-maxillary and sub-lingual glands in the Chorda Tympani: those for the Parotid pass through the lesser superficial petrosal nerve, and leave the skull with the auriculo-temporal branch of the 5th. He failed to confirm Œhl's statement that irritation of the central end of the vagus produces a flow of saliva.

LIVER. Austin Flint (*New York Medical Journal,* Jan. 1869) has made a number of observations which generally confirm Pavy's views regarding the Glycogenic function of the liver.

Eye.

A. von Hippel and A. Grünhagen (*Archives für Opthalmologie,* XIV. 3, pp. 219—258; abstract in *Centralblatt,* 1869, p. 166) communicate new experiments regarding the influence of nerves upon the intra-ocular pressure. They were chiefly performed on cats. By means of a canula inserted in the cornea, a Mercury Manometer was brought into communication with the anterior chamber. Curara was given to prevent movement of the animal.

Those branches of the third nerve which go to the extraocular muscles increase the intraocular pressure (the intraocular pressure is chiefly due to the blood-pressure, compression of the eye-ball by the recti muscles increases it); those supplying the ciliary muscle and sphincter pupillæ have no effect. Irritation of the sympathetic nerve in the neck gives rise to two very different results. At first there is, in the great majority of cases, as Adamük and Wagner have observed, an increase in the pressure. Adamük's supposition that this is due to contraction of the ciliary muscle cannot be true, for this muscle is supplied by the motor oculi, and not by the sympathetic. Grünhagen attributed the rise in pressure to compression of the eyeball by contraction of the orbital muscle, which it supplied by the sympathetic. Recently, Adamük thought that it is due to contraction of the pale muscular fibres described by H. Müller in the Choroid. The authors have, however, irritated the posterior part of recently extirpated eyes, and notwithstanding powerful contraction of the dilator pupillæ, the pressure remained the same. And further, they have not been able to see any muscular fibres in the choroid apart from the ciliary muscle. They adopt Grünhagen's explanation—that the rise in pressure is due to contraction of the orbital muscle—because they could prevent the rise in pressure by drawing the eye forwards so as to remove it from the influence of the muscle, and when sometimes the irritation of the sympathetic did not alter the pressure—this took place when the eye was pushed a little deeper into the orbit. The second result of stimulating the sympathetic is a lowering of the pressure. This sometimes takes place at once, more commonly however it follows the increased pressure due to the above-mentioned cause. With Adamük they ascribe the fall to contraction of intraocular vessels. The rise in pressure which follows stimulation of the sympathetic varies from 1—6 millimetres of a column of mercury, while the fall varies from 9—10 mm.

Their experiments as to the influence of the general blood-pressure upon the intraocular pressure show that there is a very close relation between the two. A change in the one is accompanied by a like change in the other. They think that it is not the sympathetic, but the trigeminus, which is the cause of the tension of the eyeball (increased intraocular pressure) in glaucoma, for irritation of this nerve increased the pressure, whether by producing increased secretion or simply dilated vessels, they are unable to say. (That irritation of the trigeminus nerve is the cause of glaucoma is a theory which was first advanced by Donders.) They observed no change in the pressure follow the application of extract of calabar bean to the conjunctiva.

DR GAMGEE'S REPORT.

Physiological Chemistry.

BLOOD.

ON SOME PROPERTIES OF HÆMOGLOBIN AND METHÆMOGLOBIN.— Under this title Dr Preyer (*Pflügers Archiv. f. Phys.* 1868, pp. 395—454) furnishes a large amount of information relating to the physical and chemical properties of the blood-coloring matter; his object being apparently to ascertain carefully some points which had been overlooked in the description of the substance by previous writers and by himself. The reporter can only allude to some of the results which interested him particularly on reading this paper, which must be carefully perused by all who are interested in the subject.

The author in discussing the physical properties of hæmoglobin makes some theoretical observations on the crystallographic relations of the blood-crystals of various animals. He draws attention to the curious fact that in spite of a different crystalline form the optical properties, as ascertained by the spectrum, are absolutely the same throughout the whole range of the animal kingdom. From man down to the earth-worm the blood-colouring matter presents exactly the same absorption bands and furnishes when decomposed substances having identical spectra. The action of cyanide of potassium on the blood of the earth-worm is, for instance, exactly the same as on that of man. The crystals of hæmoglobin are, as Preyer shews, all doubly refracting; they all possess, when seen suspended in water, a silky lustre. With regard to the colour of hæmoglobin the author remarks that it may vary between the shade of arterial and that of venous blood, the most oxygenised crystals having the beautiful colour of arterial blood, whilst the crystals of reduced Hb have the dark purple tint of venous blood. The latter crystals are pleochromatic, whilst the former are not. Similarly solutions of reduced hæmoglobin are dichrotic, whilst those of O-Hb are not. The author points out that the dichroism of venous blood is quite independent of the carbonic acid which it contains. Preyer maintains that the merit of pointing out these facts relating to the dichroism of Hb must be given to Brücke and not to Rose, who merely discovered that alkaline solutions of haematin possess this property.

The author describes most carefully the spectrum of solutions of hæmoglobin of different strength when a stratum 1 centimetre broad is examined. It will be remembered that he was the first to suggest the quantitative determination of hæmoglobin in blood by means of the spectroscope.

Solutions containing from 0·003 to 0·009 parts p$ shew very faintly one absorption band. Solution of 0·01 p$ shew two absorption bands, both very feeble. When a solution containing 0·09 p$

is examined the difference in intensity between the two bands is very perceptible. With a solution containing 0·8 p⅜ there is only a broad dark field ; both absorption bands have coalesced and in addition to the red from *a* to near *D* there is only a green stripe observable between *b* and *F*, but near *b*. This green stripe is not seen if the solution contain 0·9 p⅜, but is obviously much more distinctly seen if the solution contain 0·7 p⅜ of hæmoglobin. Solutions containing more than 7·3 p⅜ of hæmoglobin allow no light at all to pass. The solution containing 0·8 p⅜ of hæmoglobin is taken as the normal solution for comparison in determining the per centage of Hb in the blood. Preyer states that the chemical reaction of hæmoglobin is invariably acid, and describes the methods to be used in determining the point.

Hæmoglobin, although a crystalline substance, does not diffuse through parchment paper.

When pure hæmoglobin does not possess the slightest fibrinoplastic properties.

Under the heading of 'Action of heat on Hæmoglobin' the author states that when a small quantity of Na_2CO_3 is added to a solution of Hb, no coagulation takes place though the fluid be heated to 100"C. At 54°C the substance is however obviously decomposed, as the solution becomes of a dark brown-red colour, and exhibits the bands of hæmatin in alkaline solution instead of those of O–Hb. The fluid is alkaline, and remains clear after boiling.

At the temperature at which the decomposition takes place, it is probable that hæmoglobin splits up into hæmatin and albumen, and the author thought it would be interesting to determine what quantity of sodium carbonate had to be added in order to prevent the coagulation by heat. As a mean of two observations he found that one gramme of Hb dissolved in distilled water required 0·0238 grammes of Na_2CO_3. from which he concludes that probably one molecule of sodium must react upon three molecules of hæmoglobin in order to produce the non-coagulating compound. The author has studied the action of the following acids upon hæmoglobin :

phosphoric	acid.	acetic	acid.	lactic	acid.
phosphorous	...	formic	...	citric	...
sulphurous	...	butyric	...	tartaric	...
oxalic	. .	propionic	...	malic	...
monochloracetic	...	metaphosphoric	...	succinic	...
phosphomolybdic	...	benzoic	...	carbolic	...
gallic	...	hydrochloric	...	uric	...
nitric	...	hippuric	...	sulphuric	...
pyrogallic	...	carbonic	...	chromic	...

Substantially the action of all these acids upon haemoglobin appears to be similar in so far as can be ascertained by the spectrum. Some however precipitate the haemoglobin, and upon the occurrence of a precipitate and its characters Preyer bases a classification of their action, for which I must refer the reader to the original paper.

The action of the alkalies and of some alkaline solutions upon haemoglobin is next examined, and the action which they exert is shewn to be more uniformly similar than in the case of the acids. The results of the examination of a large number of salts and of some organic fluids upon solutions of haemoglobin is then stated, and lastly a section is devoted to the consideration of Methämoglobin.

COMPOSITION OF THE GASES OF THE BLOOD IN APNOEA.—Paul Hering (*Inaugural Dissertation*, Dorpat, 1867. Abstracted in *Central-blatt*, 1868, No. 38) has made comparative analyses of the gases of the blood of healthy cats, and of cats in which he had induced apnoea. He obtained as the mean of six experiments on the arterial blood of healthy cats $32 \cdot 81$ $p\frac{0}{0}$ of gases, containing $9 \cdot 92$ $p\frac{0}{0}$ of oxygen, $21 \cdot 91$ $p\frac{0}{0}$ of CO_2, and $0 \cdot 98$ $p\frac{0}{0}$ of N. Having induced apnoea in other 6 cats he found in three out of the six that the O was not materially altered in quantity, whilst in the remainder it was diminished ($8 \cdot 83$ $p\frac{0}{0}$), but, the CO_2 was diminished, being only $11 \cdot 44$ $p\frac{0}{0}$.

Pflüger (*Archiv*, pp. 61—106) has in a most interesting paper on the cause of the movements of respiration, given the results of his own observations on the composition of the gases of the blood of asphyxiated animals, which in no way support Hering's statements. He examined the blood of dogs during normal respiration, and then induced dyspnoea by causing the dogs to breathe nitrogen. About half-a-minute after the commencement of the nitrogen inhalation, blood was allowed to flow from an artery into an absorption tube filled with mercury; by agitating the mercury the blood was defibrinated, and when necessary kept cool by means of ice. From this tube the blood was transferred to a second calibrated tube filled with mercury, which communicated by means of a stop-cock with the exhausted receiver of the mercurial pump. The blood before and after the induction of dyspnoea was exhausted in two separate pumps. The following are the results obtained in the case of two dogs.

1st Dog.	O.	CO₂.	N.	
Before the N-dyspnoea..	18·6	− 24·8	− 1·2	At 0° C. and 1 Metre pressure
During „ „	2·6	− 25·7	− 1·2	„
½ Minutes after „	17·1	− 24·5	− 1·2	„
1½ minute after „	18·1	− 25·3	− 1·5	„
Again, during „	1·5	25·5	1·5	„
After „ „	18·1	17·4	1·2	„
2nd Dog.				
Before tracheotomy	14·35	36·9	1·35	„
During N-asphyxia	0·20	29·9	1·0	„
After recovering by means of artificial respiration.	14·45	29·6	0·7	„
Again during N-dyspnoea	2·20	25·3	0·8	„

These results shew that dyspnoea is not *necessarily* connected with an increase in the quantity of carbonic acid, for this is not constantly observed, but is rather connected with a diminution of oxygen. The idea of Thiry, that during the respiration of gases not containing oxygen there is an increase in the quantity of CO_2, is shewn to be correct, only oxygen having the power of removing the CO_2 of blood. The author thinks it probable that the phenomena of dyspnoea and asphyxia are due to the action of easily oxidizable substances which would be burnt off during active respiration, but which accumulate in the blood during sluggish respiration.

As the researches of Traube, Thiry, and others had shewn that animals might be asphyxiated by the inhalation of mixtures of O and CO_2, the author determined the composition of the gases of the blood under these circumstances.

The animals experimented upon were made to breathe a mixture composed of 70 p $\frac{0}{0}$ of oxygen, and 30 p $\frac{0}{0}$ of CO_2. The following are the results of the analysis of the gases of the blood:

	O.	CO_2	N.	
Before tracheotomy......	14·4	29·8	1·2	vols. p $\frac{0}{0}$ at 0° C. and 1 Metre pressure
During CO_2-dyspnoea...	16·8	56·8	1·4	,, ,,
After respiration of air...	16·15	27·5	1·7	,, ,,
Renewed CO_2-dyspnoea	16·9	53·9	0·0	,, ,,

As during CO_2-dyspnoea the oxygen of the blood may be actually increased in quantity, we must attribute occurrence of dyspnoea to the excess of carbonic acid, and admit that both a want of oxygen, and an increased quantity of carbonic acid, may exert an exciting action upon the respiratory apparatus.

INFLUENCE OF ACIDS ADDED TO BLOOD UPON THE GASES CONTAINED IN IT.—Pflüger and Zuntz (*Pflüger's Archiv*, pp. 361—374) have examined the statement made in the previously quoted thesis on apnoea by Paul Hering, to the effect that phosphoric acid when added to the blood does not, like tartaric acid, lead to a portion of the oxygen being fixed. Hering indeed recommended that this acid should be added to the blood, previous to the determination of the gases; Pflüger and Zuntz now shew that blood which has been treated with phosphoric acid yields the same quantity of carbonic acid, but less oxygen than blood which has not been similarly treated; the diminution in the quantity of oxygen being very great in the cases where a decided excess of acid was employed. It appears therefore that during the splitting up of haemoglobin under the influence of acids, oxygen is retained in stable combination by one of the products formed.

STATE OF COMBINATION OF THE CARBONIC ACID OF BLOOD.—N. Zuntz in an Inaugural Thesis (Bonn, 1868. Abstracted by Hermann in *Centralblatt*, 1868, No. 40) discusses many questions connected with the alkalinity of the blood, and the state of combination in which the CO_2 exists. The author believes that about 5 p$\frac{0}{0}$ of the CO_2 of blood is combined with carbonate of sodium, from 3—5 p$\frac{0}{0}$, with phosphate of sodium, the rest being in part free, in part retained with a combination of potash and haemoglobin in the blood corpuscles.

ACTION OF AMMONIA, ARSENIURETTED AND ANTIMONIURETTED HYDROGEN ON HAEMOGLOBIN.—Koschlakoff and Bogomoloff have recently examined the action of these substances on blood.

When NH_3 gas is passed through solutions of O-, or CO–Hb, the solution assumes a yellowish colour, and the absorption bands disappear entirely, without the appearance of the bands of reduced haemoglobin or of haematin.

When $As H_3$ acts upon O–Hb, reduction takes place. When acting upon CO – Hb, arseniuretted hydrogen exerts a similar action to NH_3 and PH_3; i.e. the absorption-bands disappear entirely.

When $As H_3$ acts upon alkaline solutions of haematin the two absorption-bands of reduced haematin are seen.

SbH_3 exerts a similar action to $As H_3$ on O–Hb and CO–Hb.

CO-HAEMATIN.—Dr L. Popoff (Centralblatt, 1868, No. 42) having studied the action of carbonic oxide upon solutions of haematin arrives at the following conclusions :

1. Neither the acid nor alkaline solutions of haematin suffer any change when CO is passed through them.

2. If however the solution be treated by a reducing agent (H_2S was used by the author, the solution of acid being previously treated with NH_3) at the same time that the CO is being passed through it, a new compound is obtained, which, if an ammoniacal solution of haematin be used, is deposited in the form of a flocculent red precipitate.

3. This substance is characterized by two absorption-bands very similar to those of O-Hb.

4. The precipitate very readily undergoes alteration if exposed to air.

5. The author concludes that this substance is a compound of CO with haematin (! !).

ACTION OF CYANOGEN ON BLOOD.—According to N. Laschkewitsch (Archiv v. Reichert und Du Bois-Reymond 1868, pp. 649-655), when CN is conducted through blood it not only gradually reduces the O-Hb, but prevents the reduced Hb from combining with oxygen[1].

ON THE PRESENCE OF PEPTONE IN THE SERUM OF BLOOD AND CHYLE.—Subbotin (Zeitschrift f. Rat. Medicin von Heale und Pfeufer. Dritte Reihe, Bd. 33. 1 Heft, p. 64) states that the traces of a peptone-like substance which have been found in the serum of blood, and of chyle, after the separation of the albumen which is coagulable

[1] Is it not likely that in this case a compound of the oxygenized blood colouring matter is formed with cyanogen, similar to the compounds with cyanide of potassium, and with the nitrites, and that the spectrum described as that of reduced haemoglobin is really the spectrum of the new substance? A. G.

by heat and acids, are due to the action of the latter upon Albumen. If egg-albumen be diluted with water, treated with a trace of acetic acid and boiled, the perfectly clear fluid will be found to contain a substance which, though not precipitable by acids or heat, possesses the characteristic properties of a protein body. He concludes that there is no evidence of the presence of peptone in blood.

Chemistry of Nerves.

Ranke (*Centralblatt*, 1868, No. 49) refutes the accuracy of Heidenhain's results, which appeared to contradict Funke's and his own statements with reference to the acidification of nerve substance during tetanus. He explains Heidenhain's negative results by his having employed tincture of litmus instead of delicate litmus paper; the tincture may have contained a faint excess of alkali, and thus have neutralized the feeble acidity of the nerve substance without its own colour being affected.

Heidenhain (*Centralblatt*, 1868, No. 53) insists upon the accuracy of his own statements. Ranke in his opinion has erred in instituting a comparison between the nerves of normal frogs whose blood and muscle juice were alkaline with those of tetanized frogs whose muscular juice and blood were acid.

On the Excretion of the Nitrogen of the Albuminoid Bodies which are Consumed in the Organism (*Centralblatt*, 1868, No. 41).

Sicwenow has attempted to ascertain whether in addition to the nitrogen which is excreted in the urine and fæces, there is a portion which is expired by the lungs as nitrogen-gas. He has carried out three sets of observations, each extending over ten days. The whole of the food was analysed so as to determine exactly the nitrogen ingested, as well as the amount excreted *per vesicam* and *per anum*.

The following are the results :—

	1st Series (12 days)	2nd Series (10 days)	3rd Series. (10 days)
Change in weight of body during the experiment	− 670 grms.	− 550 grms.	+ 1150 grms.
Ratio of N : C in food......	1 : 10·1	1 : 10·9	1 : 14·7 „
Total N ingested	255 grms.	190·5 grm.	193·5 grms.
N in urine	209·4 „	158·4 „	156·8 „
N in fæces	36·68 „	27·87 „	25.63 „
N not accounted for	8·86 „	4·2 „	11·14 „
or of total N there was unaccounted for	3·47 p ⁰∕₀	2·28 p. ⁰∕₀	5·75 p. ⁰∕₀

In both the first sets of experiments the nitrogen unaccounted for is in proportion to the total nitrogen ingested so small that the deficit may fairly be considered to fall within the limits of experimental error.

In the third series the increase in the weight of the body may explain the want of balance between the ingested and excreted nitrogen. The author is of opinion that the nitrogen which is contained in food leaves the body entirely in the urine and fæces.   In the above experiments the ratio between the nitrogen excreted *per anum* and *per vesicam* was almost constantly the same viz. 5.7 : 1 ; 5·68 : 1 ; 6·0 : 1.

Urine.

URINE PIGMENT.—De Jaffe (*Centralblatt*, 1869, No. 12) finds that when solutions of urinary pigment are treated with chloride of zinc a beautiful green fluorescence is observed, which disappears if an acid be added, and reappears on again rendering the fluid alkaline.

It will be remembered that De Jaffe had been led to suspect the identity of urinary colouring matter with a product of the action of acids on bile ; he now finds that the action of chloride of zinc on the bile-colouring matter in question is identical with that which it exerts on urine.

ALBUMEN IN URINE.—Gerhardt (*Deutsche Archiv f. Klin. Med.* 1868 ; *Centralblatt*, 1869, No. 11) has found that occasionally the urine of patients suffering from Bright's disease contains an anomalous form of albumen which is not precipitated by heat or nitric acid.

DR FRASER'S REPORT.

Physiological Action of Medicinal and Poisonous Substances.

ARSENIC.—An important memoir has been published by Dr Jules Lolliot (*Étude Physiologique de l'Arsenic*, Paris, 1868) on the physiological action of Arsenic; but so much valuable matter is included in this research that it is impossible to give a satisfactory abstract within the limits at our disposal.   The general views of the author may, however, be expressed in the following manner: Arsenic checks oxidation and tissue-combustion, and it restrains nutrition ; for during its administration the temperature is lowered, and the excretion of urea by the kidneys and the exhalation of carbonic acid by the lungs are diminished.   In poisonous doses, it causes fatty degeneration of the liver, kidneys, and even of the muscles.   These effects, and several others that are noticed, are referred by Dr Lolliot to an action of arsenic on the blood-corpuscles (hæmoglobin?), in virtue of which it, to a certain extent (and in common with antimony and phosphorus), takes the place of oxygen.   In consequence of this substitution the oxidizing power of the blood-corpuscles is diminished ; and as they cannot therefore furnish to the various organs a sufficient allowance of the elements essential to their nutrition, these organs undergo, with large doses of arsenic, a retrogressive transformation which is manifested by fatty degeneration.

BROMIDE OF POTASSIUM.—To the numerous recent investigations on Bromide of Potassium Dr F. A. Saison contributes an additional one of considerable merit and interest (*Du Bromure de Potassium et de son Antagonisme avec la Strychnine,* Paris, 1868).   His experiments on the lower animals point out that two principal and dominant actions are always produced by large doses of this salt: diminution of cerebral activity and impairment of motion followed by paralysis. The paralysis is due to an action on the spinal cord and on afferent and efferent nerves, and not to one on muscles. Saison appears to consider, in opposition to several previous observers, that the afferent (sensory) nerves are not always paralysed at an early stage in the poisoning; but that, sometimes, they retain their conductivity even until a few seconds before death. The heart escapes the poisonous action entirely. He agrees with previous observers in maintaining that the sympathetic nerve-system is powerfully affected, the vascular nerves being so energetically stimulated that the minute blood-vessels are often contracted to such a degree as to become completely closed. The action both on the central nerve-organs and on the nerves themselves (periphery) may be explained by this effect on the blood-vessels; interference with nutrition consequent on contraction of blood-vessels being in both cases the cause of paralysis. Saison has also studied the physiological action of bromide of potassium on man; and this portion of his brochure is of special interest to the physician. The *motor-nerve system* is always the first to be affected, and while, in many cases, weakness merely may be produced, in others there may be almost absolute loss of motor power. The effects on *sensibility* are less constant, and no instance of complete anæsthesia appears to have been met with by any observer. *Cerebral activity* is impaired almost as promptly and invariably as motricity; and like that of the latter this impairment is met with in very varying degrees, from slight feebleness of intellectual activity even to idiocy. Somnolence is very constantly produced both by large and small doses; and after the latter, many observers have described various cerebral effects of a more serious character. The principal effects that are produced by large doses on the *special senses* are slight blindness, with, occasionally, temporary amblyopia, and diminution in the acuteness of hearing or even decided deafness: but these are comparatively rare effects. Numerous observations exist to prove that the *generative function* is weakened or even rendered impossible by this salt. This inconvenience usually disappears soon after the administration is stopped, but sometimes it remains long afterwards. Epileptics seem able to take large quantities without any impairment in their genital functions. In the majority of cases the *heart* is unaffected, and where any change is observed it invariably consists of a diminution in the number of the contractions, and frequently also of an improvement in the regularity of the heart's action. The *temperature* is scarcely ever affected, and when it is an extremely slight diminution is observed. The *minute blood-vessels* are always contracted, and the peripheral circulation thereby diminished. Saison attributes the emaciation, which is sometimes produced after a long continued administration, to this influence on the circulation. The *respiratory movements* are but little affected in man. The *secretions* are very slightly influenced. That of the kidneys is somewhat augmented; that of the salivary glands neither increased nor diminished;

and that of the sebaceous glands faintly diminished. On the *digestive system* several marked effects are observed: the appetite is increased, and constipation is always produced. In conclusion, all the functions that are under the control of the sympathetic system are modified in accordance with an excitation of that system, and those under the control of the cerebro-spinal in accordance with a diminution in its activity.

Dr Saison believes that strychnia is the substance which has the strongest claims to be regarded as the antagonistic in action to bromide of potassium. The former, he asserts, dilates blood-vessels, and in this way increases the excitability of the reflex centres; the latter contracts blood-vessels, and thus diminishes this excitability. His experiments have demonstrated that strychnia-convulsions may be impeded in their manifestation and lessened in their violence by the bromide. The antagonism is not, however, a perfect one; for while bromide of potassium diminishes cerebral activity, strychnia has no influence whatever on the brain.

THE SULPHATES OF POTASH, SODA, AND MAGNESIA.—MM. Jolyet and Cahours publish an investigation (*Archives du Physiologie*, No. 1, 1869, p. 113), in which certain questions connected with the physiological action of the above substances are examined. They confirm the previous statement of Blake, Grandeau, Bernard, and others, that salts of potash are extremely poisonous, and have a primary paralysing action on the heart and on striped muscles generally. Their experiments with the sulphates of soda and of magnesia were performed for the purpose of ascertaining if these neutral salts act as cathartics when they are exhibited by injection into the veins. With the former salt they obtained the following results: "1. That sulphate of soda does not purge when it is injected into the veins; and 2. that this salt tends to produce hæmorrhage, and retards the progress of cicatrisation by diminishing the coagulability of the blood." With sulphate of magnesia, similarly administered, they found that, though the stools were sometimes liquid and tinged with bile-pigments, no proper purgation was caused. Jolyet and Cahours contradict the assertion of M. Rabuteau that the salts of magnesia are as devoid of poisonous properties as those of soda. In their experiments, doses of sulphate of soda, varying from 150 to 230 grains, could be injected into the blood-vessels of dogs without causing death; whereas doses of sulphate of magnesia, varying from 30 to 92 grains, invariably caused sudden ("presque foudroyante") death. By some experiments on frogs they have arrived at the conclusion that sulphate of magnesia has an action similar to that of curara on motor nerves.

MORPHIA.—In reviewing the facts ascertained, in a somewhat fragmentary investigation into the physiological action of Morphia, Dr Gscheidlen (*Untersuchungen aus dem physiologischen Laboratorium in Würzburg*, Drittes Heft, 1868) states his results in the following manner: 1. Morphia, in small doses, elevates the excitability of the motor nerves of muscles; and in large doses it diminishes this excitability. 2. Acetate of morphia at first increases the excitability of the sensory nerves (1 and 2 refer specially to frogs). 3. Acetate of morphia acts by first stimulating, and, then, abolishing the functions of all the nerves that influence the circulation. 4. It at once lowers the activity of the respiratory centres in the *medulla oblongata*. 5. In small doses, it at first elevates the temperature of the body; in toxic doses, it at once lowers it. 6. It does not affect the striped muscles. Gscheidlen concludes his paper by pointing out that this investigation does not include all the actions of morphia, and by promising to overtake the many points that have been omitted on some future occasion.

PAPAVERINE.—In the last number of this *Journal* (p. 228) we gave an abstract of some researches by Dr Leidesdorf on the action of Papaverine; according to whom this active principle of opium acts as a narcotic and soporific and produces muscular relaxation. These results are contradicted in a more recent research by Dr Hofmann (*Wiener Med. Wochenschr.* XVIII. 58, 59, 1858). This author, in the first place, subjected himself to some experiments with hydrochlorate of papaverine. He took, on three successive days, doses of 1·8, 3·7, and 5·5 grains, but after the first two doses no distinct symptom was observed. About an hour-and-a-half after the third dose, he suffered from severe hiccup, which disappeared in six minutes, and was followed by epigastric pain; and, on the disappearance of this, he experienced acute frontal headache, without any sensation of muscular relaxation or weakness. He thus collects together the results of his numerous experiments with this salt: 1. Papaverine occupies an extremely low position as a narcotic, for every other narcotic alkaloid produces decided hypnotic symptoms when given in so large a dose as five-and-a-half grains. 2. This dose of papaverine, however, does not cause the slightest hypnotic symptom. 3. Papaverine does not cause muscular relaxation. 4. Its effects are not cumulative, for when administered, during several days, in successively increasing doses, it produces neither sleep nor muscular relaxation. 5. Papaverine has no action on the pulse, respirations, nor animal temperature. 6. It does not produce constipation; nor has it any influence on the excretion of urine, neither its total quantity nor the quantity of the urea it contains being increased[1].

PHYSOSTIGMA (Calabar Bean).—A valuable paper has been published by Drs Arnstein and Sustschinsky, of Moscow, on the method in which Physostigma affects the cardiac nerves (*Untersuchungen aus dem physiologischen Laboratorium in Würzburg;* Drittes Heft, 1868,

[1] The investigations on Papaverine resemble those on several of the other active principles of opium in the great discrepancy of the results of different investigators. The explanation of this is probably to be found in the impurity of these alkaloids, even when obtained from some of the best manufacturers, their separation having been imperfectly effected, so that one principle frequently contains a notable admixture of another. F.

pp. 81—106). Their results are the following :—1. Calabar bean does not paralyse the musculo-cardiac ganglia in the heart. 2. The sympathetic nerve retains its power of increasing the rapidity of the heart's action when irritated by galvanism ; and, accordingly, it likewise is not paralysed. 3. The central portion of the vagus is either very little or not at all affected by Calabar bean. 4. On the other hand, a well-marked influence is exercised upon the peripheral terminations of the vagus, their excitability being considerably elevated ; and on this depends the stoppage of the heart's action in poisoning by Calabar bean[1]. 5. Even with large doses, the death of the animal (with artificial respiration) occurs without previous paralysis of the vagus. 6. The increase of the excitability of the peripheral terminations of the vagus is the consequence of a direct action on these terminations, and not of any indirect action produced by alteration in the blood-pressure. 7. The prolonged after-action and the independent involvement of the peripheral terminations of the vagus indicate the possession by these of a physiological function that is to a certain degree independent of a special (ganglionic) histological structure. 8. In corresponding doses, atropia and Calabar bean act antagonistically on the vagus.—We have also to draw attention to the very important investigation of Dr Hermann Roeber (*Ueber die Wirkungen des Calabarextractes auf Herz und Rückenmark*, Berlin, 1868). We shall content ourselves with stating briefly the arguments advanced against the fourth result of Arnstein and Sustschinsky, and with mentioning the principal results contained in the summary at the conclusion of this paper. In reference to the influence of physostigma on the heart's movements, Roeber states (p. 51) that " Fraser and Tachau assume a paralysis of vaso-motor nerves ; Lenz, Arnstein and Sustschinsky an irritation of the regulator ; v. Bezold and Götz an irritation of both cardiac nerve-centres. My observations lead me to confirm Fraser and Tachau." * * * " Arnstein and Sustschinsky concluded that there is an increase of the excitability of the vagus, chiefly from the circumstance that after poisoning with Calabar, stoppage of the heart by irritation of the vagus took place

---

[1] This statement is at variance with my results and also with those of Dr Roeber (an abstract of whose elaborate investigation is given immediately after this one). It is extremely difficult to understand how a mere increase in the excitability of the peripheral cardiac terminations of the vagi can be the cause of the cardiac paralysis in poisoning by physostigma Without entering into a discussion of this explanation, its improbability will be at once seen if we bear in mind that the heart is affected by physostigma as readily after division of the vagi as before it. Now, were this explanation correct, such division should greatly diminish the action on the heart, for it removes that organ from all central and reflex inhibitory influences.

Near the commencement of their memoir (p. 85), Drs Arnstein and Sustschinsky complain that a paper I published in the second number (May, 1867) of this Journal does not contain sufficient experimental proof of the results that are given. They have unfortunately overlooked the footnote in p. 328, where it is explained that those results are taken from an investigation communicated to the Royal Society of Edinburgh. This investigation has since been published in the *Transactions* (xxiv. part iii., 1866—67, pp. 715 —787) ; by referring to which it will be found that all the results I state are supported by detailed experimental proof. F.

on a greater distance of the coils" (of an induction apparatus) "from one another than before the poisoning." According to Roeber, this argument is insufficient, for the same result would be obtained if the excitability of the vaso-motor nerves was diminished. "In support of their view, A. and S. also state that direct irritation of the sympathetic in the neck after the poisoning is always able to produce a further increase in the number of the pulsations by from 32 to 40." As to this, it is suggested that notwithstanding an effect upon the sympathetic, its excitability is not removed but only weakened, if the doses are not too large. This diminished excitability shows itself by slowing, and not by completely stopping, the heart's action; and it is easy to understand how during its existence strong electric currents may still excite the sympathetic centres in the heart to increased activity. The other important points examined in this able investigation are referred to in the following statement of results :—1. *The principal action of Calabar bean consists of a diminution and final abolition of the activity of the ganglionic elements of the spinal cord*[1]*;* and, indeed, the ganglionic groups lying in the grey substance in the anterior cornua, which conduct motor impulses from the brain to the periphery, are first affected, and, then, the elements of the grey substance lying in the posterior cornua, which conduct sensations of pain to the brain. 2. *By this destruction of function in the grey substance there is produced a complete loss of the motility and of the reflex activity of the spinal cord, as well as complete loss of the sensation of pain;* while the sensation of touch and the so-called muscular sensation remains till the death of the animal. 3. Besides this action on the spinal cord, *Calabar bean possesses a specific action upon the heart's movements,* which by small doses are only slowed, but by large doses are completely stopped. *This action of the poison depends on a diminution of the excitation and final paralysis of the excito-motor centre.* 4. *The impairment of respiration,* which especially occurs with small doses, *is either the consequence of the sudden disturbance of the heart's action, or of destruction of the motility of the respiratory muscles,* produced by paralysis of the spinal cord. 5. The poison increases the secretion of tears and saliva. 6. *The increase of defæcation, which has been observed after Calabar bean poisoning, is the consequence of tetanus of the stomach and gut,* the cause of which has still to be more accurately determined. 7. *The motor and sensory nerves, at the time of the commencement of the development of the spinal-cord action, are not altered in their excitability;* later, there occurs a paralysis, or a more rapid death, of the intra-muscular terminations of the former. 8. *The fibrillary muscular twitching,* especially conspicuous in mammals, and occurring immediately after the administration, *may be explained by a local irritation of the termination of the motor nerves preceding their paralysis.* 9. *The pupils are strongly contracted,* both by the external application and (with large doses) by the internal administration of Calabar bean. Still more accurate experiments have to be instituted as to the cause of this phenomenon.

[1] The italics of this and the following sentences are the Author's.

VERATRIA.—M. Prévost in a valuable paper (*Recherches Expéri-mentales Relatives à l'action de la veratrine*; and *Journ. de l'Anatomie* par M. Robin, 1868, p. 206) divides the symptoms of veratria action into three periods :—1st, a period of *excitation*; 2nd, a period of *spasms*; 3rd, a period of *resolution*. The first and third of these have already been fully and accurately described by Kölliker, Schroff, Fauchey, and Ollivier and Bergeron; but M. Prévost states much that is both interesting and important in reference to the second division. In the first place, he shows that veratria lessens the force of the heart's contractions; but it differs from the majority of cardiac poisons in so far that its primary action is not on the heart, but on the other striped muscles, in which spasmodic contractions are excited. Thus, the action on the heart is always preceded by the action on the general muscular system; and this occurs even where the poison is directly applied to that organ. The convulsions that are produced in frogs by this action on the muscular system have been accurately contrasted with those produced by strychnia, in the following manner :—

In strychnia-poisoning.

1. Convulsions occur at the com-mencement.
2. The initial convulson is suc-ceeded by a series of convul-sions.

3. Extremely slight peripheral excitation causes a convul-sion.
4. The most feeble peripheral excitation always originates general convulsions.

5. Convulsions disappear on de-struction of the spinal cord.

6. Convulsions cease in limbs se-parated from the trunk, and consequently from the spinal cord. In parts so separated, excitation of nerve trunks or of muscles cause merely nor-mal contractions.
7. Convulsions occur in limbs separated from the circulation by ligature of blood-vessels, provided the nerve-trunks are intact.

In veratria-poisoning.

1. Spasmodic contractions occur at the commencement.
2. The initial contraction is pro-longed, and usually terminates in a series of faint fibrillary twitches.
3. It is difficult to originate spas-modic contractions by peri-pheral excitation.
4. Excitation often causes con-tractions that are altogether limited to the excited regions; occasionally, however, the con-tractions are general.
5. Spasmodic contractions may be caused even after destruc-tion of the spinal cord, by irritation of either the nerves or the muscles.
6. In limbs separated from the trunk, and consequently from the spinal cord, spasmodic con-tractions may be caused by ir-ritation of the nerve-trunks or of the muscles.

7. No spasmodic contractions oc-cur in limbs separated from the circulation by ligature of blood-vessels.

From numerous experiments, Prévost has satisfied himself that neither the central nor peripheral nervous system has any direct influence on the phenomena of the second stage of veratria-poisoning, but that, during this stage, this alkaloid acts simply by increasing, and slightly modifying, the functional activity of the muscular system. This action is succeeded by diminution, and, if the dose be a large one, by destruction of muscular contractility. Prévost did not obtain any distinct evidence of an action on the sensory nerves.

THE METHYL AND ETHYL DERIVATIVES OF ATROPIA, CONIA AND STRYCHNIA. CHEMISTRY AND PHYSIOLOGY.—In continuing their investigations on the connection between chemical constitution and physiological action, Drs Crum Brown and Fraser have published an abstract of some researches on the physiological action of the salts of the ammonium basis derived from atropia and conia (*Proc. R. S. Ed.*, 18th Jan., 1869, p. 461). The atropia-derivatives examined were the iodides and sulphates of methyl-atropium and of ethyl-atropium. The authors find that the action of these substances on the sympathetic system is essentially the same as that of atropia, while the action on the cerebro-spinal nervous system is different. The principal effects produced by atropia on the latter system are excitation of the spinal cord, and paralysis of the motor and sensory nerves. In their previous paper, the authors showed that the spinal-stimulant action of strychnia, brucia, thebaia, codeia, and morphia is not possessed by the ammonium bases derived from the alkaloids, but that, in its place, these bases possess a markedly different paralysing action on the peripheral terminations of motor nerves. They now announce that a similar change occurs in the methyl and ethyl derivatives of atropia. These derivatives are more powerful paralysing substances than atropia itself; as they combine with its ordinary paralysing action an additional amount, bearing some ratio to the absent spinal-stimulant action of the natural base. Probably for these reasons the salts of methyl- and ethyl-atropium are fatal to the lower animals in much smaller doses than the salts of atropia. The latter portion of this paper treats of the chemical properties and physiological action of various salts of conia, of methyl-conia, and of dimethyl-conium. It was found that the salts of conia and of methyl-conia very closely resemble each other in action and in poisonous activity; and the symptoms that were observed agree with the descriptions of the effects of conia by the more trustworthy of previous observers. In rabbits, the most obvious of the effects were stiffness of the limbs, causing difficulty in moving about; spasmodic starts; distinct increase of reflex excitability; gradually increasing paralysis with diminution and, afterwards, disappearance of the reflex excitability; and, finally, death by asphyxia. In frogs, the symptoms are mainly those of paralysis, and the authors confirm the observations of Kölliker and Guttmann, that this paralysis in the case of conia is due to a curara-like action. They further find that methyl-conia also acts by paralysing the terminations of motor nerves. The salts of dimethyl-conium differ from those of conia and of methyl-conia in never directly producing convulsant effects, and in being much less active as poisons.   In rabbits and frogs, the symptoms were invariably those of paralysis ; and, in the latter animal, the authors have demonstrated that this paralysis is due to an action on the terminations of motor nerves.   MM. L. Pélissard, F. Jolyet, and André Cahours, communicated a paper on the physiological action of ethyl-conia and iodide of diethyl-conium, compared with that of conia, to the Academy of Sciences at Paris (*Compt. Rend.* 1869, p. 149), on the same date as Brown and Fraser communicated their paper to the Royal Society of Edinburgh.   Both researches agree in all essential particulars.   The French physiologists found that " the introduction of the radical ethyl into conia abolishes the stage of convulsions that precedes paralysis in the poisoning by this alkaloid; this result being chiefly manifest in poisoning by iodide of diethyl-conium, when the animal falls deprived of all power of voluntary movement, without the occurrence of the slightest convulsive symptom."   They also found that ethyl-conia and diethyl-conium paralyses the vagi nerves; but this action is likewise possessed by conia.   They assert that of the three substances, conia is the most active as a poison, then ethyl-conia, and, finally, diethyl-conium; the last never having produced complete paralysis.   (It will be seen from this investigation, and from the latter portion of that of Brown and Fraser, that ethyl conia and diethyl-conium differ in poisonous activity from methyl-conia and dimethyl-conium ; the former derivatives of conia being less active than the latter.   This difference occurs between the ethyl- and methyl-derivatives of the majority of the alkaloids, and it is very conspicuous with those of strychnia.   It seems to be greatly due to a comparative slowness in the absorption of the ethyl-compounds, a character which renders them less suitable than the methyl-compounds for comparison with the natural alkaloid.) —In an earlier paper, MM. Jolyet and Cahours describe some of the physiological effects of the iodides of methyl-strychnium and of ethyl-strychnium (*Compt. Rend.*, 2 Nov. 1868, p. 904).   In all important points they confirm the previous researches of Brown and Fraser (of which they were unaware at the time of their communication). They, however, assert that, besides paralysing motor nerves, these substances produce feeble convulsant and tetanic symptoms analogous in character to those of strychnia.   (There can be no doubt that the discrepancy between the last statement and the results of Brown and Fraser is due to the French physiologists having employed substances that were not absolutely pure.   It is obvious that the presence of a minute trace of unacted-on strychnia will manifest its presence by such results as are described by MM. Jolyet and Cahours.)

ON THE INSUSCEPTIBILITY OF PIGEONS TO THE TOXIC ACTION OF OPIUM.—Dr Weir Michell, an American physiologist to whom we are indebted for numerous important and laborious researches, has lately drawn attention to the insusceptibility of Pigeons to the toxic action of opium (*Amer. Journ. of Med. Sc.*, 1869, p. 37).   Having had occasion to produce sleep in pigeons, he administered to them doses of various preparations of opium, but failed in producing the desired effect. Astonished at this failure, he endeavoured to discover what amount of opium was required to kill these birds. He thus states his results:—"Pigeon took eighty drops of black-drop internally; no effect except a tendency to keep quiet; no signs of stupor; no change of pupils; feathers ruffled, as is common with these birds when sick from any cause. Pigeon received forty-two drops of black-drop under skin of groin. Symptoms the same as in the last case. Neither of them slept at all, and both were well the next day. Pigeon received under skin, in three localities, in all, two grains of sulphate of morphia, dissolved in water slightly acidulated with acetic acid. No effects were seen other than those described in the former cases. Pigeon took, internally, three grains of sulphate of morphia, dissolved; recovery without notable symptoms. Pigeon took, at 8·30 A.M., two hundred and seventy-two drops of black-drop. He retained it during an hour, but at 12 was found to have vomited an unknown amount of it, by estimate at least half; recovered after remaining all day quiet in the corner of his cage; not asleep, and capable of being easily roused, and then able to execute every usual movement, as flying, walking, and the like. The final experiment seems to me decisive. To a large pigeon, which, within the two preceding days, had swallowed forty-two drops of black-drop, I gave, between two P.M. and six o'clock, *twenty-one* grains of powdered opium in soft pills of three grains each. Except the usual tendency to remain quiet, none of the common evidences of opium poisoning appeared, and the pigeon was well and active the next day." Dr Weir Michell confesses his inability to offer any satisfactory explanation of this immunity [1]. Dr Richardson of London has repeated

---

[1] This example of insusceptibility is one among many that have already been described, and which strongly indicate the necessity for greater attention being directed to the study of *comparative toxicology*. Such insusceptibilities may be divided into two great classes:—1st, Those that are dependent on causes for which absolutely no explanation can be suggested by the knowledge we at present possess of normal and pathological physiology, among which may be placed the immunity of the serpent to its own venom; and 2ndly, those that are dependent on special varieties of organization in animals of different species, among which, probably, may be placed the insusceptibility of pigeons to opium. Many of the examples that must at present be included in the first class are probably founded on erroneous observation; conspicuous among which is the asserted immunity of hedgehogs to the poisonous influence of prussic acid. The examples included in the second class may be explained by functional and structural differences in animals of different species. Thus *ceteris paribus* if the activity of absorption in one animal be greater than in another, the same poison will affect the former more violently than the latter; or if the activity of elimination in one animal be greater than in another, the same poison will affect the former less violently than the latter. Differences of structure, also, will obviously affect the actions of poisons. So-called "cerebrants," among which is included opium, act more violently in animals whose cerebral lobes are well developed than in those where they are present in a comparatively rudimentary form; and for a similar reason, strychnia produces convulsions in all animals that possess a distinctly differentiated central reflex organ. Opium probably produces its principal effects on the brain indirectly through its primary action on the vascular system. Whatever may be the exact nature of

a number of these experiments and made several additional ones, which confirm the correctness of Dr Mitchell's observations (*Brit. and For. Med. Ch. Rev.*, April, 1869, p. 538).

VENOM OF THE COBRA-DI-CAPELLA AND OF THE VIPER.— Professor Vulpian has made a number of experiments on frogs, rabbits, and rats with some cobra venom obtained from Dr Shortt of Madras (*Archives de Physiologie*, No. 1, 1869, p. 123). He found that it gradually diminishes the functional activity of the central nerve-organs, and so produces a condition resembling somnolence. In frogs, the effects are somewhat analogous to, but less energetic than, those of curara; the conductivity of motor nerves being destroyed before ideo-muscular contractility. The blood-heart continues to beat for some time after death, but the lymph-hearts are paralysed at a comparatively early period. Vulpian frequently examined the blood of poisoned animals, but he has not been able to confirm Professor Hulford's observation that this poison causes a rapid production of numerous molecular bodies in the blood. He has satisfied himself that the cobra poison may be absorbed by the mucous membrane at the upper portion (fauces) of the digestive track of frogs.—A note by MM. Cherou and Goujou was communicated to the French Academy by Professor Robin (*Compt. Rend.*, 9 Novembre, p. 962), in which these authors state that they caused a viper to bite a rabbit, and on its death, obtained from the region that had been bitten a quantity of a red serosity, some of which they injected under the skin of a second rabbit with the result that death occurred in it also. From these experiments they conclude that venom has the property of modifying the fluids of the poisoned animal in such a manner as to convert them into poisons.

this action, it will be produced in all animals that possess minute blood-vessels whose condition is regulated by a nerve apparatus analogous to that present in mammals, &c. But cerebral symptoms will be manifested chiefly in animals where the brain is of greatest developement, and only so slightly as to be scarcely distinguishable in those where the brain is rudimentary. F.

Professor Huxley made a communication (a brief abstract of a paper) on the homologies of the incus and malleus. He had been led to reconsider this subject and to make further investigations in consequence of the recent observations of Professor Peters of Berlin, who maintains the opinion held by Oken and Cuvier that the quadrate bone is the homologue of the tympanic, and who conceives that he has traced Meckel's cartilage in the crocodile through the articular part of the lower jaw up to the stapes. Professor Huxley's investigations lead him to the conclusion that this is a mistaken observation. A pneumatic duct from the quadrate bone, and not Meckel's cartilage, traverses the articular bone at the part specified. Continuing his researches in other animals, and especially in the singular Lizard *Sphenodon*, (or *Hatteria*), he had been led to modify the views he previously held. Instead of regarding the incus as the homologue of the quadrate, he now considers it to form part of the second visceral arch, and to be represented, in Birds and Reptiles, by a Ligament or a cartilage connected with the stapes. He regards the malleus as the representative of the quadrate, the *articulare* of the lower *Vertebrata* not being represented by bone in the *Mammalia*. In Fishes he considers the incus to be represented by the "hyomandibular" or "suspensorial" element. He laid much stress upon the portio dura of the 7th nerve and the representative of the chorda tympani as guides to the determination of the homologies of the bones and the components of the visceral arches.

Professor Humphry was glad that Prof. Huxley renounced the view of the homology of the quadrate and the incus, but was unwilling to admit that the quadrate is the homologue of the malleus. Such a transference of an auditory ossicle to the masticatory apparatus was, he thought not, in accordance with the laws of morphology, forasmuch as the several parts of each organ in the ascending series of animals are usually supplied by development from the organ itself and not by borrowing from other organs. He thought it more probable that the articular part of the oviparous jaw is represented by the condyloid part of the mammalian jaw which in the foetal state is largely composed of cartilage, and that the quadrate is formed from some of the parts in the line of the lower jaw and the skull than that the auditory ossicles are transferred to this region. He suggested that the inter-articular cartilage of the temporo-maxillary joint may represent the quadrate bone, just as the inter-articular cartilage of the sterno-clavicular joint represents the omo-sternal bone of certain rodents.

Mr Parker had been investigating this matter in Amphibians, and his researches led him to agree with the views propounded by Prof. Huxley which he regarded as very important.

INDEX TO VOL. III.

CAMBRIDGE : PRINTED BY C. J. CLAY, M.A., AT THE UNIVERSITY PRESS.

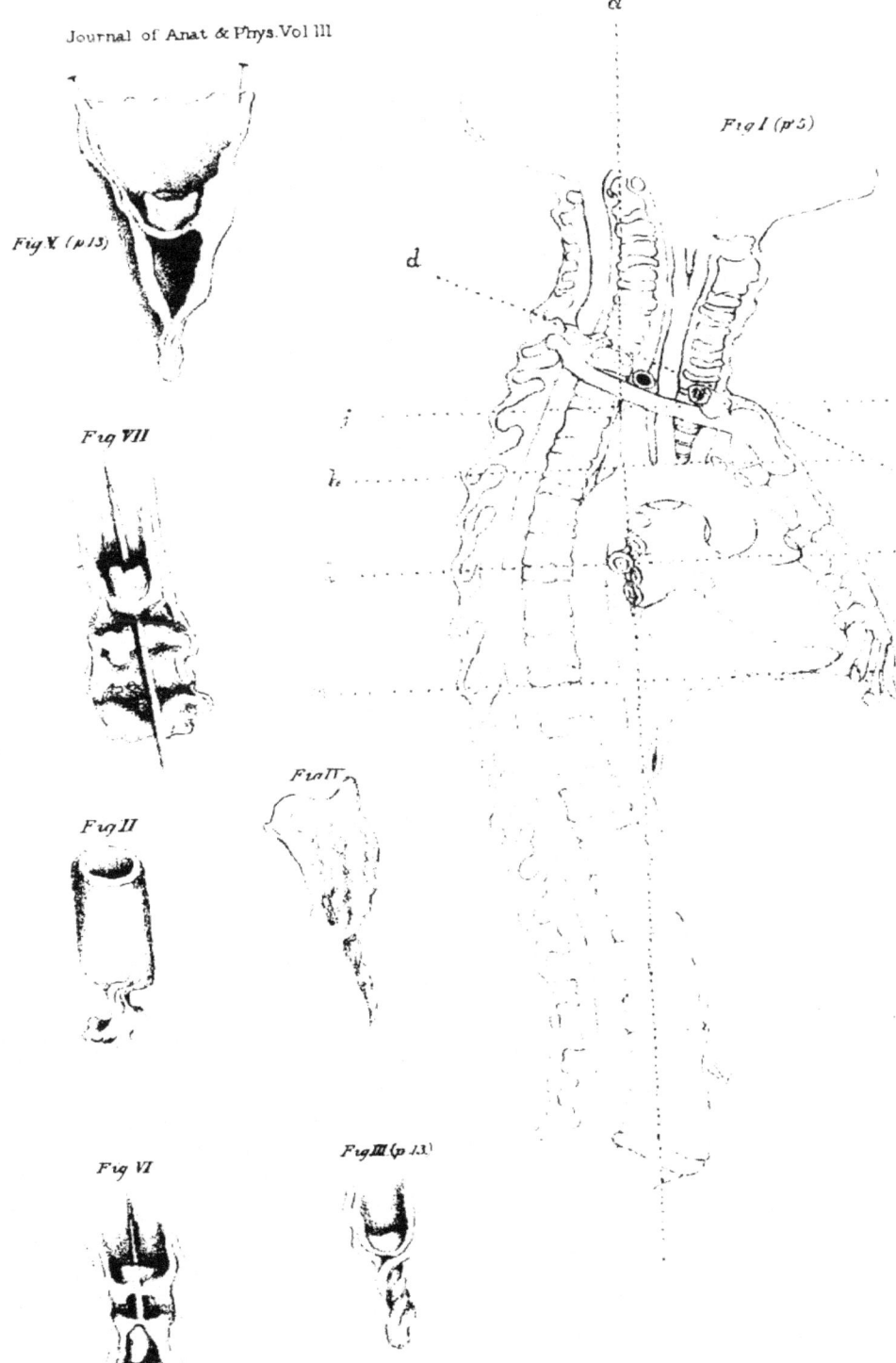

Fig V. (p 13)

Fig VII

Fig II

Fig IV

Fig VI

Fig III (p 13)

Fig I (p 5)

a

d

i

k

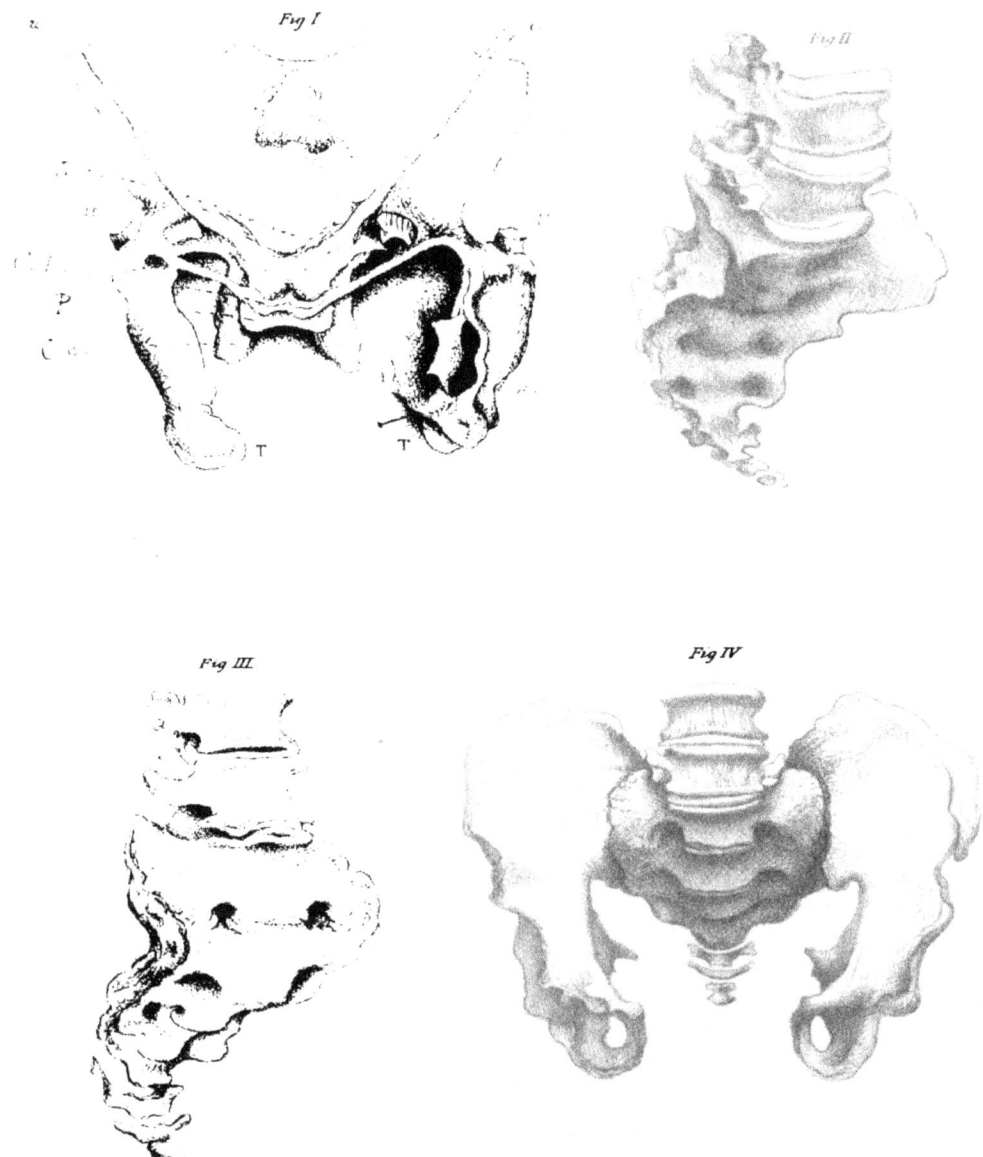

Fig I

Fig II

Fig III

Fig IV

ECTOPIA VESICÆ *(p 87)*

Fig II   Fig I

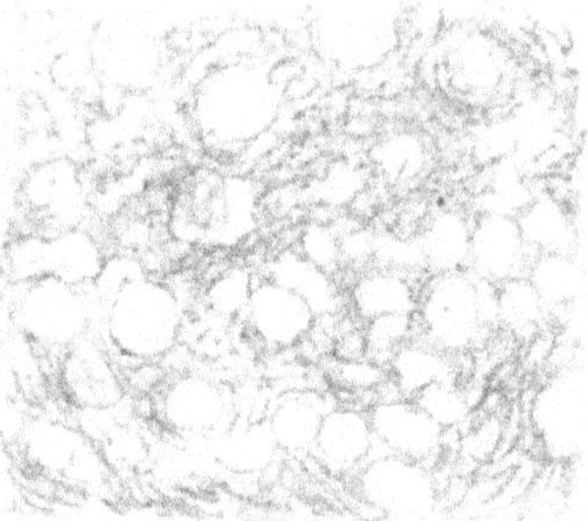

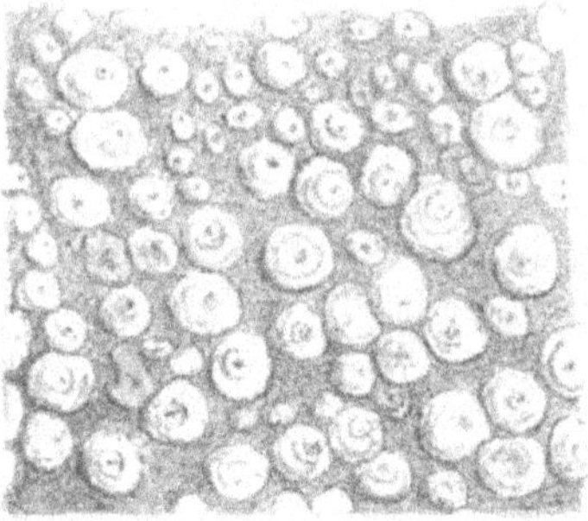

Fig V

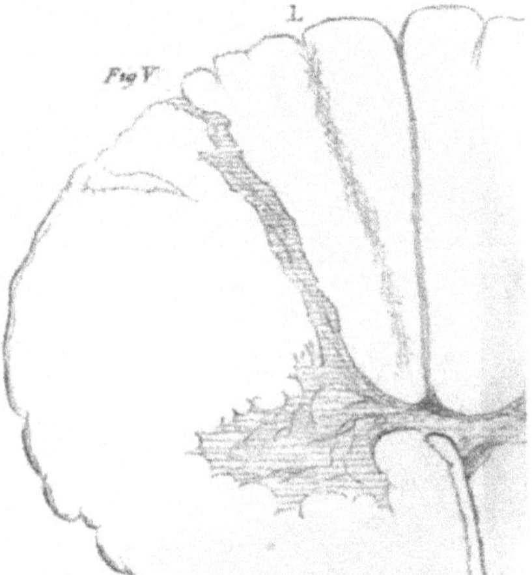

Fig VI   L

L

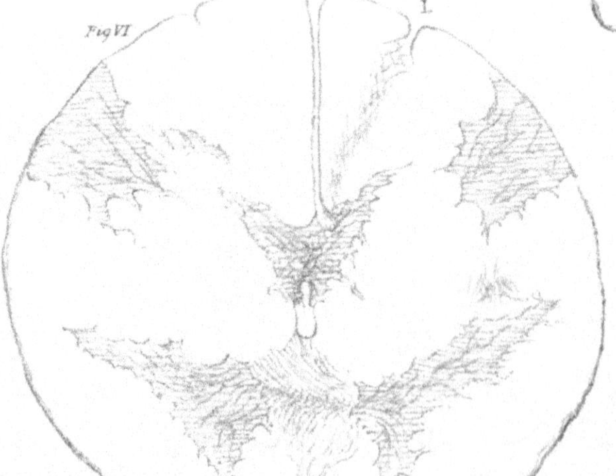

SPINAL
AFTER AMPUT...
LIMBS

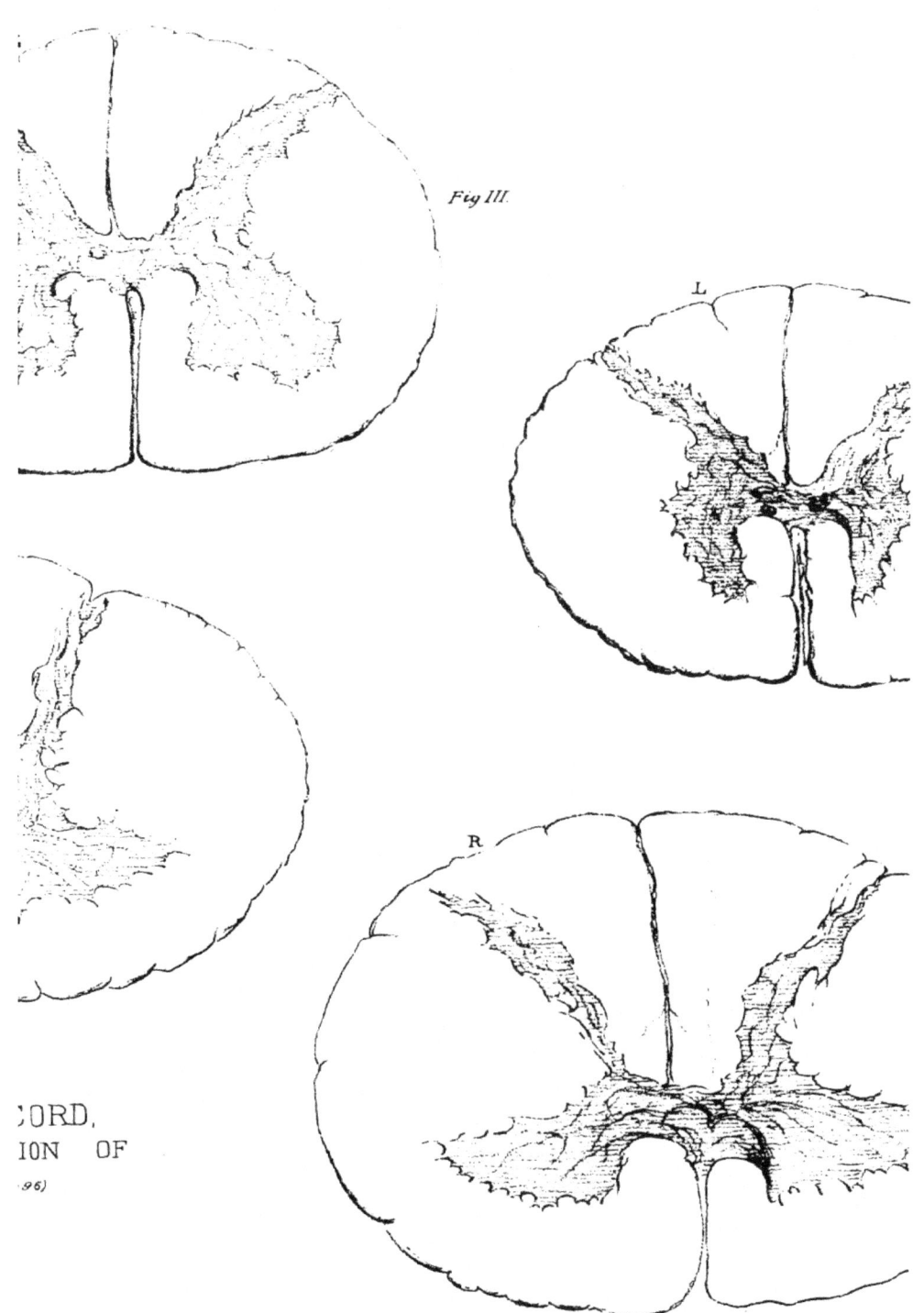

Fig III.

L

R

Pl. IV

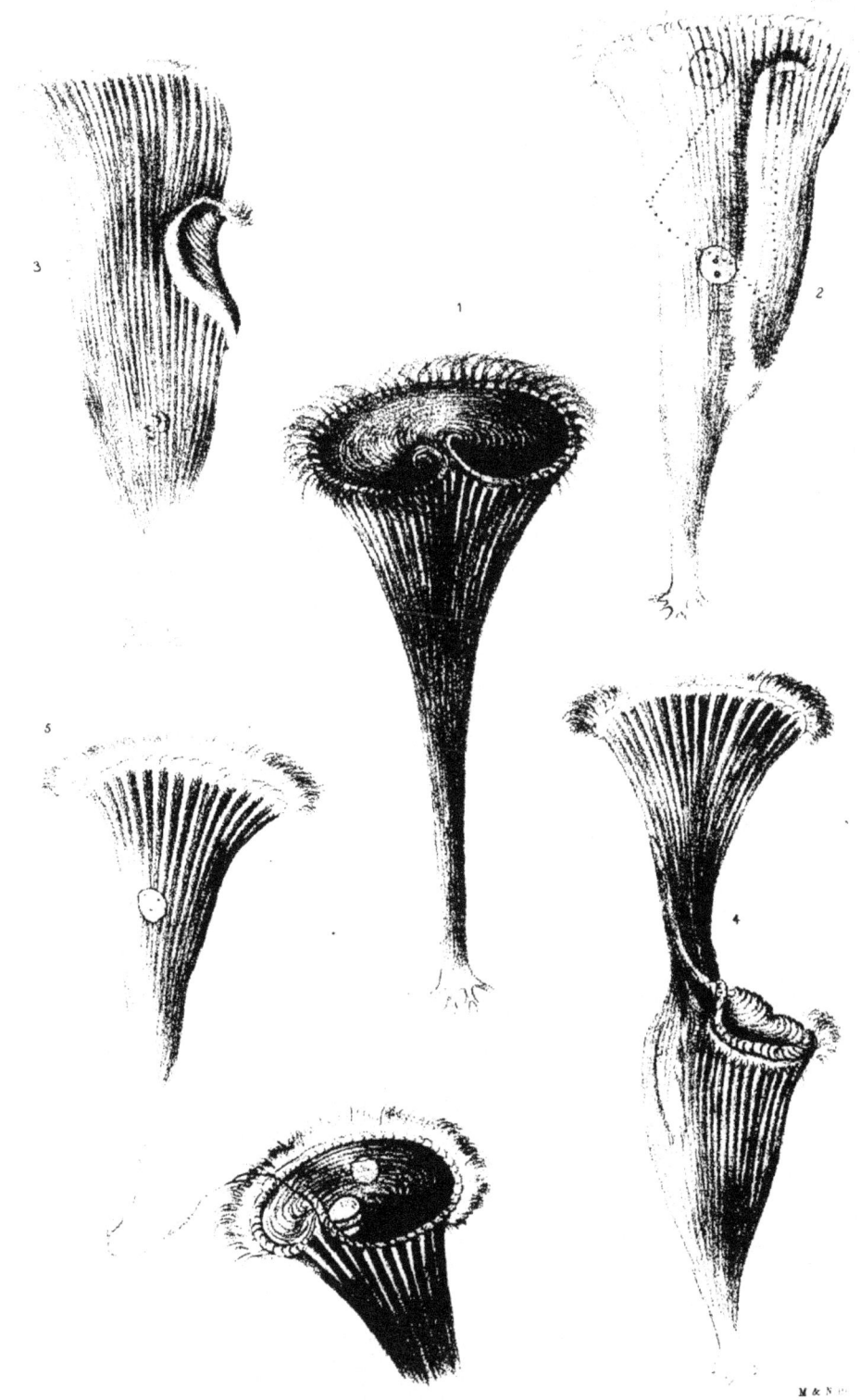

STENTOR

STENTOR (p 294)

Pl VIII

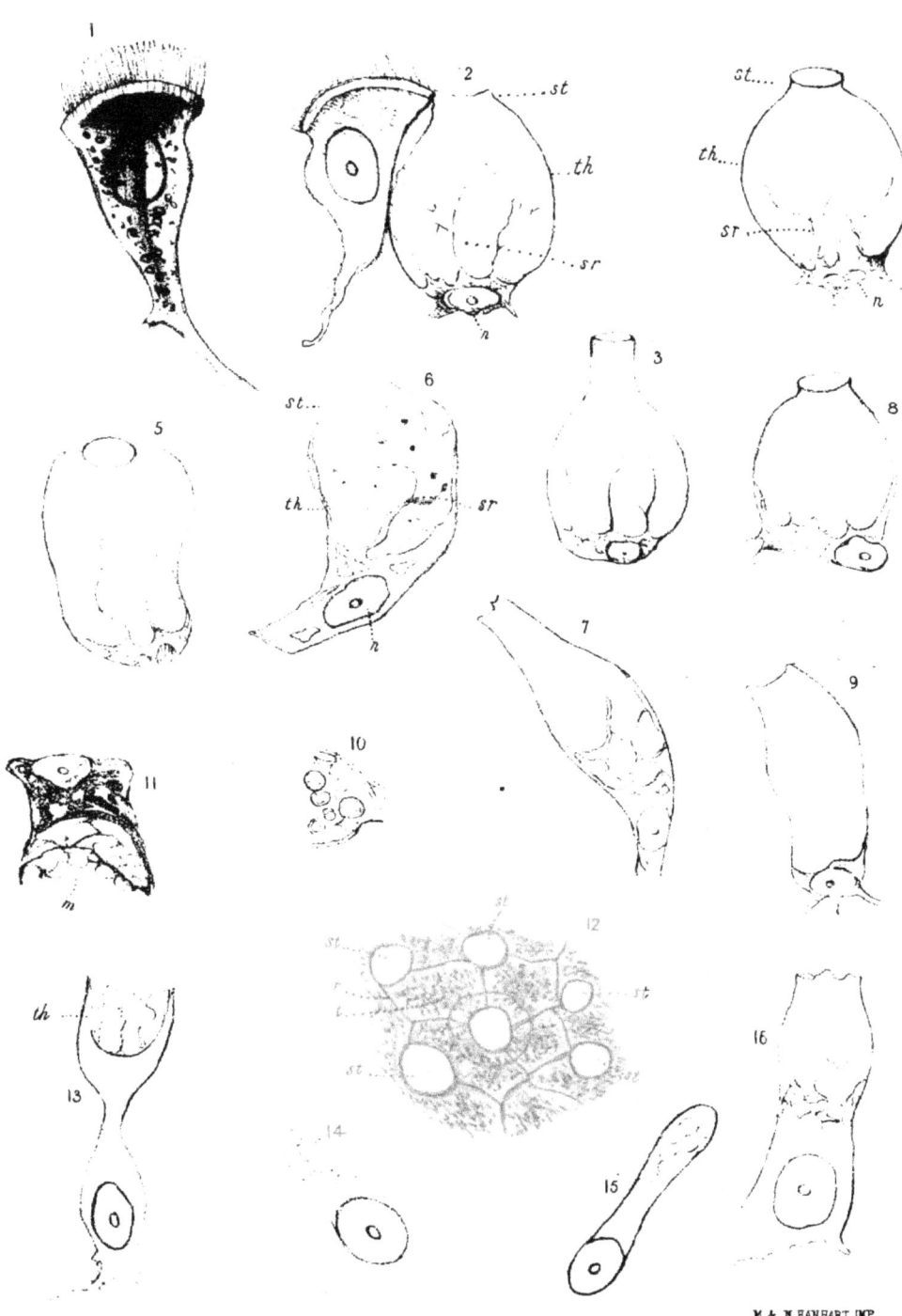

M & N HANHART IMP

EPITHELIUM OF FROG'S THROAT.(*p 399.*)

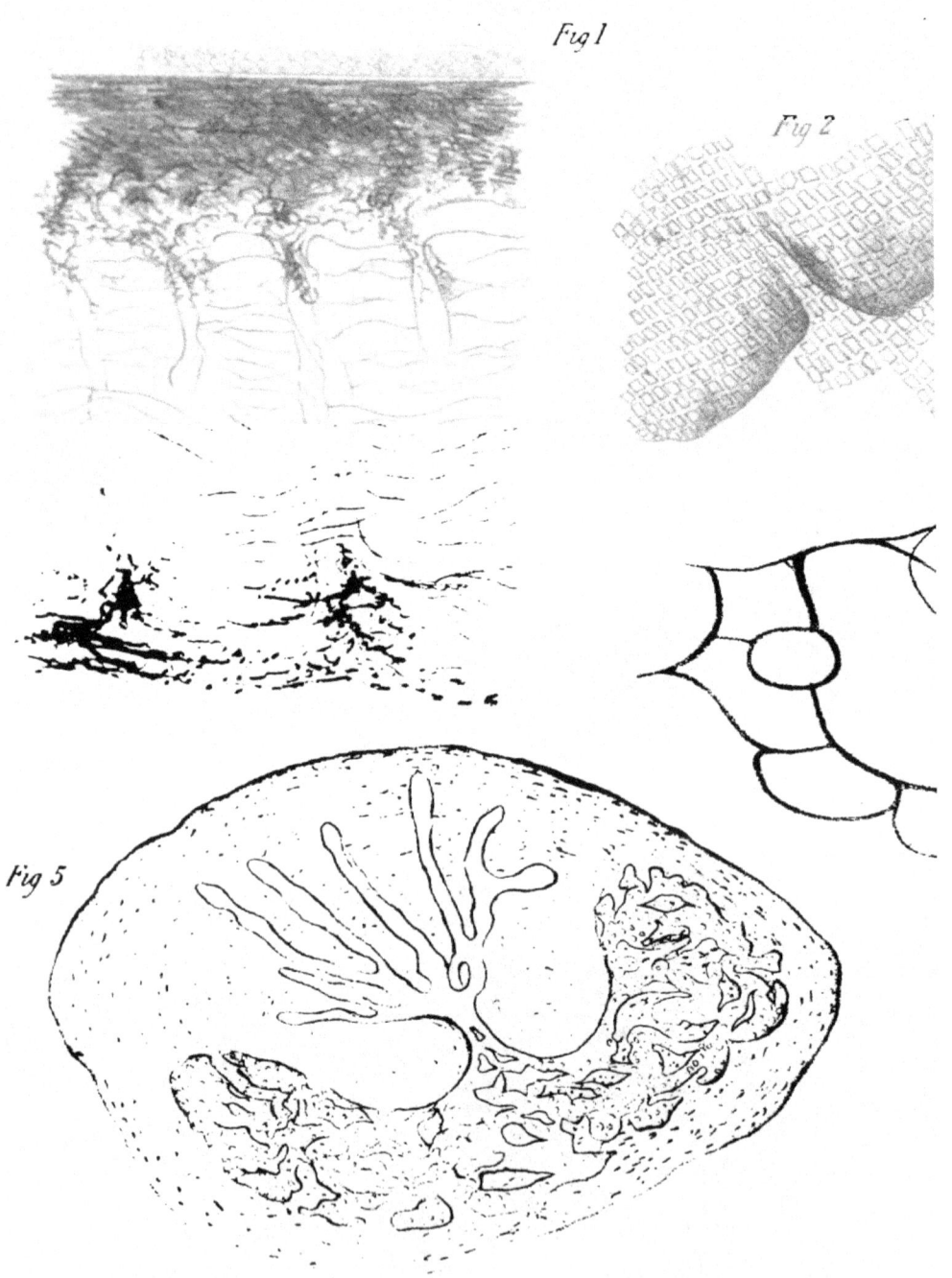

Fig 1

Fig 2

Fig 5

LIZARDS

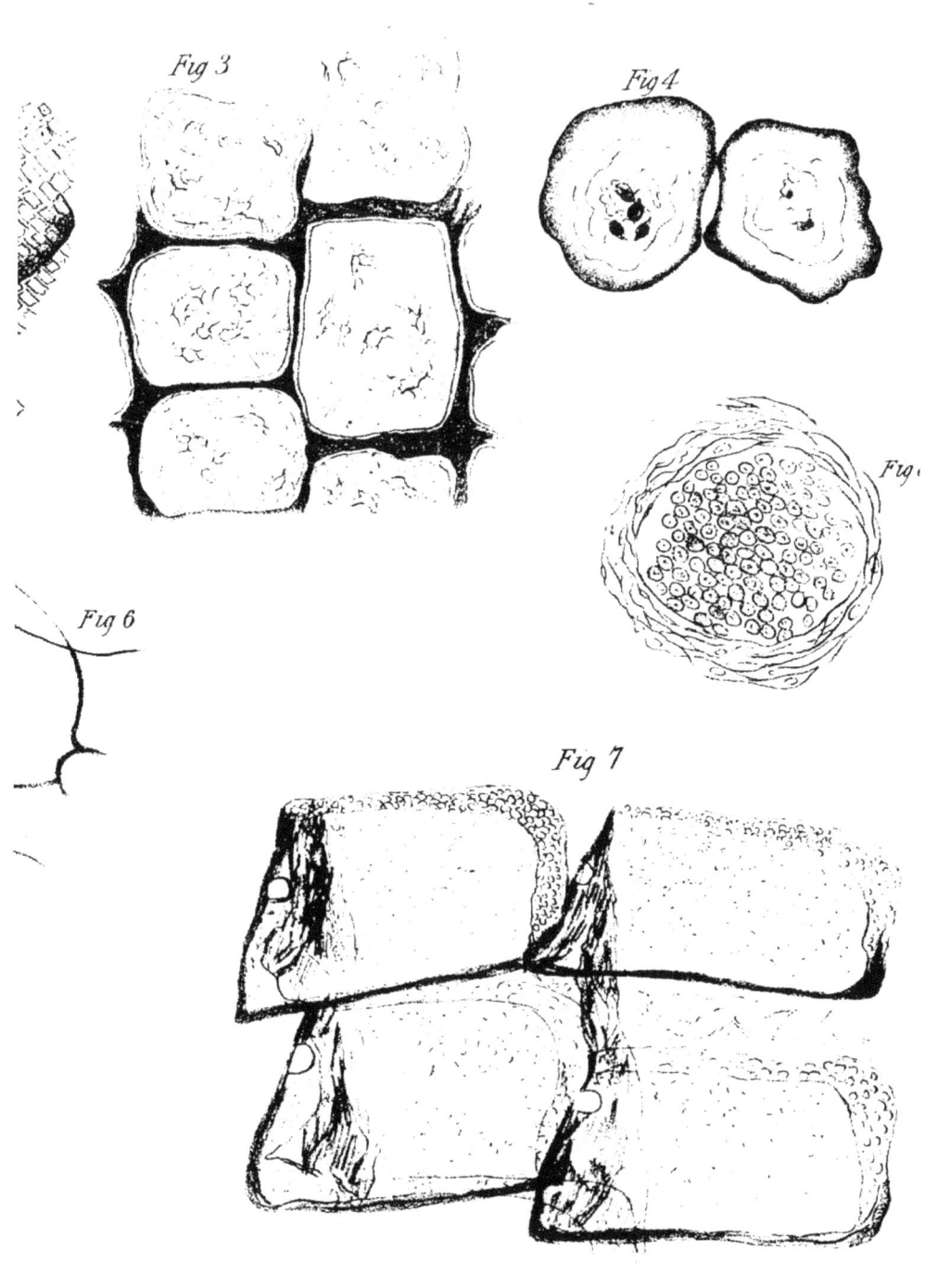

Fig 3

Fig 4

Fig ·

Fig 6

Fig 7

M & N HANHART IMP

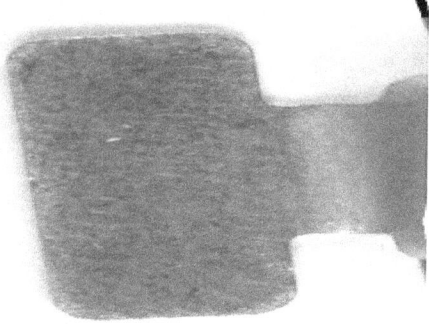

CIRCU

CIRCULATED

Check Out More Titles From HardPress Classics Series In this collection we are offering thousands of classic and hard to find books. This series spans a vast array of subjects – so you are bound to find something of interest to enjoy reading and learning about.

Subjects:
Architecture
Art
Biography & Autobiography
Body, Mind &Spirit
Children & Young Adult
Dramas
Education
Fiction
History
Language Arts & Disciplines
Law
Literary Collections
Music
Poetry
Psychology
Science
…and many more.

Visit us at www.hardpress.net

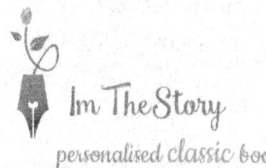

Im The Story

personalised classic books

"Beautiful gift.. lovely finish.
My Niece loves it, so precious!"

Helen R Brumfieldon

⭐⭐⭐⭐⭐

UNIQUE GIFT

FOR KIDS, PARTNERS
AND FRIENDS

Timeless books such as:

Kids

Alice in Wonderland · The Jungle Book · The Wonderful Wizard of Oz
Peter and Wendy · Robin Hood · The Prince and The Pauper
The Railway Children · Treasure Island · A Christmas Carol

Adults

Romeo and Juliet · Dracula

Highly Customizable

Change Books Title

Replace Characters Names with yours

Upload Photo He's inside page

Add Inscriptions

Visit
Im The Story.com
and order yours today!

CPSIA information can be obtained
at www.ICGtesting.com
Printed in the USA
BVHW081606120819
555665BV00013B/970/P